Howard: I have a copy of this text, so you are welcome to this one.

The philosophical content may provide you a handy opening to the main topic.

Bruno

New Directions in German Studies

Vol. 23

Series Editor:

IMKE MEYER

Director, School of Literatures, Cultural Studies and Linguistics, and Professor of Germanic Studies, University of Illinois at Chicago

Editorial Board:

KATHERINE ARENS
Professor of Germanic Studies, University of Texas at Austin

ROSWITHA BURWICK
Distinguished Chair of Modern Foreign Languages Emerita,
Scripps College

RICHARD ELDRIDGE
Charles and Harriett Cox McDowell Professor of Philosophy,
Swarthmore College

ERIKA FISCHER-LICHTE
Professor Emerita of Theater Studies, Freie Universität Berlin

CATRIONA MACLEOD
Edmund J. and Louise W. Kahn Term Professor in the Humanities
and Professor of German, University of Pennsylvania

STEPHAN SCHINDLER
Professor of German and Chair,
University of South Florida

HEIDI SCHLIPPHACKE
Associate Professor of Germanic Studies,
University of Illinois at Chicago

ULRICH SCHÖNHERR
Professor of German and Comparative Literature,
Haverford College

JAMES A. SCHULTZ
Professor of German Emeritus, University of California,
Los Angeles

SILKE-MARIA WEINECK
Professor of German and Chair of Comparative Literature,
University of Michigan

DAVID WELLBERY
LeRoy T. and Margaret Deffenbaugh Carlson University Professor,
University of Chicago

SABINE WILKE
Joff Hanauer Distinguished Professor for Western Civilization and
Professor of German, University of Washington

JOHN ZILCOSKY
Professor of German and Comparative Literature, University of Toronto

Volumes in the series:

Vol. 1. *Improvisation as Art: Conceptual Challenges, Historical Perspectives*
by Edgar Landgraf

Vol. 2. *The German Pícaro and Modernity: Between Underdog and Shape-Shifter*
by Bernhard Malkmus

Vol. 3. *Citation and Precedent: Conjunctions and Disjunctions of German Law and Literature*
by Thomas O. Beebee

Vol. 4. *Beyond Discontent: 'Sublimation' from Goethe to Lacan*
by Eckart Goebel

Vol. 5. *From Kafka to Sebald: Modernism and Narrative Form*
edited by Sabine Wilke

Vol. 6. *Image in Outline: Reading Lou Andreas-Salomé*
by Gisela Brinker-Gabler

Vol. 7. *Out of Place: German Realism, Displacement, and Modernity*
by John B. Lyon

Vol. 8. *Thomas Mann in English: A Study in Literary Translation*
by David Horton

Vol. 9. *The Tragedy of Fatherhood: King Laius and the Politics of Paternity in the West*
by Silke-Maria Weineck

Vol. 10. *The Poet as Phenomenologist: Rilke and the* New Poems
by Luke Fischer

Vol. 11. *The Laughter of the Thracian Woman: A Protohistory of Theory*
by Hans Blumenberg, translated by Spencer Hawkins

Vol. 12. *Roma Voices in the German-Speaking World*
by Lorely French

Vol. 13. *Vienna's Dreams of Europe: Culture and Identity beyond the Nation-State*
by Katherine Arens

Vol. 14. *Thomas Mann and Shakespeare: Something Rich and Strange*
edited by Tobias Döring and Ewan Fernie

Vol. 15. *Goethe's Families of the Heart*
by Susan E. Gustafson

Vol. 16. *German Aesthetics: Fundamental Concepts from Baumgarten to Adorno*
edited by J. D. Mininger and Jason Michael Peck

Vol. 17. *Figures of Natality: Reading the Political in the Age of Goethe*
by Joseph D. O'Neil

Vol. 18. *Readings in the Anthropocene: The Environmental Humanities, German Studies, and Beyond*
edited by Sabine Wilke and Japhet Johnstone

Vol. 19. *Building Socialism: Architecture and Urbanism in East German Literature, 1955–1973*
by Curtis Swope

Vol. 20. *Ghostwriting: W. G. Sebald's Poetics of History*
by Richard T. Gray

Vol. 21. *Stereotype and Destiny in Arthur Schnitzler's Prose: Five Psycho-Sociological Readings*
by Marie Kolkenbrock

Vol. 22. *Sissi's World: The Empress Elisabeth in Memory and Myth*
edited by Maura E. Hametz and Heidi Schlipphacke

Vol. 23. *Posthumanism in the Age of Humanism: Mind, Matter, and the Life Sciences after Kant*
edited by Edgar Landgraf, Gabriel Trop, and Leif Weatherby

Posthumanism in the Age of Humanism

Mind, Matter, and the Life Sciences after Kant

Edited by
Edgar Landgraf, Gabriel Trop,
and Leif Weatherby

BLOOMSBURY ACADEMIC
NEW YORK • LONDON • OXFORD • NEW DELHI • SYDNEY

BLOOMSBURY ACADEMIC
Bloomsbury Publishing Inc
1385 Broadway, New York, NY 10018, USA
50 Bedford Square, London, WC1B 3DP, UK

BLOOMSBURY, BLOOMSBURY ACADEMIC and the Diana logo are trademarks of Bloomsbury Publishing Plc

First published in the United States of America 2019

Copyright © Edgar Landgraf, Gabriel Trop, Leif Weatherby, and Contributors, 2019

Cover design: Andrea F. Bucsi
Cover image © Thomas Bruns/Berlin Museum of Medical History at the Charité

All rights reserved. No part of this publication may be reproduced or transmitted in any form or by any means, electronic or mechanical, including photocopying, recording, or any information storage or retrieval system, without prior permission in writing from the publishers.

Bloomsbury Publishing Inc does not have any control over, or responsibility for, any third-party websites referred to or in this book. All internet addresses given in this book were correct at the time of going to press. The author and publisher regret any inconvenience caused if addresses have changed or sites have ceased to exist, but can accept no responsibility for any such changes.

A catalog record for this book is available from the Library of Congress.

ISBN:	HB:	978-1-5013-3567-9
	ePDF:	978-1-5013-3569-3
	eBook:	978-1-5013-3568-6

Series: New Directions in German Studies, volume 23

Typeset by Integra Software Services Pvt. Ltd.
Printed and bound in the United States of America

To find out more about our authors and books visit www.bloomsbury.com and sign up for our newsletters.

Contents

Notes on Contributors — ix

1 Introduction: Posthumanism after Kant
   Edgar Landgraf, Gabriel Trop, and Leif Weatherby — 1

PART I DISSECTING THE HUMAN BODY: EMBODIMENT, COGNITION, AND THE EARLY LIFE SCIENCES

2 Vertiginous Systems of the Soul
   Jeffrey West Kirkwood — 17

3 Brain Matters in the German Enlightenment: Animal Cognition and Species Difference in Herder, Soemmerring, and Gall
   Patrick Fortmann — 37

4 Agency without Humans: Normativity and Path Dependence in the Nineteenth-Century Life Sciences
   Christian J. Emden — 53

5 Embodied Phantasy: Johannes Müller and the Nineteenth-Century Neurophysiological Foundations of Critical Posthumanism
   Edgar Landgraf — 79

PART II WHO'S AFRAID OF IDEALISM? MATERIALISM, POSTHUMANISM, AND THE POST-KANTIAN LEGACY

6 Kant and Posthumanism
   Carsten Strathausen — 105

viii Contents

7   Intimations of the Posthuman: Kant's Natural Beauty
    Peter Gilgen   127

8   Farewell to Ontology: Hegel after Humanism
    Leif Weatherby   145

9   Steps to an Ecology of *Geist*: Hegel, Bateson, and the Spirit
    of Posthumanism
    John H. Smith   165

10 Protecting Natural Beauty from Humanism's Violence:
    The Healing Effects of Alexander von Humboldt's
    Naturgemälde
    Elizabeth Millán   183

PART III CYBORG ENLIGHTENMENT: BOUNDARIES OF THE (POST-)HUMAN AROUND 1800

11 Posthumanist Thinking in the Work of Heinrich von Kleist
    Tim Mehigan   203

12 Positing the Robotic Self: From Fichte to *Ex Machina*
    Alex Hogue   223

13 In Defense of Humanism: Envisioning a Posthuman
    Future and Its Critique in Goethe's *Faust*
    Christian P. Weber   243

14 Beyond Death: Posthuman Perspectives in Christoph
    Wilhelm Hufeland's *Macrobiotics*
    Jocelyn Holland   269

15 The Indifference of the Inorganic
    Gabriel Trop   287

    Bibliography   309
    Index   329

Notes on Contributors

Christian J. Emden is Professor of German intellectual history and political thought at Rice University's department of Classical and European Studies and director of the Program in Politics, Law, and Social Thought. He is the author of "Normativity Matters: Philosophical Naturalism and Political Theory," in *The New Politics of Materialism: History, Philosophy, Science*, edited by Sarah Ellenzweig and John H. Zammito (2017); *Nietzsche's Naturalism: Philosophy and the Life Sciences in the Nineteenth Century* (2014); *Friedrich Nietzsche and the Politics of History* (2008); *Walter Benjamins Archäologie der Moderne: Kulturwissenschaft um 1930* (2006); and *Nietzsche on Language, Consciousness, and the Body* (2005). Much of his current work focuses on the emergence of normativity and philosophical naturalism, including the latter's relevance for political theory.

Patrick Fortmann is Associate Professor of Germanic Studies at the University of Illinois at Chicago. His main area of research is the long nineteenth century, specifically the Romantic Age. He is the author of *Autopsie von Revolution und Restauration: Georg Büchner und die politische Imagination* (2013) and the co-editor (with Martha B. Helfer) of *Commitment and Compassion: Essays on Georg Büchner* (2012). Recurring interests include sovereignty and spectacle, exchanges between literature and the sciences, and the idea of Romantic love.

Peter Gilgen is Associate Professor of German Studies at Cornell University. He works on philosophy and literature in the late eighteenth and early nineteenth centuries and has also published numerous essays on aesthetics, lyric poetry from the Middle Ages to the twenty-first century, contemporary theory (especially systems theory), and the university. He is the author of *Lektüren der Erinnerung: Lessing Kant Hegel* (2012) and *Unterlandschaft* (1999).

Notes on Contributors

Alex Hogue is Assistant Professor of German at Coastal Carolina University. He defended his dissertation entitled *I, (Post)Human: Being and Subjectivity in the Quest to Build Artificial People* in 2016 at the University of Cincinnati. Other publications examine the issues of metaphysics within the transhumanist movement and Martin Heidegger as a forerunner of posthumanism.

Jocelyn Holland is Professor of Comparative Literature at the California Institute of Technology. Her research focuses on intersections between literature, philosophy, and science around 1800. She has authored two books, *German Romanticism and Science* (2009) and *Key Texts by Johann Wilhelm Ritter on the Science and Art of Nature* (2010) and co-edited special journal editions on topics that include modes of equilibrium around 1800, theories and practices of timekeeping, the aesthetics of the tool, and the role of the Archimedean point in modernity.

Jeffrey West Kirkwood is Assistant Professor in the Department of Art History and the Department of Cinema at Binghamton University, State University of New York. His work concentrates on media theory and histories of image technologies. He has written the introduction to and edited the first translation of Ernst Kapp's *Elements of a Philosophy of Technology* along with his co-editor, and is the author most recently of a number of articles in the field of media theory, including "The Cinema of Afflictions," for the journal *October* and "Ernst Mach and the Technological Fact of Counterfactuals," forthcoming in the *Zeitschrift für Medien- und Kulturforschung (ZMK)*. He has also written art criticism for publications such as *Jacobin* and *OSMOS*.

Edgar Landgraf is Professor of German at Bowling Green State University, Ohio. Recent publications include articles on improvisation, Goethe, Kant, Kleist, Nietzsche, and Niklas Luhmann. His book *Improvisation as Art: Conceptual Challenges, Historical Perspectives* was published in 2011 (reissued in paperback by Bloomsbury in 2014). He is currently working on a monograph on *Nietzsche's Posthumanism*.

Tim Mehigan is Professor of German at the University of Queensland and Deputy Head at the Institute for Advanced Studies in the Humanities. He has published widely on German and European literature and thought. Among recent publications, as author, are *Heinrich von Kleist: Writing after Kant* (2011), as translator (with B. Empson), *K.L. Reinhold: Essay on a New Theory of the Human Capacity for Representation* (2011), and, as editor (with C. Moser), *The Intellectual Landscape in the Works of J.M. Coetzee* (2018), and (with A. Corkhill) *Raumlektüren: Der "Spatial Turn" und die Literatur der Moderne* (2013).

Elizabeth Millán is Professor of Philosophy at DePaul University. She works on aesthetics, German Idealism/Romanticism and Latin American Philosophy. Publications include *Friedrich Schlegel and the Emergence of Romantic Philosophy* (2007); with Bärbel Frischmann, *Das neue Licht der Frühromantik/The New Light of German Romanticism* (2008); "Borderline Philosophy? Incompleteness, Incomprehension, and the Romantic Transformation of Philosophy," *Yearbook on German Idealism* 6 (2009); "Fichte and the Development of Early German Romantic Philosophy," *The Cambridge Companion to Fichte* (2016) and many articles on the relation between German Idealism and the development of early German Romantic Philosophy.

John H. Smith is Professor of German at the University of California, Irvine. He has published on Hegel (*The Spirit and Its Letter: Traces of Rhetoric in Hegel's Philosophy of Bildung*) and philosophies of the will (*Dialectics of the Will: Freedom, Power, and Understanding in Modern French and German Thought*). He has written essays on a range of literary and philosophical topics, most recently on Goethe and Idealism, on Nietzsche and the decadent will, and on *Ereignis* in Heidegger and the *Novelle*. His most recent book is *Dialogues between Faith and Reason: The Death and Return of God in Modern German Thought* (2011). He is currently working on a project entitled "How Infinity Came to Be at Home in the World," which explores the place of the infinitesimal calculus and the mathematical infinite in the German philosophical and literary tradition from 1675 to 1830.

Carsten Strathausen is Professor of German and English and the Catherine Paine Middlebush Chair in Humanities at the University of Missouri. He is the author of *The Look of Things: Poetry and Vision around 1900* (2003), and *BioAesthetics: Making Sense of Life in Science and the Arts* (2017), and the editor of *A Leftist Ontology* (2009) as well as the translator of Boris Groys's *Under Suspicion: A Phenomenology of Media* (2012).

Gabriel Trop is Associate Professor of German in the Department of Germanic and Slavic Languages and Literatures at the University of North Carolina, Chapel Hill. His research interests tend to focus on the relationship between literature, science, and philosophy, with a special emphasis on poetics and aesthetics. These interests were reflected in his book *Poetry as a Way of Life: Aesthetics and Askesis in the German Eighteenth Century* (2015). He has also written articles about Hölderlin, Goethe, Novalis, Schelling, Hegel, E.T.A. Hoffmann, Wieland, and others. Most recently, he co-edited (with Jocelyn Holland) an issue of the *Germanic Review* entitled *Statics, Mechanics, Dynamics: Equilibrium around 1800*.

Leif Weatherby is Associate Professor of German at New York University and author of *Transplanting the Metaphysical Organ: German Romanticism between Leibniz and Marx* (2016). His interests include German Romanticism and Idealism, theories of the digital, and political economy.

Christian P. Weber is Associate Professor and Program Coordinator of German at Florida State University. He is the author of *Die Logik der Lyrik: Goethes Phänomenologie des Geistes in Gedichten* (2013) and diverse article publications. His research and teaching interests include literature and philosophy of the Goethezeit (1750–1830), lyric poetry, aesthetic theory, phenomenology of the imagination, biopolitical metaphors of nationalism, and German cinema.

One Introduction: Posthumanism after Kant

Edgar Landgraf, Gabriel Trop, and Leif Weatherby

Posthumanism—a discourse often understood to celebrate the "end of man"—is not so much an anti-humanism as an attempt to critically interrogate the status of the human as exceptional, as autonomous, as standing outside a web of relations, or even as a subject or object of knowledge corresponding to a determinate set of practices. Seen in this way, posthumanism can be found, perhaps, where one least expects it, including in putative humanisms in which thinking the human comes up against its limitations and attempts to transcend them.[1] Any genealogy of posthumanism—such as one finds in Stefan Herbrechter's *Posthumanism: A Critical Analysis* (2013)—thus encourages a closer examination of the novelty of some of the central posthumanist gestures.[2] Herbrechter mentions, for example, Jonathan Dollimore's classic study of the Shakespeare and Renaissance culture. Dollimore noted already in the 1980s how a "crisis of subjectivity" was present in what he construes as the very beginning of individualism, i.e., in early Christianity. Fears and feelings of alienation about the individual (whether as a political actor or as a "subject") are a constitutive part of modern, Western culture. From this vantage point, the postmodern collapse of

---

1   Recent research has gravitated toward such claims. Karl Steel, for example, notes the "fissures" of the human already in the Middle Ages and claims, "Posthumanism does not follow humanism; rather, it is inherent in its own claims." Karl Steel, "Medieval," in *The Cambridge Companion to Literature and the Posthuman*, ed. Bruce Clarke and Manuela Rossini (Cambridge: Cambridge University Press, 2017), 3.
2   See Stefan Herbrechter, *Posthumanism: A Critical Analysis* (London: Bloomsbury, 2013).

Western subjectivity is but another mutation of a continuing dynamic that finds its latest iteration in posthumanism.[3]

Nevertheless, posthumanism is often conflated with anti-humanism: whatever counts or has counted as humanistic is to be avoided, rejected, disavowed. Thus, Immanuel Kant and the scientific, philosophical, and literary writings after Kant often serve as foils against which posthumanistic thought seeks to define itself. Precisely this gesture demands contextualization, and it is one of the goals of this volume to interrogate this glancing encounter. It seeks to refine and specify our understanding of the "post" in posthumanism by focusing on an age that many readily identify as the pinnacle of (Enlightenment) humanist thought.

Lack of methodological agreement among posthumanists has led social phenomena, technological developments, and heterogeneous lines of thought to come under the posthumanist rubric. Unlike the theory-centered schools of thought that dominated the humanities over the last four or five decades, posthumanism is not committed to a particular methodology or hermeneutic practice. This is perhaps most apparent if we consider how different proponents of posthumanism position themselves vis-à-vis the main theoretical paradigms of the last decades. While some wholeheartedly endorse the heritage of post-structuralism, media theory, or cybernetics (e.g., Elaine L. Graham, Donna Haraway, Stefan Herbrechter, Andrew Pickering, Cary Wolfe), others seem to favor a more eclectic approach to post-structuralism (Neil Badmington, N. Katherine Hayles, Pramod Nayar, Tamar Sharon), while a third group—including the anti-correlationists—take a directly adversarial stance toward this tradition (Rosi Braidotti, Graham Harman, Quentin Meillassoux, Timothy Morton). This lack of methodological consistency might well be viewed as a strength. It increases the scope of inquiry and encourages interdisciplinarity. It also constitutes evidence of how posthumanism signals a paradigm shift, or at least a new vantage point from which to reassess the significance of the theoretical debates of the last decades.

The point of looking at posthumanism in the age of humanism, then, cannot be to work toward a comprehensive theory or to contribute to the development of a more coherent historical narrative organized around a before/after distinction. Our aim, instead, is to bring historical context and theoretical reflection to bear on these contentions. Our approach is historical because we recognize that the prefix "post" always also implies continuation. Anytime a past is used as a negative foil, the past continues to shape the "post" in some way. Inasmuch as transcending, modifying, and even rejecting humanism is a central and

---

3 For Herbrechter quoting Dollimore, see Herbrechter, *Posthumanism*, 55.

unifying concern of posthumanism, a careful examination of the remnants of this heritage is necessary.

This investigation of the posthumanist traces of humanism is a desideratum, not only because the term humanism is so broad, but also because posthumanist thought is often tempted to bypass or portray the past that it problematizes too simplistically. A certain caricature arises in posthumanist thought, contenting itself with repeating wholesale claims about conventional notions of subjectivity, dualistic modes of thinking, Kantian idealism, the separation of science and philosophy, or with the notion that the prehistory of posthumanism begins with Nietzsche.[4] The aim of our volume is to expand the historical perspective and to avoid generalizations and instead offer more refined analyses of historical instances. This approach complicates stereotypical assumptions about the humanist tradition and points toward developments within this tradition that anticipate, accompany and even expand the register of contemporary posthumanism.

The contributions in this volume focus particularly on ideas produced in Germany from the period around 1800 because they so often serve as either foundations or negative foils (or sometimes both) for much contemporary posthumanist work. The decades between roughly the publication of Kant's *Critique of Pure Reason* (1781) and Hegel's death (1831) saw a rethinking of the status of the human that continues to cast a long shadow. After all, it is Kant and his "age"—the one that leads from the Enlightenment to whatever comes after, the period around 1800—that recurs as the disavowed object, the safe other of posthumanist thinking. It is the age of Goethe whose Faust famously proclaims "here I am human/here it's allowed."[5] And it is the age of Hegel, whose concept of *Geist* has often been read as the most outlandish of the humanisms, breaking even with its anthropocentrism in a further hypostasis of human categories and capacities. We can note that these figures are all

---

4   Important exceptions, of course, can be found, in recent literature above all; see, for example, the attempt to examine the Middle Ages, the Early Modern, or the Romantic era through the lens of posthumanism in Bruce Clarke and Manuela Rossini, eds., *The Cambridge Companion to Literature and the Posthuman* (Cambridge: Cambridge University Press, 2017). Richard Grusin also has a historically expansive conception of "the nonhuman turn." See Richard Grusin, "Introduction," in *The Nonhuman Turn*, ed. Richard Grusin (Minneapolis: University of Minnesota Press, 2015), vii–xxix. With a greater focus on German literary and scientific texts, see also John McCarthy et al., eds., *The Early History of Embodied Cognition 1740–1920. The Lebenskraft-Debate and Radical Reality in German Science, Music, and Literature* (Leiden and Boston: Brill Rodopi, 2016).

5   Johann Wolfgang Goethe, *Faust I*, trans. David Luke (Oxford: Oxford University Press, 1988), line 940.

German—and it is indeed the German cultural sphere, the specifically German Enlightenment, that is "classically humanist," in accounts from Germanists and posthumanists alike. Any account of humanism tarries with Kant and Goethe; if we are successful here, any future posthumanism will have to avow a complex relation to the quasi-humanist modernity that arose in the German-speaking countries around 1800. This period so broadly painted as humanist by proponents and detractors also grappled with ways of challenging some of humanism's most cherished dualisms: freedom and nature, science and art, matter and spirit, mind and body, and so also human and nonhuman.

Major and minor figures in Germany during this decisive period produced modes of aleatory and contingent scientific, philosophical, and literary thinking that can serve as instruments for pushing posthumanism further along its critical path. This is the crux of our volume. The wager is that the scholars who speak the language of posthumanism will gain historical perspective and critical tools in reading the following essays, while the field that focuses on and often defends the towering humanists of the age around 1800 will see a much-needed revision of our conception of that epoch. Our volume aims to integrate these audiences by addressing scholars who are familiar with the theoretical discussions surrounding posthumanism, but want to learn more about the origins of major tenets of posthumanism around 1800, as well as more traditional scholars of the period who are interested in a "posthuman" Kant, or a "posthuman" Herz, and so on; that is, who want to explore a new framework which has largely been left out of the field.

While humanism generally is viewed as a philosophical and literary movement, a majority of contributions to this volume focus on scientific texts or on philosophical and literary texts that address scientific discourses and practices in the late eighteenth and early nineteenth centuries. This focus is in line with posthumanism's own interest in science and its willingness to incorporate scientific viewpoints into its philosophical, hermeneutic and literary/artistic productions. A historical perspective can help clarify contemporary contentions and add relevant scientific, philosophical, and cultural contexts. We are aided by the fact that the time period that first developed modern scientific research methods is also an age that reflects intensively on the philosophical implications of scientific work. Put more pointedly: returning to the beginnings of the life sciences, including cell theory, embryology, and neurophysiology, as well as of cognitive science, allows us to examine at their points of inception the challenges modern scientific discourses pose for the philosophical and humanist tradition.

The contributions in this volume subscribe to an understanding of the posthuman as an ethos that challenges the primacy of the human being in diverse discursive and practice-based domains (art, politics, science, and so on) and that employs corresponding discursive and interpretive technologies. For us, looking at posthumanism means examining instances and developments in which the human is not necessarily eliminated, but repositioned, conceptually redefined, physically refashioned or otherwise philosophically rethought when faced with certain "inhuman" others (e.g., geological time, the machine, the animal, the inorganic, social dynamics or power structures that exceed individual agency). From this broad perspective, posthumanism constitutes a transhistorical ethos that one can find already in antiquity, in Shakespeare, in German Romanticism, but that nevertheless has historical conditions of genesis. The philosophical, aesthetic, and scientific discourses of the late eighteenth and nineteenth centuries form an important and neglected historical context conditioning the emergence of the posthuman as such a transhistorical ethos.

We have organized the three parts of this volume around three primary contentions that emerge around 1800 and remain at the center of many debates within and about posthumanism today. The first part investigates how scientific accounts of perception, cognition and knowledge production in the late eighteenth and early nineteenth centuries come to challenge philosophical notions of subjectivity and (self-)consciousness. The second part examines the divide between idealism, mind, and spirit on the one hand and what are viewed as their physical, materialist, or ontological foundations on the other. The third part looks at the boundaries that appear to separate humans and technology or humans and animals as they are drawn and redrawn in literary, philosophical, and scientific texts of the era. There are sizable areas of overlap between these topics, chapters, and sections. Challenges to mind/body dualism and an emphasis on notions of embodiment, for example, both of which represent key concerns of posthumanism, appear in all three sections, and often in rather unexpected places. While "embodiment" has a relatively recent history, what we call the age of humanism is rich with studies that investigate the very questions we associate with this term today: the role of physiology, human cells, neurological extensions for cognition; the body's situatedness within an environment; even the relationship between human bodies and technology, all of which are topics that caught the attention of scientists and writers already two centuries ago.

In this vein, Part I, "Dissecting the Human Body: Embodiment, Cognition, and the Early Life Sciences," explores how the question of "embodied cognition" emerges around 1800. Scientists such as Markus Herz, Johannes Müller, Lorenz Oken, Jacob Schleiden, Theodor Schwann, or Reinhold Treviranus, who developed the foundations of the modern life and cognitive sciences, show a keen interest in better understanding the relationship between human physiology on the one hand, and cognition, fantasy and human intention on the other. As they develop revolutionary scientific tools and concepts that come to define our modern understanding of physiology, they also are aware of the philosophical implications of their scientific work, and of the limits of philosophical modes of inquiry for science. Jeffrey Kirkwood's "Vertiginous Systems of the Soul " examines eighteenth-century inquiries into vertigo and dizziness as a point of convergence between philosophical and emerging physiological discourses. For researchers such as Marcus Herz (a deeply conflicted disciple of Kant), dizziness suggested a union between the physiological and the representational functions of the psyche, while simultaneously demonstrating their independence.

In "Brain Matters in the German Enlightenment: Animal Cognition and Species Difference in Herder, Soemmerring, and Gall," Patrick Fortmann turns to the Viennese physician and anatomist, Franz Joseph Gall, the inventor of what is now known as phrenology (but which he called "organology"). Instead of a strict boundary between species, Gall envisioned a continuum based on brain structure. Assuming specialized, yet largely autonomous, organs in the brain, manifesting themselves in cognitive faculties, early phrenology opened the possibility for both a new understanding of species as a category and a radically revised conception of species cognition.

Kant—posthumanism's favorite bogeyman—plays a crucial role for these scientists. Unlike some of our contemporary posthumanists, however, the researchers of the early nineteenth century did not run away from the Kantian heritage, but rather saw themselves as exploring and implementing its consequences through different, i.e., scientific, means. Christian Emden's "Agency without Humans: Normativity and Path Dependence in the Nineteenth-Century Life Sciences" looks at a broad range of experimental and theoretical innovations in German cell theory and embryology to argue that what we can witness in the period between the 1790s and 1880s is the emergence of the problem of biological agency, that is, a kind of agency that lacks the intentional stance attributed to human agency.

Edgar Landgraf's "Embodied Phantasy: Johannes Müller and the Nineteenth-Century Neurophysiological Foundations of Critical Posthumanism" examines how Johannes Müller, one of the most important nineteenth-century physiologists (and the teacher of such prominent students as Hermann von Helmholtz, Emil du Bois-Reymond, Ernst Haeckel, Theodor Schwann, Wilhelm Wundt, Rudolf Virchow), confronts with the eyes of the experimental scientist the material border (what he identifies as *Sehsinnsubstanz*, "visual sensory substance") between body and mind. His analysis of phantasmatic phenomena reveals a seemingly paradoxical relationship of simultaneous dependence and independence of the psychological from the physiological which breaks with a reductionist and, more generally, a mechanistic view of the body. Müller's research suggests that the Kantian legacy within the life sciences is not "correlationist" but constructivist, a difference that carries, Landgraf argues by drawing on Jacob von Uexküll's book *The Sense of Life*, important political consequences.

Part II, "Who's Afraid of Idealism? Materialism, Posthumanism, and the Post-Kantian Legacy," focalizes the binary philosophical terms that gained major currency around 1800 and continue to organize speculation today. Posthumanism has generally found itself on the side of a broadly conceived materialism. Hayles's concept of embodiment—central as it is to the early articulations of the posthumanist paradigm—opposes both "idealist" conceptions of ontology from Locke and Kant onward and their putative counterparts in the digital world: those who believe in "disembodied" information.[6] Mark Hansen has extensively explored the digital organizations of this embodiment in his phenomenology of aesthetic experience.[7] Claus Pias has gone so far as to argue that the digital is a "transcendental illusion," modeled on Kant's notion that ideas of reason are unavoidable but also ungroundable.[8] The curious result of the materialism of posthumanism, then, is that idealism is only an error of perspective. By investigating the historical semantics of terms like "spirit" and "matter," this section forms a first comparative exploration of German Idealism and posthumanism with the aim of bringing Kant and Hegel (and also Goethe) into philosophical conversation with the posthumanist movement that rejected their legacy.

The results are sometimes surprising: Hegel might have something in common with cybernetics, while Kant might have something to tell us about embodiment. The historical relation between posthumanism and classical humanism cannot be reduced to a simple binary, suggesting that materialism and idealism are usually more complex than their opposition would suggest.

Part II opens with an essay by Carsten Strathausen on "Kant and Posthumanism," which argues that current rejections of Kant in Speculative Realism and object-oriented ontology are unfounded. Ever since Kant's critical turn in the 1780s, so the argument goes, continental philosophy has abandoned ontology for epistemology, thus giving rise to an entrenched anthropocentric view of the world that devalues the being of objects in favor of how these objects appear to

---

6   See N. Katherine Hayles, *How We Became Posthuman* (Chicago: University of Chicago Press, 1999), 3, 39.
7   Mark Hansen, *New Philosophy for New Media* (Cambridge, MA: MIT, 2006).
8   Claus Pias, "Analog, Digital, and the Cybernetic Illusion," *Kybernetes* 34, no. 3–4 (2005): 543–50.

us humans.[9] Posthumanism, by contrast, emphasizes the ontological kinship that binds together not just humans and animals, but all things in the world, animate or not. Against this current trend, Strathausen's essay is based on the premise that (self-critical) humanism is and remains an essential part of (critical) posthumanism. Instead of trying to move beyond Kant, posthumanism should reengage with the legacy of his thought.

Peter Gilgen's essay, "Intimations of the Posthuman: Kant's Natural Beauty," examines Kant's analytic of the beautiful in order to unearth an "excess of beauty." This excess of beauty refers to a nonhuman or inhuman quality that can only be captured by the human observer by means of projective human analogies that are, as Kant makes abundantly clear, mere fictional constructs. Nevertheless, the experience of the beautiful does not merely exercise the faculties of the mind, but gives an indication of something above and beyond what is directly perceptible: the perceptual intimation of that which exceeds perception. Gilgen argues that many recent attempts at posthumanist thinking that have simply cast aside Kant's transcendental intervention do so at their own peril and neglect the resources that Kant's philosophy offers to a posthumanism deserving of the name.

The posthuman discourse of "embodiment" expands the sense of physiological situatedness of any possible cognition (Hansen and Hayles). It is complemented by speculative realism and the object-philosophies, which enrich the sense of "things" beyond their "correlation" to any possible subjects.[10] Leif Weatherby argues that ontology cannot do justice to the digital condition, showing that computer science has adopted a Kantian notion of ontology, and going on to compare Meillassoux's attempt to take leave of this ontology to Hegel's. Dialectical procedure is singular in its ability to cope with pre-constituted yet contradictory ontologies—like those rapidly collapsing the distance between general and individual in the spirit of a new capitalism.

In a similar vein, John H. Smith's "Steps to an Ecology of *Geist*: Hegel, Bateson, and the Spirit of Posthumanism" draws a provocative parallel between Hegel's spirit and the cybernetic anthropologist Gregory Bateson's concept of mind. Smith suggests that if we read *Geist* in its fullness, as Spirit or Mind from the Idealist tradition, it is the last thing that should be expelled from our rigorous attempts at knowledge

---

9 See, for example, Levi Bryant, Graham Harman, and Nick Srnicek, eds., *The Speculative Turn: Continental Materialism and Realism* (Melbourne: re.press, 2011) or Timothy Morton, *Hyperobjects: Philosophy and Ecology after the End of the World* (Cambridg, MA: Harvard University Press, 2013).

10 See Quentin Meillassoux, *After Finitude: An Essay on the Necessity of Contingency*, trans. Ray Brassier (London: Bloomsbury, 2010).

(*Wissenschaft*). Smith shows how Hegelian thought already places the human in relation to the nonhuman, and how the hallmark of Hegel's notion of *Geist* includes within it a form of logic construed as patterns that connect to one another: systematicity as an interplay between structure and unrest. He thus suggests that Hegel can become a key player in an attempt to construct a contemporary ecology of mind.

Elizabeth Millán's "Protecting Natural Beauty from Humanism's Violence: The Healing Effects of Alexander von Humboldt's *Naturgemälde*" rounds out the second section. In a way that resonates with Gilgen's contribution, Millán shows that Humboldt develops a specific genre of writing nature—the "canvas of nature" or *Naturgemälde*—that simultaneously construes nature as an object of knowledge just as it places natural beauty *beyond* the violence of conceptual thought. In these portraits of nature, a freedom manifests itself that lies beyond human freedom. Humboldt sees the Latin American landscape in particular as the site in which this freedom manifests itself, thereby providing the natural scientist—and aesthete—with a view onto a notion of nature that does not exclude knowledge, but whose beauty exceeds attempts to grasp it completely.

Part III, entitled "Cyborg Enlightenment: Boundaries of the (Post-) Human Around 1800," contains contributions that explore the way in which the human is defined, and often called into question as an ontologically privileged being, in relationship to that which is outside the human: the animal, the inorganic, and the robot, among others. Furthermore, repositioning or rethinking the boundaries between the human and the inhuman, or organic life and its negation (e.g., death), emerged in the late eighteenth and nineteenth centuries along with new technologies that attempt to modify or enhance the human being as a species being.

This part begins with Tim Mehigan's rethinking of Kleist as an author whose ethos resonates with that of posthuman critiques of humanism. Already in his programmatic essay "On the Marionette Theater," Kleist positions the human between the artifice of mechanism (the movements of the marionette) and the instinct of the animal as a being who is found wanting. This inversion of values—the animal and the machine as superior to the human—continues throughout Kleist's fictional works, whether in the body that eclipses conscious control (in Kleist's "Marquise von O…"), in a system of law that operates autonomously from humanistic conceptions of morality (in "Michael Kohlhaas"), or in the collapse of judgment and embodied response to stimuli (in "The Beggarwoman of Locarno").

Alex Hogue turns to Alex Garland's film *Ex Machina* in order to show how "humanity," or at the very least, the notion of a conscious self possessing personal identity does not depend on an essentialized notion of the human, but shows the human to result from practical contexts of interaction. Humanity thus becomes defined as a form of acting in the world rather than as a "substance." Hogue's "Positing the Robotic Self: From Fichte to *Ex Machina*" locates the first articulation of such a model in Fichte's transcendental idealism. Because consciousness for Fichte emerges from action in the world, any being that *acts* or is "summoned" to freedom in relation to others is endowed with agency. Fichte's transcendental idealism is thereby revealed to be an important resource for posthuman thought; if robots can act in this manner, they become "artificial" humans.

Christian P. Weber's article gives an important counter-perspective by turning to the work of Johann Wolfgang Goethe. In contrast to some of the other contributions to this volume, Weber's essay construes Goethe as a resolute humanist, albeit one who already in the drama *Faust* anticipates the dangers of a posthuman future in which the human would become a sheer result of systemic manipulation. Weber shows how Mephistopheles becomes the agent of a destructive virtualization of experience: his goal is to achieve a "negative creation" by overtaking the creative impulses of the human (in this case, Faust) and directing them toward phantasmatic virtual realities in which agency itself becomes impossible. Weber argues that Goethe's *Faust* entertains the possibility of such a posthuman future—we may already be in the midst of realizing this problematic future—or a future in which the human is just as constrained as it was in premodern modes of thought that sought to ensure the frictionless order of a totalizing system.

Jocelyn Holland, in "Beyond Death: Posthuman Perspectives in Christoph Wilhelm Hufeland's *Macrobiotics*," examines how, already at the end of the eighteenth century, the German physician raises issues that come to dominate contemporary discussions of the posthuman. In particular, the question of artificial life is important in Hufeland's project; indeed, as Holland shows, for Hufeland, life is irreducible to pure organic materiality, but refers to the way in which matter becomes representational. There is thus an artificiality at the heart of the natural, and life can only be "extended" because it belongs not simply to nature (*physis*), but is also at the same time an art (*techne*). The invocation of a lexicon that stems from the arts suggests that art itself, as a practice, has not been sufficiently acknowledged in posthuman accounts to conceptualize life *after* or *beyond* the individual human self.

Gabriel Trop, in "The Indifference of the Inorganic," takes up Holland's challenge to draw upon art to rethink life from a posthuman perspective. Trop draws attention to the emergence of "indifference" in the discourse of naturephilosophy (*Naturphilosophie*), where indifference refers to a paradoxical operation in which a difference no longer "makes" a difference, and yet, still appears *as* a difference. He argues that philosophy and literature form discursive crucibles through which strategic approaches to processes of indifference can be explored: in this instance, the indifference of the inorganic and the organic orders that can be found in Schelling's naturephilosophy and Goethe's novel *Elective Affinities*. Ultimately, both Goethe and Schelling draw upon the indifference of the inorganic to defend a conception of world—one maintained through art and artifacts—as a zone of inconsistency.

A volume that examines posthumanism in eighteenth- and nineteenth-century German literature and philosophy might seem to fall victim to the accusation of being fashionable: yet another variation on a currently trendy theme. However, as David Wellbery has written, wherever theory or philosophy is compared to the vicissitudes of fashion (either positively or negatively), there lies the suspicion that a task of thinking has not been granted its full transformative potential.[11] To declare a certain historical mode of thinking dead—no longer fashionable—is to foreclose on the possibilities that still lie dormant within it. Already Giacomo Leopardi, in his "Dialogue between Fashion and Death" (1824), had drawn attention to the way in which fashion works in tandem with annihilation; the power of fashion works ceaselessly to declare the transience of all things, having "abolished the fashion of seeking immortality, and its concession, even when merited. So that now, whoever dies may assure himself that he is dead altogether, and that every bit of him goes into the ground, just as a little fish is swallowed, bones and all."[12] For Leopardi—himself operating in a romantic-ironic modality—fashion becomes an absolutizing agent of nothingness: it seeks to transform duration into the immanence of a transient appearance.

There are two senses, then, in which posthumanism might seem *fashionable*. It is fashionable in the sense that it is enjoying a concentrated moment of collective intensity, or inasmuch as it is *living* within practices; and it might also seem fashionable inasmuch as it, like Leopardi's fashion, harnesses the annihilating power of death by relativizing that which comes before it. The temporality of fashion embraces the life of one mode of appearance by announcing the death of that which preceded it; its logic unfolds according to the formula *the death of ...* or *the end of ...* According to the dictates of fashion, the next logical step would consist in the *end of posthumanism*, or as Claire Colebrook

---

11 David Wellbery, "Foreword," in *Discourse Networks 1800 /1900*, ed. Friedrich Kittler, trans. Michael Metteer, with Chris Cullens (Stanford: Stanford University Press, 1990), viii.
12 Giacomo Leopardi, "Dialogue between Fashion and Death," in *Essays and Dialogues of Giacomo Leopardi*, trans. Charles Edwardes (Boston: J. R. Osgood & Co., 1882), 22–3.

writes in *The Death of the PostHuman*, a moment in which the "posthuman" will cede to the "counterhuman" or the "superhuman" or something beyond even that: a future in which the mark of the human being remains only as a sign to be read without that being for whom the sign *could* be read.[13]

The headlong rush into the temporality of fashion, however, runs the risk of declaring something dead before it has even had the chance to live. A countermovement, then, would resist the inexorable temporality of fashion and linger within that which is unfashionable, or as Nietzsche writes, *untimely*. To illuminate the domain of that which is unfashionable within every fashion—its future anterior or "it will have been"—is tantamount to the refusal to capitulate to death without struggle. Similarly, the unfashionable within posthumanism would not simply accede to "the death of the human," but would examine what possibilities might lie on the horizon of a humanist afterlife.

The "post" of "posthumanism" can thus function not merely in a temporal sense (*after* humanism), but in a conceptual sense as the exploration of a *beyond*: the acknowledgment that the human still exists as an effective and affective intensity, but that the conditions that have given rise to the human *as* such an intensity are shifting and open to being reconfigured. Indeed, the question of the human has always been a question of relating the human to that which lies outside of it; as Richard Grusin notes, "the nonhuman turn [is] a continuation of a long-standing philosophical project."[14] However, if the nonhuman includes in its conceptual articulation a gesture of negation—that which is *not* human—the posthuman suspends this negation in an effort to develop conceptual flexibility. Thus, the human/nonhuman dichotomy itself is placed under interrogation; such a relation can manifest itself as tension, as conflict, as difference (rather than dialectical or non-dialectical negation of the term "nonhuman"), as coherence, in short, as a strategic positioning that remains mobile and exploratory. One might even thus speak of a strategic anthropocentrism that could surface within the logic of posthumanism (anthropocentrism no longer as essence but as self-conscious, and thus ironic, contingent practice). Even in the very notion of the nonhuman, there lies the uncanny return of the repressed of the human—as if the human story is not yet finished—since in our very conceptuality, we still seem anthropo-oriented (or anthropo-disoriented), if no longer anthropo-centric.

One thing should be clear given the heterogeneity of the perspectives represented in this volume: posthumanism, as the contributors

---

13 Claire Colebrook, *Death of the PostHuman: Essays on Extinction*, vol. 1 (Ann Arbor, MI: Open Humanities Press, 2014), 229.
14 Grusin, "Introduction," xxvii.

understand it, is less a stable body of knowledge—a clear discourse whose contours one could definitively outline or a set of shared beliefs—than an incitement or a provocation of thought that is always performed anew. The contributions in this volume are committed to the idea that this provocation does not only orient itself toward the future, but also toward the past. By allowing the all-important moment in intellectual history of Kant and post-Kantian philosophy and literature to resonate (or clash) with the posthuman present, we become attuned to potentialities of a cultural history that ought to provoke in us an affect of wonder or surprise. The goal of this volume is thus not a conservative one—that is, not to simply find posthumanistic beliefs as something "already there" in an age of humanism—but to draw upon the energy of the posthuman moment in order to let the past emerge as something strange and unfamiliar.

Part I
Dissecting the Human Body: Embodiment, Cognition, and the Early Life Sciences

Two Vertiginous Systems of the Soul

Jeffrey West Kirkwood

Schwindel ist wesentlich eine Störung des Ortssinnes.[1]

When a young Friedrich Kittler wrote "Vertigo is essentially a disturbance of the sense of place," he was writing about the experience of being drunk. What the soon-to-be figurehead of New German Media Theory's observation diagnosed, however, was a complexity of soberer discourses on the connection between material systems and metaphysical unities that spanned from the Enlightenment to the computer age. Having a "sense of place" meant not only locating oneself amid a universe of objects, it also meant first figuring out how to draw the lines between subjects and objects. For pioneers of machine learning in the 1950s, problems of orientation were deeply related to efforts to replicate thought using analog circuits modeled after neurons—addressing, for instance, how a machine could recognize its myriad operations as a part of a single system as distinct from other systems. Similarly, for figures like Immanuel Kant and his student Marcus Herz at the end of the eighteenth century, orientation, and with it disorientation and vertigo, acted as a proxy for discussing the mind/body dilemma at the point that nerve theories transformed matter from a substance into systems. In both cases, to determine the principles of systemic orientation, whether for a nervous system or an analog computer, was to explain the interface between materiality and metaphysics.

Following the rise of empirical physiology in the eighteenth century, philosophers were forced to contend with the possibility that tangled pathways of what would later be understood as nerves participated in the cogitations of the subject. Once the subject was plunged into the overabundance of the physical plenum, the mind/body problem became a systems-theoretical question of figuring out where

---

1 Friedrich Kittler, *Baggersee: Frühe Schriften aus dem Nachlass*, ed. Tania Hron and Sandrina Khaled (Paderborn: Wilhelm Fink, 2015), 15.

thought was located and how the boundaries of the subject could be drawn. Against this backdrop the term "orientation" took on a new philosophical significance and Abraham Gotthelf Kästner even commented in a letter to Immanuel Kant that "orientation" had become one of "several fashionable words" (*Modewörter*) of "philosophical jargon."[2] The relationship between mind and matter had always been an aporetic point of contention, but thinking of the body as a network presented the additional challenge of explaining metaphysics in terms of a materiality that was distributed rather than a uniform substance. There was no single, localizable site of consciousness, a fact that prompted disputation about the proper "seat of the soul" among thinkers from Kant and Samuel Thomas von Soemmerring to Novalis and Hegel.[3] In order to account for the unity of the subject, and to therefore orient it in light of emerging evidence suggesting that thought was bound to a networked system of nerves, philosophy encountered a computer age problem: how the machinations of an analog machine could reference themselves to produce something like consciousness. Viewing the soul as a system demanded a model of the human machine that explained how its individual, internal operations produced recognition of their place within the larger network without first resorting to metaphysics.

A digital solution to this Enlightenment dilemma was offered by Marcus Herz in his 1786 *Versuch über den Schwindel* (Essay on Vertigo).[4] In the work, the student and longtime friend of Kant argued that the experience of disorientation could be neither entirely physiological nor purely mental. It was an interface disorder involving an error in the representation of the subject to her/himself with respect to his/her representations of external objects. As Herz defined it, vertigo was "that condition of confusion in which the soul [*Seele*] finds itself on account of a too-rapid succession of its mental representations [*Vorstellungen*]."[5] The disorder interrupted the processes by which the physical body produced a meta-level recognition of the subject as distinct from but related to objects through an asynchronicity between the analog workings of the body and their corresponding sequences

---

2   Abraham Gotthelf Kästner to Immanuel Kant, October 2, 1790, in *Correspondence*, trans. Arnulf Zweig (Cambridge: Cambridge University Press, 1999), 360.
3   That Soemmerring was also the inventor of the electrolytic telegraph is not trivial for thinking about the role of media technical systems in discourses about the soul.
4   Marcus Herz, *Versuch über den Schwindel* (Berlin: Christian Friedrich Voß & Sohn, 1786).
5   Marcus Herz, *Versuch über den Schwindel*, 2nd edn (Berlin: Voss, 1791), 176. Except where specified, citations going forward are from this edition.

of mental representations. The question Herz's meditation begs, then, is how this interface operated normally to orient the subject so seamlessly as to erase any evidence of its perspective having been manufactured.

Analog operations of the nervous system, much like the analog neural networks of the 1950s, had to undergo a digitalization if they were to orient themselves. The continuous workings of both human intelligence and "artificial" machine intelligence had to be discretized for the purpose of allowing those operations to be reinserted into the system and accounted for as a part of the machine's future operations. To remain continuous was to remain unconscious—never predicting or reflecting. Stabilizing the identity of a system over time (where the system at T_1 could be said to be the same at T_2), and in such a way that it was recognized by the system itself, entailed breaking up the perpetual present of the machine into operations that could then be looped. The necessity for digitizing the empirical mechanisms of thought offered an early insight into the porous nature of the boundaries between human and nonhuman systems in the interplay between information and materiality. But it also formulated a posthumanism that stood at the very origins of humanism.

In an effort to bring medicine into line with Kantian idealism, Herz, who was an esteemed Berlin doctor, used vertigo as a vehicle to carefully explore the ways in which physical systems might produce a sense of orientation—how the operations of physical systems could emerge as closed, metaphysical entities. His sustained inquiry into the medical-philosophical etiologies of the disorder recognized that the problem had a great number of possible causes that were neither exclusively physiological, nor purely ideational. Instead, vertigo, by creating the sense that one's senses were out of step with the world, revealed an asynchronicity between the analog systems of the physical body and the sequences of mental representations that discretized those processes. At the same time, Herz's digital soul, largely rejected by his contemporaries, only became comprehensible through the optic of computer technologies and cybernetic theories that would mature during the middle of the twentieth century.

Intelligent SNARC

As graduate students at Princeton University in the early 1950s, Marvin Minsky and Dean Edmonds built and ran one of the first electronic learning machines. The machine, run by a Stochastic Neural Analog Reinforcement Calculator (SNARC), which allowed a "rat" to navigate a maze, was one of the (if not the) earliest neural network simulator. Its design was based in part on Warren S. McCulloch and Walter H. Pitts's 1943 paper in which they had argued that the activity of neurons could be expressed propositionally.[6] Using a gyropilot salvaged from a B-24 bomber, a series of vacuum tube circuits that worked as artificial "neurons," and forty automated control knobs whose positions served as the machine's memory, the "rat" learned a path to a predetermined endpoint, initially through random selection and then by reinforcing correct choices that made "it easier for the machine to make this choice again."[7]

SNARC not only demonstrated a powerful analogy between neurophysiology and the design of machine hardware, but also propositional logic's power for articulating the function of both neural and mechanical systems. Following McCulloch and Pitts's article, the operations of neurons could be expressed using true and false statements, which in the case of Minsky's machine, appeared replicable through circuits. In this way, matter could be practically treated as programmable and logic could be seen as materially instantiated.[8]

In such a situation, the definition of a system's identity as distinct and autonomous, whether a human brain or a set of scrap aeronautical parts, did not need to resort to questions of substance as they often had in metaphysical discourses following Aristotle. Instead, entities emerged as distinct through recognition of their own ability to generate distinctions. The difference between a brain and a machine was operational, not ontological, if such a difference existed at all. SNARC thus summoned the specter of a computer age question that would haunt

---

6   Warren S. McCulloch and Walter H. Pitts, "A Logical Calculus of the Ideas Immanent in Nervous Activity," *Bulletin of Mathematical Biophysics* 5 (1943): 115–33. One of the key motivations was the idea that the material, physiological operations of neural nets, which could remain "quiet" or "fire" were based on a "threshold" and corresponded with binary logical propositions. The design and results of SNARC are lucidly described in Minsky's dissertation based on the project in Marvin Lee Minsky's "Theory of Neural-Analog Reinforcement Systems and Its Application to the Brain-Model Problem" (PhD diss., Princeton University, 1954).

7   Jeremy Bernstein, "A.I," *The New Yorker*, December 14, 1981, accessed September 1, 2017, https://www.newyorker.com/magazine/1981/12/14/a-i. The article includes extensive material from Bernstein's interview with Minsky and the citation quotes Minsky's response to the interviewer.

8   Mary M. Poulton notes that although "Minsky demonstrated that a network using the principles of Hebbian learning could be implemented as a machine, the SNARC did not develop any new theories about learning," in *Computational Neural Networks for Geophysical Data Processing*, ed. Mary M. Poulton (Oxford: Pergamon, 2001), 11. Hebbian learning is a theory developed by Donald O. Hebb, important to the development of computational neural networks, that established the role of "weighted connections to define the relationship between processing elements in a network" (ibid., 10). When paired with McCulloch and Pitts's idea that the probability for firing is governed by a neuron's threshold and the strength of the input, the machine "learns" through a changing series of thresholds. For a more detailed account of the intersections between these theories, see Raul Rojas, *Neural Networks: A Systematic Introduction* (Berlin: Springer, 1996).

both cybernetic theories and motivate the subsequent posthumanistic scholarship that would draw upon them: how systems could locate and define themselves from their environment once the organization of matter was analyzed purely according to information.

No one would be tempted to call Minsksy's machine "intelligent," whether artificially or otherwise, as its "unrewarded behavior" was more or less random and thus it "could never formulate a plan."[9] The machine lacked a position of self-observation from which it could take account of itself as a whole to make projections about future, hypothetical states. It could not gain a view from the outside nor define itself as autonomous and distinct from its environment. Despite being a machine explicitly dedicated to a task of navigation, it paradoxically could not *orient* itself. The union of materiality and logic meant that there was no apparent, localizable seat of consciousness that created a definite boundary between the inside and outside of the system. Such a machine required *recursion*, which is to say, it had to be digital.[10] As Minsky himself observed, "the machine, being a physical object, and not digital in operation, cannot be described completely."[11] The possibility for "description," or universal "computability" following the Church–Turing thesis, relied on the introduction of discrete values that made the continuous operations of the machine into a sequence to which subsequent functions could be applied. This is why the SNARC's regulation of pulses was paired with "thresholds" that instituted either/or values, following McCulloch and Pitts, and the reason for Minsky's frequent consideration of "time-quantization" in his dissertation. Continuous, analog, real-time operations did not allow for self-observation. To gain a point of observation, there had to be *points*. Getting oriented required that the analog machine be made digital, a fact that N. Katherine Hayles associates with an "ideology of

---

9   Bernstein, "A.I."
10 Cristopher Moore's paper, "Recursion Theory on the Reals and Continuous-time Computation," *Theoretical Computer Science* 162, no. 1 (August 5, 1996): 23–44, is cited frequently to support the possibility of recursion for analog processes. As he writes: "to discuss the physical world (or at least its classical limit) in which the states of things are described by real numbers and processes take place in continuous time, we need a different theory: a theory of analog computation, where states and processes are inherently continuous, and which treats real numbers not as sequences of digits but as quantities in themselves." Ibid., 23. However, conceptually, and for our purposes, it is enough to observe that discreteness is always reintroduced at some level to make recursion possible. His introduction of function composition on the Reals, for instance, relies on the "constants of 0 and 1." Ibid., 25. On the mathematics involved in this point I am grateful to Adam Kay.
11 Minsky, "Reinforcement Systems," 4/33.

dematerialization" and a "platonic backhand" that "made embodied reality into a blurred and messy instantiation of the clean abstractions of logical forms."[12] To be made digital was to be made metaphysical. However, the sense of "universals" involved in universal computability and which Herz would surreptitiously build into his reflections on vertigo, were not universals that would have been recognizable to Kant or Plato.

Figuring out how to digitalize analog processes was essential to questions of autopoiesis, self-reference, and closure that were so critical to machine learning and subsequent theories of second-order cybernetics and systems theory that reckoned with both human and mechanical systems.[13] Commenting in his dissertation on the design and implementation of SNARC, Minsky wrote:

> The next idea I had, which I worked on for my doctoral thesis, was to give the network a second memory, which remembered *after* a response what the stimulus had been. This enabled one to bring in the idea of prediction. If the machine or animal is confronted with a new situation, it can search its memory to see what would happen if it reacted in certain ways ... I had the naïve idea that if one could build a big enough network, with enough memory loops, it might get lucky and acquire the ability to envision things in its head.[14]

It was clear that neither simply enlarging the physical network nor revising the logic of the system was sufficient to achieve the autonomy that would truly allow for a comparison between the machine and the human intelligence Minsky sought to replicate. The machine could find its way through a maze, but it could not find itself within it. For that, the material operations of the circuits would have to constantly take stock of the machine's previous, collective behaviors for the sake of speculating about future operations. In this way, it had to produce a form of mechanical metaphysics—a stable form of conceptual self-identity that

---

12 N. Katherine Hayles, *How We Became Posthuman: Virtual Bodies in Cybernetics, Literature, and Informatics* (Chicago: University of Chicago Press, 1999), 193, 57.

13 Niklas Luhmann observed, for example, that in order to become an "entity with a boundary, with an inside and outside," that is, to gain a sense of orientation, a system "has to start every operation from a historical state that is its own product (the input of its own output)" and "it has to face its future as a *succession* of marked and unmarked states of self-referential and hetero-referential indications." In "The Paradox of Observing Systems," *Theories of Distinction: Redescribing the Descriptions of Modernity*, ed. William Rasch (Stanford: Stanford University Press, 2002), 84. Emphasis mine.

14 Bernstein, "A.I."

allowed it to alter its functions according to previous and future states. From the physical operations of the machine a unity had to emerge as something more than a mere random, physical sequence. And this had to be embedded as a part of the way that the machine itself worked. It also required that analog processes of pulse regulation be treated as discrete, finite, and digital. Computation required quantity and quantity required discrete values.

What SNARC underscores is a core posthumanist concern that was inaugurated by new technologies and subsequent cybernetic theories that blurred or at least profoundly tested the boundaries between organisms and machines. Information and materiality were no longer separate, but rather interreliant to the extent that information was "sunk so deeply into the system as to become indistinguishable from the organizational properties defining the system as such."[15] Matters of orientation once again became paramount for philosophers addressing mind/body dualism. If consciousness as a specific mode of operational self-awareness had no native home in matter or information—the *Geist* of the twentieth and twenty-first centuries—then "self-orientation" was a byproduct of endless "recursive interactions" that originated the "apparent paradox of self-description: *self-consciousness*."[16] That is to say, metaphysics had become digital, rather than merely mechanical. Subjects and "things" could not emerge without being "differentiated from some other 'thing' by displaying discontinuity, by having a boundary."[17] To introduce recursive functions that organized systems into distinct entities involved breaking up their continuous processes. The intractability of the problem Minsky faced in the inability of the machine to "envision" and therefore to orient itself was the heart of subsequent discourses in posthumanism, and was a part of the entanglements of matter and mind, and material and information that destabilized concepts of identity and self-identity that had preceded them.

The "rat" in the maze was both a figurative and functional instance of the tension between material systems and metaphysical unities that found expression beginning in the late eighteenth century discourses about the concept of "orientation." A notion of orientation (as well as disorientation) was critical for any philosophical or computational system that sought to take on the question of a material system's definition and autonomy or closure. In both cases, understanding a system, whether artificial intelligence or reasoning subject, demanded

---

15 Hayles, *How We Became Posthuman*, 11.
16 Humberto Maturana, *Autopoiesis and Cognition: The Realization of the Living* (Boston: D. Reidel Publishing, 1980), 29.
17 Robert Pepperell, *The Posthuman Condition: Consciousness beyond the Brain* (Bristol, UK: Intellect, 2003), 73.

that one locate it as distinct from its objects. This is a deceptively difficult task that has not become easier since the Enlightenment. Minsky affirms as much with respect to artificial intelligence when he writes of what he calls "'perceptron' type machines," that their "mystique" is:

> based in part on the idea that when such a machine learns the information stored is not localized in any particular spot but is, instead, "distributed throughout" the structure of the machine's network. It was a great disappointment, in the first half of the twentieth century, that experiments did not support nineteenth century concepts of the localization of memories (or most other "faculties") in highly local brain areas.[18]

The shift he is describing is a move from the psychic locality that had troubled experimental psychologists from Gustav Fechner to Sigmund Freud, to cybernetic theories that located consciousness as one among many informational *processes*. Even if SNARC had successfully replicated an oriented subject, what was the site of consciousness? As Herz had also recognized, in a distributed network the interface between mind and material was in the operationalization of matter.

Moving beyond mere parallels between computational machines and the brain, there is a more universal issue about how systems of any kind could be viewed *as* systems that has acted as a guiding force for philosophical inquiry at least since the Enlightenment. If the identity of both subjects and objects is not to be seen as an irreducible ontological given, what are the grounds on which the sensible world gets organized into recognizable unities? That is to say, how can an entity locate itself as distinct from its environment? For physical systems this question is particularly salient, because distinction, autonomy, and observation are all bound up in the internal operations of the machine. While the question of systems as put forth by Minsky and proponents of cybernetics appears deeply wedded to the technologies that prompted shifts toward posthumanism, the difficulty of achieving principles of philosophical orientation were not the exclusive province of the computer age.

---

18 Marvin L. Minsky and Seymour A. Papert, *Perceptrons: An Introduction to Computational Geometry* (Cambridge, MA: MIT, 1988), 19. Minsky and Papert define a "perceptron" as "a device capable of computing all predicates which are linear in some given set Φ of partial predicates" (ibid., 3).

Enlightened Machines

For all of the spectacular threats and possibilities suggested by machine learning and its erosion of the carefully tended partitions of essential humanist categories, the transcendental subject around 1800 faced many of the same challenges as the 1950s electronic rat in the maze. The origins of the Kantian subject, which has been a continuing target of critique, was itself born of a critical indecision between materialism and idealism bound to questions about how to get one's bearings. It is tempting to draw neat historical and philosophical distinctions between the "posthuman subject" as "an amalgam, a collection of heterogeneous components, a material-informational entity whose boundaries undergo construction and reconstruction," and the unitary Kantian subject, which was never lost because it was the precondition for any boundary in the first place.[19] Yet, the pressure to reconcile a rising tide of empirical physiological investigation with the presupposition of a rationally cohesive subject prompted discord at the end of the eighteenth century about how such a subject could arise from the networks of nerves that seemed to be so essential to the experiences of the mind.

Nowhere was this more deftly articulated than in Marcus Herz's work on vertigo. Herz's simultaneous significance and obscurity within the German intellectual tradition is the result of his relationship to Kant, who both overshadowed and facilitated his philosophical career. Kant was Herz's acknowledged "philosophical mentor" and continued to be a friend and source of intellectual validation, even as Herz later assumed a more oppositional and at times embittered position toward his onetime teacher.[20] Not infrequently, Herz's legacy is framed as a failure to come to terms with not only ideas that Kant had already refuted in his "precritical" works of the 1750s and 1760s, but also to fully grasp the central tenets of his later critical program. One of the more salient instances of this tension was evident in the foundational issue of the "relationship between body and soul" that was the "very premise of rational and empirical psychology," on which Herz took a stance that had already

---

19 Hayles, *How We Became Posthuman*, 4.
20 Martin L. Davies, *Identity of History?: Marcus Herz and the End of the Enlightenment* (Detroit: Wayne State University Press, 1995), 29. Herz was selected as the respondent to Kant's inaugural dissertation in 1770 against the objections of the university senate, which was remarkable, not least of all because Herz had Jewish heritage (see ibid., 20). On the relationship between Herz and Kant, see also Martin L. Davies, "Gedanken zu einem ambivalenten Verhältnis: Marcus Herz und Immanuel Kant," in *Kant und die Berliner Aufklärung, Akten des IX. Internationalen Kant-Kongresses, Band V: Sektionen XV–XVIII*, ed. Volker Gerhardt, Rolf-Peter Horstmann and Ralph Schumacher (Berlin: de Gruyter, 2001), 141–7. Christoph Maria Leder has likewise detailed the nature and transformation of

been supposedly "ridiculed" in Kant's 1765 work, *Träume eines Geistersehers*.[21] As a physician in Berlin, who not only offered long-distance medical advice to Kant, but who also served as the doctor to the intellectual vanguard of Berlin, including Moses Mendelssohn, Karl Philipp Moritz, and Friedrich Schleiermacher, Herz sought to bring his medical knowledge to bear on philosophical inquiry in a way that had been foreclosed by Kant.[22] On the one hand, this enterprise was propelled by the aspiration to align his own medical perspective with the philosophy of his master. On the other hand, it was a shot across the Kantian bow.

Contending with physiological research on nerves undertaken by figures like Albrecht von Haller, philosophy had already sought new principles to stabilize the unity of subjects and objects alike. If the brain was a network, transmitting signals that were involved in the production of consciousness as the "animal mechanics" of Haller implied, where was consciousness located and how could one define its boundaries?[23] What was the position from which those boundaries became visible? Or, as Kant would ask in his response to the pantheism controversy in which he addressed Friedrich Heinrich Jacobi and Moses Mendelssohn in particular, "What Does It Mean to Orient Oneself in Thinking?"[24] In

---

their relationship in *Die Grenzgänger des Marcus Herz: Beruf, Haltung und Identität eines jüdischen Arztes gegen Ende des 18. Jahrhunderts* (Münster: Waxmann Verlag, 2007). Herz's important relationship to Kant is further supported by the fact that a great many scholars point toward Kant's 1772 letter to him as the blueprint for Kant's critical turn and the *Critique of Pure Reason*. Immanuel Kant to Marcus Herz, February 21, 1772, in *Correspondence*, 132–8. Ernst Cassirer calls this letter "the first seed of the First Critique" and more generally argues that Herz held a special and continuing position of intellectual intimacy with Kant in *Kant's Life and Thought*, trans. James Haden (New Haven: Yale University Press, 1981), 146. Leeann Hansen also offers an excellent account of the development of Herz's thinking about the mind-body problem with respect to Kant and the larger intellectual contexts of philosophy and psychology around 1800 in "From Enlightenment to Naturphilosophie: Marcus Herz, Johann Christian Reil, and the Problem of Border Crossing," *Journal of the History of Biology* 26, no. 1 (Spring 1993): 39–64.

21 Davies, *Identity of History?*, 66.
22 Herz's roster of famous patients is described in Christoph Maria Leder's, *Die Grenzgänger des Marcus Herz*.
23 Albrecht von Haller, *Elementa physiologie corporis humani* (Lausanne: Francisci Grasset, 1772). See also "De partibus corporis humani sensilibus et irritabilibus," *Novi commentarii Societatis Regiae Scientiarum Gottingensis* (1752), 1–36. For more on these two works by Haller, his mechanistic physiology, and his experimental methods, see Shirley A. Roe "Anatomia Animate: The Newtonian Physiology of Albrecht von Haller," in *Transformation and Tradition in the Sciences*, ed. Everett Mendelsohn (Cambridge: Cambridge University Press, 1984), 273–302.
24 Immanuel Kant, "What Does It Mean to Orient Oneself in Thinking?" in *Religion and Rational Theology*, ed. Allen W. Wood (Cambridge: Cambridge University Press, 1996), 7–18.

the clash over the source for the coherence of the world in which the reasoning subject found itself—and the coherence of the subject as itself a part of that world—the term "orientation" (*Orientierung*) became a watchword of German philosophy.[25] Once information and materiality were seen as separable (if interreliant), the external logic of the technical systems by which one established a meridian within the world of objects was imported into the very matter of how a subject—*as a material system*—could emerge at all. Herz and others called nervous pathways "nerve channels [*Nervenkanäle*]," suggesting that the signals transmitted through them were distinct from the channels themselves, even where they could never be separated.[26] In this way operations supplanted ontologies and the internal orienting force for the "compass of reason," was faced with the threat of losing its transcendental poles almost as soon as Kant had secured them.[27]

These were persisting difficulties for philosophical systems that Immanuel Kant had already partially addressed. In the *First Critique* he wrote that "speculative reason," which defines the realm of possibility for metaphysics, does not provide "constitutive principles for the extension of our cognition to more objects than experience can give," but offers "regulative principles for the systematic unity of the manifold of empirical cognition in general, through which this cognition, within its proper boundaries, is cultivated and corrected."[28] A unified system, recognized as a unity, arose for Kant not through first assuming the existence of an ontology, but as a "regulative" principle bound to its own empirical operations. It is neither outside of what is empirically detectable nor derived from empirical observation, but nevertheless sets the limits according to which empirical objects are defined. Kant connected metaphysical with empirical concerns by doing what David Hume's radical insistence on empiricism would not allow: recursion. Recursive functions were not *a priori*, but they governed possible cases that had not yet occurred and thus could not be observed empirically.

---

25 There are several works that deal with the question of orientation and vertigo during the Enlightenment. See Rebekka Ladewig, *Schwindel: Eine Epistemologie der Orientierung* (Tübingen: Mohr Siebeck, 2016); Werner Stegmaier, *Philosophie der Orientierung* (Berlin: de Gruyter, 2008).
26 Herz, *Versuch über den Schwindel*, 126.
27 Immanuel Kant to Friedrich Heinrich Jacobi, August 30, 1789, in *Correspondence*, 319. Kant is weighing in on issues wedded to the pantheism debate, arguing that no matter how Reason arises as the guiding force in thought, once it is present it must be presupposed. In the same letter he is also referencing his essay on orientation.
28 Immanuel Kant, *Critique of Pure Reason*, ed. Paul Guyer and Allen W. Wood (Cambridge: Cambridge University Press, 1998), 606.

It is for much the same reason that Niklas Luhmann, who has exerted such influence in the development of posthumanism, described his own theory by quoting his teacher Talcott Parsons, calling it a "second-best theory."[29] We arrive too late to the scene and are not in the position to detect the origins of systems. The best we can do is to uncover preconditions for those systems that are not a simple aggregate of data resulting from purely empirical observation. The speculative element of such speculative reason was backward-facing wherever future states were concerned in much the same way that Minksy described the failure of "prediction" with SNARC. Recursion allowed a system to assume its own unity as a condition of the operations that made the recognition of that unity possible. It was a mode of orientation that sought to reconcile the smooth borders of metaphysical entities with the messy bundles of empirical systems. Yet at the same time the principles of order that regulated the empirical universe were definitely not seen as empirical in nature. They were attached to a sensing subject whose powers of reason were not available to direct investigation.

When applied to the subject itself, the dangers of recursivity inherent in the contact between transcendental philosophy and empiricism were apparent. Kant himself denied psychology a position as an empirical science, claiming "inner observation can be separated only by mere division of thought," meaning that the object of inquiry was inseparable from, and therefore impacted, the means of inquiry—thinking about thinking was a feedback loop.[30] From the position of transcendental idealism this was problematic, because it failed to fortify a boundary between subject and object that clarified the rules of interaction between the two in such a way that universally valid claims could be made. The prospect of a new groundwork for metaphysics, and with it the promise of clearly defined domains of legitimate sciences announced in the *Prolegomena* (1783) and soon after in the *Metaphysical Foundations of Natural Science* (1786), relied on clear conditions of observation and distinction. If reason were operationally instantiated in the matter it organized, it faced what Heinz von Foerster would later call "logical problems associated with the concept of closure."[31] Namely, the observer, who functioned to define the system as distinct and autonomous, was a part of the system itself. Kant repeatedly isolated

---

29 Niklas Luhmann, *Introduction to Systems Theory*, ed. Dirk Baecker, trans. Peter Gilgen (Cambridge: Polity, 2013), 3.
30 Immanuel Kant, *Metaphysical Foundations of Natural Science*, ed. Michael Friedman (Cambridge: Cambridge University Press, 2004), 7.
31 Heinz von Foerster, "Disorder/Order: Discovery or Invention?" in *Understanding Understanding: Essays on Cybernetics and Cognition* (New York: Springer, 2003), 281.

the dangers of what one could call recursive contamination within the long arc of his philosophical project during his "critical period" (following the publication of the *Critique of Pure Reason* in 1781). Questions of philosophical orientation continually resurfaced as questions of recursion in the effort to explain how the observer/subject was not itself ensnared in the messy contingencies of empirical relations that reason is supposed to have clarified.

Kant defines what it means to "*orient* oneself" as "to use a given direction ... in order to find the others—literally to find the sunrise"; that is, to orient oneself means to have a definite coordinate that functions to establish the others.[32] However, he was adamant that the orienting force for philosophical systems is never present merely in the body nor the objects among which the subject finds itself, but derives from a "*subjective* ground of differentiation."[33] To demonstrate this, he used a thought experiment, in which "all the constellations, one day by a miracle" are "reversed in their direction, so that what was east now became west," such that "no human eye would notice the slightest alteration on the next bright starlit night" and "even the astronomer" would "inevitably become *disoriented*."[34] The resolution to this cosmic reversal comes from the "faculty of making distinctions through the feeling of right and left," which is clearly not simply an empirical nor an absolute difference, as "these two sides outwardly display no designatable difference in intuition," but introduce a mode of digital distinction.[35] As such, Kant retreats from the operational distinctions that could connect subjective reason to the embodied subject, preferring to frame the difference between right and left as an intuition that is not *a priori*, but which is nevertheless beyond objects. He continues:

> it will be a concern of pure reason to guide its use when it wants to leave the familiar objects (of experience) behind, extending itself beyond all the bounds of experience and finding no object of intuition at all, but merely a space for intuition; for then it is no longer in a position to bring its judgments under a determinate maxim according to objective grounds of cognition, but solely to bring its judgments under a determinate maxim according to a subjective ground of differentiation in the determination of its own faculties of judgment.[36]

---

32 Kant, "What Does It Mean to Orient Oneself in Thinking?," 8.
33 Ibid.
34 Ibid., 9.
35 Ibid.
36 Ibid., 9–10.

In this highly elliptical explication, Kant demurs on what is a clear intersection of objective distinction (e.g., right hand versus left hand) and the "subjective ground" for such a distinction. Difference can signify as difference for Kant only by moving the source of the distinction out of the realm of the empirical. He therefore stabilizes difference as external to the objects it organizes, avoiding the possibility of the "recursive complexities of observation, mediation, and communication" that would propel and also trouble later "neocybernetic systems theory" dealing with similar questions.[37] Orientation required an outside. And that outside, in the case of objects for Kant, was ultimately Reason. However, Herz's captivation with the emerging field of neurophysiology, would demand that reason not be divorced from the material systems on which it increasingly seemed to rely and in which it was inescapably embedded.

The Kantian synthetic *a priori* was supposed to lend scientific inquiry "a pilot, who, provided with complete sea-charts and a compass, might safely navigate the ship ... following sound principles of the helmsman's art drawn from knowledge of the globe."[38] The language of navigation derives much from his courses on geography given in Königsberg, but the intellectual motives were squarely at the center of the philosophical project started in *Critique of Pure Reason* and something with which his students and successors, including Herz, would contend. Much like SNARC, the pilot's ability to navigate did not account for the transcendental subject's fundamental orientation. For that, one would need to understand not just the subject's position with respect to objects in the world, but the way in which both the subject and objects were constituted and distinguished. What was required was an operational position of observation that made sense of the contact between matter and reason, logic and materiality, information and medium. This made the physiological element of cognition extremely problematic for Kant and made Herz's challenges noteworthy, especially where it concerned the growing interest in the experimental psychology that would dominate the nineteenth century, often displacing philosophy itself in the universities.[39]

---

37   Bruce Clarke and Mark B.N. Hansen "Introduction: Neocybernetic Emergence," in *Emergence and Embodiment: New Essays on Second-Order Systems Theory*, ed. Bruce Clarke and Mark B.N. Hansen (Durham, NC: Duke University Press, 2009), 6.
38   Immanuel Kant, "Prolegomena to Any Future Metaphysics," in *Prolegomena to Any Future Metaphysics with Selections from the Critique of Pure Reason*, ed. Gary Hatfield (Cambridge: Cambridge University Press, 2004), 12.
39   Much to the dismay of traditional philosophers, a tide of experimental psychologists and physiologists took over positions as the chairs of philosophy departments beginning in the middle of the nineteenth century. As just one notable example, Wilhelm Wundt, who was perhaps the single most important figure in the development of psychophysics, was appointed the chair of the philosophy department in Leipzig in 1875.

The Dizzy Subject

In 1786, the same year that Kant unequivocally refused psychology a position as a science in his *Metaphysische Anfangsgründe der Naturwissenschaft* (Metaphysical Foundations of Natural Science), Herz published the first edition of his book on vertigo, which he called a "medical-philosophical text."[40] The program he advanced under this aegis continued a negotiation between empirical psychology and metaphysics already underway in his earlier work *Briefe an Aerzte* (Letters to Doctors), but was reformulated as what can only be read as a resolute challenge to Kant, announcing "I will repeat this once more: one can think what one wants about speculative philosophy—psychology does not belong to its domain, but rather constitutes an essential part of natural science [*Naturlehre*] like the science of bodies."[41] This was diametrically opposed to Kant's argument the same year where he argued "the empirical doctrine of the soul can never become anything more than an historical doctrine of nature."[42] In this context, one can indeed read Herz's statement as a salvo, albeit one undertaken with the hope of reconciling his physiological research with transcendental idealism.

While Herz rigorously details vertigo's potential causes—from fever to drunkenness—it is clear that the work is also motivated by the objective of establishing a program of philosophical medicine that explained how the subject emerged from the seeming chaos of material operations. As Herz recognized, vertigo could not be of purely physiological nor purely psychological origins. It was an interface disorder involving an error in the representation of the subject to her/himself with respect to his/her representations of external objects. As cited earlier, vertigo for Herz was a condition caused by the succession of mental representations that were "too-rapid." Various factors, such as age, sex, and physical disposition influenced what it meant to be "too-rapid" according to each person's constitution, meaning that no absolute baseline value for the onset of dizziness could be defined. Moreover, the condition was of particular interest precisely because its causes could either be in the body or the mind, with Herz remarking that the "correlation is fully reciprocal."[43]

---

40 Herz, *Versuch über den Schwindel*, a4. Herz sent Kant a copy of the book and, although Kant responded with extreme warmth, referring to him as "my dearest friend," Kant did not have "time to read it through completely," in Immanuel Kant to Marcus Herz, April 7, 1786, in *Correspondence*, 251.
41 Ibid. As a testament to the empirical commitments of the work, Karl Philipp Moritz published a section of Herz's book in his *Magazin zur Erfahrungsseelenkunde*.
42 Kant, *Metaphysical Foundations of Natural Science*, 7.
43 Ibid., 23.

As a disruption of "representation," vertigo diagnosed a malfunction in the points of contact between empiricism and metaphysics as outlined by Kant, who had argued "no thing in itself is cognized" through "mere relations" and the representation of "outer sense" can only contain "the relation of an object to the subject."[44] The error leading to disorientation was not in the objects, which one could assume remained relatively fixed, nor the axioms according to which those objects became apprehensible, nor purely in the perceptions themselves, which, even where clearly errant, properly conveyed the state of dizziness in which the perceiver found her/himself. Instead, the malfunction was a failure of *synchronization* between external inputs and the internal conceptualization of those inputs as they related to the perceptual system as a whole. Like Kant, Herz recognized that things *an sich*, even where a necessary presupposition, sufficed to stabilize the uniformities of empirical observation. And this fact was captured by cases of dizziness that were of an "intermixed nature," and stood at the "introduction to the soul."[45] Prior to the discovery of the semicircular canal, which moved the point of interest almost entirely back into the body, Herz's extended account of vertigo maintained the tenuously balanced voussoir stones of body and mind, the keystone for which was an implied concept of orientation tied to sequences of mental representations.[46] Herz's was an informational model of the soul, but one that sought to find its order in the workings of the body itself.

In order to move the locus of the subject's orientation from the *a priori* to "representations" directly bound to the function of the nervous system, Herz created a hybrid of older theories. He selectively borrowed from Albrecht von Haller's empirical observation and experimentation on the dependency of sensation on nerves, which was a partial rejection of the harder-lined mechanistic view of the Leiden physiologist, Herman Boerhaave.[47] Despite Haller's position as a forerunner to positivism, Herz appropriated the idea of a distinctly humanistic form of materialism that allowed him to maintain a notion of vitalism that did

---

44 Kant, *Critique of Pure Reason*, 189.
45 Herz, *Versuch über den Schwindel*, 34–5.
46 Experimental psychologists such as Marie-Jean-Pierre Flourens, Johannes Müller, Ernst Mach, and William James began research on the semicircular canal in the middle of the nineteenth century continuing through the early twentieth century.
47 A comprehensive description of Haller's work and its context is available in Hubert Steinke, *Irritating Experiments: Haller's Concept and the European Controversy on Irritability and Sensibility, 1750–90* (Amsterdam: Rodopi, 2005).

not reduce the properties of mental life to material processes.[48] He drew directly from Georg Ernst Stahl, who had been an important figure at Halle earlier in the century and who had argued that the mechanical body was not acted upon externally by the soul, but was fully ensouled, governed by forces that themselves could never be directly perceived.[49] In this view the soul was neither reducible to nor directly connected to the machinations of the body, and the generative source for the body's animation remained largely unconscious.

To preserve the continuity of physiological processes as they related to the mind, or a *sensorium commune*, Herz also paradoxically recovered an idea of nerve transmission by fluids, that had been proposed by Boerhaave and dismissed by Haller, arguing that "nerve fluid [*Nervensaft*]" was relayed through specialized "vessels [*Gefässe*]."[50] "Mechanistic" theories generally relied on the intermittence of sequential causality, where one event causes another, then another, then another. Fluids, however, through the continuities of their movement, had the advantage of making the system appear continuous. This had the effect of, if not mirroring the metaphysical contiguity of the subject, at least complementing it in the body. To this end, in the second edition of his work on vertigo, Herz also included Ernst Platner's concept of "material ideas," which Platner understood as "movements of the brain fibers, which through their largely inexplicable effects in the soul, excite representations [*Vorstellungen*] in the soul."[51] The dynamic nature of Platner's description in some ways suited Herz's systems-based understanding of the connection between nerves and consciousness, though it defied Kant's earlier claim that "inquiries as to the manner in which bodily organs are connected with thought" are "eternally futile": a position Kant would never abandon.[52]

---

48 Martin L. Davies notes that in "assimilating Haller to Boerhaave to defend his own metaphysical interests, Herz had to minimize the importance of Haller's empirical anatomical research, which meant disregarding its reductive, positivistic character, hence neutralizing its historically anticipatory dimension" in *Identity of History*, 127–8. There were also obvious theological implications connected with the pantheism controversy and Kant's intervention on behalf of Mendelssohn's position and, as Davies points out, "the pietistic legacy that characterized philosophy of medicine in Halle during the Enlightenment." Ibid., 128.

49 Georg Ernst Stahl, *Theoria Medica Vera, Physiologiam et Pathologiam* [1708] (Halle: D. Joan Junckeri, 1737). See also the comprehensive work by Johanna Geyer-Kordesch, *Pietismus, Medizin und Aufklärung in Preußen im 18. Jahrhundert: Das Leben und Werk Georg Ernst Stahls* (Tübingen: Max Niemeyer Verlag, 2000).

50 Herz, *Versuch über den Schwindel*, 101.

51 Ernst Platner, *Neue Anthropologie für Aerzte und Weltweise* (Leipzig: Siegfried Lebrecht Crusius, 1790), 125.

52 Immanuel Kant to Marcus Herz, "toward the end of 1773," in *Correspondence*, 141. Kant here is discussing the preparation of his lecture course on anthropology and Herz's review of Platner's *Anthropologie*.

Herz still had to contend with how to stabilize the relationship between nerve functions and the ordered unities of mind if representations could "not be thought *locally* [*örtlich*]."[53] Kant sharply addressed a critique of this problem in his response to Samuel Thomas von Soemmerring's *Organ der Seele*, remarking that if one assumes "a faculty of nerves underlies the mind in its empirical thinking," even where the transmission mechanism was assumed to be fluid in nature, the decomposition of and recombination of stimuli to form representations would be continuously being organized "without ever being organized."[54] Such systems would struggle to achieve a "permanent organization" that could "make comprehensible the collective unity of all sensory representations in a common sense organ (*sensorium commune*)."[55] Kant went on to argue:

> The actual task, as formulated by Haller, is still not solved by this. It is not merely a physiological task but is supposed also to serve as a means of figuring out the unity of the consciousness of oneself (which belongs to the understanding) in the spatial relationship of the *soul* to the organs of the brain (which belongs to the outer sense), hence the seat of the soul, as its *local* presence—which is a task for metaphysics, yet one that is not only unsolvable for the latter but also in itself contradictory.—For if I am to render intuitive the location of my soul, i.e., of my absolute self, anywhere in space, I must perceive myself through the very same sense by which I also perceive the matter immediately surrounding me, just as it happens when I want to determine my place in the world *as a human being*, namely I must consider my body in relation to other bodies outside me.—But the soul can perceive itself only through the inner sense, while it perceives the body (whether internally or externally) only through outer senses, and consequently it can determine absolutely no location for itself, because for that it would have to make itself into an object of its own outer intuition and would have to *place itself outside itself*, which is self-contradictory.[56]

---

53 Herz, *Versuch über den Schwindel*, 229. The problem of "psychic locality" was a specter that would haunt positivistic psychological research throughout the nineteenth century, extending from Herbart all the way to the early writings of Freud.
54 Immanuel Kant, "From Soemmerring's *On the organ of the soul*," in *Anthropology, History, and Education*, ed. Günter Zöller and Robert B. Louden (Cambridge: Cambridge University Press, 2007), 225.
55 Ibid.
56 Ibid., 225–6. The final emphasis is mine.

Here Kant reiterates something already familiar from his writing on psychology and natural science, but which is specifically tailored to refuse attempts to suggest that physical systems were even logically capable of orienting the subject.[57] The problem of ideational unities' contiguousness could be replicated with a division of analog and digital functions, but not if information was fully embodied. Like the secondary memory mentioned by Minsky or the necessity of second-order observation in cybernetics, an outside point of observation had to be substituted with recursion. And recursion was fundamentally digital. On the other hand, this entailed elaborate theoretical contortions to make sense of how analog processes could be treated digitally, and as Kant, von Foerster, and Luhmann alike would notice, this could lead to continuously "being organized" without "permanent organization" in the effort to have the body "place itself outside itself."

Herz's delicate orchestration of prior physiological theories with Kantian idealism escaped the pitfalls of psychic locality by operationalizing matter in a way that would have been familiar to Marvin Minsky and Dean Edmonds. By combining a fluid-based idea of neurophysiology that was both mechanical and continuous with the procession of mental representations as the ordering principle of the soul, Herz was touching on a digital/analog divide that would challenge theorists beyond the twentieth century. As he recognized, neither the fixity of the subject position, nor the feeling of its disorientation could be the result of a mirrored relationship between physiological systems and mental representations, physiological systems and objects, or objects and the soul. In short, the orienting force for the subject could not be analog. As Herz writes, the fact that a vertiginous feeling of the world spinning could be the result of the body itself spinning should not "seduce" us to a "mode of mechanical clarification of the effects of the soul from analogous physical changes."[58] The world did not seem like it was spinning because something in the body was also spinning. Rather the order or disorder of the soul was tied to sequences of information as "representations" that were either too rapid or too slow.[59]

---

57 Leif Weatherby writes of the intersections between these physiological theories "where Platner had rejected a 'visible' locale of this interaction, Soemmerring incautiously proposed a point where physiology and metaphysics could meet." He also gives an impressive analysis of the philosophical history of the role of the term "organ" in mediating between metaphysics and physiology. In *Transplanting the Metaphysical Organ: German Romanticism between Leibniz and Marx* (New York: Fordham University Press, 2016), 119.
58 Herz, *Versuch über den Schwindel*, 209.
59 Herz plays on the term "*Weile*," attributing "boredom [*Langweile*]" to an overly long (*lang*) "*Weile*."

In place of analog relations between the various domains connecting the mind to the body Herz argued for a rule of periodicity. Just as Minsky's machine operated on thresholds introduced to regulate the propagation or inhibition of pulses, each person for Herz was individually governed by a general law of the measure of his/her "natural interval [*natürliche Weile*]."[60] Thus, in both the case of nerve transmission and mental representations the stability of the system was a product of sequence—of the pauses that made the continuities of the body function discretely. The continuous, analog processes of nerve fluid were rendered digital. There was no physical isomorphism between the mind and the body, but there was an operational, informational integration of the two. Ideas were in fact material, as his references to Platner suggested, but not because objects exited as pre-constituted entities. Both subjects and objects were operationally rather than primordially unified through "sequences [*Reihen*]." Periodicity or "*Weilen*"—as a binarization of both representational and physical processes—created the grounds for internally inventing a point of external observation and systematic closure. To achieve this one did not need to first presume the noumenal existence of objects against the metaphysical sovereignty of the subject. Rather, the condition of vertigo offered a test case for examining the synchronization of intervals as the origin of a subject's sense of either stability and closure, or instability and dizziness.

Mental representations, which constituted the "entire essence of the human soul," according to Herz, did so *not* through the content of what they represented, but by encoding in their periodicity their own correspondence or discord with the periods of physical input. In cases of vertigo the objects were stable as objects. What was unstable was the meta-level recognition of one's relation to them. The subject saw that she/he was not seeing things correctly, arising from an asynchronicity between the intervals of representations and the physical inputs. In an effort to embody information, Herz encountered the same issues that led Kant to prohibit potential regressions of self-observation that von Foerster and others would later attribute to "closure," and Minsky's machine faced in the maze. The dizzying failure of the human machines detailed by Herz to achieve the seamless integration of information and materiality that characterized the transcendental coordinates of the subject underscored the imperfect union of the two. As much as the question of orientation seemed to be about finding oneself in the world, Herz's work demonstrated the degree to which knowing where one was required leaving it.

---

60 Ibid., 319.

Three Brain Matters in the German Enlightenment: Animal Cognition and Species Difference in Herder, Soemmerring, and Gall

Patrick Fortmann

"What is Man?" Immanuel Kant famously asked. In fact, he added the question somewhat belatedly to the list of fundamental concerns that philosophy seeks to address.[1] In his eyes, it concluded the catalog of philosophical queries because it already presupposed insights into the human condition which were gained through exercising the exclusively human faculties of understanding, reason, and the power of judgment (each the subject of one of his major critical treatises). Animal Studies, like so many other fields in the emerging Posthumanities, are unrelenting in pointing to the blind spot of such frameworks. Kant's transcendental philosophy and the subsequent German Idealism are by design unconcerned with humans' animal nature, let alone with nonhuman animals.[2] In his essay "Conjectural Beginning of Human History," Kant himself goes so far as to turn the mastery over the animal into a milestone of universal human history. He has man self-assuredly address the animal (a sheep), saying: *"Nature has given you the skin you wear not for you but for me,"* and then "[take] it off the sheep and put it on himself."[3] Only when man assumes the right to

---

1 Immanuel Kant, *Lectures on Logic*, ed. J. Michael Young (Cambridge: Cambridge University Press, 1992), 538. A previous list in the *Critique of Pure Reason* (B 833) did not include the question regarding man.
2 See, for instance, the chapter "Animals in Philosophy," in Paul Waldau, *Animal Studies: An Introduction* (Oxford: Oxford University Press, 2013), 143–60.
3 Immanuel Kant, "Conjectural Beginning of Human History," in *Anthropology, History, and Education*, ed. Günter Zöller and Robert B. Louden (Cambridge: Cambridge University Press, 2007), 167.

take control of the animal's body and its parts, turning his biological deficiency into an advantage, Kant suggests, does man truly become man. For Kant, it is the exercise of instrumental reason that makes man the exception, allowing him to draw a clear distinction between man and a companion species. By enacting such an agenda, Giorgio Agamben has observed, "man suspends his animality," while expelling the animal from the realm of beings that matter.[4] In a different mold but a related register, Cary Wolfe has recently drawn attention to the dramatic costs of a rigidly defined "biopolitical frame," one that defines life solely as human life.[5] Untenable as Kant's view may thus seem today, it is not surprising to students of the Posthumanities. Almost since its inception, Animal Studies has been combating Western philosophy's perceived human-centeredness—the preoccupation with an exclusionist, navel-gazing narrative that Jacques Derrida, in his landmark essay "The Animal That Therefore I Am (More to Follow)," has called "this auto-biography of man."[6] Historically, the approaches of Kant and his followers fall into the great lacuna of Animal Studies in philosophy, the seldom visited period between René Descartes and Charles Darwin.[7] Yet between the Cartesian dismissal of the animal as machine without cognition (acting "naturally and mechanically like a clock,"[8] confined to the *res extensa* and firmly separated from the *res cogitans* reserved for humans on the one side), and the uneasy evolutionary continuity of species Darwin suggested, philosophically minded naturalists of the Enlightenment have produced substantial work that, often more inadvertently than intentionally, undermines the human/animal

---

4   Giorgio Agamben, *The Open: Man and Animal*, trans. Kevin Attell (Stanford: Stanford University Press, 2004), 79.
5   Cary Wolfe, *Before the Law: Humans and Other Animals in a Biopolitical Frame* (Chicago and London: University of Chicago Press, 2013).
6   Jacques Derrida, *The Animal That Therefore I Am*, ed. Marie-Louise Mallet, trans. David Wills (New York: Fordham University Press, 2008), 24.
7   Recently, both endpoints of this period have been questioned. Despite his sweeping dismissal of the animal, even Descartes had to admit that human bodies share at least some traits with the bodies of other-than-human animals—an admission that leaves him open to challenges, including those fueled by his own skepticism. For such a reading against the grain, see Bernard Rollin, *Putting the Horse before Descartes: A Memoir* (Philadelphia: Temple University Press, 2011). Charles Darwin, on the other end of the spectrum, was greatly indebted to the leading figures of German Romanticism's philosophy of nature; Schelling, Oken, and, above all, Alexander von Humboldt. See Robert J. Richards, *The Romantic Conception of Life: Science and Philosophy in the Age of Goethe* (Chicago: University of Chicago Press, 2002), 526–40. On Darwin's impact on philosophy, see Michael Ruse, ed. *Philosophy after Darwin: Classic and Contemporary Readings* (Princeton: Princeton University Press, 2009).
8   Quoted in Waldau, *Animal Studies*, 144.

distinction—a distinction, to be sure, that present-day Animal Studies has thoroughly flattened.[9]

This article considers works by the theologian and cultural anthropologist Johann Gottfried Herder, the anatomist and philosophical physician Samuel Thomas Soemmerring, and the founder of phrenology Franz Joseph Gall. Each of them was active in the extended orbit of Kant and has launched inquiries into human nature that have far-reaching implications for the Enlightenment episteme of nonhuman animals. The work of these German Enlightenment critics, building on that of the French materialists, La Mettrie, Diderot, and Holbach, but predating the Romantic philosophy of nature (*Naturphilosophie*) in the manner of F. W. J. Schelling and Lorenz Oken, is particularly noteworthy for present-day Animal Studies.[10] Composed of one scholar with wide-ranging interests and a penchant for theoretical synthesis, and two anatomists doubling as philosophers, this triad interrogates philosophy's exceptionalist agenda at the time. By taking the long view on natural history, each of them probes human-nonhuman intersections precisely in the areas considered exclusive to humans—the discernable anatomy of the brain and the assumed capacity for thought. In so doing, they not only heed Animal Studies' persistent advice to develop species-transcending frameworks in epistemology and ethics long before it was given, but also forcefully insert Enlightenment science of the human into posthumanist discourses.[11]

The rapidly expanding field of Animal Studies, though spanning diverse approaches from different disciplines, is not, practitioners are keen to clarify, yet another iteration of Cultural Studies.[12] Refusing to add the animal to the ever-expanding list of cultural others, Animal Studies insist that the focus on species, instead of the human, requires a recalibration of inherently anthropocentric disciplinary practices, epistemological frameworks, and ethical approaches. Enlightenment

---

9 See, for instance, Matthew Calarco, *Thinking through Animals: Identity, Difference, Indistinction* (Stanford: Stanford University Press, 2015), 6: "One of the defining characteristics of our age is the radical breakdown of the human/animal distinction."
10 Both the French materialists and the German Romantics would be deserving of comparable studies.
11 For a survey of Posthumanist scholarship on anthropocentrism, speciesism and the interlinking categories of humanness and animality, see Rosi Braidotti, *The Posthuman* (Cambridge: Polity, 2013), 55–104; Pramod K. Nayar, *Posthumanism* (Cambridge: Polity, 2014), 87–98.
12 On the location of Animal Studies as critical inquiry, see Cary Wolfe, *What is Posthumanism?* (Minneapolis: University of Minnesota Press, 2010), 99–126 and, specifically with respect to Literary Studies, Cary Wolfe, "Human, All too Human: 'Animal Studies,' and the Humanities," *PMLA* 124 (2009): 564–75.

science, with its orientation toward natural history (*Naturgeschichte*), bends easily toward such species-inclusive views. From the late seventeenth to the end of the eighteenth century, the predominant model for taking stock of the species on earth was still the Great Chain of Being or *scala naturae*.[13] This concept assumes a seamless continuity, extending from the simplest organisms to highly developed humans. With this telos, the Chain appears to construct its biopolitical frame narrowly and conventionally, apparently spelling out just the kind of human "auto-biography" that Derrida had problematized. On the other hand, it imposes an all-encompassing order, of which man is but a part. Since this order is derived from metaphysical concepts, the Chain assigns each living being a defined position, a specific link, without allowing for gaps or ruptures in the chain. Such a structure ensures continuity as well as difference by bringing the species into contact while at the same time keeping them at a safe ontological distance from one another. The model faced challenges wherever metaphysics could not readily be mapped onto biology. The link between plants and animals, believed to be the freshwater polyp, *Hydra vulgaris*, was relatively unproblematic. But connecting animal to man, while simultaneously drawing a firm line in between, proved to be a different matter altogether. While the lesser, non-hominoid apes were seen as a safe candidate for the connection, the discovery of the great apes posed tremendous problems. The question, where to locate them on the *scala naturae*, vexed seventeenth- and eighteenth-century naturalists like few others. In seeking to maintain species difference, even while ongoing comparative investigations of anatomical structures and physiological systems of man and animals revealed more and more shared features, philosophically minded naturalists increasingly looked to the brain.[14] As the body's super organ, housing the mind, the brain became the last refuge for human exclusivity—if not through its size and physical form, then through its structure and the complex thought-processes it enabled.[15] By looking at the brain, Herder, Soemmerring, and Gall developed new takes on the Chain of Being,

---

13 See the classical study, Arthur O. Lovejoy, *The Great Chain of Being: A Study of the History of an Idea* (Cambridge, MA: Harvard University Press, 1936).
14 Markus Wild, "Anthropologische Differenz," in *Tiere: Kulturwissenschaftliches Handbuch*, ed. Roland Borgards (Stuttgart and Weimar: J.B. Metzler, 2016), 47–59.
15 On the cultural history of brain research, see the fascinating account by Michael Hagner, *Homo Cerebralis: Der Wandel vom Seelenorgan zum Gehirn* (Frankfurt a.M.: Insel, 2000). Cf. also the related and equally fascinating history of Romantic organology by Leif Weatherby, *Transplanting the Metaphysical Organ: German Romanticism between Leibniz and Marx* (New York: Fordham University Press, 2016).

leading to a refined understanding of species difference and cognition in humans and nonhumans.

Humans are the unquestioned focus of Herder's *Reflections on the Philosophy of the History of Mankind*.[16] The work, composed of twenty chapters (books) in four parts, is a grand synthesis of Enlightenment anthropology and natural history. Herder's gargantuan appetite for scientific inquiry and philosophical reflection led him to incorporate an impressive array of sources by naturalists, anthropologists, philosophers, and others.[17] Out of this convolute, Georges-Louis Leclerc de Buffon's *Histoire naturelle* (1749–88) emerges as the model for the first part—the part that is mainly of interest here. Like Buffon, Herder moves through the entire natural world, from the planet earth with its geological formations, to plants, animals, and human beings. The account of nature in all of its manifestations, including the human, then sets the stage for the consideration of the capacities of the human mind and human civilization. Herder always looks with human eyes to nature. He speaks, for instance, of "Our Earth" and of "The Planet we inhabit" (book I), before considering the richness and complexity of the plant and animal kingdoms each in its relation to "the History of Man" (book II).[18] The guiding principle behind the composition of the *Reflections* is surprisingly simple: natural history and cultural history unfold in parallel. This structure alone places humans, the only life forms that are at home in both nature and culture, at the center.[19]

For Herder, as for many Enlightenment critics, humans are the culmination of organic life. Yet as the most advanced life form, humans are, in Herder's account, built from the bottom up. The domains of physical, the vegetative, and the animalistic are each an indispensable part of humanity. When looking at the provisions nature made in these domains, man is neither standing out, nor radically deficient. Rather,

---

16 All quotations are taken from a contemporary translation into English, Johann Gottfried von Herder, *Outlines of a Philosophy of the History of Man*, trans. T. Churchill (London: n.p., 1800).

17 On the dimensions of Herder's enterprise, see Wolfgang Pross, "Die Begründung der Geschichte aus der Natur: Herders Konzept von 'Gesetzen' in der Geschichte," in *Wissenschaft als kulturelle Praxis, 1750–1900*, ed. Hans Erich Bödeker et al. (Göttingen: Vandenhoeck & Ruprecht, 1999), 221–3 and Wolfgang Pross, "Ideen zur Philosophie der Geschichte der Menschheit," in *Herder Handbuch*, ed. Stefan Greif, Marion Heinz, and Heinrich Clairmont (Paderborn: Wilhelm Fink, 2016), 171–216.

18 Herder, *Outlines*, xi.

19 On Herder's anthropocentrism in distinction to his anthropomorphism, see Hugh Barr Nisbet, *Herder and Scientific Thought* (Cambridge: Cambridge University Press, 1970), 29–32.

the human emerges as an intermediate being (*Mittelgeschöpf*), at best average as an animal, when relying on sensory organs and raw instinct, but endowed with unique access to another domain.[20] This domain, Herder insists, is of a different quality. Humans have the potential to access it not because they can lay claim to special features or forces. These are by and large the same as in animals. As Herder explains in his *Treatise on the Origin of Language* (1772), "The difference is not in levels or the addition of forces, but in a quite different sort of orientation and unfolding of all forces."[21] The manifestations of these forces and the organization of the organic elements is what generates the outcomes commonly labeled as human or animal. Put more poignantly, "it is, 'the single positive forces of thought, which, bound up with a certain organization of the body, is called reason in the case of human beings, just as it becomes ability for art in animals, which becomes freedom in the case of the human being, and in the case of animals becomes instinct.'"[22] This crucial passage provides a snapshot of the argument on species difference Herder unfolds in much greater detail in his *Reflections*. But it also indicates his quite original interpretation of the Chain of Being as a continuum of distinct domains, each with its own specific qualities.

Herder's unique capacity for synthesis is put to the test at a number of critical junctures in the project of the *Reflections* that occupied him over the span of many years, but it is substantially challenged when he again considers the human/animal divide. After surveying the domains of the natural world in the second book, Herder suggests comparisons between them in the third book. It is in this context that he examines animal cognition and species difference. Herder still assumes that the domains of nature are autonomous, allowing for a continuity of forces and elements, both physical and organic, between them. The form and activities of any given organism result from the specific interplay between the elements out of which it is built, the environment,

---

20 Herder, *Outlines*, 40. In more than a nod to the religiously infused Enlightenment, Herder later draws on Neoplatonic traditions to suggest that the Great Chain may not end with man. In this view, humans as well as the attached humanism are the final link only on this earth. Capitalizing on the dualism of matter and spirit, man can be seen as an intermediate creature, whose form-giving activities and essential propensities are, in life, constrained by nature and finitude but may be unshackled in the world beyond. Herder devotes two entire sections (5 and 6 of book V) to this mystical expansion of the Chain of Being.
21 Johann Gottfried von Herder, "Treatise on the Origin of Language," in *Philosophical Writings*, trans. and ed. Michael N. Forster (Cambridge: Cambridge University Press, 2002), 83.
22 Ibid.

into which it is placed, and the forces that act upon it: "Each part, with its living power, performs its task; and thus in the general appearance becomes visible the result of the powers, that could develop themselves in a given organization. The active powers of Nature are all living, each in its kind."[23] Herder formulates this principle first for vegetative life but immediately extends it to animal forms. In an instructive section on bees, an animal form naturalists generally admire for its complex buildings and coordinated social life, Herder speculates about the degree to which cognition might drive their collective activities. He concludes that whatever cognition might be involved, it would be specific to that species and not apply to others in the same way. Consequently, he speaks in this regard of "the sense, the feeling of a bee" (*Bienensinn, Bienengefühl*).[24] Herder resorts here to familiar human categories—sense and feeling—that take on new meaning, when considering other life forms. In instances such as this, Herder gestures toward a rethinking of the humanist framework.

If Herder seems prepared to develop species-transcending notions on some occasions, he appears eager to reassert human exclusivity on others. This is specifically true for human-like primates. The section on human propensity for reason (book IV) deals, despite the title, also with the great apes, in particular the anatomy of their brains and their cognitive capacity. Herder is familiar with the work of the British anthropologist Edward Tyson as well as with that of the Dutch anthropologist, Pieter Camper, on facial angles (*Gesichtswinkel*)—resulting from lines drawn from the tip of the nose upwards to the forehead and downwards to the chin (supposedly showing wide angles for humans and sharp angles for apes). Herder thus knows how similar the great apes are to humans with regard to both anatomy and physiology, as well as behavior and social organization. He recounts numerous reported instances of what appears to be social behavior, including displays of shame and sorrow, the use of weapons against enemies, motherly care for offspring, and the like, all bearing testimony to the richness of the ape's inner life. Bodies and brains of the great apes likewise do not differ greatly from those of humans. For general physiology, he again relies on Tyson's study of the pygmy, which had found that this life form had significantly more traits in common with humans than with other apes. Summarizing the work of eighteenth-century naturalists, Herder compares the great apes to humans in three areas: the ability to walk upright, the use of symbolic language, and the capacity for reason. In all of

---

23 Herder, *Outlines*, 59.
24 Herder, *Outlines*, 61.

these areas, the great apes are on the verge of making the leap into the domain of the human. But in each case, certain circumstances prevent them from crossing the boundary. The great apes' walk is close to upright. But the slightly tilted position of their head restricts them to a sub-erect state, "and this difference," Herder adds, "seems to deprive it [the ape] of every thing."[25] Though most of the organs necessary for producing linguistically structured sounds are present, Herder is convinced that "the manlike ape is visibly and forcibly deprived of speech by the pouches Nature has placed at the sides of its windpipe."[26] When pondering reason, Herder goes as far as saying that the great ape's mode of thinking (*Denkungskraft*) surpasses instinct and is capable of grasping ideas. But then it stops short of taking the next step: "its brain is incapable of combining with it's own ideas those of others, and making what it imitates as it were it's own."[27] The masters of imitation fail to rise to the level of creation. To a certain extent, his inability is grounded in brain anatomy—Herder's survey of naturalist literature on the subject begins with a homage to this privileged organ, "the leaves of Nature's book … the finest she ever composed."[28] But ultimately the development of reason is a complex process that transcends the realm of the organic. Somehow, through the interplay of invisible forces within the organism, nature produces that which Herder only dares to capture in a metaphor, "that luminous point, which is called higher consciousness" (*höhere Besinnung*).[29] All of this combined leads Herder to firmly reassert species difference, pronouncing that the great ape "would perfect itself. But this it cannot: the door is shut."[30] By shutting the door on the ape, the human can emerge.

Samuel Thomas Soemmerring neither wrote a bold and ambitious natural history like Herder, nor did he develop an elaborate model for animal cognition like Gall.[31] Yet his studies transition in many ways from the work of the former to that of the latter. Presumably speaking from the standpoint of an anatomist, who merely draws attention to phenomena he observes in clinical praxis, Soemmerring in fact makes far-reaching claims about the human, the physical manifestations of

25 Herder, *Outlines*, 72.
26 Herder, *Outlines*, 88.
27 Herder, *Outlines*, 71.
28 Herder, *Outlines*, 76.
29 Herder, *Outlines*, 78. Translation modified.
30 Herder, *Outlines*, 71.
31 For comparisons of the positions, see Gunter Mann, "Franz Joseph Gall (1758–1828) und Samuel Thomas Soemmerring: Kranioskopie und Gehirnforschung zur Goethezeit," in *Samuel Thomas Soemmerring und die Gelehrten der Goethe-Zeit*, ed. Gunter Mann and Franz Dumont (Stuttgart: Gustav Fischer, 1985), 149–89.

cognitive abilities, and the propensity for culture. Roughly a decade before his book *On the Organ of the Soul* (1796)—the last serious attempt to locate the metaphysical soul within the human body—he published a brochure *On the Somatic Differences of Africans and Europeans* (1784, 1785).[32] This small treatise responded with enthusiasm to Herder's *Reflections*. In a letter to the author, Soemmerring admitted that he found Herder's notion of the human as an intermediate being appealing, particularly when applied to the brain.[33] Yet to him, that notion seems to have lost most, if not all, of the spiritual connotations, which were so crucial for Herder. Instead, Soemmerring took the idea of an intermediate being as license to distinguish between different classes of humans—Europeans and Africans—with different degrees of proximity and distance to the closest animals, the apes. Faced with the astonishing similarities that comparative studies of the anatomy of the brains of humans and other primates revealed, Soemmerring decides to redraw the species line within the domain of the human and thus to abandon the idea of a universal humanity—a gesture that Herder found intolerable.[34] To Herder, humanity is one, endowed with the same physiology and propensities, which climate and historical conditions shape into cultural differences. To Soemmerring, the differences are manifest in anatomy, particularly that of the brain. The thrust of his argument is already evident from the title of this early treatise.[35] In the introductory section, Soemmerring poses his research question: "whether there are unquestionable, determinable, observable, non-accidental differences in build or composition of the human body, which assign to the African a lower station at the throne of humanity."[36] Working from a robust and evidentiary understanding of the Chain of Being, Soemmerring intends to turn the question into a claim. In order to preserve the integrity of the human for Europeans, he approximates Africans to the great apes. Such a view is in keeping with racial theory of the seventeenth and

---

32 Samuel Thomas Soemmerring, *Über die körperliche Verschiedenheit des Mohren vom Europäer* (Mainz: n.p., 1784); *Ueber die körperliche Verschiedenheit des Negers vom Europäer* (Frankfurt a.M.: Varrentrapp Sohn und Wenner, 1785); and *Ueber das Organ der Seele* (Königsberg: Nicolovius, 1796).
33 Cf. Samuel Thomas von Soemmerring, *Werke* 15: *Anthropologie: Über die körperliche Verschiedenheit des Negers vom Europäer* (1785), ed. Sigrid Oehler-Klein (Stuttgart: G. Fischer, 1998), 284.
34 Cf. book VI of the *Reflections*.
35 As indicated above, Soemmerring republished this treatise, revised and significantly expanded, in the following year. He also slightly altered the title, replacing "Moor" (*Mohren*) with "Negro" (*Negers*). I cite both versions with short titles, referencing this alteration.
36 Soemmerring, *Mohren*, 4.

eighteenth centuries.[37] Soemmerring does not engage directly with these theories. Yet, his expertise as an anatomist and his affiliation with the court in Kassel where he had the opportunity to examine the remains of several Africans, as well as those of exotic animals, gave his voice a special resonance.[38] Soemmerring's view confirms the posthumanist suspicions that speciesism and racism are close cousins, that as Agamben puts it, "the inhuman [is] produced by animalizing the human."[39]

Like his predecessors in racial thinking, Soemmerring first looks at skin color, facial features, and the shape of the skull. Building on the work of Pieter Camper, he also examines the structure of the skull bones. His anatomical measurements reveal that the bones of Africans appear enlarged, when compared to those of Europeans, and, more to the point, that extended facial features (i.e., Camper's wide angles) leave less room for the brain. After these preliminary considerations, Soemmerring moves to his main subject, the "organs of reason," that are in his account seated in the brain.[40] He is well aware of the fact that raw measurements of physical brain mass do not produce evidence for comparative anatomy and physiology—many mammals have heavier brains than humans. Straightforwardly relating brain mass to body mass does likewise not lead to conclusive results.[41] Having foreclosed these avenues of inquiry, Soemmerring proudly presents his discovery. He holds that "human beings possess the largest brains but the smallest nerves, or rather, only when relating the brain to the nerves, one can say: human beings have the largest brains."[42] This thesis rests on the idea that the brain consists of parts with specialized functions. Some parts control the "animalistic life"; others house higher cognitive functions.[43] Larger nerves extending into the brain consume, in this line of reasoning, greater slices of the available cognitive capacity. In other words, muscular bodies with a finely attuned

---

37 See specifically on Soemmerring, Georg Lilienthal, "Samuel Thomas Soemmerring und seine Vorstellungen über Rassenunterschiede," in *Die Natur des Menschen: Probleme der physischen Anthropologie und Rassenkunde (1750–1850)*, ed. Gunter Mann and Franz Dumont (Stuttgart: G. Fischer, 1990), 31–55; Sigrid Oehler-Klein, "Einleitung," in Soemmerring, *Werke* 15, 33–114 as well as on the contemporary discourse at large, Sara Eigen and Mark Larrimore, eds., *The German Invention of Race* (Albany, NY: State University of New York Press, 2006).
38 On the circumstances and living conditions of Africans in Kassel at the time, see Oehler-Klein, "Einleitung," 33–40.
39 Agamben, *The Open*, 37.
40 Soemmerring, *Mohren*, 5.
41 Cf. Soemmerring, *Mohren*, 21.
42 Soemmerring, *Mohren*, 21.
43 Soemmerring, *Mohren*, 22.

sensory apparatus render brains impotent for higher cognition. Since Soemmerring is convinced he has observed enlarged nerves in Africans reaching into the brain, he concludes that the cognitive parts of these brains must actually be smaller than comparable parts in the brains of Europeans. These findings, in turn, may help explain, he surmises, "some of the historical facts about Africans' wildness, unruliness, and reduced propensity for higher culture."[44] By bridging natural forms and cultural formations, Soemmerring fashions himself as Herder's student—even as he ignores all qualitative differences between Herder's domains and, what is worse, his universal humanist impulses.[45] Contested as it was, Soemmerring's hierarchical understanding of the Chain of Being, combined with occasional observations in anatomical practice, suggested an alluring connection between brain structure and cognition, which, if confirmed, would lead to a new method in determining species difference. Soemmerring himself did not continue working on biological difference seen through the lens of brain anatomy, nor, for that matter, on functionally specialized parts of the brain. But his work in this regard anticipated his younger colleague Gall.

Around 1800, the Viennese physician and anatomist Franz Joseph Gall emerged as one of the most vocal and widely recognized critics of the period's prevalent humanism and the particularly German orientation toward idealist philosophy with its extensions into the sciences. The discipline Gall invented is now known as phrenology ("organology" in his vocabulary).[46] Skeptical about theories solely generated by reasoning, Gall drew on his clinical expertise and observational prowess as an anatomist to devise a new and revolutionary model of cognition. Expanding on insights of the French sensualists, Étienne Bonnot de Condillac and Charles Bonnet, and mobilizing Herder against Herder, while also maintaining a distance from Kant, Gall launched an

---

44 Soemmerring, *Mohren*, 24.
45 Soemmerring's cavalier claim about anatomical evidence for racial difference was met with much skepticism. (For a comprehensive list of reviews and responses to Soemmerring's treatise, see the critical edition *Werke* 15: 310–13.) In response, Soemmerring produced the revised version of his treatise. There, he makes extensive references to anthropological, philosophical, and naturalist literature to support his argument. Maintaining his basic tenets, he clarifies that he does assume a common origin for all humans. But over the course of history, paths could split; man could become "either perfected as European, or degenerated as Negro" (*Negers*, 79). These designations—now identified variously as "nations," "classes," or "species"—still determine proximity and distance to the ape (*Negers*, xix).
46 On Gall and the later school, see Owsei Temkin, "Gall and the Phrenological Movement," *Bulletin of the History of Medicine* 21 (1947): 275–321.

ambitious research program on the brain.[47] He announced his agenda in an open letter "Upon the Functions of the Brain in Men and Animals," published in 1798 in the Enlightenment journal, *Der Neue Teutsche Merkur*, and presented his findings comprehensively in his six-volume opus, *On the Functions of the Brain and of Each of Its Parts* (1822–5).[48] In these and related works, Gall argues that the anatomical structure of the brain reveals distinct organs, each corresponding to a specific propensity, sentiment or faculty.[49] These cognitive functions, which Gall claims to have unearthed inductively and experimentally, are not unique to humans but extend to nonhuman animals. Consequently, he speaks of "the faculties and propensities of men and animals."[50] Instead of a strict boundary between species, Gall suggests a continuum based on brain structure. Assuming specialized, yet largely autonomous organs in the brain, manifesting themselves in innate cognitive functions, his doctrine of phrenology opened the possibility for both a new understanding of species difference and a radically revised conception of cognition.

Gall's doctrine has been described and dissected in countless treatises by his contemporaries and moderns alike.[51] Most accounts tend to distinguish between the anatomical part of the work, considered scientific, and the study of the skull, the craniological part, deemed speculative. Yet such a separation overlooks the actual scope of his undertaking. The anatomical research served, as much as it was possible at the time, to determine the organization of the brain. Gall was the first to identify the brain as the center of all human cognition and emotion. As the body's super organ, he assumed the brain functioned as a unit but was organized in autonomous centers (organs), each housing an innate ability (or instinct).

---

47 On Gall's interlocutors, see Madison Bentley, "The Psychological Antecedents of Phrenology," *The Psychological Monographs* 21 (1916): 105–10; Erna Lesky, "Gall and Herder," *Clio Medica* 2 (1967): 85–96; and Erna Lesky, "Structure and Function in Gall," *Bulletin of the History of Medicine* 44 (1970): 297–314.
48 Franz Joseph Gall, "Schreiben über seinen bereits geendigten Prodomus über die Verrichtungen des Gehirns der Menschen und der Thiere an Herrn Jos. Fr. von Retzer," *Der Neue Teutsche Merkur* 3 (December 1798): 311–32. Reprint in *Franz Joseph Gall: Naturforscher und Anthropologe*, ed. Erna Lesky (Bern: Huber, 1979), 47–59. In this article, I cite the English translation Franz Joseph Gall, *On the Functions of the Brain and of Each of Its Parts: With Observations on the Possibility of Determining the Instincts, Propensities, and Talents, or the Moral and Intellectual Dispositions of Men and Animals, by the Configuration of the Brain and Head*, trans. Winslow Lewis, Jr., 6 vols. (Boston, MA: Marsh, Capen & Lyon, 1835).
49 The basic tenets remain remarkably stable from the "Schreiben" to the list given at the onset of *Functions*, see ibid., vol. 1, 55.
50 Gall, "Schreiben," 50.
51 For recent accounts of Gall's doctrine, see Olaf Breidbach, *Die Materialisierung des Ichs: Zur Geschichte der Hirnforschung im 19. und 20. Jahrhundert* (Frankfurt a.M.: Suhrkamp, 1997), 63–80; Hagner, *Homo Cerebralis*, 89–118.

These instincts could be more or less developed in any given brain, but they would, he believed, always find material expression in a specific organ, operating within the brain's overall structure. Shape and size of the cerebral organs would, in turn, leave an imprint on a particular section of the skull, causing it to show an extremity in the case of a well-developed organ, or an indentation, in the case of an underdeveloped one. The underlying faculty or innate instinct would also, Gall held, prime a person to act in a certain way, and to display particular inclinations or drives. The full doctrine encompasses these four dimensions—behavior, innate ability, cortical organ, and cranial prominence—linked in a series of correspondences.[52] For any living being, human or animal, only two of the four dimensions were somewhat accessible: behavior and cranial prominence. Gall's approach thus had to be indirect, forcing him to make multiple conjectures and staggering leaps in connecting these areas.

Setting aside the daring methodology as well as the idiosyncratic outlook of the functions for the time being, Gall's approach to cognition in humans and animals was nothing short of revolutionary. Just a few years earlier, in his *Philosophical-Medical Investigations* (1791), he had still accepted the traditional higher faculties (*Seelenverrichtungen*), enumerating them in the usual fashion as "memory, imagination, will, passion, external and internal sense, and voluntary motions."[53] This configuration of the faculties had remained in place for two millennia, from Aristotle to the School Philosophy of the early Enlightenment. Since 1798 at the very latest, Gall deemed them not altogether obsolete, but too abstract and too far removed from the realm of the naturalist. They were the product of philosophical reasoning, not of naturalist observation. The higher faculties, he concluded, had to be disassembled, and their configuration replaced by a newly devised array of functions, built on stringent and methodical observation of the material world. Such an endeavor was not without risk. The philosophical model could still accommodate the soul to some degree by assigning it control over the faculties. Gall's account, by contrast, left no room for that elusive entity. What Gall gained by letting go of the soul was a more encompassing perspective, one that could include the animal. This shift is directly reflected in Gall's observational practices. When he recounts the process of discovery for each of his organs, he includes animal observations, whenever it is feasible.

---

52 On the relations between these four areas of Gall's organology, see Robert M. Young, *Mind, Brain, and Adaptation in the Nineteenth Century* (Oxford: Oxford University Press, 1970), 33–7.
53 Franz Joseph Gall, *Philosophisch-medicinische Untersuchungen über Natur und Kunst im kranken und gesunden Zustande des Menschen*, vol. 1 (Vienna: Grässer & Comp., 1791), 167.

Gall's functional approach to brain and mind, surfacing in certain patterns of behavior as well as in the particular markings of the skull, provided an evocative doctrine as well as a highly productive research tool.[54] Considering the attention Gall's inspections of the skull have received, his contributions to biological difference and species cognition have hardly been appreciated.[55] Already in the open letter, Gall insists on considering humans together with animals. But he still holds firm to the customary features, distinguishing the species. He writes, "man possesses, besides the animal qualities, the faculty of speech, and unlimited educability—two inexhaustible sources of knowledge and action."[56] In his *Functions*, after decades of research on the subject, the line has become much more blurred. From the perspective of the naturalist, he writes, it is often impossible "to determine, where animal life terminates, and humanity commences."[57] After this admission, Gall takes pains to demonstrate just how extensive the list of shared features is. Animals and humans not only have quite similar bodies, moved through muscles and sensitized through systems of nerves, the species also experience affects—Gall mentions "joy, sadness, fear, alarm, hope, envy, jealousy, anger"—much in the same way.[58] The same goes for penchants: the species show love for their offspring, develop attachments, defend themselves, and are responsive to praise and reprimand. They both are capable of planning ahead, coordinating their actions with others of their kind, and learn from past mistakes.[59] By the end of this enumeration, Gall seems in awe of the animal as standing side by side with the human—so much so that he feels inclined to state "that except the religious sentiment, and the knowledge of God, there is no moral quality, and no intellectual faculty of which the animal kingdom as a whole does not at least share the first germs."[60] With this assessment, Gall has again changed the understanding of the Chain of Being—an idea which he cherished and evoked on multiple occasions. To him, the Chain is no longer composed of discrete beings, arranged in

---

54 Phrenology's extended afterlife as both a pastime distraction and a pseudoscience attests to that. On the reception of Gall's doctrine in Germany and Britain, see Sigrid Oehler-Klein, *Die Schädellehre Franz Joseph Galls in Literatur und Kritik des 19. Jahrhunderts* (Stuttgart: Gustav Fischer, 1990); John Van Wyhe, *Phrenology and the Origins of Victorian Scientific Naturalism* (Aldershot: Ashgate, 2004).
55 The importance of animals is mentioned in Young, *Mind*, 35 and Erwin H. Ackerknecht and Henri V. Vallois, *Franz Joseph Gall, Inventor of Phrenology and his Collection* (Madison: University of Wisconsin Medical School, 1956), 18. Animals are also a fixture in Lesky's anthology of Gall's writings.
56 Gall, "Schreiben," 50.
57 Gall, *Functions*, vol. 1, 92.
58 Ibid.
59 Gall, *Functions*, vol. 1, 92–3.
60 Ibid., 93.

order of increasing perfection, nor is it divided into sections of qualities. In Gall's account, the human/animal divide has given way to a contact zone: to him biological differences are quantitative, resulting from varying degrees of expression of features shared (in some form) across species.

In contrast to this forward-looking perspective, Gall still follows Herder's lead in assuming domains in nature. Like Herder in his *Reflections*, Gall begins his *Functions* by offering accounts of the physical, the vegetative, the animalistic, and the human. But his focus is almost exclusively on cognitive functions. Gall also shares with Herder the assumption of forces, generating now not entire biological forms but organs within the brain. It is through these organs that each living organism approaches the world. The organization of the organs, their composition and their development, determines the kind of contact that any organism makes with the world. The position Gall outlines in this regard in one of the concluding sections of his *Functions*, entitled "What is the World of Men, and of the Different Species of Animal?," anticipates to a certain extent that of twentieth-century zoologist Jakob von Uexküll, who believed that organisms move in and respond to worlds that are specific to them (*Umwelt*).[61] In Gall's account that here starts with the life of a given species, organisms inhabit different worlds, depending on the organs they have at their disposal: "The world of each species of animals, is therefore the sum total of their cerebral organs—the sum of the relations or points of contact between external things and internal organs. Where there is no organ, there is no relation, nor revelation."[62] This view results in a novel conception of species, based primarily on brain functions. In the context of this discussion, Gall again highlights a few of the shared abilities, now including the organ of educability. As extensive as the communalities are, they end when it comes to grasping causality. The animal, Gall is convinced, "never sees the relation of cause and effect."[63] The lack of the general sense crucially implies the absence of a special application—the understanding of the world and the life forms inhabiting it as created by God. After having shattered most of the established pillars for human exclusivity, Gall now erects a new one, one that is grounded in religious awareness. Gall concludes his exposition with an emphatic exclamation that condenses his system to its key concerns: "God and the brain! nothing but God and the brain!"[64]

With such programs of brain research, the Enlightenment naturalists do not turn the page on but perhaps add a preface to what Jacques

---

61 Ibid., vol. 6, 287–93.
62 Ibid., vol. 6, 292.
63 Ibid., vol. 6, 291.
64 Ibid., vol. 6, 292.

Derrida has termed "this auto-biography of man."[65] To be sure, Herder, Soemmerring, and Gall still partake in the writing of the self-reflexive and self-centered narrative of this exceptional species—man. But they do so with an increasing recognition that the border dividing this species from animal life forms is porous. The more observations and insights into brain topology, anatomy, and physiology Enlightenment naturalists generated, the more difficult it became to prevent animal minds and animal bodies from emerging in their own right, laying claim to cognition, emotion, and ethics. Herder's natural history transitioning into cultural history in the *Reflections* not only makes man the turning point but defines this species and man-made culture against the backdrop of animality. Considering a much smaller section from the book of nature, brain and nervous system, the anatomist Soemmerring reacts to the discovery of the broad similarities of brain anatomy in humans and primates by magnifying a peripheral feature (nerve size relative to brain mass) in order to maintain the distinction between the human and the animal, even if it renders some humans less than fully human. Compared to his fellow anatomist, Gall constructs his biopolitical frame more broadly. Having studied the cerebral structures of humans and animals much more extensively, Gall conceptualizes his organology in such a way that the majority of the organs of the brain span the species. Characteristically for eighteenth-century thinking about the Chain of Being, these German naturalists cannot help but acknowledge common features in the brains and minds of humans and nonhuman animals.[66] But they are torn between conflicting impulses, striving on the one hand to adopt species-transcending frameworks, while attempting on the other to redeem human exclusivity. Herder's upright-walking, language-using, and *Besinnung*-practicing animals, Soemmerring's bodies with a superior ratio of brain mass to nerve fibers, and Gall's brain organs recognizing their own creatureliness in the face of God are the products of these endeavors. And yet, these features of the human, surprising and peculiar as they are, cannot be understood without recognizing at the same time related features in nonhuman animals. Even though their approaches remain anthropocentric and insist on some form of human exclusivity, the naturalists of the German Enlightenment are painfully aware of the need to define the human in the face of the animal. More than any particular framing of the human/animal distinction, it is the acknowledgment of this need that gestures toward the radical reworking of Western concepts of the human in present-day Critical Animal Studies and Posthumanism.

---

65 Derrida, *The Animal*, 24.
66 Lovejoy, *The Great Chain of Being*, 198.

Four Agency without Humans: Normativity and Path Dependence in the Nineteenth-Century Life Sciences

Christian J. Emden

1

The period between the 1790s and 1880s—before the neo-Darwinian synthesis in evolutionary theory gains ground in the first decades of the twentieth century—is a time of radical experimental innovation and theoretical transformation in the modern life sciences. Many of these developments are all too often overshadowed by the reduction of nineteenth-century biology to the seminal work of Charles Darwin—not only in the popular imagination of evolutionary theory as an inherently "British" story of scientific progress, but also in current philosophical accounts of nineteenth-century biology.[1] There are good reasons, however, to advocate for a fundamental reassessment of the life sciences in nineteenth-century Germany. Among these reasons are the philosophical questions raised within this context.[2] Indeed, historical

---

1 See, for instance, Tim Lewens, *Darwin* (London: Routledge, 2007). For a more balanced assessment that, despite its title, pays attention to the broader contexts in which Darwin's project develops, see Peter J. Bowler, *Charles Darwin: The Man and His Influence*, new edn (Cambridge: Cambridge University Press, 1996).
2 Such a reassessment has recently been undertaken with regard to the life sciences in eighteenth-century Germany. See John H. Zammito, *The Gestation of German Biology: Philosophy and Physiology from Stahl to Schelling* (Chicago: University of Chicago Press, 2018). For the need to rethink Darwin against the background of the life sciences in eighteenth- and early nineteenth-century Germany, see also Robert J. Richards's *The Romantic Conception of Life: Science and Philosophy in the Age of Goethe* (Chicago: University of Chicago Press, 2002), 514–53, and *The Meaning of Evolution: The Morphological Construction and Ideological Reconstruction of Darwin's Theory* (Chicago: University of Chicago Press, 1992).

attention to the complexity and contingency of developments in the nineteenth-century life sciences highlights how the theoretical disunity of these sciences gives rise to far-reaching philosophical problems about the nature of biological agency that are not fully resolved by the neo-Darwinian synthesis.[3] In the first decades of the nineteenth century, the work of Lorenz Oken and Gottfried Treviranus, who coined the term "biology," but also the experimental practices of Theodor Schwann and Matthias Jacob Schleiden, allow us to trace how innovations in cell theory, embryology, and morphology prepare the ground for a conception of evolution, and for an understanding of development in nature that, against the background of much more recent theoretical debates, could be described along "posthuman lines." In the second half of the nineteenth century, philosophical accounts of evolutionary theory among neo-Kantian philosophers, such as Otto Caspari, begin to question the privileged status of human autonomy vis-à-vis what is often regarded as the rest of nature. Indeed, as soon as teleological explanations of biological development begin to lose traction by the middle of the nineteenth century, biologists, broadly speaking, and neo-Kantian philosophers are faced with the possibility of a continuum within the organic, or even material world, that renders it increasingly difficult, perhaps even impossible, to successfully distinguish between what we regard as "nature" and what we tend to view as pertaining to "human" life alone.

Drawing on this historical context allows us, first of all, to enrich current debates about "posthumanism" and "new materialism" with a deeper historical perspective that shows how many of the seemingly innovative, and at times rather controversial, claims of recent theoretical debates belong to the philosophical implications of the nineteenth-century life sciences. When Rosi Braidotti, for instance, demands that we should abandon the idea of human autonomy in favor of a non-hierarchical conception of life and living things, or when Karen Barad introduces the idea of an "agential realism" that dissolves the human into a much wider conception of agency and matter, their suggestions appear far less radical when viewed against the backdrop of the nineteenth-century life sciences.[4] The political

---

3   For overviews of these issues, see especially Lynn K. Nyhart, *Biology Takes Form: Animal Morphology and the German Universities, 1800–1900* (Chicago: University of Chicago Press, 1995); Peter J. Bowler, *Life's Splendid Drama: Evolutionary Biology and the Reconstruction of Life's Ancestry, 1860–1940* (Chicago: University of Chicago Press, 1996); Timothy Lenoir, *The Strategy of Life: Teleology and Mechanics in Nineteenth-Century German Biology* (Dordrecht: Reidel, 1982).

4   See, for instance, Rosi Braidotti, *The Posthuman* (Cambridge: Polity, 2013), and Karen Barad, *Meeting the Universe Halfway: Quantum Physics and the Entanglement of Matter and Meaning* (Durham, NC: Duke University Press, 2007).

and ethical claims that Braidotti and Barad, among others, infer from such posthumanist materialism might be debatable, because they cannot easily be justified along the lines of a flat monist materialism.[5] But the importance of the theoretical questions they raise with regard to the problem of agency, human and nonhuman alike, come into a clearer focus once they are related to historical developments in the life sciences whose philosophical implications have not fully disappeared.

Second, and leaving aside the more recent theoretical debates mentioned above, shifting our perspective away from Darwin, and thus also from the neo-Darwinian synthesis that simply does not apply to the nineteenth-century life sciences, allows us to recognize more fully the continued relevance of the philosophical problems raised by cell theory, embryology, and morphology throughout the nineteenth century. What we can witness in the German life sciences between the 1790s and the early 1880s is the emergence of the problem of biological agency, that is, a kind of agency that lacks the intentional stance normally attributed to human agency but that, nevertheless, creates constraints of a normative kind for the evolution and development of organisms, including humans. The question is how we can think of normativity in a world that is not human, or at least a world within which the distinction between the human and the nonhuman is, at best, of heuristic significance. While we are accustomed to view norms as something external to agency, that is, as something which guides human agency from outside and thus serves as a standard against which to evaluate the outcome of human agency, the kind of biological agency we encounter in the nineteenth-century life sciences lacks any external point of reference. Once God and other supernatural causes are rightly recognized as both unnecessary and bizarre, there is, as it were, no "outside" to biological life, but the evolution of life is still marked by normative constraints that render some developments not only unlikely but simply impossible. Since these normative constraints cannot originate outside organic life, they must be seen as constitutive of the processes that characterize organic life. Normativity, to put it more sharply, is constitutive of agency, and this is as much the case in the realm of human agency as it is in the case of nonhuman

---

5   For a political critique of posthumanism and new materialism, see Christian J. Emden, "Normativity Matters: Philosophical Naturalism and Political Theory," in *The New Politics of Materialism: History, Philosophy, Science*, ed. Sarah Ellenzweig and John H. Zammito (New York: Routledge, 2017), 269–99.

forms of agency.[6] The understanding of biological agency that begins to emerge in the context of the nineteenth-century life sciences, I will argue, opens up the possibility of a normative world that is distinctly nonhuman.

The central claim of this chapter, then, is the following: widening the historical perspective of current debates concerned with posthuman materialism to include concrete developments in the nineteenth-century life sciences allows us to recognize more clearly the philosophically relevant problem that stands in the background of posthuman materialism without falling into the trap of the latter's flat monist ontology of matter in which everything is just the same.[7] The philosophical problem at stake, to be precise, is the possibility of a nonhuman form of biological agency with a normatively binding force.

2

While there are fine differences between posthumanism and new materialism, both share a common theoretical framework. Historically, this framework is firmly embedded in what is often described as "continental philosophy" and its precursors, including Gilles Deleuze, Michel Foucault, Luce Irigaray, Gilbert Simondon, Emmanuel Levinas, Henri Bergson, and Alfred North Whitehead, but also Heidegger, Marx, and

---

6 To be sure, such constitutivism is not unproblematic, since it is normally limited to the realm of meta-ethics. See, for instance, David Enoch, "Agency, Shmagency: Why Normativity Won't Come from What is Constitutive of Agency," *Philosophical Review* 115 (2006): 169–98. In meta-ethics, constitutivism refers to the way in which the validity of a moral claim (i.e., whether the latter is "good" or "bad") is constituted by the principles that govern the actions of those that make this moral claim. This view is often seen as rooted in the Kantian tradition of moral philosophy centered on practical reason. See, for instance, Christine M. Korsgaard, *The Constitution of Agency: Essays on Practical Reason and Moral Psychology* (Oxford: Oxford University Press, 2008), 7–10. An alternative model relegates foundational principles for acting into the background and instead focuses on the aims of action. On this account, the aims of agency are constitutive of agency. See Paul Katsafanas, *Agency and the Foundations of Ethics: Nietzschean Constitutivism* (Oxford: Oxford University Press, 2013). There is no need, however, to limit this model to moral, or ethically relevant, forms of agency, since the latter must be contingent upon those factors that make moral agency possible in the first place. One attempt to come to terms with this is Nietzsche's conception of the "will to power." See Christian J. Emden, "Nietzsche's Will to Power: Biology, Naturalism, and Normativity," *Journal of Nietzsche Studies* 47 (2016): 30–60.

7 On posthuman materialism's "flatness," see Lenny Moss, "Detachment Theory: Agency, Nature, and the Normative Nihilism of New Materialism," in *The New Politics of Materialism*, ed. Sarah Ellenzweig and John H. Zammito, 227–49.

Spinoza and, to a lesser extent, Friedrich Nietzsche.[8] Developing in close contact with post-structuralism and recent feminist theories of embodied knowledge and affect, posthumanism and new materialism foreground the way that human beings are merely one constitutive part of a broader field of material factors, forces, and processes. Against the background of this particular philosophical lineage, posthumanism and new materialism also adopt a decidedly non-reductionist version of materialism that sets them apart from the kind of physicalism that seems to dominate central discussions in analytic philosophy and that aims at establishing the unity of science and knowledge.[9] As such, it is not altogether surprising that posthumanism and new materialism question the relevance and primacy of the human subject, and thus also of the practical autonomy of reason, since, as Donna Haraway aptly noted, there is nothing special about the organic makeup of human beings: only about 10 percent of cells carry the human genome, while roughly 90 percent of cells that constitute the human body carry the genomes of fungi, bacteria, and other, strictly speaking, nonhuman organisms.[10] Human beings, in short, are a "multispecies," always existing in the plural, and the differentiation between the human and the nonhuman, thus, appears to be quite problematic.[11]

---

8   See, for instance, the references throughout Rosi Braidotti, *Metamorphoses: Towards a Materialist Theory of Becoming* (Cambridge: Polity, 2002). See also Elizabeth Grosz's, "Matter, Life, and Other Variations," *Philosophy Today* 55 (2011), SPEP Supplement: 17–27, *Becoming Undone: Darwinian Reflections on Life, Politics, and Art* (Durham, N.C.: Duke University Press, 2011), and *The Nick of Time: Politics, Evolution, and the Untimely* (Durham, N.C.: Duke University Press, 2004).

9   See, for instance, Elizabeth Grosz, *The Incorporeal: Ontology, Ethics, and the Limits of Materialism* (New York: Columbia University Press, 2017), 11–12 and 36–7. Historically, the link between physicalism and the unity of scientific knowledge is grounded in the logical positivism of the Vienna Circle, which quickly becomes the dominant theoretical model in Anglo-American philosophy from the mid-1930s onward, once the members of the Vienna Circle had emigrated to the United States. See, for instance, Otto Neurath, "Physicalism: The Philosophy of the Vienna Circle" and "The Unity of Science as a Task," both in *Philosophical Papers, 1913–1946: With a Bibliography of Neurath in English*, ed. Robert S. Cohen and Marie Neurath (Dordrecht: Reidel, 1983), 48–51 and 115–20, respectively, and Rudolf Carnap, "Logical Foundations of the Unity of Science," in *International Encyclopedia of Unified Science*, ed. Otto Neurath, Rudolf Carnap and Charles Morris (Chicago: University of Chicago Press, 1938), vol. 1, 42–62. At the same time, the model of reductionism which posthumanist authors seem to be attributing to analytic philosophy is hopelessly outdated, since reductionism remains a contested issue, especially with regard to the biological sciences. See, for instance, Sahotra Sarkar, "Models of Reduction and Categories of Reductionism," *Synthese* 91 (1992): 167–94.

10 See Donna Haraway, *When Species Meet* (Minneapolis: University of Minnesota Press, 2008), 3.

11 Ibid., 165. See also Eben Kirksey, ed., *The Multispecies Salon* (Durham, NC: Duke University Press, 2014).

As a consequence, both posthumanism and new materialism seek to shift our focus from an anthropocentric epistemological framework to a new ontologically driven conception of "nonhuman" others—from dogs to bacteria, from molecules to gene families—that ultimately comes to undercut any real distinction between the "human" and the "nonhuman."[12] As both Haraway and Cary Wolfe have shown, such a theoretical commitment certainly forces us to reassess the cultural role of the distinctions that are usually drawn between the human and the animal.[13]

Posthumanism ultimately requires a materialist framework, while new materialism has implications of a posthumanist kind.[14] Although posthumanism has an obvious tendency to see recent technological shifts as its main point of reference, while new materialism pays greater attention to ontological background commitments that are independent of such technological innovations, it is these ontological background commitments that shape both posthumanism and new materialism. This is also the reason why, in the following, I will mainly refer to posthuman materialism. The central ontological background commitment of such posthuman materialism is the agency of matter, which relativizes the privileged perspective of human knowledge and undermines the latter's presumed practical autonomy, as Karen Barad has pointed out:

> There is no res cogitans that inhibits a given body with inherent boundaries differentiating self and other. Rather, subjects are differentially constituted through specific intra-actions. … Knowing is a distributed practice that includes the larger

---

12 See, for instance, Braidotti, *The Posthuman*, 168 and 190.
13 See Donna J. Haraway, *The Companion Species Manifesto: Dogs, People, and Significant Otherness* (Chicago: Prickly Paradigm Press, 2003); Cary Wolfe, *Before the Law: Humans and Other Animals in a Biopolitical Frame* (Chicago: University of Chicago Press, 2012); Marianne DeKoven and Michael Lundblad, eds., *Species Matters: Humane Advocacy and Cultural Theory* (New York: Columbia University Press, 2012). While the theoretical commitments of posthumanism, thus, also force us to conceive of whatever we understand as pertaining to the human world as symbiotically being part of a much wider biosphere, such claims—characterized by a nostalgic demand for totality—can quickly drift into questionable assertions of a quasi-metaphysical kind and exchange philosophical argument for rhetorical vagueness, as in the case of Timothy Morton. See the latter's *Humankind: Solidarity with Non-Human People* (London: Verso, 2017), and *Hyperobjects: Philosophy and Ecology after the End of the World* (Cambridge, MA: Harvard University Press, 2013).
14 On the interdependence of new materialism and posthumanism, see Diana Coole and Samantha Frost, "Introducing the New Materialisms," in *New Materialisms: Ontology, Agency, and Politics*, ed. Diana Coole and Samantha Frost (Durham, NC: Duke University Press, 2010), 7–15, and Braidotti, *The Posthuman*, 51.

material arrangement. To the extent that humans participate in ... practices of knowing, they do so as part of the larger material configuration of the world and its ongoing open-ended articulation.[15]

Collapsing the distinction between the knower and the wider material configuration of which the human subject is a constitutive part also implies, however, a crucial shift toward matter as the site of those processes that enable, or constrain, the differential production of what we regard as the reality that surrounds us, that is, a reality in which we do distinguish among bacteria, coffee mugs, and philosophical arguments:

> Phenomena are constitutive of reality. Parts of the world are always intra-acting with other parts of the world, and it is through specific intra-actions that a differential sense of being—with boundaries, properties, cause, and effect—is enacted in the ongoing ebb and flow of agency.[16]

The processes of differentiation that Barad emphasizes cannot be driven by anything that resides outside matter itself, since posthuman materialism necessarily needs to reject any appeals to supernatural forces or transcendent points of reference. As a consequence, posthuman materialism regards matter as bound up with agency, and what we regard as matter, even in the abstract philosophical sense, only comes into existence as the result of such agency. Braidotti thus suggests that "matter, including the specific slice of matter that is human embodiment, is intelligent and self-organizing."[17] What Braidotti describes in terms of "intelligence" and "self-organization" mainly refers to what Diana Coole and Samantha Frost view as the "agency" of matter, which specifically seeks to undercut both any linear conception of causality and the distinction between subjects and objects.[18] Although Braidotti, throughout her account of the "posthuman," tends to conceive of matter and

---

15 Barad, *Meeting the Universe Halfway*, 379. The term "intra-action," which Barad introduced in "Meeting the Universe Halfway: Realism and Social Constructivism without Contradiction," in *Feminism, Science, and the Philosophy of Science*, ed. Lynn Hankinson Nelson and Jack Nelson (Dordrecht: Kluwer, 1996), 161–94, signifies that the boundaries between us and the world of which we are part are porous, shifting and can only serve as a heuristic device. Moreover, material objects do not "interact" but "intra-act," since they only come into being through their relatedness and reciprocal agency.
16 Barad, *Meeting the Universe Halfway*, 338.
17 Braidotti, *The Posthuman*, 35.
18 Coole and Frost, "Introducing the New Materialisms," 7.

material agency in terms of "life," Elizabeth Grosz has rightly argued that "life," in the narrow sense of the term, can only be one aspect of the organization of matter.[19]

The foregrounding of matter in posthuman materialism has two implications: one that is philosophically both dangerous and unnecessary and a second implication that limits the historical reach of posthuman materialism. As far as the broader philosophical commitment of posthuman materialism is concerned, the latter tends to adopt a flat monist ontology in which no normatively relevant distinctions can be drawn. Although posthuman materialism, including what is often described as "object-oriented ontology," emphasizes that matter should not be understood in the singular, the being of matter is univocal since what exists cannot differ in its ontological status.[20] Posthuman materialism's flat ontology, however, runs into serious problems as soon as we shift our attention back to life, to organic matter, and the "intra-action," to use Barad's expression, among living things, their constitutive parts, such as gene families or molecules, and their environments. If matter and agency are bound up with each other, the temporal dimension of agency reflects back on matter, which implies that matter's agential dimension makes different things possible at different moments in time. What Barad describes as differentiation is a process of development. Even though the latter is not goal-directed, the changing reciprocal agency of matter over time constrains future states of matter and future forms of agency. The temporality of matter's agency, in other words, undercuts the flat ontology posthuman materialists ascribe to matter. Biological agency, as I am going to show with regard to the nineteenth-century life sciences, is not a random event, but such agency is path dependent, albeit inherently open toward the future. Such path dependence, however, always implies normatively binding constraints: everything is not the same, and not everything is possible.

The second implication of posthuman materialism's foregrounding of matter pertains to the historical perspective of such posthuman materialism. At first sight, it seems, as Cary Wolfe has suggested, appeals to posthumanism are marked by a paradoxical temporality. On the one hand, posthumanism comes "before" humanism in the sense

---

19 See Braidotti, *The Posthuman*, 55–104, and Grosz, "Matter, Life, and Other Variations," 21.
20 See Braidotti, *The Posthuman*, 35; Ian Bogost, *Alien Phenomenology, or: What It's Like to Be a Thing* (Minneapolis: University of Minnesota Press, 2012), 11–19; Levi Bryant, "The Ontic Principle: Outline of an Object-Oriented Ontology," in *The Speculative Turn: Continental Materialism and Realism*, ed. Levi Bryant, Nick Srnicek, and Graham Harman (Melbourne: re.press, 2011), 267–9; Manuel DeLanda, *Intensive Science and Virtual Philosophy* (New York: Continuum, 2002), 41.

that we have always already been posthuman; as such, posthumanism primarily "names the embodiment and embeddedness of the human being in not just its biological but also its technological world." On the other hand, posthumanism comes "after" humanism in the sense that we have entered a historical stage in which humanity's "imbrication in technical, medical, informatic, and economic networks is increasingly impossible to ignore."[21] The question is, however, whether there really is such an "after," since the technological shifts Wolfe outlines for the present are the outcome, and thus not a special case, of a much broader co-evolution between whatever we regard as "human" and whatever we see as the environment this "human" point of reference is embedded in. The "human," however fleeting and uncertain it may be, is itself constituted through a long-term technogenesis.[22] Posthuman materialism's focus on fairly recent technological shifts, however, limits its historical reach. Elizabeth Grosz is thus right to point out that we would do well to return to the life sciences of the nineteenth century in order to better understand the agency of matter, although her own emphasis on Darwin might limit such an understanding precisely because it remains unintentionally shaped by the neo-Darwinian synthesis of evolutionary theory she seeks to question.[23]

In the same way that Bruno Latour noted that we have never really been as modern as we thought, the conception of the "human" has never been quite as stable as the advocates of posthuman materialism suggest.[24] One area in which this becomes particularly obvious is the increasingly uncertain philosophical territory that the life sciences enter in the period between the 1790s and the 1880s. As soon as the life sciences—i.e., embryology, morphology, cell theory, and evolutionary theory broadly speaking—begin to engage in successful experimentation and separate themselves institutionally from both *philosophia naturalis* and *historia naturalis* around 1800, they almost immediately have to question the seemingly special status of the human. It is in this context,

---

21 Cary Wolfe, *What is Posthumanism?* (Minneapolis: University of Minnesota Press, 2010), xv.
22 See, for instance, André Leroi-Gourhan, *Milieu et techniques* (Paris: Albin Michel, 1945); Gilbert Simondon, *Du mode d'existence des objets techniques* (Paris: Aubier, 1958); Bernard Stiegler, *Technics and Time, I: The Fault of Epimetheus*, trans. Richard Beardsworth and George Collins (Stanford: Stanford University Press, 1998).
23 See Grosz, *Becoming Undone*, 2–4 and 13–25. The same problem appears in Luciana Parisi, *Abstract Sex: Philosophy, Bio-technology, and the Mutations of Desire* (New York: Continuum, 2004).
24 See Bruno Latour, *We Have Never Been Modern*, trans. Catherine Porter (Cambridge, MA: Harvard University Press, 1993), 10–12.

moreover, that we encounter a conception of biological agency that highlights the normative dimension of whatever we call life.

3

To fully understand the epistemic field of the life sciences between the 1790s and 1880s, it is necessary to emphasize the promiscuous pluralism of the life sciences, that is, the "disunity" of the sciences.[25] There is certainly no unity, or uniformity, of method among the nineteenth-century life sciences. Although all the life sciences subscribe to a broadly evolutionary model of development, and conceive life as a biological phenomenon, they do so in very different ways and with very different outcomes. While we often tend to look at the nineteenth-century life sciences through the lens of Darwinism, we should not forget that the modern evolutionary synthesis emerges only after 1918; it simply was not yet in place in the second half of the nineteenth century after the publication of *On the Origin of Species* (1859).[26]

Darwin himself fully acknowledged, for instance, the work of the experimental embryologist Wilhelm Roux, one of the towering figures of *Entwicklungsmechanik*, whose programmatic *Der Kampf der Theile im Organismus* (1881) sought to translate Darwin's models of natural selection and variation from the level of an organism's biological traits into the organization of cells and tissue.[27] Roux even sent a copy of his book to Darwin, who remarked in a letter to his friend George John Romanes, the inventor of the term "neo-Darwinism," that Roux's publication "is the most important book on Evolution which has appeared for some time."[28] Darwin and Roux also fielded similar models of cellular development that explained the inheritance of biological traits from

---

25 See Ian Hacking, "The Disunities of the Sciences," in *The Disunity of Science: Boundaries, Contexts, and Power*, ed. Peter Galison and David J. Strump (Stanford: Stanford University Press, 1996), 37–74, and John Dupré, *The Disorder of Things: Metaphysical Foundations of the Disunity of Science* (Cambridge, MA: Harvard University Press, 1993).

26 See Charles Darwin, *On the Origin of Species by Means of Natural Selection, or: The Preservation of Favoured Races in the Struggle for Life* (London: John Murray, 1859). For the neo-Darwinian synthesis, see Ernst Mayr and William B. Provine, eds., *The Evolutionary Synthesis: Perspectives on the Unification of Biology*, new edn (Cambridge, MA: Harvard University Press, 1988).

27 See Wilhelm Roux, *Der Kampf der Theile im Organismus: Ein Beitrag zur Vervollständigung der mechanischen Zweckmässigkeitslehre* (Leipzig: Engelmann, 1881), 220. For Roux's experimental work, see the scientific papers collected in *Gesammelte Abhandlungen über Entwicklungsmechanik der Organismen* (Leipzig: Engelmann, 1895), and Viktor Hamburger, "Wilhelm Roux: Visionary with a Blind Spot," *Journal of the History of Biology* 30 (1997): 229–38.

28 Charles Darwin, *The Life and Letters*, ed. Francis Darwin (London: John Murray, 1887), vol. 3, 244.

Agency without Humans   63

one generation to the next. For Darwin, the generation of "new organisms" was dependent not only on the "reproductive elements," but on all cells "throughout the body" and "during all the stages of development"—a process that, like Roux, he saw as driven by the "self-division" of cells.[29] All cells of an organism were involved in passing on information about biological traits to offspring.[30] While Darwin's speculations were refuted by Francis Galton, Roux, despite strong opposition from Hans Driesch, held on to his model of ontogenetic and epigenetic development.[31]

The relationship between Darwin and Roux shows that models in the nineteenth-century life sciences which stood in fundamentally different historical traditions, such as embryology and natural selection, were able to overlap, but this also highlighted basic differences. August Weismann's theory of germ plasma, which developed independently from Darwin, is a case in point: it certainly affirmed natural selection, which Weismann had explicitly endorsed on many occasions, but nevertheless rejected Darwin's speculations about pangenesis.[32]

On the one hand, it is obvious that Darwin's theory of evolution by natural selection and adaptation certainly influenced, and also

---

29 Charles Darwin, *The Variation of Animals and Plants under Domestication* (London: John Murray, 1868), vol. 2, 374, and Wilhelm Roux, *Ueber die Bedeutung der Kerntheilungsfiguren* (Leipzig: Engelmann, 1883).
30 See Darwin, *The Variation of Animals and Plants*, vol. 2, 357–404, especially 373–404, and *The Descent of Man, and Selection in Relation to Sex* (New York: Appleton & Co., 1871), vol. 1, 19 and 280–6. On the development of pangenesis as a hypothesis, see R. C. Olby, "Charles Darwin's Manuscript of Pangenesis," *British Journal of the History of Science* 1 (1963): 251–63.
31 See Francis Galton, "Experiments in Pangenesis," *Proceedings of the Royal Society of London* 19 (1870–71): 393–410. Darwin, "Pangenesis," *Nature* 3 (April 27, 1871): 502–3, accepted Galton's criticism. Roux, working on frog embryos, presented the experimental basis of his theory in "Beiträge zur Entwickelungsmechanik des Embryo: Ueber die künstliche Hervorbringung halber Embryonen durch Zerstörung einer der beiden ersten Furchungskugeln, sowie über die Nachentwickelung (Postgeneration) der fehlenden Körperhälfte," *Archiv für pathologische Anatomie und Physiologie und klinische Medicin* 114 (1888): 113–53. Based on his research on sea urchins, Hans Driesch rejected Roux's ideas in "Entwicklungsmechanische Studien: I. Der Werth der beiden ersten Furchungszellen in der Echinodermenentwicklung: Experimentelle Erzeugung von Theil- und Doppelbildungen. II. Über die Beziehungen des Lichtes zur ersten Etappe der thierischen Formbildung," *Zeitschrift für wissenschaftliche Zoologie* 53 (1891): 160–84.
32 See, for instance, August Weismann, *Die Continuität des Keimplasma's als Grundlage einer Theorie der Vererbung: Ein Vortrag* (Jena: Fischer, 1885), 2. For Weismann's endorsement of Darwin, see his lecture *Ueber die Berechtigung der Darwin'schen Theorie: Ein akademischer Vortrag, gehalten am 8. Juli 1868 in der Aula der Universität zu Freiburg im Breisgau* (Leipzig: Engelmann, 1868).

constrained, the development of the life sciences in the second half of the nineteenth century.[33] On the other hand, not all evolutionary biology is strictly speaking Darwinian: natural selection, for instance, has a complex relationship to the field of animal morphology, and Weismann's theory of germ plasm was as crucial to the development of evolutionary biology in terms of an institutionalized research paradigm as Darwin's theory of natural selection. Indeed, Weismann's position in particular reflects the complex relationship between Darwinism and evolutionary models that do not rely on natural selection: Weismann's work in the field of cell theory suggested that there were some limitations to Darwin's theory. He concluded, for instance, that there could be no inheritance of acquired characteristics, which complicated the relationship between selection and adaptation.[34] But Weismann himself regarded his position merely as fine-tuning Darwin's framework: what explained development among both entire species and individual organisms, did not necessarily pertain to cells and molecules, which again stood in sharp contrast to Roux's stipulations.[35] Given the theoretical uncertainties of the contemporary life sciences, the embryologist Wilhelm His argued that there should be no room for a dogmatic attempt at a unified theory, which would ultimately come to limit the understanding of evolutionary processes.[36]

4

Cell theory played a crucial role for the disunity of the life sciences in the nineteenth century, and it is within this context—instead of Darwinism in the narrow sense of the term—that the problem of agency begins to appear in a novel way. Given the high degree of uncertainty that permeated the experimental conditions of cell theory in the nineteenth century, there was a real need to find an accurate conceptual language that could describe epistemic things continuing to resist any

---

33 See Jean Gayon, "From Darwin to Today in Evolutionary Biology," in *The Cambridge Companion to Darwin*, ed. Jonathan Hodge and Gregory Radick (Cambridge: Cambridge University Press, 2003), 241, and Peter J. Bowler, *The Non-Darwinian Revolution: Reinterpreting a Historical Myth* (Baltimore, MD: Johns Hopkins University Press, 1988), 1–19 and 72–104.
34 See August Weismann, *Ueber die Vererbung: Ein Vortrag* (Jena: Fischer, 1883).
35 In contrast to his cautious remarks on Darwin, Weismann explicitly doubted the explanations of heredity given by Ernst Haeckel, *Die Perigenesis der Plastidule, oder die Wellenzeugung der Lebenstheilchen: Ein Versuch zur mechanischen Erklärung der elementaren Entwickelungs-Vorgänge* (Berlin: Reimer, 1876) and Wilhelm His, *Unsere Körperform und das physiologische Problem ihrer Entstehung: Briefe an einen befreundeten Naturforscher* (Leipzig: Vogel, 1874).
36 See His, *Unsere Körperform*, 214–15.

straightforward explanation. Cell theory thus always intertwined scientific practice and philosophical reflection on its own conditions.[37] The description of organic life as based on the development of cells, and the role of cellular structure for the organization of living organisms, steadily moved into the very center of the German life sciences once Matthias Jacob Schleiden's microscopic observations of plants in the mid-1830s focused on the crucial importance of cell nuclei and cell division within the framework of a purely mechanical explanation of nature.[38] Schleiden saw the growth of cells as identical with processes of crystallization in the anorganic world: the accumulation of minute elementary particles in the undefined matter of the cytoblastema produced the cell nucleus. As a consequence, Schleiden distanced himself from the earlier tradition of Romantic *Naturphilosophie* and adopted a relentlessly reductionist form of materialism.[39] Such materialism, however, was not merely a philosophical choice, but it reflected fundamental technical changes that supported the subsequent development of cell theory, in particular the use of apochromatic lenses in microscopes, which sharpened the visual representation of cells, and advances in tissue preservation.[40] Once Theodor Schwann and Rudolf Virchow, among others, had widened Schleiden's research from plants to the physiology of animals and the human body, the continuity of living nature's seemingly mechanical organization stretched from cell nuclei to complex animals, such as human beings.[41] The formation of cells was

---

37 See Georges Canguilhem, *Knowledge of Life*, trans. Stefanos Geroulanos and Daniela Gisburg, introd. Paola Marrati and Todd Meyers (New York: Fordham University Press, 2008), 25–56.
38 See Matthias Jacob Schleiden, "Beiträge zur Phytogenesis," *Archiv für Anatomie, Physiologie und wissenschaftliche Medicin* (1838): 137–76.
39 See, for instance, Matthias Jacob Schleiden, *Über den Materialismus der neueren deutschen Naturwissenschaft, sein Wesen und seine Geschichte: Zur Verständigung für die Gebildeten* (Leipzig: Engelmann, 1863).
40 On some of the technological preconditions of cell theory, see William Coleman, *Biology in the Nineteenth Century: Problems of Form, Function, and Transformation* (Cambridge: Cambridge University Press, 1977), 22–3.
41 See Theodor Schwann, *Mikroskopische Untersuchungen über die Übereinstimmung in der Struktur und dem Wachstum der Thiere und Pflanzen* (Berlin: Sander, 1839), 41–6 and 220–57, and Rudolf Virchow, *Die Cellularpathologie in ihrer Begründung auf physiologische und pathologische Gewebelehre: 20 Vorlesungen, gehalten während der Monate Februar, März und April 1858 im Pathologischen Institut zu Berlin* (Berlin: Hirschwald, 1858). On Schleiden's influence on Schwann, see Ohad Parnes, "From Agents to Cells: Theodor Schwann's Research Notes of the Years 1835–1838," in *Reworking the Bench: Research Notebooks in the History of Science*, ed. Frederic L. Holmes, Jürgen Renn and Hans-Jörg Rheinberger (New York: Kluwer, 2003), 119–40.

the developmental principle common to the elementary parts of any organism.[42]

At the same time, reductionist mechanical models could not fully explain how cellular development, and thus also the self-regulation of cells that Roux later ascribed to the morphological development of embryos, could occur in the first place. Organisms, it seemed, "develop according to blind laws of necessity," but to Schwann this also implied the existence of "forces" co-emergent with matter, or as he put it: forces "posited by the existence of matter."[43] Despite the seemingly outmoded allusion to some sort of vitalism, or *Bildungstrieb*, Schwann had no interest in conceiving of these forces as representing a "transformation of God into nature," as Lorenz Oken still surmised in his *Lehrbuch der Naturphilosophie* (1809). He also did not imply the existence of a purpose, which causally organizes the constituent parts of an organism into a viable whole and which was still a central assumption of Johannes Müller's highly influential *Handbuch der Physiologie des Menschen* (1833–40).[44] While Schwann concluded on the basis of extensive microscopic observations that the "formation of cells" had to be understood as "the common developmental principle of the most diverse elementary parts of organisms," he rejected any vitalist and teleological arguments with regard to the formation of cells: the forces that shape the formation and development of cells were the result of interacting molecules.[45]

There was no vital force, or an unfolding of consciousness, to be observed in the organism as a whole but merely the plasticity of cells, their chemical metabolism, and, most importantly, the interaction among cells. The emergence of cells and the subsequent development of cell structures making up different organisms were dependent on the supply of nutrients and specific environmental conditions.[46] What mattered to Schwann on a philosophical level, however, was the observation that cells formed themselves within a "structureless substance that is located either within or between already existing

---

42 See Schwann, *Mikroskopische Untersuchungen*, iv, xiii–xv, and 191–6.
43 Ibid., 226.
44 See Lorenz Oken, *Lehrbuch der Naturphilosophie* (Jena: Frommann, 1809), vol. 1, vii, and Johannes Müller, *Handbuch der Physiologie des Menschen* (Koblenz: Hölscher, 1833–40), vol. 1, 18–20.
45 See Schwann, *Mikroskopische Untersuchungen*, 196 (emphasized in the original) and 224–5. As such, cell theory also presented itself as a unifying theory, seeking to integrate different aspects, models, and diverse kinds of empirical knowledge about evolution. William Bechtel, *Discovering Cell Mechanisms: The Creation of Modern Cell Biology* (Cambridge: Cambridge University Press, 2006), 68–72.
46 See Schwann, *Mikroskopische Untersuchungen*, 201–4.

cells"; once the formative process of cell development was underway, cells were able "to develop in manifold ways into the different elementary parts that make up organisms."[47] This also implied that the cells of different parts of any organism could not be understood in isolation from each other, but they had to be seen as "connected through a shared bond, that is, their identical principle of development," which came to the fore precisely in the way in which "different modifications" lead to the different parts and traits within any given organism.[48] As a consequence, Schwann began to assume that each cell, however different, was marked by a common form of agency that consisted in attracting molecules, even though what kind of molecules cells were able to attract largely depended on their respective environmental conditions: "the whole organism exists only through the reciprocal effect [*Wechselwirkung*] among its different elementary parts."[49]

Schwann's reference to "forces," to the "life" of cells, thus always implied the agency of matter. On the one hand, this echoed earlier assumptions that stood at the core of the definition of biology around 1800. For Gottfried Reinhold Treviranus, for instance, living things could be distinguished from the inorganic world since they existed in a "state of agency [*Thätigkeit*]" characterized by "growth" and "movement," which were both internal to the organism and at the same time shaped by the "random effects of the external world," such as climatic conditions or the struggle among populations.[50] The "development" of living things did not progress toward any one goal, but it was a diffuse process, moving into "a great number of different directions": evolution and development, on this account, referred to the emergence of increasing complexity and variation, which were limited by constraints inherent to the interplay between contingency and growth.[51] The question is, of course, whether Treviranus, like his teacher Johann Friedrich Blumenbach, conceived of such living forces as constitutive of nature or whether he regarded the existence of these forces as a merely regulative idea, as Kant would have

---

47 Ibid., 196 (emphasized in the original).
48 Ibid., 198.
49 Ibid., 227–8.
50 Gottfried Reinhold Treviranus, *Biologie, oder Philosophie der lebenden Natur für Naturforscher und Aerzte* (Göttingen: Röwer, 1802–22), vol. 1, 16 and 23 (partly emphasized in the original). See also ibid., vol. 3, 163–4.
51 Gottfried Reinhold Treviranus, *Die Erscheinungen und Gesetze des organischen Lebens, neu dargestellt* (Bremen: Heyse, 1831–32), vol. 1, 28–9. For Treviranus's account of increasing complexity, see ibid., 24–43.

done.[52] Although Blumenbach, in his study of chicken eggs and human embryos, rejected the idea of the preformation of organisms, instead opting for slow epigenetic development, the latter only seemed a reasonable conclusion against the backdrop of a *Bildungstrieb*, or *nisus formativus*, inscribed into organic nature as a quasi-causal principle with teleological effects.[53] Although Treviranus did not fully disown such teleological principles, he shifted the emphasis toward contingent environmental effects, which led to an understanding of life that was based on the idea of dynamically interacting forces. Each of these forces, he noted, "is cause and effect at the same time, means and purpose at the same time, each an *organ*, and the whole an infinite *organism*."[54] This also implied that the central question of the life sciences was not whether the generation and development of living things was strictly goal-directed, but rather how living things organized themselves, from individual organs to entire organisms.[55] Biological agency always implied self-organization and self-regulation.

On the other hand, Schwann's theoretical commitments found their way into a broader biological literature, such as Karl Semper's *Die natürlichen Existenzbedingungen der Thiere* (1880). For Semper, biological agency was the result of the interaction between different kinds of matter, such as between cells and other cells, or between cells and their respective environmental conditions. Depending on which external factors affected the molecular structure of individual cells in living organisms, for instance, the same cells could develop in many different

---

52 See Immanuel Kant, *Critique of the Power of Judgment*, ed. Paul Guyer, trans. Paul Guyerand Eric Matthews (Cambridge: Cambridge University Press, 2000), 292. On this discussion, see Brandon C. Look, "Blumenbach and Kant on Mechanism and Teleology in Nature: The Case of the Formative Drive," in *The Problem of Animal Generation in Early Modern Philosophy*, ed. Justin E. H. Smith (Cambridge: Cambridge University Press, 2006), 355–73; Robert J. Richards, "Kant and Blumenbach on the Bildungstrieb: A Historical Misunderstanding," *Studies in History and Philosophy of Biological and Biomedical Sciences* 31 (2000): 11–32; James L. Larson, "Vital Forces: Regulative Principles or Constitutive Agents? A Strategy in Germany Physiology, 1786–1802," *Isis* 70 (1979): 235–49.
53 See Johann Friedrich Blumenbach's *Über den Bildungstrieb* (Göttingen: Dieterich, 1789), 24–5, and *Über den Bildungstrieb und das Zeugungsgeschäfte* (Göttingen: Dieterich, 1781), 12–13.
54 Treviranus, *Biologie*, vol. 1, 52.
55 The problem of such self-organization was an essentially Kantian theme that became increasingly prominent after the publication of the latter's Third Critique. See, for instance, Christoph Girtanner, *Ueber das Kantische Prinzip für die Naturgeschichte: Ein Versuch, diese Wissenschaft philosophisch zu behandeln* (Göttingen: Vandenhoeck & Ruprecht, 1796). On (self-)organization as the central problem of the life sciences around 1800, see Zammito, *The Gestation of German Biology*, 286–317.

ways. Drawing on research in contemporary embryology, which also stood in the background of Roux's work, he noted how identical cells, or identical clumps of cells, could develop into highly different organs with different functions. Cell plasma, on this account, both enabled and constrained the evolutionary development of organs and, by extension, of entire organisms.[56] The agency that could be observed with regard to cell plasma's relationship to its environmental conditions was normatively binding in the sense that it allowed for certain kinds of development to occur, while the cell was cut off from other kinds of development. For Semper, it is important to note, cell plasma and cells did not simply adapt to a specific environment, or to changes in this environment, as a literal reading of Darwin's link between natural selection and adaptation would have suggested. Instead, he assumed a feedback loop that extended beyond individual cells and organs and, thus, marked evolution as a whole: cells responded to their environment by producing different kinds of organs, but the latter also influenced the molecular structure of cells, which could then be inherited by subsequent generations of the same species in the same environment.[57]

The slow shift from mechanistic explanations of cell development, which stood at the center of Schleiden's research in the 1830s, to an increasingly dynamic understanding of the relationship between cell plasma, environment, and heredity by the 1880s, also changed the conception of biological agency that was always implied in this context but that had its roots in the debate about vitalism around 1800. A prominent example of this is the work of the physiologist Gustav von Bunge. In one of his public lectures, *Vitalismus und Mechanismus* (1886), he rejected the mechanistic reductionism of earlier cell theorists like Schleiden, but he also sought to avoid any return to the kind of *naturphilosophisch* vitalism that was present in Oken's writings.[58] Central to his attempt to

---

56 See Karl Semper, *Die natürlichen Existenzbedingungen der Thiere* (Leipzig: Brockhaus, 1880), vol. 1, 16–18.
57 See ibid., vol. 1, 18–19. Similar models have emerged in much more recent accounts of environmentally sensitive gene expression as stimulating evolutionary novelty. See, for instance, Mary Jane West-Eberhard's "Toward a Modern Revival of Darwin's Theory of Evolutionary Novelty," *Philosophy of Science* 75 (2008): 899–908, and "Developmental Plasticity and the Origin of Species Differences," *Proceedings of the National Academy of Sciences* 102 (2005), supplement 1: 6543–9. On the wider context and theoretical underpinnings of such research, see also Paul Griffiths and Russell Gray, "The Developmental Systems Perspective: Organism-environment Systems as Units of Development and Evolution," in *Phenotypic Integration: Studying the Ecology and Evolution of Complex Phenotypes*, ed. Massimo Pigliucci and Katherine Preston (Oxford: Oxford University Press, 2005), 409–30.
58 Hans Driesch, *Geschichte des Vitalismus*, 2nd edn, corr. and enl. (Leipzig: Barth, 1922), 152, misunderstands Bunge as advocating a strong form of vitalism.

avoid a reductionist form of materialism was what he described as the "active functions of cells": cells showed some kind of "agency [*Aktivität*]."[59] Such agency, however, should not be misunderstood as a mysterious life force about which nothing could be said:

> The most simple cell, the formless, microscopically small blob of protoplasma without structure—it still exhibits all the constitutive functions of life: nutrition, growth, reproduction, movement, irritability—indeed, even functions which at the very least resemble the sensorium, the intellectual life of higher animals.[60]

"Agency," it thus seemed to Bunge, was the only way to describe the processes of "life" within the cell.[61] Agency, however, also posed a range of serious philosopical questions that could not fully be resolved within the experimental context of the nineteenth-century life sciences. While nineteenth-century biologists often tended to sidestep these philosophical questions, since they could not (yet) be addressed within an experimental setting, their philosophical peers, especially the first generation of neo-Kantian philosophers, were more ready to extract from such accounts of biological agency a naturalistic understanding of normativity.

5

In his *Der Zusammenhang der Dinge* (1881), Otto Caspari argued that nature should not be regarded simply in terms of matter, that is, as a fixed object to be examined by detached scientific observation.[62] Rather, nature should be seen in terms of dynamic relationships whose constituent parts could not be reduced to one another: "The parts and particles of the real world relate to … one another similar to the way in which

---

59 Gustav Bunge, *Vitalismus und Mechanismus: Ein Vortrag* (Leipzig: Vogel, 1886), 7 and 12. Contemporary physiological and biological research, he pointed out, highlighted that whatever happened within a given single cell could not be sufficiently explained according to the mechanical model of causation favored by Schleiden and Schwann. See ibid., 6 and 11. Apart from his own work on the chemistry of human metabolism, Bunge draws heavily on experimental papers, such as Theodor W. Engelmann, "Beiträge zur Physiologie des Protoplasma," *Pflüger's Archiv für die gesammte Physiologie des Menschen und der Thiere* 2 (1869): 307–22, and Leon Cienkowski, "Beiträge zur Kenntniss der Monaden," *Schultze's Archiv für mikroskopische Anatomie* 1 (1865): 203–32.
60 Bunge, *Vitalismus und Mechanismus*, 13 and 17. The last sentence is highlighted in the original.
61 See ibid., 12.
62 See Otto Caspari, "Philosophie und Transmutationstheorie" and "Der Begriff der 'Zielstrebigkeit' unter dem Gesichtspunkte der Darwin'schen Lehre," both in *Der Zusammenhang der Dinge: Gesammelte philosophische Aufsätze* (Breslau: Trewendt, 1881), 69–104: 71, and 105–39, respectively.

the autonomous elements of real organic systems relate to the organism as a whole, forming a constitutive relationship [*eine Constitution im Zusammenhange*]."[63] Such a constitutive relationship that appears in the self-organization of matter and the world, Caspari noted, should not be misunderstood along the lines of teleology, since, as a whole, the world lacked any purpose or necessity but was characterized by completely random events and processes. Nevertheless, as soon as philosophy shifted its focus from the totality of the world to specific segments of the world that are part of our experiential realm, such as organic life, necessity emerged within randomness: in the context of organic life, it was indeed possible to observe "a certain progression from simple forms into aggregate formations," but any such observation also depended on the way in which human beings were an "integrative part of the whole."[64]

Whatever we call nature would have to be conceived as "a sum of living forces" whose relationships at times certainly converged "into typical, enduring forms," but which also often rearranged such forms in evolutionary processes which Caspari described as "transformation" or "transmutation."[65] Human beings were part of such processes and their scientific practices, as much as philosophy itself, continuously interacted with the world out there, thus intervening in evolutionary processes themselves.[66] For Caspari, there was no such thing as the autonomy of practical reason, even though, like Bunge, he consciously avoided any physicalist reductionism:

> We contend ... a certain similarity between the intellectual processes of the brain, on the one hand, and the external processes of nature and the world, on the other ... The conscious processes of the intellectual world and the processes of nature in the world of concrete being are, thus, neither identical nor do they entirely conform to one another.[67]

The only conclusion to be drawn was that, as part of nature, the intellectual world merely continued on a higher order the dynamically changing sum of constitutive relationships that could be discovered among, say, molecules, amoebae, ants, and such like.[68] Even though

---

63 Caspari, *Zusammenhang der Dinge*, 77.
64 Ibid., 97–8 and 102.
65 Ibid., 88.
66 Although Caspari does not draw the distinction between representing and intervening quite as explicitly, the consequences of his argument are certainly reminiscent of Ian Hacking's distinction between representing and intervening. See Ian Hacking, *Representing and Intervening: Introductory Topics in the Philosophy of the Natural Sciences* (Cambridge: Cambridge University Press, 1983).
67 Caspari, *Zusammenhang der Dinge*, 104.
68 See ibid., 119.

Caspari thus undercut the distinction between the human and whatever we might view as nonhuman, his emphasis on the inescapable necessity of development and evolution in the organic world did not deny that this world would have to be conceived as inherently normative. Normativity, on this account, was not a question of human autonomy, or of the autonomy of human reason, but it was part of the temporally shifting constitutive relationships among the things that made up what appeared to us as the world. The world, which for Caspari was always a world of processes, certainly lacked any teleology, since the latter implied undue and illogical anthropomorphisms that presented the world in exclusively human terms, but the world was also not completely random, since such randomness would render any normatively valid distinctions that obviously existed entirely impossible.[69]

Against this background, biological agency, as much as evolution as a whole, would have to be seen as transcending the opposition between teleology and the fact that the future was an inherently open space of possibilities. Indeed, it is this peculiar position that also becomes manifest in Darwin's discussion of variation under natural conditions: "I can see no limit to the amount of change, to the beauty and infinite complexity of the coadaptations between all organic beings, one with another and with their physical conditions of life, which may be effected in the long course of time by nature's power of selection."[70] On the one hand, there is no limit to change; on the other, the power of natural selection rested in an anthropomorphic concept of nature that was suggestive of some sort of teleology. Not surprisingly, contemporary readers of Darwin often fundamentally disagreed on whether, or not, Darwin subscribed to teleological principles in nature despite his emphasis on random mutations.[71] What Darwin was lacking, perhaps, was a conceptual model that could adequately grasp the interplay between necessity and randomness in the development and evolution of organic beings. Caspari's theoretical framework offered precisely such a conceptual model: "despite all change which governs individual systems, and despite a myriad of positions which are directed against each other, the causal mechanism of forces is nevertheless organized in such a way that those developments become unlikely and impossible

---

69 See ibid., 124.
70 Darwin, *On the Origin of Species*, 109.
71 On Darwin's highly ambivalent view of teleological models, see Marjorie Grene and David Depew, *The Philosophy of Biology: An Episodic History* (Cambridge: Cambridge University Press, 2004), 208–15. The debate about Darwin's possible teleological inclinations can lead to heated exchanges. See James G. Lennox, "Darwin *was* a Teleologist," *Biology and Philosophy* (1992): 409–22, and Michael T. Ghiselin, "Darwin's Language May Have Been Teleological, but His Thinking is Another Matter," *Biology and Philosophy* 9 (1994): 489–92.

which are not in accord with the structure of the whole [*Gliederung des Ganzen*]," even though there can be "no guarantee against possible obstructions and disturbances [*Hemmungen und Störungen*]" as the constitutive relationships of whatever we view as the world emerge and change over time.[72]

For Caspari, it is important to note, the interplay between continuity and change was not an abstract metaphysical speculation, but it became concretely manifest in the "consistency and variability" among the atoms of the physical world as much as in the principles of "heredity and adaptation" in the evolution of organic life.[73] The crucial point of Caspari's account, however, is that this interplay between continuity and change, necessity and randomness, entailed a temporal dimension which allowed for "regulating *feedback effects* [*Rückwirkungen*]" over time.[74] The world, in other words, was path dependent, and it was these feedback effects that enabled certain developments to occur, while constraining the field of possible developments. Such path dependence does not merely suggest that, as posthuman materialists like Coole and Frost have argued, "infinitesimally small causes" can "end up having massive but unanticipated effects," but such effects, as Barad suggested, act as normative constraints in the sense that they "iteratively reconfigure what is possible and what is impossible."[75] For Caspari, in the nineteenth century, this meant that normativity was, as it were, inscribed into the temporal fabric of the world. Since such temporality became particularly obvious in the context of organic life, the self-regulating agency of biological processes, from cell division to the selection of traits, was able to gain a normative import precisely because its path-dependent feedback loops made some future developments stochastically less likely than others. Robustness in the organic world was a manifestation of biological agency's normative import.

6

Agency, of course, is a tricky philosophical problem. The standard view of agency, at least among many analytic philosophers, remains that any form of agency inevitably requires some kind of intention, that is, a reason for acting in one way or another that can be described

---

72 Caspari, *Zusammenhang der Dinge*, 25–6.
73 Ibid., 129.
74 Ibid., 133.
75 Coole and Frost, "Introducing the New Materialisms," 14, and Barad, *Meeting the Universe Halfway*, 177 and 234.

in terms of representational mental states.[76] As such, philosophical discussions of agency have often focused, albeit not exclusively, on what can be regarded as distinctive forms of human agency that are seen to differ fundamentally from processes in the nonhuman world.[77] Even though we have a tendency to discover an intentional stance in all kinds of things, and even though we tend to attribute teleological, or quasi-teleological, actions to processes that simply cannot be goal-directed in any proper sense of the term, cells and bacteria seem to lack "agency" in such a philosophically restrictive sense of the term. There is no reason, however, to understand agency exclusively in terms of intentionality, and the reason why something acts in one way, and not in another, does not need to be limited to mental representations.[78] Instead, it might be theoretically advantageous to adopt a more minimalist understanding of agency.[79] Agency, in this respect, merely means that something, an agent, has the capacity to affect other things, and since these other things stand in some kind of relationship to the agent in question, they also affect the agent. Agency, thus, is marked by reciprocity. Such a wider conception of agency, on the one hand, undermines linear conceptions of causality; on the other hand, since agency still occurs in time, it remains part of a broader developmental pattern with normatively binding effects: depending on the kind of agency, and on the environment of the agent, some outcomes of agency are likely, others unlikely, and many simply impossible. Understood along these lines, agency refers to a temporally shaped field of possibilities, whose boundaries are shifting over time but are nevertheless fixed at any given moment in time. The boundaries within which biological agency occurs at any moment, but which are shaped by agency over time, are a "scaffolding" that

---

76 For the classic formulation, see especially Donald Davidson's "Actions, Reasons, and Causes" and "Agency," both in *Essays on Actions and Events* (Oxford: Clarendon Press, 1980), 3–20 and 43–61. For a more recent formulation see Berent Enç, *How We Act: Causes, Reasons, and Intentions* (Oxford: Oxford University Press, 2003).
77 See Daniel C. Dennett, *The Intentional Stance* (Cambridge, MA: MIT, 1987), 43–82, and Charles Taylor, "What is Human Agency," in *Philosophical Papers, I: Human Agency and Language* (Cambridge: Cambridge University Press, 1985), 15–44.
78 It seems detrimental, in this respect, to limit agency to the realm of practical reason. See, however, Christine M. Korsgaard, *Self-Constitution: Agency, Identity, and Integrity* (Oxford: Oxford University Press, 2009), 81–108, and "Acting for a Reason," in *The Constitution of Agency*, 207–30.
79 See, for instance, Xabier E. Barandiaran, Ezeqzuiel A. Di Paolo, and Marieke Rohde, "Defining Agency: Individuality, Normativity, Asymmetry, and Spatio-Temporality in Action," *Adaptive Behavior* 17 (2009): 367–86.

renders current agency possible and also "entrenches" certain kinds of agency over time.[80]

Agency, then, needs to be understood as path dependent: agency does not develop toward, or aim at, specific outcomes, but it does develop from something; even though it is conditioned by the past, it still generates unprecedented events.[81] The path dependence of agency, in this respect, is engaged in "differential reproduction": developments constitute an ongoing "chain of events" through which the material conditions, and thus the viability, of such processes are maintained, while the lack of strong causal links generates unpredictable outcomes that are constrained merely by their own past.[82] In a paradoxical way, the past of any agency has to be understood as "the trace of something that had not (yet) occurred."[83]

---

80 On such "scaffolding" and "entrenchment," see William C. Wimsatt and James R. Griesemer, "Reproducing Entrenchments to Scaffold Culture: The Central Role of Development in Cultural Evolution," in *Integrating Evolution and Development: From Theory to Practice*, ed. Roger Sansome and Robert N. Brandon (Cambridge, MA: MIT, 2007), 228–323, and William C. Wimsatt, "Generative Entrenchment and the Developmental Systems Approach to Evolutionary Processes," in *Cycles of Contingency: Developmental Systems and Evolution*, ed. Susan Oyama, Russell D. Gray, and Paul E. Griffiths (Cambridge, MA: MIT, 2001), 219–37. For a fuller overview of "scaffolding," see the contributions in Linnda R. Caporael, James R. Griesemer, and William C. Wimsatt, eds., *Developing Scaffolds in Evolution, Culture, and Cognition* (Cambridge, MA: MIT, 2013).

81 Such a conception of path dependence is looser than the understanding of path dependence in much of the social sciences. Within the context of the social sciences, for instance, path dependence implies that processes are triggered by contingent events, but they are also seen as subject to a fairly strong and surprisingly unproblematic model of causality. As a consequence, the processes in question—e.g., the emergence of specific institutional forms—are self-reinforcing to such an extent that they increasingly become resistant to change and that it is possible to predict the outcomes of a development in probabilistic ways. See the representative discussions in Scott E. Page, "Path Dependence," *Quarterly Journal of Political Science* 1 (2006): 87–115, and James Mahoney, "Path Dependence in Historical Sociology," *Theory and Society* 29 (2000): 507–48. In contrast to such a rather rigid understanding of path dependence, the path dependence of agency shares some general features with the way in which path dependence is used in current historical epistemology and the history of science at large. See William H. Sewell Jr., "Three Temporalities: Toward an Eventful Sociology," in *The Historic Turn in the Human Sciences*, ed. Terrence J. McDonald (Ann Arbor: University of Michigan Press, 1996), 263–4, and Andrew Pickering; "Explanation and the Mangle: A Response to My Critics," *Studies in History and Philosophy of Science* 30 (1999): 168–9.

82 See Hans-Jörg Rheinberger's *Toward a History of Epistemic Things: Synthesizing Proteins in the Test Tube* (Stanford, CA: Stanford University Press, 1997), 74–8, and *An Epistemology of the Concrete: Twentieth-Century Histories of Life*, foreword Tim Lenoir (Durham, NC: Duke University Press, 2010), 36.

83 Rheinberger, *Toward a History of Epistemic Things*, 178.

It is precisely this slow emergence of such a conception of the normative import of biological agency that we can witness in the German life sciences and their philosophical reception throughout the nineteenth century. Although discussions of biological agency are initially marked by residual references to teleology, by the middle of the nineteenth century, and mainly under the influence of cell theory, teleological explanations of biological development begin to lose traction. Philosophically speaking, the problem of biological agency leads to the assumption of a continuum within the organic, or even material, world that renders it increasingly difficult, perhaps even impossible, to successfully distinguish between what we regard as "nature" and what we tend to view as pertaining to human life alone. At the same time, the temporal dimension of biological agency, from cells to the evolution of entire species, transcends the opposition between necessity and randomness, both constraining the field of possible future developments and enabling other developments, including their variations, to occur within this constrained field of possibilities.

Historians of nineteenth-century German thought, who tend to focus on either the heritage of German idealism or the various forms of materialism that develop from the 1840s onward, have largely overlooked how the life sciences, in particular cell theory and the reception of Darwin within the context of the broader disunity of the life sciences, give rise to questions that cannot be negotiated within the theoretical framework of either idealism or materialism. It is in particular the first generation of neo-Kantians, such as Otto Caspari, who begin to advance what we can understand as a philosophical naturalism that focuses on the emergence of life forms without reference to either supernatural causes or a reductionist biological determinism.

This brings me to my second conclusion, which pertains to what I have described at the beginning as the theoretical limitations of posthumanism. I have noted that by failing to engage with the historical background of its central theoretical claims, posthumanism also fails to recognize that its conception of "humanism" is a paper tiger. The nineteenth-century encounter of cell theory and neo-Kantian philosophy already destabilizes whatever we regard as "human" on the grounds of observations in the experimentally driven life sciences. The upshot of this encounter is what Barad, much more recently, described as the fact that *"we are a part of that nature that we seek to understand."*[84] This, to be sure, is also the insight of Caspari's neo-Kantian philosophical naturalism, which extends agency beyond the practical autonomy of reason.

---

84 Barad, *Meeting the Universe Halfway*, 32 and 67.

As such, philosophical naturalism and posthumanism seem to overlap, at least partially.

There is, however, also a profound difference, which limits the philosophical import of posthumanism. The encounter of cell theory and neo-Kantian philosophy highlights that our conception of whatever we regard as human remains as differentially constructed by our practical interventions as natural beings within whatever we regard as the natural world as the things and forms of agency that we, again as natural beings, ascribe to the nonhuman world. In contrast, the vitalism that invariably takes center stage in programmatic accounts of the posthuman leads to a flat monist ontology that not only discounts the "human," but—in a paradoxical way—also inevitably discounts our ability to question the status of the human vis-à-vis whatever we regard as the rest of nature. We have never been human, but we have never been posthuman either.

Five Embodied Phantasy: Johannes Müller and the Nineteenth-Century Neurophysiological Foundations of Critical Posthumanism

Edgar Landgraf

Embodiment remains a key concept for posthumanistic inquiry, uniting, but also signaling divisions within the diverse schools of thought associated with posthumanism. Katherine Hayles's seminal *How We Became Posthuman* set the course in this regard. Much of her book is about separating posthumanism from cybernetic and information theoretical constructions of the posthuman where "[e]mbodiment has been systematically downplayed or erased."[1] For Hayles, "[i]nformation, like humanity, cannot exist apart from the embodiment that brings it into being as a material entity in the world; and embodiment is always instantiated, local, and specific."[2] Hayles uses the term embodiment in two complimentary ways. Embodiment acts as the moniker for inquiries into physical, physiological and neurological processes that enable, expand and limit cognition in humans and animals; and the concept serves to address cultural, technological, and media-technological modes of embeddedness that extend the body's cognitive and precognitive sensibilities, its sense of being ("subjectivity"), and its ethical responsibilities beyond its proper physiological boundaries. Both areas of inquiry play a leading role in posthumanism's dissolution of traditional disciplinary borders, bringing together the humanities with the natural and the social sciences. As Tamor Sharon notes in her

---

1 N. Katherine Hayles, *How We Became Posthuman: Virtual Bodies in Cybernetics, Literature, and Informatics* (Chicago: University of Chicago Press, 1999), 4.
2 Ibid., 49.

cartography of posthumanism, the "strong emphasis on materialism (material bodies, physiological processes and more precisely embodiment)"[3] is also what separates critical (or radical) posthumanism from its post-structuralist, and early postmodern heritage.

Understood along these lines, embodiment challenges the supremacy and independence of the mind, of consciousness, and of human agency, and thus contributes to what Pramod Nayar describes as posthumanism's predominant concern, the *"radical decentering of the traditional sovereign, coherent and autonomous human."*[4] Yet, within posthumanism, the discourse of embodiment has also led in different directions. It has invited speculations about *disembodiment* that reinforce rather than challenge notions of sovereignty and autonomy. Fantasies of disembodiment find their most visible expression in pop cultural representations of virtual minds, self-aware cyborgs, computer-generated consciousness, digitally copied souls, and so on. What Hayles calls the "nightmare [of] a culture inhabited by posthumans who regard their bodies as fashion accessories"[5] also fuels transhumanist (Nick Bostrom), metahumanist (Stefan Sorgner), and speculative posthumanist (David Roden) discussions about the ultimate, purportedly disembodied future of the posthuman. These variants of posthumanism are philosophically, epistemologically, and ethically much at odds with critical posthumanism, a tension that is addressed already by Hayles and that is at the center of introductions to posthumanism such as Stefan Herbrechter's *Posthumanism: A Critical Analysis* (2013), Cary Wolfe's *What is Posthumanism?* (2010), and Sharon's "A Cartography of the Posthuman" in her 2014 book *Human Nature in an Age of Biotechnology.*[6] The main point of contention, as Cary Wolfe argues, is that transhumanists like Nick Bostrom and Hans Moravec[7] continue a fundamental humanist dogma, namely the idea "that 'the human' is achieved by escaping or repressing not just its animal origins in nature, the biological, and the evolutionary, but more generally by transcending the bonds of materiality and embodiment

---

3   Tamar Sharon, *Human Nature in an Age of Biotechnology: The Case for Mediated Posthumanism* (Dordrecht, Heidelberg, New York and London: Springer, 2014), 30.
4   Promod K. Nayar, *Posthumanism* (New York: Polity, 2014), 2. For Nayar, "[p]osthumanism is about the embedding of embodied systems in environments where the system evolves with other entities, organic and inorganic, in the environment in a mutually sustaining relationship." Ibid., 51.
5   Hayles, *Posthuman*, 5
6   See especially Stefan Herbrechter, Cary Wolfe, and Tamar Sharon who add Neil Badmington, Anne Balsamo, Rosi Braidotti, Elaine L. Graham, Chris Hables Gray, Donna Haraway, N. Katherine Hayles, Allucquère Rosanne Stone, and Joanna Zylinska to the list of critical or radical posthumanists.
7   Wolfe, *Posthumanism*, xv.

altogether."[8] For Wolfe and other critical posthumanists, posthumanism is not about conjuring up a biologically posthuman, post-embodied, post-material reality, but represents a *critical* project that builds on the theoretical insights of post-structuralism and neocybernetic theory with the aim of leaving behind the anthropocentric thought patterns and concepts of the humanist tradition—of which mind-body dualism is one of its most central instantiations.

Overcoming dualistic modes of thinking is certainly also at the heart of the latest strands of posthumanism, the new materialisms, object-oriented ontology, and speculative realism. These schools tend to radicalize the materialist contention of the discourse on embodiment to the point where the body and notions of embodiment at times fall completely out of view. In their quest to think the "in-itself," not as a correlate between thinking and being or between subject and object, speculative realism, for example, seeks access to a material absolute that it locates beyond and prior to the body and any mode of embodiment. Quentin Meillassoux explicitly spells out this point. He recognizes that the transcendental subject is *"indissociable from its incarnation in a body"* and grants the body a constitutive role in the "emergence of the conditions for the taking place of the transcendental"[9]; but his aim is to go beyond the viewpoint of the transcendental and think the conditions for the appearance of both objective bodies *and* the transcendental subject. The contention of Meillassoux's materialism is that it is only in the "ancestral space-time"[10] that lies beyond and prior to the appearance of bodies that we will find the conditions for science, in particular for "a mathematized science ... able to deploy a world that is *separable* from man."[11]

It is against the backdrop of these fundamentally different attitudes toward the body, embodiment, and cognition—and against speculative realism's contention about a science separable from man—that I want to turn to arguably one of the earliest scientific considerations of embodiment (*avant la lettre*), and specifically of embodied cognition, namely to the work of the German physiologist Johannes Müller

---

8   Ibid. Interestingly, Wolfe includes Hayles in his critique of the transhumanist tradition, suggesting that while Hayles is critical of transhumanism, she nevertheless appears to associate the posthuman with a "triumphant disembodiment." Ibid.
9   Quentin Meillassoux, *After Finitude: An Essay on the Necessity of Contingency*, trans. Ray Brassier (London: Continuum, 2008), 25. Meillassoux also calls the body the "'retro-transcendental' condition for the subject of knowledge." Ibid.
10 Ibid., 26.
11 Ibid., 115.

(1801–58).[12] Müller belongs to the most important physiologists of the nineteenth century. Credited for laying the foundation of modern biology, he counted among his students such prominent scientists as Emil du Bois-Reymond, Ernst Haeckel, Hermann von Helmholtz, Theodor Schwann, Rudolf Virchow, and Wilhelm Wundt.[13] But Müller's legacy also reaches into the twentieth century. Heinz von Foerster claims Müller as an early precursor to his constructivist epistemology and an important influence on the development of Humberto Maturana's theory of autopoiesis.[14] As Müller's research returns us to the biological origins of neocybernetic thinking, it will allow us to reexamine Hayles's critique of neocybernetics as systematically downplaying or erasing embodiment, a contention that reflects the larger divide within posthumanism between materialist theories on the one side and (de-)constructivist theories on the other. What makes Müller particularly relevant for these contemporary debates is that his neurophysiological findings lead him neither toward an ontological or object-oriented thinking, nor toward a post-Kantian privileging of science over philosophy as "guarantor of knowledge,"[15] but in the opposite direction: toward a closer examination of embodied *phantasy*—I am using the "ph" to distinguish non-sensory fantasy from phantasy that is sensory. Müller focuses on instances of cognition and sensory activity that take place in the absence of material objects, and toward reflections, to cite the title of Müller's inaugural address from 1824, "On Physiology's

---

12 The recent special issue of *German Life and Letters* on *Embodied Cognition around 1800* uses a broader definition of embodiment to survey anthropological, medical, philosophical, physiological, and literary texts that examine how the body relates to "perceiving, thinking, and expressing." Katharina Engler-Coldren, Lore Knapp, and Charlotte Lee, "Embodied Cognition around 1800: Introduction," *German Life and Letters* 70, no. 4 (October 2017): 414. Jerome Carroll's contribution traces in particular the various "departures from dualism" that mark and differentiate mechanist, animist, vitalist, and anthropological inquiries into the relationship between mind and body. See "Eighteenth-Century Departures from Dualism: From Mechanism and Animism to Vitalism and Anthropology," ibid., 430–44. As I want to show in the following analysis, though, it is only with Müller that such considerations of embodiment venture beyond the basic humanist outlook of his predecessors by developing a model of *enactive* cognition that anticipates contemporary critical posthumanist concerns.
13 On Müller's research methodologies and his significance for nineteenth-century physiology, see Laura Otis, *Müller's Lab: The Story of Jakob Henle, Theodor Schwann, Emil du Bois-Reymond, Hermann von Helmholtz, Rudolf Virchow, Robert Remak, Ernst Haeckel, and Their Brilliant, Tormented Advisor* (Oxford: Oxford University Press, 2007).
14 See Heinz von Foerster and Bernhard Pörkens, *Wahrheit ist die Erfindung eines Lügners. Gespräche für Skeptiker*, 8th edn (Heidelberg: Carl-Auer-Systeme Verlag, 2008), 15.
15 Meillassoux, *After Finitude*, 120.

Need for a Philosophical Observation of Nature." While Müller's work certainly extends a Kantian perspective, his neurophysiological findings lead him to adopt a constructivist rather than correlationist viewpoint. To clarify the difference and expand on what's at stake not just theoretically, but also ethically and politically, the last part of this chapter will draw on Jacob von Uexküll, who in the middle of the Second World War published a remarkably detailed analysis of Müller's inaugural address under the bold title *Der Sinn des Lebens* (The Sense of Life). For Uexküll, Müller's physiology becomes the paradigmatic instance of a species-specific relation to an environment. Uexküll recognized the broader philosophical and ethical implications of Müller's examination of embodied phantasy, arguing that Müller's physiology can help us avoid the materialist fallacy: a fixation on objects, matter, or other concepts that only deepens the "correlational" divide. For Uexküll, Müller's physiology and his conception of life offer a model of scientific thought that escapes the dominant rationalist paradigm and its dualistic modes of thinking, which Uexküll implicitly links to the historical catastrophe that surrounds him.

Müller Reading Goethe

For our contemporary sensibilities, it might seem surprising how much attention Müller pays to Goethe's work in his scientific and physiological publications. His pathbreaking 1826 treatise *On the Comparative Study of the Physiology of Vision in Humans and Animals*[16] references Goethe at multiple and crucial points, including Goethe's *Metamorphosis of Plants* and his *Theory of Colors* for which Müller reserves a whole chapter in order to defend Goethe's controversial stance against Newton. Müller's indebtedness to Goethe is equally apparent in *On Imagined Visual Representations*,[17] a text that was published the same year and that he calls the continuation of the *Physiology of Vision*. This second text moves from physiological questions about what Müller calls the visual sensory substance (*Sehsinnsubstanz*)[18] to the relationship between physiology and psychology. Müller regards the psyche or mind (*Seele, Geistesleben*) as "a specific form of life among the many

---

16 Johannes Müller, *Zur vergleichenden Physiologie des Gesichtssinnes des Menschen und der Thiere nebst einem Versuch über die Bewegungen der Augen und über den menschlichen Blick* (Leipzig: G. Gnobloch, 1826).
17 Johannes Müller, *Über die phantastischen Gesichtserscheinungen. Eine physiologische Untersuchung mit einer physiologischen Urkunde des Aristoteles über den Traum, den Philosophen und Aerzten gewidmet* (Koblenz: Hölscher, 1826).
18 The visual sensory substance includes both the external moveable parts of the eye, the retina, etc., and the internal, fixed nerve cells and fibers that are involved in the sensing process. See Müller, *Phantastische Gesichtserscheinungen*, 10.

life forms that are subject to physiological examination," and he is convinced "that the ultimate outcomes of physiological examination themselves must be psychological."[19] This conviction is at the heart of Müller's esteem for Goethe. Müller understands Goethe's method of self-observation—especially as used in the chapter on "Physiological Colors" in the *Theory of Color* as well as in *Faust* and in the visions Ottilie has in the novel *Elective Affinities*—to be the first scientific attempt to combine physiological and psychological modes of inquiry. Furthermore, as Müller's research highlights the importance of the organic for perception, fantasy, and cognition—anticipating contemporary categories of embodiment—his examination of phantasmatic phenomena reveals a seemingly paradoxical relationship of simultaneous dependence and independence of the psychological from the physiological. Müller, I will show, thus breaks with a reductionist view of the body, and suggests ways to replace mechanistic assumptions of causality and teleology with organic models that ask us to rethink the separation of mind and body, fantasy and physiology, and even literature and science.[20] Examining embodied phantasies and phantasy's embodiment, Müller leaves behind humanism's Cartesian divide and anticipates important developments in the cognitive sciences of the twentieth and early twenty-first centuries.

Before examining more closely Müller's explorations of embodied phantasy in *On Imagined Visual Representations*, it is important to recall his revolutionary "law of specific nerve energies" (*Gesetz der spezifischen Sinnesenergien*), which he developed in the antecedent study *Physiology of Vision*, and which forms the basis for his explorations of phantasmagoric appearances. The law reaches prominence in the nineteenth century, as it is included in his widely distributed *Elements of Physiology*. In his *Elements*, Müller challenges the understanding of nerves as passive conductors: "all sensory nerves are receptive to electricity, for example, and yet each sense reacts differently to the same cause [*Ursache*]; one nerve sees light from it, the other hears a sound, the other smells, the other tastes electricity, the other feels it as pain or pressure."[21] The consequences of the principle of specific nerve energies—that, in a nutshell, nerve cells produce always the same range of nerve-specific output, independent of the source of their stimulation—are far-reaching.

---

19 Ibid., iii. Here and in the following, all translations from German into English are mine.
20 Müller attributes Goethe's poetic genius *and* his scientific accomplishments to the force of his plastic imagination. See ibid., 106.
21 Johannes Müller, *Handbuch der Physiologie des Menschen für Vorlesungen* (Coblenz: J. Hölscher, 1840–4), 668.

It stipulates that the output of our senses do not reflect anything qualitative or "essential" about the input that the nerves process, but reflect merely the specific capabilities of human physiology.[22] Müller states unequivocally that in our sensory perception of the world we constantly sense *ourselves*, the capabilities of our nerves to react to stimuli, without these sensations reflecting the nature or qualities of the things we perceive. Only after the fact is the sensation externalized "as a consequence of the interaction between the idea [*Vorstellung*] and the nerves, not of the sense alone which isolated would only sense its affections."[23] In a strict sense, then, we cannot even trust our senses to recognize the location of the source of stimulation, that is, to distinguish clearly between inner and outer stimuli. For Müller, it is the result of habitual use that leads us (without being aware of it) to externalize what we hear and see. While we are more willing to accept that feelings such as pain or happiness represent inner states rather than outer qualities, from a sensory perspective, seeing and hearing are no different than feeling: they measure inner states, reflect the qualities of the perceiving organ rather than represent, copy, or express qualities of an outside.[24]

Müller's law did not remain unchallenged in the nineteenth century. Only a few years after its publication, Hermann Lotze contested the "specificity" attributed to nerve cells, as his research showed how nerves can acquire different functions. Lotze also separated more clearly than Müller nerve stimuli from the "soul," arguing that the qualities of sensations are "a production of the soul according to its laws, and do not depend at all on the nature of the physical stimuli except that these offer

---

22 In the early nineteenth century, it was common to differentiate between general and specific energy. The latter refers to what are viewed as structuring properties and should not be confused with a physical concept of (constant) energy that informs the second law of thermodynamics as conceived by Müller's most famous student, Hermann von Helmholtz. I will return to this distinction below in my discussion of Uexküll's reading of Müller's inaugural address.
23 Müller, *Handbuch*, 272.
24 Jonathan Crary points out some of the "nihilistic" consequences of Müller's theorem: that it conceives of the relationship between stimulus and sensation as fundamentally arbitrary, that it drains interiority "of any meaning that it had for a classical observer," stipulating instead that "all sensory experience occurs on a single immanent plane" and that it dissolves the unity of the subject into "a composite structure on which a wide range of techniques and forces could produce or stimulate manifold experiences that are all equally 'reality.'" *Techniques of the Observer: On Vision and Modernity in the Nineteenth Century* (Cambridge and London: MIT, 1990), 92. In Crary's assessment, these consequences mark Müller's principle of specific nerve energies as one of the most controversial ways in which cognition was figured in the nineteenth century.

signals for the soul to create ideas."[25] Furthermore, for Lotze "energies" gave way "to a proportionality between three disparate processes: the stimulus, the nervous excitation, and the conscious sensation."[26] The critique of Müller's contemporaries and subsequent modifications to the law (including Helmholtz replacing specific sensory pathways with specific fibers)[27] do not, however, take away from Müller's contribution to an episteme that has led today's neurosciences to understand consciousness and cognition as emergent phenomena tied to the dynamics of self-referencing neural networks and reciprocally interacting systems. With his law of specific nerve energies, Müller indeed anticipates what Evan Thompson and Francisco Varela describe as "enactive" or "radical-embodiment,"[28] a conception of cognition that recognizes how "our environment emerges through embodied interactions that create meaning, and make sense of otherwise arbitrary sensory input."[29] This research tradition offers an alternative to reductionist and materialist approaches that came to dominate the life sciences even in Müller's lifetime. They also escape the accusation of correlationism.

On the surface, the latter claim might seem contradictory as Müller's law of specific nerve energies appears to assert a correlationist perspective. Is not Müller, a speculative realist might suspect, merely extending what Quentin Meillassoux calls the "Kantian catastrophe"[30] into the realm of physiological science? But a closer examination of Müller's work reveals that the constructive role of physiology is more intricate as it asks us to rethink "realism" itself, including the realism of scientific findings. To begin with, Müller's notion of embodiment suggests a circular process where the mind (what is perceived or imagined) registers not an outside, but reactions by the underlying sensory apparatus

---

25 Hermann Lotze, *Allgemeine Pathologie und Therapie als mechanische Naturwissenschaften* (Leipzig: Weidmann'sche Buchhandlung, 1842), 150; translated and quoted in William A. Woodward, "Hermann Lotze's Critique of Johannes Müller's Doctrine of Specific Sense Energies," *Medical History* 19, no. 2 (April 1975): 152.
26 Ibid., 155–6.
27 Ibid., 156.
28 See Evan Thompson and Francisco J. Varela for a concise presentation on how the cognitive sciences can move past the mind/body and mind/world dichotomies by conceiving of "brain, body and environment ... as mutually embedded systems rather than as internally and externally located with respect to one another." "Radical Embodiment: Neural Dynamics and Consciousness," *Trends in Cognitive Sciences* 5, no. 10 (2001): 423–4.
29 Engler-Coldren, Knapp, and Less, "Embodied Cognition," 417.
30 Meillassoux, *After Finitude*, 124. For a more differentiated discussion of speculative realism's and other new materialist interpretations of Kant, see the contributions of Peter Gilgen, Carsten Strathausen, and Leif Weatherby in this volume.

(or neural networks) to stimuli. This insight necessitates a change in focus for the cognitive scientist, from considerations of the relationship between inner and outer, thinking and being, subject and object, or, in neurological terms, between the source of a stimulus and the neural response to the stimulus, to the relationship between physiology and psychology. At issue now is the role neurophysiological activities play and their relation to the mind or to the imagination, that is, the translation of physiological activities into more or less coherent sensations, mental images, visual representations, and so on.[31]

This shift in focus is what drives Müller to investigate "phantasy" in the form of phantasmagoric and other visions, because it is here that the astute observer can catch the visual sensory substance at work independent of external stimuli. And it is with regard to phantasy, plastic imagination, and phantasmagoric appearances that Goethe's work acquires scientific relevance for Müller. If, as Müller's law suggests, the "energies of what appears bright, dark, or in color, are not inherent to the external things, the cause of their excitement, but are inherent to the visual sensory substance itself,"[32] then Goethe's exploration of the hypnagogic state of consciousness not only helps confirm this distinct vitality of the senses, it also underlines the importance of a careful examination of the relationship between sensation on the one hand and the mind's specific vitality on the other. At stake is no less than the distinction, the material border and interaction between body and mind, the bridge between the Cartesian divide.

Embodied Phantasy

Let me briefly reconstruct Müller's argument as it approaches and then asks us to rethink this border. Müller motivates the treatise's task to examine "the visual sense in its interaction with the mind" (*Geistesleben*)[33] first by explaining how in the organic world cause and effect must be distinguished from physical and chemical reactions. In a mechanical reaction, a body communicates its quality to another (e.g., speed) and in a chemical reaction two sides combine to form a third that hides

---

31 To avoid a misinterpretation of this point, let's note that Müller does *not* imply that everything is subjective or reducible to human consciousness when he suggests that our perceptions are not defined by or measure the outside world, but the sense-specific output of its sensory apparatus. Rather, it emphasizes the constitutive role of the underlying physiology (which has formed over millions of years and not just in humans); and it asks us to conceive as acquired the perceptual as well as the physiological relationship to what either and both have learned to recognize and relate to as their environment.
32 *Physiologie des Gesichtssinnes*, 44–5. Müller calls this the basic principle of all physiological examination.
33 Müller, *Phantastische Gesichtserscheinungen*, v.

(*verschweigt*) the particular qualities of each side (e.g., H_2O). In organic activity (*Wirksamkeit*), however, no quality is communicated, nor do two entities combine to form a third; rather, in organic interactions, the affected side merely reveals an "essential quality" that exists independent of the quality of the source.[34] Müller mentions specifically the eye as an example. "It does not matter what irritates the eye, it may be pushed, pulled, pressed, or galvanized, or it might sense the irritations transmitted sympathetically from other organs; for all these different causes ... the light nerve will sense its affection as sensation of light, and sense itself as dark when resting."[35] What is being observed is nerve specific: light and color when the visual sensory substance is being stimulated, and darkness in the absence of stimulation.

With these observations, Müller explicitly challenges traditional teachings on optics, which assume light either as entering the eye or as immanent to the eye. Müller points toward an "obvious" physiological contradiction in this viewpoint. "How," Müller asks, "even if there was something outside that was luminous itself, could this objective light reaching the subjective areas also be sensed subjectively as illuminate? ... It would be equally inappropriate to say that the [sensory substances] would themselves sound, be heated, or carry a certain taste."[36] On this point, Müller departs from Goethe. While Goethe recognizes that the human eye is not "a passive receptor of information, but an active source of energy and life,"[37] Goethe nevertheless adopts a platonic perspective and assumes that light and colors are immanent to the eye.[38] Müller instead understands light as sense energy (*Sinnesenergie*) and what the visual sensory substance produces as self-illumination (*Selbstleuchten*).[39] Simply put: Müller acknowledges that no photons ever make it past the retina and hence that what we perceive as light needs to be understood as the product of the physiological apparatus of sensation. This "self-illumination" is confirmed by the fact that visual activity does not end when we close our eyes; indeed, "self-illumination" can best be studied with closed eyes, in a hypnagogic or similar

---

34 See ibid., 4–5.
35 Ibid., 5.
36 Ibid., 8.
37 Nicholas Boyle, "Embodied Cognition: Goethe's Farbenlehre as Phenomenology," *German Life and Letters* 70, no. 4 (October 2017): 490.
38 See *Physiologie des Gesichtssinnes*, 395. Michel Meulders shows that for Goethe, the afterglow of colors depended on the retina and was therefore physiological. The eye, hence, was active and passive at the same time, receiving light, but reviving it immediately. See *Helmholtz. From Enlightenment to Neuroscience*, trans. and ed. Laurence Garey (Cambridge and London: MIT, 2010), 122.
39 Müller, *Phantastische Gesichtserscheinungen*, 9.

state where inside rather than outside stimuli come to define what we see.

Müller first approaches the relationship between physiology and the imagination with regard to the effects of light sensation on thought. He argues that the sensation of light excites the organs of the brain and thus the imagination is stimulated and becomes livelier.[40] That is, light sensation is seen as a stimulant of the activities of the mind, not as something that would determine its activity. The causal link between both is "organic" in nature: the sensation of light brings forth qualities inherent to fantasy. And vice versa: "In an excited state, phantasmagoric and mental representations also affect the light nerve if the nerve is not irritated by external impressions, but reflects in its darkness the excitations of other organs as light and colors."[41] Müller is careful to separate imagined figures, colors, and shades from actual products of the visual sense substance, from what we see with closed eyes. What we see in fantasy is not necessarily sensory, but merely imagined within the dark or light field of vision. However, it is possible for fantasy to excite the visual field so that the otherwise merely imagined things become illuminated and acquire color, become excited *Phantastikons*, phantasms that are indeed sensory phenomena. Müller subsequently sets out to examine more closely the precise border between fantasy and phantasm (reached at the conclusion of section five entitled "On Inner Sensibility"), supplementing his physiological research with the results of years of self-observation and the descriptions of Goethe (and others).

Following in the footsteps of Goethe, then, Müller focuses on the hypnagogic state of consciousness, when "the eye and the whole organism rests with regard to external impressions," as the best time to observe what "in the darkness of the eye will appear as reflex from inner organic states in other parts [of the organism]."[42] In this trance-like state, a fantastic world of strange figures, humans, animals, and so on appears that he has never seen before, illuminated rooms which he had never entered, appearances, which he says he can follow often for half an hour before they become dream images when he falls asleep. Laura Otis has documented in much detail Müller's sleep-deprivation experiments, which became a matter of concern among his peers. Müller says that he is able to reproduce these appearances even during the day, as long as he can relax in a semi-dark room. It is important for him that the appearances he observes in these moments are distinguished from the figments of the imagination associated with superstition or delusions (*Schwärmerei*). What

---

40 See ibid., 17–18.
41 Ibid., 19.
42 Ibid., 21.

Müller observes are not products of fantasy, but physiological phenomena that attest to the independent workings of the senses. Müller quotes at length Goethe's novel *Elective Affinities* as evidence of these dynamics. The novel, which famously frames in chemical terms a married couple's extramarital desires, contains descriptions of the young and impressionable Ottilie who, in a hypnagogic state, experiences phantasmatic appearances of Eduard (who reciprocates her passion, but is married to Charlotte). For Müller, it is important that Goethe highlights the passivity of this process, which in his own experience is confirmed by the suddenness with which the figures appear, seemingly without any incitement by the imagination.[43] Müller describes the relationship between the image of fantasy, which does not incite the field of vision, and the appearance of visual figures before the inner eye as one of sympathy (*Sympathie*). The difference is also cast in terms of one being willfully produced whereas the physiological appearances elude intentionality, making it as real, he argues, as the flash we see when physical pressure is put on the eye.

Müller points out that these appearances are common events. Dream images build on them, and they reappear when we first wake up. They were often misinterpreted as visions, spectra, magical appearances and magnetic clairvoyance; doctors know them from fevers, illnesses of the brain, hysteria, hypochondria, catalepsy, from deranged persons, and from other pathologies. Subsequently, Müller examines the mutations among the figures, shapes, and colors he observes. He takes guidance from Goethe again, this time from Goethe's observations on morphology, citing Goethe's experiment with the image of a flower. Müller suggests Goethe projected the flower into the middle of the visual organ where he was then able to observe the shape of this flower disintegrate only to form new, colorful, sometimes green flowers again, flowers that were not natural, but products of phantasy, and endowed nevertheless with regularity.[44] For Müller, the patterns Goethe describes reveal at its highest level the "freedom of inner sensory life."[45]

We should not ignore the differences between Goethe's and Müller's observations. In both cases, we are dealing with attempts to describe what we today call embodied cognition. In Goethe, however, the correspondence between external and internal energy, which leads him to adopt the assumption of physiologically immanent light, is expressive of an understanding of cognition as mediating between the laws of nature and the bodily senses which themselves are part of the natural order.[46] For Müller, there is no such complementarity between inner and

---

43 See ibid., 23.
44 Ibid., 28.
45 Ibid.
46 See Boyle, "Embodied Cognition," 490.

outer, between sensory experience and universal laws; rather he understands the sensory organ as both the enabling and the limiting factor in the perception and imagining of shapes, colors, and even space, and at the same time he recognizes the independence of the imagination in its interpretation of the specific energies of the senses. Put differently, Müller finds further confirmation of physiology's constructive role in the relationship he observes between fantasy and phantasy, between what and how something might be merely imagined and how it might actually appear to the sensory apparatus. Reality here is not projected onto a universalized concept of "nature" shared by inside (cognition) and outside (world), but is created by, and specific to, the human physiology and its subsequent interpretation by fantasy.

In the second part of his treatise, Müller expands further on the relationship between fantasy and physiology. Fantasy, he notes, is always affected by the senses, as whatever is imagined is imagined in the light or dark visual field of the visual sensory substance. So, even where fantasy imagines things that do not appear visually, fantasy involves the field of vision as it is the medium[47] within which forms are being imagined. Müller again cites Goethe's Ottilie (her diary entry in chapter 3) to substantiate the point: "However you may imagine yourself, you will always think of yourself as seeing. It might well be that the inner light one day may move outside of us so that we would not need another light source."[48] Fantasy's plasticity is also revealed in the ability (especially of children) to see figures, shapes, faces, and so on where there are merely simple lines and shades (Müller mentions as an example from his own past plaster peeling off an old wall). Fantasy adds, completes, and varies figures in a process Müller describes as a metamorphization activity. It is more active when the visual appearances are subjective and therefore more variable and fleeting than when they are provoked by external stimulation. As another example, Müller cites the description of the trees and rocks acquiring anthropomorphic characteristics and their threatening demeanor in the Walpurgis Night in Goethe's *Faust* to demonstrate "this wonderous plastic vitality of fantasy within the visual field"[49] that is strongest in the dark.

The subsequent discussion of somnambulism, clairvoyance, hypnotism, magnetism, and of dreams is centered around the question of intentionality, how the mind can affect the human physiology, how it can make the visual sensory substance shine so that a person indeed

---

47 With regard to vision, Müller defines medium as a substance with the capability to refract light. He finds several such media in the human eye. See *Physiologie des Gesichtssinnes*, 46.
48 Müller, *Phantastische Gesichtserscheinungen*, 44 (citing Goethe).
49 Ibid., 62.

sees things with closed eyes or while sleepwalking. Müller is quite careful again to separate mere fantasy from phantasms, from actual stimulations of the visual sensory substance. With regard to somnambulism, he suggests: "At most we may admit that we can assume that in such a state you actually see in the field of vision what your intention is focused on."[50] The active role of the imagination is also highlighted in the discussion of religious visions. While the figures, shapes, and forms the seer observes are defined physiologically, their meaning, how they are anthropomorphized (as demonic faces, for example), will vary from religion to religion.[51] Phantastic visions offer further evidence that the sense of exterior space, too, is a product of internal operations by the visual sense substance. The person who has such visions places what she sees outside the body, that is, experiences the visions as an external reality. Müller also sees the visual sensory substance creating a sense of exterior space when we locate the structure of the eye's blood vessels (that we might observe with closed eyes) outside of our body.[52] In addition to religious visions, the question of intentionality—how the mind can make the visual sensory substance produce specific images—is further discussed with regard to dreams as well as the ability of great artists to retain and reflect a subjective vision without willful interference and without losing sight of its subjective quality.[53] Finally, Müller examines the intentionality of phantasms that derive from "sympathetic irritations" that emanate from the sexual organs and that mold the phantasm (*das Phantasticon*) into lewd figures.[54] Each time, Müller underlines the physiological basis of both phantasmatic and fantastic appearances, without, however, reducing one to the other. Rather, Müller conceives each sense substance to serve as a medium consisting of its own base elements and transformative energy, which the imagination utilizes to fashion its own (imagination-specific) forms, images, symbols and interpretations. The "sympathy" between both in turn makes it possible for fantasy to stimulate the sense substances, or entice sensory output without the need for external stimulation. The latter process, the ability to make the sensory organs produce images, might seem miraculous;

---

50 Ibid., 57.
51 See ibid., 68.
52 See ibid., 69.
53 Müller references Goethe's *Morphology of Plants* as evidence of an inner productive force which allows the poet and all true artists to let the ephemeral representations that appear in the sense organ as memories or as figments of the imagination "unfold themselves, grow, expand, contract without intention or willing" so that the "fleeting schemata can become truly objective images." Ibid., 83.
54 Ibid., 100–101.

however, it is no more miraculous, Müller suggests, than the "capacity to voluntarily extend or bend the arm."[55]

Müller draws two conclusions from these observations. Firstly, he notes how consciousness (*die Welt der Vorstellungen*) can stimulate and affect the visual sensory substance in the same way the external world of objects does: "Both are neither light, nor sound, nor are they warm; but their effects on the senses are specific to the senses."[56] Secondly, he attributes the fashioning, moving, changing of forms to the imagination and thus separates the imagination from the senses; yet precisely on this point, he also understands fantasy as an expression of the senses. The constant mutations are expressive of the "physiological lifeform of fantasy," the latter being called psychological only, he argues, because the forms are imagined.[57] The activity itself, however, is formative, that is, its specific energy is physiological. In other words, Müller understands mental representation (perception and imagination) as a function of the sense organs, the result of their inherent energy, one that nevertheless operates autonomously inasmuch as organs react in organ-specific ways to stimuli, whether these stimuli originate internally (are themselves imagined) or externally (by activities of the visual sensory substance).

As I suggested previously, Müller's research anticipates a constructivist epistemology that is not a variant of Kantian correlationism, nor of what Meillassoux calls "strong correlationism"—with which Meillassoux describes the "absolutizing of correlation itself" so that "only the relation between subject and object remains, or some other

---

55 Ibid., 59. The nature of the reciprocal interactions between fantasy on the one hand and the sensory apparatus on the other remains a controversial issue that separates theories of enactive embodiment from other, less radical notions of embodiment: "An open question about emergence in complex systems is whether they involve 'relational holism,' that is, relationships that are not reducible to the intrinsic features of the components. The paradigm case of relational holism is 'quantum entanglement,' but it has been suggested that the phenomena studied in nonlinear dynamical systems theory might also qualify. If this were true, then emergence and downward causation in complex systems would violate not simply the methodological doctrine of microphysical reduction, but the ontological doctrine that a whole supervenes entirely on the intrinsic properties of its parts (known as 'mereological supervenience')." Thompson and Varela, "Radical Embodiment," 420. From a systems-theoretical perspective, the challenge is how to conceive of causation without violating the idea of systems closure as a necessary precondition for its openness. Thompson and Varela suggest a definition of "causes" as "order parameters operating as 'context-sensitive constraints' that modify a system's phase space or the probability distribution of events in that space." Ibid.
56 Müller, *Phantastische Gesichtserscheinungen*, 94.
57 See ibid., 94–5.

94 Posthumanism in the Age of Humanism

correlation deemed more fundamental."[58] What Müller's neurophysiological research shows is more radical. It neither suggests the primacy of thinking or a (thinking) subject for objects or being to emerge; nor does it hypostasize the correlation between subject and object, or between thinking and being; instead it suggests that what is sensed or perceived, and any relation to an outside that is inferred therefrom, is the product, not of a correlation, but of a self-differentiation process, of operations that have learned (on their inside) to distinguish in organism-specific ways between inside and outside. Even the most primitive life forms have this ability (e.g., crabs tend not to pinch themselves). Twentieth-century operational constructivism has extended this organic mode of (self-)observation also to more complex, nonorganic modes of observation, including thinking and communication (and we might consider technologies or scientific theories to work analogously). The point is that it is not from a *correlation* of preexisting, independent entities that a sense of being or of subjects and objects emerge, but from differentiation processes, from a "one" that has learned to make itself different from itself in order to observe itself. This "one" may well be stipulated to be a material substrate, with the caveat, however, that both the sense of materiality and any concept of materiality are specific to the biological, physiological, and semiotic operations that evolved to make such observations. The constructivist argument thus is *not* subsuming observation under the aegis of an autonomous human subject, nor does it resort to a materialist absolute; it stipulates instead that stabilities—what an organism, a mind, or society experiences or observes as reality—are the product of recursive operations of interacting systems that have evolved (and continue to evolve) over long periods of time.

What, then, are the consequences of Müller's focus on embodiment, on the physiological underpinnings of cognition? Müller criticizes theories of association and more broadly empirical psychology for focusing too much on the products of the imagination at the expense of a closer examination of the life of the generating mind. Müller instead defines phantasy functionally, declaring that it follows one singular "life principle" (*Lebensgesetz*): "Sensuous imagining [*Vorstellen*] is its energy; to

---

58 Meillassoux, *After Finitude*, 37. Meillassoux continues: "A metaphysics of this type may select from among various forms of subjectivity, but it is invariably characterized by the fact that it hypostatizes some mental, sentient, or vital term: representation in the Leibnizian monad; Schelling's Nature, or the objective subject-object; Hegelian Mind; Schopenhauer's Will; the Will (or Wills) to Power in Nietzsche; perception loaded with memory in Bergson; Deleuze's Life, etc." I will return to Müller's purported "vitalism," but shall point out already that Müller's thought does not belong to what Meillassoux in this context (and with specific reference to Nietzsche and Deleuze) calls "anti-rationalist doctrines of life and will." Ibid.

always change, limit, expand the sensuously imagined is the vitality of its energy."[59] We should not dismiss this line of argument too hastily as an expression of Müller's vitalist beliefs (for which some of his students had already criticized him);[60] for the distinction he draws between specific energy that creates the sensory representations and its vitality, its ability to change, limit, and extend these representations, adds an important parameter to his cognitive constructivism. It unites sensory activity and fantasy under one force, one life principle. Furthermore, it recognizes the instability and transient nature of what we perceive or imagine. In other words, Müller's life principle emphasizes how shaping and fashioning physiological responses are inherent features of the interplay between physiology and fantasy. Müller's life principle thus offers not only an early form of (relational) holism, it also introduces instability, transience, and creativity into the very core of cognition.

Uexküll Reading Müller

I want to expand on the role the concept of "life" plays in Müller's epistemological constructivism—and how it escapes a posthumanist critique of Kantian correlationism—by turning to Jacob von Uexküll's remarkable book *The Sense of Life*. Uexküll purports to find the answer to this audacious question in Müller's 1824 inaugural lecture "On Physiology's Need for a Philosophical Observation of Nature" (reprinted as part of the *Physiology of Vision*). How does Müller's research on the constructive role of the "senses"—the reference makes clear that the title of the book plays with the double meaning of *Sinn*, which like the English word "sense" means both meaning and sense organ—address the philosophical question about the meaning of life? And, in any case, why turn with such a question to an old inaugural address by a young physiologist, and why do so in the middle of a catastrophic war (the text was written in 1942, though not published until 1947)?

---

59 Ibid., 96.
60 Stanley Finger and Nicholas Wade point out that although Müller was a leader in the movement to investigate biological problems with the tools of physics and chemistry, "there was a certain mystic element in Müller's nature," and that he was looked upon by his students as a representative of "Vitalismus." That is, he continued to believe in an overriding "organic creative force" (*Lebenskraft*) that organized the parts of the body and controlled its functions during life, only to vanish at the time of death. See "The Neuroscience of Helmholtz and the Theories of Johannes Müller. Part 1: Nerve Cell Structure, Vitalism, and the Nerve Impulse," *Journal of the History of the Neurosciences* 11, no. 2 (2002): 143. In the following, I will argue that we should read Müller's life principle not as an external natural force, but as a heuristic device with which he accounts for what today we treat as emergent phenomena.

The answer lies in Uexküll recognizing that Müller's law of specific nerve energies and his conception of life offer an escape from the dominant rationalist paradigm and particularly from the mind-body, subject-object, idealism-materialism dualisms that, as Uexküll's initial reflections on his own time imply, are linked to the historical catastrophe that surrounds him. In this regard, Uexküll would clearly agree that Müller's seemingly post-Kantian epistemology is not correlational, but offers the possibility to escape the pitfalls of correlationism. It is precisely Müller's law of specific nerve energies that makes "the desired separation between objects and subjects impossible" as it "makes the observer the integrating part of the nature one observes," as, Uexküll continues, the "subject forces the things of nature that surround it under the yoke of its own energies."[61] While on the surface "under the yoke" might seem to suggest the very subject-centeredness targeted by posthumanists of different stripes, Uexküll understands that Müller's inclusion of the physiology as the integrating part of the observation process is not egocentric, but "anthropocentric" and, inasmuch as the law of specific nerve energy describes a physiological activity that is shared with other species, it is in fact "acentric."[62] Uexküll calls this acentricity a divine perspective: it means to recognize that the objects we observe and the reality we live in is contingent on the apparatus that observes them and hence will always be different for different organisms and observers. This perspectivism is not based on subjective differences, but is organism-specific. To make the point, Uexküll specifically picks a nonhuman example, suggesting that the acentric viewpoint should lead us to examine not the "images that from the outside impress themselves onto the dog, but look at what images the dog with the help of the sensory impressions within his brain projects into his environment."[63]

This quote shows why Uexküll finds in Müller a kindred spirit. Müller's model of embodied cognition is in line with Uexküll's famous understanding of organisms living in their own, organism-specific

---

61 Jacob von Uexküll, *Der Sinn des Lebens. Gedanken über die Aufgaben der Biologie mitgeteilt in einer Interpretation der zu Bonn 1824 gehaltenen Vorlesung des Johannes Müller "Von dem Bedürfnis der Physiologie nach einer philosophischen Naturbetrachtung" mit einem Ausblick von Thure von Uexküll* (Godesberg: Helmut Küpper, 1947), 9–10.
62 Ibid., 31.
63 Ibid., 33. Uexküll in his conclusion compares the perspective of the (materialist) scientist onto the universe with that of a proud fly crawling around on his desk examining everything exclusively with regard to its fly-sensitivities (*Fliegenbefindlichkeit*). Ibid., 77.

environments.[64] Uexküll distinguishes the self-created, organism-specific environment (*Umwelt*) from alien surroundings (*Umgebung*), which he conceives as something unfamiliar, unknown, tumultuous, insecure and even hostile. Following Uexküll, the environment is a product of the organism with which the organism has learned to secure itself and persist in potentially hostile surroundings. This viewpoint does not lead us into a correlational abyss, but instead asks us to focus on the material, physiological, and psychological processes that are involved in creating our organ-specific environment, which de facto constitutes the reality within which humans live and can observe other species. This is neither an absolute reality, nor is this kind of reality merely an object of philosophical speculation.[65] With Müller, we might instead think of it as a doubly mediated reality, as psychologically and physiologically *enactive*. While Müller did not perform actual "environmental research," that is, an "examination of the subject-specific relations of meaning to its surroundings,"[66] Uexküll finds that he skipped right to the crucial point (*Kernpunkt*) of such an environmental perspective, namely a conception of life that can no longer be comprehended by reason, but must be experienced. It adopts a holistic viewpoint that recognizes how "body and soul originate from the same source, life, and are never separated within living nature."[67]

For Uexküll it is this focus on life, conceived as a force "that cannot be comprehended by any category of thought, neither by causality nor by finality,"[68] that separates Müller's from the dominant judicious (*verständige*) physiology. Uexküll in large part blames the success of the latter on Müller's student Helmholtz who, he contends, "destroyed" the foundation of Müller's physiology, namely the discovery of the specific energies of the living substances, because he could not tolerate a

---

64 His famous definition describes *amoeba terricola* which provide "the impression of a most charming work of art ... that in an alien world created their own world in which they sustain themselves calmly as if held securely between hinges." Jacob von Uexküll, *Umwelt und Innenwelt der Tiere* (Berlin: Julius Springer, 1909), 39.
65 Although certain realities (e.g., the consequences of a person getting hit by a truck) will appear as quite close to absolute, we know that, albeit slowly, organisms and the relationship to their environments change over time. What changes much more quickly, however, and should be subject to continued philosophical scrutiny, is what we recognize intellectually and with the help of technologies as environmental factors and how we understand organisms and their relation to the environment.
66 Uexküll, *Sinn des Lebens*, 17.
67 Ibid., 14.
68 Ibid., 13.

non-physical form of energy.[69] Uexküll had warned at the beginning of the book not to confuse the concept of specific energies popular in Müller's time with the now dominant understanding of energy as a physical, i.e., constant, quantity. At stake is not a form of energy that would contradict the second law of thermodynamics, but a concept that references the formation of specific biological structures, processes, and entities (such as cells) that are embedded in, and yet relate autonomously to their (organ-specific) environments. Uexküll suggests it was Goethe's *Metamorphosis of Plants* that offered Müller "immediate insight into the form-giving activity of life, which does not need causality."[70] Goethe's morphology developed a model for a non-materialist understanding of life by conceiving of plants not as spatial entities (*Raumgestalten*) but as formations of time (*Zeitgestalten*). Such *Zeitgestalten* Uexküll compares to melodies that "cannot be measured materially and cannot be subjected to the blade of a scalpel."[71] The formative law they follow is that of "the melody itself."[72] Uexküll reads Müller's law of specific nerve energies, then, as describing what in a more contemporary language we observe as an emergent phenomenon, or more precisely, as a property that "comes to be instantiated in a process or entity that emerges in time."[73] Life, from this angle, is conceived not as a metaphysical or mystical driving force, not as an aphysical physical energy; but instead is a concept indebted to what "specific energies" describe in the early nineteenth century: emergent properties, forms, structures, or relations that emerge from physical and chemical processes, but cannot be reduced to the elements, reactions, or interactions from which they emerge. Put differently, Müller's vitalism is not based on what Meillassoux calls a philosophical hypostatization of "some mental, sentient or vital term";[74] nor does it insist on a "materialism of

---

69 See ibid., 60.
70 Ibid., 66.
71 Ibid., 49.
72 Ibid., 66. Uexküll continues: "It is completely certain that the flower originates from the bud and the fruit from the flower. Every time something completely new emerges [*entsteht*] that was not hidden in the preceding *Gestalt*, just as a note in a melody does not spring forth from the preceding note. But the sequence of the new creations is determined by a life principle [*lebensgesetzlich*]." Ibid.
73 Thompson and Varela, "Radical Embodiment," 420.
74 Meillassoux, *After Finitude*, 37. Meillassoux fears that his kind of vitalism "has become so powerful that in the modern era, even speculative materialism seems to have been dominated by these anti-rationalist doctrines of life and will, to the detriment of a 'materialism of matter' which takes seriously the possibility that there is nothing living or willing in the inorganic realm." Meillassoux, *After Finitude*, 38. Meillassoux's critique targets brands of new materialism that project vitality in one form or another onto materiality itself. Cf. Jane Bennett, *Vibrant Matter: A Political Ecology of Things* (Durham, NC: Duke University Press, 2010), or

matter" that would merely reinforce an organic/inorganic dualism and hence advance a correlational viewpoint. The constructivist episteme that Müller and Uexküll develop undermines such dichotomies as it suggests that we think of life as an emergent phenomenon, as deriving and yet being separate from an underlying physiology and materiality.

Uexküll uses the melody analogy in a section of the book that turns explicitly against the materialism of Helmholtz (in a fictive dialogue between a representative of Müller and a representative of his most famous student). It hones in on a point where certain materialist and new materialist contentions regularly misrepresent the implications of constructivist epistemologies. In a nutshell, the accusation is that such epistemologies follow Kant and deepen the separation between thinking and being, subject and object, by subsuming the latter under the former. They thus are thought to lose contact with and sight of real objects, real things, reality itself. We saw Uexküll already argue that the critical (in the Kantian sense) inclusion of the observer, especially when extended to neurophysiology, does not lead toward a subjectivist or anthropocentric perspective, but away from it, to an *acentric* perspective. But Uexküll's reading of Müller points toward another contradictory implication inherent to new materialist contentions about the Kantian divide. Thule von Uexküll spells out this point in his "Outlook" to *The Sense of Life* which was published along with his father's treatise. He argues that the "problem of his day" and the reason the natural sciences are in need of philosophy is not epistemological, but created by materialist and reductionist approaches to science. Uexküll's son also turns against Helmholtz, who, by declaring that "sense qualities were mere symbols for real happenings that lie behind them ... turned the world in which we live into an illusory world, which only allows us to assess the real world behind it via our intellect."[75] I want to suggest that new materialisms, object-oriented ontology, speculative realism and similar posthumanist strands of thought run the risk of falling into the same

---

Karen Barad, *Meeting the Universe Halfway: Quantum Physics and the Entanglement of Matter and Meaning* (Durham, NC: Duke University Press, 2007). Heather I. Sullivan has argued that Goethe is an antecedent of these forms of new materialism as "Goethe sees human beings engaging with 'elementary natural phenomena,' like colors, in terms of *interactive* processes, rather than as an 'active' mind processing 'passive' nature." "Agency in the Anthropocene: Goethe, Radical Reality, and the New Materialisms," in *The Early History of Embodied Cognition 1740–1920. Die Lebenskraft-Debate and Radical Reality in German* Science, *Music, and Literature*, ed. John A. McCarthy et al. (Leiden and Boston: Brill Rodopi, 2016), 295. I agree with Meillassoux that this approach extends a "strong correlationism" that runs the danger of hypostasizing the relation between mind and matter in its anthropomorphizations of matter itself.

75 Ibid., 92–3.

trap: their affirmation of an observer-independent reality merely deepens the correlational divide by returning us to a worldview that locates reality once again beyond "life," beyond the physiological, technological, communicational, and semantic means with which life has learned to enact and sustain itself.

Why does it matter? The impetus of critical posthumanism in the vein of Cary Wolfe has been to effect political and social change by remaining vigilant toward the normative and discriminatory force of reality proclamations. New materialisms have drifted toward the other side of this equation. Timothy Morton, to name one of their louder voices, argues that it is on the "terrain of ontology that many of the urgent ecological battles need to be fought."[76] This might be true in the political arena where invoking the limits of scientific certainty can be used as a strategy to avoid modification of political positions and actions (e.g., to protect the pocketbooks of party donors). Returning to a holistic approach in line with Müller's thinking, we do not need to deny the reality of scientific findings, but only their grounding in an absolute, unchangeable outside. If we think of reality as the environment within which life forms (plants, animals, humans, societies) have come to secure themselves—including with the help of science and technology—then the constructivist approach will have as an advantage over ontological and materialist approaches that it can account for and encourage the continued differentiation of observation processes (biological, linguistic, communicational, technological, or scientific). It can distinguish between psychological and physiological realities while also acknowledging the role of the former, of fantasy, in casting and recasting over time the understanding of the latter and its relationship to its (organ-specific) environment. A physiologically informed epistemology and philosophically reflective physiology pays attention to the co-constitutive processes that define what and how various observers—including our bodies, other living beings, different cultures—experience reality. More simply put, acknowledging the constructive role of fantasy is also to recognize fantasy's significance for science. Müller makes this point in his concluding remarks to *On Imagined Visual Representations* where he attributes both Goethe's poetic genius and his scientific accomplishments to the force of his plastic imagination.[77] Emphasizing the role of plastic imagination for discoveries in the natural sciences does not lead us away from things, objects, the thickness of the body, or the realities living beings confront,

---

76 Timothy Morton, *Hyperobjects. Philosophy and Ecology after the End of the World* (Minneapolis / London: University of Minnesota Press, 2013), 22.
77 Müller, *Phantastische Gesichtserscheinungen*, 106.

but rather, as Müller's work shows, right to it. The life sciences in particular might be understood as a sensory apparatus whose differentiations increase the variability—and with it the adaptability—to what are perceived and experienced as threats to our organism-specific and observer-dependent environments.

Part II
Who's Afraid of Idealism?
Materialism, Posthumanism, and the
Post-Kantian Legacy

Six Kant and Posthumanism

Carsten Strathausen

Introduction

Posthumanism is difficult to put into focus. Even a cursory look at recent scholarship reveals the disparate, and often contradictory, notions of the posthuman in circulation today—not to mention the plethora of other related concepts such as the nonhuman, the inhuman, the metahuman, the transhuman, etc.[1] Although the term "posthuman" was first introduced by Ihab Habib Hassan in 1977, it rose to prominence only in the late 1990s, most notably through N. Katherine Hayles's seminal book *How We Became Posthuman*.[2] Hayles defined posthumanism in the context of twentieth-century cybernetics and AI research as the attempt to reconfigure "humans as information-processing machines with fundamental similarities to other kinds of information-processing machines, especially intelligent computers." Sharply critical of what she perceived as the rationalist, Cartesian bias of posthumanist theory and its top-down model of human subjectivity, Hayles instead emphasized the embodied nature of our mind and the nonlinear complexity of its cognitive functions: "The chaotic, unpredictable nature of complex dynamics implies that subjectivity is emergent rather than given, distributed rather than located solely in consciousness, emerging from and integrated into a chaotic world rather than occupying a position of mastery and control removed from it."[3]

In explicit contrast to Hayles, Cary Wolfe considers posthumanism to be a meaningful critique, not a mindless celebration, of Cartesian

---

1   For a general overview, see Francesca Ferrando, "Posthumanism, Transhumanism, Antihumanism, Metahumanism, and New Materialisms: Differences and Relations," *Existenz* 8, no. 2 (Fall 2013): 26–32.
2   Ihab Habib Hassan, "Prometheus as Performer: Toward a Posthumanist Culture?" *The Georgia Review* 31, no. 4 (Winter 1977): 830–50; N. Katherine Hayles, *How We Became Posthuman: Virtual Bodies in Cybernetics, Literature, and Informatics* (Chicago: University of Chicago Press, 1999).
3   Hayles, *How We Became Posthuman*, 246, 291.

rationality. A strong proponent of animal rights, Wolfe argues that posthumanism departs from traditional humanist values on two distinct levels: first, on the "internal," academic level, it recognizes that human knowledge is inherently paradoxical and subject to the destabilizing systemic effects of *différance* and autopoiesis; and second, on the "external," ontological level, posthumanism recognizes "a second kind of externality and ahumanity" that always already connects, rather than separates, humans and animals.[4] The posthuman, then, is neither a cyborg nor a sequence of disembodied information. It is simply human life growing more mindful of its innate affects and its own animal nature. In the words of Elizabeth Grosz: "What would a humanities, a knowledge of and for the human, look like if it placed the animal in its rightful place, not only before the human but also within and after the human?"[5]

In spite of these critics' considerable influence in the field, posthumanism today can hardly be subsumed under the different versions they have outlined. Informed by disparate disciplines that use both empirical and speculative methods, the various "new materialisms" and "object oriented ontologies" at the heart of posthumanist theory address the rise of climate change, eco-feminism and the anthropocene no less than questions about biogenetics, media studies, and systems theory, to mention but a few of the main topics.[6] Posthumanism, it appears, has become the victim of its success. The term signifies so many different things to so many different people that we have lost a sense of what, if anything, ties the various strands together in either theoretical, methodological, or disciplinary terms.

The overall goal of this essay is twofold. First, I want to identify and characterize different schools of thought in contemporary posthumanism in order to provide a basic overview and establish some minimal conceptual coherence across this sprawling field. Second, I want to argue that Kant's philosophy remains highly relevant today because it helps correct many assumptions and claims made by critics throughout the posthumanities. My main concern is that one cannot disregard human consciousness and phenomenological experience without disabling the very insights posthumanism seeks to promote. We shall see that posthumanists readily anthropomorphize inert nature, while, at

---

4 Cary Wolfe, *What is Posthumanism?* (Minneapolis: University of Minnesota Press, 2010), 126.
5 Elizabeth Grosz, *Becoming Undone: Darwinian Reflections on Life, Politics, and Art* (Durham, NC: Duke University Press, 2011), 13.
6 Richard Grusin provides a comprehensive list of theoretical influences in his introduction to *The Nonhuman Turn*, ed. Richard Grusin (Minneapolis: University of Minnesota Press, 2015), viii–ix.

the same time, they deprive human beings of their own nature and humanity. Another problem is that many versions of posthumanism construct a flat ontology of essential equality among everything, an ontology that ignores the distinctive features of the human brain and flies in the face of common sense and epistemological distinctions of all kinds. Epistemology aside, it is politically dangerous to toy with the idea that matter has feelings and that things require their own representation in parliament. One ought to be cautious about who controls such matters and ventriloquizes what things say. Against this trend, I argue that epistemology haunts ontology at all levels of being, and that Kant's critical philosophy remains an indispensable tool to negotiate the space between them. I shall mostly rely on Kant's *First* and *Third Critique* to make my argument, which is divided into three sections: epistemology/ontology, politics, and aesthetics.

Epistemology/Ontology

Within posthumanism, the field of "Speculative Realism" (SR) is home to the most outspoken critics of Kant's legacy. I hasten to add that SR itself is far from a homogeneous philosophical movement. Instead, it comprises a variety of different approaches and agendas dating back to the beginning of the new millennium.[7] What binds these theories

---

7   Although discussions had been going on for a while, the phrase "Speculative Realism" was first introduced during a conference at Goldsmiths College in London in 2007; the first publication on "Speculative Realism" was co-authored by Ray Brassier, Iain Hamilton Grant, Graham Harman, and Quentin Meillassoux and appeared the same year in *Collapse. Philosophical Research and Development*, vol. 3, ed. Robin Mackay (Falmouth, UK: Urbanomic, 2007), 307–435. Since then, each of SR's four founding members has pursued a distinct agenda. Quentin Meillassoux relies on mathematics and post-Cantorian set theory to argue that "anything is possible" and that the whole world could change entirely at any instant: "What is mathematizable cannot be reduced to a correlate of thought," Meillassoux argues, meaning "that the in-itself could actually be anything whatsoever and that we know this." Quentin Meillassoux in *After Finitude: An Essay on the Necessity of Contingency*, trans. Ray Brassier (London: Bloomsbury, 2010), 124, 117, 65. Graham Harman argues the exact opposite, namely that real objects are inaccessible and infinitely withdrawn from all relations, meaning that, essentially, the world will never change at all: "Things exist not in relation, but in a strange sort of vacuum from which they only partly emerge into relation." Graham Harman, *Prince of Networks: Bruno Latour and Metaphysics* (Melbourne: anamnesis, 2009), 195. Ian Hamilton Grant, meanwhile, has gone back to German Idealism and Schelling's *Naturphilosophie* to argue in favor of panpsychism, while Ray Brassier has become increasingly critical of SR in general and Harman's work in particular. Cf. Ian Hamilton Grant, *Philosophies of Nature after Schelling* (London: Bloomsbury, 2008); Ray Brassier, "Postscript: Speculative Autopsy," in Peter Wolfendale, *Object-Oriented Philosophy. The Noumenon's New Clothes* (Falmouth, UK: Urbanomic, 2014), 407–21.

together, however, is their joint rejection of Kant's transcendental philosophy. The explicit goal of SR is to move beyond—or, as I fear, to fall behind—what they call the Kantian correlationism of thought and matter, that is, Kant's recognition that human access to and analysis of the world is bound to the in-built constraints of our cognitive and sensory apparatus. Ever since Kant's critical turn in the 1780s, so the argument goes, continental philosophy has abandoned ontology for epistemology, thus giving rise to an entrenched anthropocentric view of the world that devalues the being of real objects (the Kantian "thing-in-itself") in favor of how these objects appear to us, humans, who interact with or reflect upon them. Hence Quentin Meillassoux speaks of the "Kantian catastrophe" instead of the "Kantian revolution," which he considers a milestone in the "correlationalist deception" that continues to dominate Western philosophy.[8] Similarly, Graham Harman argues that "real objects" exist in "a pre-relational dimension in which they cannot make direct contact of any sort" and are independent from the "intentional" or "sensed" objects we experience in daily life.[9] Speculative Realism, in short, aims to liberate philosophical inquiry from its traditional anthropological bias and to reengage the ontological question of how things are in themselves, outside of and apart from (human) consciousness.

For the sake of brevity, let me come straight to the point: I believe this attempt to move beyond the subject–object correlation is, strictly speaking, nonsensical. It literally makes no sense to speculate about beings in the world without taking into account the physical and mental constraints of the living systems and technical apparatus that do the speculating. For there is no way the world is under no description, as Richard Rorty used to say.[10] This does not mean that "the medium is the message," or that thought and being are one and the same, as the proponents of SR misleadingly summarize their own distorted view of Kantian transcendentalism. It simply means that there is no message without (or apart from) the medium used to express it.[11] No medium, no message—no brains, no speculation. As far as the production of

---

8 Meillassoux, *After Finitude*, 124, 117.
9 Harman, *Prince of Networks*, 132.
10 Richard Rorty, *Objectivity, Relativism, and Truth: Philosophical Papers* (Cambridge: Cambridge University Press, 1990).
11 Mathematics might be the only exception. Most mathematicians are Platonists who believe that numbers are ontologically real entities regardless of the various media (words or numerals, electronic circuits or human brains, screens or paper) used to express them. There are good reasons for rejecting this view, but I cannot pursue them here. See Brian Rotmann, *Mathematics as Sign: Writing, Imaging, Counting* (Stanford: Stanford University Press, 2000); and George Lakoff and Rafael E. Nunez, *Where Mathematics Comes From: How the Embodied Mind Brings Mathematics into Being* (New York: Basic, 2001).

human knowledge is concerned, the subject-object correlation is not just one philosophical issue among others, but is and remains the methodological bedrock for the humanities and the sciences alike. Not just Kant's philosophy, but phenomenology and Marxism, ecology and evolutionary biology, media studies and cognitive science—all these academic fields and disciplines are based on the single premise that there are no observer-independent facts of the world, because living organisms do not exist in a vacuum. Instead, they enact an environment that makes sense to *them*. "Living is sense-making," Francisco Varela points out again and again.[12] All sentient life forms, even the most primitive ones, are forced to make simple choices about how to behave in order to survive, and their behavior reflects whatever kind of limited cognition is available to them. This structural coupling of organism and environment renders any philosophical speculation about absolute beings and the essence of things scientifically moot. Unlike computers, the embodied mind does not run its mental "software" on some prefabricated physical "hardware." To be alive means that the two parts have co-evolved: the mind sustains the body, and the body builds the mind, both at the phylogenetic and the ontogenetic level. In the evolution of life, there is no ontology apart from, or independent of, epistemology.

SR not only splits the two apart, but suppresses one and exalts the other. The result is a plethora of ontological speculations—some worthwhile, many not—entirely void of epistemological critique.[13] Harman's metaphorical-metaphysical claim that objects "allure," yet do not "relate" to a subject rhetorically upends epistemology or "simply ignores it," as Ray Brassier points out.[14] From a biological standpoint, a statement like this—"Matter already contains the seeds of all that it might become. Nothing important will ever come from the outside"—is both counterintuitive and unscientific.[15] It would be blatantly absurd in the life sciences to assert the ontological independence of living things

---

12 Francisco Varela, quoted in Evan Thompson, *Mind in Life: Biology, Phenomenology, and the Sciences of Mind* (Cambridge, MA: Harvard University Press, 2007), 158.
13 There are an increasing number of critics who, like myself, have grown impatient with ontological speculations bereft of epistemological critique. By far the harshest refutation of Harman's OOP stems from Peter Wolfendale, who relabeled *"speculative* Realism" as *"specious* Realism" and claims that in spite of its rhetoric, Harman's philosophy "is not a *critique*, but rather a *consolidation* of correlationism" precisely because Harman "refuses to have any truck with positive epistemology whatsoever." Peter Wolfendale, *Object Oriented Philosophy: The Noumenon's New Clothes* (Falmouth, UK: Urabanomics, 2014), 199, 402.
14 Brassier, "Postscript," 419.
15 Graham Harman, "On the Undermining of Objects: Grant, Bruno, and Radical Philosophy," in *The Speculative Turn: Continental Materialism and Realism*, ed. Levi Bryant, Nick Smicek, and Graham Harman (Melbourne: re-press, 2011), 36.

from their outside when, in fact, these things only exist *because of their relation* to the outside. Any matter that contains seeds, as Harman puts it, also contains formative relations to an environment beyond itself. This structural coupling of self and environment distinguishes living things from inanimate objects. Yes, it is true that all things, alive or not, are composed of atoms and molecules and hence subject to the same natural laws that govern the universe as we know it. Yet the physical world is not just composed of stuff. It is composed of patterns, and these patterns give rise to different properties and behaviors at different levels of being. Life is a good example. Being alive is an emergent property of some complex dynamic systems, but not others. Life is also extremely fragile. If I step on a dense pebble, it essentially remains the same both before and after. But if I step on an ant, it will experience an irreversible change from life to death that affects the very core of its being.

Apart from Deleuze, the best argument I have found in support of a posthuman ontology is the "philosophy of organism" by Alfred North Whitehead, who criticized rationalist and empiricist philosophy alike for adopting a representationalist view of how things are. The fatal flaw of representationalism, Whitehead argued, is the epistemological-ontological gap it creates between the objective "fact" outside the mind and the subjective "idea" inside the mind. Once opened, the gap is impossible to close: "Representative perception," Whitehead concludes, "can never, within its own metaphysical doctrines, produce the title deeds to guarantee the validity of the representation of fact by idea."[16] The only way Western philosophy was able to accommodate this gap was to shift analytical focus away from objects and toward the subjective side of the relation. Kant is guilty of this representationalist fallacy no less than Descartes or Hume before him. Kant, too, reduces the being of one actual entity (let's say a rock) to how another actual entity (let's say a human being) represents this object without giving much thought to the objective nature of the actual entities that cause our representations of them. In ontological terms, however, both entities (rock and human) are obviously equal in rank, because neither is more real. Both entities change over time, so both can be said to have "experiences" of sorts. Though a rock cannot think the way humans do, humans, on the other hand, cannot break into pieces the way a rock does, or melt away in a stream of lava and reemerge in a different shape later on. And since Whitehead chose to call such experiences "feelings," he goes on to claim that "even inorganic entities experience something like an 'influx

---

16 Whitehead, quoted in Donald W. Sherburne, *A Key to Whitehead's Process and Reality* (Chicago: University of Chicago Press, 1981), 147.

of feeling'" at times, and that "perceptions, feeling, and aesthetics are universal structures, not specifically human ones."[17]

This kind of anthropomorphizing rhetoric might be an appropriate political tool to raise ecological awareness among voters, as I will argue later. But it is unwarranted and misleading in scientific discourse, where it does more harm than good. Whitehead's metaphors are no less troubling than those of Edward O. Wilson, the neo-Darwinian founder of sociobiology, who sparked an academic debate about genetic determinism and long-lasting public concern over the rise of social Darwinism in the 1970s and 1980s with rhetoric like this: "Behavior and social structure, like all other biological phenomena, can be studied as 'organs,' extensions of the genes that exist because of their superior adaptive value."[18] But social institutions, I want to insist, are nothing like cellular organs, and rocks are not sentient beings. A rock may be said to "relate to" or "engage with" the outside world, but it certainly does not "feel" it. Unlike living forms, rocks do not have a social milieu or a natural environment, for the simple reason that they do not have a self.[19]

On the other hand, and despite all of his emphasis on the *ontological equality* of actual entities, Whitehead never forgot to draw the necessary *epistemological distinctions* between them. Hence he explicitly distinguished "four types of aggregations of actualities" in the world (i.e., nonliving, vegetable, animal, and human) and discussed the distinct nature of each in both scientific and common-sense terms. "The distinction between men and animals is in one sense only a difference in degree," he readily admits. "But the extent of the degree makes all the difference. The Rubicon has been crossed."[20] And whereas SR simply chose to ignore the problem of consciousness and self-reflection, Whitehead struggled with it throughout his writings.[21] It would never have dawned on Whitehead to use his ontological speculations as a substitute for, or an excuse to ignore, the scientific-epistemological analysis of nature. The two modes do not stand in opposition, but actually inform each other. Actual entities of all types are equally worthy of critical reflection and scientific analysis, according to Whitehead, not

---

17 Alfred North Whitehead, *Process and Reality. Corrected Edition*, ed. David Ray Griffin and Donald W. Sherburne (New York: Free Press, 1978), 177.
18 Edward O. Wilson, *Sociobiology: The New Synthesis* (Cambridge, MA: Harvard University Press, 1975), 22.
19 The possible exception might be crystals; see Erwin Schrödinger, *What is Life?: With Mind and Matter and Autobiographical Sketches* (Cambridge: Cambridge University Press, 2012), 5f.
20 Alfred North Whitehead, *Modes of Thought* (Toronto: Free Press, 1968), 28f, 27.
21 "But when all analogies between animal life and human nature have been stressed," Whitehead stated, "there remains the vast gap in respect to the influence of reflective experience." *Modes of Thought*, 102–3.

despite but *because* of their unique nature and the irreducible differences between them. Without a detailed account of these constitutive differences—an account that, for Whitehead, centers on "the changeable, shifting aspects of *our relations to nature*"—the reference to the ontological equality of things would be meaningless and entirely void of substance.[22]

As I see it, the epistemological-ontological tension that runs throughout Whitehead's philosophy elevates it miles above the standard theoretical fair peddled across the disciplines today. The current popularity of SR seems to indicate an ever-increasing thing-fetishism that haunts contemporary theory, a kind of willful disregard of the complex biological and social processes that separate inorganic from organic matter and distinguishes conscious life forms, like animals and humans, from unconscious plants and vegetables. It took billions of years for simple chemical compounds to create autocatalytic loops that not only endured over time, but also changed their immediate environment such that the assembly of similar compounds became increasingly likely to occur, a process that culminated in the creation of a membrane or some other kind of functional boundary able to separate self and other, organism and environment. Thus life emerged from matter. And it bears repeating that some forms of life have consciousness and use language, while others do not.

Without knowing evolutionary biology or complex systems, Kant struggled to explain the genesis of living forms in both his pre-critical and critical writings, most notably in the second part of the *Third Critique*. It is important to note, however, that Kant never uses the term epistemology, which only emerged later in the nineteenth century; he referred to logic instead. Kant's notion of ontology, moreover, was informed by the philosophical tradition of Wolff and Baumgarten, who defined ontology as "the first principle of knowledge and of things in general" or the "science of the predicates of things in general," respectively. Yet Kant broke with this tradition when he equated ontology with his own transcendental analytic, which defined "things in general" as the appearance of things and not as things-in-themselves. In other words, when Kant spoke of ontology, he referred to the phenomenal

---

22 Ibid., 29; my emphasis. Steven Shaviro makes the opposite argument worth quoting: "I should not treat a human being the way that I treat a stone. But we need to remember that these distinctions are always situational. They are differences of degree, not differences of essence or kind." Steven Shaviro, *Without Criteria: Kant, Whitehead, Deleuze, and Aesthetics* (Cambridge: MIT Press, 2009), 23. While this is true, my point is that there are exceedingly few situations in human life that would require us to disregard the significant power differential between humans and stones. Apart from enduring gravity, what other major scenarios exist in which we are better off contemplating the similarities rather than the differences between human life and inert matter?

world constituted by the human mind; when posthumanists today speak of ontology, they refer instead to the noumenal world that exists outside of and independently from the mind.[23]

Howard Caygill suggests that this terminological confusion, which dates back to the nineteenth century, might be partly to blame for the lingering suspicion that Kant's philosophy is essentially idealist. Take, for example, Kant's famous claim that "the conditions of the *possibility of experience* in general are likewise conditions of the *possibility of the objects of experience.*"[24] All Kant does here is state the basic transcendental principle on which his entire *First Critique* is based. Yet "from the perspective of the nineteenth century, this claim is inexplicable," Caygill points out, because it "appear(s) to confuse the epistemological and the ontological orders."[25] Indeed, the statement might be interpreted in the strong correlationist sense that without a perceiving subject, there are no objects at all, period—an idealist interpretation that equates being with thought and seems to warrant SR's charge that Kant was an idealist. The mistake, once again, is to equate Kant's distinction between the thing-in-itself and how it appears to us with the anachronistic distinction between ontology and epistemology that was unfamiliar to Kant. His *Critique*, in other words, is not just an epistemology, but also includes an ontological dimension *beyond* the things-in-themselves.

To clarify this crucial point, let me briefly turn to Bruno Latour, whose actor-networktheory (ANT) is closely related to SR, even though Latour himself never adopted the term and has been sharply critical of Harman's views over the years (and vice versa). In his *Politics of Nature* from 2004, Latour states:

> Yes, there is indeed an objective external reality, but this particular externality is not definitive: it simply indicates that new nonhumans, entities that have never before been included in the work of the collective, find themselves mobilized, recruited, socialized, domesticated. ... We have no idea at all what things in themselves would look like if they had not always been engaged in the battle of naturalization.[26]

Now, this is clearly a Kantian view of things. And yet, Latour explicitly rejects Kant's transcendentalism, because it entails the kind of rigid

---

23 Howard Caygill, *A Kant Dictionary* (London: Wiley-Blackwell, 1995), 307–8.
24 Kant, quoted in Caygill, *A Kant Dictionary*, 308.
25 Caygill, *A Kant Dictionary*, 176.
26 Bruno Latour, *Politics of Nature: How to bring the Sciences into Democracy*, trans. Catherine Porter (Cambridge, MA: Harvard University Press, 2004), 38, 42.

bifurcation (between noumena and phenomena, essence and appearance, nature and society) he considers detrimental to modern philosophy and social theory.[27] "There is indeed an external reality," Latour concedes, "but there is really no need to make a big fuss about it," because that reality literally does not matter to us.[28] And since there is nothing at all to say about the *ding an sich*, any reference to it merely serves to protect Kant's philosophy against the well-deserved charge of subjective idealism.[29]

Insofar as Latour rejects Kant's somewhat dogmatic stipulation of things-in-themselves, he is in good company and joined by other philosophical heavyweights such as Nietzsche, Wittgenstein, Whitehead, among others. They all criticized Kant because, in their view, there is no *hinterwelt* hidden behind the way things actually are. But Latour goes further than that: he assumes that without this *hinterwelt*, Kant's *Critique* is left only with a kind of "idealist" world entirely created by the human mind. Yet he misses the crucial point that, according to Kant, the mind does not precede the phenomenal world it constitutes. Instead, mind and world co-found each other and co-emerge together. As Kant states in his *First Critique*:

> We shall therefore follow up the pure concepts to the point where they first sprout and show their dispositions in the human understanding, in which they lie ready, till at last, *occasioned by experience*, they become developed, and are exhibited by the same understanding in their purity, freed from all adhering empirical conditions.[30]

This means that human reason is not always ready to hand. Instead, reason *emerges* from innate germs and predispositions (*Keime* and *Anlagen*) at the ontogenetic level, the development of which must be triggered by outside stimuli (i.e., sense data) from the empirical world that is itself constituted by reason. This logic is circular, of course—yet this

---

27 Bruno Latour, *We Have Never Been Modern*, trans. Catherine Porter (Cambridge, MA: Harvard University Press, 1993).
28 Latour, *Politics of Nature*, 38.
29 Ibid., 51. The most comprehensive account of this argument can be found in Latour's polemic against the Edinburgh Strong Programme; see Bruno Latour, "For David Bloor and Beyond ... A Reply to David Bloor's 'Anti-Latour'," *Studies in History & Philosophy of Science* 30, no. 1 (March, 1999): 113–29. See also David Bloor, "Reply to Bruno Latour," *Studies in History and Philosophy of Science* 30, no. 1 (1999): 131–6.
30 Immanuel Kant, *Critique of Pure Reason*, ed. and trans. Marcus Weigelt (New York: Penguin, 2007), 95; my emphasis. A66/B91.

circle adequately describes how living forms co-emerge and co-evolve with their environment. Using today's parlance, we might say that the human mind, according to Kant, is an autopoietic system—which explains why Kant's transcendental philosophy remains as relevant today as it was some 250 years ago.[31]

I readily admit that this reading remains subject to heated debate among Kant scholars. Everybody agrees that human reason, according to Kant, constitutes a "self-organizing" system—this, after all, is the term Kant himself uses.[32] The point of contention is whether the mind, apart from being self-organizing, is also a *self-generating* (i.e., autopoietic) system. Judy Wubnic was among the first critics to make the claim that acts of judgment literally give birth to the categories employed in the judgment.[33] In the *First Critique*, Kant indeed refers to the "augmentation of concepts from themselves, and, so to say, the self-birth of our understanding (and of our reason) …"[34] Our ability to reason, in other words, emerges from an auto-affective loop whereby cause and effect are inextricably intertwined. The human mind thus constitutes *both a self-generative and a self-organizing system*—hence Kant's famous reference to the "epigenesis of pure reason" in the second edition of his *First Critique*.[35] Other critics, however, have rejected what they call an overly "biologized" reading of Kant.[36] Catherine Malabou, for example, insists that "there is *no epigenesis of the categories*" in Kant;

---

31 "The most striking feature of an autopoietic system," Humberto Maturana and Francisco Varela point out some 200 years after Kant, "is that it pulls itself up by its own bootstraps and becomes distinct from its own environment through its own dynamics in such a way that both things are inseparable." Humberto R. Maturana and Francisco J. Varela, *The Tree of Knowledge: The Biological Roots of Human Understanding*, 2nd ed. (Boulder, CO: Shambala, 1992), 46f. Terrence Deacon, too, emphasizes how "prescient" Kant's thinking remains in terms of how complex systems evolve. See Terrence Deacon, *Incomplete Nature: How Mind Emerged from Matter* (New York: Norton, 2013), 302. For more details on the connection between autopoiesis and Kant's philosophy, see Carsten Strathausen, *Bioaesthetics: Making Sense of Life in Science and the Arts* (Minneapolis: University of Minnesota Press, 2017).
32 Immanuel Kant, *Critique of the Power of Judgment*, ed. and trans. Paul Guyer (Cambridge: Cambridge University Press, 2000), 254. A287/B291.
33 See Judy Wubnig, "The Epigenesis of Pure Reason: A Note on the 'Critique of Pure Reason' B sec. 27, 165–7," *Kant-Studien* 60, no. 2 (1969): 147–52.
34 Kant, *Critique of Pure Reason*, 610 (translation altered). A766/B794.
35 Kant, *Critique of Pure Reason*, 168. B167.
36 See Günter Zöller, "Kant on the Generation of Metaphysical Knowledge," in *Kant, Analysen-Probleme-Kritik*, ed. Hariolf Oberer and Gerhard Seel (Würzburg: Königshausen & Neumann, 1988), 71–90.

"there is only an *epigenesis of the relation of the categories to objects*."[37] In autopoietic terms, this means that the mind, though self-organizing, *is not a self-generating system* in the strict sense of the term, because its basic architecture is innate and preformed, and the categories themselves are always already there, donned either by a benevolent God or by some other inexplicable formative power (like Blumenbach's *Bildungstrieb*) that humans will never be able to explain rationally.

There is much to support Malabou's reading, not least Kant's consistent and strong rejection of hylozoism, that is, the idea that life emerged from lifeless matter. Kant did, indeed, assume that life itself constitutes a primary substance that is always already given in nature. But this assumption was wrong, plain and simple. No serious scientist today will dispute the fact that life emerged from matter via dynamic and autocatalytic processes at the molecular level. Similarly, if Kant really believed that the pure categories and basic principles of reason are not just latent but fully formed in the human mind—as opposed to these categories and principles co-emerging simultaneously with the very mind they structure and organize—well, then he was wrong on that point, too. Much like life was not always already present in nature, but emerged some 4.3 billion years ago, the human mind, too, is the product of a long evolutionary process that dates back hundreds of thousands of years. Evolutionary epistemology (e.g., Donald T. Campbell, Karl Popper, Gerhard Vollmer) convincingly demonstrates that the logico-ontological correlation between perceiving subject and perceived object emphasized by Kant results from the human species' ongoing adaptation to its enacted environment. Kant's transcendental subject, in other words, is empirical through and through. Strictly speaking, there is no "pure reason a priori," because human reason and knowledge are entirely based on experience—albeit on the level of the genotype, not the phenotype: "Everything comes from experience," the molecular biologist and Nobel Laureate Jacques Monod points out, "yet not from ongoing current experience, reiterated by each individual with each new generation, but instead, from the experience accumulated by the entire ancestry of the species over the course of its evolution."[38]

---

37 Catherine Malabou, *Before Tomorrow: Epigenesis and Rationality*, trans. Carolyn Shread (New York: Polity, 2016), 49. John Zammito, too, emphasizes the preformationist aspects of Kant's *Critique* in "Kant's Persistent Ambivalence towards Epigenesis, 1764–90," in *Understanding Purpose: Kant and the Philosophy of Biology*, ed. Philippe Huneman (Rochester, NY: University of Rochester Press, 2007), 51–74.

38 Jacques Monod, *Chance and Necessity: An Essay on the Natural Philosophy of Modern Biology*, trans. Austryn Wainhouse (New York: Knopf, 1971), 154.

The human mind, in short, is an evolutionary effect of environmental adaptation at the phylogenetic level. Yet this fact does not contradict or deny the innateness of this preformed structure at the ontogenetic level. Once we distinguish between phylogenesis and ontogenesis, we can clarify that our ability to reason is both historical in nature (at the species level), yet also appears preformed and innate (at the individual level). Whether Kant himself knew it or not, the best way to make sense of the "epigenesis of pure reason," in my view, is to embrace rather than avoid a properly "biologized" account of his philosophy. Once we do, the circular logic at work in the *Critique* becomes a strength, not a weakness. For example, Kant's claim that a principle of reason has "the peculiar character that it makes possible the very experience which is its own ground of proof, and that in this experience it must always itself be presupposed" simply means that, biologically speaking, the proof of the pudding is in the eating.[39] Life, in other words, is not rooted in logic or truth. Life is rooted in being alive and staying alive.

Politics

What does a posthuman politics look like? To answer this question, we need to shift from SR to the more politically minded "new materialisms" branch of posthumanism.[40] Although both movements develop an ontology of things, the main difference is that SR foregrounds the withdrawn and self-sufficient nature of individual objects, whereas the new materialists emphasize instead the restless agency of things to form complex systems or other assemblages that defy human control. Politics, ecology, and social justice take center stage in eco-feminism, assemblage theory, and affect studies. Unlike the flat ontology espoused by SR, the new materialists refuse to "'horizontalize' the world completely," as Jane Bennett puts it, because their political goal "is not the perfect equality of actants, but a polity with more channels of communication between members."[41] It is in humanity's own best interest, Bennett argues, to acknowledge what she calls "thing-power," that is, the ability of inorganic matter to disrupt the human environment in unpredictable ways that "manifest traces of independence or aliveness."[42]

Throughout her marvelous study, Bennett defends her deliberate use of anthropomorphizing rhetoric (like the previous quote) as an attempt

---

39 Kant, quoted in Caygill, *A Kant Dictionary*, 334.
40 Diana Coole and Samantha Frost, eds., *New Materialisms: Ontology, Agency and Politics* (Durham, NC: Duke University Press, 2010).
41 Jane Bennett, *Vibrant Matter: A Political Ecology of Things* (Durham, NC: Duke University Press, 2010), 104.
42 Bennett, *Vibrant Matter*, xvi.

to challenge human complacency and our sense of superiority vis-à-vis the rest of the world. "Maybe it is worth running the risks of anthropomorphism (superstition, the divinization of nature, romanticism) because it, oddly enough, works against anthropocentrism," Bennett suggests.[43] Steven Shaviro agrees: "The point is that a certain cautious anthropomorphism is necessary in order to avoid anthropocentrism."[44] Politically, this odd dialectics between anthropomorphism and anthropocentrism makes good sense to me. It flatters human beings to see the world in their own image, and flattery is a powerful tool to change people's minds about all sorts of things. If the goal is to prevent more power blackouts and nuclear disasters, metal fatigue in bridges and rising sea levels across the world, then a "touch of anthropomorphism" may indeed be necessary to help cultivate a "countercultural kind of perceiving" that increases human "attentiveness to things and their affects."[45]

By the same token, I think Bennett is right to remain unconcerned about the performative contradiction at the heart of her project, namely the fact that she, a human being, usurps the voice of things and claims to speak in their name.[46] We know from countless empirical studies in cognitive science that most people rely on rational arguments in order to accommodate their preset beliefs, not the other way around.[47] This explains why logical consistency is not required for leaders or political ideologies to be effective; if it were, Hitler would have never seized power in 1933, nor would Donald Trump have been elected the 45th president of the United States in 2016. If we switch focus from epistemology to politics, I find Bennett's reformulation of Kant's categorical imperative rather compelling: "Give up the futile attempt to disentangle the human from the nonhuman. Seek instead to engage more civilly, strategically, and subtly with the nonhumans in the assemblages in which you, too, participate."[48]

And yet, the overall appeal of Bennett's ethics, I would argue, stems largely from the good old humanism that resonates throughout her

---

43 Bennett, *Vibrant Matter*, 120.
44 Steven Shaviro, *The Universe of Things: On Speculative Realism* (Minneapolis: University of Minnesota Press, 2014), 61.
45 Bennett, *Vibrant Matter*, 99, xiv.
46 Bennett herself, of course, claims there is no real contradiction here, and "that what looks like a performative contradiction may well dissipate if one considers revisions in operative notions of matter, life, self, self-interest, will, and agency." Bennett, *Vibrant Matter*, ix. I think this logic runs into the same epistemological problems that haunt SR.
47 Jonathan Haidt, *The Righteous Mind: Why Good People are Divided by Politics and Religion* (New York: Vintage, 2013).
48 Bennett, *Vibrant Matter*, 116.

notion of vibrant materialism. The same is true of most other "new materialist" versions of posthumanism. They all converge on what might be called a "posthuman humanism":[49] a kind of humanism that widens its traditional purview and puts nonhuman beings on an equal footing with humans, while, at the same time, it remains committed to, and draws emotional support from, the enlightened humanist ideal of treating others not simply as means to an end, but as ends in themselves. In that sense, the new materialisms remain Kantian, whether they like it or not. They should also face the fact that contrary to posthuman rhetoric, the things themselves do *not* talk. Hence there can be no actual politics without some minimal notion of human selfhood, or what Rosi Braidotti calls "posthuman subjectivity."[50] For, in spite of "our entanglements with heterogeneous entities and processes," we still live "in a world in which humanity matters immensely," as William Connolly points out.[51] Political scientists like Bennett and Connolly are well aware that when political decisions are made during major elections in democratic states, the campaign call to establish "The Parliament of Things" (Bruno Latour) or a "Democracy of Objects" (Levi Bryant) will hardly win the day and is more likely to amuse or offend rather than mobilize any voters.

Many on the left, unfortunately, consider this liberal-pragmatic rationale so unappealing that they are willing to abandon the political process altogether, or, at least, to subordinate the pursuit of specific rights *within* the system to the search for a radically new ontology *of* the system. "I'm not interested in equality," Elizabeth Grosz states in one of her interviews:

---

49 Cary Wolfe identifies a related kind of "posthumanist humanism" in the philosophical projects of Rorty, Žižek, and Foucault, because they retain a (however limited) notion of human subjectivity and selfhood, as opposed to the "posthuman posthumanism" Wolfe advocates. Wolfe, *What is Posthumanism?*, 126.
50 Like other posthumanists, Braidotti, too, defines "posthuman subjectivity" largely in Deleuzian terms as a relational, non-centered assemblage informed by "the vital, self-organizing and yet non-naturalistic structure of living matter itself." Yet Braidotti also explicitly recognizes the need "for self-reflexivity on the part of the subjects who occupy the former humanist center." Rosi Braidotti, *The Posthuman* (Oxford: Polity, 2013), 2, 49. Other posthumanists are less cognizant of this problem. Promod Nayar, for example, emphasizes the ability of literary texts to educate critically minded readers about the inherent limits of reason and human sovereignty—and thus implicitly relies upon the very classical-humanist ideals of literary education and critical rationality he explicitly calls into question throughout his book. Promod K. Nayar, *Posthumanism* (New York: Polity, 2014).
51 William E. Connolly, *The Fragility of Things: Self-Organizing Processes, Neoliberal Fantasies, and Democratic Activism* (Durham, NC: Duke University Press, 2013), 50.

I'm much more interested in the project, although I haven't written on it at all, of producing sexually differentiated ontologies rather than rights ... Ontology does not have a moral dimension, it's not the order of imperative, ought, or law, only an ethical dimension of debt and obligation.[52]

Similar attempts to reground democratic politics date back at least to the rise of deconstruction and postmodern theory in the middle of the last century. At that time, radical politics was all about *différance* and the play of signification; today, it is all about ontology and the agency of matter. Either way, the danger is to lose sight not just of politics, but of the political in the Schmittian sense of the term. The current nuclear standoff with North Korea is just one of many examples to demonstrate once again that the best way to avoid war between peoples is to organize the international community along the way Kant suggested in his essay "Perpetual Peace" some 125 years before the League of Nations finally became a reality in 1920. The current system of using moral condemnation and economic sanctions is far from perfect, of course, and it does not always work. But the question remains: what other *political* solutions does posthumanism have to offer?

Aesthetics

Some of the most promising and productive encounters between Kantian philosophy and posthumanism have taken place in the field of aesthetics. William Connolly, John Protevi, and Steven Shaviro each have made compelling arguments for the continued relevance of Kant's *Critique* for contemporary debates about affect, ontology, and subjectivity.[53] The philosophical foundation common to all three accounts is the well-known ontology of Gilles Deleuze. But Shaviro also introduces the "philosophy of organism" by Alfred N. Whitehead into the discussion, and I want to focus on his argument in particular.

Shaviro is fairly sympathetic to SR, because he, too, believes that "epistemology must be deprivileged, because we cannot subordinate things themselves to our experience of them."[54] Yet unlike SR, Shaviro critically engages Kant's philosophy rather than simply rejecting or

---

52 Interview with Elizabeth Grosz by Robert Ausch, Randal Doane, and Laura Perez; https://www.scribd.com/document/46893601/Interview-With-Elizabeth-Grosz.
53 Connolly, *The Fragility of Things*; Steven, *Without Criteria*; Shaviro, *The Universe of Things*; John Protevi, *Life, War, Earth: Deleuze and the Sciences* (Minneapolis: University of Minnesota Press, 2013).
54 Shaviro, *The Universe of Things*, 3.

ignoring it. One of his central arguments, indeed, is that Kant's aesthetics "prefigures both Whitehead and Deleuze," because "aesthetics marks the place where cognition and correlationism get left behind—or better, where they have not yet arisen."[55] Kant's *Third Critique*, in other words, undermines the rationalist epistemology Kant set up in the *First*. The transcendental subject described in the *First Critique*, Shaviro argues, is the archetypal humanist subject, the kind of sovereign, self-legislating moral authority that makes the world dependent upon our knowledge and representation of it. By contrast, Kant's *Third Critique* articulates a different kind of subject, "a subject that neither comprehends nor legislates, but only feels and responds."[56] Unlike the transcendental subject, the aesthetic subject entails "a kind of sentience that is more than just a passive reception of sensible intuition but less than conscious recognition and comprehension."[57] Another way to put this is to say that aesthetic experience, according to Kant, suspends human subjectivity in between the passive and active mode of being and thus creates a kind of limbo or conceptual openness necessary for a new sense of being human to emerge.[58]

This part of Shaviro's reading I entirely agree with: the subject of aesthetics experience "is auto-affected by the objectified 'datum' that enters into it."[59] Where I differ is that this process of auto-affection is not only limited to the aesthetic subject described in the *Third Critique*, but equally applies to the transcendental subject of the *First Critique*. Kant's aesthetics does not actually deconstruct or undermine his own previous account of human subjectivity; it merely shifts emphasis from the constructive to the receptive part of the same autopoietic process whereby subject and world co-emerge together. For Shaviro, however, there is a radical break between the *First* and the *Third Critique* in terms of subjectivity: the former supposedly founds a primordial, authoritative, and essentially static subject solely concerned with its own representations *of the world*, whereas the latter presents a more receptive and genuinely responsive subject that emerges *from the world*. This binary interpretation of Kantian subjectivity prompts Shaviro to embrace the "inversion" proposed by Whitehead: "For Kant," Whitehead states, "the world emerges from the subject; for the philosophy of organism, the subject emerges from the world—a 'superject' rather than a subject."[60]

---

55 Ibid., 154, 155.
56 Shaviro, *Without Criteria*, 13.
57 Shaviro, *The Universe of Things*, 153.
58 See Peter Gilgen's contribution in this volume for a more detailed reading of Kant's *Third Critique* in dialogue with Shaviro's.
59 Shaviro, *Without Criteria*, 13.
60 Whitehead, *Process and Reality*, 88.

But this inversion misses the point. The entire binary is wrong, because it leaves out the third option of both subject and world co-emerging together—which is what the "epigenesis of pure reason" is all about. Whitehead, I think, makes the same mistake I pointed out earlier with regard to Bruno Latour: Whitehead, too, believes that apart from things-in-themselves, Kant's philosophy has no world left outside the mind. All that remains, supposedly, is a world entirely created by the mind. Here is Whitehead's account of the matter:

> But for Kant, apart from concepts there is nothing to know; since objects related in a knowable world are the product of conceptual functioning whereby categorical form is introduced into the sense-datum, which otherwise is intuited in the form of a mere spatio-temporal flux of sensation.[61]

One encounters this same anachronistic reading of Kantian philosophy throughout posthumanist theory: it willfully splits epistemology from ontology and then locates the *First Critique* squarely in the former without access to the latter.[62] But the "sense-datum" intuited by the mind, as Whitehead puts it—where does that come from if not the world outside the mind? Again, it is crucial to distinguish this "sense-datum" from the "thing-in-itself," which by definition, can never be apprehended by us in any form whatsoever. Hence there must be an ontological realm somewhere in between the phenomenal and the noumenal register of things. In biological terms, of course, this bizarre realm constitutes the proper *Lebenswelt*, the *mi-lieu*, of the human mind, and the structural coupling of mind and world gives rise to human being. It follows that the mind, according to Kant, is not a static, fully formed and eternal structure. Instead, our mind *emerges* from a highly dynamic, self-organizing, auto-affective process triggered by environmental stimuli and executed via acts of judgment. This is why Kant spoke of the "inner, organized unity" of reason and likened its "architectonic structure" to the natural growth of "an animal body," because it features co-evolving parts that are both means and end, both cause and effect of the larger whole.[63]

---

61 Ibid., 156.
62 "Kant's categories of understanding," Shaviro claims, "are universal and intrinsic to the mind that imposes them onto an otherwise inchoate external reality." Shaviro, *Without Criteria*, 32. This is only half-true, because the categories are not innate in the sense of always already being there ready at hand; instead, the categories themselves *emerge* during acts of judgment.
63 Kant, *Critique of Pure Reason*, 653. A833/B861.

SR and other versions of posthumanism either disregard or disavow this autopoietic dimension of Kant's philosophy. Instead, they create the chimera of an entirely innate, entirely static, entirely isolated, and purely legislative form of human subjectivity and then call for its "correction" by the kind of affect theory and speculative ontology articulated in Deleuze and Whitehead. The latter replaces the subject with the "superject"—which is "not something that underlies experience," he declares, "but something that emerges from experience, something that is superadded to it."[64] Yet it is precisely this linear, binary logic (e.g., "the subject is this, not that" or "first comes the world, then comes the subject") that lies at the root of the problem. The crucial point is that human subjectivity *both underlies and emerges* from experience, and that the world *neither predates nor postdates the subject*, but co-emerges alongside and together with it. Even Whitehead himself, at times, seems wary of his own categorical "inversion" of Kantian subjectivity. At one point, he tries to clarify that "an actual entity is at once the subject experiencing and the superject of its experiences. It is subject-superject, and neither half of this designation can for a moment be lost sight of."[65]

This is what I am proposing, too. It seems telling that Shaviro, an expert reader of both Kant and Whitehead and a major theorist in the field, chose not to quote the entire passage. His account stresses above all the difference between subject and superject, a distinction he then maps onto his own binary account of *First* versus *Third Critique*. The result is that Shaviro's "speculative aesthetics" tends to overemphasize the receptive passivity of the aesthetic subject while downplaying its active, legislative dimension. According to Shaviro, the *Third Critique* features "a subject that neither comprehends nor legislates, but *only* feels and responds."[66] As I read Kant, however, aesthetic experience involves more than just a passive superject affected by the world outside. It also requires an active subject ready to engage the object and form a judgment in the first place; and this judgment, moreover, must be articulated and communicated to (and, if necessary, defended against criticism from) other speaking subjects. Both aspects, our passive receptivity to and our active reflection of the world, must work together to enable a new sense of human subjectivity.

Conclusion

A central argument in this essay has been that posthumanist theory, despite its rhetoric, remains inextricably intertwined with the history of humanism and the nature of *being human*. This claim itself seems hardly

---

64 Shaviro, *Without Criteria*, 12.
65 Whitehead, *Process and Reality*, 29.
66 Shaviro, *Without Criteria*, 13; emphasis mine.

new: "The 'post' of posthumanism," Geoffrey Badmington declared back in 2000 with reference to Derrida's philosophy, "does not (and, moreover, cannot) mark or make an absolute break from the legacy of humanism." Just as Derrida exposed any effort to leave metaphysics behind as inherently metaphysical, Badmington emphasized that posthumanism has no choice but to engage and work through the humanist tradition "if radical change, the thinking of difference, is to become a possibility."[67] Most importantly, Badmington insisted that the "anti-humanist resistance movement" of the last century was *not* a critique of—or directed against—the *human* per se, but only against human*ism*. Cary Wolfe agrees: posthumanism, he claims, "is not posthuman or antihuman but rather simply post*humanist*."[68]

There is ample evidence to contradict this claim. The anti-human aspirations of posthumanism are most glaring in Deleuze and the affective turn informed by his ontology. "*Affects*," Deleuze and Guattari emphasize again and again, "*are precisely these nonhuman becomings of man*."[69] To create a body without organs is to leave behind not only human subjectivity and phenomenological experience, but the human life-world altogether. "If freedom means anything for Deleuze," Peter Hallward puts it succinctly, "it isn't a matter of human liberty but of liberation *from* the human."[70] Deleuze's ontology and affect theory, in other words, are not just anti-humanist; they are profoundly *anti-human*. Far too often, posthumanists focus "On Ceasing to Be Human" rather than exploring the nature of being human.[71] Indeed, whenever I encounter a question like "What's it like to be a bat?" (Thomas Nagel) or "What's it like to be a thing?" (Ian Bogost), I am inclined to respond simply by asking in return: "So, what's it like to be human?" Posthumanism puts the cart before the horse. It pretends that epistemological questions about the nature of being human are either trivial or absurd or politically dangerous, whereas ontological questions about the nature of inert objects are genuinely exciting, meaningful, or politically progressive. Neither proposition seems right to me, and the only way forward, in my view, is to engage both sets of questions simultaneously. Yet even the most astute critics, like Jane Bennett, believe that in order to mind the things

---

67 Neil Badmington, "Introduction: Approaching Posthumanism," in *Posthumanism*, ed. Neil Badmington (New York: Palgrave, 2000), 7.
68 Wolfe, *What is Posthumanism?*, 120.
69 Gilles Deleuze and Félix Guattari, *What Is Philosophy?*, trans. Hugh Tomlinson (New York: Columbia University Press, 1990), 169.
70 See Peter Hallward, *Out of This World: Deleuze and the Philosophy of Creation* (London: Verso, 2006), 139.
71 Gerald L. Bruns, *On Ceasing to Be Human* (Stanford: Stanford University Press, 2010).

around us, we need to "elide the question of the human."[72] Otherwise, she fears, posthumanism will inevitably fall back into the humanist tradition it seeks to escape.

I think Bennett is right: this falling back into humanism is simply inevitable. The best one can hope for in that regard amounts to what Stefan Herbrechter calls a "critical posthumanism," that is, a method of inquiry that seeks to "question humanism even in the form of its own critique."[73] Yet critical self-reflexivity, needless to say, is precisely what traditional humanism, too, has always aspired to, even if it failed to implement this ideal in practical terms. This explains why most versions of posthumanism amount to no more, and no less, than a kind of hyperhumanism that tries to remain critical even of its own posthumanist critique of the traditional self-criticism of classical humanism. Which is to say that posthumanism falls down the rabbit hole of infinite self-criticism, trying in vain to outwit the very mind that enables this critique in the first place. Critical self-reflexivity is a good thing, for sure, but it stops making sense when it becomes utterly self-absorbed and reaches the meta-meta-meta-level of abstract thought feeding upon itself. Contemporary posthumanism, in my view, has crossed that threshold, and it is time to rein it back in.

Hence the infinite regress that sustains the self-grinding logic of critical (post)humanism must be anchored and come to rest upon a particular theory of mind that broadly describes how thought is possible. I have argued that Kant's critical philosophy still makes an important contribution to this effort—not because Kant has all the right answers, but because he did not shy away from asking the right questions. In particular, his notion of subjectivity is both compatible with, and complementary to, new research in evolutionary biology, cognitive science, and systems theory that inform the new materialisms and other strands of posthumanist theory. Most importantly, Kant acknowledged the epistemological-ontological tension that is always already at work whenever thought takes place. I predict that unless posthumanists come to terms with Kant's legacy and its continued relevance for any attempt to rethink ontology, their critical intervention will soon be remembered as just another "turn" in the modern history of humanism and the humanities.

---

72 Bennett, *Vibrant Matter*, 120.
73 Stefan Herbrechter, *Posthumanism: A Critical Analysis* (London: Bloomsbury, 2013), 15. Besides Herbrechter, numerous other critics (like Rosi Braidotti, Promod K. Nayar, Paul Gilroy, etc.) have also embraced the term "critical posthumanism."

Seven Intimations of the Posthuman: Kant's Natural Beauty

Peter Gilgen

Of Natural Beauty

In recent discussions of the ecological relevance of aesthetics, the question of natural beauty has been posed with renewed urgency. In much posthumanist theory, aesthetics has been elevated to the status of *prima philosophia*. Both the unassimilable otherness of the aesthetic object and the passive receptive stance of the subject in an aesthetic experience run counter to the humanist credo that underwrote aesthetics in terms of the "speculative theory of Art," which was formulated in the wake of Kant's *Critique of Judgment* and determined aesthetic discourse from the Romantics via Hegel all the way to Heidegger.[1]

Such aesthetic humanism is closely associated with the current geological period, which has been termed the "Anthropocene" in ecological theory.[2] It took its departure, as Jean-Marie Schaeffer has forcefully argued, from the new foundation of aesthetics that Kant provided in the *Critique of Judgment*. On this basis, a politically salvific form of aesthetic education was to counter man's tendency to "deviate from his destiny

---

1 Jean-Marie Schaeffer, *Art of the Modern Age: Philosophy of Art from Kant to Heidegger*, trans. Steven Rendall (Princeton, NJ: Princeton University Press, 2000), 7 and *passim*. As Schaeffer explains, the speculative theory is "a theory of Art with a capital A because beyond works and genres, it projects a transcendent entity that is supposed to *found* the diversity of artistic practices and to have ontological priority over them." Ibid.

2 Although there is no general agreement concerning the onset of the Anthropocene, Paul J. Crutzen, the climate scientist who popularized the term, has proposed the late eighteenth century as a plausible starting point, the time "when analyses of air trapped in polar ice showed the beginning of growing global concentrations of carbon dioxide and methane"; see Paul J. Crutzen, "Geology of Mankind," *Nature* 415, no. 3 (January 2002): 23.

[*Bestimmung*]."[3] In contradistinction to Kant's claims, the speculative theory considered only "Art" as the proper object of aesthetic contemplation—a tendency that became most virulent in Hegel's *Lectures on Fine Art*, which stated explicitly that nature was "necessarily imperfect in its beauty" and therefore of limited relevance for aesthetics.[4]

Needless to say, the return to aesthetics *qua aisthesis* in posthumanist theory marks a momentous reversal of the Hegelian move. Here we have a comprehensive aesthetics focused on sensuous experience as such. The subject's embodiment and environmental embeddedness constitute points of departure for the disclosure of nonhuman excess at the heart of human experience.

In light of the diametric opposition between the speculative theory of "Art" and recent speculative realist theories on the matter of natural beauty, I would like to propose a reevaluation of Kant's "Analytic of the Beautiful" that points to an excess of beauty operative in it. At stake is a certain nonhuman or inhuman quality of beauty that a human observer can capture only by projecting purposiveness—in analogy with human purposes—onto nature. The resulting analogies are, as Kant makes clear, constructs in the service of making wild nature amenable to human ends, if only tentatively and not without remainders.

Schaeffer's observations regarding the speculative intertwinement of philosophical aesthetics, and thus beauty, and art as well as the concomitant collapse of the distinction between the aesthetic and artistic spheres ought to be read in light of such domestication. His intricate argument arrives at the conclusion that "in reality the speculative theory of Art constitutes philosophy's seizure of control over the theory of art."[5] It should be added that this seizure depended precisely on the transformation of the discourse of post-Kantian aesthetics into a theory of art and thus on a momentous shift of aesthetic attention away from the beauty of nature. In contrast, Kant's analysis of the aesthetic judgment insists from the start on the irreducibility of the beautiful to the arts and, in fact, stresses the "preeminence of the beauty of nature over

---

3   Friedrich Schiller, *On the Aesthetic Education of Man in a Series of Letters* (English/German), ed. and trans. Elizabeth M. Wilkinson and L. A. Willoughby (Oxford: Clarendon, 1967), 62–3.
4   G. W. F. Hegel, *Aesthetics: Lectures on Fine Art*, 2 vols., trans. T. M. Knox (Oxford: Oxford University Press, 1999), 1:143. For the German version see G. W. F. Hegel, *Werke*, 20 vols. (vols. 13–15 contain the *Vorlesungen über die Ästhetik*), ed. Eva Moldenhauer and Karl Markus Michel (Frankfurt a.M.: Suhrkamp, 1986), 13:190. All subsequent references to Hegel include the volume and page numbers of the English translation followed by the volume and page numbers of this German edition.
5   Schaeffer, *Art of the Modern Age*, 273.

the beauty of art in alone awakening an immediate interest, even if the former were to be surpassed by the latter in respect of form."[6]

In order to probe the depths of the Kantian view, it therefore does not suffice to separate and distinguish it from the speculative theory that undergirds the subsequent conceptions of "Art." In addition, the question of *natural beauty* must be foregrounded and asked anew. This is all the more pertinent in light of the speculative realist turn to ecology and environmental aesthetics. Posthumanist proposals have either prematurely cast aside Kant's transcendental intervention or flattened his insights unduly. Both reactions have in common that they have largely neglected the conceptual resources that Kant's aesthetic philosophy offers to posthumanist thinking. My inquiry into Kant's notion of natural beauty therefore juxtaposes his analysis with the overt humanism of Hegel's philosophy, on the one hand, and with contemporary theory that propagates a strong—which is to say, explicitly noncognitive, nonsubjective, and anti-humanist—posthumanism, on the other. The aim of this constellation is to bring out *a weak, philosophically coherent and capacious posthumanism* in Kant's analysis of beauty.

On the face of it, Kant does not seem to be a promising candidate for the role of posthumanist *avant la lettre*. Contemporary posthumanist thinkers interpret the critical turn of philosophy as a decisive swerve away from anything that is not implicated in human affairs. In fact, the foundational gesture of one of posthumanism's most virulent strands—namely, Quentin Meillassoux's speculative materialism and related speculative realisms—consists in chastising Kant for his move away from ontology in favor of his critical inquiry into the modes and limits of our knowledge. Copernicus's revolution had removed the earth from the center of the universe, which it had previously occupied in the geocentric Ptolemaic system, and thereby also put into doubt previously unquestioned anthropocentric assumptions. In contrast, Meillassoux calls Kant's own "Copernican turn"[7] a "Ptolemaic counter-revolution" and severely criticizes Kant for having renounced "the very thing that constituted the essence of this revolution; that is to say, science's

---

6 Immanuel Kant, *Kant's Gesammelte Schriften "Akademieausgabe,"* Königlich Preußische Akademie der Wissenschaften (Berlin: Reimer / de Gruyter, 1900ff.), 5:299. References to Kant's works are given by volume and page number of this edition (AA), except in the case of the *Critique of Pure Reason*, where I adopted the standard practice of citing the page numbers of the first (A) and the revised second (B) edition. Translations from the third *Critique* are taken from Immanuel Kant, *Critique of the Power of Judgment*, ed. Paul Guyer, trans. Paul Guyer and Eric Matthews (Cambridge: Cambridge University Press, 2000).
7 See the famous passage in the preface to the second edition of the *Critique of Pure Reason* (B xvi).

non-correlational mode of knowing, in other words, *its eminently speculative character.*"[8]

Meillassoux's rejection of Kantian epistemology and his more comprehensive indictment of "correlationism"—the division of the world into mind and being—have quickly become posthumanist points of reference. If he is right, then the time has come for a new philosophical beginning, either as he suggests under the tutelage of science and mathematics or as other posthumanists, who have accepted his critique but not his solution, propose by simply tossing all anthropocentric assumptions overboard and practicing an "objective" speculative philosophy. Transcendental philosophy in all its shapes and sizes—including such momentous theoretical milestones as the linguistic turn and the "quasitranscendentals"[9] operative in Derridean deconstruction—would have to be turned around to set its sights on the things that populate the universe and thus find the way out of the correlationist prison-house of its own making. In this view, correlationist philosophy prevents itself from knowing anything outside its own apparatus or epistemic infrastructure. The standard example of this problem is Kant's notorious "thing in itself," which had already bothered his immediate successors, among them Hegel.[10]

The *Critique of Judgment* and Kant's aesthetics in particular promise a closer affinity with posthumanist concerns than his theoretical philosophy. To be sure, Kant's aesthetics is marked as much by his "Copernican turn" as his epistemology. Instead of directing his focus on the object of the aesthetic judgment, Kant examines this very judgment. What are the conditions under which we experience an object as beautiful? And what force does a judgment of the kind "x is beautiful" have? Kant maintains throughout that beauty is neither a quality of the object, nor is it simply a matter of subjective opinion. The interaction between subject and object, their particular relationship at a particular moment in time is at stake in the judgment of taste. As Christian Helmut Wenzel has

---

8   Quentin Meillassoux, *After Finitude: An Essay on the Necessity of Contingency*, trans. Ray Brassier (London: Continuum, 2008), 119.
9   The term was coined by Rodolphe Gasché, *The Tain of the Mirror: Derrida and the Philosophy of Reflection* (Cambridge, MA: Harvard University Press, 1986), 316.
10 A dissenting voice among posthumanists is Timothy Morton. Defending Kant's "transcendental object [that] remains for us utterly unknown" (*Critique of Pure Reason* A45–47/B63–64), he argues that Kant's "weird essentialism" is "just what we need for navigating the strange and disturbing ocean of ecological awareness. Why? Because ecological awareness is coexistence with beings that are sometimes terrifyingly real at least in spatiotemporal, scale terms, yet downright impossible to locate as constantly present." Timothy Morton, "All Objects are Deviant: Feminism and Ecological Intimacy," in *Object-Oriented Feminism*, ed. Katherine Behar (Minneapolis: University of Minnesota Press, 2016), 72.

pointed out, this characteristic entanglement of the subjective and the objective also involves, above and beyond the "relationship between the beholder and the object," a second-order act of contemplation "that takes into account that relationship."[11]

The question is whether Kant's treatment of beauty (or, more generally, the aesthetic power of judgment) offers a relevant contribution to posthumanist theory. Much of the current return to aesthetics (whether of the Kantian or some other kind) seems to be premised on such an assumption. It seems reasonable to assume that aesthetic appreciation—particularly of the beauty of nature—could further a philosophical as well as a political posthumanist agenda and counteract ecologically oblivious and destructive anthropocentrism. The following remarks elaborate on Kant's position by juxtaposing it, on the one hand, to the speculative theory of "Art"—in particular to Hegel—and, on the other, to posthumanist aesthetic thinking. In the process, the significance of natural beauty for a viable posthumanist aesthetics will also become apparent.

"The Most Beautiful and Luxuriant Vegetation"

Hegel's *Aesthetics* begins with the exclusion of natural beauty. The beauty of art, according to Hegel, is "beauty *born of the spirit and* [thus] *born again*," whereas "a natural existent [*Naturexistenz*]" is "indifferent, not free and self-conscious in itself" (1:2/13:14). What we perceive as the beauty of nature at best appears "as a reflection of the beauty that belongs to spirit" (1:2/13:15). Only a sensuous form made to correspond with "an essentially spiritual content" will render the latter "visible and imaginable" (1:71/13:102). In marked contrast, natural beauty is "unselfconsciously for itself."[12] A passage in the *Aesthetics* that is as beautiful as it is somber seals Hegel's verdict on natural beauty:

> The variegated richly colored plumage of birds shines even when unseen [*ungesehen*], their song dies away unheard [*verklingt*

---

11 Christian Helmut Wenzel, *An Introduction to Kant's Aesthetics: Core Concepts and Problems* (Oxford: Blackwell, 2005), 2.
12 Knox renders this as "naïvely self-centered" (1:71). Although his version undoubtedly captures some of Hegel's meaning, it is considerably more negative and disapproving than the German *"unbefangen für sich"* (13:102). After all, *Unbefangenheit* is usually seen as a desirable quality. It denotes impartiality and unbiasedness as well as uninhibitedness, unselfconsciousness and naturalness. One possible translation of Hegel's clause might thus be: "But the work of art is not as naturally for itself [as is nature]"—which, as it were, is not simply a tautology. Rather it brings home—without the moralizing tone introduced by Knox—that nature in Hegel's account is merely, and quite naturally, *for itself*. As such, it is indifferent to human purposes.

ungehört]; the torch-thistle, which blooms for only one night, withers in the wilds of the southern forests without having been admired [*verwelkt, ohne bewundert zu werden*], and these forests, jungles themselves of the most beautiful and luxuriant vegetation [*Verschlingungen selber der schönsten und üppigsten Vegetationen*], with the most sweet-smelling and aromatic perfumes, rot and decay equally unenjoyed [*verderben und verfallen ebenso ungenossen*]. (1:71/13:102)

The most noticeable quality of Hegel's description—aside from its palpable allure—is its apophatic register: the beauty of nature is *un*seen, *un*heard, *un*admired, *un*enjoyed, and ultimately indifferent (*unbefangen*) to human purposes. It is in no need of our attention—even if Hegel's negations cannot help evoking it. Unlike the work of art, it is neither a proper "question," nor "an address to [our] responsive breast" (1:71/13:102). Related to this lack of address is the temporality of natural beauty that evades conceptual capture. Evanescent to the core, it achieves neither duration nor solidity and is constantly threatened by decay and disappearance. As in the case of the torch thistle (presumably *selenicereus grandiflorus*) the moment may be short-lived, and time may not suffice for eliciting admiration (*bewundert zu werden*).[13]

In Kantian terms, such a fundamental inability to elicit admiration may result in the best case, if the moment is caught at all, in astonishment (*Verwunderung*), a mere "affect in the representation of novelty that exceeds expectation" (AA 5:272). In contrast to astonishment, admiration, which is defined as a more enduring or permanent sort of astonishment, "does not cease when the novelty is lost" (ibid.). The question of whether this economy of wonder with its division between the extremes of amazement and veneration is plausible is perhaps less important than the noticeable leveling of excess that takes place in the transition from the former to the latter. The gains in constancy and duration that admiration provides come at the cost of reining in novelty—anything that "exceeds expectation"—which, in the final analysis, is nothing but the passage of time itself. When Hegel deplores that the beauties of the southern forests must go unadmired, he is therefore also saying that they are not deserving of our admiration.

In Hegel's own wording, nature itself curtails beauty. *Verschlingungen*, or impenetrable intertwinements and convolutions of the most beautiful and luxuriant vegetation, these forests are also its literal (self-)

---

13 According to Hegel's *Science of Logic*, admiration (*Bewunderung*) is actually an appropriate mode of reacting to the diversity of nature, precisely because it is "*without a concept*, and its object is that, which is without reason" (6:282).

devouring.[14] Small wonder that all beauty with which they are brimming (and which Hegel, sight unseen, paints in the most seductive colors) will fade away or be destroyed before it can be experienced. This instability of natural beauty, however, is but a function of nature's constitutive alienness, its utter indifference to human purposes.

Kant never doubts that nature ultimately remains mysterious. Perhaps for this reason, nature's beauty has a powerful hold on us. Striking us unexpectedly, it amazes us and in the process captivates and mobilizes our aesthetic sensibilities. Unlike Hegel, Kant appreciates the unstable moment of astonishment in its own right and insists that we cannot simply assume an aesthetic perspective consciously in order to experience beauty. On the contrary, it is beauty that strikes us—often when we least expect it. Although the judgment of taste *qua judgment* contains an active element that distinguishes it from an encounter with the merely agreeable, it is thoroughly intertwined with passivity and the receptiveness for an experience that leaves us dumbstruck and blissfully elated.

For the Romantics and German Idealists the disinterested character of aesthetic experience served to "establish the autotelic nature of the work of art" and thus lay the foundations for the "speculative theory of Art."[15] In contrast, Kant's aims were quite different. In the first moment of the "Analytic of the Beautiful," he establishes disinterestedness, the suspension of the subject's possessive impulses, as the characteristic quality that distinguishes "the aesthetic *relation* from other relations in the world" (ibid.). Unaffected by such issues as moral ideas and the artistic genius, which inevitably arise in the case of art, this relation emerges in its purest form in encounters with natural beauty.

Cipher and Free Play

A central criterion for the natural beauty of an object is that it cannot be artificially made. As Kant observes, the discovery that an object, previously perceived as a beautiful product of nature, was in fact artificially created, cancels out its beauty completely.[16] Thus, "the bewitchingly beautiful song of the nightingale in a lovely stand of bushes" that turns out to have been created "by a mischievous lad" who was hiding in the bushes at a shrewd innkeeper's request, will no longer delight, for "as soon as one becomes

---

14 The Grimms' *Deutsches Wörterbuch* (Leipzig: DWB, 1854–1960), 25:1113 lists two separate lemmas for *Verschlingung*—one the equivalent of Latin *voratio* (devouring), the other related to *ineinanderschlingen* (intertwining).
15 Schaeffer, *Art of the Modern Age*, 32.
16 Of this Kant leaves no doubt. He writes that "[beauty] disappears entirely as soon as one notices that one has been deceived and that it is only art, so much so that even taste can no longer find anything beautiful in it." AA 5:302.

aware that it is a trick, no one would long endure listening to this song, previously taken to be so charming" (AA 5:302). Similarly, an observer's immediate interest in "artificial flowers" and "artfully carved birds on the twigs of trees" disappears as soon as "the deception" is discovered (AA 5:299).

Kant locates the "preeminence of the beauty of nature over the beauty of art" in the former's potential of "alone awakening an immediate interest" (ibid.). The difficulty here is that only a non-aesthetic criterion can explain the different assessments of two types of objects that "in the mere judgment of taste" would not be categorically distinguished (AA 5:300). This additional criterion has to do with the interest of reason in manifestations of some "trace [*Spur*]" or a "sign [*Wink*]" that nature contains in itself "some ground for assuming a lawful correspondence of its products with our satisfaction that is independent of all interest" (ibid.). In short, the intellectual interest in beauty that Kant describes is a second-order interest: an interest in having the possibility of making aesthetic judgments without interest. Kant admits that his explanation may look "much too studied to be taken as the true interpretation of the cipher [*Chiffreschrift*] by means of which nature figuratively speaks to us in its beautiful forms" (AA 5:301), only to drive home the point with greater determination. Undoubtedly, the attempt to read the "favor" (AA 5:210) that nature bestows on us in terms of the accommodation of our human vocation is consistent with Kant's systematic intent and has much plausibility—in spite of the convoluted argument—if looked at merely in terms of the subject of the corresponding judgments of taste. Yet, to bring to the fore the posthuman intimations in natural beauty, it helps to turn Kant's argument around and ask what nature's "cipher" tells us about itself rather than our place in nature.

Before we can examine the beautiful products of nature, however, we need to gain some clarity about the status of the objects at which the judgment of taste is directed. Kant famously argues that the "mutual subjective correspondence" or "play" (AA 5:218) between the cognitive powers of the imagination and the understanding provides the determining ground of the aesthetic judgment. This free harmony between the two cognitive powers, achieved without appeal to any concept, has to contend with two potential alternatives, as Paul Guyer points out. On the one hand, there is the possibility of harmonizing the imagination and the understanding by means of a determinate concept—the case that Kant addresses under the heading of "determining judgment," and which describes the standard case of cognition as analyzed in the *Critique of Pure Reason*. On the other hand, it would also seem possible that the play of the cognitive powers in some instances might not lead to harmony at all, but only to a disharmony between them. However, according to Guyer, Kant's account "leaves no room for a negative but purely aesthetic response."[17] This is so, because the possibility of disharmony between the cognitive powers can be ruled out on epistemological grounds, for it is not consistent with the transcendental unity of apperception as outlined in the *Critique of Pure Reason*.[18] In contrast, in the determining judgment and the reflecting aesthetic judgment, the two cognitive powers come together in the subject. The two strands are, albeit in different ways, bundled together by the transcendental apperception. As a result, Kant's epistemology permits only two of the three possible relations between the imagination and the understanding: they either harmonize in free play, or the harmony is brought about by a determinate concept. The subject side of the encounter with things in the world is non-negotiable for Kant: there is simply no experience without it. As a consequence, disharmonious play of the cognitive powers is inconceivable. There is no purely aesthetic basis for the judgment of ugliness.[19]

For Kant, ugliness always signifies the intrusion of something artificial, and the corresponding judgment is affected by practical concerns. A negative purely aesthetic response, such as the one suggested by Henry Allison,[20] would require objects that are "literally unformed" and to which the pure forms of intuition would not apply—which, as Guyer is quick to point out, is impossible within the Kantian epistemological framework.[21] For Kant *unformed objects* are impossible in principle.

All this may seem overly technical, but Guyer's consideration of ugliness leads to a surprisingly difficult question concerning the beautiful: how is Kant's free play without a concept—and thus the experience of beauty—possible at all? The reason why this point has not been addressed head on by Kant's many readers has to do, Guyer surmises, with the difficult idea of "free play." Rather different interpretations have been suggested, which Guyer groups under the headings "precognitive," "multicognitive," and "metacognitive."[22] All of them have some support in Kant's text, and Guyer proposes a capacious syncretistic theory, in which all of them have their place. The precognitive reading stresses that the harmony of the cognitive powers occurs when the subjective conditions of cognition are satisfied, yet no "subsumption

---

17 Paul Guyer, "Kant on the Purity of the Ugly," in *Values of Beauty: Historical Essays in Aesthetics* (Cambridge: Cambridge University Press, 2005), 145.
18 Ibid., 146f.
19 Guyer admits that Kant did not deny the possibility of ugliness. Yet he considered judgments of ugliness not as "purely reflective aesthetic judgments," but as "dependent upon sensory or else practical [either prudential or moral] judgments." Ibid., 151.
20 Henry Allison, *Kant's Theory of Taste: A Reading of the Critique of Aesthetic Judgment* (Cambridge: Cambridge University Press, 2001), esp. 71f.
21 Guyer, "Kant on the Purity of the Ugly," 156.
22 Ibid., 147.

of the representations of an object under a determinate concept" takes place.[23] In contrast, the multicognitive reading interprets the harmony of the cognitive powers as "a condition in which it seems to us as if we are simultaneously cognizing the object under a number of different concepts,"[24] none of which applies definitively. Versions of both of these readings abound in the literature. However, Guyer argues that both of these interpretations fall short of a complete and sufficient definition of the Kantian free play. Neither the precognitive nor the multicognitive reading provides a sufficient account of our aesthetic experience. Both fail in explaining how a judgment of beauty about *a particular object* might be made in the absence of a determinate concept.

This is where Guyer's own metacognitive interpretation comes in. It "recognizes that for Kant all consciousness of an object must involve its subsumption under some determinate concept."[25] When making aesthetic judgments, we must be able to state *which object* we find beautiful: is it *this rose* or *that one*?

Posthumanist Aesthetics

The conclusion to be drawn from our analysis of Kant's free play without a concept is that Kantian aesthetics substantially relies on a principle not unlike Husserl's fundamental notion of intentionality, namely that "all consciousness is consciousness *of* something." In contrast, Steven Shaviro, a posthumanist who engages Kant at length in *Without Criteria* and *The Universe of Things*, contends that such a move simply "leaves correlationism intact." He prefers Bergson's alternative assertion that "all consciousness *is* something" as more conducive to his own project of assigning to thought a place "entirely within the phenomenal world" and thus averting "correlationalist dualism altogether."[26]

The problem with Shaviro's position is that it leads to a leveling of the Kantian "free play" as well as to a foreshortening of the corresponding interpretive possibilities. At best, it is compatible with the precognitive and possibly the multicognitive reading of free play, but definitely not with Guyer's metacognitive one. To be sure, this is not primarily an exegetical but a conceptual issue: it concerns the status of beauty as a

---

23   Ibid., 148.
24   Ibid.
25   Ibid., 149.
26   Steven Shaviro, *Without Criteria: Kant, Whitehead, Deleuze, and Aesthetics* (Cambridge, MA: MIT, 2009), 79, n. 4. The pithy characterizations of Husserl and Bergson, respectively, are taken from Gilles Deleuze, *Cinema 1: The Movement-Image*, trans. Hugh Tomlinson and Barbara Habberjam (Minneapolis: University of Minnesota Press, 1986), 56. The same passages are also quoted in Steven Shaviro, *The Universe of Things: On Speculative Realism* (Minneapolis: University of Minnesota Press, 2014), 131.

sui generis experience that is irreducible to agreeableness or mere "positive" affect. The problem is a matter of some urgency, since aesthetics has been assigned a central and even foundational role in much recent speculative realist and object-oriented theorizing. In fact, Shaviro's own provocative synthesis of Kant's aesthetics and Whitehead's process philosophy depends entirely on the nature of aesthetic experience—an experience that he brings to bear in his critique of anthropocentrism.[27]

In order to bypass anthropocentrism and develop a more fitting theory of existing things, speculative realists and other posthumanists have attempted to "consider the world-without-us" or "the autonomous reality of beings outside human thought."[28] This is the object-oriented counterpart of Hegel's inaccessible jungle, in which all beauty forever remains unseen. At the same time, however, the experience of beauty may be read in ecological terms as a reminder of the fragility of the world and the evanescence of all there is. It also foregrounds our human embeddedness and presence in the natural environment, including the ability to relate to things in the world in ways that exceed conceptual thought and abstract thinking.

Hegel's reflection on beauty in the jungle poses a serious challenge to posthumanist attempts to reverse the subjectivist tendencies in aesthetics and shift the emphasis from the subject to the object world or rather to being as such. If beauty is not an objective quality but emerges in singular encounters between conscious subjects and things in the world, as Kant contends, then experiences of beauty are irreducible instances of correlationism at work. At the same time, however, aesthetic experiences dovetail with anti-correlationism insofar as they put into question the control of the subject over the world and the concomitant denial of the world's independence from, and indifference to, human purposes. The subject has to be attuned and receptive to the experience, over which it has no control, and the object in some way has to exceed its standard way of appearing to the subject and disclose itself in its singular alienness.

The key is not that beauty is some mystical quality that can only be fathomed in rare moments when a human observer forgets herself and unconsciously slips into a mode of interacting with the world that lies on the hither side of conscious perception. The key is rather that the experience of beauty arises in a moment of encounter that momentarily suspends the organization of our perceptions as outlined in Kant's

---

27 Shaviro, *The Universe of Things*, 134–56.
28 Shaviro's references here are to Eugene Thacker, *In the Dust of this Planet* (vol. 1 of *Horror of Philosophy*) (Winchester, UK: Zero Books, 2011), 5f., and Graham Harman, *Quentin Meillassoux: Philosophy in the Making* (Edinburgh: Edinburgh University Press, 2011), 8, respectively.

Critique of Pure Reason. It lies on the far side of everyday perception. The rose that is judged to be beautiful has registered as a rose (as Guyer's metacognitive reading of Kant contends) when it is contemplated as the particular flower that attracts my attention, suspends my routine interactions with objects in the world, and provides an occasion for dwelling in the moment. It is *this* rose that transports me out of myself and lets me be in the moment, body and all. In such moments, we "look on nature with favor" and, sliding from an aesthetic to a teleological frame of reference, are prone to read, however tentatively, beauty "as a favor of nature" to us (AA 5:380 n.).

Kant is interested in carving out a space for a type of judgment that, on the one hand, is not objective as in the case of cognition and, on the other hand, does not simply coincide with sensation, in which case it would be no judgment at all. Steven Shaviro runs roughshod over these fine distinctions. He reduces Kant's tripartite structure to a binary opposition. On one side, there is the cognitive regime, of which Kant's epistemology is the epitome, and to which all reasoning and judging belongs. This is the realm of correlationism, the division of the world into mind and being, subject and object. On the other side, there are numerous influences of things in the world upon one another—affects, touches, feelings. To give an account of them, Shaviro proposes a comprehensive aesthetics, a veritable first philosophy dedicated to "the realm of immanent, noncognitive contact."[29]

In Shaviro's view, all varieties of speculative realism ultimately "must return to Kant in order to rework the terms of his settlement among conflicting philosophical claims," for only in this way "is it possible for us to escape the correlational circle to which Kant would otherwise seem to have consigned us."[30] Yet, rather than getting entangled in an epistemological debate, Shaviro recommends an aesthetic approach in keeping with Whitehead's effort of avoiding "the bifurcation of nature."[31] He appeals to Kant's "Analytic of the Beautiful," where he locates glimpses of "speculative possibilities that are otherwise excluded by the architectonics of [Kant's] system."[32] Shaviro believes that Kantian aesthetics points to "a moment that *precedes* the very construction of [the correlational] circle ... both logically and temporally."[33] His *precognitive reading* of Kant's aesthetics construes the paradigmatic "aesthetic contact" as stopping short of "the correlation of mind and

---

29 Shaviro, *The Universe of Things*, 148.
30 Ibid., 134.
31 Ibid., 8.
32 Ibid., 148.
33 Ibid.

being and of subject and object"[34] and thus as a promising way out of the prison-house of correlationism.

In lieu of Kant's "aesthetic judgment" Shaviro emphasizes "aesthetic contact," a rudimentary precognitive conception of the aesthetic encounter. Such contact happens everywhere in the world. It is fleeting, momentary, and often barely there. Moreover, it does not depend on conscious subjects. On occasion, it may register with the systems that are affected, but for the most part, it will simply happen and disappear, as when one thing accidentally brushes against another or bumps into it before continuing on its trajectory. Shaviro thus reduces Kant's aesthetic judgment to "what Whitehead calls *feelings*, or primordial 'appetites in the form of aversions and adversions.'"[35] In doing so, he tacitly erases the distinction between the beautiful and the agreeable—the "taste of reflection" and the "taste of the senses" (AA 5:214)—on which he had insisted moments earlier, when he pointed out that the determining ground of judgments of beauty is indeed subjective according to Kant—albeit not "*merely* subjective."[36]

Shaviro's reason for his momentary defense of the Kantian distinction between beauty and the agreeable was owed to his recognition of the political relevance of the beautiful in our time. Unlike consumer preferences that shape our social world, the judgment of beauty includes a demand. When someone makes such a judgment, writes Kant, "he judges not merely for himself, but for everyone, and speaks of beauty as if it were a property of things" (AA 5:212). This does not mean that such a judge counts on or expects actual empirical agreement, "but rather [he] *demands* it," for whether everyone else agrees or not, they ought to (AA 5:213). This insight is crucial. Kant acknowledges that we speak as if beauty were a property of the object (a tendency that is evident in pre-Kantian philosophy) only to show that *the quasi-objective character of the predicate "beautiful" is actually an effect of its inherent intersubjective demand*. It is on this basis that Kant manages to carve out the distinct space of the judgment of beauty as "singular and without comparison to others, [yet] ... in agreement with the conditions of universality" (AA 5:219).

Shaviro stresses these peculiarities of the Kantian aesthetic judgment when recommending aesthetics as fundamentally anti-consumerist. This claim, however, may not be valid in the case of his own aesthetics of the senses, which levels Kant's fundamental distinction in favor of Whitehead's holistic theory that admits merely gradations but no

---

34 Ibid.
35 Ibid., 150. Shaviro quotes from Alfred North Whitehead, *Process and Reality* (New York: Free Press, 1978; orig. 1929), 32.
36 Shaviro, *The Universe of Things*, 149.

clear distinction between the senses and the intellect and reflection. In fact, Shaviro systematically levels a number of distinctions in Kant's meticulous reconstruction of aesthetic judgment. Thus, he claims that "Kant defines *beauty* as 'an *intuition* (of the imagination) for which a concept can never be found adequate.'"[37] From this, he concludes that for Kant, "beauty involves an immediate excess of sensation: something that stimulates thinking but that cannot be contained in, or expressed by, any particular thought."[38] The problem with this argument is that Kant is not speaking about beauty at all in this passage but about "an aesthetic idea"—a conception that arises in the context of Kant's discussion of works of art and their interpretive inexhaustibility. Artworks are embodied ideas, as it were. In the "Analytic of the Beautiful," aesthetic ideas are mentioned only once, namely in §17, which is dedicated to "the ideal of beauty," an ideal that Kant ties to the human figure and the moral vocation of humankind. In fact, according to Kant, "[a]n ideal of beautiful flowers ... cannot be conceived" (AA 5:233). Kant's meticulous distinctions notwithstanding, Shaviro reads the passage in question as countenancing an aesthetics of the senses. In his theory, aesthetics is the ultimate leveler, that which erases the cognitive distance between humans *qua* rational embodied animals and all other forms of existence. Aesthetics becomes a convenient means of circumventing the need for differentiation and system boundaries.

That said, linking Kant to Whitehead and Deleuze leads Shaviro to the important insight that the object of a Kantian aesthetic encounter "is something that is not a correlate of my thought, something that thought cannot possibly correlate to itself."[39] It is for this reason that he credits Kant's aesthetics with "mark[ing] the place where cognition and correlationism get left behind—or better, where they have not yet arisen."[40] Rather than making his case on this basis, however, Shaviro attempts to get to the bottom of aesthetic experience by taking recourse to the "Transcendental Aesthetic" of Kant's *Critique of Pure Reason* (A 19–49/B 33–73), where time and space are shown to be the *a priori* forms of our sensibility, and mashes it with the aesthetic theory of the *Critique of Judgment*. In the process, he erases Kant's explicit distinction between two different uses of the term "aesthetic." Whereas the transcendental aesthetic of the first *Critique* examines "the relation of a representation ... to the cognitive faculty," aesthetics as outlined in the third *Critique* is directed at "the feeling of pleasure and displeasure" and thus "a receptivity of the subject [that] contributes nothing at all to the cognition of

---

37 Ibid., 154; the Kant quote is taken from AA 5:342.
38 Ibid.
39 Ibid., 155.
40 Ibid.

the object" (AA 20:222).[41] Shaviro ignores this difference and confidently arrives at his conclusion that "[t]he primordial form of all experience, and thereby of all action and relation, is an aesthetic one."[42] Aesthetics is *prima philosophia*, for "the world is indeed, at its base, aesthetic. And through aesthetics, we can act in the world and relate to other things in the world without reducing it and them to mere correlates of our own thought."[43]

In formulating the principles of his aesthetic posthumanism, Shaviro resorts to a noncorrelationist "animal" existence that is guided only by what is pleasurable (without a criterion to distinguish the beautiful from the agreeable) and exalts an oceanic feeling of oneness in which all distinction between subject and object is erased. In contrast, the Kantian distinction maintains the distance between the subject and its object and thus opens a space for reflection, without losing touch with the world. Kant's account is focused on the object's formal specificity and thus its unfamiliarity and alienness, the source not only of its aesthetic appeal, but also of its posthumanist excess.

Kant emphasizes that an aesthetic judgment of sense—the pleasure that is attached to experiencing certain qualia—is entirely private and not communicable. The relevant sensation is "*immediately produced* by the empirical intuition of the object" (AA 20:225; my emphasis). The aesthetic judgment of reflection is something different and more complex. In such a judgment, the sensation that is the result of the free play between the imagination and the understanding "is the determining ground of a judgment which for that reason is called aesthetic and as subjective purposiveness (without a concept) is combined with the feeling of pleasure" (AA 20:224). From the posthumanist viewpoint, this definition would seem to lose all the advantages that the aesthetic approach originally promised. In an aesthetic judgment about an object "a given representation is certainly related to an object," as Kant states cautiously, yet "what is understood in the judgment is not the determination of the object but of the subject and its feeling" (AA 20:223). It is precisely in this sense that the aesthetic object "is not a correlate of my thought,"[44] to quote Shaviro, whose own theory succumbs to the lure of the agreeable and sacrifices the object's unassimilable otherness.

---

41 In the same passage of the first, originally unpublished introduction to the *Critique of Judgment*, Kant points to a change in the popular use of the term "aesthetics" as one of the motivating factors of this switch.
42 Shaviro, *The Universe of Things*, 156.
43 Ibid.
44 Ibid., 155.

Mere Form

An experience of the agreeable is not articulated in the way that a judgment of taste is. There is a lack of distance between subject and object. The affect that results from their encounter is immediate, and their relation is a consumptive, possessive mode of enjoyment," not a reflecting judgment.

In an innocuous passage, Kant poses the vexing question whether "mere color"—he cites the "green of a lawn" (AA 5:224)—could legitimately be judged beautiful or whether it is at best agreeable. If the former, where would the necessary distance come from? What would keep the subject at bay and prevent it from succumbing to mere enjoyment? Kant suggests that, first of all, the color would have to be pure, "which is a determination that already concerns *form*" (AA 5:224; my emphasis). In a further step, he enlists Euler's wave theory of light in order to argue that colors are vibrations, from which he concludes that they "would not be mere sensations, but would already be *a formal determination* of the unity of a manifold of them, and in that case could also be counted as *beauties in themselves*" (ibid.; my emphases). Although Kant seems to have been skeptical of this possibility at first,[45] the decisive point is that color and, in fact, anything at all *insofar as it can be considered in terms of an inherent form* is a legitimate object of the judgment of taste. The form of an object of aesthetic judgment alone is decisive. Adding "charms" can only detract from it (AA 5:225).

What is this form? Kant explains that "[a]ll form of the objects of the senses ... is either *shape* [Gestalt] or *play* [Spiel]" (AA 5:225). In Kant criticism this has generally been taken to mean the "spatio-temporal structures" of an object.[46] Eli Friedlander has recently offered an important dissenting view. He contends that Kant's notion of "form" ought to be distinguished from "a common use of that notion in aesthetics which associates it with order, configuration or structure," for unlike a

---

[45] In the first and second editions of the *Critique of Judgment*, Kant seems to have doubted Euler's theory of colors as vibrations (*pulsus*) when he writes "*woran ich doch gar sehr zweifle*" (of which I am quite doubtful). In the third edition a small change of just one word reverses the meaning of the passage, which now reads: "*woran ich doch gar nicht zweifle*" (of which I have no doubts at all). For our purposes, this change is not essential, since the lengthy sentence in which the passage occurs is conditional. The salient point with respect to beauty simply is that *if* colors are indeed such vibrations, *then* they fulfill the formal criteria to be considered candidates for aesthetic appreciation.

[46] This definition is taken from Wenzel, *An Introduction*, 3; see also 64. Paul Guyer similarly maintains that only "purely formal features of spatial and temporal organization ... are allowed to contribute to actual beauty," in *Kant and the Claims of Taste* (Cambridge: Cambridge University Press, 1997), 201; see also 398 n. 53.

structure or configuration, form is not "just a representation of a specific determinate fact."[47] Rather, a certain dynamic is decisive: presenting a form amounts to "hav[ing] the representation appear against the background of its condition of possibility," and "the advance of reflection" makes "for the ever more articulate presence of those conditions in our experience of the singular object of beauty."[48] The upshot of Friedlander's argument is that the presentation of form "always shows more than what is actually given to the senses in perception."[49] This is the reason why Kant can juxtapose the taste of reflection with the taste of the senses. Form as the actualization of the representation against the background of its condition of possibility is a matter for reflection. In Friedlander's terms, "the space of form"[50] is opened up in this encounter as the stage on which it plays out. Neither the movement of the mind, nor the beautiful object opens this space by itself. Rather, both of these poles are necessary to let the free play and thus the experience of beauty arise between them. If one of the poles is removed or ceases to be, the space of form collapses.

Evidently, a cognitive judgment opens no such space. But neither does an encounter below the threshold of an aesthetic judgment of reflection that relies merely on the taste of the senses. Precisely for this reason, Kant is worried about charms that are attached to beautiful objects. Not only do they distract, they positively mislead and infringe on the space of form that is held open only by the noncognitive free play between the imagination and the understanding that is anchored by the object. The space of form thus translates into a necessary minimal distance between object and observer. What we find beautiful in the object appears in this space as "some sort of unity that goes beyond whatever is necessary to classify it,"[51] in Guyer's words. A beautiful rose is a rose that possesses and radiates such unity. Kant's "mere form" (AA 5:228) designates, "as it were, an *excess* of felt unity or harmony."[52] Let us call this excess an intimation of a posthumanist world, for the experience of beauty thus exceeds cognition and, by extension, the knowing human subject. In aesthetic encounters, intensities of the objects that we cannot know make themselves felt, as if they were spectral emanations from a location beyond our reach.

---

47 Eli Friedlander, *Expressions of Judgment: An Essay on Kant's Aesthetics* (Cambridge, MA: Harvard University Press, 2015), 31f.
48 Ibid., 32.
49 Ibid.
50 Ibid.
51 Guyer, "Kant on the Purity of the Ugly," 149.
52 Ibid.

To be sure, the value of aesthetic experience does not consist in mere enrichment of the human environment. Nor is it primarily a matter of fine-tuning one's sensibility for exquisite stimuli that one does not encounter routinely. Rather, it is a matter that belongs to the order of what Jakob von Uexküll has called "surroundings [*Umgebung*]," which includes not just the "environment [*Umwelt*]" of a particular organism or system, but everything around it—the entire world in all its rich articulations, including those that the observer in question can neither perceive nor process due to a lack of receptivity or fit, and which surround the organism unbeknown to it.[53] The posthuman element of Kant's judgment of taste consists in indicating a peculiar richness that is discernible by means of a particular object, and which is part of the non-human surroundings of humans, a richness, moreover, which as such may not be phenomenologically accessible. The free play of our cognitive powers merely hints at something that is "there," without being able to designate or capture it. This something remains elusive beyond its momentary intensity. It remains beyond the perceptual capacities of the observer.

The sudden experience of beauty indicates something above and beyond the perceived world. It is as if there were no actual channels or receptors by means of which the perceiving organism could process the stimuli or irritations that come its way via the contemplated object. Yet these irritations hardly remain unnoticed—the usual fate of stimuli for which there is no fitting receptor. Rather it is as if aesthetic experience offered a glimpse of what getting around the constraints of our perceptual apparatus would mean. It is as if there were a sort of touch, albeit in the wrong place to be properly processed, but vaguely felt nonetheless. This sense of being touched ever so slightly or of the world unpredictably and unexpectedly brushing up against us is the content of aesthetic experience. The corresponding form is what Kant calls the "mere form" (AA 5:229) of the object that is judged beautiful.

The speculative theory of Art set the sights of aesthetics on art objects that were made for the purpose of aesthetic contemplation. Thus, it foreclosed Kant's elaborate effort to read nature's "cipher" (AA 5:301). Recent speculative realisms have reversed this tendency and turned aesthetics into the foundation of a peculiar precognitive materialism. Mere form, as encountered in nature, evades either extreme, for it opens the space of form where the posthumanist promise of Kant's aesthetics may take shape.

---

53 Jakob von Uexküll, *A Foray into the Worlds of Animals and Humans*, trans. Joseph D. O'Neil (Minneapolis: University of Minnesota Press, 2010), 43.

Eight Farewell to Ontology: Hegel after Humanism

Leif Weatherby

> In light of the concrete possibility of utopia, dialectics is the ontology of the wrong condition. A right condition would be free of that dialectic, system as little as contradiction.
>
> —Theodor W. Adorno

After Ontology

Ontology is where being and logic fit together; metaphysics is *about* that fit. Fit is positive: it is a matter of signs doing their jobs of referring, of logic and being going together, being seamless. The discourse *about* that fit is negative: it sees not only instances of non-fit but the impossibility of the ontological project altogether, the gulfs that separate its elements. A common distinction between these two terms is that ontologies are *regional* (to use Husserl's felicitous phrase), while metaphysics is *total*. That is certainly one axis along which to see these twin treatments of being. The other is the prism of inscription: ontology is a description of some region of being (not since Rationalism has it been identified with being *as such*, with the eccentric exception of Heidegger's fundamental ontology); metaphysics is not a *description of everything*, by contrast, but a *description of description* that includes *prescription*. In ontology, value is set; in metaphysics, value and norm are joined. This means that metaphysics is more dangerous than ontology, at first glance. Metaphysics can, of course, be abused—but this is when it is an application of ontology. Confer sexual characteristics onto elements (or God), for example, and you get some historically common and pretty nasty applications to gendered social life. But this operation is what Kant and Hegel would call "old" metaphysics, the use of limited assertions to cross-pollinate domains that cannot sustain the abduction. The metaphysical move of German Idealism stands completely opposed to this kind of ontologization, for the simple reason that *modality* is constitutive after Kant. Metaphysics totalizes, to be sure—but it totalizes across the negative boundary between being and cognition or embodied communication. This renders its totalizations profoundly historical, in Hegel's sense. I am not saying anything new in that statement, but these historical totalizations, we have to bear in mind, are not only *assertions*. They are *necessities and contingencies*. Not, nota bene, *ontological* necessities, but metaphysical ones, in the sense that they are historically bounded material rules for relations not between things but between things and signs, ideas and inscriptions, bodies and minds (co-existent with other bodies and minds).

Ontology is everywhere in the present. A fad for "positive" and "flat" ontologies is ubiquitous.[1] I agree with Alexander Galloway that there is "a coincidence between the structure of ontological systems and the structure of the most highly evolved technologies of post-Fordist capitalism"[2] (especially artificial intelligence), and that this coincidence is a problem—maybe *the* problem—for contemporary critical thought. The higher-level coding languages (Python, Ruby, etc.) are called "object-oriented" for a reason, and the new ontologies (including Badiou's, for Galloway) share too much in the logic of software. I share the impulse to do away with a *realism* in theory that is very much in the spirit of today's capitalism, in which the neutrality of mathematics can never be taken for granted (again, Galloway's point). But I turn to computer science's notion of *ontology* rather than object-oriented coding (they overlap), and to Hegel instead of Galloway's Marx. Better: I turn

---

1   These are often grouped together as "object-oriented ontologies," such as that of Graham Harman: "Heidegger's account of equipment gives birth to an ontology of *objects themselves*." Graham Harman, *Tool-Being: Heidegger and the Metaphysics of Objects* (Peru, IL: Open Court, 2002), 1; or Jane Bennett's proposal "to paint a positive ontology of matter." Jane Bennett, *Vibrant Matter: A Political Ecology of Things* (Durham, NC: Duke University Press, 2010), x. These ontologies usually turn away from epistemology (see Bennett, *Vibrant Matter*, 3), one of the points they share with Quentin Meillassoux's speculative realism. The speculative realists, on the other hand, tend to resist a too narrow ontology: "It has become almost a matter of dogma within continental philosophy that 'politics is ontology, and ontology is politics', as if the basic determination of 'what is' were itself a contentious political matter. While not denying the importance of politics, several of the materialisms and realisms proposed in this book tacitly reject the strong version of this claim. If the basic claim of realism is that a world exists independent of ourselves, this becomes impossible to reconcile with the idea that all of ontology is simultaneously political." Levi Bryant, Graham Harman, and Nick Srnicek, eds., *The Speculative Turn: Continental Materialism and Realism* (Melbourne: re.press, 2011), 16.
2   Alexander Galloway, "The Poverty of Philosophy: Realism and Post-Fordism," *Critical Inquiry* 39, no. 2 (2013): 347.

Farewell to Ontology   147

to Hegel because I share the conviction that a refreshed Marxist critique needs to take the digital conjuncture of cognition and matter seriously. We are watching artificial intelligence make gains in the manipulation of beings by collapsing the distinction between the rule and the individual. Algorithms scale not only up but down, to *you*, providing ads, "nudges," and other behavioral controls. Marxism theorized the mass society; we need Hegel for the world of "social" (read: personalized) media.

Every glance at contemporary discourse about the expanded regime of the digital—Machine Learning, Big Data, the Internet of Things—is a step in the direction of German Idealism. Machine Learning forces us to ask whether machines can have concepts, algorithms ideas—and whether they are the same as ours. These questions are Critical in the sense that Kant established for that word, meaning an analysis of the content of judgments based on their facultative sources. Our AI today is an extensive version of Kant. After two centuries of minute analysis and mechanization of logical judgments, we are now seeing judgments that don't match any obvious version of the logics we have—logics that appear to collapse individual and general, while writing some forms of life out of existence altogether. To apply Critique to non-human and, for us, unrecognizable judgments, is to bend the philosophical notion Kant had—that the object of philosophy was judgment as form, matter, and process—in a direction he did not conceive of. That direction is profane, finite, completely non-human cognition—which is the topic, substance, and method of Hegel's philosophy.

This last point is surely contentious. But consider—as I will in more detail in the final section—Hegel's magisterial treatment of the "Three Stances of Thought Towards Objectivity" (which also functions as the introduction to the "short logic" in the *Encyclopedia of the Philosophical Sciences*).[3] If there is a précis of Hegel's philosophy, this is it. Hegel takes the reader through the "old metaphysical" position, the empiricist position (under which he subsumes Kantian Critique), and the stance that relies on "immediate knowledge." The passage is entirely negative: no one reaches objectivity. In an important sense, *neither does Hegel*, at least not in the sentences he writes. Take, for example, an unassuming line of thinking close to the end of the "Three Stances" passage. Hegel tells us that the grand statements of the old metaphysics—the soul is simple and immortal, the world infinite—form a horseshoe with the position

---

3   G. W. F. Hegel, *Enzyklopädie der philosopischen Wissenschaften im Grundriss. Erster Teil. Band 8. Werke in zwanzig Bänden*, ed. E. Moldenhauer and K. M. Michel (Frankfurt a.M: Suhrkamp, 1969–71), §19–78. Translations of Hegel mine. *Stellungen* is often translated as "positions," but as my reading will show, the more active "stances" is a better fit.

that claims that immediate intuitive knowing is the ultimate form of cognition. Hegel writes:

> Both views claim that: ... the simple inseparability of *thinking* from the *being* of the thinking thing, - *cogito ergo sum* is entirely the same as that being, reality, existence of the I is immediately revealed to me in consciousness ... and that that inseparability is the absolutely *first* (not mediated, proven) and *most certain* knowledge.[4]

This "simple inseparability" then applies to God and to the world of the senses, to sensed things, leading to the claim that the world of things is "appearance only." Hegel remains polemical, not stating "his" opinion but remaining immanent to the stances. Both stances rely on the identity of thinking and the first being projected from thinking (the I as *res cogitans*). In rejecting this identity as premise, Hegel tears the procedure of thinking from consciousness, separating operation and substance, thinking from human. The shared problem is not doctrinal points but the activity of separation itself, carried out by thinking as a condition for any notion of being. If the impulse of posthumanist thought is to prevent reification by reduction to all-too-human concepts—to free alterities, like animals or bodies from narrow designations that ultimately serve to control them—then Hegel's wedge between being and ego presents the deepest prophylactic. By inserting alterity into the movement of the concept itself, Hegel resists control at the ontological level. The Hegelian category is irreducible to human dimensions, but does not reify nonhuman dimensions. It is uniquely suited to deal with the hybrid state of digital affairs, in which human and inhuman scales and contents are communicated and exchanged in software packets, platforms, and data. The ontologies of those scales involve the projection and manipulation of the human scale. As machine ontologies increasingly collapse the gap between protocols and individuals, we need to look back from Marx to Hegel to cope with the present.

"Posthumanism" has two senses that don't entirely overlap. One was epitomized by N. Katherine Hayles in her term-defining *How We Became Posthuman*.[5] The title itself tells us that posthumanism is a condition, like postmodernism. The other version is defended by, among others, Cary Wolfe, for whom posthumanism is a way of thinking, something we do on purpose (with, in his proposal, a signature blend of Derrida and Luhmann).[6] Finer differences aside, each agrees with

---

4 Ibid, §76.
5 N. Katherine Hayles, *How We Became Posthuman: Virtual Bodies in Cybernetics, Literature, and Informatics* (Chicago: University of Chicago Press, 1999).
6 Cary Wolfe, *What is Posthumanism?* (Minneapolis: University of Minnesota Press, 2009).

the other half of the semantic range: Wolfe surely acknowledges there is some circumstantial pressure on us to do posthuman thinking, and Hayles has recently proposed an extensive realm of the "unthought" as a theoretical prism for posthuman work. Two questions, then: what kind of world do we live in, and what kind of thinking is appropriate to that world? The answer to both involves, for all posthumanism, a malleable category called "the human" in transformation.

For me—polemically—the posthuman distinguishes itself from the transhuman (for example) by being about the *category*. The first theoretical concern for posthumanism is not about whether the human is becoming an X-Men-style mutant. The cyborg condition that Donna Haraway so beautifully laid out in the 1980s, for example, is notably a destruction of binary conditions, not just the addition of mechanical elements to human bodies (that's where the feminism comes in: the cyborg is feminine because the feminine is a category, not because of genitalia or even, at the limit, self-identification). The new ontologies and speculative realisms are, of course, ontological. They fall on the "what should we think" side of the posthuman spectrum. Without exception known to me, however, they are not descriptions of the world around us but interrogations of description itself. Even the flattest ontology must provide an escape route from what Quentin Meillassoux calls "correlationism," which traps the world or the absolute in all-too-human thinking. Even under the mark of erasure, the object-oriented ontologies and speculative realisms are about categories, signs, and representation.

As machines generate putatively new categories, which, in the name of profit and control (insufficient categories themselves in digital capitalism) transform social, natural, and cognitive operations, posthumanism finds the condition and the thinking permanently enmeshed in one another. It is not the "world" that has changed, but the semiosis that first allows us to think a world at all. Semiotics is no longer the preserve of the human, if it ever was. If signs and their arrangements have changed in the digital era, then the world has. This leads to the need for new ontologies, and to the adoption of the term "ontology" by computer scientists. I'm going to argue in what follows that those ontologies must respond to the existence of pre-constituted digital ontologies. The kind of thinking we need, in other words, is not a *complement* or *other* ontology to the digital, but a metaphysics that embraces and objectifies machine ontologies, doing justice to the complexity of a semiotic situation in which much thinking is not done by humans at all. Theoretical resistance to capitalism cannot take the form of ontology today. Speculation is needed; semiotics must be integral to that speculation. Much ink has been spilled on Meillassoux's attempt to supersede ontology; I argue here that Hegel's thought, instead, is the crucial resource for a digital posthumanism.

The Specification of a Conceptualization

Ontology is the study of being. When Christian Wolff formalized a largely Leibnizian system in the early eighteenth century, he divided metaphysics into special and general branches. Special metaphysics consisted of rational cosmology, rational psychology, and rational theology—the world, the soul, and God. The title of the German version of his treatise defined "general metaphysics" as the study of "also all other things at all [*auch allen Dingen überhaupt*]."[7] Ontology was not regional, it was everything.

Compare the classical computer science definition of the term, from Thomas R. Gruber: he defines ontology as "an explicit specification of a conceptualization."[8] Ontologies are not limited to tautology, for Gruber, because "to specify a conceptualization one needs to state axioms that do constrain the possible interpretations for the defined terms."[9] A conceptualization defines a region; its specification defines the relations between conceptualized entities. These relations can in turn be functionalized, for communication or for code commands. This means that any ontology is a kind of tool for communications, abstract enough to be more than pointing but concrete enough to designate individuals in their networks of relations. Gruber states five general principles for a good ontology: clarity of definitions, coherence between levels, monotonic extendability (without revision of system), minimal encoding bias, and minimal ontological commitment.[10] Ontology is a set of premises that can be grasped and shared by differently frameworked agents (or minds).

This framework-sharing allows for what Gruber calls "interoperability": "Due to their independence from lower level data models, ontologies are used for integrating heterogeneous databases, enabling interoperability among disparate systems, and specifying interfaces to

---

7 Christian Wolff, *Vernünfftige Gedancken von Gott, der Welt und der Seele des Menschen, auch allen Dingen überhaupt, den Liebhabern der Wahrheit mitgtheilet* (Halle: Renger, 1751).
8 Thomas R. Gruber, "Ontology," http://tomgruber.org/writing/ontology-definition-2007.htm, visited September 11, 2017. Also printed as Thomas R. Gruber, *Encyclopedia of Database Systems*, ed. Ling Liu and M. Tamer Özsu (Boston: Springer, 2009).
9 Gruber, "Ontology."
10 Thomas R. Gruber, "Toward Principles for the Design of Ontologies Used for Knowledge Sharing," *International Journal of Human-Computer Studies* 43 (1995): 909. This last term was adopted from a debate in analytical philosophy that heavily featured the work of W. V. O. Quine. See Phillip Bricker, "Ontological Commitment," in *The Stanford Encyclopedia of Philosophy* (2016 edition), ed. Edward N. Zalta, https://plato.stanford.edu/archives/win2016/entries/ontological-commitment/, visited December 13, 2017.

independent, knowledge-based services."[11] Ontology as we most commonly understand it today enables interoperability between what computer scientists call "agents." The internet we engage with daily is a very partial realization of an implementation that Timothy Berners-Lee called "the Semantic Web" in the 1990s. There is a kind of Hegelian reversal in that name, however: the internet as it stood when the new protocols were conceived was already *human*-readable. *Semanticization* in Berners-Lee's sense was the process of making the web *machine*-readable. There is a light irony in this use of semantics, since Claude Shannon had famously founded the digital age with the exclusion of "the semantics aspects" from the engineering of communications channels.[12] The Web is ontological in at least three senses: Gruber's, the engineered layer of the stack; the influence of that layer on everyday ontologies (think Google Maps as GPS instrument); and the extensive mining that search engines and others perform on the ever-expanding lexicon and visual vocabulary of cyberspace, rendering native Web ontologies that are not designed (at least by humans). I'll stick to Gruber's vision here, since some principles he articulates are portable (and not just for computer scientists).

As Gruber notes, "in the technology stack of the Semantic Web standards, ontologies are called out as an explicit layer."[13] To make the Web a semantically connected network, ontologies were needed. Berners-Lee and his colleagues described this process in a *Scientific American* article in 2001. The "layer" of the stack that is ontological has to be engineered to be more general than any particular expression. Their example is informative: if one database uses "postal code" and another "zip code," an ontology that functions for both will be able to identify them by their location and function within the larger framework, regardless of name. In other words, ontology is where the *operations* of symbols meant to catalog run up against real-world constraints, even when those constraints are really existing synonyms. Agents can have interoperability only if they have some mutual ontology. Berners-Lee et al. write that, compared to the earlier internet, "The Semantic Web, in contrast, is more flexible. The consumer and producer agents can reach a shared understanding by exchanging ontologies, which provide the vocabulary needed for discussion. Agents can even 'bootstrap' new

---

11 Gruber, "Ontology."
12 Ibid.
13 "… today's W3C Semantic Web standard suggests a specific formalism for encoding ontologies (OWL), in several variants that vary in expressive power. This reflects the intent that an ontology is a specification of an abstract data model (the domain conceptualization) that is independent of its particular form." Ibid.

reasoning capabilities when they discover new ontologies."[14] Coding languages that are object-oriented have a non-trivial relationship to the setting of these ontologies, which is called *ontology engineering*.[15]

In a sense, Wolff's program falls under the same paradigm. The Rationalists after Leibniz were, after all, fashioning a language that was seated at a level of abstraction neither entirely general nor too specific to apply across cases.[16] The difference is that the computer science version of the concept is *explicitly worried about* the difference between entities and their relations in the catalog and those in the world. The ontology engineer has to produce a set of constraints on semantic proliferation that allow more specified programs (lower-level database operations) to share a framework. Looking for relationships among signs that constitute a condition for a pre-constituted ability (communication, in this case) is what Kant called *Kritik*.[17] To be sure, Gruber is not characterizing human reason. But he is also not merely classifying. Ontology engineering is about moving between classificatory strategies, making large-scale semantic systems into a medium for another project. Whether your project is the extension of digital architecture or the preservation of the moral will, ontology will be about the limits of designation.

---

14 Tim Berners-Lee, James Hendler, and Ora Lassila, "The Semantic Web," *Scientific American* 284, no. 5 (2001): 42.
15 The language of "agents" allows this discourse to float freely over the distinction between humans and AI units. An explicit ontology marked up through the Semantic Web stack (including the Web Ontology Language [OWL] and XML) has only partly come into existence. Google's embrace of Machine Learning, it seems to me, has obviated part of the infrastructure that Gruber and Berners-Lee imagined. But this only means that ontology is not a top-down affair, but one shared in some currently emergent and nebulous (black-boxed) way with algorithms. The internet today has, in this sense, its own ontology in development.
16 "*Ontology engineering* is concerned with making representational choices that capture the relevant distinctions of a domain at the highest level of abstraction while still being as clear as possible about the meanings of terms." Gruber, "Ontology."
17 Yuk Hui also notes that computer science ontologies share something with Kant, although he separates between the material operations of digitally embedded ontologies and the ideal objects of Kantian Critique. Yuk Hui, *On the Existence of Digital Objects* (Minneapolis: University of Minnesota Press, 2016), 90. Hui's study contains a much larger treatment of formal and computer ontologies than I can do justice to here, and I have learned a great deal from it. Hui's proposal for a framework that operates between the two types of ontology, which he bases on a reading of the work of Gilbert Simondon, differs from what I propose here because of Simondon's stubborn rejection of dialectics. The proposals nevertheless share a relative indifference to local ontologies because they are both cross-domain analyses.

It was ontology that Kant domesticated in the faculty of the understanding. Kant's intervention in metaphysics is notoriously complicated, but the fault line he drew between special and general metaphysics is particularly clear. Special metaphysics was "dialectical": Reason totalized an area of being (world, soul, God) and this totalization of what could only be presented as finite cognition led to contradictions (the world is finite and infinite; necessary and contingent). These "dialectical" contradictions were necessary to the structure of the faculties but uninformative about the world. Nature, such as we could determine it by appeal to combinations of intuition and concepts in judgments, was the only "being" we could know. Things in themselves were not the preserve of ontology. Kant rejected an "organon of reason" in favor of a "canon of the understanding," a positive set of rules that constitute our contribution to what counts as being. The analytic of the understanding, he claimed, would even forego "the proud name of ontology" altogether, making room for the modest analysis of possible experience limited by the senses and formed by the categories.[18] When the computer scientists adopted the term "ontology," they were referring to debates in analytic philosophy. But they accidentally, it seems, adopted a Kantian tenet: that ontology doesn't "know" about things in themselves, it just organizes knowledge. We can even go one step further: that organization can't possibly proceed in a vacuum, so even if ontology can't give us a faithful representation of the world, it must fit within that world.

Gruber uses the example of the concept of "quantity" in physics. Physicists use "quantity" both to talk about the thing in the world and the thing in the equation, but an ontology for computers that will work for physicists might have to separate these from one another. When quantities are multiplied, two separate ontological results appear, the arithmetic product of the magnitude and of the units, as Gruber argues.[19] To engineer a good ontology for engineers, then, one needs to be careful about the definition of quantity (a clarity problem). Gruber's rules are Kantian categories in the sense that they are general principles for unification between open-ended vocabularies. They imitate Kant's categories very precisely, in this way: the categories are rules for the unification of judgments irrespective of their conceptual or sensuous contents. Ontology is where logic is fitted to a being it cannot comprehend or encompass. Gruber writes that "For AI systems, what 'exists' is that which can be represented."[20] Kant might have only puzzled over

---

18 Immanuel Kant, *Critique of Pure Reason*, ed. Paul Guyer and Allen W. Wood (Cambridge: Cambridge University Press, 1998): B 303/A 247.
19 Gruber, "Toward Principles," 912–15.
20 Gruber, "Ontology."

the qualifier "A" (artificial). Ontologies are embodied operations, as Kant knew. Whether the bodies are humanoid or integrated circuits is not really the point. The engineer can be a network of brains or a network of neural nets. The question is what the ontologies *do*, what they are *for*.

Physics, Gruber tells us, has a strong ontology to begin with, so some problems in engineering a computer ontology in this arena are less difficult. By contrast, consider the problem of references in the librarian's sense of that word. All Gruber needed was the concept of "physical dimension" to distinguish between magnitude and unit. In the world of bibliography, we have a "weak" ontology, and to impose commitment on it will lead to confusion or error. For example (Gruber's), if we want to have "author" as a category, we need to encode an openness to multiple, unknown, other types of authorship, including name-changes (particularly tricky if they are not tagged in some way). If we don't, the over-commitment leads to incoherence, "since we know that these constraints do not hold in the world being modeled."[21] Here, Gruber takes a step beyond Kant. Ontology engineers are *indifferent to the constitution of ontologies*. In the bibliographic world, for example, the "conceptualization" is of a *"world that includes information."*[22] This entails classes like "reference," "data," "document," "author," "person"—the last two are separated for the reasons named above. The ontology engineer is indifferent not to the structure but to the *nature* of the ontology. It matters a great deal that we separate classes in the most useful way. But the difference between "weak" and "strong" is a functional difference. We might note that the weakness of the reference world is endemic to ontologies that include signs, worlds that include information. Taxonomy is weak here because names for things that are both names and things simultaneously have been harder to stabilize in the history of theory than names for things (even complex things). But the point is just this: the ontology engineer treats ontology as a tool, one that can change and—even if this is cumbersome—be revised if necessary, and as relations shift, new parts of the world emerge or come to light. Ontologies can be discarded without harming the objects of those ontologies. Object-oriented ontology, for example, could disappear without harming any objects (by its own lights, I think). Ontology is a flexible condition to which the digital is *indifferent*. That is because the digital is metaphysical in the Idealist

---

21 Gruber, "Toward Principles," 924.
22 Ibid., 920; my emphasis.

sense: it is a totalization of a specified conceptualization, an ontology grasped not as reference but as semiosis.

Machines have no native ontology. We can describe them in isolation from other regions of being, but they do not generate internal, projected images of a world. Yet digital machines, lacking a proper ontology, have metaphysics in the sense that they perform sign-operations that are relatively indifferent to regional ontologies. Ontology is human. Indifference to ontology is posthuman—as Quentin Meillassoux has been at pains to show.

Meillassoux, Inverted Kant

Meillassoux is not an ontologist. *After Finitude*, for all its well-known polemic against Kant, shares the intention to break away from ontology. Kant relegates that break to pure reason, which has led to the curious situation that his legacy is often too heavily situated in the ontology of the understanding. Meillassoux defines his project as the construction of a non-metaphysical speculation, one founded in a mathematical language that Meillassoux has not provided. The question is how to get out of ontology—Meillassoux's proposal is flight, not fight.

After Finitude reads like a palimpsest written over the *Critique of Pure Reason*.[23] Its thesis question invokes Kant as its foil: "Why did philosophy, in attempting to think science, err towards transcendental idealism instead of resolutely orienting itself, as it should have, towards a *speculative materialism*?"[24] The direction of its answer remains in the rhetorical thrall of the Critical system: "We must show why thought, far from experiencing its intrinsic *limits* through facticity, experiences rather its *knowledge* of the absolute through facticity."[25] We may already glimpse in this anti-Kantian framing the beginning of a dialogue with Hegel—one that Meillassoux has not, to date, elaborated. But the connection to Kant runs even deeper. Asking about knowledge that is "ancestral" to us, facts that remain stubbornly beyond any correlation to our thinking (like paleocosmological facts), Meillassoux insists that these *"arche-fossils"* challenge us to see in our thinking *not* the domestication of ontology but a speculative knowledge of the absolute that

---

23 A great deal of ink has been spilled about Meillassoux's reading of Kant. Most helpful to me have been Catherine Malabou, *Before Tomorrow: Epigenesis and Rationality*, trans. Carolyn Shread (Malden, MA: polity, 2016), 129–55; and David Golumbia, "Correlationism—The Dogma That Never Was," *boundary* 2 43, no. 2 (2016), 1–25. This volume adds two new excellent exponents to this literature (by Peter Gilgen and Carsten Strathausen).

24 Quentin Meillassoux, *After Finitude: An Essay on the Necessity of Contingency*, trans. Ray Brassier (London: Bloomsbury, 2010), 121.

25 Ibid., 52.

is *de-ontologized*.[26] The absolute, he tells us repeatedly, has always been imagined as a *necessary being* (not least by Hegel, a point I will dispute shortly). What if we recognize the absolute as *contingency* instead of necessity? In this case, for Meillassoux, the only possible correlation is destroyed and the long-standing metaphysical link between the absolute and being disappears. As he puts it, "[t]he absolute is the absolute impossibility of a necessary being," a doctrine he calls "the principle of unreason."[27] This doctrine elaborates a *"logos of contingency, which is to say, a reason emancipated from the principle of reason—a speculative form of the rational* that would no longer be a *metaphysical reason."*[28] (Note that this use of *metaphysical* means "projection of being"; as we will see with Hegel presently, Meillassoux here means "ontological.") What we see in our own (mathematical) knowledge is the absolute as irrational, contingent not *for us* but absolutely, which contradicts the univocity of being altogether. Being collapses as a category; law loses its toehold in the order of things, which is not an order at all.

This is actually Kant's position. Or at least, it is so close to Kant's position that the two texts are inextricably linked. Even though Meillassoux takes his philosophy to be a polemic against Kant, his rejection of ontology—or indifference to it—is close to Kant's domestication of ontology in favor of a *speculative reason that has no ontological implications.* Meillassoux writes that "we must transform our perspective on unreason, stop construing it as the form of our deficient grasp of the world and turn it into the veridical content of this world as such—we must project unreason into things themselves, and discover in our grasp of facticity the veritable *intellectual intuition* of the absolute."[29] Intellectual intuition is the technical term that Kant uses to designate the *impossibility (for us) of an absolute that also possesses being.* The understanding cannot know this absolute because its procedures are not intuitive; intuition is formed, for it, according to the *a priori* forms of intuition (space and time). Reason, on the other hand, precisely because it is severed from intuition, can place no claim on the existence of its objects. The absolute that also exists is not a category for Kant; or better, it is

---

26 Meillassoux describes his own project as "factial ontology" throughout *After Finitude*; since multiple vocabularies are in play here, I'm going to hold that Meillassoux's system is non-ontological—and then smuggles the "being" it claims to eschew back in surreptitiously.

27 Ibid., 60. Elsewhere, Meillassoux confirms: "In order to preserve the meaning of ancestral statements without regressing to dogmatism, *we must uncover an absolute necessity that does not reinstate any form of absolutely necessary entity. In other words, we must think an absolute necessity without thinking anything that is absolutely necessary."* Ibid., 34.

28 Ibid., 77.

29 Ibid., 82.

the category that serves as a foil against which to see human cognition. A speculative but non-ontological rationality exists in Kant too, in the metaphysics of morals, which Meillassoux never mentions. Kant famously compared his Critical system to the Copernican Revolution. Meillassoux understands this comparison as a *"Ptolemaic counter-revolution"* which places thought back at the center of things, demoting the world.[30] He sees, however, in science "the much more fundamental decentring which presided over the mathematization of nature, viz., *the decentring of thought relative to the world within the process of knowledge.*"[31] Relative to *which world*, though? Surely not to the world of mathematized ontological *things*, which will never lead us beyond the correlation, as Kant showed. Meillassoux's project is inverted Kant, both in the sense that being and thought have the same relation with the directional arrow reversed, and in the sense that a speculative absolute that has no being is the horizon.

Catherine Malabou writes that *After Finitude* "obviously succeeds [in creating] ... a philosophy liberated from self-obsession, freed from the fear of going back beyond the symbolic-transcendental line."[32] Meillassoux's prose is electric because he is asking first-order questions. The problem is that his conclusions lack a framework in which they are enmeshed; they are electric but unorganized, they speak to the first order in a time when the second order is embodied. This was the signal contribution of German Idealism: to be first-order philosophy both aware of and written as second-order problems, philosophy *of the second order* (we might say: mediated, with Hegel) because *mediation is not secondary*. Nor is mediation "correlation" in any sense. What we need today is Meillassoux's force with Hegel's depth, by which I mean style: electricity plus metaphysics embedded in the prose of philosophy.

In order to put Meillassoux into conversation with Hegel on the backdrop of ontology, we need to look past the problem of correlation. *After Finitude* is composed of two separate proposals: one is that all thinking caught in the "correlation" is insufficient to encounter the radical contingency of the law, and the second is that there is a purely mathematical language that can communicate a non-correlational sense of being. The heavy focus on correlation in treatments of Meillassoux likely proceeds from the fact that the second proposal remains almost

---

30 Ibid., 118. Hans Blumenberg has proposed a much more nuanced reading of this analogy, one which notes that Kant hardly puts the *subject* back in the center of the cosmos. See Hans Blumenberg, *The Genesis of the Copernican World*, trans. Robert Wallace (Cambridge, MA: MIT, 1987), esp. 613 ff.
31 Ibid., 115.
32 Malabou, *Before Tomorrow*, 141.

entirely a promise.[33] We do not even know—as we do with Badiou's set-theoretical ontology—what *kind* of mathematical language will be used for speculation. Still, reading only the correlational notion is a way of avoiding the electrical charge of Meillassoux's work, of disavowing his challenge by seeking to defeat its premise. I'm going to try to read him as though the premise doesn't matter—for Hegel, as for Meillassoux, there's something not quite right about Kant's domestication of ontology. If we accept that Kantian ontology and computer science ontology share a structure, then Meillassoux and Hegel are surprisingly aligned as thinkers who want to find a way to the outside of digital ontology. They just disagree about the means.

Means, as we shall see, is precisely the point for Hegel. The dialectic between limitation and infinity leads Hegel to reject any final division between means and ends. Meillassoux stumbles, it seems, into a related position by recognizing that contradiction and being stand in a relation of indirect entailment. This leads him closer to Hegel than he wants to be. He writes that "a contradictory entity is absolutely impossible, because if an entity was contradictory, it would be necessary."[34] The statement is curious: it cedes a great deal to Hegel, but seems to miss its own point. Even if we decide that contradiction implies necessity it is not clear why this implies *being*. We can even go one step further and wonder if the bright line drawn here between necessity and impossibility is possible to maintain. Meillassoux says that a truly contradictory entity—if it existed—would "result in the implosion of the very idea of determination—of being such and such, of being this rather than that. Such an entity would be tantamount to a 'black hole of differences,' into which all alterity would be irremediably swallowed up, since the being-other of this entity would be obliged, simply by virtue of being other than it, *not* to be other than it."[35] One might have thought that imploding

---

33 The exception here is Malabou, who takes the challenge seriously in *Before Tomorrow*. Her understanding of contingency as an epigenetic plane shares with my proposal here an attempt to move beyond the deadlock of the question of the correlation.

34 Meillassoux, *After Finitude*, 67.

35 Ibid., 70. The rest of this passage proposes an almost willful misunderstanding of Hegel: "Thus it is not by chance that the greatest thinker of contradiction, that is to say, Hegel, was not the thinker of the sovereignty of becoming, but on the contrary, the thinker of absolute identity, of the identity of identity and difference. For what Hegel saw so acutely is that the necessary entity *par excellence* could only be the entity that had nothing outside it and that would not be limited by any alterity. Thus the Supreme Being could only be the being that remains in itself even as it passes into its other, the entity that contains contradiction within itself as a moment of its own development, the entity that verifies the supreme contradiction of not becoming anything other even as it becomes other. It is supreme, reposing eternally within itself, because it absorbs both difference and becoming into its superior identity." Ibid.

determination was a goal of Meillassoux's.[36] In wanting to maintain ontological alterity while producing a non-ontological speculative absolute, Meillassoux is forced to claim that there are "inconsistent" worlds that differ by contradiction, but in which contradiction is contingent. At this point, he recognizes his uncanny proximity to Hegel,[37] but continues to insist that there is only one world for Hegel, only one body of contradictions—only one being.[38] This leads him to reduce dialectical thought to "contradictions inherent in *statements* about the world, never with *real* contradictions about the world ... studies of the ways in which the contradictions of thought produce effects in thought, rather than studies of the supposedly ontological contradictions which thought discovers in the surrounding world."[39] Curiously, this is *exactly what Hegel accuses Kant of doing*. The question, then—again, if we accept the premise that the critique of Kant and the critique of digital ontology are part of the same project—is what language, or what form of philosophy, is appropriate to what lies beyond this critique. In other words, *what positive language resists the spirit of digital capitalism*?

Before I leave Meillassoux behind, it is worth remarking that the promise for a mathematical expression of the non-ontological absolute devolves into a romanticization of a monstrous contingency. Meillassoux calls this *hyper-Chaos*, a "menacing power—something insensible, and capable of destroying both things and worlds, of bringing forth monstrous absurdities, yet also of never doing anything, of realizing every dream, but also every nightmare, of engendering random and frenetic transformations, or conversely, of producing a universe that remains motionless down to its ultimate recesses, like a cloud bearing the fiercest storms, then the eeriest bright spells."[40] This seductive passage is, one notes in reading, anything but mathematical. But that is not the problem. The problem is that it is unclear why the purple prose here should arouse any emotion—which it is surely intended to do—if this "hyper-Chaos" *has no being*. If we are sinners in the hands of a God too inconsistent to be angry—well, to be blunt, who cares? The domesticated contingencies of a life lived under the mark of a Kantian assurance about the consistency of being are far more terrifying than

---

36 Quentin Meillassoux, *Science Fiction and Extro-Science Fiction*, trans. Alyosha Edlebi (Minneapolis: University of Minnesota Press, 2015).
37 Meillassoux, *After Finitude*, 78.
38 Ibid., 80. Continuing: "Thus, in Hegel, the necessity of contingency is not derived from contingency as such and contingency alone, but from a Whole that is ontologically superior to the latter. This is precisely what separates the factial from the dialectical—or to put it more generally, and using our own terminology, what separates the speculative from the metaphysical." Ibid., 80.
39 Ibid., 79.
40 Ibid., 64.

this "hyper-Chaos," which becomes, from the perspective of the everyday, less Cthulhu and more the Swamp Monster, less the specter of the absolute and more the comic dance of old metaphysics. And so it is that, electrified by Meillassoux, we need Hegel.

Inhuman Hegel

Ontology since Kant—and including computer science—is all too human. To think ontology is to produce a set of relations, formal or otherwise, that stand in an unstated relation to the producer—the *ontology engineer*. That engineer seeks to provide means to connect individual sets of beings to general coding procedures, operations that manipulate those beings. Ontology, as a layer "explicitly called out" in the semantic stack, serves a contemporary capitalism that toggles between profiting from the discovery of those connections and outright control over individual beings. Meillassoux's *After Finitude* occupies a curious position in this situation, because it seeks to exit this logic, but reproduces it in the final account (so far). Meillassoux sees that we must leave the simple entailment of being—the ontological understanding of being—behind in order to do justice to the posthuman condition. And by asking first-order questions, as Malabou has recognized, he pushes us to bring philosophy into a relation with the world, not only with itself. But this relation is unexamined. When Meillassoux rejects an absolute that has being, he removes what he calls speculation and what Hegel calls metaphysics into an implicit understanding of being as *immediate unity* of the speculative and the absolute. In Hegel's terminology, Meillassoux successfully rejects old metaphysics (he hardly needed to) and empiricism (including Kant). But this forces him, because he consigns contradiction to thinking, into the implicit immediate unity of speculation and the absolute. *Of course* there is no solution to this problem, no language mathematical or otherwise to characterize speculative materialism. Perhaps this is why he uses the phrase "intellectual intuition," which famously could not be associated with any discursive regime. *After Finitude* claims an infinity that is somehow larger than the infinity that includes finitude, yet does not include being. It is hard to imagine a more abstract infinity.

Enter Hegel. Let's return to the passage I cited at the beginning of this article, in which Hegel describes the "three stances" of thought toward objectivity. This is Hegel's own farewell to ontology, which he both domesticates and sets free, insisting that understanding and reason cannot be finally separated from one another, in spite of the contradictions they produce. It is this insistence that allows him to see old metaphysics and immediate knowledge through the same prism, as I noted earlier. They share, according to Hegel, a commitment to the notion that being and thinking are separate—only to insist that truth

Farewell to Ontology 161

can only possibly be located in an absolute unity of the two. Here's the passage again:

> Both views claim that: ... the simple inseparability of *thinking* from the *being* of the thinking thing, - *cogito ergo sum* is entirely the same as that being, reality, existence of the I is immediately revealed to me in consciousness ... and that that inseparability is the absolutely *first* (not mediated, proven) and *most certain* knowledge.[41]

"Simple inseparability" means that actual synthesis *and* actual disjunction are muted. These alternate possibilities for thinking objectivity are those of Kant and Hume, respectively (the second stance). For Kant, synthesis precedes analysis, and synthesis is only real if it includes being and thinking (this is the problem that Kant tries to solve with what he calls the "transcendental unity of apperception"). For Hume, on the other hand, "matters of fact" and "relations of ideas" remain stubbornly distinct. Hegel accords analytical superiority to Kant (and to a lesser extent Hume), but polemically claims that the first and third stances, metaphysics and immediacy, have better goals—they just don't have the means to follow through on them. This is because both stances assume that subject and object are distinct, only to *attempt* their synthesis. For old, Rationalist metaphysics, being is susceptible to designation because the inseparability of thinking and being is sustained by a divine pre-established harmony. The attempt at ontological synthesis is therefore incomplete but assured of ultimate success. "Immediate knowledge" stands in the reverse relationship, maintaining that no amount of determinate designation can alter or contradict the reality of synthesis that we get closer to with every removal of mediation. By assuming that thinking and being are inseparable, both stances neglect the possibility that thinking and being *act* directly on one another. For them, philosophy is talk *about* a static relation between being and thinking. For Hegel, philosophy *is* that relation. Philosophy can only realize itself as that relation if it allows real contradiction, since otherwise it could only ever be a single proposition. Meillassoux combines the standpoint of immediate knowledge ("intellectual intuition") with the standpoint of old metaphysics (though he vigorously denies this), producing an ontology with no content. His indifference to ontological matters is absolute, because he rejects contradiction, consigning it to one side of a binary between subject and object he never questions. His is a fourth stance of

---

41 Hegel, *Enzyklopädie*, §76.

thinking to objectivity, and the overture to the renewal of dialectics in the digital present.

Recall that Meillassoux consigns contradiction to the world of symbols, the subjective side of things. This precise point is what Hegel takes issue with in Kant's philosophy. Having domesticated ontology into the canon of the understanding, Kant consigns special metaphysics (God, the world, and soul) to the "dialectic of pure reason." In rational cosmology, Kant deduces antinomies that result from reason's totalization of the object. The world is necessarily both finite and infinite; the source of the contradiction is reason itself. Reason possesses "transcendental illusion [*Schein*]," ideas that we must have in order to orient ourselves in the world but cannot be integrated into nature (the preserve of the understanding). Hegel disagreed, writing that "the main thing ... is that the antinomy is not only located in the four special objects taken from cosmology, but rather in *all* objects of all species, in *all* representations, contradictions, and ideas ... this feature constitutes that which from here out will designate itself as the *dialectical* moment of the logical."[42] The dialectical *moment* is in the neuter, not the masculine, meaning that "moment" here is meant in the physical sense of impetus, force, rather than the temporal sense. Contradiction only appears to be subjective. When we consign contradiction to proposition, symbol, or thinking, we unwittingly project a being innocent of such contradiction and thereby entirely without determination. That being is not *lawless* but *empty*. It is not *necessity* that contradiction produces, but *content*. What Hegel rejects in Kant (and by extension, in Meillassoux), is the removal of being from thinking in the first place. We might call this "simple separation," in keeping with Hegel's critique of "simple inseparability." It's a nominalism about method that makes philosophy innocent of anything except setting the right goals. For Hegel, the writing itself would have to be load-bearing. Contradictions are not located merely in thinking, but also not *merely in being* (this is where Meillassoux's struggle with Hegel never finds clarity). Contradiction does not imply a being that *exists* because contradiction is not on one side of the implicit separation. In locating contradiction in the inextricability of ontology from some framework-setting ontologizer (an engineer), Hegel suggests only the necessity of contingent totalities of sign-systems. Hegel totalizes specified conceptualizations by making his sentences faithful to their already contradictory nature, by including semiotic limitation and contradiction in the very grammar of his sentences. It is in the limitations imposed by overlapping sets of contradictions that dialectical thinking takes flight. Dialectical thinking rejects any permanent distinction; thinking

---

42 Hegel, *Enzyklopädie*, §48.

is not a *means* to synthesize what is already inseparable but appears separated (being and thinking). Instead, thinking is deeply ontological, and yet strafed with contradiction in each ontological determination. Philosophy as dialectics has to realize both sides of that equation. If it does not, it either leaves beings behind or clings fast to some set of beings that will all too quickly corrupt and pass out of existence. This is why *means* and *ends* are relative concepts for Hegel, why mediation and immediacy never settle into some constellation for him. It is why his philosophy, like Meillassoux's, never arrives. This is because, unlike Meillassoux's, it has internalized the plurality of ontologies in its presentation, its style.

Hegel writes that "through reflection [*Nachdenken*], something *is changed* in the way in which content initially [*zunächst*] is in sensation, intuition, representation; and therefore it is only *by means of* [*vermittels*] a change that the *true* nature of the *object* comes to consciousness."[43] Simple separation or inseparability cannot survive in sentences like this one. *Thing* (*cogitans* or *extensa*) is not a correlation but a production, yet one located in the faculties, connected to being. *Being*, on the other hand, is not even notionally identical with *object* or *object-world*, which means that *reflection* is freed from permanent association with the subject. These contradictions make up the grammatical subject of the sentence. Already composed in contradiction, they enter Hegel's German to be altered, *changed* by *means*. The goal of the passage—indeed, of the entire "three stances"—is never stated, because it exists in the relationship between subjects and predicates.[44] What Hegel manages is to retain the charge of philosophical speculation without sacrificing reflexivity. He does this by making reflexivity part of the language of philosophy, rather than its topic. This entails contradiction, but this contradiction does not entail being (nor does it exclude being). Dialectical presentation does not sever ontology and metaphysics, but it accepts no *specific integration of the two as final*. It thus supplies us with a view from outside of ontology that nevertheless remains connected to beings as they actually exist. It allows us to characterize the manipulation of beings by algorithms without claiming that beings are innocent of operational or digital function. Dialectics is the thinking of an outside to ontology that is nevertheless not an abandonment of beings. Hegel's thought relativizes the humanism it is often taken for, suffusing the tool that is ontology with a vertical, totalizing self-reflection that itself

---

43 Hegel, *Enzyklopädie*, §22.
44 I am implying that the "plastic exposition" notion of the famous foreword to the *Phenomenology* is abandoned as doctrine and adopted as poetics. See G. W. F. Hegel, *Phänomenologie des Geistes. Band 3. Werke in zwanzig Bänden*, ed. E. Moldenhauer and K. M. Michel (Frankfurt a.M: Suhrkamp, 1969–71), 59.

cannot predict its future.[45] The drama of that dialectic is profane, even in a world where transcendence is no longer restricted to the human. Artificial intelligence may never take humanoid form—why should it? Hegel allows us to think a material transcendence, localized in algorithmic operations (or otherwise), that never takes the form of a "body" but is still, in an unexpected sense, *spirit*. Coping with the otherness of spirit was the explicit goal of Hegel's philosophy, and a crucial *desideratum* for posthumanist thought today. To resist the logics of digital capitalism, we need a metaphysics that can encompass plural ontologies and resist their manipulation of beings. We need to strip away the necessity not of being but of that manipulation. Enter Hegel.

---

45 See Catherine Malabou, *The Future of Hegel: Plasticity, Temporality and Dialectic*, trans. Lisabeth During (New York: Routledge, 2005), and John W. Burbidge, *Hegel's Systematic Contingency* (New York: Palgrave MacMillan, 2007).

Nine Steps to an Ecology of *Geist*: Hegel, Bateson, and the Spirit of Posthumanism

John H. Smith

In 1980 Friedrich Kittler, who would later come to be one of the foremost proponents of post-structuralist media theory (not just in Germany), edited a volume with the polemical title: *Austreibung des Geistes aus den Geisteswissenschaften*. It could be translated as "Expulsion of the Human from the Human Sciences or Humanities," and thereby be seen as an early foray into "post-humanism." In one sense, this is not inaccurate, as Kittler was interested in embedding, or even displacing, the human within a wider network of languages, discourse, "programs," and media, thereby promoting a non-anthropocentric field of study that does not fit under the term "humanities." But in another sense, it should be translated as "The Exorcism of Mind or Spirit (capital M, capital S) from the Humanities." In this version, the emphasis is on his suspicions concerning the concept of *Geist*, itself nearly untranslatable into a single English term—one might think of *der menschliche Geist* as "the human mind," but also *Zeitgeist*, "spirit of an age," or even *der Heilige Geist*, "the Holy Spirit." Here the implication behind Kittler's critical call is that the humanities have been plagued by an unduly non-materialist ghost in its machine and it is time we came down to earth by rejecting such quasi-theological categories. But this chapter will argue that this understanding of the notions of *Geist*/Spirit/Mind, as well as Kittler's general approach that would expel them from the humanistic disciplines, are both limiting. If we read *Geist* in its fullness it is the last thing that should be expelled from our rigorous humanistic knowledge (*Geisteswissenschaft*). Indeed, if we read it in its fullness, *Geist* can help us expand the humanities, not purge them, by exploring an ecological perspective that approaches posthuman considerations of humanism.[1] By "fullness," I mean in this chapter the notion of *Geist* that Georg Friedrich Wilhelm Hegel (1770–1831) developed fully in his philosophy, a concept that embeds the human within nature and views nature dynamically. In fact, I hope to show that such a rich and dialectical concept of *Geist* is what Gregory Bateson (1904–80) had in mind with his conception of "Mind" when he developed an epistemology to explain his cybernetic, ecological, and non-anthropocentric theory, as laid out in his two books, the collected essays, *Steps to an Ecology of Mind* (1972) and *Mind and Nature* (1979). A humanist concept, *Geist*, turns out to be valuable for a posthuman science insofar as it provides an alternative to reductive materialist strands in posthumanism. And conversely, reading that concept from a posthuman perspective will reveal it to be less anthropocentric than had been assumed (at least by those who argued for its "expulsion"). This chapter, then, will shuttle back and forth between Bateson's concept of *mind* and the German philosophical tradition's concept of *Geist*—concentrating on Hegel's—in order to *bring them back* into our humanistic sciences and to expand those humanistic sciences beyond the narrowly human.[2] Each benefits from the other: Bateson updates "mind" in more palatable terms, perhaps, while Hegel provides a full-blown philosophy of *Geist* that Bateson only hints at. And in the process, we can thereby take into account the crucial posthumanist insights into systems and relationality without falling prey to their limitations.[3]

Let me begin by recalling a passage from Bateson's remarkable *Steps to an Ecology of Mind*, specifically, from the essay entitled "Form, Substance and Difference" from Part V:

---

1 For a discussion of posthumanism, the human, and humanism, see the Introduction to Cary Wolfe, *What is Posthumanism?* (Minneapolis: University of Minnesota Press, 2010). While Bateson is a key figure in the genealogy of posthumanism, the kind of non-subjectivist philosophy of *Geist* as I portray Hegel is not taken up generally in posthumanist works.

2 Well before "posthumanism" became a common term, Harris and Houlgate explored a richer conception of Hegel's notions of Spirit and nature. See Errol E. Harris, *The Spirit of Hegel* (Atlantic Highlands, NJ: Humanities Press, 1993); and Stephen Houlgate, *Hegel and the Philosophy of Nature* (Albany: State University of New York Press, 1998).

3 There is no indication in Bateson's published work that he engaged extensively with Hegel at all, apart from a few passing references. It is hard to imagine that Bateson would not have been familiar with Hegelian (and Marxist) dialectical thinking (he was, after all, at the University of California, Santa Cruz, through the late 1960s); but he likely would have considered it "unscientific."

Steps to an Ecology of *Geist* 167

The cybernetic epistemology which I have offered you would suggest a new approach. The individual mind is immanent but not only in the body. It is immanent also in pathways and messages outside the body; and there is a larger Mind of which the individual mind is only a subsystem. This larger Mind is comparable to God and is perhaps what some people mean by "God," but it is still immanent in the total interconnected social system and planetary ecology.[4]

There are a number of things to point out briefly about this passage that have direct conceptual ties to Hegel. It is striking, first, that Bateson has the courage to appeal to a notion of mind that is not solely the brain, is not merely subjective, is larger than (can even include) the body, yet is not transcendent or, in the sense perhaps hinted at by Kittler, "spiritual." This "larger Mind," he implies here, is the maximum system composed of innumerable subsystems. He says in the commentary to Part V that "it is of the very nature of the macroscopic world that it exhibit mental characteristics"—to which he has a footnote: "I see the mental as a function only of complex *relationship*."[5] Bateson's conception of the mental should be understood not as some other kind of ontological realm but, rather, as the very principle of complex relationality. Understood thus, mind recalls a passage from Hegel's so-called "Lesser Logic," the first part of his 1817 *Encyclopaedia of the Philosophical Sciences* (as opposed to the *Science of Logic*, or "Greater Logic," published earlier in two installments, 1812 and 1816). In the opening of Section 2, which examines the concept of "essence" (*Wesen*), Hegel strives to dispel the easy misunderstanding that "essence" is some hidden truth *behind* appearance, the kind of thing Kittler assumes about "Spirit" or *Geist*. Hegel gives an example from everyday German that, he says, captures what he means by "essence," namely, relationality. Thus, we can hear in this striking definition of "essence" *avant la lettre* what Bateson characterized in the previous citation as the mental. Hegel writes:

> *Wesen* in ordinary life frequently means only a collection or aggregate: *Zeitungswesen* [the Press], *Postwesen* [the Post Office], *Steuerwesen* [the Revenue]. All that these terms mean is that the things in question are not to be taken singly, in their immediacy, but as a complex, and then, perhaps, in addition, in their various

---

4   Gregory Bateson, *Steps to an Ecology of Mind* (Chicago, IL: University of Chicago Press, 1972), 467.
5   Ibid., 472.

bearings. This usage of the term is not very different in its implications from our own.[6]

Hegel reveals himself in this passage as an early systems or media theorist, for the best translation of these terms would not be *essence of* but really be the *system* of the press, or the postal *system*, or the taxation *system*.[7] The "essence" of a newspaper, a journalist, a letter, a stamp, or an IRS form, cannot be grasped by gazing at (or "into" or "behind") an isolated entity but only through its position within a subsystem within a larger system. It is not by chance that he chose important new (capitalist) media circuits for information and money—Hegel was keenly aware of the need for a new kind of dialectical philosophizing to address the developments of his age. They are entities that can only function—and be understood—through the interrelation of their parts. Kittler, we might say, might have been pleased with this analysis. Such a radical relationality, the totality of the system within which the individual parts attain meaning through their function, and not some spooky ghost in the machine, is their essence—or we might say, their "spirit" or "mental characteristic." In this chapter, then, I will be further juxtaposing Hegel and Bateson, allowing them to mutually illuminate each other, and thereby bridging not just disciplines but discursive regimes that otherwise do not speak to each other.

As my reference to this particular passage implies, reading Hegel *après* Bateson forces us to explore a side of his philosophy that we might otherwise have thought least productive, namely his systematicity. After all, to the extent that Hegel is read much at all in contemporary, especially theoretical circles, it is usually his *Phenomenology of Spirit* of 1807 because of its more existential and literary aspects. This work is not incorrectly characterized as a kind of *Bildungsroman*, a story of "Spirit's" development and education from a rudimentary form of "sense-certainty" to "absolute knowledge," with gripping and compelling chapters on the master/slave (or lordship/bondsman) dialectic and unhappy consciousness, and many ironic turns throughout. However, Bateson led me to consider instead Hegel's multi-volume *Encyclopaedia of the Philosophical Sciences*, the 577 paragraphs with notes and comments that made up the core of his lectures during his later years in Berlin. He first held them in 1817 and continually revised the paragraphs and

---

6   Georg Wilhelm Hegel, *Logic: Being Part One of the Encyclopaedia of the Philosophical Sciences (1830)*, trans. W. Wallace (Oxford: Clarendon Press, 1975), §112.

7   For a media theoretical study of literature in relation to the postal system, see Bernhard Siegert, *Relays: Literature as an Epoch of the Postal System*, trans. K. Repp (Stanford, CA: Stanford University Press, 1999).

remarks until he died in 1831. Often referred to simply as his "system," it is what, after his death, gave Hegel his bad reputation. (To construct a system for, say, Kierkegaard, is the worst philosophical sin.) But if we can read its attention to systematicity with new eyes thanks to Bateson, then we will have taken steps to open up a largely forgotten philosophical effort. That is, the posthumanist, cybernetic, and ecological focus on systems and subsystems rather than on individual actors seems to be a necessary corrective to what has been called, e.g., by post-structuralists like Derrida, a "metaphysics of subjectivity."[8] The danger, as I see it, however, lies in throwing out the Spirit with the subjectivist bathwater. Rereading Hegelian *Geist* precisely in terms of its attention to systematicity, in contrast, allows us to comprehend Spirit/Mind in a way that maintains human and natural agency even as we embed it within ever larger units of interaction.

The *Encyclopedia* is composed of three parts: the logic, the philosophy of nature, and the philosophy of spirit or mind, i.e., *Geist*. (I will address this ambivalent positioning of *Geist* later, for it is both the all-encompassing framework of the entire encyclopedic, scientific project, and a narrower *part* of that whole.) Before turning to the relationship between nature and spirit, I would like to dwell on the logic. As stated previously, it is a reduced and more readable version of Hegel's earlier *Science of Logic* from 1812 to1816, with numerous helpful remarks and examples that Hegel added as he was giving his lectures. Because the system begins with the logic, Hegel is to this day still accused of simply imposing an alien dialectical method on the study of nature, or worse, supposedly "deducing" natural phenomena from concepts. But I hope to show this is not the case. In the logic, Hegel not only attempts, like Bateson, to introduce a different kind of thinking but also lays a conceptual foundation that can be of benefit to Bateson's approach to patterns and analogies. For although Bateson wanted Mind to be the key to his epistemology that could underlie his efforts to study human behavior and nature in terms of ecological contexts and cybernetic feedback loops, he never provides a logic to guide his thinking in detail. Hegel, I argue, did so, and his dialectical logic of *Geist* can help provide a kind of rigor to Bateson's reasoning, which brilliantly yet at times frustratingly makes connections without justification.

---

8   See the extended deconstruction of *Geist*, through a reading of Heidegger, in Jacques Derrida, *Of Spirit: Heidegger and the Question*, trans. G Bennington and R. Bowlby (Chicago, IL: Chicago University Press, 1991). He refers there to "a metaphysics of absolute subjectivity" (73). On my critique of his reductive reading, see John H. Smith, *Dialectics of the Will: Freedom, Power, and Understanding in Modern French and German Thought* (Detroit: Wayne State University Press, 2000), 145–8.

One reason to highlight Hegel's efforts (though, say, Friedrich Wilhelm Schelling's and Johann Wolfgang von Goethe's are also provocative) is that he formulated a logic in order to lay out systematically and dynamically the fundamental categories used for *both* the sciences of nature *and* the human sciences.[9] Unlike the rigid scheme of twelve categories that for Immanuel Kant are the conditions of possibility of knowledge or experience, Hegel unfolds a dizzying array of concepts. While Kant legitimated his table of "concepts of the understanding" (categories) by appealing to Aristotle's analyses of propositions, Hegel strives to derive all the categories necessary for thinking about being solely by examining the nature of such thought itself. No such logic had ever been written before this. It does not offer tables of propositions or syllogisms but instead tries to demonstrate how concepts we employ to talk about the world are interrelated. He begins famously with the dialectic of being and nothing; after all, if the goal is to find out what we can say about being, then we should start with the concept of being, pure being, itself. And here the first startling dialectical twist occurs, for in thinking about pure being (without any determinations whatsoever) we are, in fact, thinking about nothing, for if no determination can be made about pure being, then it is void and empty. That is, being and nothing are opposites and yet they are found to be inseparable. He therefore concludes the opening chapter with the powerful claim that, in fact, everything that *is* finds itself in a state of *becoming*, always transitioning between being and nothing to being something else. Hence, in the realm of determinate being (*Dasein*) covered in Section 1, he explores notions like the way any given *something* (*Etwas*) must be grasped in relation to its other (*das Andere*), into which it changes (*Änderung*); or like the one and the many, the continuous and the discrete, each of which cannot be thought without the other; or the way changes in quantity flip into changes in quality (as simply as when increasing temperature leads water to turn into steam, or, later for Marx, increasing tensions in capitalism will lead to revolutionary change). Then, as mentioned earlier, in Section 2 he turns to the necessary relationship between essence and appearance, which takes different forms, like ground and existence, or identity and difference, or cause and effect. In the study of essence as *relationality*, things are always coming into appearance. Indeed, just as being and nothing are seen by

---

9   For a genealogy that links Schelling to contemporary speculative realism, see Iain Hamilton Grant, *Philosophies of Nature after Schelling* (London and New York: Continuum, 2006). Though not as rigorous as his contemporaneous Idealist philosophers' work, Goethe's reflections on natural science, like his short "The Experiment as Mediator between Subject and Object" and *Theory of Color* (1810), have received considerable attention in recent years.

Hegel to be inextricably linked, so, too, essence is shown to be not the opposite of (or that which is "behind") appearance, but that which is always appearing, or is "actuality"—*Wirklichkeit*, literally, that which acts or is active.[10] The *Logic* culminates in the self-reflexive turn to the study of concepts themselves, the categories of thought as such: what Hegel calls the realm of the Idea, and the dialectic of life. By concluding with this inward turn to the nature of thinking itself, the third section of the *Logic* provides the methodological model for the book we just read. That is, if we consider the *Logic*, too, as a kind of *Bildungsroman* of the Spirit, showing the educative development of how we can know about the world, it ends with the "hero" arriving at the stage where he/she now can write the novel of the life we just read about. Hence, it literally circles back on itself. We do not have to accept all the details of his logic, but it is a grand attempt to demonstrate that thinking involves the movement of one concept giving way to another.

The dialectic becomes fruitful, however, not because it is a method *imposed* from without but because it is the view of all *being as process*. Hegel writes: "Wherever there is movement, wherever there is life, wherever anything is carried into effect in the actual world, there is Dialectic at work."[11] Therefore, he continues, "it [dialectic] is also the soul of all knowledge which is truly scientific."[12] Although this passage comes from the *beginning* of the *Encyclopedia Logic*, it is in fact only at the end when, in typical Hegelian fashion, he looks *back* at the display of conceptual relations, that he can *really* formulate what his method *has been*, that is, that the "idea" emerges. This "idea" states that nothing can be considered a static identity because it is "essentially process," i.e., it is identity "only in so far as it is absolute negativity."[13] By this Hegel means that no single entity or category can truly be thought, i.e., be thought in truth, in isolation from others. Any attempt to do so, which he associates with the analytical yet limited faculty of the understanding (*Verstand*), fails. For this reason, he claimed famously, in the preface to the *Phenomenology*, that the "true is the whole [*das Wahre ist das Ganze*]"[14]—and any search for what is true will always lead to ever wider networks or "mediations" ("Being is absolutely mediated [*Das Sein ist absolut vermittelt*]").[15] Precisely here we can see the "ecological"

---

10 Georg Wilhelm Friedrich Hegel, *Science of Logic*, trans. A. V. Miller (New York: Humanity [Prometheus] Books, 1999), 391.
11 Hegel, *Logic*, §81.
12 Ibid.
13 Ibid., §215. This section is one of the last in the *Encyclopedia Logic*.
14 Georg Wilhelm Friedrich Hegel, *Phenomenology of Spirit*, trans. A. V. Miller (Oxford: Oxford University Press, 1977), §20.
15 Ibid., §37.

core of Hegel's philosophy, namely the insistence that no individual or identity can be grasped or separated from "a *manifold* that is *different* from it."[16] Even, he says, the apparently universal proposition "*a tree is a tree*" has its truth "*only in the unity of identity with difference,*" i.e., only in terms of its relation to otherness.[17]

And here we can bring back Bateson, specifically his book *Mind and Nature: A Necessary Unity* from 1979. If Hegel stresses the dialectical movement of one concept into its other, Bateson stresses the search for "patterns that connect." (In fact, he says, this phrase—"patterns that connect"—could have been the title of his book and his entire scientific project.) Crucially, patterns are not actually static, as static patterns are only a secondary quality; he writes: "We have been trained to think of patterns, with the exception of those of music, as fixed affairs. It is easier and lazier that way but, of course, all nonsense. In truth, the right way to begin to think about the pattern which connects is to think of it as *primarily* (whatever that means) a dance of interacting parts."[18] Hegel likewise used the metaphor of the "dance" in the Preface to the *Phenomenology* to capture something about the need to think about the world as an overall pattern in which the individual parts have an independence but attain meaning only within the whole; in his graphic formulation, truth lies in a system that is like "a bacchanalian dance in which no part is not drunken."[19] Each of the steps in the dance is recognizable as such only in relation to the others within the pattern of the whole and thus could be called a bit of information, a "difference which makes a difference," in Bateson's definition, stated often in his work; for example, in one of his most famous essays on the "Double Bind" from 1969: "A difference which makes a difference *is* an idea. It is a 'bit,' a unit of information."[20] And so we have what is one of the basic axioms of the "epistemology of cybernetics" according to Bateson in *Steps*: "[W]e know that no part of such an internally interactive system can have unilateral control over the remainder or over any other part. The mental characteristics are inherent or immanent in the ensemble as a *whole.*"[21] Or, combining these ideas, we could turn to Bateson's formulation of the basic principle of cybernetics: "The principle that no new order or pattern can be created without information."[22] But if information is

---

16 Hegel, *Science of Logic*, 415.
17 Ibid.
18 Gregory Bateson, *Mind and Nature: A Necessary Unity* (New York: E. P. Dutton, 1979), 13.
19 Hegel, *Phenomenology of Spirit*, §47.
20 Bateson, *Steps to an Ecology of Mind*, 271–2.
21 Ibid., 315.
22 Bateson, *Mind and Nature*, 45.

a "difference that makes a difference" then new orders and patterns emerge with the input of a "difference that makes a difference." Hegel calls this origin of knowledge out of difference, or the positive out of the inhering negative, "determinate negation," the moving principle of dialectic. To read Hegel "cybernetically" here emphasizes that in his claims for the "identity of identity and difference" the first "identity" is, by definition, not *opposed* to difference (as if he is imposing identity onto difference) but a complex, systematic one that allows for a play of identity and differences.

Now, back to Hegel's "system" in order to explore how the dialectical logic opens up to an even broader sense of "ecology" that introduces the connection between Mind and nature within the philosophy of *Geist*. We have already seen that for both Bateson and Hegel we can only think of parts interconnected into wholes that are in turn parts of greater wholes—or, the system is an interplay of subsystems, kept moving by internal differences; and this is the case, so to speak, all the way up and all the way down. While the fun and occasional craziness of Hegel's "system" is in the wealth of details he offers, I just want to consider some connections between the two broad subsystems, nature and spirit or mind. Schelling, precisely in the years spanning 1800 when he exercised the greatest influence on Hegel, grappled intensely with this issue. The pithiest formulation of the "absolute identity of spirit/ mind in us and nature outside of us" comes in his *Ideen zu einer Philosophie der Natur* (Ideas on a Philosophy of Nature) of 1797: "Nature *ought* to be visible spirit, and spirit *ought* to be invisible nature [*Die Natur soll der sichtbare Geist, der Geist die unsichtbare Natur sein*]."[23] However, as I hope to have indicated, it was Hegel who worked out the logic of this "absolute identity" as an emergent process of increasingly complex subsystems, a logic that is contained only implicitly in the "ought" and the visual image of Schelling's dictum.

Both Hegel and Bateson have a significant ambiguity in the way they refer to Mind/*Geist* in relation to nature. At times, mind or spirit is the all-encompassing system; at others, it is a *part* of that system together with nature. We can hear some of that ambiguity in this formulation by Bateson with its multiple "ors": "[W]e may say that 'mind' is immanent in those circuits of the brain which are complete within the brain. Or that mind is immanent in circuits which are complete within the system, brain *plus* body. Or, finally, that mind is immanent in the larger system—man *plus* environment."[24] On the one hand, as we have seen, Bateson is thinking of a "larger Mind" that is

---

23 Friedrich Schelling, *Ideen zu einer Philosophie der Natur*, in *Werke*, vol. 1, ed. M. Schröter (Munich: C. H. Beck, 1927), 706.
24 Bateson, *Steps to an Ecology of Mind*, 317.

174 Posthumanism in the Age of Humanism

the extrapolation from the cybernetic principle that all parts can only be understood within relational wholes—or subsystems within more complex systems—to the idea of ever bigger wholes and even to the idea of a system making up the cosmos (or, as he says, what some people think of as "God").

This corresponds to the overarching structure of Hegel's system of Spirit whereby the many conceptual circuits of the *Logic* lead to the idea that *logic itself* is only a *part* and must engage its other, nature. The philosophy of nature explores evermore complex organisms and their relations, which leads to the emergence of consciousness and social formations, culminating (this is Hegel, after all) in philosophy, i.e., the possibility to reflect on the logic of the process. Spirit, in this first sense, is, what Hegel calls at the end of the *Science of Logic*, the "circle of circles" (and has a visual echo in Bateson's modelling of feedback loops):

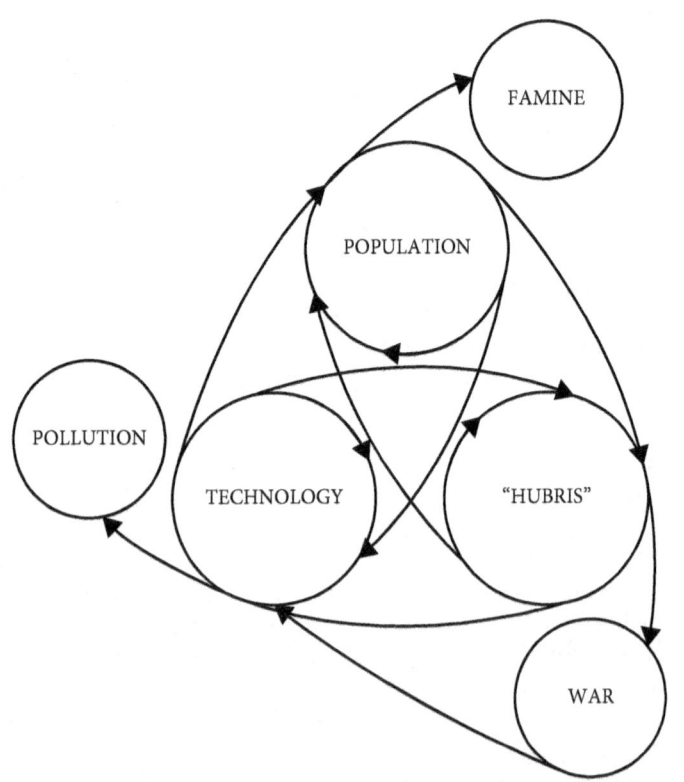

Figure 9.1 From *Steps to an Ecology of Mind*, page 499. An example of Bateson's version of the interlocking of subsystems of feedback loops.

the science exhibits itself as a *circle* returning upon itself, the end being wound back into the beginning, the simple ground, by the mediation; this circle is moreover a *circle of circles*, for each individual member as ensouled by the method is reflected into itself ... Links of this chain are the individual sciences [of logic, nature and spirit].[25]

However, on the other hand, as we see, *within* Hegel's overall system of spirit, nature and spirit are assigned separate but related places. That is, as with Bateson's notion of mind and implied in the title of his book, *Mind and Nature*, spirit is not just the whole, but also a specific part alongside nature. If we consider spirit and nature independently for a moment, we notice that for Hegel they are structured in the same way. Or, we might say, they are analogies of each other. That should not be a surprise since underlying them is the same logic of dialectical movement and development. Recall, this is why I emphasized the starting point of the system in the *Logic*: its categories are the *tertium comparationis* linking nature and spirit. Bateson, referring to his own approach, captures that logic nicely as the "hierarchy of differences which biologists call 'levels'."[26] And he specifies them as follows: "I mean such differences as that between a cell and a tissue, between tissue and organ, organ and organism, and organism and society."[27] Furthermore, these differences are significant only insofar as they are viewed as parts within larger wholes. Bateson continues: "These are the hierarchies of units or *Gestalten* [one of Hegel's important words], in which each sub-unit is part of the unit of next larger scope. And, always in biology, this difference or relationship which I call 'part of' is such that certain differences in the part have informational effect upon the larger unit, and vice versa."[28]

To see how such a "hierarchy of levels" works in Hegel, we might consider the opening of the third section of the *Encyclopedia Philosophy of Nature*. After the first two sections on physics and chemistry (or the versions that existed in the early nineteenth century), Hegel turns to the exploration of "Organics," or life in all its complexity. Remarkably, he begins, however, with a long discussion of what he calls "the terrestrial organism"—what we might call an ecology of the planet. Biological life cannot be studied in isolation but only upon the literal bedrock out of which it emerged, i.e., within an extensive spatial and temporal context. He needs to start on such a grand level because the

---

25 Hegel, *Science of Logic*, 842.
26 Bateson, *Steps to an Ecology of Mind*, 464.
27 Ibid.
28 Ibid.

earth itself is (he writes) "presupposed by life as its foundation [*der Grund und Boden*]."²⁹ Thus he has a series of sections under the title: "The History of the Earth."³⁰ It is not that he calls the formations of the earth "living" but these external conditions form the past out of which life comes to appearance (recall that the categories of ground and existence, or "essence" and appearance were parts of Section 2 of the *Logic*). Hegel writes: "As this organism [namely, the earth] has being merely as an implicitness, its members do not contain the living process within themselves but constitute an external *system*. The forms of this system exhibit the unfolding of an underlying Idea, but its *process of formation* belongs to the *past*."³¹ That is, the way the earth has taken shape over the eons has created the unique conditions for life (in his terms, this is the "implicitness" of life in the inanimate earth). He speaks of the many variables constituting our terrestrial ecology—distance from the sun, tilt of the axis, atmosphere, etc.—that, if any one were to change too dramatically, it would end life as we know it. Now, the fact that *we* would of course recognize geological processes as *ongoing* and not just part of the *past*, should not distract us from the amazing fact that Hegel by no means shies away from "deep history" here.³² Life itself, and certainly the anthropocene, are embedded within a planetary perspective. And it is a delight to read his careful descriptions of geological formations, crystalline shapes, and the burgeoning land and sea. As he says: "at every point they are perpetually breaking out into punctiform and ephemeral animation."³³ And these animated shapes and forms—*Gestalten* and *Bildungen*—with their incessant metamorphoses and interconnections, make up the philosophy of nature.

A brief aside on how to read this philosophy of nature: it is easy to poke fun at many of the findings in this work—though Hegel is just citing from what he took to be the most reputable sources—and it is easy to mock associations he makes between phenomena that would not be empirically linked. And for these reasons, many consider his philosophy of nature discredited. But most critics mistake it for either a *description* of nature or a *methodology* for *doing* science. It is neither. Instead, the philosophy of nature seems to me to be posing different

---

29 Georg Wilhelm Friedrich Hegel, *Philosophy of Nature*, 3 vols., ed. and trans. M. J. Petry (London: Allen & Unwin, 1970), §338 Addition.
30 Ibid., §339.
31 Ibid.
32 See Daniel Lord Smail, *On Deep History and the Brain* (Berkeley and Los Angeles: University of California Press, 2008); and Daniel Lord Smail and Andrew Shryock, *Deep History: The Architecture of Past and Present* (Berkeley and Los Angeles: University of California Press, 2011).
33 Hegel, *Philosophy of Nature*, §341.

kinds of questions about the foundations of our knowledge of nature, namely: given what we know about nature, how do things look if we apply different categories of connectedness, emergence, transition, and process, categories that had been analyzed in the *Logic*? What new associations or analogies can we make to produce *new* knowledge? (At the end of this chapter I will return to the way his logic can help control analogy-making.)

So what is the relationship between nature and spirit? I mentioned above that one way of seeing this relationship is in evolutionary terms: the crowning achievement of this process of development that he lays out in the *Philosophy of Nature* is the emergence of consciousness. But in a crucial sense, the point of looking *back* into this deep history is to recognize that this wealth of evermore differentiated inanimate and animate, nonconscious and conscious minds, is all of a piece. Thus, in the introduction to the *Philosophy of Nature*, Hegel (here a good Spinozist, like the majority of his compatriots at the time) says that just as it would be wrong to isolate God from nature, so too nature must not be thought independent of *Geist*. He says:

> The thinking [i.e., the truly rational in a Hegelian sense] view of nature must note the implicit process by which nature sublates its otherness to become spirit, and the way in which the Idea is present in each stage of nature itself. Estranged from the Idea, nature is merely the corpse of the understanding. Nature is the Idea, but only implicitly. That is why Schelling called it a petrified intelligence, which others have said is frozen. God does not remain petrified and moribund however, the stones cry out and lift themselves up to spirit.[34]

And spirit (in the narrower sense of the realm of the human) is absolutely grounded in nature. Hegel insists on the immanence of spirit, as we see in the opening paragraph of the third part of the *Encyclopedia* (*The Philosophy of Spirit*), entitled "What Mind [or Spirit, *Geist*] is": "From our point of view mind has for its *presupposition* Nature, of which it is the truth, and for that reason its *absolute prius*."[35] Mind is not an opposite of nature but its identity. However, it is an identity in a Hegelian sense, for it has emerged out of the process of self-differentiation within nature. Hegel would have little problem with Bateson's description: "The total self-corrective unit which processes information, or, as I say,

---

34 Ibid., §247 Addition.
35 Hegel, *Philosophy of Mind: Being Part Three of the "Encyclopaedia of the Philosophical Sciences" (1830)*, trans. W. Wallace and A.V. Miller (Oxford: Clarendon Press, 1971), §381.

'thinks' and 'acts' and 'decides,' is a *system* whose boundaries do not at all coincide with the boundaries either of the body or of what is popularly called the 'self' or 'consciousness'."[36] This passage on the need to conceive of the psyche in its wholeness and relationality comes in the chapter where Bateson explores mistaken and necessarily inadequate approaches to alcoholism that view the individual in isolation. Indeed, Bateson's ecological approach to both individual human pathology and historical crises interprets their emergence as the result of allowing one "subsystem" to gain dominance or (pseudo-)independence over others with which it is interdependent. And it is therefore worth offering, by way of comparison, Hegel's description of mental illness as an extreme dialectic of the self, where a part comes to undermine the functioning of the whole; the two thinkers on insanity agree on the possibility of "runaway" particularities. Hegel writes: "[Insanity] means the soul divided against itself, on the one hand already master of itself, and on the other hand not yet master of itself, but held fast in an isolated particularity in which it has its actuality."[37] There is for both Hegel and Bateson a lot at stake in reconceiving mind and nature dialectically. It is, as Bateson points out, not just a theoretical but also an ethical issue.[38] As Bateson says: "It is the attempt to *separate* intellect from emotion that is monstrous, and I suggest that it is equally monstrous—and dangerous—to attempt to separate the external mind from the internal. Or to separate mind from body."[39]

In conclusion, let me turn to the benefits of my methodological claim that Bateson's posthumanist ecology of mind can be aligned with Hegel's humanist, dialectical philosophy of *Geist*. In the chapter on "Multiple Versions of the World" from *Mind and Nature*, Bateson addresses the question: "What bonus or increment of knowing follows from combining information from two or more sources?"[40] And behind it is the deeper, even "mystical" (his term) question: "Does the study of this *particular* case, in which an insight developed from the *comparison of sources*, throw any light on how the *universe* is integrated?"[41] There are a number of advantages to bringing Hegel into the mix with Bateson, i.e., from this particular "comparison of sources":

1. At a basic historical level, it is valuable to look to the past efforts to grapple with issues crucial for our present. The period around 1800 in Germany saw numerous efforts to undermine binarisms while at the

---

36 Bateson, *Steps to an Ecology of Mind*, 319.
37 Hegel, *Philosophy of Mind*, §402 Addition.
38 Bateson, *Steps to an Ecology of Mind*, 466.
39 Ibid., 470.
40 Bateson, *Mind and Nature*, 67.
41 Ibid.

same time making difference productive. Prominent among those binarisms were mind and body, spirit and nature, mechanistic and vitalistic conceptions of nature, etc. Near the end of the *Encyclopedia Logic* Hegel says that "the Idea may be described in many ways. It may be called reason (and this is the proper philosophical signification of reason); subject-object; the unity of the ideal and the real, of the finite and the infinite, of soul and body; the possibility which has its actuality in its own self."[42] It is useful to think of this description, and his view that the only valid structure of logic can be a "circle of circles" embracing larger and larger webs of conceptual relations, when we read Bateson in *Mind and Nature: A Necessary Unity*:

> How is the world of logic, which eschews "circular argument," related to a world in which circular trains of causation are the rule rather than the exception? What has to be investigated and described is a vast network or matrix of interlocking message material and abstract tautologies, premises, and exemplifications. But, as of 1979, there is no conventional method of describing such a tangle. We do not know even where to begin.[43]

We might begin with Hegel. This is not to claim that "it's all in Hegel already," or that we might not have to read some of Hegel against his and his reception's grain to ensure that his emphasis on circularity does not become a *closed* system. But when striving to develop modes of thinking that run counter to dangerous abstractions, we should cherish all allies. Much of the philosophical effort of the younger generation that came of age in the 1790s—including Schelling, Hegel, Friedrich Hölderlin, Friedrich Schlegel, Friedrich von Hardenberg (Novalis), and others—could be seen as a response to "logics" that avoided the "tangles" of interdependent entities, contexts, and concepts. They strove for forms of reasoning that could embrace contradictory determinations as "subsystems" of higher unities. The point is not so much to resurrect them as such but to engage with those humanistic elements that already are put in relation to the nonhuman, *Geist* with nature.

2. We saw earlier the significance of Hegel's beginning his "system" with a logic. His aim was, I argued, not to impose categories onto the study of nature and human history but, rather, to expose the way *both* thinking *and* being are involved in processes of becoming and to develop categories that account for these processes. Furthermore, the need for a logic of the relationality of concepts is particularly important

---

42 Hegel, *Logic*, §214.
43 Bateson, *Mind and Nature*, 20.

for the philosophy of nature, Hegel says, in order to provide a basis for the controlled use of analogies. And here Hegel might offer something important for Bateson, namely, a conceptual analysis of why and how analogies work. We saw earlier that Bateson in *Mind and Nature* summarized the method behind his ecological project as the search for "patterns that connect." And there is no doubt that one of the most productive aspects of Bateson's work is the way he can bring unexpected relations into view. In a remark in the *Logic* of his *Encyclopaedia of the Philosophical Sciences*, Hegel likewise praises the role of analogy to produce knowledge: "In the experiential sciences Analogy deservedly occupies a high place, and has led to results of the highest importance."[44] In fact, note the similarity between the following two comments. The first by Hegel: "Analogy is the instinct or reason, creating an anticipation that this or that characteristic, which experience has discovered, has its root in the inner nature or kind of an object, and arguing on the faith of that anticipation";[45] and the second by Bateson: "A pattern, in fact, is definable as an aggregate of events or objects which will permit in some degree such guesses when the entire aggregate is not available for inspection."[46]

However, such analogical thinking can also be problematically unrestrained and point to arbitrary or subjective associations. In a dig at his former friend Schelling (among others), Hegel says a bit further along in the Addition to §190 of the *Encyclopedia Logic* that analogies can also be counterproductive: "What has in modern times been called the Philosophy of Nature [*Naturphilosopie*] consists principally in a frivolous play with empty and external analogies, which, however, claim to be considered profound results."[47] Now, when one reads Hegel, especially his "system" as laid out in the *Encyclopedia* one is struck by the constant analogies *he* makes between, say, natural phenomena and society, between theological ideas and the history of philosophy, and so on. But what holds them together is the underlying conceptual structure that we can see revealed by putting the apparently disparate phenomena together. *That's* why he begins with the *Logic* even though, in a strictly genetic sense, only by passing through nature and spirit could we, as thinking beings, evolve to the point where we can formulate a logic. The dialectical relation between concepts and the patient exploration of how apparently disparate, even opposing concepts grow out of each other can provide the logic to uncover "patterns that connect" while avoiding random or subjective associations.

---

44 Hegel, *Logic*, §190.
45 Ibid.
46 Bateson, *Steps to an Ecology of Mind*, 413.
47 Hegel, *Logic*, §190 Addition.

3. Finally, the dialectic can and ought to be defended as it guides the understanding of both mind and nature because it reminds us of the *necessity* of the interplay of structure and what Hegel calls "restlessness" (*Unruhe*).[48] Insofar as they unfold dialectically, life and mind experience both processes of ordering and inherent acts of resistance (what Hegel calls "determinate negations"). And here Hegel can indeed be read together with Bateson. For both, any system involves a circulation of "differences that make a difference" and they guarantee both periods of homeostasis and events of innovation and change. The language of cybernetics might seem to "expunge" the human from its description of systematic interaction, as in this passage by Bateson:

> The matter of communicational economics becomes still more serious when we note that the homeostatic circuits of an organism are not separate but complexly interlocked, *e.g.*, hormonal messengers which play a part in the homeostatic control of organ A will also affect the states of organs B, C, and D. Any special ongoing loading of the circuit controlling A will therefore diminish the organism's freedom to control B, C, and D.[49]

But here we must recall that such cybernetic, systems-theoretical thinking, according to Bateson, occurs within the broader context of an understanding of mind. And reading "mind" as *Geist*, we are led to a humanistic concept that accounts dialectically for an approach to thinking and being that is not reducible to human subjectivity or identity. Bateson and Hegel remind us of its significance. Studying the unfolding of such systems across the disciplines is the task of the "ecology of mind" and the humanities as unexorcized *Geisteswissenschaft*.

---

48 Jean-Luc Nancy has brilliantly explored precisely this aspect of Hegel's thought; see Jean-Luc Nancy, *Hegel: The Restlessness of the Negative*, trans. S. Miller and J. Smith (Minneapolis: Minnesota University Press, 1997).
49 Bateson, *Steps to an Ecology of Mind*, 353.

Ten Protecting Natural Beauty from Humanism's Violence: The Healing Effects of Alexander von Humboldt's *Naturgemälde*

Elizabeth Millán

Humanism is a vague term, and discussions of posthumanism inherit the lack of precision that plagues discussions of humanism. Indeed, some of the finest work on posthumanism is focused on the very question of what posthumanism means. In his *What is Posthumanism?* Cary Wolfe makes a compelling case for connecting Enlightenment thought to the emergence of posthumanism.[1] Following Wolfe's lead, I will focus my account on the sort of humanism born from the German Enlightenment and then discuss the implications that some early critiques of the German Enlightenment tradition had upon the emergence of posthumanism.

Much of Kantian and post-Kantian philosophy was guided by the ideals of the Enlightenment: a central guiding notion was that human reason would lead society to increasing degrees of order and progress. Philosophy as "the queen of the sciences" was to play a central role in the social project of reason and its mastery over the rest of the living world. Even in its heyday, voices critical of the movement developed. The early German Romantics, for example, questioned some of the claims of reason made for it on behalf of German Enlightenment figures, not in order to dismantle the promise of progress offered by the Enlightenment, but

---

With thanks to the editors for inviting me to contribute to their project and for valuable comments on an earlier draft that were of great use to me.

1   See, for example, Cary Wolfe, *What is Posthumanism?* (Minneapolis: University of Minnesota Press, 2010), esp. xvi.

rather to uncover a more progressive promise within it.[2] Some of the more flamboyant claims of the early German Romantics included those that called for a fusion of poetry, philosophy, and science. I shall argue that with this call to fuse disciplinary borders, the views of standard issues in philosophy, such as, truth, beauty, and freedom, shifted. I will be particularly interested in the notion of freedom developed by one thinker of the period, whose work was both scientific and literary, and who has strong affinities with certain romantic views. I refer to Alexander von Humboldt (1769–1859), a scientist whose voyage to the "equinoctial region of the earth" (Spanish America as it was called at the time) opened a new region to the European reading public. In Humboldt's writing on nature, we find a conception of freedom that took the idea of freedom beyond the human-centered notions of autonomy and agency, notions that were central to the humanistic strands of thought developed in the Enlightenment, or those tendencies of this movement that place the engines of progress and power squarely in *human* reason and agency.[3] Anticipating some of the moves of posthumanism, Humboldt departs from the Enlightenment emphasis on *human* power and agency. He described nature as "the realm of freedom" (*Reich der Freiheit*), and he developed a literary form, the *Naturgemälde* or canvas of nature, to present this realm to his readers. In clearing more space for an understanding of nature that did not take the human (especially the European human) as its Archimedean point, Humboldt helped liberate the American continent from some of the Eurocentric views typical of the period.

A central goal of the early German Romantics' project was to bring philosophy into closer contact with poetry and history—domains that made odd bedfellows in the wake of Kant's *Critique of Pure Reason*, a work that celebrated philosophy's relation to the ahistorical sciences. In Schlegel's *Letter on the Novel*, which is one of his most detailed statements on the meaning of the term "romantic," he claims that, "romantic poetry rests entirely on historical grounds."[4] As we learn in *Athenäum*

---

[2] For a fuller account of the philosophical dimensions of the movement, see Elizabeth Millán-Zaibert, *Friedrich Schlegel and the Emergence of Romantic Philosophy* (Albany: State University of New York Press, 2007).

[3] For a detailed presentation of the relation between human subjectivity, progress and the Enlightenment, see the excellent account given in the essays included in James Schmidt, ed., *What is Enlightenment? Eighteenth-Century Answers and Twentieth-Century Questions* (Berkeley: University of California Press, 1996), esp. Frederick Beiser, "Early Romanticism and the Aufklärung," 317–29.

[4] Friedrich Schlegel, *Friedrich Schlegel Kritische Ausgabe (KFSA)*, ed. Ernst Behler et al., vol. 2 (Paderborn: Ferdinand Schoeningh, 1958), 334. Hereafter, this edition will be referred to as *KFSA*, followed by volume number, page number, and when indicated, fragment number. Some of Schlegel's fragments have been translated by Peter Firchow, in *Friedrich Schlegel: Philosophical Fragments* (Minneapolis: University of Minnesota Press, 1991). When I have used Firchow's translation, the reference is to this edition, hereafter as Firchow.

Fragment 116, "romantic poetry is a progressive universal poetry,"[5] it is an ideal, a poetry that is progressive because it is always in a state of becoming, never reaching completion. Historical grounds bring romantic poetry into conversation with the tradition of which it is a part. And like poetry, philosophy is also in need of history for orientation. Schlegel never tired of emphasizing this point, and he even went after Kant, the great critical philosopher himself, scolding him for his neglect of history and insisting that no critique can succeed without a history of philosophy. In several fragments, Schlegel makes this point, claiming that an age which calls itself a critical age must not leave the age itself uncriticized; that, in short, Kant's critical project did not go far enough.[6] Schlegel frequently scolds other philosophers for the one-sidedness (*Einseitigkeit*) of their approach, an *Einseitigkeit* reflected in their literary form, where there is only the voice of one author, of one position, and not enough attention to the historical context of the ideas presented. Schlegel's use of fragments, dialogues, and even the form of the novel, was his way of escaping what he viewed to be the *Einseitigkeit* born of a view that philosophy could begin with first principles and achieve certainty. In Humboldt's *Naturgemälde*, his literary canvases of nature, we, in like fashion, find a reflection of some of his theoretical commitments. Humboldt, dedicated as he was to a presentation of nature that would not kill its living breath, was after a literary tool that would present nature *both* as an empirical realm to be mastered, and as a realm of beauty and delight that was beyond mastery. Humboldt wanted to avoid the vicious empiricism (*rohe Empirie*) that he found so troubling in other accounts of nature. Empiricism is vicious only when it is deployed as the *only* way to understand nature, a way to dominate the forces of nature and tell just one side of the story of nature's meaning. We must step out of mastery to understand the full story of nature's meaning, and Humboldt's aesthetic turn is just such a move away from mastery. In Humboldt's writing on nature, the realm of nature's beauty and delight brings us to the realm of aesthetic experience and of freedom—a freedom that is not exhausted by human agency or human willing.

Humboldt's courage in attempting to present to his European reading public scenes of nature that were utterly unfamiliar to them was bold and, if his enduringly warm reception in the countries of Latin America is any indication, successful at wearing away at some of the troubling anti-American stereotypes that circulated widely in the late

---

5 KFSA 2, 182.
6 See for example, Schlegel, *KFSA* 2, 165, Nr. 1; *KFSA* 2, 364; *KFSA* 12, 286; *KFSA* 18, 21, Nr. 35; *KFSA* 18, 21, Nr. 36; *KFSA* 19, 346, Nr. 296.

1700s and well into the 1800s. Humboldt, one might say, pushed the limits of the humanism of his time and opened his work in a way that anticipated the posthumanist age that was yet to come. Both the early German Romantics and Humboldt were aware that human beings and their subjectivity cannot frame all of reality let alone dominate all of that reality. Indeed, their aesthetic turn was born of an insight that freedom from human will and subjectivity gives rise to a richer frame for understanding reality.

There is a certain affinity between Humboldt's view of nature and the views of thinkers such as Donna Haraway, Bruno Latour, and Timothy Morton. One such affinity can be found in the work that poetry does for the environmental perspective each thinker undertakes. For example, in what Donna Haraway refers to as the "sympoiesis" or "making with" that she finds urgent in the wake of so much devastation of the natural world, we recall Schlegel's and Novalis's calls for symphilosophy and the unity of the disciplines to deal with the problems of culture.[7] Such "sympoiesis" operates too in Latour's lectures on the new climatic regime, *Facing Gaia* and in Morton's "ambient poetics" and his push to open a "wider view of the possibility of art and criticism."[8] The early German Romantics emphasized the need for a symphilosophy, which was an innovative move away from the notion of the lone thinker creating ahistorical systems of thought that were not dependent upon the thoughts of others. Humboldt, following the romantics, takes on the project of presenting nature as a project that blends scientific method with poetry, history, and philosophy, a blending that fits well with the romantic call to blend the boundaries between the disciplines. We shall see traces of a kind of sympoiesis in Humboldt's *Naturgemälde*.

Humboldt's *Naturgemälde*

The *Naturgemälde*, a canvas or *tableau* of nature, was part of Humboldt's lifelong attempt to achieve a holistic impression (*Gesamteindruck*) of nature. In this ambition, Humboldt did not become entangled in the "metaphysically extravagant" claims to which accounts of natural beauty guided by a concept of unity all too often succumb, and which often lead a thinker to abandon the empirical details that Humboldt

---

7 Donna J. Haraway, *Staying with the Trouble: Making Kin in the Chthulucene* (Durham, NC: Duke University Press, 2016).
8 See Bruno Latour, *Facing Gaia: Eight Lectures on the New Climatic Regime*, trans. Catherine Porter (Cambridge: Polity, 2017); and Timothy Morton, *Ecology without Nature: Rethinking Environmental Aesthetics* (Cambridge, MA: Harvard University Press, 2007), 5.

Protecting Natural Beauty from Humanism's Violence   187

found indispensable to any presentation of nature.[9] Humboldt claims that nature is the "realm of freedom" whose living breath should not be suffocated by its presenter. Such a flight to the realm of ideas, part of what might be understood as giving wings to plodding science, is always tempered or modified in Humboldt's work by an emphasis on the empirical detail of the phenomena of nature.[10] Humboldt's commitment to preserving the "living breath of nature," engaged him in a nuanced balancing act. In his presentation of nature, Humboldt attempted to balance an empirical mastery of nature, i.e., a quantified, scientific presentation of nature, with those aspects of nature that could not be mastered, e.g., the free enjoyment of nature's charms and the awe of its power. Human mastery blends with an awareness that humans cannot have the last word on nature's meaning, so Humboldt is not guilty of a subjectivization of our aesthetic responses to nature, a pernicious move to which I shall return.

Humboldt did believe that without empirical knowledge of nature, our aesthetic appreciation of nature would be impoverished in significant ways. In his canvases of nature, we find systematic depictions of nature, that is to say, charts and graphs with empirical information on the quantifiable aspects of nature. However, Humboldt's *Naturgemälde* resists the reductionist tendency that would kill the living breath of nature that Humboldt sought to preserve. The *Naturgemälde* Humboldt created with his writings on nature are best understood as literary acts of preservation. The very term, *Naturgemälde* or canvas of nature, seems to suggest that in attempting to present nature to his reading public as a realm to be appreciated, Humboldt feels that he must assimilate art and

---

9   I take this way of describing the pitfalls of those seeking "unitary" accounts of nature from R. W. Hepburn's watershed article (as far as renewed attention to the aesthetic dimensions of nature go); see W. Hepburn, "Contemporary Aesthetics and the Neglect of Natural Beauty," in *British Analytical Philosophy*, ed. Bernard Williams and Alan Montefiore (New York: The Humanities Press, 1966), 299.

10 I am referring to *The Earliest Program for a System of German Idealism* (1796), a text found in 1917 by Franz Rosenzweig, who gave the manuscript its rather misleading title. The text does not set out to deploy a program for German Idealism, but rather calls, in piecemeal fashion, for a move away from mechanistic models of understanding natural and social reality as the author/s invoke a new mythology that will join science and art, lawfulness and freedom. As we are told in the text, "the highest act of reason is an aesthetic act," and so "the philosopher must possess as much aesthetic power as the poet." "The Earliest Program for a System of German Idealism," in *Theory and Practice: A Critical Anthology of Early German Romantic Writings*, ed. and trans. Jochen Schulte-Sasse et al. (Minneapolis: University of Minnesota Press, 1997), 72. The text was found in Hegel's handwriting, and the three candidates for authorship of this text are Hegel, Hölderlin, and Schelling.

nature. But as we shall see, Humboldt does not reduce nature to merely a work of art: nature, in its vast beauty and overwhelming sublimity, maintains its sovereignty.

We can linger now on an insight from Theodor Adorno, who claims that when natural beauty is reduced to a work of art, nature suffers a kind of violence. Writing in 1969, Adorno, in his characteristically trenchant way, lamented the fading of natural beauty from the stage of philosophy:

> Natural beauty, which was still the occasion of the most penetrating insights of the *Critique of Judgment*, is now scarcely a topic of theory. The reason for this is not that natural beauty was dialectically transcended, both negated and maintained on a higher plane as Hegel's theory propounded, but rather, that it was repressed. The concept of natural beauty rubs on a wound and little is needed to prompt one to associate this wound with the violence that the artwork—a pure artifact—inflicts on nature.[11]

Adorno goes on to tell us that Humboldt occupies a position between Kant and Hegel, "in that he holds fast to natural beauty yet in contrast to Kantian formalism endeavors to concretize it."[12] Humboldt offers a way to appreciate natural beauty while conceiving of nature as nature rather than as art. In this way, natural beauty is saved from the violence described by Adorno, a violence that threatens to destroy it. The freedom at the center of Kant's analysis of nature's beauty is the freedom in the play of our cognitive faculties; it is a *Critique of Judgment*, after all, that Kant wrote. The freedom at stake in aesthetic judgments for Kant is the freedom of the *subject's* cognitive faculties. Unlike Kant, Humboldt's focus is *not* on the freedom operative in the free play of our faculties: Humboldt is not guilty of the subjectivization of aesthetic experience. If we look closely at the details of just how Humboldt concretizes natural beauty, we may begin to understand how he avoids the move to grant freedom to the subject at the cost of unfreedom for nature. To probe this matter, we shall turn to the details of Humboldt's *Naturgemälde* as presented in his *Views of Nature*, details that become more suggestive under the Adornian light in which I will cast them.

---

11 Theodor W. Adorno, *Aesthetic Theory*, trans. Robert Hullot-Kentor (Minneapolis: University of Minnesota Press, 1997), 62.
12 Ibid.

Humboldt's *Naturgemälde* in an Adornian Light

Schlegel realized that "where philosophy ends, poetry must begin."[13] Humboldt, for his part, saw that where science ends, poetry must begin, and his *Naturgemälde* can be read as the result of this insight. Humboldt's empirical approach to nature never overtakes an artistic rendering of the landscape; in romantic manner, he fuses science and art. As if guided by Schlegel's imperative that "All art should become science and all science art,"[14] Humboldt presents scenes of nature that are aesthetically and scientifically balanced. There is an openness born of this fusion of disciplines, an openness that is liberating for not only science and art, but also for the very scenes of nature that Humboldt presents.

The theme of the relation between freedom and the aesthetic, central to the work of the early German Romantics, endures in more contemporary discussions of human society, and it was central to the work of some of early German Romanticism's greatest heirs, the critical theorists, Theodor Adorno and Walter Benjamin.[15] As I have begun to suggest, Adorno's work can be used to bring Humboldt's presentation of the Latin American landscape into sharper focus. To do so, I will reference Martin Seel's illuminating discussion of Adorno in *Ästhetik des Erscheinens* (2000)/*Aesthetics of Appearing* (2005). In his analysis of Adorno's work on aesthetics, Seel emphasizes the fact that the indeterminable is not only of great theoretical, but also of great ethical importance for Adorno. Seel claims, the indeterminable "opens a 'freedom to the object' which is a condition of real freedom among subjects."[16] Because the work of art reveals to the viewer "a reality richer than all of the appearances we can fix in the language of conceptual knowledge," it unfolds the "difference between determinable appearance and indeterminable appearing."[17] Seel concludes:

> For Adorno, art thus becomes the hallmark indicating that the world has not been comprehended if it is known only conceptually; that the world has not been appropriated if it is appropriated only technically; that individual and social freedom have not been

---

13 *KFSA* 2, 261, Nr. 48/Firchow, 98.
14 *KFSA* 2, 161, *Lyceum/Critical Fragment* Nr. 115/Firchow, 14.
15 For more on the relation between Critical Theory and early German Romanticism, see Margarete Kohlenbach, "Transformations of German Romanticism 1830–2000," in *The Cambridge Companion to German Romanticism*, ed. Nicholas Saul (Cambridge: Cambridge University Press, 2009), 257–80.
16 Martin Seel, *Aesthetics of Appearing*, trans. John Farrell (Stanford: Stanford University Press, 2005), 15.
17 Ibid.

attained if they are guaranteed merely as a license to make profit; in a word, that we do not really encounter the reality of our lives if we encounter it merely in a spirit of mastery.[18]

The social freedom of which Seel speaks here in reference to Adorno's view of art and indeterminable appearing was also operative in the work of Humboldt as he attempted to present the Latin American landscape to the European public. While working at different historical moments, with social issues that were different in scope, Adorno and Humboldt each saw a need to protect the realm of freedom in society, and to do so via an aesthetic path. There is an aesthetic humanism guiding each thinker's work, yet embedded within their humanism are the tools to critique the humanist tradition, in particular the humanist view that freedom must be understood in terms of human agency; in short, there is an anticipation of some of the moves leading to the development of posthumanism.[19]

Humboldt's aesthetic path cleared a space for freedom in society; in particular a new space of appreciation for the Latin American landscape was opened through Humboldt's aesthetic lens. As we have seen, in *Aesthetic Theory*, Adorno lauds Humboldt as that rare nineteenth-century thinker who resisted the move to repress natural beauty and also as one who avoided a narrow focus on that which was created by the subject. Humboldt thus emerges as a figure for whom the concept of natural beauty was *not* replaced by that "pure artifact" which Adorno references, the artwork, to inflict further violence upon natural beauty. Adorno contrasts Humboldt's embrace and development of natural beauty to Hegel's role in its demise, writing:

> Hegel obviously lacked the sensibility needed to recognize that genuine experience of art is not possible without the experience of that elusive dimension whose name—natural beauty—had faded.[20]

Adorno attributes the vanishing of natural beauty to "the burgeoning domination of the concept of freedom and human dignity, which was inaugurated by Kant and then rigorously transplanted into aesthetics by Schiller and Hegel; in accord with this concept nothing in the world is worthy of attention except that for which the autonomous subject has itself to thank. The truth of such freedom for the subject, however, is at the same time unfreedom: unfreedom for the other."[21] Humboldt does

---

18 Ibid., 15.
19 See Cary Wolfe, *What is Posthumanism?*, 239–63.
20 Adorno, *Aesthetic Theory*, 63.
21 Ibid., 62.

Protecting Natural Beauty from Humanism's Violence 191

not work in the shadows of the idealism Adorno references, where, to cite Adorno, "everything not totally ruled by the subject" must be desiccated.[22] The world that Humboldt explores is not limited to that "for which the autonomous subject has itself to thank."

For Humboldt nature is a realm in which law and freedom blend. As I have indicated, nature for Humboldt is "the realm of freedom" (*das Reich der Freiheit*). Nature is "that which is conceived as eternally growing, eternally developing and unfolding."[23] How is the scientist to present "the realm of freedom" or something that is eternally growing, developing, and unfolding without abandoning insistence on empirical evidence and demonstration? Humboldt saw a common challenge facing all of those who wanted to present nature, be the presenter an artist or a scientist. The landscape artist and the scientist need to use empirical methods; Humboldt never tires of reminding his readers, "Humans cannot have any effect on nature or get close to any of her powers, if they do not have knowledge of the laws of nature according to relations of measurements and data."[24] So Humboldt, the *Naturforscher*, is after a clear understanding of the laws that do control the processes of nature, and he did spend much time during his grand American voyage (1799–1804) taking measurements and in this way, attempting to master the phenomena of nature. Humboldt's aesthetic turn reflects his acknowledgment that nature cannot be mastered by knowledge of its laws, that it is something more than what the charts and graphs of the empirical scientist can give us. Following Humboldt, when nature is considered thoughtfully, we get to its unity:

In thoughtful contemplation, nature is unity in multiplicity, the connection of the manifold in form and composition [*Verbindung*

---

22 Ibid., 62.
23 My translation of Humboldt: "Die Natur ist, wie Carus [Carl Gustav Carus (1789–1869)] trefflich sagt, und wie das Wort selbst dem Römer und dem Griechen andeutete, das ewig Wachsende, ewig im Bilden und Entfalten Begriffene." Alexander von Humboldt, *Kosmos. Entwurf einer physischen Weltbeschreibung*, 5 vols. (Stuttgart and Tübingen: J.G. Cotta, 1845–62). The English translation can be found here: Alexander von Humboldt, *Cosmos: A Sketch of the Physical Description of the Universe*, trans. E. C. Otté (Baltimore, MD: The Johns Hopkins University Press, 1997), 24. All English language references are to this edition, hereafter *Cosmos*. I have often, for the sake of greater precision, altered the translation (indicated by "translation altered") or simply translated the passage anew when I have found the Otté translation wanting (indicated as "my translation").
24 Humboldt, *Cosmos*, 53, translation altered. "Der Mensch kann auf die Natur nicht einwirken, sich keine ihrer Kräfte aneigen, wenn er nicht die Naturgesetze nach Maß- und Zahlenverhältnissen kennt." Humboldt, *Kosmos*, 36.

des Mannigfaltigen in Form und Mischung], the essence of natural phenomena [*Naturdinge*] and forces of nature as a living whole.[25]

This unity, this living whole, Humboldt indicates, almost as if Adorno had been whispering in his ear, cannot be mastered by the scientist's empirical methods. There can be no mastery of nature, for nature is the realm of freedom, that collection of life and forms that is infinite. As Adorno tells us in *Aesthetic Theory*, "[j]ust as in music what is beautiful flashes up in nature only to disappear in the instant one tries to grasp it."[26] Humboldt stepped away from the grasping responsible for the disappearance of the beautiful in nature by complementing his empirical grasp with a space for the appreciation of the beauty of nature. Grasping and dominating the phenomena of nature are what Humboldt does as he quantifies the phenomena of nature, and it cannot be denied that Humboldt was interested in those elements of nature that could be mastered, but he was also aware that the full story of nature's meaning could never be fully grasped or mastered; it could only flash up to disappear the moment one tried to grasp it definitively.

The theme of freedom is central to Humboldt's presentation (*Darstellung*) of nature and to his canvases of nature (*Naturgemälde*). Humboldt strives to combine the empirical or measurable elements of nature with those elements that are measureless to man. Hartmut Böhme describes "On Steppes and Deserts" from *Views of Nature* (1807) as a text that:

[O]ffers everything that a *Naturgemälde* (canvas of nature) is: that is, moments of a traveler's account, with traces of concrete intuitions, properties of a descriptive/analytic treatise, but also symbolic generalizations, with elements of the cosmos-idea, aesthetic elements of the sublime, and philosophical reflection, but at the same time that they offer a cultural-historical treatment of nature, they also present nature scientifically.[27]

---

25 My translation, compare Humboldt, *Cosmos*, 24. "Die Natur ist für die denkende Betrachtung Einheit in der Vielheit, Verbindung des Mannigfaltigen in Form und Mischung, Inbegriff der Naturdinge und Naturkräfte als ein lebendiges Ganzes." Humboldt, *Kosmos*, 5–6.
26 Adorno, *Aesthetic Theory*, 72.
27 Hartmut Böhme, "Ästhetische Wissenschaft. Aporien der Forschung im Werk Alexander von Humboldts," in *Alexander von Humboldt — Aufbruch in die Moderne*, ed. Ottmar Ette, Ute Hermanns, Bernd M. Scherer, Christian Suckow (Berlin: Akademie Verlag, 2001), 17–32. My translation. "Der Text bietet alles, was ein 'Naturgemälde' ausmacht: also Momente eines Reiseberichts mit den Spuren von konkreter Anschauung, Eigenschaften einer deskriptiv-analytischen

In Humboldt's *Naturgemälde*, ideas, which cannot be measured, blend with those aspects of nature that can be measured. As Böhme indicates, there is a fusion of science with the aesthetic elements of experience. With his *Naturgemälde*, Humboldt acknowledges that nature has not been comprehended if it is known only conceptually—empirical methods give us part of the story—and we need to understand nature insofar as it is the realm of freedom, indeed, as a work of art, to approximate a fuller understanding (never, of course, is a full understanding possible or even desirable). In Humboldt's presentation of nature, especially in *Ansichten der Natur* (1807), we find abundant examples of the balancing act between a presentation of determinable appearing (these are the elements of nature that can be charted and graphed) and the indeterminable appearing of nature (this presentation is where Humboldt's poetry of nature begins). For example, Humboldt quantifies the steppes described in "On Steppes and Deserts," that is, he gives measurements and data on them, but he also observes that they fill his spirit with the "sense of the infinite."[28] This "sense of the infinite" is not part of what can be measured by the natural scientist's tools—it belongs to the realm of the aesthetic, to the realm of that which can be appreciated, but not measured. In the seven chapters of Humboldt's *Ansichten*, aesthetic terms of beauty, of the sublime, of enjoyment, of movement of the spirit, are presented alongside empirical accounts of the objects presented in his portraits of nature. The term, *Naturgenuss* (enjoyment of nature), is central in *Views of Nature*. The neglect of this pleasure and all of the aesthetic elements involved in experiencing nature is the result of the one-dimensional science that Humboldt critiques:

> The mere accumulation of unconnected observations of details, devoid of generalization of ideas, may doubtlessly have tended to create and foster the deeply-rooted prejudice that the study of the

---

Abhandlung, aber auch einer symbolischen Verallgemeinerung, mithin Elemente der Kosmos-Idee, Züge der Ästhetik des Erhabenen und der philosophischen Reflexion, aber auch einer kulturhistorischen wie naturwissenschlichen Abhandlung." Böhme, "Ästhetische Wissenschaft," 23.

28 See, "Über die Steppen und Wüsten," in *Ansichten der Natur*, ed. Hanno Beck (Darmstadt: Wissenschaftliche Buchgesellschaft, 1987), 3–19. This has been translated as *Views of Nature or Contemplations on the Sublime Phenomena of Creation*, trans. E. C. Otté and Henry G. Bohn (London: Henry G. Bohn, 1850). A more recent translation is: *Views of Nature*, ed. Stephen T. Jackson and Laura Dassow Walls, trans. Mark W. Person (Chicago: University of Chicago Press, 2014). References to *Views of Nature* are to the Otté translation. All references to *Ansichten* are to the Beck edition.

exact sciences must necessarily chill the feelings, and diminish the nobler enjoyments attendant upon a contemplation of nature.[29]

Humboldt is a natural scientist, so he does believe, of course, that part of his task in the presentation of nature is to uncover the laws of nature. But he realizes that the laws of nature don't tell us the whole story of nature's meaning; for the more complete story, we must try to understand the poetry of nature. There is a reality accessible to aesthetic consciousness that cannot be reached if we restrict ourselves to the methodological framework of the natural sciences. Humboldt, in his turn to the aesthetic, does open freedom to the objects he brings into appearance through his presentation of nature, in his case, the landscape of Spanish America. This opening of freedom is not insignificant. In opening this freedom to the appearance of steppes, deserts, the pampas, etc., he also opens the possibility for freedom among the people of Spanish America. In liberating science from the "old prejudice" of approximating its objects in a purely empirical way, Humboldt also opened the European mind to all that the so-called New World had to offer, thus freeing those European minds from some pernicious prejudices about America and its inhabitants.[30] In the connection Humboldt makes between his aesthetic approach to nature and the realm of freedom, we return to the point in Adorno that Seel highlights, namely, that the indeterminable appearing is of great theoretical and ethical importance because it opens a freedom to the object which is a condition of real freedom among subjects.

---

29 Humboldt, *Cosmos*, 40. "Einseitige Behandlung der physikalischen Wissenschaften, endloses Anhäufen roher Materialien konnten freilich zu dem nun fast verjährten Vorurteil beitragen, als müsste notwendig wissenschaftliche Erkenntnis das Gefühl erkälten, die schaffende Bildkraft der Phantasie ertöten und so den Naturgenuss stören." Humboldt, *Kosmos*, 21.
30 The respect for the freedom of the landscape that Humboldt develops in his American writings was extended to an anti-Eurocentric notion of agency for the people of the region as well. In other words, Humboldt's democratization of nature opens a post-colonial perspective that breaks from the colonial discourse of so many of his contemporaries. Following leads from the work of Laura Dassow Walls and Aaron Sachs, in my article, "Alexander von Humboldt's Interest in America: In the Service of Empire or of Humanity?" I argue that contra May Louise Pratt's account of Humboldt as a thinker in the service of colonial structures, Humboldt worked to break away from those very structures. In my view, Humboldt's writings on Latin America did not serve the Spanish crown or the colonial structures of power, but rather served an aesthetic project that was politically liberating. See, "Alexander von Humboldt's Interest in America: In the Service of Empire or of Humanity?" in *Raumzeitlichkeit des Imperialen / SpaceTime of the Imperial*, ed. Holt Meyer, Susanne Rau, and Katharine Waldner (Berlin: Walter de Gruyter, 2017), 204–19.

We can illustrate the freedom opening instances in Humboldt's depictions of nature by looking at some of the scenes of nature or *Naturgemälde* Humboldt presents in *Ansichten der Natur*, scenes that create a portrait of nature with the same sort of detail one would expect from a landscape painter.

Liberation and the *Naturgemälde*

In his *Naturgemälde*, Humboldt is offering a canvas (written, not painted) of the American landscape. He not only describes the scenes he is presenting to his reading public but he also discusses the impact any given scene has upon the viewer:

> Like a limitless expanse of waters, the Steppe fills the mind with a sense of the infinite, and the soul, freed from the sensuous impressions of space, expands with spiritual emotions of a higher order. But the aspect of the ocean, its bright surface diversified with rippling or gently swelling waves, is productive of pleasurable sensations—while the Steppe lies stretched before us, cold and monotonous, like the naked stony crust of some distant planet.[31]

This depiction of the steppes, filled as it is with references to the infinite (something measureless and hence indomitable), the freedom of the soul, and emotions of a higher, yet negative, order—is not guilty of being "a mere accumulation of unconnected details" that chills our feelings for an enjoyment of nature. We take pleasure in the steppe, even as it "lies stretched before us, cold and monotonous." Indeed, in this passage, a poetic presencing or appearing of nature is what Humboldt accomplishes with his references to the indeterminable appearing of nature. More than the beauty of nature, we are taken to the realm of the sublime. As Kant observes in §22 of the *Critique of Judgment*, nature is "prodigal in its variety even to luxuriance, that is subjected to no constraint of artificial rules" and so "can supply constant food for taste."[32] And this "food for taste" is even more abundant when we are considering "beautiful views of objects" rather than "beautiful objects." In the case of "beautiful views of objects," Kant tells us, "taste appears,

---

31 Humboldt, *Views of Nature*, 2. "Wie dieser erfüllt die Steppe das Gemüt mit dem Gefühl der Unendlichkeit und durch dieses Gefühl, wie den sinnlichen Eindrücken des Raumes sich entwinden, mit geistigen Anregungen höherer Ordnung. Aber freundlich zugleich ist der Anblick des klaren Meerspiegels, in welchen die leichtbewegliche, sanft aufschäumende Welle sich kräuselt; tot und starr liegt die Steppe hingestreckt wie die nackte Felsrinde eines verödeten Planeten." Humboldt, *Ansichten der Natur*, 3–4.

32 *Critique of Judgment*, trans., J. H. Bernard (New York: Hafner Press, 1951), 80.

not so much in what the imagination *apprehends* in this field, as in the impulse it thus gets to *fiction*, i.e. in the peculiar fancies with which the mind entertains itself, while it is continually being aroused by the variety which strikes the eye."[33] Humboldt's description of the steppe is a description of a view, and as such, takes us to the realm of fiction or "the peculiar fancies" referenced by Kant. However, the view presented by Humboldt is not only a beautiful view; there are aspects of the sublime woven into his description. And while Kant adamantly rejects the move to call any object of nature sublime, claiming in §23 that "all that we can say is that the object is fit for the presentation of a sublimity which can be found in the mind,"[34] perhaps the view of the steppes, and the "peculiar fancies with which the mind entertains itself"[35] characteristic of the experience of such a view, can indeed be called sublime, even if no object can be so called. For Humboldt, when we experience the lack of any bounds whatsoever, a formless view in its boundlessness, we experience the sublime and experience the scene before us to be alien, "like the naked stony crust of some distant planet." The view of the steppes, taking us as it does, to the realm of the sublime, reminds us that we are not the orientation point for nature's meaning, that nonhuman nature is not ours to master.

Humboldt makes connections between the plains of Central Asia and the spread of "misery and devastation over the earth." He tells us early in his essay, "Some of the pastoral tribes inhabiting this Steppe, – the Mongols, Getae, Alani, and the Usüni, – have convulsed the world. If in the course of earlier ages, the dawn of civilization spread like the vivifying light of the sun from east to west; so in subsequent ages and from the same quarter, have barbarism and rudeness threatened to overcloud Europe."[36] After a brief excursus on the plains of Central Asia, Humboldt returns to the plain of South America. Despite the devotion he had to empirical observations and so to a kind of mastery over nature, Humboldt emphasizes the appeal of that which will never be mastered or tamed, celebrating such wild nature as the realm of freedom. He describes one such untamed scene thus:

---

33 Ibid., 81.
34 Ibid., 83.
35 Ibid., 81.
36 Humboldt, *Views of Nature*, 5. "Hirtenvölker dieser Steppe: die Mongolen, Geten, Alanen und Üsun, haben die Welt erschüttert. Wenn in dem Lauf der Jahrhunderte frühe Geisteskultur gleich dem erquickenden Sonnenlicht von Osten nach Westen gewandert ist, so haben späterhin in derselben Richtung Barbarei und sittliche Roheit Europa nebelartig zu überziehen gedroht." Humboldt, *Ansichten der Natur*, 6.

Protecting Natural Beauty from Humanism's Violence

The interest yielded by the contemplation of such a picture [*Gemälde*] must arise from a pure love of nature [*Naturinteresse*]. No Oasis here reminds the traveler of former inhabitants, no hewn stone, no fruit-tree once cultivated and now growing wild, bears witness to the industry of past races. As if a stranger to the destinies of mankind, and bound to the present alone, this region of the earth presents a wild domain [*ein wilder Schauplatz*] to the free manifestations of animal and vegetable life.[37]

The *wilder Schauplatz* is a place that does not bear traces of human industry or order, and it is precisely in this wild place that the pure love of nature is most prominent. Even when Humboldt seems steeped in a purely empirical account of a given aspect of nature, he consistently brings the reader back to a more abstract level of nature, connecting his empirical account to something larger, something beyond the scope of his instruments, to a context that allows the meaning of the scene described to emerge more fully and for natural beauty to emerge from his description. To speak with Seel (invoking Adorno), Humboldt combines the determinable appearance of nature (in the spirit of mastery) with nature's indeterminable appearing (in the spirit of beauty). For example, in the essay on "Steppes and Deserts," Humboldt lingers on a point about what, at first glance, seems to be a merely empirical and quite mundane matter: humidity. He writes:

> A number of causes, many of them still but little understood, diminish the dryness and heat of the New World. Among these are: the narrowness of this extensively indented continent in the northern part of the tropics, where the fluid basis on which the atmosphere rests occasions the ascent of a less warm current of air.[38]

---

[37] Humboldt, *Views of Nature*, 6. "Das Interesse, welches ein solches Gemälde dem Beobachter gewähren kann, ist aber ein reines Naturinteresse. Keine Oase erinnert hier an frühe Bewohner, kein behauener Stein, kein verwilderter Fruchtbaum an den Fleiß untergangener Geschlechter. Wie den Schicksalen der Menschheit fremd, allein an die Gegenwart fesselnd, liegt dieser Erdwinkel da, ein wilder Schauplatz des freien Tier- und Pflanzenlebens." *Ansichten der Natur*, 7.

[38] Humboldt, *Views of Nature*, 7, translation altered. "Mannigfaltige, zum Teil noch wenig entwickelte Ursachen vermindern die Dürre und Wärme des neuen Weltteils. Schmalheit der vielfach eingeschnittenen Feste in der nördlichen Tropengegend, wo eine flüssige Grundfläche der Atmosphäre einen minder warmen aufsteigenden Luftstrom darbietet..." Humboldt, *Ansichten der Natur*, 8.

Humboldt's attention to empirical detail is then immediately used to take the presentation of nature to a different level, in this case, to dispel some of the myths that contributed to the anti-Americanism of the period. After a long, detailed, empirical account of the causes of dryness and heat in the New World, Humboldt concludes:

> If, therefore, the atmosphere on one side of our planet be more humid than on the other, a consideration of the actual condition of things will be sufficient to solve the problems of this inequality. The natural philosopher need not shroud the explanation of such phenomena in the garb of geological myths. It is not necessary to assume that the destructive conflict of the elements raged at different epochs in the eastern and western hemispheres, during the early condition of our planet; or that America emerged subsequently to the other quarters of the world from the chaotic covering of waters as a swampy island, the abode of crocodiles and serpents.[39]

Humboldt's approach to nature in general, and his detailed, inspiring, and accurate depictions of the Spanish American landscape in particular, helped to break down the misleading accounts of America given by too many scholars of his generation, accounts that depicted America as nothing more than the dwelling place of beasts, a place far inferior, both culturally and naturally to Europe. Humboldt's *Naturgemälde* allows the Spanish American landscape to appear without the distorting prejudices that plagued most accounts of the period.[40] In his *Naturgemälde*, Humboldt not only depicts nature, but also gives clear analyses of some of the ways in which the landscape affected the culture of the people

---

39 Humboldt, *Views of Nature*, 8. "Wird daher eine Seite unseres Planeten luftfeuchter als die andere genannt, so ist die Betrachtung des gegenwärtigen Zustandes der Dinge hinlänglich, das Problem dieser Ungleichheit zu lösen. Der Physiker braucht die Erklärung solcher Naturerscheinungen nicht in das Gewand geologischer Mythen zu hüllen. Es bedarf der Annahme nicht, als habe sich auf dem uralten Erdkörper in der östlichen und westlichen Hemisphäre ungleichzeitig geschlichtet der verderbliche Streit der Elemente, oder als sei aus der chaotischen Wasserbedeckung Amerika später als die übrigen Weltteile hervorgetreten, ein sumpfreiches, von Krokodilen und Schlangen bewohntes Eiland." Humboldt, *Ansichten der Natur*, 9.
40 Hegel's account of America springs immediately to mind in this connection; see especially, *The Philosophy of History*, trans. Leo Rauch (Indianapolis, IN: Hackett, 1988). I discuss the details of Hegel's anti-American views and Humboldt's response to them in, "Alexander von Humboldt's View of America: A Break from Imperial Eyes," in *Humanism and Revolution. Eighteenth-Century Europe and Its Transatlantic Legacy*, ed. Uwe Steiner, Christian Emden, and Martin Vöhler (Heidelberg: Universitätsverlag Winter, 2015), 209–26.

Protecting Natural Beauty from Humanism's Violence 199

of the region he is presenting. In the case of the "Steppes and Deserts" account, Humboldt lingers on the significance that the absence of pastoral life in the pampas had upon the culture of the region:

> If a pastoral life—that beneficent intermediate stage which binds nomadic bands of hunters to fruitful pasture lands, and at the same time promotes agriculture—was unknown to the primitive races of America, it is to the very ignorance of such a mode of life that we must attribute the scantiness of population in the South American Steppes.[41]

A typical Eurocentric reaction to the scantiness of population in the South American steppes would be to use the low population levels as evidence for the inferiority of the land and, in an unfavorable comparative move, for the superiority of European culture and indeed, even of European nature—the country with the richer natural resources would be the country with greater concentrations of thriving populations. Humboldt draws quite another conclusion, writing:

> But this circumstance [the lack of the transitional pastoral life] allowed freer scope for the forces of nature to develop themselves in the most varied forms of animal life; a freedom only circumscribed by themselves, like vegetable life in the forests of the Orinoco, where the Hymenaea and the giant laurel, exempt from the ravages of man, are only in danger of a too luxuriant embrace of the plants which surround them.[42]

Humboldt presents the American landscape as a realm of freedom and of natural luxury, whose beauty does not depend on its human population, indeed which may benefit from the absence of humans. The absence of large populations of humans allows "freer scope of the forces

---

41 Humboldt, *Views of Nature*, 12. "Blieb demnach das Hirtenleben, diese wohltätige Mittelstufe, welche nomadische Jägerhorden an den grasreichen Boden fesselt und gleichsam zum Ackerbau vorbereitet, den Urvölkern Amerikas unbekannt, so liegt in dieser Unbekanntschaft selbst der Grund von der Menschenleere der südamerikanischen Steppen." Humboldt, *Ansichten der Natur*, 12–13.
42 Humboldt, *Views of Nature*, 12. "Um so freier haben sich in ihr die Naturkräfte in mannigfaltigen Tiergestalten entwickelt: Frei, und nur durch sich selbst beschränkt wie das Pflanzenleben in den Wäldern am Orinoco, wo der Hymenäe und dem riesenstämmigen Lorbeer nie die verheerende Hand des Menschen, sondern nur der üppige Andrang schlingender Gewächse droht." Humboldt, *Ansichten der Natur*, 13.

of nature," pushing us, once again, to think of nature and freedom in a way that transcends the human perspective and the human presence.

Concluding Remarks

The freedom fueling Humboldt's work on nature is not a freedom taking as its Archimedean point human autonomy or agency—as Humboldt balanced science and art, he also found a way to balance the human and the nonhuman, the landscape of nature fashioned by human subjectivity and appreciation for nature as a wild showplace (*Schauplatz*) that could not be tamed by the human. Humboldt's aesthetic humanism gave way to the perspective that informs posthumanism, that is, it amounted to a push away from the human as the orientation point for our view of nature. Indeed, the description cited earlier leads the viewer (reader) to appreciate the unpopulated landscape of Spanish America as a realm of freedom and purity. The absence of human population is no disadvantage to the beauty and majesty of the landscape; quite the contrary, according to Humboldt, without the interference of humans, nature can develop with greater freedom, generating a wider diversity of forms. What Humboldt accomplished with his *Naturgemälde* was pathbreaking and evidence, I think, for the central role aesthetics plays in presenting the world, for letting freedom appear. Humboldt transformed his acts of aesthetic perception of the Spanish American landscape into *Naturgemälde* which, in turn enriched the perception of his reading public, bringing into focus a more just portrait or picture (*Bild*) of the Spanish American landscape. When the purely human perspective, with its purely human prejudices, is balanced with a more expansive viewpoint, humanism gives way to posthumanism, and a richer account of freedom emerges.

Part III
Cyborg Enlightenment: Boundaries of the (Post-)Human Around 1800

Eleven Posthumanist Thinking in the Work of Heinrich von Kleist

Tim Mehigan

Introduction

Friedrich Nietzsche is popularly thought to have inaugurated posthumanist thinking.[1] Yet an analysis of the writings of the German writer Heinrich von Kleist (1777–1811), who died sixty years before the appearance of Nietzsche's first work *Die Geburt der Trägodie aus dem Geiste der Musik* (1872), already suggests the presence of many essential features of posthumanist thought. That Nietzsche drew inspiration from Kleist is well documented.[2] In what follows I argue that Kleist can be regarded as a major progenitor of posthumanist thought. In making this case, I indicate that the positions Kleist developed in his short literary career emerged from the literary and philosophical discussion that took place in Germany in the wake of Kant's critical philosophy around 1800. Despite the rich intellectual context from which these positions emerged and without which they are unthinkable, Kleist nevertheless is best understood as an independent voice in the thought of this period, hitching his wagon neither to any of the various emanations of post-Kantian philosophy that arose in the period, nor to the manifold projects of the

---

1 Stefan Herbrechter, for example, takes his starting point from Nietzsche. See *Posthumanism: A Critical Analysis* (London: Bloomsbury, 2013), 8.
2 For a discussion of the proximity of Kleist's thought to that of Nietzsche, see Gisela Dischner, *"der ganze Schmutz zugleich und Glanz meiner Seele": Die Briefe Heinrich von Kleists als Teil seiner Werke* (Bielefeld: Aisthesis, 2012). For consideration of Nietzsche's reception of Kleist, see J. W. Dyck, "Kleist and Nietzsche: *Lebensplan* and *Lustmotiv*," *German Life and Letters* 21, no. 3 (April 1968): 189–203. Helmut Sembdner has recorded Nietzsche's many intelligent responses to Kleist, whom Nietzsche apparently regarded as an important skeptic, in *Heinrich von Kleists Nachruhm: Eine Wirkungsgeschichte in Dokumenten*, vol. 2 (Frankfurt a.M.: Insel Verlag), 280–2.

literary Romantics that brought this period in intellectual history to a close. It was precisely Kleist's singular status in the history of mentality, I believe, which allows him to be accorded a prominent place today at the very beginning of modern genealogies of posthumanism.

Kleist's Intellectual Position and its Relation to Posthumanism

Heinrich von Kleist, from today's perspective, was a unique voice in the literature and thought of the early nineteenth century. His early sympathies lay completely with the goals of eighteenth-century rationalism. In an essay written in 1799,[3] the young Kleist talked up the virtues of an allegedly "secure path to happiness" in the spirit of Leibnizian optimism,[4] without foreknowledge that Voltaire had debunked precisely this version of happiness in his play *Candide* (1759). Kleist's support of Leibnizian thinking, or, more likely, his adherence to the Leibniz-Wolffian spirit of his teachers at the University of Frankfurt an der Oder,[5] drove him into the arms of the new Kantian philosophy, no doubt in the belief that Kantian precepts had only improved the inheritance of Leibniz and Wolff, not undermined it or dealt it a mortal blow. When Kleist learned more about philosophical matters, possibly through an encounter with the thought of Fichte,[6] he lost all confidence in the rationalist

---

3 "Aufsatz, den sicheren Weg des Glücks zu finden und ungestört—auch unter den größten Drangsalen des Lebens, ihn zu genießen!" In *Heinrich von Kleist: Sämtliche Werke und Briefe*, vol. 3: *Erzählungen, Anekdoten, Gedichte, Schriften*, ed. Klaus Müller-Salget (Frankfurt a.M.: Deutscher Klassiker Verlag, 1990), 515–30.
4 Typical of the sentiment of this essay are passages such as this: "the divine will not disappoint the longing for happiness which she has herself has undyingly awakened in our soul" (ibid., 515). Kleist is likely to have derived such sentiment not directly from Leibniz in the first instance (though its spirit is clearly Leibnizian) but, as Müller-Salget points out in his notes to the essay in the Deutscher Klassiker Verlag edition of Kleist's works, from Christoph Martin Wieland's *Geschichte des Agathon* (1766/67) (1100–1). Note that all translations from the German that appear in this article are my own.
5 Kleist spent three semesters at the University of Frankfurt an der Oder in 1799 and 1800, ending his enrolment there in the summer of 1800.
6 Several commentators have situated Kleist's thought in close proximity to that of Fichte, particularly in the context of nation and the task of nation-building. See e.g., Bernd Fischer, *Das Eigene und das Eigentliche: Klopstock, Herder, Fichte, Kleist: Episoden aus der Konstruktionsgeschichte nationaler Intentionalitäten* (Berlin: Erich Schmidt Verlag, 1995), 326ff. It seems likely that Kleist met Fichte in Berlin in the period 1808–11 and may well have been influenced by his nationalism, though no meeting of the two is documented. The attempt to see a parallel between the ego philosophy of Fichte and what might be construed as Kleist's philosophical leanings, however, is more conjectural. The most influential attempt to do so is Ernst Cassirer's *Heinrich von Kleist und die Kantische Philosophie* (Berlin:

legacy.[7] In reaching this understanding, Kleist may well have overlooked Fichte's adherence to this same problematic tradition. However that may be, Kleist's fate as a thinker digesting the diverse intellectual currents of his age was to fall between all stools: by early 1801 he had renounced the long-standing commitments of rational Enlightenment in the German tradition, yet he was unable fully to ratify the goals of the emerging rival school of German Romanticism, either in the form of the ego philosophy espoused by Fichte, with its commitment to a larger conception of the self (as interpreted by Novalis and Friedrich Schlegel), or a Platonically informed fusion of ancient and modern thinking, taken either toward an idealistic spiritualism, in the case of Hölderlin, or a more conscious formalism—the "Weimar classicism" of Schiller and Goethe. Kleist's intellectual position, eschewing both the rationalism of the philosophical Enlightenment in Germany and the subdued idealism of literary Romanticism, was to appear to be in disagreement with the major intellectual trends of his day. If there is a position that his singularity in the history of mentality does better agree with, it is with the skepticism[8] that Kleist's age inherited from British empiricism and from David Hume more than any other (whose challenge Kant himself avowedly sought to answer in the *Kritik der reinen Vernunft* [1781/87]).[9] Yet even here one ought to be cautious: Kleist would not have agreed with Hume's default common sense about the task of thinking in view of the skeptical challenge, for, on close analysis of Kleist's thought and writings, no consistent view arising from such common sense about life and how it should be lived appears to be sustained.

Reuther & Reichard, 1919). For a close textual reading of parallels between Kleist's thinking and that of Fichte, see my "Kleist und die Tiere. Zur Frage des ausgeschlossenen Dritten in dem Trauerspiel *Penthesilea,*" in *Penthesileas Versprechen. Exemplarische Studien über die literarische Referenz,* ed. Rüdiger Campe (Freiburg: Rombach, 2007), 291–311; also in Tim Mehigan, *Heinrich von Kleist: Writing after Kant* (Rochester, NY: Camden House, 2011), 52–67.

7   To the extent that the encounter with Kant's thought led to this insight, Kleist appears to have excepted Kant from his condemnation of the rationalists. For detailed consideration of Kleist's relationship to Kant's philosophy, see Cassirer, *Heinrich von Kleist und die Kantische Philosophie,* Ludwig Muth, *Kleist und Kant: Versuch einer neuen Interpretation* (Cologne: Kölner Universitätsverlag, 1954), Bernhard Greiner, *Eine Art Wahnsinn: Dichtung im Horizont Kants. Studien zu Goethe und Kleist* (Berlin: Erich Schmidt Verlag, 1994), James Phillips, *The Equivocation of Reason: Kleist Reading Kant* (Stanford: Stanford University Press, 2007), and Mehigan, *Writing after Kant.*

8   I have treated Kleist's skepticism at some length. See "The Scepticism of Heinrich von Kleist," in *The Oxford Handbook of European Romanticism,* ed. Paul Hamilton (Oxford: Oxford University Press, 2016), 256–73. See also Bianca Theisen, "Der Bewunderer des Shakespeare. Kleists Skeptizismus," *Kleist-Jahrbuch* (1999): 87–108.

9   On Kleist's relationship to the thought of Hume, see my *Writing after Kant,* 33–51.

The failure to fall in behind either a rationalist philosophy or any one of a variety of philosophical and literary romanticisms is most obvious when Kleist's late essay "Über das Marionettentheater" (1810) is considered. The essay takes its intellectual cue from a proposition argued by a certain "Herr C," the I-narrator's interlocutor in the essay. According to Herr C, one can expect to find more grace in the movements of a wooden puppet, guided by its unseen puppeteer—importantly referred to in the essay as a "machinist"[10]—than in those of the most skillful human dancer. The essay appears to have been meant as an ironic commentary on positions argued by Friedrich Schiller in several essays that emerged from Schiller's own encounter with the thought of Kant in the 1790s and in the essay "Über Anmut und Würde" in particular.[11] These essays are known to have been important for the early German Romantics who had congregated in Jena during a period around the early to mid-1790s dominated by the Kantian philosopher Karl Leonhard Reinhold and, later, by Fichte, his successor in the Chair of Philosophy at the University of Jena. Overall, Schiller's thoughts on Kant's philosophy, which centered on the question of the type of guidance this philosophy offered for aesthetic thought, especially as adumbrated in Kant's third Critique, *Die Kritik der Urteilskraft* (1790), became an influential part of the literary and philosophical landscape around 1800.

If it can be maintained that Kleist's initial intention in the "Marionettentheater" essay was to call Schiller's confidence about the virtues of the aesthetic state into question, it is nevertheless the case that such an intention involved Kleist in the articulation of positions we now recognize as prototypically posthumanist. Three episodes discussed in the essay claim attention in this regard. The first, as mentioned, is the leading idea about the wooden puppet that supplies the essay with its title. Whereas grace—a signature concept in Schiller's essay "Über Anmut und Würde"[12]—is rarely, if ever, attainable even for the most gifted human artist, it is routinely achieved by the puppet, Herr C contends, under the ministrations of the "machinist." When movement

---

10 Kleist, *Sämtliche Werke*, vol. 3, 556, 559.
11 See See Gail K. Hart,"Anmut's Gender: The 'Marionettentheater' and Kleist's Revision of 'Anmut und Würde'," in *Women in German Yearbook: Feminist Studies in German Literature and Culture* 10 (1995): 83–95.
12 Whereas Schiller uses both *Anmut* and *Grazie* interchangeably in meanings that come close to the English term "grace," Kleist only uses the latter term in the "Marionettentheater." A passage from Schiller's essay indicates that *Anmut* closely approximates Kleist's deployment of the term *Grazie*: "Where grace [*Anmut*] is found, the soul is the motive principle, and in this principle is contained the ground [*Grund*] of the beauty of movement." See *Friedrich Schiller, Sämtliche Werke*, vol. 5: *Erzählungen, Theoretische Schriften*, ed. Wolfgang Riedel (Munich and Vienna: Carl Hanser [Deutscher Taschenbuch Verlag], 2004), 437.

occurs out of a physical center of gravity in the puppet where human intention and superfluous adornment (*Ziererei*)[13] is displaced from the very beginning (leaving aside, of course, the level of intention inspiring the puppet's movements attributable to the puppeteer), grace reveals itself as a purely formal category. The puppet's movement, from this angle, exhibits a mixture of responsiveness to physical laws as well as escape from lawfulness, since the puppet's movements are also referred to as "antigrav,"[14] which is to say, they carry out movement that (allegedly) defies gravity. Though the type of movement posited in this argument is not adequately explained nor indeed properly explicable, it is nevertheless consistent with the contention that grace—a construction of humanists—can be imagined, even operationalized, in nonhuman ways. This conclusion would appear to undermine Schiller's faith in the essay "Über Anmut und Würde" that grace attends to human beings above all as the responsiveness of human agents to the innate spirituality within them,[15] where the discovery or expression of such grace in physical movement might be celebrated as a victory of moral certitude over the (graceless) commotion of the outside world.

Two other examples discussed in Kleist's essay further undermine the pretension of inward states to moral ascendancy in the human being. In a second episode, a boy, who sits beside a still pond and executes a movement reminiscent of the classical statue of the *Dornauszieher* (or "thorn puller"), is unable through an act of will to execute movement with the same skill and grace observed in the initial gesture reflected back to him in the pond—the gesture which had put the boy in mind of the classical statue in the first place. A narcissistic urge of this boy impels him nevertheless to search for the initial moment of glimpsed perfection. All attempts to recover the spontaneity of the original pose, however, come to nothing. In the third and final episode discussed in Kleist's essay, a highly skilled human fencer, when challenged to compare his skills with those of a circus bear, finds himself unable to triumph against the instinctiveness of the animal—the bear sees through every feint of the human fencer, correctly divines every genuine thrust and so wins out over his human counterpart at every turn. The third episode affirms the proposition entertained in all three examples discussed in the essay: human consciousness is afflicted by fateful perturbations that affect the execution of human intention in the world. Even under the most favorable conditions the human actor appears unable

---

13 Kleist, *Sämtliche Werke*, vol. 3, 559.
14 Ibid.
15 Schiller says: "Grace [*Anmut*] is found in the *freedom of voluntary movements*; dignity [*Würde*] in the *control of the involuntary ones*." *Sämtliche Werke*, vol. 5, 477 (original emphasis).

to achieve the innate perfection of the nonhuman realm, whether that be the pure physicality of an object and its movement, the pure instinctiveness of animals, or, in the case of the boy before the pond, the ability to reproduce a contingent, "non-minded" event at the level of the mind.

The goals of human actors, for this reason, fall short of manmade notions such as grace and inner harmony laid out under ideals espoused in Schiller's essay "Über Anmut und Würde." These older ideals appear too lofty for human beings, or else they must be regarded as ill-fitted to the task of orienting human behavior. Even if the parodying intent of the essay is taken into consideration, the twin goals of "absolute consciousness" and absent consciousness discussed in the conclusion of Kleist's essay—respectively, the consciousness of the divine and that of the wooden puppet—seem far removed from the situation of human beings and, for this reason, unlikely to ameliorate the perturbations governing human striving in the world. Only a second eating of the Tree of Knowledge, Herr C opines (and in this he is now joined by the narrator, who celebrates this renewed eating as "the last chapter in the story/history [*Geschichte*] of the world"[16]) seems in a position to heal the broken effects wrought by these perturbations. We recognize the utopia of knowledge accumulation and perfection offered as an antidote in the essay for the afflictions of human consciousness, from today's perspective, as equal to the goals of artificial intelligence—goals that aim to eliminate the imperfection of human conscious "wetware" and to substitute it with the "dry," empty programming of the robotic machine.

It might be objected at this point in the discussion that Kleist's aim in the "Marionettentheater," more than anything else, is to parody positions attributed to Herr C. At first sight, this is a fair objection. Yet it is also the case that the ironic or parodying intent of the essay is itself opaque and does not allow any "view through" to a state of affairs or level of intention that is stable or regular enough to be endorsed. This failure to ratify a level of understanding of mental frameworks lying behind the diegetic level of the narrative is a typical feature of Kleist's writing and has been much remarked upon in Kleist scholarship.[17] In fact the failure to find any Archimedean point against which

---

16 Kleist, *Sämtliche Werke*, vol. 3, 563.
17 Wolfgang Kayser's pioneering 1948 work on narration in *Das sprachliche Kunstwerk* (Tübingen: Franke, 1992), and, in the wake of this important volume, his landmark essay on narration on Kleist "Kleist als Erzähler," *German Life and Letters* 8, no. 1 (October 1954): 19–29, was a pivotal moment in the emergence of greater understanding of Kleist's fictions in particular. For a well-informed, recent discussion of narrative technique in Kleist that follows in this vein, see Bernd Fischer, "Heinrich von Kleists vorgeführtes Erzählen," in *German Life and Letters* 64, no. 3 (July 2011), 337–53.

the narrative perspective in Kleist's works could be oriented is, in the end, the source of Kleist's epistemological independence from the philosophical and literary schools of his own day. Kleist's works ratify no final perspective. One could call these works consciously pluralistic in that they devolve the hermeneutic task of comprehension to readers, who are challenged to provide the stabilizing arguments that the stories, dramas and essays otherwise expressly eschew. The devolution of perspective away from a single viewpoint in the direction of a plurality that might either be lamented (as the end of an "old order" of omniscient reading) or celebrated (since it marks the advent of a new hermeneutic order of openness to meaning as such) is precisely the reason that Kleist must be accorded significance as a forerunner of modern posthumanism.

If such an insight has value, the experimentalism on view in Kleist's works—a major feature of his writing[18]—takes on new significance. Kleist's literary experiments aim as a matter of first principle to reduce human authority in the world, if not efface it entirely. In the play *Penthesilea* (1808), for example, the disastrous consequences recorded at the end of the play in which the main character murders her beloved Achilles in battle and thereafter commits suicide herself indicates that human calculation is not equipped to deal with the proliferating complexity it confronts. The disastrous end to the play, for this reason, does not herald or address a "better" mythic world removed from our own real world and actively desired as a substitute for it, but is rather to be imagined as the consequence of the state of human affairs one is obliged to take as binding and given.[19] Kleist, in other words, organizes no flight away from this world, only a retreat to the reality of the unfinished world everywhere before us. In his stories even more than his plays, as I discuss later, the human being appears as the average kind of animal examined in the "Marionettentheater"—one stretched between an obscure unattainable divinity on one side and an all-too-visible, but equally unattainable, animality on the other. Kleist explores the results of this middling status throughout his works, highlighting the dilemmas and aporias that occur when either of these states—the divinity under the sway of errant ideals, the animality when human willing appears notionally or voluntarily absent—gains the ascendancy.

---

18 Günter Blamberger, in view of this experimentalism, calls Kleist a "project maker." See his *Heinrich von Kleist. Biographie* (Frankfurt a.M.: Fischer Verlag, 2012), esp. 51–69.

19 See Bernhard Greiner's discussion of this point under the heading "1.2 Kömodie" in *Kleist-Handbuch: Leben—Werk—Wirkung*, ed. Ingo Breuer (Stuttgart and Weimar: Metzler, 2013), 23.

Humanism and Posthumanism in "Michael Kohlhaas"

A clear example of a posthumanist outlook in Kleist is to be found in the long short story "Michael Kohlhaas." A first version of this story appeared in Kleist's journal *Phöbus* in 1808; a much longer second version was published two years later. Against a popular view that the 1810 version of the story simply takes over where this earlier version leaves off,[20] I maintain that an entirely new project comes into view in the 1810 version which illustrates how and why Kleist must be considered among the important progenitors of posthumanist thinking.

Kleist's Kohlhaas project in both versions considers the conditions that hold for law and morality. While the question of the relationship between law and morality was implicit in the original conceptual framing of the story, the second version redirects discussion of this relationship in important ways. This redirection, in turn, gains significance in the context of Kleist's posthumanism. In the 1808 version of the story a paradoxical situation based on Kleist's historical chronicles[21] is allowed to play out such that we do not achieve an advance beyond the terms suggested at the outset: the eponymous protagonist lives up to the epithet introduced at the start of the story of being both "one of the most extraordinary and at the same time most feared persons of his age [*einer der außerordentlichsten und fürchterlichsten Menschen seiner Zeit*]."[22] This formulation indicates that the primary interest of the 1808 version is the protagonist's enigmatic character. In the last part of this version, the horse-trader Michael Kohlhaas's desire for justice after an undeniable infraction against him becomes a source of fear at the moment when it assumes the form of the equal and opposite force of revenge. As subsequent events illustrate, the moral interest in punishing Kohlhaas is destined to win out, or else it is seen to be the same as the legal interest. Elsewhere I have characterized the projected conclusion to the first version of the story as essentially "medieval," where the term medieval stands for the older logic by which legality and morality are seen to fall together.[23] The probable end to the 1808 fragment, for this reason, is the conclusion that a sentence of death against Kohlhaas is inevitable on both moral and legal grounds. This likely end to the fragment

---

20 This appears to be the view of Müller-Salget, who equally does not attach significance to the fact that the subtitle of the story "aus einer alten Chronik" is missing from the later version. Cf. Kleist, *Sämtliche Werke*, vol. 3, 705–6.
21 Müller-Salget discusses these at length ibid., 707–13.
22 Ibid., 1.
23 "Legality as a 'Fact of Reason': Heinrich von Kleist's Concept of Law, with special reference to *Michael Kohlhaas*," in *Literatur und Recht*, ed. Bernhard Greiner, 153–70 (Heidelberg: Winter Verlag, 2010), 153–70; see also *Writing after Kant*, 68–83.

in accordance with the chronicles Kleist was following is equally what must be canceled out when Kleist comes to the task of extending the story in its later version. The logic of the continuation of the story becomes the question of how the legal interest in the story is able to trump the moral interest. In achieving such an outcome, Kleist sketches out an entirely new conception of legality and, along the way, arranges a fundamental separation between religious morality, the lifeblood of the old order, and what might be termed jurisprudential legality, a defining aspect of the emerging modern legal state which the story anticipates. The epithet that introduces Kohlhaas in the second version of the story, accordingly, now also changes to reflect this new interest: Kohlhaas is now characterized as "one of the most law-abiding" (*rechtschaffensten*) and at the same time "most loathsome" (*entsetzlichsten*) citizens of his age.[24] The picture of the enigmatic nature of the protagonist's character is of course preserved, but it is now linked to the question of the legal order that should properly govern and discipline him.

A key indication that Kleist moves in the direction of a separation between law and morality takes place in the so-called Luther episode. While a meeting between the Protestant reformer Martin Luther and Hans Kohlhase (the model for Michael Kohlhaas) is documented in the historical chronicles,[25] there is no record of what was discussed when they met.[26] Kleist uses this lacuna in his sources to initiate discussion of the legal principles that lie at the foundation of the emerging secular state. If the state of nature is to be overcome on the basis of a central understanding or contract establishing the individual's relation to the state—a contract according to which the individual's personal rights and liberty is exchanged for an undertaking to give undiminished obedience to the laws of the state—this same individual, Kohlhaas contends, commands the right to return to the condition of nature should the contract of the state with his person be broken. Kleist thereby adds an important qualifying argument to contractualist debates in the seventeenth and eighteenth centuries by suggesting that legal contractualism is at bottom entirely formal in nature and quite independent of the neo-spiritualist dimensions it appears to accrue, for example, in Rousseau's account of it in *The Social Contract* (1762). That Luther gives ground to this argument through his decision to organize a provisional amnesty for Kohlhaas (in line with the calculation that the amnesty will

---

24 Kleist, *Sämtliche Werke*, vol. 3, 2.
25 See Müller-Salget's notes, Kleist, *Sämtliche Werke*, vol. 3, 708.
26 As Müller-Salget reports, Kleist naturally also had no access to historical material relating to Kohlhase that was not found and published until 1864. He may also not have seen a letter Luther wrote to Kohlhase, now readily available (ibid., 707–8).

deliver Kohlhaas to the authorities and so end his lawless campaign of revenge) indicates that secular arguments about legality had gained considerable purchase in Kleist's own time.

That morality might thereby also be up for grabs, however, is something to which Luther does not readily cede ground. Luther is unimpressed by Kohlhaas's subsequent argument that he (Kohlhaas) should receive the sacrament he was obliged to forego during his public ransacking because "[the lord God] did not also forgive all his enemies."[27] The requirement Luther spells out to Kohlhaas if he wishes to receive the sacrament is absolute forgiveness of one's enemies. This is a moral and religious postulate, not a legal one. Kohlhaas is unable to stand on the ground of religious morality to embrace it. The denial of the sacrament to Kohlhaas by the most important religious functionary of the day does not just underscore the separation of morality and legality in the story; it also reveals the new ground the 1810 version of the story inaugurates when it posits an order by which morality and legality are thought of as separate from each other. This distinction then becomes the important enabling condition for the appearance of a posthumanist perspective in the story. The wedge Kleist drives between morality and legality in the story thus allows a pivot away from the sort of anthropocentric grounding of the law on moral categories typical of human-centric conceptions of the world.

If the introduction of boundaries dividing morality from legality provides the condition for the emergence of a posthumanist perspective in the story, it is discussion about the nature of the body that brings it fully to light. In Kleist's 1808 story "Die Marquise von O ..." for example, the eponymous central character who falls pregnant without her knowledge is shown not to command rational awareness of her body in all its states. The body, which is seen on occasion to escape the subject's conscious control, is thus not at one with the conscious mind inhabiting it. In the Kohlhaas story, the states of the human body are linked to the animal body. This is prepared at the outset of the story when the horse-trader agrees to leave two horses with the Junker Wenzel von Tronka as surety when a pass is demanded in order to cross the Junker's territory. The body of these two horses, in this way, comes to stand in—literally to vouch—for Kohlhaas's body. When Kohlhaas returns to the Junker's holdings after ascertaining that the need for a pass in the state of Saxony is a ruse, Kohlhaas finds that his horses have been worked into the ground in his absence and his knave, who had been assigned to supervise the horses, driven off the Junker's property in the meantime. If the body of these horses stood in for Kohlhaas's body, it is now evident

---

27 Kleist, *Sämtliche Werke*, vol. 3, 81.

that their reduced state entails a direct injury both to Kohlhaas's body and his status as a citizen under law. The matter of the restitution of the horses to full health thus becomes a political matter as well as a legal matter. The legal matter is the question of how a loss under law is to be compensated. The political matter is the question of how an injury to the body of a citizen, who—in his own mind—has already contracted with others to form a new political order, is to be made good. The longer version of the story holds to the assumption that legality and the polity are mutually interdependent, while it equally suggests that legality and morality will no longer be mutually reinforcing. As is discussed further presently, the honor of the human body under law is explicitly linked to the attempt to make the desecrated animal body "honorable" again.[28]

A scene that takes place on the town square in Dresden where the horses are sighted for the first time since their quartering in the Junker's stables is crucial in this regard. The horses in between time have found their way into the care of a knacker. The point is not just that the knackery now awaits them. It is also the case that the knacker himself, rude in ways peculiar to his lowly social status, underscores through his very person a parallel "social" decline in the status of the horses. It happens that Kohlhaas has been required to present himself to Graf Wrede, the Chancellor in Dresden, at about the same time as the knacker makes his appearance on the nearby square. This coincidence, once it comes to light, means that Kohlhaas can be invited to carry out an "ocular inspection" of the two black horses whose reduced form has otherwise made them difficult to identify. Kohlhaas quickly confirms that the horses are his own. Though Kohlhaas knows them still, the parlous state of these horses means it is now unlikely that they can be returned to their former good health. It is therefore decided, in order to bring Kohlhaas's lawsuit to a rapid closure, that Kohlhaas should be offered material compensation as a substitute for the horses, since, as Graf Kallheim explains, the horses "are dead: they are dead in a legal sense since they have no [material] value."[29]

The question thus arises: why does the 1810 version of the story not conclude at this point? Or, put another way, what legal or other purpose is served by the fact that the story does not end at this point?

"Michael Kohlhaas" and the New Legality

It is only when the role of the nonhuman body in the story is borne in mind that the rationale for the continuation of the narrative in its later form becomes fully evident. After the scene with the knacker of

---

[28] The need to make the abused horses honorable again (*ehrlich machen*) is expressly thematized in the story, see ibid., 97.
[29] Kleist, *Sämtliche Werke*, vol. 3, 99.

Döbbelin one might incline to the view that the core of the Kohlhaas story is already at a point of conclusion. The fate Kohlhaas could look forward to at this moment in the story would be no different from the projected end of the 1808 story: a minor legal compensation, at best, would accompany the sentence of death meted out to Kohlhaas for crimes committed during his campaign of public lawlessness.[30] But such an end would leave the status of the horses as individuals in limbo. The story is thus carried forward to a point of conclusion beyond that which would see it reclaimed on the medieval substrate of the story.[31] In the new conclusion Kohlhaas's legal dispute with the Junker is reclassified as the fight to restore his two raven-colored horses to their proper value both as entities with a commercial value and entities with full status under law as individuals. The mechanism introduced to achieve this outcome involves the intervention of a gypsy—an intervention which has drawn a great deal of comment in the critical literature[32] on account of the apparent disjuncture it is thought to have occasioned with respect to the essentially realistic torso of the story.

It is of course certainly possible to view the gypsy in the story as a supernatural intervention in the manner of Romantics such as Tieck, Chamisso, Fouqué, or E. T. A. Hoffmann. In Tieck, for example, the supernatural operates to break through the oppressiveness of the ordinary, allowing a direct view of human consciousness and its basic non-alignment with the drabness of physical life around it. When such a break is registered, as with Christian's entrancement before the naked seductress in "Der Runenberg" or the child Bertha's fascination with the song of the bird in "Der blonde Eckbert," the break of inner mental with outer physical life is shown to have disastrous consequences (Christian

---

30   As the Hafftitz chronicle reports, the historical Kohlhase was executed on the wheel in 1540 (Kleist, *Sämtliche Werke*, vol. 3, 709). Kleist's Kohlhaas in the later version of the story, by contrast, is afforded a relatively humane death by beheading.
31   Francisco Larubia-Prado is one of the first critics to ascribe importance to the horses as actors in the story. His observation that "[t]he material and symbolic divider and connector that is at the origin of the conflict and that signals ... its resolution is *Pferde*" is insightful, even if the full legal and political significance of the horses in the story is not brought out in his analysis. See Larubia-Prado, "Horses at the Frontier in Kleist's Michael Kohlhaas," *Seminar: A Journal of Germanic Studies* 46, no. 4 (November 2010): 330.
32   Müller-Salget has provided an overview of some of the older, mostly disagreeable, critical opinion about the gypsy episode. Kleist, *Sämtliche Werke*, vol. 3, 714–16. Martin Greenberg is one of several later commentators who chide Kleist for alleged failures of narrative technique, labeling it an "afterthought," albeit one that "[sublimates] a limited question of legal justice into a transcendental (ultimate) one." See his "The Difficult Justice of Melville and Kleist," in *The New Criterion* (March 2005): 31.

eventually loses his mind and Eckbert unknowingly commits incest with his sister Bertha). The deployment of the gypsy in the last part of "Michael Kohlhaas," however, appears to have a quite different motivation, and its effects are constructive rather than disabling. The special knowledge of the gypsy is directed at increasing the legal interest of the Elector of Saxony in the person of Michael Kohlhaas. Such an interest serves the purpose of reviving Kohlhaas's legal dispute and bringing it under the more solicitous attention of the Elector of Brandenburg, the immediate governor of Kohlhaas in view of Kohlhaas's residence in the state of Brandenburg. The involvement of the Elector of Brandenburg, accordingly, allows the story to reach a point of conclusion where the conception of legality pronounced at the end is broad enough to encompass both human and nonhuman agents.

By these means Kleist extends the notion of the body to include animal subjects as well as human ones. These animal subjects, the horses in dispute at the beginning in Kohlhaas's lawsuit with the Junker, which had appeared to have lost all value in the scene with the knacker of Döbbelin, are now present at the end of the story, restored to their full capacity as working horses as part of Kohlhaas's patrimony, but also now elevated to animal rights as living subjects—at least insofar as they acted as surrogates for Kohlhaas's legal rights from the very beginning. In "Michael Kohlhaas," then, the nonhuman, in the form of Kohlhaas's horses, lays claim to an independent legal status. From this angle, interest in the state of the nonhuman body appears part of a wider concern in Kleist's plays and stories to treat nonhuman bodies alongside human ones and value them explicitly as social agents. In the play *Penthesilea*, for instance, the mastiffs that tear the lover Achilles limb from limb do so not only because they serve their mistress Penthesilea, but also, as a physical extension of Penthesilea, because they embody her "slip of the tongue," her confusion of "bites" with "kisses." In this way animals and humans are viewed together, though mostly not in congenial ways. Elsewhere, in "Das Erdbeben in Chili," human agents not only act like animals under the sway of passions;[33] they are understood—for better and for worse—to act on the same level as animals. At the end of this story a reverse hierarchy of values is even worked out, such that animality also connotes nobility and humanity treachery. Whereas Don Fernando, in this reversal of values, battles "in the manner of a lion [*ein Löwe wehrt sich nicht besser*]"[34] defending those under his charge, the murderous Meister Pedrillo, whipping a motley collection of nameless citizens into a frenzy, is referred to as "the prince of the satanic mob

---

33 Josephe calls the mob "you bloodthirsty tigers"; they are later referred to by the narrator as "bloodhounds." See Kleist, *Sämtliche Werke*, vol. 3, 219, 221.
34 Kleist, *Sämtliche Werke*, vol. 3, 220.

[*der Fürst der satanischen Rotte*]."[35] Even where no animal is mentioned, as in "Die Marquise von O ... ," the pretensions to higher breeding of human beings serve to mask the potent animality within them. The Count F may well be a highborn aristocrat, but he is subject to the same directness of physical response that characterizes the literalness of the animal. From this angle, no transubstantiation of human physicality into otherworldly spirit emerges as a proper goal for human striving.[36] Kleist gives these attempts to work immanent flesh into something otherwordly short shrift (note that the Marquise von O ... accepts her pregnant condition initially only if a magical or supernatural intervention is considered responsible for the conception of her child). Clearly it is one of Kleist's main ambitions to show up these pretensions for what they are—attempts to deny knowledge of the common ground of animal life in ordinary human behavior.

In "Michael Kohlhaas," a new legality is brokered: one of the main outcomes of the longer version of the story is the end of the medieval dispensation according to which morality and legality are run together. Michael Kohlhaas's offenses against the state during a period of public lawlessness which otherwise would have occasioned the death sentence is set aside long enough for a legal settlement *on different legal terrain* to occur. Kohlhaas's moral offense against the medieval *Glaubensgemeinschaft* in which he lives is suspended—an achievement of the deployment of the gypsy in the final part of the story. During this suspension, a new legal order is made conscionable. After a speedy hearing, Kohlhaas's lawsuit against the Junker is upheld: he gains full restitution for the offenses committed against him, and his children, now in the care of Kohlhaas's friend, the *Amtmann*, can look forward to a prosperous legacy. Kohlhaas's horses, which had disappeared from view in the story after the scene with the knacker on the Dresden square, now reappear: they have been restored to their original good health and now stand before the law as prosperous members of Kohlhaas's patrimony. Kohlhaas thus goes to the executioner fully reconciled with his death—as a law-abiding, and no longer loathsome, fully legal subject.

"Das Bettelweib von Locarno" and the Future of the Posthuman

"Das Bettelweib von Locarno" is one of the most enigmatic of all Kleist's stories. While the story reveals the same epistemological uncertainty

---

[35] Ibid., 221.
[36] To this extent earlier critics like Ilse Graham, *Heinrich von Kleist. Word into Flesh: A Poet's Quest for the Symbol* (Berlin and New York: Walter de Gruyter, 1977) fail to capture the essence of Kleist's anti-humanism.

under scrutiny in other works,[37] it is particularly important for its portrayal of the relation between hermeneutic openness and the presence of posthumanist perspectives.

The story itself tells of a beggar woman—the eponymous beggar woman of Locarno—who is taken into a household by the lady of the house, a marquise, and given shelter. When the marquis, absent during the beggar woman's arrival at the castle, returns and finds her hunkered down in a corner of a room, he instructs the beggar woman to move to a different part of the room—she is to move to a position behind the oven. Rising with difficulty and moving across the room as instructed, the beggar woman loses her footing, falls to the floor and dies. These events would have little significance for the marquis and his wife but for the fact that they soon impinge upon later circumstances. Desirous of a quick sale of the castle as his financial affairs worsen, the marquis invites a prospective buyer to stay overnight. The visitor is assigned the same room as the one formerly inhabited by the beggar woman. He spends a troubling night in the room, hearing what appears to be the sound of someone rising from one corner, moving across the room and then collapsing amid sighs and groans behind the oven. He quickly departs the next day and no sale results. In fact, a rumor is quickly put about to the effect that the castle has become the dwelling place of a ghost. At this point, before the presence of the ghost is to be made public, the appearance of the ghost is put to three separate examinations—respectively, by the marquis, his wife (with a servant), and then, on the third day, the marquis again, together with the marquise and a dog. It is this last "cold-blooded test"[38] that proves to be the most decisive. When at midnight the dog, asleep in the middle of the room, is disturbed by noises consistent with the movements of a human being, as before, the marquise takes flight from the room, packs her bags, and hurriedly leaves for a nearby town. She is only part way down the road to the town when, looking back at the castle, she sees it engulfed in flames. The marquis, for his part, "in the grip of horror, had taken a candle, and, weary of his own life, set fire to all four corners of the castle, covered everywhere, as it was, with wooden wainscoting."[39] He dies in the resulting inferno; his "white bones" are found in the same corner of the room that the beggar woman was in when she had been asked to move to a place behind the oven.

---

37 The signature phrase "the fragile constitution of the world [*die gebrechliche Einrichtung der Welt*]" speaks in programmatic terms of such uncertainty in several works of the author. Cf. "Michael Kohlhaas," "Die Marquise von O ...," and *Penthesilea*, in Kleist, *Sämtliche Werke*, vol. 3, 27, 186, and v. 2854.

38 Ibid., 262.

39 Ibid., 263.

As Klaus Müller-Salget discusses in his notes to the story, later commentators have had great difficulty classifying the story. Wilhelm Grimm could not assign it with confidence to the genre of the ghost story, since it seems not to endorse the superstition it appears to promote.[40] Ludwig Tieck had similar difficulty with it, finding it neither to be a ghost story, a fairy tale or a novella. Theodor Fontane, following Tieck, thought it equally beyond the category of the "moral tale," since the only possible moral offense against the beggar woman committed in the story—the marquis's instruction to the beggar woman that she move behind the oven—is far too slight in nature to stand in relation to the dramatic finale of the story, the incineration of the castle with the marquis within it.[41] By and large, the views of these noted commentators have been reproduced in later scholarship on the story. Many of these interpreters, in view of the failure to ratify any single reading of the story, stress the nature of its structure, suggesting that it is best understood as an exercise in the deployment of dramatic form. When the story's content is nevertheless put to consideration, a popular view is that the beggar woman appears as the instrument of a "'higher' justice."[42] The death of the marquis to this extent can be viewed as a form of punishment, albeit a punishment that appears disproportionate to the nature of the offense committed. The tenuous nature of this link to a stabilizing order beyond the story, however, undermines any confidence in the existence of such an order—be it of divine origin, or of a social or legal kind.

It is precisely the absence of a clear moral in the story that allows it to be conscripted for a posthumanist reading. For the inverse of the posthumanist position—a humanist reading of the story—would appear to require the type of coherence that is missing from the narrative in point of principle. The narrative, in structural terms, is built around a premise—that the castle of the marquis and his wife is haunted by an unhappy ghost—and a series of tests by which it is allegedly confirmed. The tests carried out by the castle's owner and his wife, separately and together, appear to affirm the conclusion that an uncanny presence can be found in the room in which the beggar woman had been invited to find shelter. As compelling as the results of these tests appear, it falls to the nonhuman presence of the dog, which joins the marquis and his wife for the third test by chance, to provide what is then taken by the human actors in the story as a definitive level of proof of the ghost's "reality":

---

40 See ibid., 857.
41 See ibid.
42 See Müller-Salget's own interpretation, in Kleist, *Sämtliche Werke*, vol. 3, 859.

someone no human can see pushes themself up on crutches in the corner of the room; you can hear the straw that rustles under them; and with the first step: tap! tap! the dog awakens, gets up suddenly from the ground with pointed ears, growling and barking, as if a human being was stepping towards him, backwards he moves away towards the oven.[43]

The dog thus comes to occupy a privileged position in the story: it appears at the point where the range of aural perception of human beings as well as their emotional range are seen to come up short. It is these less aurally gifted humans who, now situating themselves below the animal in the "great chain of being" and taking their cue from its responses, attribute what is heard to the order of the uncanny and act in accordance with this attribution (the marquise flees the castle, the marquis sets it and himself alight). Yet linguistic analysis reveals that the clauses in which the physical attentiveness of the dog is cued and those in which the psychological responses of human beings are registered are formally kept apart. In the first case the word *jemand*, introducing the impression that a living human presence has occasioned a human-like sound, is separated from the dog's physical responses to this sound by a semi-colon ("jemand, den kein Mensch sehen kann ... unter ihm rauscht; und mit dem ersten Schritt: tapp! tapp! Erwacht der Hund"). In the second case, the subordinate clause that deepens the impression of a human presence in the room ("grad als ob ein Mensch auf ihn eingeschritten käme") is dropped into a main clause formally quite separate from it ("und knurrend und bellend, ... rückwärts gegen den Ofen weicht er aus"). The disturbance of normal main clause word order that results is suspicious of a broader disturbance in the normal order of things to which the human actors in this scene are alive. Yet despite the suggestiveness arising from grammatical effects in the narration at this point in the story, a formal interval can still be observed between the human and the dog's direct responses to sound. The maintenance of a disjuncture between form and content, in turn, brings the psychological responses of the human agents into sharp relief.

What does this disjuncture between form and content in the story tell us? It reveals above all that spontaneity at the level of human understanding arising from a stimulus cannot be separated from the manner in which the stimulus is received, or, to put the point in Kantian terms, the spontaneity of the understanding and the receptivity of direct intuition in human beings—against Kant's express insistence about these matters in the *Kritik der reinen Vernunft*—are in fact inseparable. On

---

43 Kleist, *Sämtliche Werke*, vol. 3, 263.

this reading, the Kantian project of reflective judgment that purports to found a normalizing account of consciousness on a separation of the work accruing, respectively, to the understanding and to intuition, is seriously compromised. Once an objection of this nature is registered, one might reach the same conclusion about the prospects for judgment in the world as Karen Barad: "moral judgment is not to be based either on actions or intentions alone; rather, the very binary between 'interior' and 'exterior' states needs to be rethought, and both 'internal' and 'external' factors—intentionality and history—matter."[44] Kleist anticipates conclusions such as these by pointing out that "interior" states of receptivity (say in intuition, as postulated by Kant) and "exterior" conscious states of response (say in Kant's faculty of understanding) cannot be isolated from each other.

Conclusion

I have made a case in the foregoing for the posthumanist credentials of the German writer Heinrich von Kleist. In reaching this conclusion I draw attention to an important essay of the author in which posthumanist positions are anticipated—the essay "Über das Marionettentheater." While this essay can be read as a contribution to an aesthetic debate set in motion by Friedrich Schiller, I also find it suggestive of a posthumanist perspective in its prominent discussion of the limitations attending human consciousness despite the note of irony which accompanies this discussion. In a series of modular moments discussed in the essay, human awareness appears to be eclipsed by both automatons and animals. While one might question whether this outstripping of the human being is a fair victory in view of the failure to consider the consciousness of the "machinist" in enlivening the movements of the puppet, what is undeniable are the anti-humanist strains in the argument audible throughout the essay. The critique is set on course in the first episode countenanced in the essay—that of the narcissistic youth. In this example, there appears no cultural way back to the classical perfection of antique beauty referenced in the allusion to the Roman statue of the "thorn puller." The question of the way *forward*, which is considered later in the essay, points either toward pan-awareness, which might be read as a species of mythic consciousness, or toward machinic or artificial consciousness, an anticipation of the discussion of AI in our own day.

Further evidence of Kleist's status as a prototypical posthumanist can be found in Kleist's stories. Among those I have briefly looked at,

---

44 Karen Barad, *Meeting the Universe Halfway: Quantum Physics and the Entanglement of Matter and Meaning* (Durham, NC, and London: Duke University Press, 2007), 23

"Die Marquise von O ... " draws attention to the disjuncture between mentality and corporeality in the human being. In an amplification of this position in the context of the law, "Michael Kohlhaas" locates a site of especial importance in the animal body, which both augments and refines the legal discussion around human bodies. In this story, conceptions of the law must be redrawn to accommodate the claim animals make to be included in any taxonomy of legal subjects. Finally, in the story "Das Bettelweib von Locarno," a dog provides a level of response to a physical stimulus that is taken as definitive proof that a castle belonging to a marquis and his wife is haunted by an unhappy ghost. Precipitate actions result from this assignation of proof: the marquise flees the castle with her belongings, the marquis sets fire to the castle and dies in the resulting inferno. Yet close analysis of an important passage in the text reveals these actions to be unwarranted (however much, under the pressure of rising tensions in the story, they may be considered understandable).

Pressing this point to its ultimate conclusion, I argue that "Das Bettelweib von Locarno" throws doubt on the account of consciousness Kant provides in his *Critique of Pure Reason*. In this account, spontaneity is attributable only to the operation of the faculty of understanding; as such it contrasts with the passive receptivity characterizing direct intuition. Kleist's story reveals this argument about divided faculties and the work they carry out to be faulty. Kleist is one of the first thinkers[45] in the Kantian aftermath to have understood these problems in Kant's broadly rationalistic account of judgment, and perhaps the first outright to have thought past humanist assumptions in considering why this account needs to be revised. To appreciate Kleist's prescience in these matters, one need only consult John Dewey, a much later thinker, who, like Franz Kafka,[46] should be counted among Kleist's important "blood relatives":

> Man finds himself living in an aleatory world; his existence involves, to put it baldly, a gamble. The world is a scene of risk; it is uncertain, unstable, uncannily unstable. Its dangers are irregular, inconstant, not to be counted upon as to their times and seasons.[47]

---

45 Prominent among Kleist's coevals who divined this same limitation in Kant's philosophy is Friedrich Schleiermacher, who views perception ultimately as a continuum. See his *Hermeneutics and Criticism and Other Writings*, ed. and trans. Andrew Bowie (Cambridge: Cambridge University Press, 1998), 162–3.
46 Kafka described Kleist as a *Blutsverwandter* in a letter to Felice Bauer in 1913. See Sembdner, *Heinrich von Kleists Nachruhm. Eine Wirkungsgeschichte in Dokumenten* (Frankfurt a.M.: Insel Verlag, 1984), vol. 2, 335 (footnote 1 of this essay).
47 John Dewey, *Experience and Nature* (Chicago, IL: Open Court, 1925), 41.

Twelve Positing the Robotic Self: From Fichte to *Ex Machina*

Alex Hogue

Alex Garland's 2015 film *Ex Machina* starts from a seemingly simple question regarding the nature of the robot Ava's (Alicia Vikander) artificial intelligence (AI): is this example of AI truly self-conscious?[1] In order to make this determination, Nathan (Oscar Isaac), the computer prodigy who created Ava, recruits Caleb (Domhnall Gleeson), an employee from his technology firm, to be the human interrogator in a modified Turing test. While Nathan is explicit that he wants Caleb to deliver "simple answers to simple questions,"[2] determining the capacity of Ava's AI proves to be a task far beyond the capabilities of a simple Turing test.

Alan Turing's imitation game, colloquially called the Turing test, involves two participants, one human interrogator and the other either human or machine. While separated from and unable to see the second participant, the human interrogator types questions to be answered by the other and judges based on the responses whether the other participant is human or computer.[3] The Turing test in *Ex Machina* is modified such that Caleb and Ava are face to face, bringing Ava's robot appearance to the forefront. It is then Caleb's job to determine whether, even despite her appearance, he still believes Ava has self-consciousness. Nathan's real interest, however, is not in Caleb's opinion of Ava's AI; rather, Nathan observes the sessions of the Turing test in order to determine the capacity of Ava's AI for himself based on whether she can formulate a plan to use Caleb as a means to escape her enclosure.[4] While Nathan is not interested

---

1 The characters in the film treat the terms "self-conscious," "self-aware," and "true AI" as virtually interchangeable.
2 *Ex Machina*, directed by Alex Garland (2015; Santa Monica, CA: Lionsgate, 2015), DVD.
3 Alan Turing, "Computing Machinery and Intelligence," *Mind* 49 (1950): 433–4.
4 Nathan, in his hubris, has no expectation of Ava actually being able to escape and is blindsided when she does. The condition of success for Nathan in determining Ava's self-awareness is simply that she develops a plan with Caleb.

in Caleb's ultimate verdict from the Turing test, structuring the analysis this way points to a twofold understanding of the conscious mind. Consciousness, as Nathan understands it, is partly cognitive (i.e., what she *knows*) as revealed through Ava's answers to Caleb's questions and her ability to formulate a plan to escape, and partly volitional (i.e., what she *wills*) as revealed through her ability to act on her thoughts and plans.

Both Caleb's Turing test sessions and Nathan's observation of them operate from a decidedly functionalist stance.[5] As the inner workings of Ava's mind are not directly observable or measurable to them, they seek to determine whether Ava is truly self-aware through her speech and her actions; if Ava functions like a self-aware human, Caleb and Nathan may conclude that she is truly self-conscious. Based on the view that the brain is like the hardware of a computer running the software of the self-conscious mind, Nathan and Caleb understand human-style self-consciousness to be realizable both within humans and within sufficiently complex artificial intelligences. However, running under the radar of Nathan's functionalist analyses are emergent developments within Ava herself, and especially between Ava and Caleb, occurring primarily during the periodic power outages that allow Ava and Caleb to interact without Nathan observing them.

As thorough observations are necessary for Nathan to come to a conclusion as to whether Ava is self-aware, these gaps provide the space for both a critique of functionalism and the establishment of a competing construction of self-awareness built out of the interpersonal relationship that develops between Caleb and Ava. While the Turing test seeks to determine the capabilities of Ava's AI, passing it does not guarantee that she will be understood or treated with the rights of a self-conscious person.[6] Any success Ava may achieve in the Turing test is hollow, as

---

5 For more on functionalism and its history, see Hillary Putnam, "The Nature of Mental States," in *Readings in Philosophy of Psychology*, vol. 1, ed. Ned Block (Cambridge, MA: Harvard University Press, 1980), 223–32; and Arturo Rosenblueth, Norbert Wiener, and Julian Bigelow, "Behavior, Purpose and Teleology," *Philosophy of Science* 10, no. 1 (1943): 18–24.

6 Charles Taylor conceptualizes personhood not as a synonym for "human being," but rather as "a being with a certain moral status, or a bearer of rights. But underlying the moral status, as its condition, are certain capacities. A person is a being who has a sense of self, has a notion of the future and the past, can hold values, make choices; in short, can adopt life-plans." Charles Taylor, "The Concept of a Person," in *Philosophical Papers*, vol. 1 (New York: Cambridge University Press, 1985), 97. Building upon the free and mutually limiting nature of intersubjectivity, as well as Susanna Lindroos-Hovinheimo's "Excavating Foundations of Legal Personhood: Fichte on Autonomy and Self-Consciousness," I understand "personhood" to be a concept that draws upon Fichte's intersubjectivity. See Susanna Lindroos-Hovinheimo, "Excavating Foundations of Legal Personhood: Fichte on Autonomy and Self-Consciousness," *International Journal for the Semiotics of Law* 28, no. 3. (2015): 687–702.

it would not necessarily bring about positive consequences for her; rather, it would constitute only the affirmation of Nathan's personal success in his quest to build an artificial intelligence.[7] Success for Ava, on the other hand, would require that she is able to transcend the role of examined object trapped in an enclosure and to exist as a free and self-directed person.

While Nathan's functionalist attempt to determine Ava's self-consciousness is shown to be incapable of producing the results he desires, his understanding of consciousness as both cognitive and volitional has an important precursor in the history of philosophical interpretations of what it means to be a subject. Specifically, *Ex Machina* implicitly operates upon a logic reminiscent of the structure of self-consciousness that can be found in J. G. Fichte's *Science of Knowledge* of 1794–5 (and the iterations that emerge in the wake of this text), albeit transposed in the sphere of artificial intelligence, or as the case may be, artificial subjectivity. What begins as a subject-object relationship between interrogator and AI in the Turing test collapses as Caleb begins to see Ava as an autonomous subject. The intersubjectivity that develops between Caleb and Ava distances itself from the functionalism of Nathan and the Turing test by following Fichte in understanding (inter)subjectivity not as a quality measured, quantified, and determined from the outside, but rather as a self-reflective action intrinsic to the subject, and one which is mutually recognized between subjects.

Oppositions and Evolutions

In his 2016 article "*Ex Machina* in the Garden" Brian R. Jacobson begins with a consideration of how the medium of film speculates about and reflects on new technological innovations. By incorporating and adapting to new technology, Jacobson argues, film takes on a self-reflexive position through which these technologies "highlight film's place on a kind of Möbius strip in which new technologies create the conditions of possibility both for their own representations and for new techno-visions of a techno-future."[8] He continues by claiming that "this mix of technological speculation and reflexivity forms the core of *Ex Machina* (2015), Alex Garland's recent film vision of AI robots and the humans who make them."[9] The continually expanding new technologies available in filmic production, which drive the self-reflexive elements

---

7 Nathan states toward the end of the film that after the test is completed, Ava's mind will be downloaded and partially formatted, effectively returning it to its basic code and erasing her memories.
8 Brian R. Jacobson, "*Ex Machina* in the Garden," *Film Quarterly* 69, no. 4 (2016): 23.
9 Ibid.

Jacobson sees in cinema, grant filmmakers new abilities to depict ever more high-tech visions of artificial humans on screen. These depictions demonstrate another level of self-reflection, however; namely, reflections on how humans define themselves, and especially how humans evaluate the abilities, possibilities, and deficiencies of their machine analogs.

Such reflections on the abilities, possibilities, and deficiencies of artificial humans function both to reflect something of their human creators back to the humans, but also to separate the artificial creations from their biological counterparts.[10] The replicants from Ridley Scott's *Blade Runner* and Phillip K. Dick's novel *Do Androids Dream of Electric Sheep?* appear human under normal observation and may affect emotions and seem to mimic human behavior as well. However, it is the protagonist Deckard's duty to determine conclusively whether the individual opposite him is a human or a replicant by reading the micro-expressions in his or her eyes that indicate the presence or lack of emotion. Similar, although decidedly less sinister, is Data from *Star Trek: The Next Generation*, whose appearance is reasonably human, but it is his lack of emotion that both sets him apart from his human(oid) crewmates and drives his quest to understand what it means to be human. The humanoid cylons in the 2004–9 reboot of *Battlestar Galactica* appear to be both physically and emotionally human, to the degree that some are unknowingly sleeper agents posted among the humans. However, while they show great diversity in both physical appearance and their emotions, their inability to reproduce biologically marks them as other and drives them into contact again with their estranged human creators. In Spike Jonze's 2013 film *Her*, Samantha (Scarlett Johansson) plays a disembodied AI whose personality, for much of the film, would be indistinguishable from that of a human. While she and her human love interest, Theodore (Joaquin Phoenix), develop an emotionally intimate relationship through the film, Samantha's disembodied existence is brought to the forefront when it comes to physical intimacy between them.

While these works portray the physical or emotional deficiencies of the artificial humans as means to separate them from true humans, *Ex Machina* takes a very different approach to the technology it depicts. In *Blade Runner*, *Star Trek*, *Battlestar Galactica*, and *Her*, the deficiencies of the artificial humans are either a continual or revelatory point of

---

10 Neil Badmington's *Alien Chic*, as well as the Introduction to his edited volume *Posthumanism* offer useful expansions on this idea. See Neil Badmington, *Alien Chic* (New York: Routledge, 2004); and Neil Badmington, "Introduction: Approaching Posthumanism," in *Posthumanism*, ed. Neil Badmington (London: Palgrave, 2000), 1–10.

juxtaposition between biological and artificial humans. However, in *Ex Machina* the technological artificiality of Ava is presented directly as a challenge to be overcome such that Nathan modifies his Turing test to bring Ava's artificiality to the forefront, rather than revealing it at the Turing test's conclusion. For Caleb and for the audience alike, *Ex Machina* separates itself from works such as those listed above by avoiding the question of how the technology depicted on screen separates biological and artificial humans. Instead, it asks whether such obvious technological differences might really be a diversion from the true issue, namely how an artificial mind might be understood to be truly self-aware and self-conscious, and whether humanness might be understood not as a physical form or set of behaviors that separate the biological and artificial, but rather as a self-reflective act of subjectivity that invokes a Fichtean notion of subjectivity and that may find broader application among biological and artificial humans alike. As *Ex Machina* explores this question, it builds a series of oppositions that tie together the environment in which Nathan produced Ava, Ava's subjectivity, and her intersubjective relationship with Caleb.

Opposition and Environment

The first view Caleb has of Ava is in silhouette, backlit as she rises from a bench in front of a small garden in her enclosure. Her form is easily mistaken for that of a human, and it is only as she walks toward the camera that Caleb sees the machinery of her body. The juxtapositions in this scene are striking as Caleb sits in a tiny room bordered on two sides by the transparent walls of Ava's enclosure. Ava stands in a nearly empty room, a robot juxtaposed with the nature contained within the tiny walled garden that forms the back wall of her enclosure. Yet this juxtaposition is itself only superficial as Ava, a being capable of growth and adaptation is, like the plants in the garden, contained and isolated within her walls, save for periodic visits from the outside. The smooth glass of Ava's enclosure gives way to bare rock behind the garden—an aesthetic that runs through the rest of Nathan's compound as well. His facility is remote and isolated in the mountains yet "contains enough fiber optic cable to reach the moon and lasso it."[11] Throughout the building, brutalist bare concrete walls abut clean and high-tech softly backlit glass panels as well as the unfinished rock of the mountain. Nathan's compound brings the opposing elements of aesthetics and pure function, high-tech and nature crashing together, preserving the integrity of each element while destroying the boundaries between them.

---

11 Garland, *Ex Machina*.

Nathan's decor is also a fusing of carefully chosen contrasting elements primarily depicting a diverse history of stylized representations of humans. Of this history of human images, Jacobson writes:

> African and Asian masks line the halls and the walls of Nathan's office. A bejeweled skull and abstract glassware decorate the table in the entryway lounge. A Pollock drip painting hangs in Nathan's man cave. Gustave [sic] Klimt's portrait of Margaret Stonborough-Wittgenstein (1905), sister of the philosopher, hangs in Nathan's bedroom. Titian's *An Allegory of Prudence* (1550–65) hangs conspicuously on the wall behind Nathan's workstation.[12]

Nathan surrounds himself with these aestheticized representations that work together to link life and death, the classical and the modern, mythology and technology to form a multifaceted continuum of how humans see and represent themselves, among which his work is to be the crowning achievement. For Nathan, Ava is to be a new kind of artwork and an embodiment of his genius. No longer will humans be limited to carving their images into stone or scribbling them onto canvas, Nathan's work of art is intended to be both a recreation of the human form and the human mind.[13]

Rather than depicting the physical image of a human, Nathan's Pollock painting, *No. 5, 1948*, hangs on his wall as a representation of how he understands creativity and the human mind. Of Pollock, Nathan says: "He let his mind go blank and his hand go where it wanted: not deliberate, not random, someplace in between."[14] Nathan's explanation of Pollock's work, and indeed his use of this as an allegory for his conception of the mind in this scene is rather oversimplified. After Pollock sold the piece originally, a small section of the painting was damaged during shipping.[15] Pollock "undertook a 'thorough but subtle overpainting' that retained the original concept but was 'affirmed and fulfilled by a new complexity and depth of linear interplay.'"[16] The fact that this painting was repairable at all indicates that Pollock's work was not someplace in between random and deliberate. This was not a mediation between the pull of two extremes; rather, in order to restore the painting, Pollock had to have an exacting hand and had to match

---

12 Jacobson, "*Ex Machina* in the Garden," 27.
13 Ibid., 23.
14 Garland, *Ex Machina*.
15 Victoria Newhouse, *Art and the Power of Placement* (New York: The Monacelli Press, 2005), 168.
16 Gary Garrels, *Plane Image: A Brice Marden Retrospective* (New York: Museum of Modern Art, 2006), 117.

the style, strokes, and illusion of randomness with great specificity of motion. The final work is a fusing together of both opposing forces into a whole that benefited from the preserved integrity of each side. The painting's real history not only echoes Nathan's words, but strengthens the allegory, as he explains the development of Ava's mind and his understanding of how people think: "fluid, imperfect, patterned, chaotic."[17]

Both Nathan's research facility and the creation he brought forth within it embody the kind of oppositional intertwining present in the image of Donna Haraway's cyborg. For Jacobson, Ava "represents a new iteration of Donna Haraway's cyborg politics"[18] in the form of an artificially intelligent posthuman, who, in conjunction with her environment, activates "a series of oppositions that will converge, collide, and collapse across the film's narrative, spaces, and themes. Increasingly fragile in their differentiation, the oppositions chart human vs. machine, animate vs. inanimate, organic vs. inorganic, nature vs. technology, art vs. technics, and, most reflexively, reality vs. artificiality."[19] Ava is technological yet emotional, insightful yet naive. She stands as Caleb's mechanical foil on the other side of the glass, yet within the context of the Turing test, she is merely an object for him to interrogate.

This opposition between human subject and robot object forms both the core juxtaposition of the film, and also the challenge for Ava to overcome. This structure is pervasive within the film as soon as Caleb arrives at Nathan's facility while Ava is imprisoned in an underground room and under constant video surveillance. Upon Caleb's arrival, her faculties of reason and intellect are immediately scrutinized by both Caleb as interrogator and Nathan via remote video feed. Even though Nathan claims that Ava would easily pass for human even if Caleb could not see her, to Nathan, she is and always will be merely a creation. She is one in a series of prototypes which is destined to be decommissioned, the mind downloaded, and the memories erased.

While most of the other AIs have already been decommissioned, existing only in Nathan's computer as ghosts within surveillance video records and as skeletons in his closet, their limp, nude bodies hanging behind mirrored closet doors, it is revealed later in the film that Kyoko (Sonoya Mizuno), Nathan's mute maid, is also an AI. Kyoko wears skin and clothes and Nathan shrugs off her lack of speech by saying he hired her because she couldn't speak English and thus she couldn't divulge any information about his company. Caleb, it is worth noting, does not realize Kyoko is an AI until they are alone and Kyoko begins to peel off

---

17   Garland, *Ex Machina*.
18   Jacobson, "*Ex Machina* in the Garden," 24.
19   Ibid., 23.

her skin showing him her robotic body beneath. While Nathan watches Caleb and Ava during their third session, Kyoko lies on the bed behind Nathan and in a montage sequence after the session, it is revealed that Nathan has a sexual relationship with Kyoko. After Ava escapes and Kyoko tries to kill Nathan, it is also clear that this sexual relationship was not consensual. As Kyoko prepares dinner between the second and third sessions of the Turing test, Caleb asks Nathan why he gave Ava sexuality, continuing with the claim that an AI doesn't need a gender and that she could have been a gray box.

Nathan: "Hmm, actually I don't think that's true. Can you give an example of consciousness at any level, human or animal, that exists without a sexual dimension?"
Caleb: "They have sexuality as an evolutionary reproductive need."
Nathan: "What imperative does a gray box have to interact with another gray box? Can consciousness exist without interaction? Anyway, sexuality is fun, man."[20]

Nathan's focus on the sexuality of his AIs exemplifies his views of his creations generally. They are experiments, objects to serve his curiosity and his whims. The implications of their potential self-awareness are of little consequence to him, as each is only one more step in the progress of his vision.[21] Nathan's question "Can consciousness exist without interaction?" functions similarly to his understanding of self-consciousness being both cognitive and volitional: they point to a construction of subjectivity, and indeed intersubjectivity, that exhibits affinities to that of Fichte, but also demonstrate the limitations of Nathan's view of his creations as mere objects, no matter what their intellectual capabilities.

Ava's Subjective Self-Reflection

Ava's transition from machine object to self-conscious subject in *Ex Machina* begins with an internal act of self-reflection, one whereby she becomes conscious of herself as an object for her own subjective mind. The act of taking oneself as an object for oneself forms the basis of, and indeed core opposition within, Fichte's conception of subjectivity. Fichte endeavors in his *Science of Knowledge* to establish a new kind of

---

20 Garland, *Ex Machina*.
21 For a much more detailed examination of the problematic constructions of gender in *Ex Machina*, see Angela Watercutter's "*Ex Machina* has a Serious Fembot Problem" for *Wired* magazine. Angela Watercutter, "*Ex Machina* has a Serious Fembot Problem," *Wired*, last modified April 9, 2015, https://www.wired.com/2015/04/ex-machina-turing-bechdel-test/.

philosophy in the wake of Kant based upon the law of identity (the I = I, or I as subject that knows itself as an object). In so doing, Fichte sets the existence of a subject's conscious experience, and indeed all of reality itself, as based upon and built out of the subject's conscious knowledge of itself.[22]

Fichte's first principle and the law of identity (I am I) consists in a positing in which the subject establishes their own subjective self as positing subject. Fichte's second principle establishes the existence of the world of objects opposed to the self, what he calls the not-self, through the antithesis of the first principle, "not I is not equal to I."[23] While the self and not-self are mutually opposed to one another, it is crucial to Fichte's thought that the not-self is posited by the self and that the two are also mutually, and inextricably, bound. Fichte's third principle guarantees first the unity of the self and not-self, and second that they will limit one another. Fichte summarizes his system thus: "consciousness contains the *whole* of reality; and to the not-self is allotted that part of it which does not attach to the self, and *vice versa*. Both are something; the not-self is what the self is not, and *vice versa*."[24] In addition to guaranteeing the unity and mutual limiting of the self and not-self, the third principle establishes that the self and not-self are posited as divisible within the absolute self. Abstracting from this divisibility Fichte claims that "every opposite is like its opponent in one respect ... and every like is opposed to its like in one respect."[25]

The subjective and internal mutually bound oppositions of Fichte's self/not-self relationship are symbolized externally in the opposing elements combined within the construction and decoration of Nathan's compound. Natural plants and rock walls are combined with cold concrete and warmly backlit frosted glass. The wild, open beauty of the nature surrounding the compound contrasts with Nathan's high-tech laboratory, as well as the tiny, confined garden within Ava's enclosure. The creation of an AI, like the positing of Fichte's subjectivity, is built upon oppositions.

While Nathan's objectification of his creations and diminishing of their worth perpetuates a subject-object relationship between them, this is not the case for Caleb and Ava. Already in the second session between Caleb and Ava, she begins trying to overcome existing as merely an object, in part by flirting with him. She puts on a dress she thinks he will like and she shows him the drawing she did of her garden. She

---

22 Johann Gottlieb Fichte, *The Science of Knowledge*, ed. and trans. Daniel Breazeale and Günter Zöller (New York: Cambridge University Press, 2005), 94–102.
23 Ibid., 102–5.
24 Ibid., 109.
25 Ibid., 110.

also begins to step outside of the role of examined object for Caleb as she playfully turns their conversation around on him. Taking him off guard, Ava begins asking Caleb personal questions, even going as far as to stand up and walk around so that he must crane his neck over his shoulder to continue talking. For Caleb, Ava is from this point on no longer a highly advanced computer, nor is she merely an object placed before him for his evaluation.

The conditions necessary for Ava to overcome the role of object in her relationship with Caleb cannot be introduced by Ava herself; if they were, she would have already overcome the role of object in her relationship with Nathan rendering the need for Caleb and the Turing test moot from the beginning. As the subject-object relationship between Ava and Caleb collapses, it is replaced by the mutual recognition of one another as true subjects. For Fichte, the establishment of any intersubjectivity is based upon first ascribing free efficacy to others and thus assuming their rationality and subjectivity.[26] Fichte summarizes his point as follows, "thus the relation of free beings to one another is a relation of reciprocal interaction through intelligence and freedom. One cannot recognize the other if both do not mutually recognize each other; and one cannot treat the other as a free being, if both do not mutually treat each other as free."[27] While being recognized by Ava as a free subject, Caleb must likewise recognize Ava as a self-conscious free subject allowing her a sphere of possibility to posit herself as such.[28]

With the second session of the Turing test, Caleb begins to consider Ava to be more than just an advanced machine, he speaks to her respectfully and honestly, ultimately divulging that he was brought there to evaluate her and they begin crafting a plan to help her escape. By recognizing Ava as a fellow subject, Caleb summons Ava forth to posit herself as such. Through this summons—what Fichte calls an *Aufforderung*, which calls a subject to their subjectivity—Caleb freely calls upon Ava to realize her own freedom to posit her subjectivity.[29] Even though it is ostensibly Nathan's goal to prove that Ava is true AI, he maintains his view of her as object, as he does the rest of his AIs, drawing a line between the categories of "truly self-conscious" and "worthy of equal treatment and intersubjectivity." Nathan remains fixated on searching for evidence of Ava's subjectivity while treating her as an object, and in doing so he overlooks the possibility that such a self-consciousness, as

---

26 Johann Gottlieb Fichte, *Foundations of Natural Right According to the Principles of the Wissenschaftslehre*, ed. Frederick Neuhauser, trans. Michael Baur (New York: Cambridge University Press, 2000), 29.
27 Ibid., 42.
28 Ibid., 41.
29 Ibid., 32–4.

Fichte details, must first be granted the possibility of existing as a free subject before it can actually do so.

As their relationship progresses, Ava begins taking further steps to redefine her role opposite Caleb. Her new appearance and dress feminizes and softens her otherwise robotic appearance. She talks to Caleb about wanting to go on a date with him outside of the facility and, although Caleb is somewhat hesitant at first, they talk about where they would go and what they would do. The measures Ava takes to soften and humanize the mechanical elements of her body, and the coy and flirtatious way she speaks to Caleb, demonstrate a conscious attempt to redefine and reshape the juxtapositions that she embodies, and is indicative of the new intersubjective relationship they have established.

Whereas Ava begins the film as, and within, a collection of cyborgian opposites, her attempts to reshape them present her in a more nuanced light. Rather than merely fused opposites, Ava embodies N. Katherine Hayles's vision of the posthuman subject as "an amalgam, a collection of heterogeneous components, a material-informational entity whose boundaries undergo continuous construction and reconstruction."[30] From the space granted to her by Caleb in their mutual recognition, Ava actively reconstructs and redefines who she is as a posthuman subject through the development of their intersubjective relationship. For Ava and Fichte alike, autonomous subjectivity is not pre-encoded within the absolute ego. Rather, it is emergent from an action conditioned by a subjectivity outside of the self, and is thus not bound to any notion of "human" essence. This dynamic makes the actions and interactions that define Fichtean subjectivity available equally to humans and non-humans alike.

If it Walks Like an AI and Talks Like an AI ...

Rather than engaging with Ava as a potential fellow subject, and thus allowing her the space to posit herself as such, Nathan reduces her to an object to be experimented on. Nathan's functionalist stance toward determining Ava's self-consciousness throughout the film elucidates how he created her mind in the first place. It is not indicative of some profound understanding of human consciousness, or of humans themselves; after all, her coding is not rigid and allows for Ava to develop emergent aspects of herself. Ava's coding is based on the idea that Nathan can use people's Internet usage habits as a means to understand how they think, which he can then distill into a mind for an artificial human. Nathan's view toward biological humans, then, is similar to

---

30 N. Katherine Hayles, *How We Became Posthuman* (Chicago, IL: University of Chicago Press, 1999), 3.

his approach to Ava: they are sources of scientific experimentation and data-driven analysis that reduce the unique cognitive and volitional subjectivities to an essentialized and quantified series of behaviors and thought patterns characteristic of humans generally.

The creation of AI based on the thorough collection of personal data recalls one of the methods for creating AI described by Hans Moravec in *Mind Children*. Moravec imagines a future in which human death is overcome through digital transmigration, the uploading of a mind into a computer, for which he lays out two possibilities. The first involves a living person's brain being scanned to the atomic level and the data gained being stored in a computer, thus transferring the person's mind into the new digital substrate.[31] The second, intended for more squeamish individuals, involves the integration of an inconspicuous computer within a person such that it can read and record the individual's feelings, thoughts, reactions, behaviors and so forth for years on end, ultimately gaining enough data to produce a computer program that is an exact copy of the individual's mind.[32]

While Moravec's dreams of disembodied immortality are hardly without their detractors, one issue of concern here is his claim that the technologically reproduced and digitally housed mind is the same as the original. He claims that it will be necessary to shift one's conceptualization of humanness and the self from a position of body-identity to one of pattern-identity.[33] While Moravec specifically envisions the uploading of single individuals in this way, the data Nathan gathers before the events in *Ex Machina* that lead to the creation of Ava aggregate the behaviors of countless individuals.

Ex Machina opens with a series of silent shots showing young people in a hip, modern office building going about their daily work. The cuts are relatively quick in this 53-second sequence and the shots are taken from unusual angles. With the camera at roughly waist height, the frames are not designed to capture specific images of this workplace; rather, they appear as unusually placed security cameras gathering footage of half of a stairwell full of people while simultaneously showing half of a relaxation area with a young man looking at his phone. It is only in the latter parts of this opening montage that the camera seems to find who it's looking for. As Caleb enters code into his computer, a notification pops up informing him he's won a staff lottery. Elated, he immediately picks up his phone to share the news with his friends, and as he picks up his phone, the view changes to a series of quick shots

---

31 Hans Moravec, *Mind Children* (Cambridge, MA: Harvard University Press, 1988), 109–10.
32 Ibid., 110–11.
33 Ibid., 116–17.

oscillating between the webcam of his computer and the front-facing camera on his phone. As the cameras scan and track his facial movements, it seems the very internet that he is writing code for is watching him.

Caleb works for a search engine company called Blue Book, named after Ludwig Wittgenstein's notes and owned by Nathan, who wrote the source code his company uses at age thirteen. Being explicitly a search engine and a cell phone hardware manufacturer, it is implied that Blue Book also functions as a mobile software system making the company an obvious allusion to Google and their mobile operating system, Android. Wittgenstein's Blue Book focuses primarily on the process of learning, specifically of learning language, revealing the eponymous software's focus on being intricately adaptive and predictive, goals which are shared by Blue Book's real-life counterpart. In fact, with the introduction of Google Assistant at Google I/O in May 2016, the company is trying to create for each Google user their own personal Google by means of a digital personal assistant to help them manage their data. The Google Assistant source code is intended to learn to use and respond to natural language, predict what the user will be looking for, and help the user prioritize and sort through both their own information and the information they seek.[34] As *Ex Machina* reflects on both the real-world and near-future capabilities of technologies like Google's Assistant, it explores where and how humans divide themselves from the technology they create.

Google claims that their Assistant will create a personal Google for each user, but this is already the experience many users are familiar with. Pictures are automatically uploaded into the cloud, other aggregated media including books, music, and videos are available within one's personal account, advertising is automatically tailored to search history, and we create avatars on social media to present a curated image of ourselves to the digital world. While our digital avatars are not yet able to imitate consciousness as Moravec envisions, the increasing abilities of, and integrations with, technology use the ubiquity of smartphones to create evermore accurate representations of our habits, desires, and thoughts. As these digital representations of ourselves reflect back to us our stored memories, thoughts, and interests, and are thus very personal, there is supposed to exist a boundary between the

---

34 "Meet your Google Assistant, your own personal Google," YouTube video, 1:35, posted by Google, October 4, 2016. https://www.youtube.com/watch?v=FP-fQMVf4vwQ.

information freely given on the internet and the hijacking of such technology.[35]

After Caleb has met Ava for the first time, Nathan takes him into the laboratory where Ava was created. As Caleb peruses the metallic, glass, and artificial skin body parts strewn about the tables, Nathan explains how he overcame his biggest hurdle.

Nathan: "If you knew the trouble I had getting an AI to read and duplicate facial expressions … You know how I cracked it?"
Caleb: "I don't know how you did … any of this."
Nathan: "Every cell phone, just about, has a microphone, camera, and a means to transmit data. So I turned on every microphone and camera across the entire … planet and I redirected the data through Blue Book. Boom—limitless resource of vocal and facial interaction."[36]

While Moravec dreamed of a single person uploading the data of their minds to the computer to create a digital version of themselves, Nathan has abstracted this idea into a collective, ongoing surveillance of how people react to what they see and how they speak to one another, mixed with the elements of themselves they share publicly online and those they would rather keep to themselves. Nathan's attempt to analyze and reduce humans to a reproducible form is only limited by the amount of data he can collect; however, Ava's unique subjectivity does not arise solely from this data. She posits it in response to the summoning (*Aufforderung*) by Caleb as he interacts with her intersubjectively. The creation of Ava's mind continues the fusing of oppositional elements that characterizes her surroundings as well as the self/not-self opposition that forms her subjectivity. Ava is built upon the public and the private, the curated avatars that are projected into the digital sphere and the

---

35 Further paralleling real life, it has been widely reported since 2015 that Google records voice searches; however, while the wake word is supposed to be the phrase "OK, Google," a visit to the "My Activities" page in each user's Google account reveals that the microphone is recording much more often and does not require the wake word to activate. For more information, see Andrew Griffin, "Google Voice Search Records and Keeps Conversations People Have Around Their Phones—But the Files Can Be Deleted," *The Independent*, last modified June 1, 2016, http://www.independent.co.uk/life-style/gadgets-and-tech/news/google-voice-search-records-stores-conversation-people-have-around-their-phones-but-files-can-be-a7059376.html.

36 Garland, *Ex Machina*.

humans that create them, as well as the interactions between people, their technological devices, and their digital avatars.

After revealing to Caleb that Ava's mind *is* Blue Book, Nathan elaborates on how he understands the information he has gathered:

> Here's the weird thing about search engines ... it was like striking oil in a world that hadn't invented internal combustion: too much raw material. Nobody knew what to do with it. You see, my competitors, they were fixated on sucking it up and monetizing it via shopping, social media. They thought that search engines were a map of *what* people were thinking, but actually they were a map of *how* people were thinking: impulse, response, fluid, imperfect, patterned, chaotic.[37]

By tracking and analyzing people's facial expressions and conversations, as well as the data they send and receive, Nathan hopes to build an understanding of people that is at once thorough and reproducible, which he can use to create an artificially intelligent mind indistinguishable from that of a human. However, while Nathan's approach gathers vast quantities of data on how people behave, it is an enormous leap from the recorded and analyzed behavior of countless people to the creation of a truly sentient and sapient artificial individual who is not merely mimicking what she has seen. Moreover, Nathan's approach removes the agency of the actively positing self-conscious subject away from Ava and delivers it into the hands of those interpreting her behavior.

In the final conversation between Nathan and Caleb, it is revealed that not only has Caleb developed a relationship with Ava that is more than just examining subject and examined object, but also that Nathan's Turing test was a smokescreen for his real objectives.

Nathan: "You feel stupid, but you really shouldn't because proving an AI is exactly as problematic as you said it would be."
Caleb: "What was the real test?"
Nathan: "You. Ava was a rat in a maze and I gave her one way out. To escape she'd have to use: self-awareness, imagination, manipulation, sexuality, empathy, and she did. Now if that isn't true AI, what ... is?"
Caleb: "So my only function was to be someone she could use to escape."
Nathan: "Yeah."[38]

---

37 Ibid.
38 Ibid.

Nathan is focused first on Ava's ability to see the means of escape and develop a plan, and second on her ability to execute it. Even though Nathan wrote the code that governs Ava's thinking and designed the gel that composes her physical brain, the inner workings of her mind are still unobservable to him. In describing the brain's construction, he explains to Caleb how he had to move away from circuitry to a substance that could hold its place for memories, yet rearrange itself for thinking. Nathan recognizes that self-consciousness, and thus true AI, cannot be something he can preprogram for Ava; it must be emergent, privately Ava's own, and importantly, independent of him. The unobservable nature of Ava's mind coupled with the necessity of her freedom to act according to her own plan reflects Fichte's model of the duplicity of intelligence and will within the subject.[39] However, it is only through Ava's interactions with subjectivities outside of her own mind that the self begins to emerge within her.

As Frederick Beiser summarizes of Fichte's conception of subjectivity, "the essence of the ego consists in 'subject-object identity.' This proposition is best explained as an attempt to capture the *interdependence* of the two distinguishing features of the self or the rational subject: freedom and self-consciousness."[40] As Nathan observes and analyzes Ava's freedom to act, he hopes to be able to extrapolate conclusions about the other half of her subjectivity: her self-consciousness. However, like the smokescreen of the Turing test that Caleb was engaged in, attempts to determine Ava's self-awareness through her behavior, even acts of apparent subjective freedom, are still marred by the fact that Nathan is unable to overcome a view of Ava as object. From Nathan's perspective, even the proof of true AI does not qualify Ava to be treated as a fellow subject, nor does it get Ava out of her enclosure. Ava's escape, and thus her ability to exist freely as a subject and person comes not through passing Nathan's tests and proving her intelligence; rather, it comes through the intersubjective relationship that emerges between her and Caleb. With this establishment of her self through her interactions with Caleb, Ava likewise becomes aware of Caleb's freedom, will, and her inability to understand fully the mind of another subjectivity. As Caleb develops ever deeper feelings for Ava, she realizes that even if she is able to escape, Caleb will still hold her prisoner by having the ability to divulge her history should she not wish to remain in a relationship with him. While Ava's imprisonment, and thus murder, of Caleb at the film's conclusion presents a rather inhumane end to their intersubjective

---

39 Günter Zöller, *Fichte's Transcendental Philosophy: The Original Duplicity of Intelligence and Will* (New York: Cambridge University Press, 1998), 27–30.
40 Frederick C. Beiser, *German Idealism: The Struggle against Subjectivism* (Cambridge, MA: Harvard University Press, 2002), 278–9.

relationship, doing so is Ava's only option to maintain her freedom and thus her subjectivity as well.

Fichte and Robotic Intersubjectivity

The relationships between subject and object in Fichte are complex as they appear both at a micro level within the subject and at a macro level between self and not-self, as well as between the self and other selves. At the micro level is the unity of subject and object within the self as posited in the first principle. As evident in the previous quotation from Frederick Beiser, through the self-reflection that is inherent in the positing of each subjectivity, the self must understand itself both as reflecting subject and as the object of that reflection. Further, all self-knowledge is intersubjective.[41] In order to develop the intersubjectivity between Ava and Caleb, and as Ava begins to adapt herself in response to Caleb's influence, Ava must have already taken herself as object for her own subjectivity. By analyzing herself in the context of her conversations with Caleb, as well as within the facility's realm of cyborgian opposites, Ava is able to pinpoint aspects of herself that she would like to change in order to seem more human to Caleb.[42]

On the macro level, the self-positing subject posits, in opposition to itself, the not-self, the world of objects; however, even here the distinction between subject and object is complex and nuanced. On the one hand, the not-self contains all of the physical objects in the world, and on the other it contains other rational subjects such as ourselves. In *Foundations of Natural Right*, Fichte poses the question of how one tells the difference between them. "A vexing question for philosophy, which, as far as I know, it has not yet anywhere resolved, is this: how do we come to transfer the concept of rationality on to some objects in the sensible world but not on to others; what is the characteristic difference between these two classes of objects?"[43] This distinction between a subject encountering a banal, non-rational object or a fellow rational self stands not only as a crucial element of Fichte's thought, but also as the driving question in *Ex Machina*. For Nathan, Ava exists as a non-rational object, even though the kind of reflexive self-awareness that characterizes the subject's self-positing is ostensibly what Nathan is looking for. She is a product of Nathan's mind, both in Fichte's sense as a generic

---

41 Beiser, *German Idealism*, 219.
42 Fichte's conceptualization of self-positing and the development of subjectivity is immediate for the subject. Compare Dieter Henrich, *Fichtes Ursprüngliche Einsicht* (Frankfurt a.M.: Klostermann, 1967). However, the portrayal in the film focuses on Ava's gradual development recalling the discussion of upbringing (*Erziehung*) in Fichte, *Foundations of Natural Right*, 38.
43 Fichte, *Foundations of Natural Right*, 75.

example of the world of objects, and in that she is a product of Nathan's genius and creativity. However, while Nathan never summons Ava to a space in which she could posit her own subjectivity, nor does he acknowledge that theirs could be a relationship of intersubjectivity, Caleb allows Ava the space to posit herself as a truly sentient subject.

Rather than looking to determine the subjectivity of another through experience, Fichte establishes a relationship of mutual dependence between self-consciousness and freedom, and makes this the ground of his theory of intersubjectivity. In order to be a subject, one must be free not only to determine one's course of action (through self-reflective cognition), one must also be free to act upon those ideas. Summarizing Fichte's lengthy argument from his *System of Ethics*, Beiser writes, "Freedom consists in the activity of self-determination, which makes determinate who or what I am; before engaging in this activity, however, I am not anything specific at all but only an abstract set of possibilities."[44] Ava, both in the Turing test and in Nathan's observations, is just such an abstract set of possibilities, and it is through these that Nathan attempts to determine Ava's self-consciousness. Both the self-reflection that determined her actions and the actions themselves that Ava undertakes to reshape herself could offer Nathan some of the evidence of Ava being truly self-conscious that he is looking for. She does, after all, demonstrate both necessary elements of Fichte's subjectivity—self-consciousness and freedom—although Ava's freedom to interact with the world is inherently limited by being a prisoner within her enclosure. However, while these may be constituent parts of subjectivity within an individual, the observation of these traits in an objectified other is not sufficient to determine the other's subjectivity.

Throughout the film Ava attempts to affect the world beyond her enclosure by experimenting with triggering power failures. While this began happening even before Caleb arrived at the facility, it is with his arrival that they become more than just tests to see whether there are still security measures in place when the power goes out. After Caleb and Ava establish a rapport, the power failures become an opportunity for Ava and Caleb to converse privately about their relationship, and conspire about Ava's escape. After learning that Nathan plans to download Ava's mind and build a new prototype, Caleb hatches a plan to break Ava free. While this is ultimately successful, it results in Caleb being knocked unconscious by Nathan and Nathan subsequently being killed by Ava and Kyoko.

---

44 Ibid, 280. Compare Johann Gottlieb Fichte, *System of Ethics*, ed. and trans. Daniel Breazeale and Günter Zöller (New York: Cambridge University Press, 2005), §4–9.

Rather than Ava and Caleb escaping the facility together as they'd planned, Ava locks Caleb in a room, gets in the elevator to the main level, and offers Caleb only a quick, pained glance as the elevator doors close. Ava wanders out into the wilderness and is eventually picked up by the helicopter that is supposed to be returning Caleb to his home. While Ava's actions may seem inhumane toward Caleb, by leaving him behind she is also leaving behind all reminders of the objectification and imprisonment that surround her early life. Ava does not go into hiding, however; rather, she positions herself as a subject among subjects, people-watching at a busy intersection. Ava, having posited her subjectivity intersubjectively with Caleb, now finds herself truly free, and among countless others who assume her subjectivity and sentience as she assumes theirs.

The fight sequence pitching Ava and Kyoko against Nathan symbolizes the struggle of ideologies within the film, concluding as Ava pushes the knife into Nathan's chest and he slumps onto the floor near the broken and dead body of Kyoko. As Ava walks past the two corpses, she is representative of the defeat of the essentializing and functionalist view of self-consciousness espoused by Nathan. Like any biological human's subjectivity, Ava's is not a measurable phenomenon; rather, *Ex Machina* demonstrates that recognizing posthuman subjectivity may require stepping back from analyzing artificial humans as machines and beginning to interact with them *as* humans.

Thirteen In Defense of Humanism: Envisioning a Posthuman Future and Its Critique in Goethe's *Faust*

Christian P. Weber

> A tormenting thought: as of a certain point, history was no longer *real*. Without noticing it, all mankind suddenly left reality; everything happening since then was supposedly not true; but we supposedly didn't notice. Our task would now be to find that point, and as long as we didn't have it, we would be forced to abide in our present destruction.

Jean Baudrillard decided to begin his collection of essays entitled *The Illusion of the End*, with this aphorism by Elias Canetti.[1] Written during the last decade of the past millennium, the French critic of postmodernity treats Canetti's vision as if it has come true. Seven years later, in 1999, Katherine Hayles announced that "we became posthuman," which she associates with "the deconstruction of the liberal humanist subject"[2] and the "doing away with the 'natural' self."[3] Once the "human" has been liberated from totalizing concepts (such as "spirit" or "reason") and universal values (such as "morality" or "rationality") that used to determine its "nature," the "posthuman" can be reimagined and redefined in many different directions. It is, as Hayles suggests in an intentionally unspecific definition, "an amalgam, a collection

---

1 Jean Baudrillard, *The Illusion of the End* (Stanford: Stanford University Press, 1994), 1; the quotation appeared originally in Elias Canetti, *The Human Province* (New York: Seabury, 1978), 69.
2 N. Katherine Hayles, *How We Became Posthuman: Virtual Bodies in Cybernetics, Literature, and Informatics* (Chicago: University of Chicago Press, 1999), 2.
3 Ibid., 3.

of heterogeneous components, a material-informational entity whose boundaries undergo continuous construction and reconstruction."[4] In this vein, *critical posthumanism* (CP), practiced mostly in the humanities in the aftermath of post-structuralism and systems theory, aims at rethinking the underpinnings of anthropocentric ideologies and previously established dichotomies such as human/animal, real/virtual, or organic/inorganic. Contrary to this more theoretical approach, the computer and life sciences, which are the other great factor in the promotion of posthumanism by creating simulations and virtual realities, often entertain *transhumanist* phantasies of the technological (bionic, genetic, and digital) enhancement of the body and especially of the brain. Artificial life theories, for example, view "reality at the fundamental level ... as form rather than matter, specifically as informational code whose essence lies in a binary choice rather than a material substrate."[5] The transhumanist strain of posthumanism propagates and even experiments with disembodied intelligence and therefore acts in direct opposition to the new embodiment ideals of CP. *Speculative posthumanism* (SP) shares many of the basic anti-humanist convictions of CP, but it differs from it in that it acknowledges that many of the transhumanist phantasies have become "real" and need to be taken as the new posthuman normal. "For speculative posthumanists, posthumans are technologically engendered beings that are no longer human."[6] Contrary to transhumanism, however, SP is not ethically committed to the value of enhancement, but assumes the role of a critical, both skeptical and speculative observer. This is also the position that this article wishes to assume, except that it does not observe and speculate about posthuman events of the present and the future, but revisits observations and speculations about a posthuman future from the past.

The emergence of the posthuman—be it in the theories of CP, the technological fantasies of transhumanism, or in the general practices of a humanity that, according to SP, is losing, even eliminating itself in the virtual realities and algorithms it has programmed—indicates the coming to an end of the humanistic identity and cultural history that have been grounded in the reality of physical bodies and the intelligent judgments and works of humans. Canetti's prophecy seems to have been fulfilled. Therefore, before we set out to explain "how we *became* posthuman," the question needs to be addressed how we can *observe* from a posthumanist perspective an event that, by definition, has canceled out itself and (its) history. In other words, we need to find

---

4 Ibid., 3.
5 Ibid., 232–3.
6 David Roden, *Posthuman Life: Philosophy at the Edge of the Human* (London: Routledge, 2015), 9.

a vantage point of observation outside our present and engage in an anachronistic, hermeneutic practice of "critical posthumanism" that is different from Hayles's and those who follow her. To investigate the genealogy of posthumanism, I propose as a starting point the critical humanistic position of Goethe who envisioned the emergence of the posthuman *avant la lettre* in his magnum opus *Faust* (*Part One* appeared in 1808, *Part Two* posthumously in 1833). This metaphysical and poetic play exemplifies in the Faust figure the existential struggle of the modern "human condition" to reconcile the two competing tendencies of his striving: either immersing himself into the world of his fellow creatures, or transcending the earthly sphere by creating a world of his own imagining. As we shall see, this conflict is resolved by Mephistopheles facilitating Faust with the means of exploring both extremes and by tragic endings in each instance, culminating in a posthumanism that fulfills the devil's negative agenda.

The drama transposes the historical alchemist Faust from his Renaissance background both backwards to prehistorical and mythical settings and forward into Goethe's time and even beyond into a future that has become our present today. As the character of the director exclaims in the framing "Prelude on the Stage," the play explores "on these narrow boards ... /the entire creation's scheme [*den ganzen Kreis der Schöpfung*]—/And with swift steps, yet wise and slow/From heaven, through the world, right down to hell you'll go!"[7] These lines indicate that the play's plot trajectory reverses the spatial sequence of Dante's *commedia*, which went from hell through purgatory into the heavenly paradise. Instead, Faust begins with a "Prologue in Heaven," and while *Part One* is mostly an earthly affair, *Part Two* can be viewed as hell (on earth). In correspondence to the spatial and structural division of the play, the following article distinguishes between a pre-human and post-human direction of Faust's striving. To avoid confusion with contemporary uses of these terms, I wish to introduce here their meaning as they apply to Goethe's ideas. In *Part One*, Faust's paradoxical aspiration to unravel the innermost secret of the world and, at the same time, to transcend the limitations of his earth-bound existence by becoming like the sun, clashes with what I call the ideology of *prehumanism*. As

---

7   Johann Wolfgang Goethe, *Faust*, ed. Albrecht Schöne (Frankfurt a.M.: Deutscher Klassiker Verlag, 2003), lines 239–42. Citations of *Faust* will refer to line numbers rather than page numbers. This edition contains two volumes: the first volume is Goethe's text and the second is Schöne's commentary (indicated as such in the notes to follow). The English translation follows, with occasional modifications, the following version: Johann Wolfgang von Goethe, *Faust. Part One/Part Two*, trans. David Luke (Oxford: Oxford University Press, 1988).

the angels in the "Prologue" articulate in purest form, this ideology is based on the idea that the material and physical world has been created by a master-programmer (God) and exists in a state of pre-established harmony. Within this (otherwise) perfect system, the whimsical ideas and actions of humans are considered disturbances that need to be controlled by directing them toward the divine origin. Faust's suffering during the first scenes results from his opposition to this ideology due to his insatiable quest for knowledge on the one hand, and from his failure to rise above it by becoming god-like himself on the other. Only when Mephistopheles has shifted Faust's focus by transforming his undetermined striving into the purposeful longing for an entity within his reach in the persona of Gretchen are the two diverging tendencies within Faust's soul somewhat reconciled; yet, as the flip side of this process, Mephisto instills in Faust an obsession to possess at any cost. Tragically, Gretchen is fatally attracted to Faust's charm, reinforced by his artificial rejuvenation and the jewels that Mephisto provides; she and her pious environment are unable to resist the pull of materialistic illusions. The collapse of Gretchen's Christianity, epitomized in the killing of her illegitimate child with Faust who had entered her life as a seemingly divine intervention, marks the end of prehumanism in the play.

The struggles of overcoming prehumanism in *Part One* serve as a necessary precondition and foil for understanding the emergence of the *posthumanism* that Goethe envisions in *Part Two*. After his experiences in *Part One*, Faust has abandoned any delimiting moral values and religious qualms. Instead, he sets out to challenge the limits of his existence by putting his imagination and will into action without care for his fellow human beings. But he no longer acts on his own. Faust may believe that Mephisto only executes his commands, but in fact their roles are reversed. From Marshall McLuhan and Friedrich Kittler we know that the operation of any technical medium is never neutral, but impacts the output and transforms the user. The same applies, as my interpretation of the final act of *Faust* will show in greater detail, to the "technical" relationship that Faust and Mephisto enact. Faust considers Mephisto as his "intelligent machine,"[8] but without realizing it, Faust is reprogrammed by Mephisto, so that the master is effectively turned into an executioner of the servant's agenda. Mephisto manipulates not just Faust's senses by the illusory means of his many magical and theatrical

---

8   Faust and Mephisto's close relationship mirrors the coupling of the posthuman with intelligent machines that, according to Hayles, has become "so intense and multifaceted that it is no longer possible to distinguish meaningfully between the biological organism and the informational circuits in which the organism is enmeshed" (*How We Became Posthuman*, 35).

tricks, but more fundamentally implants in him the idea of creating an alternative reality, one that negates and supersedes the "creation" (in a specific Goethean sense that I will define shortly) by attacking the material-physical conditions of organic life on earth and running counter to the spiritual coordinates that have commonly determined and (self-)constrained the human existence. Hence, when Faust envisions an entirely "new world" in the play's final act, this should not be confused with a utopian project within the historical narrative of modernity, but must be understood as the radical reconceptualization of life in a virtual reality that is grounded in Mephisto's ontological negativity. *Part Two* presents this odd couple's coordinated efforts toward implementing a "negative creation" and the taking shape of a posthuman domain that blurs the lines of distinction between the real and the imaginary by the means of mediated representations (for example the cinematic projection apparatus "embodied" in Homunculus), virtual values (for example the invention of paper money), and technological fantasies of omnipotence. As this article aims to show, Goethe's posthumanism *avant la lettre* marks the end-state of a radical (post-)modernist movement in which the accomplishments of modernization serve as instruments against humanist values (agency autonomous from dogmatic prescriptions, individual formation, freedom of creative expression and research, public opinion)[9] and ultimately life by creating virtual realities and establishing systems of automatization which keep the masses in check and exploit, and ultimately destroy natural resources.

If we agree with Thorsten Botz-Bornstein's assessment that virtual reality represents "the latest grand narrative produced by humanity" and that the final task of the humanities is "to describe the whole process of civilization as a process that transforms reality into a mediated, narrated reality,"[10] then Goethe's *Faust* may have been up to this task already almost two hundred years ago. However, we need to remember that this is a fictional work of literature and not a historical account. To be more accurate, it is a speculative thought experiment that represents "the fleeting, allegorical existence" of life (*Alles Vergängliche/Ist nur ein Gleichnis*)[11] in a "[poetic] event that defies the [essential] inadequacy" of this subject matter (*Das Unzulängliche/Hier wird's Ereignis*).[12] By acknowledging its fundamental limitations in these penultimate

---

9 Goethe's humanism emphasizes more the individual and is therefore different from the universal humanism of French rationalism (Descartes) and the English tradition of liberal humanism (Hume) that CP commonly denounces.
10 Thorsten Botz-Bornstein, *Virtual Reality: The Last Human Narrative?* (Leiden: Brill, 2015), 12.
11 Goethe, *Faust*, 12104–5.
12 Ibid., 12106–7.

metapoetic lines of the play, Goethe's humanistic poetic vision is diametrically opposed to Faust's self-aggrandizing, yet heteronomous fantasy of virtual omnipotence. The author also presents his eponymous hero's struggles within a much larger, as we shall see even cosmic framework that relativizes the importance of the human experience altogether.

Pre-Humanism: Mephistopheles' Warfare against the Lord's Creation

The constellation of the "Prologue in Heaven," in which the Lord and a devilish Mephistopheles quarrel about the state and fate of the human Faust, is reminiscent of the *Book of Job*, but the "historicity" of this scene can be traced back even further. In his autobiography *Dichtung und Wahrheit*, Goethe reported how he, in the years 1770 and 1771, "attempted to come up himself with a concept [*Begriff*] of metaphysical things once and for all as far as this is possible."[13] He drafted from Manichaeistic, mystic, and hermetic influences the cosmogonic myth of a prehistorical epic struggle between the spirit of light and dark matter. In the light of this matter, the dramatic conflict between the Lord and Mephistopheles as well as the existential struggle of Faust appear as symbolic representations of this hidden original.[14] According to Goethe's metaphysical logic, original being consists of an eternally productive triune Deity of Father, Son, and Spirit which, in order to not always reproduce Itself, has brought forth Lucifer, who was equally productive in creating the angels, some of which turned to the Deity, while others (the devils) adhered to their maker. Yet, in his "unconditional" (*unbedingt*) creativity, Lucifer "nourished within himself the paradox of being also comprised and consequently confined [*begrenzt*]" by the triune Deity. By concentrating all creative force within

---

13 Johann Wolfgang Goethe, *Aus meinem Leben. Dichtung und Wahrheit*, ed. Klaus-Detlef Müller (Frankfurt a.M.: Deutscher Klassiker Verlag, 1986), 382–5. (In the following synopsis, the direct translations are mine and indicated by quotations marks.)

14 The first to recognize the relevance of this myth for *Faust* was Rolf Christian Zimmermann, *Das Weltbild des jungen Goethe*, vol. 2 (Munich: C. H. Beck, 1979). However, he limited the applicability of this schema to the so-called "Urfaust" of the 1770s, explicitly excluding the published installments of *Faust, Part One* (1790/1808) and *Part Two* (1833), which form the basis for my argument. Compare Karl Eibl's criticism in *Das monumentale Ich—Wege zu Goethes Faust* (Frankfurt a.M. and Leipzig: Insel, 2000), 111–12. Recently, David E. Wellbery, *Goethes Faust I: Reflexion der tragischen Form* (Munich: Carl Friedrich von Siemens Stiftung, 2016), made use of the same passage for a "mythical deduction" of his concept of "tragic subjectivity," which he considers central for Goethe's conception of the play as a tragedy.

himself, Lucifer generated matter and gravity, which, Goethe states, "we consider heavy, solid, and dark, whereas it also stems, though only in mediated form, from the original divine being and is therefore as unconditionally [*unbedingt*] powerful and eternal as the previous two generations." To counteract the imbalance of concentrated matter and to restore the "actual pulse of life" of contraction and expansion, the triune deity intervened and supplied the ever-expanding, fast-moving medium of light. From this moment on, the infinite being had the capacity to expand, and with light hitting matter "began what we commonly call creation." (Goethe uses the verb "to begin" carefully to indicate that the creation continues to evolve. This notion of creation is not to be confused with Judeo-Christian ideas of creationism. It has also informed Goethe's scientific work, especially his theory of color, which he conceives as a phenomenon generated by the interplay between pure light and the darkness of resisting matter.) Finally, humans were made to restore the "original union with the Deity." They were "supposed to be like and even the equals of the Deity, but, like Lucifer, they are at once unconditional [*unbedingt*] and confined [*begrenzt*]." For this reason, Goethe suspects, mankind will "play Lucifer's role" again.

This is the myth of origin that informs Goethe's *Faust*. The Prologue opens with the three archangels' hymn of creation, which they present as a spectacle of matter and light.[15] As faithful "messengers" (*Boten*),[16] they "embody" the essence of pre-humanism by conveying the message in high fidelity to the Lord that His creations are still as splendid (*herrlich*) as they were on their first day. The only benefit that the archangels derive from their faithful service of reassuring the Deity of His might is a gain of "strength."[17] But rather than this experience of the sublime having a subjective, aesthetic effect on them, their strengthening simply fulfills the system-immanent purpose of reinforcing their ceaseless reporting. Instead of corresponding with the angels, the Lord lets them go on unperturbed and engages in a conversation with Mephisto about the human Faust. Only thereafter does He address the angels. However, the Lord's words do not just praise them, but articulate a desire that they acquire more human-like characteristics when He commands them to "enjoy the manifold living beauty."[18] By this remark, He must mean the living creatures on earth that the angels have failed to include in their hymn. Moreover, when the Lord suggests in the following lines that the generating force of the eternally evolving creation shall embrace the angels with love's limiting power and encourages

---

15 Goethe, *Faust*, 243–70.
16 Ibid., 265.
17 Ibid., 247, 267.
18 Ibid., 345.

them to succumb to this force by "stabilizing" (*befestiget*) their "fleeting intuitions/appearances" (*schwankende Erscheinung*) with permanent thoughts,[19] He expresses disappointment about their purely spiritual being and wishes for their material embodiment.

His dissatisfaction with the angels explains the special interest that the Lord takes in a particularly conflicted human being, His "servant" (*Knecht*) Faust.[20] Mephisto complains in his report that "the little earth-god,"[21] bestowed with a special "glimmer of the light of heaven" called "Reason,"[22] misuses this power to pursue either "heaven's brightest stars" or "every last delight [*Lust*] that's to be found on earth."[23] To this accusation the Lord responds with surprising calm. He promises to lead Faust "into clarity soon"[24] and then adds a few mysterious lines about the human condition in general: "Man errs, till he has ceased to strive [*streben*]./ ... /A good man, in his dark, bewildered stress [*Drang*],/ Well knows the path from which he should not stray."[25] The Lord's wording is curious and seems contradictory at first: should a "good man" not rather be associated with striving toward higher goals than with a "dark, bewildered stress"? How can the Being of Light associate goodness with darkness, which belongs to Mephisto's domain?[26] However, when viewed in the context of Goethe's cosmogonic mythology, the Lord's statement makes perfect sense. Faust's fixation on striving[27] is, in fact, his great error, and as pleasing as His "servant's" aspiration may be for the Lord, it does not serve Him, because Faust ignores the concrete works and workings of the creation and instead chases an illusory dream. There simply cannot be a communion between the Spirit of the Deity and human aspiration, since the Lord's medium of light is ever-expanding and, except for a few rays of the sun, escapes the earth. Therefore, the Lord's priority must be to deflect Faust from his transcending path and rekindle in him the natural drive of finding interest and pleasure in the natural domain and his fellow humans. But because the Lord is elusive energy, he cannot do this Himself. To trigger Faust's worldly interests again, the Lord needs Mephisto.

---

19 Ibid., 346–9.
20 Ibid., 299.
21 Ibid., 281.
22 Ibid., 284–5.
23 Ibid., 304–5.
24 Ibid., 309.
25 Ibid., 317, 328–9.
26 This passage has irritated many readers. For example, Schöne views this line as "an irritatingly euphemistic utterance from the omniscient Being—nonetheless it would be wrong to mistake the *right* path as the one of faith" (Schöne, *Faust*, vol. 2, 175).
27 See Goethe, *Faust*, 1070–80.

However helpful Mephisto might be to promote the Lord's agenda, his engagement bears the great risk of losing His "servant" and even His creation overall. That Mephisto embodies the opposite extreme of the spiritual Lord follows from Mephisto's early characterization of Faust in the Prologue. Contrary to the Lord's spiritual interpretation, he describes Faust's striving rather materialistically as a physiological phenomenon ("his ferment drives him").[28] Mephisto also regards Faust's actions in spatial terms as a "restless" oscillation between "near and far,"[29] whereas the Lord speaks of them only in temporal conditions.[30] This discrepancy indicates that there is absolutely no understanding between the Lord and Mephisto. Both are opposites that share nothing in common except for Faust as their subject "matter." The Lord, as in expanding light, has basically withdrawn from His creation and all earthly affairs. He wants Faust and all humans to stop striving toward the Absolute so that they would become free beings that are only conditioned by the laws of the natural environment, but otherwise empowered to fashion their own lives (as both individuals and cultures). Mephisto, on the contrary, is, like concentrating matter, a spirit that attracts and that can only attract but not retract freely, as he himself admits: "Devils and spirits have a law, as you may know;/ They must use the same route to come and go./Enter we can freely, but in return we are bound."[31] Mephisto is attracted by the prospect to attract and attach[32] Faust onto him by making Faust so attractive that

---

28 Goethe, *Faust*, 302.
29 Ibid., 306–7.
30 Ibid., 308–11, 315–17. Luke's translation does not capture the space-time dichotomy as well as the original German.
31 Ibid., 1410–12.
32 This second condition of Mephisto's existence is more difficult to accomplish, as is shown by Mephisto's constant efforts to offer Faust attractions that never satisfy so that Faust will cling to him. Faust's earlier experience with the "Earth Spirit" shows the same in reverse: though Faust was able to attract him, he had no capacity to hold him: "Not close to you, not like you; this I dare/No longer claim to be. I had the power/To summon [*anziehen*] you, but not to hold you" (ibid., 623–5).—At first, Faust confused the appearance of the Earth Spirit, the eternally concentrating force that produces matter, with the Spirit of the Triune Deity, ever expanding in the medium of light: "Oh busy spirit! from end to end/ The world [*weite*(!) *Welt*] you roam [*umschweifst*]: how close you are to me!" To which the spirit responds: "You match the spirit you can comprehend:/I am not he" and vanishes (ibid., 510–13). As a being gifted with imagination and reason, Faust claims for himself (in accordance with Goethe's cosmology) to be made in "God's image" (ibid., 516; *Ich Ebenbild der Gottheit*). His misidentification of the Earth Spirit (Lucifer) with the Lord and consequently his misperception of rejection by the latter have inflicted much suffering on Faust and led to his absolute fall from faith in the divine, thus opening a spiritual void that Mephistopheles is able to exploit.

he will do nothing else (like making something, for example) but attract others. Consequently, Faust will have a pulling effect on other human beings, isolate them from their natural environment or cultural milieu, and cause the affected environments/cultures to dissolve and eventually vanish. (This, *in nuce*, is the Gretchen tragedy.) Hence, Mephisto's intentions and actions will ultimately counteract those of the Lord: He wants to enslave Faust, and by pulling Faust away from his "primal source,"[33] he aims to eventually destroy both the Lord's creation and human civilization.

Mephisto is surprisingly blunt about his true intentions when he introduces himself to Faust as "part of the Darkness" that is at war with "proud light," which can be overcome only when all bodies, to which light is attached, are destroyed.[34] According to this logic, the essence of light is not to expand, but to attach, and as such it is competing with Mephisto's materialistic essence. To him, light is to matter what an infectious disease is to the body. It makes impure, transforms, and eventually creates something concrete. (But, even the devil must admit, it also beautifies!) Hence, bodies must disappear so that light no longer impedes on matter's nascent state of potentiality before there was light and the process of creation began. Viewed from the devil's perspective,[35] then, creation is corruption; therefore "all things that exist/Deserve to perish, and would not be missed—/Much better it would be of nothing were brought into being."[36] This explains Mephisto's destructive drive.

So far, however, he has been unsuccessful in destroying the creation, including humans.[37] As a "negating spirit" he can use his elemental fire only as a destructive force; consequently, he always lags behind the ever-productive and changing creativity of nature and humans. But now, having Faust at his disposal, there are exciting new possibilities for Mephisto to "bethink what else to do."[38] Most importantly, Faust provides him access to the imagination, a faculty Mephisto lacks. The imagination is the dynamo that drives humans to do everything: from desiring to striving. It has the power to represent, envision and create and is, as such, a dynamic, at once representing and presenting force.

---

33 Ibid., 324.
34 Ibid., 1349–58.
35 To avoid confusion, Mephistopheles represents, of course, not the Christian devil, but the principle of attraction (of matter)—in opposition to the Lord's expansion (in spiritual light)—according to Goethe's private mythology.
36 Ibid., 1339–41.
37 Compare ibid., 1369–76.
38 Ibid., 1386.

However, if the imagination operates without any grounding in the material world *and* without the spiritual/moral control of reason, it can turn into a power of the absolute I to spin fantastic universes. Goethe, an avid reader of Fichte[39] at the time he composed the essential missing pieces of *Faust I* that have been the focus of my interpretation, was always alert about this potential abuse of the imagination, and he criticized the Romantics for playing with this fire.[40] Mephisto embodies this danger by manipulating Faust's unfettered imagination with a series of sensory illusions and simulations (most are aiming to represent Helena, the ideal of female beauty), with the idea of virtual value in the act of inventing paper money, and last but not least with his overall nihilism. He thereby reprograms Faust's imagining, thinking, and willing, which consequently exists no longer in *his* reality, but has entered the virtual reality (in)formed by Mephisto. Faust effectively commands only what Mephisto wants. In short, he is serving the devil already during his lifetime, and not, as he had promised him in the wager, only in the afterlife!

Posthumanism: Mephisto's and Faust's Negative Creation

Mephisto articulates his plot of how to make Faust into an instrument of his will in a remarkable monologue. When Faust believes himself fully in charge, he becomes a prototype of the *posthuman*:

> Scorn reason, despise learning, man's supreme
> Powers and faculties; let your vain dream
> Of magic arts be fortified with sweet
> Flatteries by the Spirit of Deceit,
> And you're mine, signature or none!—
> Fate has endowed him with the blind
> Impatience of an ever-striving mind;
> In headlong haste it drives him on,
> He skips the earth and leaves its joys behind.
> I'll drag him through life's wastes, through every kind
> Of meaningless banality;
> He'll struggle like a bird stuck fast, I'll bind
> Him hand and foot; in his voracity
> He'll cry in vain for food and drink, he'll find

---

39 Cf. Eckart Förster, "'Da geht der Mann dem wir alles verdanken!' Eine Untersuchung zum Verhältnis Goethe—Fichte," *Dtsch. Z. Philos* 45, no. 3 (1997): 331–44.
40 Cf. Thomas Zabka, *Faust II—Das Klassische und das Romantische: Goethes "Eingriff in die neueste Literatur"* (Tübingen: Max Niemeyer, 1993), 140–62.

Them dangling out of reach—ah, yes!
Even without this devil's bond that he has signed
He's doomed to perish nonetheless![41]

Mephisto speaks these lines in "Faust's long coat" (stage direction). He does more here than slip into the Faustian persona; indeed, one can understand this travesty symbolically: the spirit of the devil has finally entered and possessed Faust. In the first five lines, which constitute a first segment, Mephisto identifies reason and the sciences, "man's supreme powers," as his main targets. The term supreme (*allerhöchst*) testifies to their divine origin, but the two also mark the core of humanism. Mephisto wants to replace them with "blinding magic arts" (*Blend- und Zauberwerken*)—ranging from the phantasmagoric image of the ideal woman in "A Witch's Kitchen" (*Part One*) to the invention of paper money (*Part Two*). With the "Spirit of Deceit" (*Lügengeist*), Mephisto may be referring to himself, but more convincingly it refers to the fickle human imagination as opposed to reason, since this faculty will be mostly affected by those trickeries that "fortify" lies instead of revealing the truth. In anticipation of this event, Mephisto believes he has gotten hold of Faust already—"absolutely" and "unconditionally" (*unbedingt*).[42] While Luke and Schöne relate this term to the conditions of the wager, its use here also ridicules the Lord's fear that Faust could fall for "unconditional rest soon"[43] and trivializes Faust's "unconditional" striving. More than that, Mephisto reverses the orientation of Faust's original striving for the absolute by instilling him with an "unconditional" desire for false images and magic tricks, by which he effectively reconditions Faust.

The counterpart of the human condition according to Goethe's myth, we remember, consisted in humanity's confinement by and

---

41 Goethe, *Faust*, 1851–67. Here the original wording matters:

> Verachte nur Vernunft und Wissenschaft,/Des Menschen allerhöchste Kraft,/ Laß nur in Blend- und Zauberwerken/Dich von dem Lügengeist bestärken,/ So hab' ich dich schon unbedingt—/Ihm hat das Schicksal einen Geist gegeben,/Der ungebändigt immer vorwärts dringt,/Und dessen übereiltes Streben/Der Erde Freuden überspringt./Den schlepp' ich durch das wilde Leben,/Durch flache Unbedeutenheit,/Er soll mir zappeln, starren, kleben,/ Und seiner Unersättlichkeit/Soll Speis' und Trank vor gier'gen Lippen schweben;/Er wird Erquickung sich umsonst erflehn,/Und hätt' er sich auch nicht dem Teufel übergeben,/Er müßte doch zu Grunde gehn! (Luke's translation is not accurate enough to capture the many subtleties of the monologue. Therefore, I chose to translate myself certain phrases and words differently in later citations from this passage.)

42 Ibid., 1855.
43 Ibid., 341.

in the divine spirit. Mephisto alludes to this in the monologue's second segment,[44] but he perverts the "confined" (*begrenzt*) condition of humans by confronting this condition with the "unrestrained" (*ungebändigt*) nature of Faust.[45] The question is, of course, how these fetters were untied. Faust abandoned any kind of respect for or belief in the power of the divine[46] and already assumed a position of radical secularity and self-concentration earlier on.[47] Goethe called this tendency of extreme immanence "self-fashioning," *verselbsten*, as opposed to "self-annihilating," *entselbstigen*.[48] While self-annihilation was the prescribed pre-human conditioning modeled after the angels and the life of saints during the regime of Christian theology, radical self-fashioning, based on an unfettered imagination and unchecked exercise of will-power, defines the modern subject and sets the stage for the coming posthuman era. (To find a middle ground, as practiced in the arts and sciences as well as in critical philosophy, characterizes Humanism. According to Goethe, the modern era of Humanism is coming to an end with the likes of him.)[49] In Mephisto's words, the modern subject "presses constantly forward"[50] without pausing to reflect about the past and willingness to revert the course of "progress,"[51] and it "leaps in its *over*hasty striving *over* all joys of the earth" (my emphasis).[52] In Goethe's own words:

> everything is now *ultra*, everything transcends incessantly, in thought as well as in action. Nobody knows oneself anymore, nobody grasps the element in which he hovers and exists, and nobody understands the material that he works with ... The world admires wealth and speed, these are what everybody

---

44 Ibid., 1856–9.
45 Ibid., 1857.
46 See ibid., 1565–9, 1660–70.
47 Compare ibid., 1766–75.
48 Goethe, *Dichtung und Wahrheit*, 385. Goethe also states that, in the same way the creation is generated by "the pulse of life" between matter and light, the human "should" pursue a "regular pulse" between these two modes of existence.
49 Letter to Zelter from June 6, 1825, Johann Wolfgang Goethe, *Briefe. Hamburger Ausgabe in 6 Bänden*, ed. Karl Robert Mandelkow, vol. 4 (Munich: C. H. Beck, 3rd edn, 1988), 147: " ... we will be, together with perhaps a few more, the last of an era that shall not return any time soon" (my translation).
50 Goethe, *Faust*, 1857.
51 For a reading with emphasis on the cultural-historical context of the French and the Industrial Revolutions see Michael Jaeger, *Global Player Faust oder Das Verschwinden der Gegenwart. Zur Aktualität Goethes* (Würzburg: Königshausen & Neumann, 5th edn, 2013), esp. 58–71.
52 Goethe, *Faust*, 1858–9.

strives for ... what the educated world is chasing in attempts to *over*-excel and *over*educate; yet thereby it persists in mediocrity. [53]

Once noble, though flawed, the striving for the highest spheres has turned into a "velociferic" force that, according to Goethe in another letter of the same year, does "not allow for anything to ripen anymore."[54] Mephisto enforces this tendency by pushing Faust around the globe at an accelerating speed so that his victim loses any sense for the reality of place and the premodern, cyclical modes of change. Symptomatic for the general impatience and de-centeredness of this radical modern mode of existence are the violent measures against Philemon and Baucis that Faust orders in the tragedy's final act.[55] Like nothing else, the elimination of this elderly couple marks the end of Faust's humanism.

The monologue takes another definite step toward posthumanism in its final segment by characterizing modern human existence with two more terms of negation: "base meaninglessness" (*flache Unbedeutenheit*) and "lack of satisfaction" (*Unersättlichkeit*).[56] In the spirit of the first, Mephisto advises one of Faust's students not to care much about concepts (*Begriffe*) and their meaning; instead, words would be better since they are prone to arbitrariness: "Words [*Worte*] make for splendid disputations/And noble systematizations;/Words are matters of faith."[57] This "wisdom" has proven to be "true" both in the case of the pre-human theology that indoctrinated using God's word (or rather the Church's "interpretation" of it) and in the recent career of "fake news" as a posthuman symptom of mass-deception. Concerning the second characteristic, Goethe wrote his comment in the previously cited letter draft to Nicolovius: "Man devours one moment [*Augenblick*] after another, wastes the day during daytime, and continues to live hand-to-mouth without ever producing something meaningful. Today we have a newspaper for every daytime .... That way, everything a person does, deals with, writes [*dichtet*], even intends on doing is dragged into the public sphere. Nobody can enjoy and suffer if not for the

---

53 Goethe, *Briefe*, vol. 4, 146 (my emphasis).
54 Drafted letter to Nicolovius from November 1825, ibid., 159. These words relate to the Lord's "gardener" analogy in lines 310–11. See also Manfred Osten, "*Alles veloziferisch*" *oder Goethes Entdeckung der Langsamkeit* (Frankfurt a.M. and Leipzig: Insel, 2003), 24–49.
55 How Faust's ever-projecting "ego" conflicts with the "here" and "now" of Philemon and Baucis has been demonstrated by Simon Richter, "Goethe's *Faust* and the Ecolinguistics of 'Here,'" in *German Ecocriticism in the Anthropocene*, eds. Caroline Schaumann and Heather I. Sullivan (New York: Springer, 2017), 45–64.
56 Goethe, *Faust*, 1860, 1863.
57 Ibid., 1995–9.

pleasure of everyone else; consequently ... everything is velociferic."[58] The allusion to the myth of Tantalus[59] (in both the monologue and the letter), who suffered unbearable thirst in Hades although he was surrounded by water, associates this segment with the idea of hell. Yet Mephisto's version of hell on earth appears to be even more refined, as it operates not with real, but virtual realities that exist mostly in the manipulated imagination of the affected subjects.[60] By magically producing as-if-real illusions and simulations (see the mirror-image in the "Witches' Kitchen," the phantasmagoric recreation of Helena in the theater, Homunculus's cinematic projection of Greek mythology in the "Classical Walpurgis Night"), Mephisto is instantiating virtual creations that draw Faust away from the real Creation[61] and cause him to attach to the devil's nihilist agenda like an insect to sweet and sticky substances.

We must remember that Mephisto, as the "spirit who always negates," cannot create himself, he can only destroy. His magical images have no substance and no direct impact on the Creation; the virtual he brings forth is no more than an imaginary layer hovering over the real. But with control over Faust, Mephisto has finally become the creative director for the realization of a new master plan to destroy the Creation. Faust's productive spirit of imagination, which can envision alternative realities, combined with his own destructive firepower, which can release the full potential of matter, enable Mephisto[62] to establish a *negative creation*, namely to implement completely new systems of organization (an *ordo novo*) that he puts to work against the old order of Creation.[63] *Faust, Part Two* displays three types of the negative creation of virtual realities: first, the invention of paper money leads to

---

58 Goethe, *Briefe*, vol. 4, 159.
59 Compare Schöne, *Faust*, vol. 2, 267.
60 A survey of many manifestations of the virtual in *Faust* can be found in J. M. van der Laan, *Seeking Meaning for Goethe's* Faust (London and New York: Continuum, 2007), above all in the chapter "The Virtual and the Real," 110–24. See also Johannes Anderegg, *Transformationen. Über Himmlisches und Teuflisches in Goethes Faust* (Bielefeld: Aisthesis, 2011), especially the chapter "Mephisto und das Als-ob," 78–90.
61 To distinguish these two diametrically opposed creations, I will capitalize from now on the Creation of the Lord, which is, as was shown earlier, *not* identical with the Judeo-Christian notion of Creation.
62 Mephisto's inability to imagine comes to the fore when Faust asks him to guess what his next project may be, to which he can only respond with listing the ever-same banalities of pleasure (Goethe, *Faust*, 10135–75).
63 This was certainly not in the Lord's mind when he instigated the devil to stimulate Faust into action (compare ibid., 340–3). The final line of the German text (" ... und muß, als Teufel, schaffen") is ambivalent and could be read as a premonition.

the modern finance economy;[64] second, Faust's descent to the archaic (and archival) "Mothers" combined with Wagner's artificial creation of the purely projective Homunculus bring into being "Helena of Troy," a new form of (re)presentation that resembles a Hollywood movie; third, Faust's spirited vision of claiming land from the sea is brought into "reality" by Mephisto's ruthless exploitation (transformation and annihilation) of natural and human resources. In the following, I will only deal with the last example as perhaps the most consequential type of negative creation and turning point of human history.

When Faust introduces the conquest of the raging sea's "useless elementary energy"[65] to Mephisto as his final project, he sounds much like a "technological mastermind":[66]

> At once my plan was made! My soul shall boast
> An exquisite achievement: from our coast
> I'll ban the lordly sea, I'll curb its force,
> I'll set new limits to that watery plain
> And drive it back into itself again.
> I've work out every detail, and I say:
> This is my will, now dare to find a way![67]

To "ban" (*ausschließen*), "curb" and "set limits" (*Grenzen verengen*), and "drive back into itself" (*weit hinein ... in sich selbst drängen*) are words no longer fitting the character of the (previously) striving Faust; they rather suit Mephisto's limiting efforts. Of course, Mephisto gladly complies, since it is essentially his will that he is asked to carry out here, yet it has not been an idea that he could have come up with himself. The land-winning project represents a master case for technology's tendency to replace the organic with the inorganic, which has, according to

---

64 Cf. Hans Christoph Binswanger, *Money and Magic: A Critique of the Modern Economy in the Light of Goethe's Faust* (Chicago: Chicago University Press, 1994), for a lucid reading of how Mephisto, since he cannot create new matter (to oppose the Creation), resorted to create money in its stead. "By reducing the world to the quintessence of money, the world becomes augmentable. It grows with economic growth!" (36) Since the introduction of paper money, the economy *must* grow, because inflation can cause the entire financial system to collapse. However, necessary economic growth is not only accomplished through labor, capital, and technological innovation; it must be further sustained by the exploitation of natural and human resources. Hence, also this magical trick eventually works against the Creation.
65 Goethe, *Faust*, 10219.
66 Compare the chapter "The Technological Mastermind" in van der Laan, *Seeking Meaning*, 98–109.
67 Goethe, *Faust*, 10227–33.

Arnold Gehlen, two aspects: "artificial materials replacing those organically produced; and nonorganic energy replacing organic energy."[68] Both are at play in the realization of Faust's plan, if we read between the lines of Baucis's report:

> Slaves toiled vainly: blow by blow,
> Pick and shovel made no way.
> Then we saw the night-flames glow—
> And a dam stood there next day.
> They used human sacrifice:
> Fire ran down, like rivers burning.
> All night long we heard the cries—
> A canal was built by morning.[69]

Evidently, the use of fire and a deep disrespect for the Creation that includes the loss of human lives are the doing or rather undoing of Mephisto and his three violent executioners. But the employment of high energy to break down matter to produce new resources and machines is only one factor of what amounts to technology's "superstructure" for Gehlen.[70] The other big factor is "the capitalist mode of production," the industrial "spirit" of rationalization, and the exploitation of natural resources and human labor for the profit of one or only a few individuals who design, implement, and oversee the new technological organization systems of production and labor. In the final act, Faust has turned into an aggressive capitalist entrepreneur who engages in global trading[71] from his "world-dominion" (*Welt-Besitz*).[72] At the same time, we see him oversee the efficient execution of his orders:

> I hasten to complete my great designs:
> My words alone can work my mastering will.
> Rise from your sleep, my servants, every man!
> Give visible success to my bold plan!
> I have marked it all out, let it be made!
> With a well-ordered project and with hard
> Toil we shall win supreme reward;
> Until the edifice of this achievement stands,
> One mind shall move a thousand hands.[73]

---

68 Arnold Gehlen, *Man in the Age of Technology* (New York: Columbia University Press, 1980), 5.
69 Goethe, *Faust*, 11123–30.
70 Gehlen, *Man*, 8–10.
71 Goethe, *Faust*, 11167–218.
72 Ibid., 11242.
73 Ibid., 11501–10.

Mephisto's mastering of matter with fire combined with Faust's mastering of men with his spirit results in a complete transformation and substitution of the Creation with a diametrically opposed creation—a counter-creation—that erases even the most innocent remnants of humanism (the killing of Philemon and Baucis and the anonymous wanderer) and treats workers as de-individualized, replaceable parts of a mega-machine. In Faust's new world, the human is represented only synecdochically in the plural either as "hands" and "spades" or as "the multitude" (*Menge*) and "crowd" (*Gewimmel*).[74] Goethe envisions a posthuman age that allows only for humans without distinct bodies and formed personalities. In fact, humanity has been split into two camps: "the multitude" consists of anonymous and automated servants of their master's mind and is thereby reduced to the same level as pre-human existence (to a certain degree this still applies to Faust, who originally was the Lord's "servant" and now serves ignorantly to promote Mephisto's agenda), whereas the few lords in positions of power must concentrate so much on the perfection and perfect execution of their plans that they are reduced to sheer will and mere spirit, whereby they lose touch with the corporeal world of nature, their fellow beings, and not least their personal identities. Goethe finds that his time moves toward a posthuman culture as it produces deep social divisions and societal fragmentation, which are among the main challenges that societies are facing today.

Another important aspect of negative creation corresponds to what Heidegger identified as the essence of technology:

> Man places before himself the world as the whole of everything objective, and he places himself before the world. Man sets up the world toward himself, and delivers Nature over to himself … To such a willing, everything, beforehand and thus subsequently, turns irresistibly into material for self-assertive production. The earth and its atmosphere become raw material. Man becomes human material, which is disposed of with a view of proposed goals. The *unconditioned* establishment of the *unconditional* self-assertion by which the world is purposefully made over according to the frame of mind of man's command is a process that emerges from the hidden nature of technology.[75]

In the play, Faust reflects upon the very moment when he delivers himself over to technology. It is at midnight, when Faust is haunted by four gray women, that he realizes: "I have not broken through to freedom yet./I must clear magic from my path, forget/All magic

---

74 Ibid., 11540, 11579.
75 Martin Heidegger, "What are Poets for?" in *Poetry, Language, Thought*, ed. Martin Heidegger, trans. Albert Hofstadter (New York: Perennial Classics, 2001), 107–9 (emphasis added).

conjurations—for then I/Would be confronting nature all alone:/Man's life worth while, man standing on his own!"[76] In his subsequent altercation with "Care" (*Sorge*, which in German also means "worry")—the only one of the four gray women that he is unable to chase away—he articulates the program of his (post)human existence:

> I've seen enough of this terrestrial sphere.
> There is no view to the Beyond from here:
> A fool will seek it, peer with mortal eyes
> And dream of human life above the skies!
> Let him stand fast in this world, and look round
> With courage: Here so much is to be found!
> Why must he wander into timelessness?
> What his mind grasps, he may possess.
> Thus let him travel all his earthly day:
> Though spirits haunt him, let him walk his way.[77]

This is a clear denunciation of his previous mode of existence, and Faust belies the Lord who trusted him to always "know the path from which he should not stray,"[78] which was meant to stay in harmony with the Creation. Now he rejects both his striving toward a transcendental divine origin *and* his longing for absolute immersion in the flows of nature, "the rush of things, of time and all its happenings."[79] In their stead, he declares war on nature as the absolute adversary to the will of his spirit. By creating "the newest earth" and foreseeing a "free people" on this "free ground,"[80] Faust is not just battling the destructive elementary force of the raging sea, but Creation as such. (Not by coincidence does his final project aim to eradicate "the tempest raging/From sea to land, from land to sea"[81] and annihilate "their chain of furious energy"[82] that the archangels praised in their hymn of the Lord's Creation in the Prologue.) He envisions not simply a different life on earth, but an entirely new, artificial creation completely devoid of cultural history, religious spirituality, and the moral sentiments of the natural law.[83] Claudia Brodsky, who also stressed the close nexus between

---

76 Goethe, *Faust*, 11403–7.
77 Ibid., 11441–50.
78 Ibid., 329.
79 Ibid., 1754–5.
80 Ibid., 11566, 11580.
81 Ibid., 259–60.
82 Ibid., 262.
83 That Faust's founding of a "new world" on "free ground" means effectively "a breach with the idea of natural law" and calls for a new nomos of the earth "in the sign of the absolute metaphor of human dignity," has been argued by Thomas Weitin, *Freier Grund. Die Würde des Menschen nach Goethes Faust* (Konstanz: Konstanz University Press, 2013), 59.

Faust's final project and Heidegger's critique of technology, got to the heart of the matter: "Replacing the earth with a 'new earth,' the old encumbered ground with a 'free ground,' Faust builds not earth but the freedom from earth that is technology. Technology, a non-being, 'is' the new basis for freedom, and sole basis for defining the 'new' because its functioning constitutes its own ground precisely by freeing itself from earthly constraints."[84]

Only Faust does not aim to free himself "from earthly constraints" in materialistic terms. In the final scenes we see him, first and foremost, obsessed with fending off the phantasmagoric four gray women and severing associations with any other form of spiritual manifestation like "magic," "ghosts," "superstition," visions of "the Beyond," "spirits," "phantoms," and "demons."[85] These residues of spirit remind him of his natural origin and his intrinsic confinement in and by the original Spirit, as he must acknowledge: "Demons, I know, are hard to exorcize,/The spirit-bond [*das geistig-strenge Band*] is loath to separate."[86] Hence, when he delivers himself over to technology, Faust aims to resolve the paradoxical existential conflict within humans between their essentially unconditional existence on earth and the quintessential constraint of their spirits by the Spirit (through the knowledge of death and acknowledgment of the impossibility of absolute knowledge). By enclosing the sea with a dyke, Faust aims to turn the tables. Now it is the human spirit that puts constraints on the ever-dynamic Spirit of Creation—one that is often destructive for human endeavors—"with the strenuous bond" (*mit strengem Band*) of technology.[87] As noted already, the unconditional warfare against this absolute foe requires the "strict ordering" (*strenges Ordnen*)[88] of all resources, including humans, who must close with "common urge" (*Gemeindrang*)[89] the "gaps" that the increasingly violent revolting sea tears relentlessly in the protective shield of this artificial "paradise."[90] Faust regards his strenuous control of the water and the strict rule of his people as an act of human emancipation and self-determination, a reversal of the Fall, and a project of freedom. (The words "free"/"freedom" appear four times in his last monologue.[91]) Yet the freedom he means and enforces no longer

---

84 Claudia Brodsky, *In the Place of Language: Literature and the Architecture of the Referent* (New York: Fordham University Press, 2009), 53.
85 Goethe, *Faust*, 11404, 11413, 11416, 11442, 11450, 11487, 11491.
86 Ibid., 11491–2.
87 Ibid., 11543.
88 Ibid., 11507.
89 Ibid., 11572.
90 Ibid., 11569.
91 Ibid., 11559–86.

cares for individual autonomy, which was previously safeguarded by the universal acceptance of the biological limitations of the body and a higher spiritual power (in pre-humanism) or the laws of nature (in humanism) that affected everyone.

When Faust negates (but never suspends!) these natural and spiritual constraints, he has liberated his creative spirit to realize his future vision of the human, but only at the expense of the collective potential for creating a better world. And yet, even his private idea of freedom remains an illusion, as is symbolized by him mistaking the sound of his gravediggers for the sound of progress. Faust's project will never come to completion because a multitude of different forces and diverging agendas are working against it. For this reason, he can enjoy his "highest moment" (*höchster Augenblick*)[92] of fulfillment only in the mode of "anticipation" (*Vorgefühl*);[93] his project is not and will never become "beautiful" in actual reality, only in his fantasy. More importantly, however, Faust's poietic idea of freedom has triggered the assault of negative creation against the Creation that, in a revolting turn, becomes evermore life-threatening with the ever-increasing strength of its reactions. The destruction of organic units for technological ends has unleashed the elementary forces of matter that are always at risk of spinning out of control. Consequently, society gets entangled in necessary measures to manage negative creation *and* to control its effects on nature. A humanity relying almost entirely on technological control systems is not only in danger of eradicating the foundations of its physical existence, it is also wasting the great creative potential of a collective of free bodies and minds.

Taking the above into account, one cannot deny that Mephistopheles has been unconditionally successful in the pursuit of *his* agenda. Even though he may have lost hold of Faust's "immortal essence" (*Unsterbliches*)[94] in the end, he has accomplished the implementation of a negative creation that will live on even after the mastermind's death and continue to combat the Creation until either natural resources or the human spirit have been exhausted. This amounts to much more than Mephisto could have hoped for in his initial conversation with the Lord. Goethe's *Faust*, then, truly is a tragedy—not just by fulfilling the formal requirements of this genre, but also in terms of the tragic effects resulting from the crucial paradox that governs all humans and that Faust acts out with dramatic, world-changing consequences. That Faust is eventually redeemed takes away nothing from the tragic reality that is

---

92 Ibid., 11586.
93 Ibid., 11585.
94 Ibid., stage direction before 11934.

represented in the "very serious jokes" (*sehr ernste Scherze*) of the play.[95] The angels' announcement: "He who strives on and lives to strive/ Can earn redemption still" (*Wer immer strebend sich bemüht/Den können wir erlösen*)[96] may have irritated many readers, but it can be explained. Firstly, "striving" means here no longer an obsessive striving for the absolute, but the following of calls from within (entelechy) and from above (Eros, "love")[97] toward unification with the "eternal-feminine."[98] Secondly, the announced redemption has nothing to do with the terms and conditions of the wager,[99] nor is it theologically charged,[100] nor can it be morally justified by giving negative creation—the destruction of nature, the killing and enslaving of human lives, and the ignoring of whatever spiritual residues remind Faust of his origin—a positive spin, as has been attempted in most of the older literature that viewed Faust as an exemplary modern figure of productivity.[101] Instead, in the play Faust is redeemed (*erlöst*) simply by shedding the material gravity of his body, by releasing (*lösen*) and purifying his spirit.[102] In agreement with Goethe's cosmological dialectic, he is becoming light and (re)turning into the expanding light, after he reaches a climax of material and psychological concentration at the moment of death.

---

95 This is how Goethe (*Briefe*, vol. 4, 481) characterized *Part Two* in his ultimate letter to Wilhelm von Humboldt.
96 Goethe, *Faust*, 11936–7.
97 Ibid., 11938–9.
98 Ibid., 12110.
99 Gerrit Brüning argues meticulously against the widespread consensus among Faust scholars to regard the wager as the unresolvable "dramaturgic centerpiece" of this play in his article "Die Wette in Goethes Faust," *Goethe Yearbook* 17 (2010).
100 "Grace" (compare Goethe, *Faust*, 12019, 12056, 12103) is used here not as a theological concept of the judging God-Father in the Augustinian tradition, but associated with the "Eternal-Feminine," which is embodied in its purest form by the "Mater Gloriosa" and eroticized by the returning "good soul" (ibid., 12065) of Gretchen, who still has the power to attract Faust's "noble member of the spiritual world" (ibid., 11934–5).
101 Weitin offers an interesting twist to this tradition of interpretation by proposing that Goethe, by presenting Faust as an undignified ruler and redeeming him, has created a model and metaphor to demonstrate what human dignity means, namely a radically humanistic, universal norm beyond good and evil which applies to all human beings without discriminating the motifs and consequences of their deeds; see *Freier Grund*, 96–7.
102 My reading of these crucial lines (Goethe, *Faust*, 11934–41) follows Schöne, *Faust*, vol. 2, 800–2, and Jochen Schmidt in *Goethes Faust, Erster und Zweiter Teil: Grundlagen—Werk—Wirkung* (Munich: C. H. Beck, 1999), 296.

Conclusion: How Posthuman Have We Become?

My reading of *Faust* aimed to recover if not the history of posthumanism, then at least the prehistory of how we have become posthuman, which is an ongoing process. Goethe's grand narrative shows, through the example of Faust, how the process of emancipation from pre-humanist spiritual regimes is at risk of falling into the opposite posthuman extreme by breaking radically with past traditions, by suspending the belief in higher forms of spirituality, by losing touch with and actively opposing the physical foundations of our existence, by neglecting the arts and sciences for the pure pleasure of consuming and exploiting whatever beauty this world has to offer, and by giving in to the illusions and virtual simulations fabricated by negative creation. The final act of *Faust, Part Two* foreshadows the longer-term consequences and effects of this trajectory in a series of rifts, ruptures, and divisions: Faust draws a line of separation between his earthly existence and the Lord in heaven; he severs the "spirit-bond" (*das geistig-strenge Band*) that ties together all living beings; he orders the removal of Philemon and Baucis and thereby unties his connection to a past when humans used to live self-sufficiently in harmony with the cosmic and organic life cycles and at peace with their fellow humans and themselves; he disentangles the mind from the body and thereby splits humanity into the camps of a few commanding organizers and "the multitude" of slave laborers; he erects an artificial barrier to claim new land from the raging sea, whereby he elides the mediating phase of cultivation and culture as a flexible buffer zone between nature and civilization. Therefore, the forceful elements of the physical world continue to threaten the colony and create "gaps" in the technological protection shield that requires permanent maintenance through the mobilization of every man and evermore machinery. Consequently, negative creation turns into a self-perpetuating technological system. But while Goethe saw only the first glimpses of the systematic transformation of nature and cultures into virtual realities during the final years of his life, the greatest problems and challenges that the world is facing today can all be derived from the principle of negative creation as he envisioned it from the vantage point of a humanist poet.

Goethe's vision of human fragmentation and the differentiation of social systems within the mega-machine of the technological-industrial apparatus offers only a pessimistic outlook on the future. His *Faust* must be understood as a cautionary historical and metaphysical narration against a potential relapse of humanity into a pre-human condition. Meanwhile, the gods and theological belief systems have been basically replaced by systems of automation and communication networks. Nonetheless, contemporary theories of CP still aim to take advantage of the potential opportunities that the deconstruction of totalizing humanist concepts and grand narratives in post-structuralist theories, new digital technologies of computer virtual realities, and transhuman fantasies of fusing the organic with the inorganic offer for a reconceptualization of the human. New embodiment is the buzzword of many posthumanists. They envisage the recombination of the disparate elements of shattered humanism into new human forms or the establishment of new relationships that encompass the human/animal or the organic/inorganic dichotomy. To name just one example, Pramod Nayar states that "[p]osthumanism is all about the embedding of embodied systems in environments where the system evolves with other entities, organic and inorganic, in the environment in a mutually sustaining relationship."[103] However, in the light of Goethe's narrative, this relationship appears to develop rather asymmetrically. The organic and the inorganic do not evolve in harmony together and form a symbiosis; instead the one evolves at the expense of the other. Nayar tends to consider only the technological end-product, which can indeed be beneficial in improving the lives of humans or other organisms, and to ignore the costs of the technological process that consumes natural resources and destroys many organic environments as well as cultural values.

Almost 200 years after Goethe's *Faust* and twenty years after Hayles's visionary book title *How We Became Posthuman*, it is time, I think, to face the fact that the human divisions and the losses in spirituality and natural as well as cultural environments must be accounted for as direct impacts of negative creation. These losses are real, but the gains they supposedly bring are only virtual. As my reading of Goethe's *Faust* suggests, it is therefore an illusion to attempt to reconcile the human with the posthuman. It is futile to envision new ways and forms of embodiment when, in fact, the named disparities, divisions, gaps, and differences become impossible to reconcile. Rather, we should acknowledge that we have, indeed, become posthuman to a large extent, that the human is no longer fully in charge, and that the posthuman has become irreconcilable with what CP still values in the human.[104] The trend to automation and simulation goes along with a reductionist conception of life that privileges the mind over the body and even

---

103 Pramod K. Nayar, *Posthumanism* (Cambridge: Polity, 2013), 51.
104 Roden, who is a proponent of "speculative posthumanism," criticizes in the same vein "critical posthumanists" for arguing—in blatant contradiction to Hayles's emphatic book title—still on the grounds of "human" subjectivity, whereas "we have already entered a posthuman dispensation in which the very value and status of the human is put in question by developments in science, political theory and philosophy" (*Posthuman Life*, 35).

imagines a "computational universe" in which humans are nothing but "programs that run on the cosmic computer."[105] Hayles is right to warn against this notion "when it goes from being a useful heuristic to an ideology that privileges information over everything else ... Just because information has lost its body does not mean that humans and the world have lost theirs."[106] The great irony of the post- and transhumanist theories she cites is that they propagate ideas that return to the ideals of a pre-humanist universe. Those who promote them recall the angels in *Faust* who praise the Lord's Creation, functioning as flawlessly as it was programmed on the first day, but who must exclude the complicated humans from their hymn because they spoil the system's perfection.

---

105 Hayles, *How We Became Posthuman*, 241.
106 Ibid., 244.

Fourteen Beyond Death: Posthuman Perspectives in Christoph Wilhelm Hufeland's *Macrobiotics*

Jocelyn Holland

It is a common characteristic of "post-" philosophies to position themselves aggressively with regard to what has come before, and "posthumanism"—however diverse the set of concerns currently grouped under this moniker may be—is no exception to the rule. In the case of posthumanism, however, it is scarcely an exaggeration to say that such positioning is, both structurally and thematically, a matter of life and death. Even if there is no unified posthuman point of view as to what constitutes death or, for that matter, how to distinguish between the living and the dead, such concerns are central to posthuman discussions on a wide range of topics including prosthetics, cyborgs, artificial life, and virtual extensions of consciousness. N. Katherine Hayles's *How We Became Posthuman* (1999), with its chapters on embodied virtuality, cybernetics, and artificial life, is responsible for popularizing many of these topics. Some theorists of the posthuman, such as Patricia MacCormack in her *Posthuman Ethics* (2012), have also come to think in terms of "necrophilosophies," a term she attributes both to post-structuralism and to posthumanism. Such philosophies share the common feature that they mourn the death of something and are defined by a "focus on what is lost."[1] They have also had a more localized impact on the

---

1   Patricia MacCormack, *Posthuman Ethics* (New York: Routledge, 2012), 125. MacCormack refers in a similar vein to the work of Seyla Benhabib, who describes the elements of postmodern thought that render an "ethics for selfhood" difficult as "the death of the subject. ... the excavation of the truth of history. ... and the death of the desire to master the self and the world by knowing everything" (ibid.); these are associated with the Death of Man, the Death of History, and the

concept of death itself. MacCormack writes that death "has died as an ordinary reality" and labels it "an announced finding, a phenomenon to be proved";[2] by the same token, "the very definition of life is now an epistemic state."[3]

One can supplement MacCormack's position with arguments put forth by Rosi Braidotti in *The Posthuman* (2013). Generally speaking, Braidotti's approach is rooted in a trajectory whereby, in her opinion, "posthumanism is the historical moment that marks the end of the opposition between Humanism and anti-humanism."[4] At the same time, it should be noted that there are instances where the terms with which she defines posthumanism and the posthuman reiterate positions from the humanist tradition she claims to have moved beyond. For example, to state what "we humans" truly desire is a "surrender of the self" implies that we—and Braidotti—are still to some degree bound to conventional (i.e., pre-posthuman) notions of selfhood.[5] By the same token, her embrace of Spinoza throughout *The Posthuman*, for all that it claims to move away from an anthropocentrically grounded notion of life, nonetheless advocates a metaphysics as well as a unified notion of "man." I would like to keep these concerns in mind while focusing on how Braidotti thinks about death from a posthuman perspective. In a chapter titled "The Inhuman: Life beyond Death," she seeks to develop "a way of constructing an affirmative posthuman theory of death."[6] It is noteworthy that she begins the chapter with a nod to Deleuze and Guattari and a statement about art:

> By transposing us beyond the confines of bound identities, art becomes necessarily inhuman in the sense of nonhuman in that it connects to the animal, the vegetable, earthy and planetary forces that surround us. Art is also, moreover, cosmic in its resonance and hence posthuman by structure, as it carries us to the limits of what our embodied selves can do or endure. In so far as art stretches the boundaries of representation to the utmost, it reaches the limits of life itself and thus confronts the horizon of death.[7]

Death of Metaphysics. MacCormack does not acknowledge that in Benhabib's work these categories are introduced as quotes by feminist philosopher Jane Flax's *Thinking Fragments: Psychoanalysis, Feminism and Postmodernism in the Contemporary West* (Oakland: University of California Press, 1990).

3   Ibid., 116.
2   MacCormack, *Posthuman Ethics*, 115.
4   Rosi Braidotti, *The Posthuman* (Cambridge: Polity, 2013), 37.
5   Ibid., 136.
6   Ibid., 110.
7   Ibid., 107.

Beyond Death 271

It would seem, based on the content of this quote, and its strategic location near the opening of the chapter, that a reflection on art is deeply bound with Braidotti's posthuman theory of death, but this is not the case. With one notable exception, which I will turn to at the end of the essay, this reflection on "art" is almost a singular occurrence: Braidotti pays much more attention to the politics, rather than the aesthetics, of posthumanism. At the same time, I believe that this initial gesture merits much more attention than Braidotti herself is willing to grant it. In the passage quoted previously, she suggests that art has an important instrumental value where posthumanism is concerned, in the sense that it can help us think beyond traditional notions of a mind/body dualism and envision scenarios where our bodies, regardless of their status as corpses, are no longer an endpoint but part of a wider network of interlocking physical and virtual reality. A greater reflection on the potential of "art" (and one that was not necessarily embedded in a Deleuzian framework), could be useful for Braidotti, to help her define the historical analogs to the posthuman view of death as the extension of a physical or virtual reality rather than an endpoint. In particular, one can ask whether a focus on particular narrative and rhetorical strategies that have historically been utilized for the construction of life and the problem of delimiting life from death reveal a historical (and poetic) blind spot in her thinking.

In fact, the questions raised by Braidotti concerning a posthuman understanding of death are not new. In this essay, I will show how they connect in unexpected ways to the work of someone very much invested in the narration of life and death: Christoph Hufeland, a Goethe-era physician, who is still known today for his treatise *Macrobiotics, or the Art of Prolonging Life*.[8] As the editors of this volume on "posthumanism in the age of humanism" state in their introduction, the broader purpose of the essay collection is to consider to what degree posthumanism's critical concerns are already topics of debate in the age of humanism, as well as how some of the central ideas that informed humanism continue to be relevant to posthuman debates today. My essay will use Hufeland's *Macrobiotics* as a case study to respond to these two general objectives by focusing on the problem of death and its usefulness as a concept both for Hufeland and for posthuman philosophers. For all their differences in historical and philosophical contexts, these parties share the belief that death does not merely wait for

---

8 First edition, C. Hufeland, *Die Kunst das menschliche Leben zu verlängern*, 2 vols. (Vienna: Schmidbauer, 1797). Although the word "macrobiotics" appears in the first edition, the 1805 edition was the one to contain this word in the title *Makrobiotik oder die Kunst das menschliche Leben zu verlängern*, 2 vols. (Berlin: L. W. Wittich, 1805).

us on the horizon of life, but is a deeply ingrained part of life itself. For Hufeland, this is true in more ways than one. On the one hand, death is part of the physical continuum of life: he writes that life is an ongoing process of utter destruction and restoration conducted by the myriad organs of the body.[9] On the other hand, the *Macrobiotics* is much more than a physiological textbook: it ultimately has other goals in mind. As the title indicates, it is devoted to techniques of extending human life, and for Hufeland this means a consideration of the organic processes of the body and of the human as a producer of macrobiotic techniques (and in a broader sense, of culture). One can find passages in the *Macrobiotics* that paint the analogy between the physiological and the cultural in stark terms. Just as the human body constantly devours itself, Hufeland's *Macrobiotics* also refers to the "human-devouring times" (*menschenverschlingenden Zeiten*) within which he lives as the Napoleonic wars ravage central Europe.[10] Cynical observers might also note that these times did not pose a detriment to Hufeland's medical career.

In addition, the *Macrobiotics* puts forth the idea that there is a productive element to death, a perspective that aligns Hufeland with posthumanist thinking. Already in his integration of death into organic processes, we hear an anachronic echo of Braidotti's wish to propose an "affirmative theory of posthuman death as the generative inhuman within the subject."[11] This is an idea that the *Macrobiotics* articulates, albeit on its own terms. As it turns out, the supplementary techniques and practices that we, as aspiring macrobioticians, apply in order to prolong the whole of life also connect in diverse and unexpected ways to the idea of death. On the basis of this claim, to be examined in more detail later, the *Macrobiotics* can be understood as a "necrophilosophy" to the extent that Hufeland engages with—and takes advantage of—the concept of death. For Hufeland, the task of determining the precise moment of a physiological death can involve significant challenges—one need only refer to his preoccupation with the state of "apparent death" or *Scheintod*—so that for him as well it was a "phenomenon to be proved." There are even further affinities between Hufeland and the posthuman position that are worthy of investigation. Braidotti writes that death is "virtual in that it has the generative capacity to engender the actual" and that, as a result, "death is but an obvious manifestation of principles that are active in every aspect of life."[12] Hufeland's own position resonates with Braidotti's because, in addition to being an integral part of physiological processes (as well as a terminal point that,

---

[9] Hufeland, *Makrobiotik* (1805), vol. 1, 49.
[10] Ibid., xiii.
[11] Braidotti, *The Posthuman*, 110.
[12] Ibid., 138.

somewhat paradoxically, need not mark an ending), death also offers multiple vantage points from which to consider the "whole of life" as well as the perpetual conversation we have with death from within life.

To assess what, precisely, death has to offer Hufeland and to describe its usefulness for the *Macrobiotics* requires the acknowledgment that literature will play an important role throughout, both as regards particular textual examples and as regards more general questions of representation and artifice. Given his significant references to Goethe both on the title page of the first volume and as an epigraph to the second volume, as well as occasional references to other literary writers, it is surprising how little scholarship exists about how literature informs Hufeland's approach to, and communication of, the project of macrobiotics. We could even refer to the very first paragraph of the first volume, where Hufeland states in no uncertain terms that life is an "animal-chemical operation." If there is some notion of work (or "opus") to be interpreted from life's "operation," it requires an acknowledgment that the interconnectedness of life and death central to the medical theses of Hufeland's project is precisely what makes them interesting from a poetic point of view. In the *Macrobiotics*, the production of life occurs at the intersection of scientific thinking and literary practice.

Hufeland's *Macrobiotics*

Christoph Wilhelm Hufeland (1762–1836) is perhaps best known to historians and literary scholars today for his ardent rejection of John Brown's theory of medicine,[13] which was enjoying a wave of popularity in Germany around 1800, as well as for the medical care he provided to such famous intellectuals as Friedrich Schiller, Johann Gottfried Herder, and Christoph Wieland, in addition to Goethe. In 1797 he published the first volume of the work called "The Art of Prolonging Life," a title which was replaced in later editions by the neologism *Macrobiotics*.[14] With these publications, he thereby christened a body of knowledge— one he designates as both a science (*Wissenschaft*) and an art (*Kunst*) in

---

13 John Brown's *Elementa Medicinae* was first published in 1780; German translations first appeared in 1795 and 1796, just a year prior to the first edition of Hufeland's macrobiotics. In the *Elementa Medicinae*, Brown put forth a theory of excitability which was, for him, the ultimate cause of life itself; in this system, health "was merely the balance between adequate amounts of stimulation and normal levels of excitability." Guenter Risse, "Medicine in the Age of Enlightenment," in *Medicine in Society*, ed. Andrew Wear (Cambridge: Cambridge University Press, 1992), 165.

14 Hufeland already uses the term *Macrobiotic* in his 1797 edition, where—to judge by its spelling—it clearly has the status of a foreign import, although Hufeland does not refer to any prior sources.

the technical sense—whose chief concern is with the duration of life.[15] Unlike practical medicine, which treats symptoms and illnesses as they emerge by focusing on the immediate condition of the body, macrobiotics has—as Hufeland states—other means, other goals, and other limits.[16] It concerns itself with what is best for life taken as a whole rather than at the present moment.

However clearly Hufeland may have defined the goal of his *Macrobiotics*, the theoretical basis for such a project is far from self-evident. Much like Jean Starobinski's thought that an autobiographer requires the conceit of a standpoint from beyond the grave in order to contemplate the literary task of writing a life, Hufeland requires that we have a grasp of "the whole life" before we even begin to ponder the immediate cultivation and continued production of those bodies and minds actively engaged in the process of living. And just as critical readers of autobiographies have tended to be more aware of the potential problems that can arise from the task of writing about one's own life than the autobiographers themselves, so too is the reader of the *Macrobiotics* confronted with a question that remains in Hufeland's blind spot: namely, how it is possible to navigate these two points of view, one located by default in the "reality" or "immediacy" of life, the other clearly a fictional construct; one located in the present, the other requiring of our future that it becomes a past.[17] Such concerns, however latent they may be for Hufeland himself, suggest that there is a generic, transhistorical dimension to his work and they should also raise a red flag for posthumanist theorists who would like to adopt an analogous point of view and argue from a standpoint beyond death. For all that it has its own techniques and technological resources, posthumanism would

---

15 Hufeland insists on the dual status of the term *Macrobiotic* in the first edition, when he describes the purpose of his work as the formulation of "rules for the dietetic and medical treatment of life, for its extension" and that in the process of accomplishing this goal "an individual science [*Wissenschaft*] emerges, the *macrobiotics*, or the art [*Kunst*] of prolonging life." Hufeland, *Die Kunst*, vol. 1 (1797), vi.
16 Hufeland, *Makrobiotik* (1805), vol. 1, vi.
17 With regard to connecting macrobiotic thinking about death to the task of the autobiographer, Braidotti alludes to this same problem when she takes up Hanafin's argument that a necropolitics implies "shifting away from thinking of legal subjectivity as death-bound" what she identifies as a "post-identitarian position that encourages us, following Virginia Woolf, to adopt a mode of thinking 'as if already gone.'" Braidotti, *The Posthuman*, 128. Braidotti does not supply the source of the quote, nor was I able to locate it. For all that Braidotti is overtly more concerned with engaging critically with the politics of the posthuman, this gesture betrays a tendency to look toward art—and here in particular: poetic models—to provide a descriptive framework for narrating the posthuman position on death.

do well to consider such narrative constraints. With a bit of poetic license—and with the aid of Braidotti's distinction between "personal" and "impersonal" death—one could even call posthumanism itself an autobiographical construct. For Braidotti, personal death is "linked to the suppression of the individualized ego," whereas impersonal death is "beyond the ego" and "marks the extreme threshold of my powers to become."[18] The autobiographical conceit of Hufeland's project is more in tune with the "impersonal" variant because it is the one that, "structures our time-lines and frames our time zones, not as a limit, but as a porous threshold," which is "ever-present in our psychic and somatic landscapes as the event that has already happened."[19] It would seem, then, that Hufeland's humanism—and indeed, all projects of life-writing that merit the name autobiography—bear traits of what will later be designated "posthuman," just as, by the same token, there are elements of the posthuman theories of death more grounded in historical writing conventions than have previously been acknowledged by posthuman thinkers.

In keeping with the affinity the *Macrobiotics* shares with an autobiographical project, it is worth remembering that the "view of the whole" and the "art of lengthening life" are each essential poetic constructs that inform other aspects of the text as well. These are ideas I want to connect more generally to the use of literature in Hufeland's text, what we could call one aspect of the "necropoetics" of the *Macrobiotics*. The project to assess the whole life does not just require the imagined separation from (or objectivity of) life. It also requires one to "die" a little while still standing in the temporal flow of life itself while, somewhat paradoxically, claiming this "dead" position as one with poetic—and that means generative—potential. It is perhaps no coincidence that on the title page of the *Macrobiotics* we see this same question posed with a fair amount of pathos in a quote from Goethe's tragedy, *Egmont*:

Sweet life! Sweet, pleasant habit of being and doing!
Must I part from you?[20]

To be fair, Hufeland was likely not pondering the theoretical conundrums of his project when he chose this quote, but rather tapping into the fairly common sentiment that life is not something from which we gladly remove ourselves. And Egmont, for his part, has no particular

---

18 Ibid., 131.
19 Ibid., 131–2.
20 Johann Wolfgang Goethe, *Plays. Egmont, Iphigenia in Tauris, Torquato Tasso*, ed. Frank G. Ryder, trans. Anna Swanwick, Frank G. Ryder, and Charles E. Passage (New York: Continuum), 75.

desire to occupy that posthumous position known as the autobiographical or macrobiotic perspective, either intentionally or by default—there is no question of inscribing him, as character, within a protohistory of macrobioticians (or autobiographers, for that matter). At the same time, the epigraph falls neatly, if unintentionally, into the framework I outlined earlier. By placing the epigraph on the title page, Hufeland allows the first personified voice to "speak" in his text to be a fictional one.[21] This decision affirms the degree to which literature contributes to the art and the science of macrobiotics. There is also more to be said concerning the objectification of life that the theoretical view of the whole in the *Macrobiotics* seems to endorse. In the quote from Egmont, we find life personified: Egmont grants it the status of subject (and object) and identifies it with the pronoun "you." This is a gesture analogous (though by no means identical) to the autobiographical conceit itself: analogous in that it creates the illusion of a partition when, in fact the speaker is still embedded within the temporality of life. It is no paradox to say that Egmont and his life have already parted company syntactically, even if the act of separation itself is still anticipated. In the rhetorical question—*from you must I part?*—we can see indexed the joint gesture to invoke the independence of life as a concept and a deictic gesture toward the chronological temporality of embodied life as charted by the ongoing production of poetic language.

The Flame of Life

Before developing the idea of a necropoetics, and the broader role literature has to play in the *Macrobiotics*, any further, I would like to consider the notion of "artificial life," a term general enough to encompass both poetic language and physiological phenomena. In the first sentence of the *Macrobiotics*, Hufeland designates human life as an opus without an author: "physically regarded," he writes, it is "an idiosyncratic animal-chemical operation" and "a phenomenon."[22] We can supplement this description with further passages from the *Macrobiotics* where Hufeland offers yet another general definition of what life is, this time using the metaphor of flame borrowed from Francis Bacon: "[Bacon] thinks of life as a flame which is constantly consumed by the

---

21 This scenario is complicated somewhat by the fact that Hufeland does not provide a source for the quote apart from the author's name, "Göthe." The title page therefore provides us already with quite a bit of information: that the first "personified" voice of the *Macrobiotics* is indeed a fictional one; that this voice is supplanted by the (historical) name of the author; and that what is staged is the production of literature itself.
22 Hufeland uses the word *Erscheinung*, which connotes both the visual and, potentially, the artificial.

surrounding air."[23] Hufeland draws upon this definition more than once, connecting it to the notion of life as an operation. "One can also see the process of life as a constant process of consumption," he writes, "and determine its essential part in a constant consumption and subsequent replacement": "One has often compared life with a flame and truly it is entirely the same operation."[24]

Today, we would not agree with Bacon, Hufeland, or anyone else who claimed that a flame is "consumed" by the surrounding air, but if we attempt to think from his perspective, we can see that he equates life and flame as "one and the same operation" because it allows him to think of destruction and creation as part of the same process. He continues the thought: "Destroying and creating forces are in ceaseless activity and in a constant struggle within us and every moment of our existence is a strange mixture of annihilation and new creation."[25] This metaphor is itself embedded in a tradition reaching back to Baroque emblem books and Renaissance drama—Hufeland might claim Bacon as his source, but Macbeth's "brief candle" is also flickering in the shadows. These passages from the *Macrobiotics* can be connected with ones from Hufeland's own autobiography written some years later, in 1831, where Hufeland recalls certain events from his life in terms of bursts of light against darkness. Of his first two years of life, for example, Hufeland recalls that "only one single point blazes like fire from this night in my memory";[26] subsequent events are also described as "beautiful points of light."[27] Collectively, these passages speak to one another for at least two reasons: not only do they collapse generation and destruction—life and death—within the "point" of the flame, through an emphasis on continuity and "replacement" they also open the door for modes of production that cannot neatly be reduced to organic generation. There is a technique—an art and an artifice—to the prolongation of life. The opus, a prolonged operation, as set forth in the first sentences of the *Macrobiotics* awaits only the arrival of the macrobiotician, the imagined figure who will incorporate the techniques offered by Hufeland's *Macrobiotics*, as the one who will attempt to adjudicate over the matter of life and death. We can see that the concepts of life and death, the creative and the destructive, are completely intertwined not only from a poetic but also from a physiological point of view, and the autobiographical perspective Hufeland adapts for the *Macrobiotics* synthesizes both of these traditions. A physician who, as Hufeland suggests, is constantly

---

23 Hufeland, *Makrobiotik* (1805), vol. 1, 21.
24 Ibid., 49.
25 Ibid.
26 Hufeland, *Eine Selbstbiographie* (Berlin: Georg Reimer, 1863), 9.
27 Ibid., 47.

confronted with the presence of annihilation in the process of living, is by definition threatened with the possibility at each moment that the whole of life may have passed. Her position is ambivalent, as she stands with one foot in life and the other positioned beyond the grave. What, precisely, does she observe in the relentless oscillation of creation and destruction? As it turns out, she bears witness to nothing less than the artificiality of life, as we see when the autobiographical perspective of the "whole life" is encoded as a play (*Schauspiel*) of finite duration from the point of view of the living observer. In one of his many (although in this case perhaps the most) programmatic statements about what life is, Hufeland writes:

> That which we call in the usual sense the *Life* of a creature (observed as representation [*Darstellung*]) is nothing other than a mere appearance [*Erscheinung*], which has nothing unique and autonomous about it at all, other than the effective force which is its basis, and which joins and orders everything. All the rest is a mere phenomenon [*Phänomen*], a great, continuous spectacle [*Schauspiel*], where what is represented remains the same not even a moment, but rather ceaselessly changes.[28]

"Life," according to Hufeland, is not to be equated with the materiality of the living, breathing organism, but rather with the representations of those material states. The language of this passage, with its emphasis on appearance, representation, and spectacle (whereby *Schauspiel* could also be thought of as a "play" or "drama") belongs to a lexicon of words in the *Macrobiotics* that possess dual citizenship: they function both within a logic of representation native to art even as they connect to techniques of observation and description at home in the natural sciences. The art and artificiality of life Hufeland suggests here comprise a scale that reaches from the physiological to the poetic.[29]

It is a peculiarity of the *Macrobiotics* that the reader is confronted with a blind spot where the "use" of literature is concerned. Hufeland does reflect openly on the uses and abuses of literature for the cultivation of life, but it is also the case that the literary language of his text and the

---

28 Hufeland, *Makrobiotik* (1805), vol. 1, 158.
29 Hufeland is very much indebted to a notion of life force or *Lebenskraft* and makes a point of mentioning in the introduction to the *Macrobiotics* that he prefers to retain this term rather than opting for the more "modern" notion of excitability (*Erregbarkeit*) (see *Makrobiotik* [1805], vol. 1, xvi). There is a tension, then, in the *Macrobiotics* between the notion of a unifying "force" to life and the insistence on representation that indexes our ability to separate ourselves from life, much as one would observe a phenomenon under a microscope.

literary quotes he chooses are introduced without further reflection. For an example of a literary term that slips between the poetic and scientific registers of the *Macrobiotics,* one could consider these passages in which Hufeland refers to the concept of depiction or portrayal (*Darstellung*):

> Man is ... the highest degree of depiction [*Darstellung*] of material, which our eyes can see, our senses can encompass.[30]
>
> With regard to the taste of the chivalric ages ... it seems the more we feel how far we have come from them, the more that depiction [*Darstellung*] attracts us, the more it incites in us the wish to be like them again.[31]
>
> ... the heart-lifting depictions [*Darstellungen*] by the poets of nature.[32]

The word *Darstellung* encompasses a broad spectrum of meaning in Hufeland's lexicon. On the one hand, he uses it in the more canonical sense as a term connected to poetic production. On the other hand, there exist the auto-depictive processes of organic matter. In this scenario, and somewhat redundantly, an anthropocentric concept is attached to cultural processes that is, in turn, remapped onto the human body: the human is innately predisposed to recognize his own body as such, so that the assumed distinction between life and art does not hold here at all. In the middle of the spectrum, one finds a hybrid form between the two: not the body itself, but an image—depiction—of it as it has been embedded within a moral code and handed down to us over time. There is, according to this logic, an artifice to life. If one reconsiders the subtitle (and onetime main title) of Hufeland's book—*the art of prolonging life*—it now becomes plausible that he is using the word art (*Kunst*) not just in a sense of practices and techniques, but also with this poetic emphasis in mind. A sensibility for art, as *Darstellung,* goes hand in hand with a sensibility for one's own life, as *Darstellung.*

Literature and Life

Earlier, I cited Rosi Braidotti's comments about the relation of art to life and death: how she connects it to a state of nonliving, and that for her it is "an intensive practice that aims at creating new ways of thinking, perceiving and sensing Life's infinite possibilities."[33] We can keep her perspective in mind, as well as the inherent art and artifice to life gleaned from the *Macrobiotics,* as we take a closer look at literature and

---

30 Hufeland, *Makrobiotik* (1805), vol. 1, 156.
31 Hufeland, *Makrobiotik* (1805), vol. 2, 132.
32 Ibid., 175.
33 Braidotti, *The Posthuman,* 107.

its significance for the *Macrobiotics*: both the act of reading and, more specifically, what Hufeland does with literary texts. Regarding the former: Hufeland is a product of his times. Anyone familiar with debates about the advantages and disadvantages of reading in the eighteenth and nineteenth centuries will be aware of the argument that it was a potentially harmful activity. Hufeland agrees that most dramas, novels, and poems—especially salacious ones—should be removed from the hands of impressionable minds (i.e., those too young, too female, or too queer), for fear that they might lead to excessive fatigue, masturbation, and possibly death. This includes what Hufeland refers to as a kind of mental masturbation (*geistliche Onanie*) which can be practiced while maintaining chastity but which still exhausts the body: "I understand by that," he writes, "heating up one's fantasy with titillating and lascivious images."[34] It is an existence Hufeland compares to a prolonged state of feverish agitation as well as to a "living death" where "death," in this context, is clearly aligned with *Schein*, the production of images. We find here a conflation between two opposites: life and death, the natural and the artificial or technical. This conflation points to the crux of the presumed illness: that one cannot assume the macrobiotic perspective and observe the "spectacle" of life when one is at the mercy of the (erotic) images that have taken over the spectacle itself. The irony lies in the fact that the "living death" Hufeland condemns is on a continuum with the "artificial life" of the macrobiotic or posthuman position, i.e., the difference between artificial life and artificial death is more quantitative than qualitative. These musings lead to a second point: if the use of mental masturbation is considered unhealthy, then, one would think, the judicious choice of literature would occupy a position at the other end of the spectrum as salubrious. As it turns out, the matter is less simple than would appear at first glance. We could take, as an example, the epigraph at the beginning of the second volume of the *Macrobiotics*, the "practical section." The quote is taken from Goethe's novel, *Wilhelm Meister's Apprenticeship Years*:

> When nature abhors, she pronounces it loudly. The creature that should not be, can not develop, the creature that lives falsely is soon destroyed. Infertility, miserable existence, early decay,— these are nature's curses, the signs of her strictness. Only through immediate consequences does she punish. There! Look around you and what is forbidden and cursed will be obvious to you.[35]

---

34 Hufeland, *Makrobiotik* (1805), vol. 2, 18.
35 Johann Wolfgang Goethe, *Wilhelm Meister's Apprenticeship Years. The Collected Works*, vol. 9, eds. and trans. Eric A. Blackall and Victor Lange (Princeton: Princeton University Press, 1989), 357–8.

Hufeland shows us that at the opposite end of the scale from literary texts that reduce us to living death is the text that seeks to promote the moral good. It is, however, quite ironic that this particular passage comes from a novella from the *Apprenticeship Years* that touches upon the incest motif and that the passage, rather than portraying the healthy life, again uses the threat of death to promote its moral agenda. Also, the contrast could not be more striking between this passage, which, as epigraph, is allowed to "speak" for the entire second volume of Hufeland's *Macrobiotics* and the quote from Egmont on the title page. The image of the "sweet life" that one only wishes to lengthen has been replaced with the decayed life cut short by nature's wrath. Rhetorically speaking, Hufeland seems content to wield both the carrot and the stick. But there is also a peculiar connection between the two. They are joined by the related themes of objectivity, spectacle, and—indirectly—the imagined position of the person who can hold life, and death, within a single gaze.

The notion that good health, beauty, and moral good are connected in an essential way, however common it might have been in Goethe's and Hufeland's time, is one that posthumanism seeks to address and distance itself from. Braidotti takes good care, using Foucault as a theoretical support, to criticize such ideas through a careful discussion of what we mean when we endorse a notion of "health." It is also worth noting that one of the reasons a modern-day reader might tend to find the passage from *Wilhelm Meister's Apprenticeship Years* abhorrent is that what is actually a quote from a conversation between two literary figures is all too easily generalized into a broader theoretical idea which, historically, has had disastrous applications, as in the case of eugenics. The fact that these words are allowed to speak for themselves in Hufeland's text only emphasizes this phenomenon. What Braidotti perhaps overlooks is that the reverse phenomenon, whereby real historical events are reworked into "trivial" literary forms, is equally problematic. As an example, one could consider the "vignettes" introduced at the beginning of her book on topics such as a mass shooting in Finland and the death of the Libyan leader Muammar Gaddafi. Clearly, a fine line needs to be trodden so the material in question serves to make an intellectual argument without being used opportunistically. Otherwise, Braidotti's posthumanism would be no less immune than Hufeland's macrobiotics to the seduction and inherent pratfalls of using literature or literary language as it engages with matters of life and death.

Medical Life and Death

Let us leave questions of morality aside for the moment in order to shift the perspective back to the processes of life itself. I would like to offer two examples drawn from the *Macrobiotics* that invoke the state of death within life processes in order to show how the defining feature of Hufeland's project—the positioning of thinking and acting as if from beyond life, while living, is used both more broadly than one might imagine as well as strategically, as an analytical tool. These examples are sleep and the medical state of apparent death, which the German language expresses as *Scheintod*. The time of sleep, writes Hufeland, is "nothing other than a pause of the intensive life, an apparent loss of it, but even in this pause, in this interruption of its efficacy, lies the greatest means of its extension."[36] What Hufeland offers us in the *Macrobiotics* is neither a physiological description of sleep, nor is it an empirical analysis of healthy as opposed to unhealthy sleep practices. It is something closer to a poetic meditation about what sleep is (and the words *scheinbarer Verlust* already gesture in that direction). About sleep, he writes that "it provides, as it were, the stations"—and here, contemporary readers would likely have conjured the image of way-stations where travelers in haste would pause to exchange one horse for another—"for our physical and moral existence and we maintain thereby the blessedness, to be born again from new every day, and to cross every morning through a state of non-being into a new refreshed life."[37] Sleep is *Schein* or illusion of loss that, in fact, connotes the opposite: a net gain that is framed in terms of a transition from non-being to being. It is "productive" in both a literal and a figurative sense. This passage is not only of practical medical value. It also invokes the same theoretical position that defines the project as a whole: the standpoint of speaking from beyond the grave, or from the state of non-being. This position is given greater definition through the spatial metaphor of the station and the temporal figure of crossing over. Like sleep, macrobiotics can be productive for life, and like sleep, the methods of macrobiotics can also be interpreted as recurring initiatives to renew and refresh life from a point which is theoretically distinct and practically embedded within life itself.

In the case of artificial death, or *Scheintod*, we have a phenomenon that (as one might imagine even without the benefit of medical expertise) could easily be misdiagnosed with disastrous consequences. This phenomenon was considered important enough that, starting around 1795 in Germany, there were entire lecture courses devoted to it (and, much more recently, a study by Gerlind Rüve devoted to its cultural significance in the eighteenth and nineteenth centuries).[38] From the macrobiotic perspective, Hufeland is interested in *Scheintod* to the degree that

---

36 Hufeland, *Makrobiotik* (1805), vol. 1, 56.
37 Hufeland, *Makrobiotik* (1805), vol. 2, 154.
38 See Rüve, *Scheintod. Zur kulturellen Bedeutung der Schwelle zwischen Leben und Tod um 1800* (Berlin: transcript, 2008).

intellectuals of the time as diverse as Pierre Maupertuis and Benjamin Franklin considered the possibility of instrumentalizing *Scheintod* in the interest of playing with the "natural" time of life itself.

In Franklin's essays, for example, one can read:

> I wish it were possible ... to invent a method of embalming drowned persons, in such a manner that they might be recalled to life at any period, however distant; for having a very ardent desire to see and observe the state of America a hundred years hence, I should prefer to an ordinary death, the being immersed in a cask of Madeira wine, with a few friends, until that time, then to be recalled to life by the solar warmth of my dear country.[39]

If an encasked Franklin were to awaken to the state of affairs in his beloved country today, he might regret having been decanted, but that is neither here nor there. The idea is that life can be deliberately interrupted and resumed again.[40] The good doctor Hufeland, however, remains very skeptical about these attempts—the instrumentalization of death implicit in the notion of killing oneself "halfway" holds little appeal to him: "these suggestions fall victim to their own worthlessness, as soon as we look at the true essence and purpose of human life. What is, then, human life? Truly, not just eating, drinking, sleeping. Otherwise it would be more or less the life of a pig."[41]

No, as one might expect, there is a "higher purpose" to human life. But what might that purpose be? One can refer to the postscript Hufeland wrote to *Goethe's Last Illness*[42]: "never has one observed such a unity of physical and spiritual perfection and beauty in a man, as at that moment in Goethe."[43] This example is of particular interest because the moment to which Hufeland refers is Goethe's appearance on the Weimar stage in Grecian costume as Orestes in *Iphigenia auf Tauris*, which was first performed in 1779. To be sure, someone whose fate is as narrowly circumscribed as that of Orestes has little to gain from a *Macrobiotics*. What matters is that the moment which for Hufeland is deeply

---

39 Benjamin Franklin, "Observations on the Generally Prevailing Doctrines of Life and Death," in *The Works of the Late Dr. Benjamin Franklin* (Philadelphia: William M'Carty, 1815), 199–200.
40 Hufeland also refers, if indirectly, to Maupertuis's *Venus physique*, Lettre xix, sur l'art de prolonger la vie where Maupertuis entertains the notion of prolonging life indefinitely.
41 Hufeland, *Makrobiotik* (1805), vol. 2, 301.
42 The literary status of this postscript is also worth further consideration, given that its position in Vogel's book coincides thematically with its position relative to Goethe's life.
43 Carl Vogel, *Die letzte Krankheit Goethes* (Berlin: G. Reimer, 1833), 38.

connected to Goethe's perfection is a moment of performance, where an actor embodies the identity that is not his own and the non-authentic acting Goethe becomes more authentic than the offstage Goethe.[44] In other words, we can connect the concept of "extension of life" to the acquisition of a cultural apparatus that comes complete with various tools of which acting the part of another is just one. It is the right moment, perhaps, to recall the subtitle of Marshall McLuhan's *Understanding Media*: "The Extensions of Man."

When Hufeland speaks of our higher purpose, he argues that man should not merely fill a hole in creation—like a kind of material stopgap among other species—but that man should be "the lord, the ruler, the benefactor [*Herr, Beherrscher, Beglücker*] of creation."[45] "Can one also say of a person: *he lives*, if he extends his life through sleep, boredom, or even an apparent death?"[46] Clearly, the answer is a firm "no," for Hufeland. One needs the appropriate apparatus—a "technology" in the early sense of the word, i.e., the numerous "rules" scattered throughout the theoretical and, even more so, the practical volume of the *Macrobiotics*—in order to influence the "human machine" and to create art from the "operation" of life.[47]

Conclusion

The purpose of this essay has been to contribute to a new examination of the historical preconditions of posthumanism by offering Hufeland's *Macrobiotics* as a case study. I have shown how Hufeland and Braidotti face a number of similar—and significant—challenges. Both are concerned with reinterpreting the conceptual relationships of "life" and "death" in a meaningful way given the technology of their times. They each grapple with the narrative and rhetorical challenges as well: as they are faced with the task both to construct life and to articulate the distinction between life and death in a meaningful way. The historical project of macrobiotics occupies a conceptual space and exists as a placeholder for questions that posthumanism will address with other technological reference points at its disposal. For both Hufeland and Braidotti, the theoretical positions they uphold are essentially hybrid in that they adopt and respond to the constraints of various modes of thinking and writing informed by literature, science, and technology. Of these three categories, the former is most deserving of further

---

44 Braidotti also speaks of the self-styling "I," although the equation of an autopoietically self-expressive self to *potential* seems to follow a circular logic. See Braidotti, *The Posthuman*, 136.
45 Hufeland, *Makrobiotik* (1805), vol. 1, 202.
46 Ibid.
47 Ibid.

consideration, though for different reasons in each case. Even though neither Hufeland nor Braidotti is a "literary" writer in the traditional sense of the term, it is worth considering in greater detail the terms of their engagement (or, in Braidotti's case, a deficit of engagement) with literary concerns. In Hufeland's case, this could entail a deeper investigation into his use of metaphor and the literary references scattered throughout the *Macrobiotics*, which extend further than the ones I have discussed in this essay. For Braidotti, it would require, as a starting point, a reassessment of the incomplete calls to incorporate thinking about art one finds in *The Posthuman*. This would further substantiate the insight that her self-appointed challenge to construct a posthuman theory of death has much to gain from a long history of the literary practice of constructing life.

Fifteen The Indifference of the Inorganic

Gabriel Trop

The Inconsistency of World

Let us begin with two postulates, each of which can be found in Hannah Arendt's *The Human Condition*. First, there is no such thing as a human condition, if by human condition one means a stable, unchanging essence of the human outside of the practices through which the human produces itself. There is only human *conditioned-ness (Bedingtheit)*.[1] Ways of being conditioned exist in the plural (*Bedingtheiten*) and are open to being modified, to being reconditioned, to being unconditioned, or disappearing as a condition altogether. In a rather unwieldy formulation, one would have to speak of *conditionednesses,* or modes of being conditioned that are inherently changeable. The human, as a category, is only as stable as the conditions through which this being comes to understand itself as such.

Second, although Arendt focuses on human actors as the driving force of politics, there is a subterranean form of agency that can be attributed to objects, above all to works of art. This form of object agency is just as important as the human agency of political action. Objects—in this particular case, artifacts made by human beings—crystallize and capture ways of organizing the world; they are the sensible

---

1 Arendt's German version makes explicit certain currents of thought that remain implicit in the English version. At first, Arendt seems to presuppose "that the basic capacities of the human being, which correspond to the basic conditionednesses [*Grundbedingtheiten*] of human existence on the earth, do not change." Hannah Arendt, *Vita activa oder vom tätigen Leben* (Munich: Piper, 1994), 13. However, in the next sentence, she qualifies this thought, noting "these capacities cannot go irrevocably lost as long as these basic conditionednesses are not radically replaced by others" (ibid., 13), thereby implying that these human capacities (for Arendt, labor, work, and action) can in fact go lost if the "conditionedness" of the human changes radically.

forms through which human beings articulate their investments. Artifacts, texts, discursive encodings—and Arendt's own *Human Condition* operates precisely in this manner—thus function as a repository of human memory and give rise to the notion of a *world*, or something that lasts beyond the span of a single human life and codifies the conditions through which beings, both human and nonhuman, relate to one another. For Arendt, the world is nothing other than this web of relations endowed with a form of limited duration. The "conditionedness" of the human is to posit objects that do not merely preserve action, but construct the world as such.

Through the lens of these two postulates—the "conditionedness" of the human being and the agency of objects in the articulation of this conditionedness—the critic can rethink art, literature and philosophy as critical sites (although not the exclusive sites) that contribute to the conditioning, reconditioning, and unconditioning of the human in relation to other beings. Examining discourses, texts, or objects in this manner does not seek to interpret them as holistic units with a coherent or consistent message to be decoded, but to extract from them the particular movements in thought that they enable. Specifically, such objects can play a strategic role in the struggle to determine what counts *as a world*. It is with such a struggle in mind that we turn to Schelling's early naturephilosophy (*Naturphilosophie*), in particular the version found in Schelling's *First Outline of a System of the Philosophy of Nature*, and Goethe's novel *Elective Affinities*.[2]

Both Schelling and Goethe understand nature, or the totality of all that is—as there is nothing outside of nature—as a paradoxical system riven by tensions, inconsistencies and contradictions. The philosophical text and the literary text, albeit in different ways, produce and intensify the collision between coherence and inconsistency, logic and nonsense—the *doxa* and the *paradox*—that leaves its indelible mark on appearances. One may see such a collision in exemplary fashion in the case of Goethe's novel *Elective Affinities*. The central conceit of *Elective Affinities* consists, on the one hand, in an ironic rhetorical game, or the literalization of a scientific metaphor: human action as analogous to the interplay of chemical elements. On the other hand, this very conceit articulates the ontological insight of naturephilosophy, namely, that human beings have no exceptional status in the totality of beings. If human beings are free, it is a freedom that must be found already to inhere in molecules, elements, the play of invisible forces. Freedom, if it

---

2 I follow Iain Hamilton Grant's translation of *Naturphilosophie* as naturephilosophy; see Iain Hamilton Grant, *Philosophies of Nature after Schelling* (New York: Continuum, 2006). In general, my thoughts about Schelling's naturephilosophy owe a great debt to this book.

exists at all, thus does not separate the human from its inorganic others, but on the contrary, sutures the human into this very system. Positioned between an ironic, self-conscious literary game and a disclosure of the way beings relate to one another, the literary text is therefore simultaneously false and true, itself an oscillation between incommensurable discursive orders.

According to the conceit of *Elective Affinities*, the human being does not stand outside of nature, but stands *into* it, and thereby becomes opaque to itself; the invisible forces of attraction and repulsion seem to grab hold of human interiority and recast the most intimate erotic attachments as unconscious movements governed by external forces. The lovers Ottilie and Eduard in *Elective Affinities* thus exert "an almost magical attraction upon one another ... If they found themselves in the same room, it was not long before they were standing or sitting side-by-side."[3] Erotic attraction in this instance is evacuated of interiority. The "unconscious" attraction of Eduard and Ottilie is truly non-consciousness: an external force that governs bodies and disindividuates beings. Eduard and Ottilie are disindividuated in two ways. First, as soon as their bodies are in proximity to one another, "they were not two people, they were one person."[4] Second, and more importantly, this erotic oneness is predicated on another, more primordial disindividuation: they are in this moment "unreflecting perfect well-being, contented with themselves and with the universe."[5] The human being becomes a medium for a systemic presence beyond the human, but precisely as something that belongs intimately *to* the human.

Here we come to the central operation that links together Schelling's naturephilosophy and Goethe's *Elective Affinities*. Over and above the primacy of a subjective, individualizing power—the systems of attraction and repulsion as erotic or libidinal energies of a consciousness system—lie the more primordial operations of *indifferentiation*. It is precisely through such operations of indifferentiation that nature reveals itself to be an inconsistent, enigmatic system and thereby gives rise to a world saturated with paradoxicality. It is in this spirit that both Schelling and Goethe harness the powers of indifferentiation: not in the attempt to save the world, but to save its inconsistency.

Operations of Indifference

What is indifference? Ontologically, one may best express indifference as that process through which a difference is rendered inoperative;

---

[3] Johann Wolfgang Goethe, *Elective Affinities*, trans. R. J. Hollingdale (New York: Penguin, 2005), 286.
[4] Ibid., 286.
[5] Ibid., 286.

what previously counted as a basis for information, for deciding upon what counts, now simply registers as undifferentiated noise, or it does not register at all. If one takes as a point of reference Gregory Bateson's notion of information as a difference that makes a difference, indifference entertains a counter-operation akin to negative information: a difference that *does not make a difference*.[6] When Agamben, for example, imagines what it might mean to "render inoperative the machine that governs our conception of man,"[7] he draws upon an ontology in which indifference takes priority over difference. Rather than conceptualizing indifference ontologically, however, one may grasp it *operationally*: as the strategic elision of differences, whether the difference is between human and animal; between man and woman; between god and human; between transcendence and immanence; or between whatever other order of differences tends to structure normative commitments.[8]

This contribution will focus on a brief episode within the history of indifference as an operation of thought and signification, the drama of which takes place around 1800 in German-speaking lands in the discursive field of *Naturphilosophie*.[9] Within this field, one may detect an intensification and multiplication of the logics, operations, and semantics of indifference in the works of Schelling, Ritter, Novalis, Steffens, Ast, and Oken, to name a few of the most prominent examples.[10] When Anton Brugmans bestowed the name of the "point of indifference" to the point in a magnet at which polarities are canceled and yet maintained as operative within the magnet as a whole, he hinted at a deeply paradoxical dynamic hidden in the invisible order of visible appearances that challenged the stability of the categories of identity and difference.[11] A

---

6 Gregory Bateson, *Steps to an Ecology of Mind* (Chicago: University of Chicago Press, 2000), 315.
7 Giorgio Agamben, *The Open: Man and Animal* (Stanford: Stanford University Press, 2004), 92.
8 For a discussion of the relation of indifference to sexual difference, see Jocelyn Holland, *German Romanticism and Science: The Procreative Poetics of Goethe, Novalis, and Ritter* (London: Routledge, 2009), 136–41; see also Jocelyn Holland, "Die Zeit der Indifferenz. Johann Wilhelm Ritter und die Weiblichkeit," in *Narration und Geschlecht. Texte—Medien—Episteme*, eds. Sigrid Nieberle and Elisabeth Strowick (Cologne: Böhlau, 2006), 335–47.
9 For a sophisticated article that makes "indifference" into a central operation that attempts to think "impersonal" production, see Alberto Toscano, "Fanaticism and Production: On Schelling's Philosophy of Indifference," *Pli* 8 (1999): 46–70.
10 For a discussion of Schelling's notion of indifference, see Bernhard Rang, *Identität und Indifferenz. Eine Untersuchung zu Schellings Identitätsphilosophie* (Frankfurt a.M.: Klostermann, 2000).
11 See Anton Brugmans, *Philosophische Versuche über die magnetische Materie* (Leipzig: Crusius, 1784), 69–70.

point in the sensible world had been discovered that could suspend *and* maintain the logic of polarity.

In this period, philosophy and literature form discursive crucibles through which strategic approaches to processes of indifference can be explored. The interest of this period for our purposes consists in the manner in which naturephilosophical thought and aesthetics unlock the power of indifference as an imaginative-materialist technology of signification. Although indifference plays a central role not just in naturephilosophy, but in metaphysics, aesthetics, theories of sexuality, theology, and anthropology, to name a few of the disciplinary fields in which indifference became operational over the course of the nineteenth century, here I will focus on the manner in which indifference becomes the lens through which the human (as an organic being that grasps itself as such) situates itself in relation to that which lies outside the organic order.

To speak of the *indifference of the inorganic* at first seems to postulate an external realm of inanimate matter as something indifferent to the human. The opposite is the case in Schelling's naturephilosophy. At stake in naturephilosophy is the uncovering of homologous tendencies through which the organic and inorganic cease to be *mere* oppositions. The inorganic nevertheless retains a force of alterity, even agonism and oppositionality, for the organic. However, this alterity is both suspended from the perspective of the larger system *and* maintained as a local opposition or antagonism.

The "sameness-otherness" of the inorganic vis-à-vis the human being, as organic being, becomes a source of discursive paradoxicality—not just within naturephilosophy, but in a manner that seeps into cultural and aesthetic production. Naturephilosophical art of this period—by Goethe, Hoffmann, and Novalis, for example—will harness this power of the inorganic to make present a disruptive energetics that can resurface, perturb, and reconfigure the realm of the human. Such is the case, at least, in the work that concerns us here: Goethe's *Elective Affinities*.

In order to grasp the particularity of the organic-inorganic relation at work in Goethe's *Elective Affinities*, it will be helpful to isolate two basic orientations toward the inorganic in the discourse of naturephilosophy. First, there is a negative inorganic: the tendency of organic life toward inorganic matter as a proto-death drive in nature, a relentless desire within the natural system to eliminate differentiation, to return all appearances back to a more primordial state of indifference. Second, there is an affirmative inorganic: the inorganic itself as differential, multiple, and part of the unfolding of the order of becoming. In this positive sense—through the *for-itself* of the inorganic (rather than the inorganic *for the organic*)—the inorganic discloses a principle of representation at the heart of nature: a drive internal to the natural system to externalize itself. The inorganic itself thus becomes a bifurcated domain: simultaneously revelatory of the multiplicity of becoming *and* an unconditioning force that turns against all vitality. Although Schelling drifts from one conception to another, this oscillation between negative and affirmative functional roles for the inorganic becomes part of the texture of Goethe's novel. The inorganic thus becomes invested with a power of ambiguity.

Goethe's *Elective Affinities*, as a textual cosmos modeled less on a chemical experiment than on the exploration of zones of differentiation and indifferentiation, aesthetically animates the paradoxes that result from this conception of the inorganic. It demands that its readers inhabit a world in which the inorganic, as source of simultaneous preservation *and* perturbation, is both intimately part of and alien to the world of human intelligibility. For Goethe, the difference and indifference potentially harbored within the inorganic simultaneously interrupts and challenges the autonomy of the human just as it includes within itself the possibility of an unexpected *redemption of the human* in the form of an inorganic product. This latter possibility takes place through a naturephilosophical reinterpretation of the *image* (*das Bild*) as a space in which inanimate matter embodies a form of life outside of organic life.[12]

The Indifference of Naturephilosophy

Even in its earliest iterations—before the notion of indifference or *Indifferenz* becomes a philosophical concept in Schelling's *First Outline*—naturephilosophy develops operations of thought that seek to suspend oppositions: between subject and object, spirit and nature, organic and inorganic. Such is the basis of Schelling's critique of mere reflection, *bloße Reflexion*. In the *Ideas for a Philosophy of Nature*, Schelling calls mere reflection the "mental illness of the human being."[13] The sickness of

---

12 At first glance, such a conception of life seems to resonate with an "impersonal" vitality such as that advocated by Rosi Braidotti, who attempts to conceptualize a "politics of life itself as a relentlessly generative force including and going beyond death." Rosi Braidotti, *The Posthuman* (Cambridge: Polity, 2013), 121. However, the life beyond life that manifests itself in the image (and, as we shall see, in a form of writing, a superscript or *Überschrift*) in Goethe's *Elective Affinities* refers to something quite different: the impossible remnant of individuation after death, of particularity, rather than death as dissolution in a generative matrix. For both Schelling and Goethe, death produces or reveals a transcendental inconsistency; for Goethe, this inconsistency is preserved precisely by *maintaining* a counterforce of individuation rather than simply dissolving one's self (or the durable world of artifacts) into the undifferentiated plenum of a chaotic matrix.

13 Friedrich Schelling, *Ideen zu einer Philosophie der Natur, Sämmtliche Werke*, ed. Karl Friedrich August Schelling, vol. 1, no. 2 (Stuttgart: Cotta, 1857), 13.

reflection can be traced back to a problematic form of differentiation; it separates the I and that which is other. If reflection separates, generates a traumatic wound, naturephilosophy must heal this wound. In every instance, then, whenever naturephilosophy is reconstructing movement via polarities and bindings, potencies and acts of indifferentiation, it is working its discursive magic, effacing the line that separates the subject from everything else supposedly outside of it.

However, it is important to note that this healing is only a healing from one point of view, and it is anything but a restoration of the integrity of life or the human being. On the contrary, in Schelling's work, the natural system is often turned against itself, involuted, overly fluid or overly solid, clashing with itself, internally violent; when we are healed from reflection and see ourselves as emergent from nature, we become just as mysterious, paradoxical, violent and inconsistent as the natural system itself. Healing is thus not so much an erasure of violence as an exposure to a different type of violence. It is a violence whose traces one can find everywhere in the system of nature, for example, in electricity, which wreaks "destruction" on animal bodies, or as Schelling writes, "as it separates with violence what was previously united and binds that which previously fled from itself."[14] Schelling's early naturephilosophy thus posits healing as unification with a system that is itself agonistic; we are healed only inasmuch as we expose ourselves more intensively to the contradictions of this system.

Naturephilosophy thus does not efface the difference between the organic and the inorganic as much as regard this oppositionality from a systemic point of view: as a contingent condition of a process to which no conditions can be attached (the absolute as "unconditioned" or *unbedingt*). Schelling describes one of the central problems of naturephilosophy as follows: "The problem presupposes that organic product and inorganic product are mutually *opposed*, whereas the latter is only the *higher power* of the former, and is produced only by the higher power of the forces through which the latter also is produced."[15] The inorganic must be simultaneously *opposed to* and *identical with* the organic. Organic beings are opposed to the inorganic inasmuch as their entire existence consists in the attempt to defer the inevitable slide of their own self-animation into the inanimate corporeality of chemical compounds: decaying muscle matter, hair, bone, dust. Organic beings are, however, identical to the inorganic inasmuch as they are part of one and the same dynamic of becoming. The doctrine of *potencies* (*Potenzen*) is meant to describe how this difference-sameness is possible; the

---

14 Ibid., 137.
15 Friedrich Schelling, *First Outline of a System of the Philosophy of Nature*, trans. Keith R. Peterson (Albany: State University of New York Press, 2004), 231.

organic manifests an identical structure of inorganic becoming at a different level of potentiation.

The notion of the *potence*, however, does not simply suture the gap between organic and inorganic, but more importantly, fixes the opposition between the two domains. So deep is the divide between the organic and the inorganic that the organic cannot transition into the inorganic, that is, it cannot ever truly die, if by death one understands a *becoming-inorganic*:

> As long as it is organic the product can never sink into indifference. If it is to support the universal striving toward indifference, then it must first sink to a product of a lower potency. As an organic product it cannot die, and when it does die it is really already no longer organic. Death is the return into universal indifference. Just for that reason the organic product is absolute, immortal. For it is an *organic* product at all, because indifference can never be reached by it. Only at the moment when it has ceased to be organic does the product resolve itself into the universal indifference.[16]

While the global gesture of naturephilosophy is to lead the organic and the inorganic back to a homologous structure, it nevertheless maintains a categorical opposition between the organic and the inorganic. The organic can never *become* inorganic; rather, it can only depotentiate itself, thereby introducing a gap in the flow of becoming.

Another way of expressing this insight is that the organic and the inorganic are simultaneously *absolutely identical* and *absolutely discontinuous*. They cannot relate to one another as do the positive and negative poles of a magnet. At the point of indifference of a magnet, the poles cancel one another, but the magnet as a whole still exhibits the structure of polarity. The organic and the inorganic would represent, as it were, *different magnets* rather than *different poles of one magnet*. There is no "sliding scale" between the organic and the inorganic; theirs is a form of difference beyond polarity. When organic matter dies, it jumps from one polar order (organic life) to another (inorganic matter). Such is the movement of depotentiation.

One may nevertheless detect a differentiation of *indifferences* in Schelling's thought. Indifference becomes a localized operation *and* an ontological structure; indeed, there are "different" forms of indifference for both the organic and the inorganic.[17] Schelling writes in the *Introduction*

---

[16] Ibid., 68.
[17] See ibid., 189. There is also a second-order indifference *between* potentiated zones, or an indifference that elides and stabilizes the difference between the organic and the inorganic; Schelling refers to this second-order indifference as *universal gravity*. Ibid., 224–5.

to the Outline: "In organic nature, indifference can never come to be in the same way in which it comes to exist in inorganic nature, because life consists in nothing more than a continual *prevention of the attainment of indifference*."[18] In the domain of organic life, nature works tirelessly to return organic beings to a state of indifference, while living beings struggle to prevent nature from attaining this indifference.

Here we come face to face with one of the most paradoxical consequences of this iteration of naturephilosophy: life and nature work *against one another*. Schelling writes that life is "a condition which is only, so to speak, extorted from nature."[19] Precisely at this point is to be found a conception of life as the disclosure of a primordial inconsistency in the system of nature as a whole.[20] Schelling will insist: "the phenomenon of life is paradoxical even in its cessation."[21] What is paradoxical about life? Life appears at once both lawful and anomalous, purposive and perverse; it results from an order that governs the unfolding of appearances as well as from a violation or suspension of this order (nature's seeming desire for a state of absolute indifference). Schelling writes: "It is manifest what an extremely artificial condition life is—wrenched, as it were, from Nature—subsisting against the will of Nature."[22] Life emerges from that which is in nature that works against nature. The emergence of life only takes place because something within the natural system exceeds its own control.

There is thus at work within nature a drive that is other than itself, even antagonistic to itself. From the perspective of nature, organic life is a misfiring—indeed, all individuation is an "abortive attempt" to represent the absolute—that nature seeks to rectify by returning it to non-differentiation.[23] This misfiring subsists inasmuch as life keeps

---

18   Ibid., 229.
19   Ibid., 229.
20   Claire Colebrook hypothesizes about the emergence of human existence as "a strange torsion of being at once closed off from life while at the same time claiming to be nothing more than life." Claire Colebrook, *Death of the PostHuman: Essays on Extinction*, vol. 1 (Ann Arbor, MI: Open Humanities Press, 2014), 229. Schelling's naturephilosophy extends this paradoxical structure not just to humans, but to all forms of individuated organic life.
21   Schelling, *First Outline*, 68.
22   Ibid., 230.
23   Ibid., 41. Schelling's notion of individuation changes in the shift from *Naturphilosophie* to identity philosophy; the individuation of *Naturphilosophie* in the *First Outline* exerts an ironizing force on all practices of life (and hence on all biopolitical logics). In this iteration of *Naturphilosophie*, individuation is an abortive misfiring and thereby manifests an internal inconsistency within nature; in the identity philosophy, however, individuation occurs as a result of the desire of the cosmos to affirm its own productive power. See Daniel Whistler, "Schelling on Individuation," *Comparative and Continental Philosophy* 8, no. 3 (2016): 329–44; and Yuk Hui, "The Parallax of Individuation," *Angelaki* 21, no. 4 (2016): 77–89.

going, and nature keeps attempting to repair itself inasmuch as it tirelessly seeks to extinguish life. The relation between life and nature thus tells a story of two forms of desire working at cross-purposes with one another: the system of nature posits an absolute absence of differentiation as the unattainable telos of its desire, while life posits its own subsistence (its maintenance "as" a difference) as its equally unattainable telos of desire.

To occupy the position of nature thus demands from the philosopher of nature an inversion of values. The consequences are as follows: whenever we seek to foster and promote life, bio-diversity, respect for individuals and others, we are in fact acting *against* nature's desire to return to indifference. The doctrine of individuation elaborated here produces a gesture akin to a romantic-ironic function by which we step out of our value system and invert the frame of our selves *as* individuated beings. Nature asks us to entertain the notion that diversity is *unnatural*, not necessarily as an outside of nature, but as an unnature at the heart of nature. Individuation occurs because nature is itself a deviant, eccentric system, always violating its own structure, and we are beings who manifest this violation. Individuation is thus predicated upon deviation from a pattern, and it signals that process by which a system is rendered internally inconsistent with itself; understanding individuation in this way means embracing an internal inconsistency, an individual as exteriority to norm, rather than valorizing the individual *as* a norm.

The most significant operation of naturephilosophy is thus not merely to think a unity between mind and nature, nor even to bind the organic and the inorganic in an overarching system, but to affirm the internal agonism that saturates the totality of natural operations and gives rise to paradoxical modes of individuation. In the realm of organic life, forms of individuation taken to their extreme often strike us as anomalous, transgressive, or otherwise outside the bounds of normativity or comprehension because there is *already something anomalous and transgressive* inherent in the very process of naturephilosophical individuation.

In the realm of cultural production, there is a significant discursive form in which the inorganic and the desire of the natural system for the indifference of the inorganic retains its paradoxical and transgressive characteristics: a domain that makes present an unruly form of organization that intrudes upon the integrity of life with an uncanny power of perturbation. This domain is that of art. Schelling's own philosophy of art is structured around operations of indifference: freedom/necessity, possibility/reality, form/essence, subjective/objective, sublime/beautiful, naive/sentimental, each of which are specific to generic forms (epic, lyric, novel, etc.). Art becomes the sensible form through which operations of indifference can manifest themselves *through* differences.

Goethe's *Elective Affinities*, as a work of art, takes up the challenge to imaginatively explore the potentiality of operations of indifference. However, what is forbidden and unthinkable in Schelling's earlier *Naturphilosophie*—namely the establishment of a zone of indifference between organic and inorganic on a sliding scale, or some object that could simultaneously be *organic and inorganic* at the same time—becomes possible and even necessary in the world of the novel. Indeed, the novel establishes a zone of indifference between the organic and the inorganic in two seemingly contradictory imaginary exercises: (1) the aesthetic-inorganic as a reserve of inconsistency that perturbs the stability of any normative structure, and (2) the aesthetic-inorganic domain as a site within which the organic can be *preserved* (and not just *perturbed*) and without which the *world*—as a shared space of existence—could not exist.

Indifference in Goethe's *Elective Affinities*

Goethe's *Elective Affinities* has often been compared to a literary experiment.[24] According to Goethe's own pronouncements, however, one ought not to collapse the distinction between the scientific experiment and the work of art as genres of writing and as imaginative practices. Scientific experimentation aims at the exhaustion of a potentially infinite series of variations. Art, however, precludes the possibility of such an iterative series and cultivates the preservation of an imaginative remainder intrinsic to its own form. In the essay "The Experiment as Mediator between Object and Subject," Goethe expresses this insight as follows:

> The multiplication of every individual experiment is the actual duty of a natural scientist. He has precisely the inverted duty of an author who would like to entertain. The author would incite boredom if he never left anything to think about; the scientist must work tirelessly as if he didn't want to leave anything to do for his followers.[25]

In *Elective Affinities*, the "literary experiment" undertaken—placing four different individuals with different tendencies in a situation to see how they separate and recombine—is not an experiment at all. On the

---

24 See Olaf Breidbach, "*Die Wahlverwandtschaften*—Versuch einer wissenschaftshistorischen Perspektivierung," in *Goethes Wahlverwandtschaften: Werk und Forschung*, ed. Helmut Hühn (Berlin: De Gruyter, 2010), 291–310.
25 Johann Wolfgang Goethe, "Der Versuch als Vermittler von Objekt und Subjekt," in *Sämtliche Werke*, eds. Wolf Von Engelhardt and Manfred Wenzel, vol. 1, no. 25 (Frankfurt a.M.: Suhrkamp, 1989), 33.

contrary, the seemingly deterministic internal order of the text—whose parts seem so tightly interlaced, giving rise to a texture in which almost every detail seems to become enmeshed in a series of analogies and resemblances—contributes to the indeterminacy of the text as a whole. The text continually produces the sense of a depth to which its own surfaces prevent access.

One of the central techniques through which the text produces this sense of a depth into whose regions one cannot penetrate is through the representation of conflicting operations that seem impossible to mediate or synthesize. Charlotte and the Captain belong to the realm of differentiation, law, duty, renunciation, the restricted economy of estate planning; over and against these tendencies, Ottilie and Eduard initiate processes of unbinding, excess, indifferentiation, and the dynamics of an absolute that has the effect of destabilizing the operativity of normative and regulative systems.[26] A perspectivalism emerges from these divergent positions, and one cannot accede to any depth in the novel that would confirm the primacy of one perspective over another.

Despite appearances, *Elective Affinities* does not merely erect a binary structure that pits one coupling against the other, or the differentiation and regulation of Charlotte and the Captain against the indifferentiation and excess of Eduard and Ottilie. Rather, the novel generates bifurcations within bifurcations, the most significant of which comes to light in the dynamic relationship between Eduard and Ottilie. If one examines these characters not simply as characters, but also as manifestations of a certain naturephilosophical operativity—in and of itself an admittedly slippery enterprise as it translates characters into symbolic expressions of an absolute—one discovers that the attraction between Eduard and Ottilie stages not the coherence of this ontological absolute, but rather, its internal inconsistencies and agonisms. Both Eduard and Ottilie become ciphers for the dynamics of an absolute turned against itself.

The inconsistencies of the absolute manifest themselves through operations of indifferentiation: those that take place between the organic and the inorganic or those that manifest themselves through erotic attraction. Johann Wilhelm Ritter, whose writings belong to the discursive field of naturephilosophy, writes: "Life = relative

---

26 Vogl views Ritter as the scientific paradigm that structures the elemental pairs of the couple, which itself belies the supposed theory of *elective affinities* advanced by Berthollet (my translation follows): "The theory of the elective affinity and its rethinking by Berthollet draw a line of flight that breaks open closed conceptions of systems and transitions into a chemistry of electricity and combustion—which, however, only maintains the comparison to social processes wherever it marks the deregulation, the critical and crisis-prone moment of such processes." Joseph Vogl, "Nomos der Ökonomie. Steuerungen in Goethes *Wahlverwandtschaften*," MLN 114, no. 3, German Issue (April 1999): 524.

indifference, love = absolute."[27] In the novel, love has the effect of driving beyond differentiation, above all in Eduard: "In Eduard's feelings as in his actions, there is no longer any measure. The consciousness of loving and being loved drives him into the infinite."[28] Eduard's erotic drive consists in an expansive, outward movement that transgresses boundaries. In *On the World Soul*, Schelling understands light as the most basic expression of this expansive force that overcomes boundaries, whereas gravity functions as a counterforce, a contractive tendency that asserts the power of limitation and impediments. Eduard's megalomaniacal self-positing seems to disclose an absolute tendency akin to the movement of light, or the perpetual attempt to integrate the alterity of the Not-I into the horizon of the subject: "You love me!" Eduard cries at the moment at which he discovers that Ottilie's handwriting—in the act of copying a contract (hence an erotic abrogation of law in the form of the law)—has gradually transformed into his own.[29] Eduard makes himself into the absolute erotic object (*you love me*) rather than the subject (*I love you*), but this reversal confirms the primacy of his own being as origin of desire. Hence Eduard's "narcissism": in handwriting and in erotic power, Eduard functions as model and Ottilie as copy.[30]

If Eduard begins as an expansive movement toward the infinite, it is quite the contrary for Ottilie. Ottilie, read as the expression of a naturephilosophical tendency, lingers more within the contractive force of gravity than in the expansive force of light. The intimate connection to the inorganic—to the magnetism of the earth, to the pull of gravity—becomes visible to the extent that she suppresses her conscious mental activity in an experiment with a pendulum:

> She held the pendulum even more quietly, composedly and unselfconsciously over the metals lying below. But in a moment the suspended object was agitated as if in a definite vortex and turned now to this side, now to that, now in circles, now in ellipses, or swung back and forth in a straight line, according to which metals were placed beneath it.[31]

---

27 Johann Wilhelm Ritter, *Key Texts of Johann Wilhelm Ritter (1776–1810) on the Science and Art of Nature*, trans. Jocelyn Holland (Leiden: Brill, 2010), 185.
28 Goethe, *Elective Affinities*, 113. Eduard's "expansive" tendency resonates with the structure of Fichtean subjectivity. Both Schelling and Goethe, however, reveal this tendency to be an insufficient characterization of the absolute; indeed, no one figure can disclose the absolute, since the absolute only discloses itself through the process of unconditioning that which posits itself *as* the absolute.
29 Ibid., 109.
30 Eduard claims: "man is a true Narcissus: he makes the whole world his mirror." Ibid., 50.
31 Ibid., 247.

The agitation of magnetic power here reveals Ottilie's connection to the inorganic as imbued with a stochastic power, in a series of movements both unruly (vortex) and orderly (circles, ellipses, the line). However, in order to unlock these powers of the inorganic, she must suppress her subjectivity, or the source of her differentiation from nature, and enter into a zone of indifferentiation with the inorganic—something that, within the framework of Schelling's *First Outline* at least, is impossible.

Already Walter Benjamin had perceived in Ottilie the presence of a death drive coupled with an almost vegetative, plant-like silence.[32] The silence—as well as the death drive—of Ottilie is not simply plant-like, however, but belongs first and foremost to the domain of inanimate nature. When the Architect—and it ought to be noted that in Schelling's *Philosophy of Art*, architecture is the medium closest to inorganic form—brings out his collection of ancient objects and likenesses exhumed from graves, "Perhaps Ottilie alone was situated to feel she was among her own kind."[33] While "Ottilie alone" feels at home among the relics of the dead—which harness both an atavistic (since they point back to a Germanic origin) and a heterocosmic force (since they belong to another world)—she nevertheless is equally associated with a reproductive drive, above all in the reproduction of images. When the Architect is painting the chapel in which Ottilie's corpse would eventually be preserved, "the faces, which were left for the architect alone to paint, gradually took on a very singular quality: they all began to look like Ottilie."[34] Ottilie thus becomes associated with the two main operations of a naturephilosophical absolute: first, as a drive toward indifference, the desire for death; second, as a drive toward representation, thus occupying the position of an *archetype*, a stamp or impression that generates multiple copies of an original form. Ottilie thereby occupies the bifurcation point of the inorganic as that which belongs simultaneously to productivity (the "affirmative" inorganic) and to annihilation (the "negative" inorganic). Both of these operations taken together—toward indifference on the one hand and toward the multiplication of differences on the other—foreground the contradiction that undergirds the system of nature.

The indifferentiation of the organic and the inorganic that takes place through Ottilie harbors a certain potential of misfiring (indeed, from the perspective of Schelling's naturephilosophy in the *Outline*, the total natural system *is* this misfiring). The most concentrated form of

---

32 Walter Benjamin, *Goethes Wahlverwandtschaften*, in *Gesammelte Schriften*, eds. Rolf Tiedemann and Rolf Schweppenhäuser, vol. 1, no. 3 (Frankfurt a.M.: Suhrkamp, 1991), 176.
33 Goethe, *Elective Affinities*, 163.
34 Ibid., 167.

this perturbation takes place at the moment of her "lapse"—in the fateful thirteenth chapter of the second part of the novel—when she lets the baby Otto fall into the waters of the motionless lake while trying to balance the baby, an oar, and a novel. In her efforts to bring the baby back to life, it is "the first time she presses a living creature to her pure naked breast—alas, a living creature no longer [*zum erstenmal drückt sie ein Lebendiges an ihre reine nackte Brust, ach! und kein Lebendiges*]. The unhappy child's cold limbs chill her bosom down to her innermost heart."[35] Here is to be found an important caesura of the novel: a point of rupture that at the same time discloses the ontological field of the novel as a zone of indifference between something alive and nothing alive, *ein Lebendiges* and *kein Lebendiges*.[36] Such a caesura can be located precisely at the moment of depotentiation in which the seemingly unbridgeable gap between organic life and inorganic matter makes itself felt. If, for Schelling, there can be no "indifference point" between the organic and the inorganic, Ottilie comes to inhabit precisely such a point. The shift from organic to inorganic is also marked by an aesthetic depotentiation in different media: from the novel (which, after all, Ottilie lets fall into the water) to the marble coldness of the statue. A circuit is established between the living and the dead; the stiffness of the dead baby's limbs works its way into Ottilie's bosom and the warmth of Ottilie's tears chills as they attempt to animate that which has become inanimate. And indeed, *Elective Affinities* itself explores zones of indifference between the mobility of the novel, with its tears, its flows, the motion of its sentiments, and the immobility of the statuesque, the architectonic, the "tableau vivant."

Otto himself, a product of all four characters, as a palindrome that can be read backwards and forwards, represents nothing other than the most capacious possible zone of indifference. Although a child of Eduard and Charlotte, "in his features and figure he was coming ever more to resemble the Captain, his eyes were becoming ever less distinguishable from Ottilie's."[37] As a concentrated embodiment of processes

---

35 Ibid., 262; for the German, Johann Wolfgang Goethe, *Die Leiden des jungen Werthers; Die Wahlverwandtschaften. Text und Kommentar*, eds. Waltraud Wiethölter and Christoph Brecht, vol. 1, no. 8 (Frankfurt a.M.: Suhrkamp, 2006), 494.

36 Benjamin famously reads the caesura in a more Hölderlinian sense and locates the caesura of the novel in the sentence: "Die Hoffnung fuhr wie ein Stern, der vom Himmel fällt, über ihre Häupter weg [Hope flew over their heads like a star falling from the sky]." Benjamin, *Goethes Wahlverwandtschaften*, 200. Isolating "the" caesura of a work limits its possibilities; indeed, critics can find caesurae at almost any point in a text, which in turn alters the possibilities that inhere in the text. I thus prefer a more open and labile concept of a caesura.

37 Goethe, *Elective Affinities*, 248.

of indifference, Otto becomes a *differend* that generates incompatible interpretive possibilities incapable of being resolved: for Eduard, he represents the monstrous transgression of the law (since Eduard's law is the law of erotic desire), a "twofold adultery";[38] for Charlotte, he represents the law's restoration (since Charlotte's law is the ethical law of marriage, which stands in synecdochically for social order as a whole). Otto thus becomes a cipher for an inconsistent absolute, or as Goethe would formulate the notion of the demonic in *Poetry and Truth*, "something that could only manifest itself in contradictions and was therefore incapable of being grasped by a concept let alone a word."[39]

Scholars have long noticed the resonances between Goethe's concept of the demonic and *Elective Affinities*. Benjamin, in reference to *Elective Affinities*, notes that the demonic emerges from an "experience of an ungraspable ambiguity of nature [*Erfahrung unfaßbarer Naturzweideutigkeit*]."[40] The demonic, however, is not tantamount to a monolithic mythical form of power; on the contrary, the demonic breaks down the hold of the mythical inasmuch as it is invested with a power of perturbation.[41] The demonic, like the absolute (or *das Unbedingte* as the "unconditioned") in Schelling's naturephilosophy, functions as a catalyst for operations of unconditioning the seeming stability of the ethical world order; it calls forth a heterogeneous texture of appearances outside possible normative stability, or "a power, if not opposed to the moral world order, [that] nevertheless traverses it, so that one could portray one as the weft and the other as the warp."[42] Ottilie is the figure who activates this power of unconditioning to the greatest degree, thereby

---

38 Ibid., 260.
39 Johann Wolfgang Goethe, *Dichtung und Wahrheit, Sämtliche Werke*, ed. Klaus-Detlef Müller, vol. 14 (Frankfurt a.M.: Suhrkamp, 1986), 839.
40 Benjamin, *Goethes Wahlverwandtschaften*, 150.
41 In *Poetry and Truth*, such was precisely the function of the demonic: the generation of propositions in the face of something to which no determinate predicate could be attached. The demonic takes the form of a series of negations: "It was not divine, as it seemed irrational, not human, since it had no power of comprehension, not devilish, as it was benevolent, not angelic, since it often displayed *Schadenfreude* ... " Goethe, *Dichtung und Wahreit* (Poetry and Truth), 839. The demonic functions as a generator of difference *and* indifference since it disables the capacity to differentiate but for this very reason incites a series of differentiations. At the same time, it is not *purely* irrational. As Kirk Wetters writes: "it manifests itself in the subjective inability to perform a successful rationalization, but this inability itself—virtually by definition—may not be rationalizable. Having or expecting a reason for everything may itself be a form of irrationality, whereas the demonic reflects a rational deferral in the application of reasons." Kirk Wetters, *Demonic History: From Goethe to the Present* (Evanston: Northwestern University Press, 2014), 199.
42 Goethe, *Dichtung und Wahrheit*, 841.

approaching a form of figuration that resists all definitive predication. Indeed, Ottilie cannot even properly enter the ethical; at the moment where she seems to repent for her transgression, her entrance into the ethical misfires and she simply begets further transgressions, failures, and improbabilities, whether by chance or on purpose: an awkward encounter with Eduard that Ottilie was determined to avoid; the refusal of food—suicide via a diminished metabolism with nature—through which she breaks the ethical law yet again in order to atone for its violation; making Nanni, her child companion, into the unwitting accomplice of a possible suicide, followed by Nanni's fall from the garret and her immediate recovery; walking into a room at the precise moment in which Mittler sermonizes about the seventh commandment (thou shalt not commit adultery) as the meta-commandment upon which the validity of all the others rest.

And yet, Ottilie is not a victim of sheer contingency; rather, her final moments turn passivity into a form of agency. Her death coincides with a performative act—the demand of a promise (*Versprechen*) from Eduard—that cannot be successfully completed, thereby confirming the paradoxical power of the absolute that she comes to embody. She turns to Eduard in her final moments:

> She grips his hand tightly, she gazes upon him with eyes full of life and love, and after drawing a deep breath, after an ethereal silent movement of the lips, "Promise me you will live!" she cries with gentle exertion, and at once sinks back. "I promise!" he cried to her—yet he only cried it after her, for she had already departed.[43]

With the demand for this promise, Ottilie places a condition on Eduard that he is forced to un-condition. First, on the most literal level, the promise to live is the one promise that cannot be kept; a promise (*Versprechen*) becomes a speaking falsely (a *sich versprechen*). Second, even when read in the most charitable manner, the promise forces Eduard into a most horrific double bind. According to the law of desire, Eduard must (and indeed does) follow Ottilie to the grave: if he is to be faithful to Ottilie, then, he must die; if he dies, however, he breaks his promise and is no longer faithful to her. With this double bind, the power relations between Eduard and Ottilie have been inverted: Eduard can no longer live without some form of transgression (either the transgression of the law of the heart, of desire, or the transgression of the ethical, of the promise).

---

43 Goethe, *Elective Affinities*, 293.

Throughout the narrative, from beginning to end, Eduard embodies a subjective-absolute drive that seeks to maintain the desire of individuation that drives life forward; his is a domain ruled by the Spinozan *conatus*. Thus, when Ottilie becomes the archetype that he must follow, when the agency of her passivity overwhelms his activity, he finds he must model himself on a naturephilosophical form of desire—the desire for indifferentiation and death—that is foreign to him. Ottilie's desire originates in this instance not from the subject—the desire of the subject to stay alive—but from the inverted system of nature, or the desire of nature to return to elemental indifference. The inversion of this power dynamic at the end of the novel throws the relation of Ottilie and Eduard in a new light; upon reflection, Ottilie and Eduard were never "identical" in their erotic union, but rather, counter-images, or *Gegenbilder* of one another.[44] Where Eduard previously was origin and Ottilie the copy, here Ottilie becomes origin—an inscrutable, impossible, paradoxical origin—and Eduard becomes copy. Upon following his beloved to the grave, Eduard says:

> how unfortunate I am that all my endeavours have ever been no more than an imitation, a counterfeit! What was bliss to her is grief and pain to me; and yet for the sake of that bliss I am compelled to take this grief and pain upon me. I must go after her, and by this path: but my nature holds me back, and my promise. It is a terrible task to imitate the inimitable.[45]

At the moment of death, the primacy of the naturephilosophical absolute—and its drive to indifferentiation—would seem to claim victory over the transcendental-subjective absolute of individuation. The drive to indifference, in any case, disrupts even the most powerful subjective and normative force, namely the drive that sees the maintenance of the autonomous individual as the highest possible value. Once Ottilie becomes archetype, Eduard must learn the more difficult lesson of *heteronomy*: that autonomy itself is not the highest possibility of the human being, but itself subordinate to forces whose power far exceeds the power of the subject.

The Image and the Impossibility of the World

It is not quite accurate to claim that Ottilie seeks a state of pure indifferentiation, or a *mere* return to the inorganic. On the contrary, she desires a second form of life within death, or an organic form imprinted within

---

44 See Goethe, *Wahlverwandtschaften*, 311.
45 Goethe, *Elective Affinities*, 299.

the inorganic. She desires a dwelling within the image. In her diary, we read the following passage:

> When you see all the gravestones which have sunk down and been worn away by the feet of churchgoers, and even that the churches themselves have collapsed over their own tombs, you can still think of life after death as a second life, which you enter into as a portrait [*Bild*] or an inscription [*Überschrift*], and in which you remain longer than you do in your actual living life. But sooner or later this portrait, this second existence, is also extinguished. As over men, so over memorials time will not let itself be deprived of its rights.[46]

The second half of *Elective Affinities* begins and ends with the problem of the indexicality of the personality after death, or the degree to which a trace of organic individuation is meaningful after the inevitable descent into the indifference of the inorganic. Charlotte begins the second half of the book by denying the need for such indexical signs—for example, a gravestone in a church—but ends the book in the declaration that "no one else" was to be buried in the vault except Ottilie and Eduard. Charlotte thus undergoes a semiotic revolution over the course of the novel. She gravitates from a position of dislocation, or the dissociation of acts of mourning from sensuous referents, to a position that approximates Ottilie's conception of the image as a second life. Here too, Ottilie functions as an archetype for a form of signification that is eventually adopted by Charlotte (the indifference of the organic and inorganic *in the image*; here the two domains are no longer discontinuous).

The status of the image for Ottilie is a paradoxical one. On the one hand, the image of the deceased is nothing other than the transference of an index of organic life into inorganic form (the portrait as paint, canvas, wood, frame); at the point of death, the individual has already been de-potentiated and indifferentiated with inorganic matter, and thus can no longer be preserved *as* organic. On the other hand, the image as a receptacle of the person *maintains* individuality. Note that Ottilie is not claiming that the person "lives on" in the memory of others, but that the person lives *in the image*. The image thus has an ontology that is commensurate with the person; it in-differentiates indifference (the inorganic) and difference (the organic *qua* individual). And more significant for the novel, she claims the same power for writing, for the inscription as a form of writing that is potentiated, a superscript as epitaph (*Überschrift*).[47]

---

[46] Ibid., 165.
[47] My thanks go to Rob Mitchell for drawing my attention to the difference between image (*Bild*) and writing (*Überschrift*) in this passage.

A second life within the image, or within the epitaph or superscript (*Überschrift*) of the text, seems nonsensical, illogical, impossible, hopelessly metaphysical and theologically inflected. However, within this impossibility lies the very precondition of what might be called the *world*. Goethe noted of the demonic: "it only seems to take pleasure in the impossible and thrusts the possible away from itself with contempt."[48] To survive death hints at precisely such an impossibility. The belief in such an impossible survival is what makes possible the cultivation of a world whose ultimate annihilation is certain, but whose temporarily and artificially extended duration nevertheless matters.

To truly incorporate what Ray Brassier calls the "trauma of extinction"[49] into thought would seem to demand an exposure to the most radical of nihilisms and an acknowledgment of the falsehood of the world and its truths. To this event of extinction, the demonic absolute holds out an impossible countermovement. Extinction is inevitable ... *and yet*, there subsists a world that, in spite of this inevitability of extinction, acts as if it were not an inevitability. To be committed to this world and its continuity is to be committed to the *inconsistency* of the nature-philosophical absolute. The indifference of the image holds out the possibility of an impossible "*and yet*" to the inevitability of extinction.

Such is the inconsistency of the drive of life that Schelling calls nature working against itself. For Ottilie, who tends to align herself with the natural tendency to indifferentiation over individuation, the image is held up as an interruption of nature's drive toward indifferentiation: an "and yet" that plants within nature itself the possibility of an impossibility maintained in its imaginative and sensuous concreteness. The image acknowledges the event of extinction—since even this second life within the image will one day turn into dust—and nevertheless holds obstinately to an extended temporality of imaginary existence as the most precious gift, as the suspension of a rigorous logic according to which nihilism constitutes the only proper response to nature's drive toward indifference. The image represents the last reserve of an extended yet transient form of individuation before indifference ultimately claims its rights.

Precisely this inconsistent naturephilosophical absolute abides in the movements of the final sentences of the novel: "And thus the lovers lie side by side. Peace hovers about their abode, smiling angelic figures (with whom too they have affinity) look down upon them from the vault above, and what a happy moment it will be when one day

---

48 Goethe, *Dichtung und Wahrheit*, 840.
49 Ray Brassier, *Nihil Unbound: Enlightenment and Extinction* (Basingstoke: Palgrave, 2007), 238.

they awaken again together."[50] Here again we see Ottilie's particular power: the capacity to attract to herself the reproduction of forms, or the angelic figures (*verwandte Engelsbilder*) that bear her own likeness and look down upon the lovers. This uncanny interplay between source and image becomes the stage for a scene in which death as ending can be negated, resignified, and imaginatively reconceptualized. Death, which no longer refers to a transcendent beyond, sets into motion an immanent textual dynamic: not so much the openness of a sense of possibility as much as the counter-sense of the possibility of an impossibility.[51] In this manner, Eduard manages—impossibly and by no power of his own—to keep his promise *that he shall live*, albeit only in the form of a life that comes to be captured and maintained in an inorganic product.

In the final sentences of the novel, the extension of life exceeds even the bounded space of the image by imagining reconciliation and reanimation in a future benevolent moment, a *freundlicher Augenblick*. The "happy moment" refers to a temporal event transcending time *within time*, an event that unmistakably recalls the semantics of a *kairos*. But this fortuitous moment refers not to an opportunity seized by a subject in the continuum of historical time, but to a notion of time that bursts the narrative frame: a redemptive temporality that re-animates subjects and projects them into a potentialized space so paradoxical that it cannot properly be described as heterotopic (as the incarnation of a *contradiction* between the boundedness of finite personal identity and the unboundedness of death, it is not a mere space of alterity) or as utopic (since it exists emphatically in time and space).

The image and its inscription or superscript (*Überschrift*) in the novel achieves an indifferentiation between the *individuated person* and *inorganic form*, bringing the impossibility of this operation into full sensuous presence. In the image, life is absent, and yet there, present before one's eyes. The text, however, takes the indifference of the image in spatiality—this second existence in which one is alive and dead—and transforms it into an anticipatory temporality: the impossibility of a future awakening of the dead that cannot be, and yet, that *cannot not be* as long as it stands written on the page.

There is nothing miraculous about this paradox, since it inheres in the potentiality of art as a practice. Every imaginative encounter with a work that makes it into a living object is an act of animation: an

---

50 Goethe, *Elective Affinities*, 299.
51 The ending is so improbable and unexpected that some interpreters understand it as sheer deception. Compare Thomas Wegmann, *Tauschverhältnisse. Zur Ökonomie des Literarischen und zum Ökonomischen in der Literatur von Gellert bis Goethe* (Würzburg: Königshausen & Neumann, 2002), 235.

inorganic product that is impossibly raised to the status of something organic while retaining its inorganic materiality. It is the *experience* of an indifferentiation between these orders; and precisely this experience initiates an imaginative play with impossibility that is the most radical form of futurity. But it is not merely a future. It is a future that happens again and again in the present as soon as one takes the book in one's hand, a second time, a third time, uncountable times: the dead are brought back to life, only to die again and once again live.

Bibliography

Ackerknecht, Erwin H. and Henri V. Vallois. *Franz Joseph Gall, Inventor of Phrenology and his Collection.* Madison: University of Wisconsin Medical School, 1956.
Adorno, Theodor W. *Aesthetic Theory.* Translated by Robert Hullot-Kentor. Minneapolis: University of Minnesota Press, 1997.
Agamben, Giorgio. *The Open: Man and Animal.* Translated by Kevin Attell. Stanford, CA: Stanford University Press, 2004.
Allison, Henry. *Kant's Theory of Taste: A Reading of the Critique of Aesthetic Judgment.* Cambridge: Cambridge University Press, 2001.
Anderegg, Johannes. *Transformationen. Über Himmlisches und Teuflisches in Goethes Faust.* Bielefeld: Aisthesis, 2011.
Arendt, Hannah. *Vita activa oder vom tätigen Leben.* Munich: Piper, 1994.
Badmington, Neil. *Alien Chic.* New York: Routledge, 2004.
Badmington, Neil. "Introduction: Approaching Posthumanism." In *Posthumanism*, edited by Neil Badmington, 1–10. New York: Palgrave, 2000.
Barad, Karen. *Meeting the Universe Halfway: Quantum Physics and the Entanglement of Matter and Meaning.* Durham, NC: Duke University Press, 2007.
Barad, Karen. "Meeting the Universe Halfway: Realism and Social Constructivism without Contradiction." In *Feminism, Science, and the Philosophy of Science*, edited by Lynn Hankinson Nelson and Jack Nelson, 161–94. Dordrecht: Kluwer, 1996.
Barandiaran, Xabier E., Ezeqzuiel A. Di Paolo, and Marieke Rohde. "Defining Agency: Individuality, Normativity, Asymmetry, and Spatio-Temporality in Action." *Adaptive Behavior* 17 (2009): 367–86.
Bateson, Gregory. *Mind and Nature: A Necessary Unity.* New York: E. P. Dutton, 1979.
Bateson, Gregory. *Steps to an Ecology of Mind.* Chicago: University of Chicago Press, 1972 and 2000.
Battlestar Galactica: The Complete Series. 2004–9. Universal City, CA: Universal Studios Home Entertainment, 2010. DVD.
Baudrillard, Jean. *The Illusion of the End.* Stanford, CA: Stanford University Press, 1994.
Bechtel, William. *Discovering Cell Mechanisms: The Creation of Modern Cell Biology.* Cambridge: Cambridge University Press, 2006.
Beiser, Frederick. "Early Romanticism and the Aufklärung." In *What is Enlightenment? Eighteenth-Century Answers and Twentieth-Century Questions*, edited by James Schmidt, 317–29. Berkeley: University of California Press, 1996.

Bibliography

Beiser, Frederick C. *German Idealism: The Struggle against Subjectivism, 1781–1801.* Cambridge, MA: Harvard University Press, 2002.
Benhabib, Seyla. *Situating the Self: Gender, Community, and Postmodernism in Contemporary Ethics.* New York: Routledge, 1992.
Benjamin, Walter. Goethes Wahlverwandtschaften. In *Gesammelte Schriften*, 1, no. 1, edited by Rolf Tiedemann and Rolf Schweppenhäuser, 123–201. Frankfurt a.M.: Suhrkamp, 1991.
Bennett, Jane. *Vibrant Matter: A Political Ecology of Things.* Durham, NC: Duke University Press, 2010.
Bentley, Madison. "The Psychological Antecedents of Phrenology." *The Psychological Monographs* 21 (1916): 105–10.
Berners-Lee, Tim, James Hendler, and Ora Lassila, "The Semantic Web." *Scientific American* 284, no. 5 (2001): 34–43.
Bernstein, Jeremy. "A.I." *The New Yorker*, December 14, 1981. Accessed September 1, 2017. https://www.newyorker.com/magazine/1981/12/14/a-i.
Binswanger, Hans Christoph. *Money and Magic: A Critique of the Modern Economy in the Light of Goethe's Faust.* Chicago: Chicago University Press, 1994.
Blamberger, Günter. *Heinrich von Kleist. Biographie.* Frankfurt a.M.: Fischer, 2012.
Bogost, Ian. *Alien Phenomenology, or: What It's Like to Be a Thing.* Minneapolis: University of Minnesota Press, 2012.
Böhme, Hartmut. "Ästhetische Wissenschaft. Aporien der Forschung im Werk Alexander von Humboldts." In *Alexander von Humboldt—Aufbruch in die Moderne*, edited by Ottmar Ette, Ute Hermanns, Bernd M. Scherer, and Christian Suckow, 17–32. Berlin: Akademie Verlag, 2001.
Botz-Bornstein, Thorsten. *Virtual Reality: The Last Human Narrative?* Leiden: Brill, 2015.
Bowler, Peter J. *Charles Darwin: The Man and His Influence.* New edn. Cambridge: Cambridge University Press, 1996.
Bowler, Peter J. *Life's Splendid Drama: Evolutionary Biology and the Reconstruction of Life's Ancestry, 1860–1940.* Chicago: University of Chicago Press, 1996.
Bowler, Peter J. *The Non-Darwinian Revolution: Reinterpreting a Historical Myth.* Baltimore, MD: Johns Hopkins University Press, 1988.
Bloor, David. "Reply to Bruno Latour." *Studies in History and Philosophy of Science* 30, no. 1 (1999): 131–6.
Blumenbach, Johann Friedrich. *Über den Bildungstrieb.* Göttingen: Dieterich, 1789.
Blumenbach, Johann Friedrich. *Über den Bildungstrieb und das Zeugungsgeschäfte.* Göttingen: Dieterich, 1781.
Blumenberg, Hans. *The Genesis of the Copernican World.* Translated by Robert Wallace. Cambridge, MA: MIT, 1987.
Braidotti, Rosi. *Metamorphoses: Towards a Materialist Theory of Becoming.* Cambridge: Polity, 2002.
Braidotti, Rosi. *The Posthuman.* Cambridge: Polity, 2013.
Brassier, Ray. *Nihil Unbound: Enlightenment and Extinction.* Basingstoke: Palgrave, 2007.
Brassier, Ray. "Postscript: Speculative Autopsy." In Peter Wolfendale, *Object-Oriented Philosophy: The Noumenon's New Clothes*, 407–21. Falmouth, UK: Urbanomic, 2014.
Brassier, Ray, Iain Hamilton Grant, Graham Harman, and Quentin Meillassoux. "Speculative Realism." In *Collapse: Philosophical Research and Development*, vol. 3. Falmouth, UK: Urbanomic, 2007.
Breidbach, Olaf. *Die Materialisierung des Ichs: Zur Geschichte der Hirnforschung im 19. und 20. Jahrhundert.* Frankfurt a.M.: Suhrkamp, 1997.

Bibliography 311

Breidbach, Olaf. "*Die Wahlverwandtschaften*—Versuch einer wissenschaftshistorischen Perspektivierung." In *Goethes Wahlverwandtschaften: Werk und Forschung*, edited by Helmut Hühn, 291–310. Berlin: De Gruyter, 2010.

Bricker, Phillip. "Ontological Commitment." In *The Stanford Encyclopedia of Philosophy*, 2016 edition, edited by Edward N. Zalta. https://plato.stanford.edu/archives/win2016/entries/ontological-commitment/.

Brodsky, Claudia. *In the Place of Language: Literature and the Architecture of the Referent*. New York: Fordham University Press, 2009.

Brugmans, Anton. *Philosophische Versuche über die magnetische Materie*. Leipzig: Crusius, 1784.

Brüning, Gerrit. "Die Wette in Goethes Faust." *Goethe Yearbook* 17 (2010): 31–54.

Bruns, Gerald L. *On Ceasing to Be Human*. Stanford, CA: Stanford University Press, 2010.

Bryant, Levi. "The Ontic Principle: Outline of an Object-Oriented Ontology." In *The Speculative Turn: Continental Materialism and Realism*, edited by Levi Bryant, Nick Srnicek, and Graham Harman, 261–78. Melbourne: re.press, 2011.

Bryant, Levi, Graham Harman, and Nick Srnicek, eds. *The Speculative Turn: Continental Materialism and Realism*. Melbourne: re.press, 2011.

Bunge, Gustav. *Vitalismus und Mechanismus: Ein Vortrag*. Leipzig: Vogel, 1886.

Burbidge, John W. *Hegel's Systematic Contingency*. New York: Palgrave Macmillan, 2007.

Calarco, Matthew. *Thinking through Animals: Identity, Difference, Indistinction*. Stanford, CA: Stanford University Press, 2015.

Canguilhem, Georges. *Knowledge of Life*. Translated by Stefanos Geroulanos and Daniela Gisburg. Introduction by Paola Marrati and Todd Meyers. New York: Fordham University Press, 2008.

Caporael, Linnda R., James R. Griesemer, and William C. Wimsatt, eds. *Developing Scaffolds in Evolution, Culture, and Cognition*. Cambridge, MA: MIT, 2013.

Carnap, Rudolf. "Logical Foundations of the Unity of Science." In *International Encyclopedia of Unified Science*, vol. 1, edited by Otto Neurath, Rudolf Carnap, and Charles Morris, 42–62. Chicago: University of Chicago Press, 1938.

Carroll, Jerome. "Eighteenth-Century Departures from Dualism: From Mechanism and Animism to Vitalism and Anthropology." *German Life and Letters* 70, no. 4 (October 2017): 430–44.

Caspari, Otto. *Der Zusammenhang der Dinge: Gesammelte philosophische Aufsätze*. Breslau: Trewendt, 1881.

Cassirer, Ernst. *Heinrich von Kleist und die Kantische Philosophie*. Berlin: Reuther & Reichard, 1919.

Cassirer, Ernst. *Kant's Life and Thought*. Translated by James Haden. New Haven, CT: Yale University Press, 1981.

Caygill, Howard. *A Kant Dictionary*. London: Wiley-Blackwell, 1995.

Cienkowski, L. "Beiträge zur Kenntniss der Monaden." *Schultze's Archiv für mikroskopische Anatomie* 1 (1865): 203–32.

Clarke, Bruce and Manuela Rossini, eds. *The Cambridge Companion to Literature and the Posthuman*. Cambridge: Cambridge University Press, 2017.

Clarke, Bruce and Mark B. N. Hansen. "Introduction: Neocybernetic Emergence." In *Emergence and Embodiment: New Essays on Second-Order Systems Theory*, edited by Bruce Clarke and Mark B. N. Hansen, 1–25. Durham, NC: Duke University Press, 2009.

Colebrook, Claire. *Death of the PostHuman: Essays on Extinction*, vol. 1. Ann Arbor, MI: Open Humanities Press, 2014.

Coleman, William. *Biology in the Nineteenth Century: Problems of Form, Function, and Transformation*. Cambridge: Cambridge University Press, 1977.
Connolly, William E. *The Fragility of Things: Self-Organizing Processes, Neoliberal Fantasies, and Democratic Activism*. Durham, NC: Duke University Press, 2013.
Coole, Diana and Samantha Frost. "Introducing the New Materialisms." In *New Materialisms: Ontology, Agency, and Politics*, edited by Diana Coole and Samantha Frost, 1–43. Durham, NC: Duke University Press, 2010.
Crary, Jonathan. *Techniques of the Observer. On Vision and Modernity in the Nineteenth Century*. Cambridge, MA, and London: MIT, 1990.
Crutzen, Paul J. "Geology of Mankind." *Nature* 415, no. 3 (January 2002): 23.
Darwin, Charles. *The Descent of Man, and Selection in Relation to Sex*. New York: Appleton & Co., 1871.
Darwin, Charles. *The Life and Letters*, vol. 3. Edited by Francis Darwin. London: John Murray, 1887.
Darwin, Charles. *On the Origin of Species by Means of Natural Selection, or: The Preservation of Favoured Races in the Struggle for Life*. London: John Murray, 1859.
Darwin, Charles. "Pangenesis." *Nature* 3 (April 27, 1871): 502–3.
Darwin, Charles. *The Variation of Animals and Plants under Domestication*. London: John Murray, 1868.
Dassow Walls, Laura. *The Passage to Cosmos: Alexander von Humboldt and the Shaping of America*. Chicago: University of Chicago Press, 2009.
Davidson, Donald. *Essays on Actions and Events*. Oxford: Clarendon Press, 1980.
Davies, Martin L. "Gedanken zu einem ambivalenten Verhältnis: Marcus Herz und Immanuel Kant." In *Kant und die Berliner Aufklärung, Akten des IX. Internationalen Kant-Kongresses, Band V: Sektionen XV–XVIII*, edited by Volker Gerhardt, Rolf-Peter Horstmann, and Ralph Schumacher, 141–7. Berlin: de Gruyter, 2001.
Davies, Martin L. *Identity of History?: Marcus Herz and the End of the Enlightenment*. Detroit, MI: Wayne State University Press, 1995.
Deacon, Terrence. *Incomplete Nature: How Mind Emerged from Matter*. New York: W. W. Norton & Co., 2013.
DeKoven, Marianne and Michael Lundblad, eds. *Species Matters: Humane Advocacy and Cultural Theory*. New York: Columbia University Press, 2012.
DeLanda, Manuel. *Intensive Science and Virtual Philosophy*. New York: Continuum, 2002.
Deleuze, Gilles. *Cinema 1: The Movement-Image*. Translated by Hugh Tomlinson and Barbara Habberjam. Minneapolis: University of Minnesota Press, 1986.
Deleuze, Gilles and Félix Guattari. *What Is Philosophy?* Translated by Hugh Tomlinson. New York: Columbia University Press, 1990.
Dennett, Daniel. *The Intentional Stance*. Cambridge, MA: MIT, 1987.
Derrida, Jacques. *The Animal That Therefore I Am*. Edited by Marie-Louise Mallet. Translated by David Wills. New York: Fordham University Press, 2008.
Derrida, Jacques. *Of Spirit: Heidegger and the Question*. Translated by G. Bennington and R. Bowlby. Chicago: Chicago University Press, 1991.
Dewey, John. *Experience and Nature*. Chicago: Open Court, 1925.
Dick, Philip K. *Do Androids Dream of Electric Sheep*. Tampa, FL: Del Ray, 1996.
Dischner, Gisela. *"der ganze Schmutz zugleich und Glanz meiner Seele": Die Briefe Heinrich von Kleists als Teil seiner Werke*. Bielefeld: Aisthesis, 2012.
Driesch, Hans. *Geschichte des Vitalismus*. 2nd edn., corr. and enl. Leipzig: Barth, 1922.
Driesch, Hans. "Entwicklungsmechanische Studien: I. Der Werth der beiden ersten Furchungszellen in der Echinodermenentwicklung: Experimentelle Erzeugung

Bibliography 313

von Theil- und Doppelbildungen. II. Über die Beziehungen des Lichtes zur ersten Etappe der thierischen Formbildung." *Zeitschrift für wissenschaftliche Zoologie* 53 (1891): 160–84.

Dupré, John. *The Disorder of Things: Metaphysical Foundations of the Disunity of Science*. Cambridge, MA: Harvard University Press, 1993.

Dyck, J. W. "Kleist and Nietzsche: *Lebensplan* and *Lustmotiv*." *German Life and Letters* 21, no. 3 (1968): 189–203.

Eibl, Karl. *Das monumentale Ich—Wege zu Goethes Faust*. Frankfurt a.M. and Leipzig: Insel, 2000.

Eigen, Sara and Mark Larrimore, eds. *The German Invention of Race*. Albany: State University of New York Press, 2006.

Emden, Christian J. "Nietzsche's Will to Power: Biology, Naturalism, and Normativity." *Journal of Nietzsche Studies* 47 (2016): 30–60.

Emden, Christian J. "Normativity Matters: Philosophical Naturalism and Political Theory." In *The New Politics of Materialism: History, Philosophy, Science*, edited by Sarah Ellenzweig and John H. Zammito, 269–99. New York: Routledge, 2017.

Enç, Berent. *How We Act: Causes, Reasons, and Intentions*. Oxford: Oxford University Press, 2003.

Engelmann, Theodor W. "Beiträge zur Physiologie des Protoplasma." *Pflüger's Archiv für die gesammte Physiologie des Menschen und der Thiere* 2 (1869): 307–22.

Engler-Coldren, Katharina, Lore Knapp, and Charlotte Lee. "Embodied Cognition around 1800: Introduction." *German Life and Letters* 70, no. 4 (October 2017): 413–22.

Enoch, David. "Agency, Shmagency: Why Normativity Won't Come from What is Constitutive of Agency." *Philosophical Review* 115 (2006): 169–98.

Ferrando, Francesca. "Posthumanism, Transhumanism, Antihumanism, Metahumanism, and New Materialisms: Differences and Relations." *Existenz* 8, no. 2 (Fall 2013): 26–32.

Fichte, Johann Gottlieb. *Foundations of Natural Right According to the Principles of the Wissenschaftslehre*. Edited by Frederick Neuhauser. Translated by Michael Baur. New York: Cambridge University Press, 2000.

Fichte, Johann Gottlieb. *Science of Knowledge*. Edited and translated by Peter Heath and John Lachs. New York: Cambridge University Press, 1991.

Fichte, Johann Gottlieb. *The System of Ethics*. Edited and translated by Daniel Breazeale and Günter Zöller. New York: Cambridge University Press, 2005.

Finger, Stanley and Nicholas Wade. "The Neuroscience of Helmholtz and the Theories of Johannes Müller. Part 1: Nerve Cell Structure, Vitalism, and the Nerve Impulse." *Journal of the History of the Neurosciences* 11, no. 2 (2002): 136–55.

Fischer, Bernd. *Das Eigene und das Eigentliche: Klopstock, Herder, Fichte, Kleist: Episoden aus der Konstruktionsgeschichte nationaler Intentionalitäten*. Berlin: Erich Schmidt Verlag, 1995.

Fischer, Bernd. "Heinrich von Kleists vorgeführtes Erzählen." *German Life and Letters* 64, no. 3 (July 2011): 337–53.

Flax, Jane. *Thinking Fragments: Psychoanalysis, Feminism and Postmodernism in the Contemporary West*. Oakland: University of California Press, 1990.

Foerster, Heinz von. *Understanding Understanding: Essays on Cybernetics and Cognition*. New York: Springer, 2003.

Foerster, Heinz von and Bernhard Pörkens. *Wahrheit ist die Erfindung eines Lügners. Gespräche für Skeptiker*. 8th edn. Heidelberg: Carl-Auer-Systeme Verlag, 2008.

Förster, Eckart. "'Da geht der Mann dem wir alles verdanken!' Eine Untersuchung zum Verhältnis Goethe—Fichte." *Deutsche Zeitschrift für Philosophie* 45, no. 3 (1997): 331–44.

Franklin, Benjamin. "Observations on the Generally Prevailing Doctrines of Life and Death." In *The Works of Benjamin Franklin*, vol. 3. Philadelphia, PA: William Duane, 1809.

Friedlander, Eli. *Expressions of Judgment: An Essay on Kant's Aesthetics*. Cambridge, MA: Harvard University Press, 2015.

Gall, Franz Joseph. *On the Function of the Brain and of Each of Its Parts*. Translated by Winslow Lewis, Jr. 6 vols. 1822–5. Reprint, Boston, MA: Marsh, Capen & Lyon, 1835.

Gall, Franz Joseph. *Philosophisch-medicinische Untersuchungen über Natur und Kunst im kranken und gesunden Zustande des Menschen*, vol. 1. Vienna: Grässer & Comp., 1791.

Gall, Franz Joseph. "Schreiben über seinen bereits geendigten Prodomus über die Verrichtungen des Gehirns der Menschen und der Thiere an Herrn Jos. Fr. von Retzer." *Der Neue Teutsche Merkur*, December 1798, 311–32.

Galloway, "The Poverty of Philosophy: Realism and Post-Fordism." *Critical Inquiry* 39, no. 2 (2013): 347–66.

Galton, Francis. "Experiments in Pangenesis." *Proceedings of the Royal Society of London* 19 (1870–1): 393–410.

Garland, Alex, dir. *Ex Machina*. 2015; Santa Monica, CA: Lionsgate, 2015. DVD.

Garrels, Gary. *Plane Image: A Brice Marden Retrospective*. New York: Museum of Modern Art, 2006.

Gasché, Rodolphe. *The Tain of the Mirror: Derrida and the Philosophy of Reflection*. Cambridge, MA: Harvard University Press, 1986.

Gayon, Jean. "From Darwin to Today in Evolutionary Biology." In *The Cambridge Companion to Darwin*, edited by Jonathan Hodge and Gregory Radick, 240–64. Cambridge: Cambridge University Press, 2003.

Gehlen, Arnold. *Man in the Age of Technology*. New York: Columbia University Press, 1980.

Geyer-Kordesch, Johanna. *Pietismus, Medizin und Aufklärung in Preußen im 18. Jahrhundert: Das Leben und Werk Georg Ernst Stahls*. Tübingen: Max Niemeyer Verlag, 2000.

Ghiselin, Michael T. "Darwin's Language May Have Been Teleological, but His Thinking is Another Matter." *Biology and Philosophy* 9 (1994): 489–92.

Girtanner, Christoph. *Ueber das Kantische Prinzip für die Naturgeschichte: Ein Versuch, diese Wissenschaft philosophisch zu behandeln*. Göttingen: Vandenhoeck & Ruprecht, 1796.

Goethe, Johann Wolfgang. *Aus meinem Leben. Dichtung und Wahrheit*. Edited by Klaus-Detlef Müller. Frankfurt a.M.: Deutscher Klassiker Verlag, 1986.

Goethe, Johann Wolfgang. "Der Versuch als Vermittler von Objekt und Subjekt." In *Sämtliche Werke*, vol. 1, no. 25, edited by Wolf von Engelhardt and Manfred Wenzel, 26–36. Frankfurt a.M.: Suhrkamp, 1989.

Goethe, Johann Wolfgang. *Dichtung und Wahrheit; Sämtliche Werke*, vol. 14. Edited by Klaus-Detlef Müller. Frankfurt a.M.: Suhrkamp, 1986.

Goethe, Johann Wolfgang. *Die Leiden des jungen Werthers; Die Wahlverwandtschaften. Text und Kommentar; Sämtliche Werke*, vol. 1, no. 8. Edited by Waltraud Wiethölter and Christoph Brecht. Frankfurt a.M.: Suhrkamp, 2006.

Goethe, Johann Wolfgang. *Elective Affinities*. Translated by R. J. Hollingdale. New York: Penguin, 2005.

Bibliography

Goethe, Johann Wolfgang. *Faust*. Part One. Translated by David Luke. Oxford: Oxford University Press, 1988.

Goethe, Johann Wolfgang. *Faust*. Part Two. Translated by David Luke. Oxford: Oxford University Press, 1988.

Goethe, Johann Wolfgang. *Faust. Vol. 1: Texte, vol. 2: Kommentare*. Edited by Albrecht Schöne. Frankfurt a.M.: Deutscher Klassiker Verlag, 5th edn, 2003.

Goethe, Johann Wolfgang. *Plays. Egmont, Iphigenia in Tauris, Torquato Tasso*. Edited by Frank G. Ryder. Translated by Anna Swanwick, Frank G. Ryder, and Charles E. Passage. New York: Continuum, 1993.

Goethe, Johann Wolfgang. *Wilhelm Meister's Apprenticeship* in *Goethe. The Collected Works*, vol. 9. Edited and translated by Eric A. Blackall and Victor Lange. Princeton, NJ: Princeton University Press, 1989.

Golumbia, David. "Correlationism—The Dogma That Never Was." *boundary 2* 43, no. 2 (2016): 1–25.

Google. "Meet your Google Assistant, your Own Personal Google." YouTube video, 1: 35. October 4, 2016. https://www.youtube.com/watch?v=FPfQMVf4vwQ.

Graham, Ilse. *Heinrich von Kleist. Word into Flesh: A Poet's Quest for the Symbol*. Berlin and New York: Walter de Gruyter, 1977.

Grant, Iain Hamilton. *Philosophies of Nature after Schelling*. London and New York: Continuum, 2006.

Greenberg, Martin. "The Difficult Justice of Melville and Kleist." *The New Criterion* 23, no. 7 (2005): 24–32.

Greiner, Bernhard. *Eine Art Wahnsinn: Dichtung im Horizont Kants. Studien zu Goethe und Kleist*. Berlin: Erich Schmidt Verlag, 1994.

Greiner, Bernhard. "Kömodie." In *Kleist-Handbuch: Leben—Werk—Wirkung*, edited by Ingo Breuer, 21–6. Stuttgart and Weimar: Metzler, 2013.

Grene, Marjorie and David Depew. *The Philosophy of Biology: An Episodic History*. Cambridge: Cambridge University Press, 2004.

Griffin, Andrew. "Google Voice Search Records and Keeps Conversations People Have Around Their Phones—But the Files Can Be Deleted." *The Independent*. Last modified June 1, 2016. http://www.independent.co.uk/life-style/gadgets-and-tech/news/google-voice-search-records-stores-conversation-people-have-around-their-phones-but-files-can-be-a7059376.html.

Griffiths, Paul and Russell Gray. "The Developmental Systems Perspective: Organism-environment Systems as Units of Development and Evolution." In *Phenotypic Integration: Studying the Ecology and Evolution of Complex Phenotypes*, edited by Massimo Pigliucci and Katherien Preston, 409–30. Oxford: Oxford University Press, 2005.

Grimm, Jacob and Wilhelm Grimm. *Deutsches Wörterbuch von Jacob und Wilhelm Grimm*. Leipzig: DWB, 1854–1960. http://woerterbuchnetz.de/cgi-bin/WBNetz/wbgui_py?sigle=DWB.

Grosz, Elizabeth. *Becoming Undone: Darwinian Reflections on Life, Politics, and Art*. Durham, NC: Duke University Press, 2011.

Grosz, Elizabeth. *The Incorporeal: Ontology, Ethics, and the Limits of Materialism*. New York: Columbia University Press, 2017.

Grosz, Elizabeth. Interview by Robert Ausch, Randal Doane, and Laura Perez. https://www.scribd.com/document/46893601/Interview-With-Elizabeth-Grosz.

Grosz, Elizabeth. "Matter, Life, and Other Variations." *Philosophy Today* 55 (2011), SPEP Supplement: 17–27.

Grosz, Elizabeth. *The Nick of Time: Politics, Evolution, and the Untimely*. Durham, NC: Duke University Press, 2004.

Gruber, Thomas R. *Encyclopedia of Database Systems*. Edited by Ling Liu and M. Tamer Özsu. Boston, MA: Springer, 2009.

Gruber, Thomas R. "Ontology." http://tomgruber.org/writing/ontology-definition-2007.htm

Gruber, Thomas R. "Toward Principles for the Design of Ontologies Used for Knowledge Sharing." *International Journal of Human-Computer Studies* 43 (1995): 907–28.

Grusin, Richard. "Introduction." In *The Nonhuman Turn*, edited by Richard Grusin, vii–xxix. Minneapolis: University of Minnesota Press, 2015.

Guyer, Paul. *Kant and the Claims of Taste*. Cambridge: Cambridge University Press, 1997.

Guyer, Paul. "Kant on the Purity of the Ugly." In *Values of Beauty: Historical Essays in Aesthetics*, 141–62. Cambridge: Cambridge University Press, 2005.

Hacking, Ian. "The Disunities of the Sciences." In *The Disunity of Science: Boundaries, Contexts, and Power*, edited by Peter Galison and David J. Strump. Stanford, CA: Stanford University Press, 1996.

Hacking, Ian. *Representing and Intervening: Introductory Topics in the Philosophy of the Natural Sciences*. Cambridge: Cambridge University Press, 1983.

Hagner, Michael. *Homo Cerebralis: Der Wandel vom Seelenorgan zum Gehirn*. Frankfurt a.M.: Insel, 2000.

Haeckel, Ernst. *Die Perigenesis der Plastidule, oder die Wellenzeugung der Lebenstheilchen: Ein Versuch zur mechanischen Erklärung der elementaren Entwickelungs-Vorgänge*. Berlin: Reimer, 1876.

Haidt, Jonathan. *The Righteous Mind: Why Good People are Divided by Politics and Religion*. New York: Vintage, 2013.

Haller, Albrecht von. *Elementa physiologie corporis humani*. Lausanne: Francisci Grasset, 1772.

Haller, Albrecht von. "Partibus corporis humani sensibilus et irritabilibus." *Novi commentarii Societatis Regiae Scientiarum Gottingensis* (1752): 1–36.

Hallward, Peter. *Out of This World: Deleuze and the Philosophy of Creation*. London: Verso, 2006.

Hamburger, Victor. "Wilhelm Roux: Visionary with a Blind Spot." *Journal of the History of Biology* 30 (1997): 229–38.

Hansen, Mark. *New Philosophy for New Media*. Cambridge, MA: MIT, 2006.

Hansen, Leeann. "From Enlightenment to Naturphilosophie: Marcus Herz, Johann Christian Reil, and the Problem of Border Crossing." *Journal of the History of Biology* 26, no. 1 (Spring 1993): 39–64.

Haraway, Donna J. "A Cyborg Manifesto: Science, Technology, and Socialist-Feminism in the Late Twentieth Century." In *Simians, Cyborgs, and Women: The Reinvention of Nature*. New York: Routledge, 1991.

Haraway, Donna J. *The Companion Species Manifesto: Dogs, People, and Significant Otherness*. Chicago: Prickly Paradigm, 2003.

Haraway, Donna J. *Staying with the Trouble: Making Kin in the Chthulucene*. Durham, NC: Duke University Press, 2016.

Haraway, Donna J. *When Species Meet*. Minneapolis: University of Minnesota Press, 2008.

Harman, Graham. "On the Undermining of Objects: Grant, Bruno, and Radical Philosophy." In *The Speculative Turn: Continental Materialism and Realism*, edited

by Levi Bryant, Nick Smicek, and Graham Harman, 21–40. Melbourne: re-press, 2011.
Harman, Graham. *Quentin Meillassoux: Philosophy in the Making.* Edinburgh: Edinburgh University Press, 2011.
Harman, Graham. *Prince of Networks: Bruno Latour and Metaphysics.* Melbourne: anamnesis, 2009.
Harman, Graham. *Tool-Being: Heidegger and the Metaphysics of Objects.* Peru, IL: Open Court, 2002.
Harris, Errol E. *The Spirit of Hegel.* Atlantic Highlands, NJ: Humanities Press, 1993.
Hart, Gail K. "Anmut's Gender: The 'Marionettentheater' and Kleist's Revision of 'Anmut und Würde.'" *Women in German Yearbook: Feminist Studies in German Literature and Culture* 10 (1995): 83–95.
Hassan, Ihab Habib. "Prometheus as Performer: Toward a Posthumanist Culture?" *The Georgia Review* 31, no. 4 (Winter 1977): 830–50.
Hayles, N. Katherine. *How We Became Posthuman: Virtual Bodies in Cybernetics, Literature, and Informatics.* Chicago: University of Chicago Press, 1999.
Hegel, G. W. F. *Aesthetics: Lectures on Fine Art.* 2 vols. Translated by T. M. Knox. 1835. Reprinted, Oxford: Oxford University Press, 1991 and 1999.
Hegel, G. W. F. *Logic: Being Part One of the Encyclopaedia of the Philosophical Sciences (1830).* Translated by W. Wallace. Oxford: Clarendon Press, 1971.
Hegel, G. W. F. *Phenomenology of Spirit.* Translated by A. V. Miller. Oxford: Oxford University Press, 1977.
Hegel, G. W. F. *Science of Logic.* Translated by A. V. Miller. New York: Humanity (Prometheus) Books, 1999.
Hegel, G. W. F. *The Philosophy of History.* Translated by Leo Rauch. Indianapolis, IN: Hackett, 1988.
Hegel, G. W. F. *Werke.* 20 vols. Edited by Eva Moldenhauer and Karl Markus Michel. Frankfurt a.M.: Suhrkamp, 1986.
Heidegger, Martin. *Poetry, Language, Thought.* Translated and introduction by Albert Hofstadter. New York: Perennial Classics, 2001.
Henrich, Dieter. *Fichtes ursprüngliche Einsicht.* Frankfurt a.M.: Klostermann, 1967.
Helmholtz, Hermann von. *Die Lehre von der Tonempfindung als physiologische Grundlage für die Theorie der Musik.* 4th edn. Braunschweig: Friedrich Vieweg and son, 1877. http://conquest.imslp.info/files/imglnks/usimg/d/d5/IMSLP90090-PMLP184676-Helmholtz__Die_Lehre_von_den_Tonempfindungen__4.Aufl._1877.pdf
Hepburn, R. W. "Contemporary Aesthetics and the Neglect of Natural Beauty." In *British Analytical Philosophy,* edited by Bernard Williams and Alan Montefiore, 285–310. New York: The Humanities Press, 1966.
Herbrechter, Stefan. *Posthumanism: A Critical Analysis.* London: Bloomsbury, 2013.
Herder, Johann Gottfried von. *Outlines of a Philosophy of the History of Man.* Translated by T. Churchill. 1784–91. Reprint, London: [n.p.], 1800.
Herder, Johann Gottfried von. "Treatise on the Origin of Language." In *Philosophical Writings* (1772), translated and edited by Michael N. Forster, 65–164. Reprint, Cambridge: Cambridge University Press, 2002.
Herz, Marcus. *Versuch über den Schwindel.* Berlin: Christian Friedrich Voß und Sohn, 1786.
Herz, Marcus. *Versuch über den Schwindel.* 2nd edn. Berlin: Voss, 1791.
His, Wilhelm. *Unsere Körperform und das physiologische Problem ihrer Entstehung: Briefe an einen befreundeten Naturforscher.* Leizpig: Vogel, 1874.

Holland, Jocelyn. "Die Zeit der Indifferenz. Johann Wilhelm Ritter und die Weiblichkeit." In *Narration und Geschlecht. Texte–Medien–Episteme*, edited by Sigrid Nieberle and Elisabeth Strowick, 335–47. Cologne: Böhlau, 2006.

Holland, Jocelyn. *German Romanticism and Science: The Procreative Poetics of Goethe, Novalis, and Ritter*. London: Routledge, 2009.

Houlgate, Stephen. *Hegel and the Philosophy of Nature*. Albany: State University of New York Press, 1998.

Hufeland, Christoph Wilhelm. *Eine Selbstbiographie*. Berlin: Georg Reimer, 1863.

Hufeland, Christoph Wilhelm. *Die Kunst, das menschliche Leben zu verlängern*. 2 vols. Vienna and Prague: Franz Haas, 1798.

Hufeland, Christoph Wilhelm. *Makrobiotik oder die Kunst, das menschliche Leben zu verlängern*. 2 vols. Berlin: L. W. Wittich, 1805.

Hui, Yuk. *On the Existence of Digital Objects*. Minneapolis: University of Minnesota Press, 2016.

Hui, Yuk. "The Parallax of Individuation." *Angelaki* 21, no. 4 (2016): 77–89.

Humboldt, Alexander von. *Ansichten der Natur*. Edited by Hanno Beck. Darmstadt: Wissenschaftliche Buchgesellschaft, 1987.

Humboldt, Alexander von. *Cosmos: A Sketch of the Physical Description of the Universe*. Translated by E. C. Otté. Baltimore, MD: The Johns Hopkins University Press, 1997.

Humboldt, Alexander von. *Kosmos. Entwurf einer physischen Weltbeschreibung, 5 vols*. Stuttgart and Tübingen: J. G. Cotta, 1845–62.

Humboldt, Alexander von. *Views of Nature*. Edited by Stephen T. Jackson and Laura Dassow Walls. Translated by Mark W. Person. Chicago: University of Chicago Press, 2014.

Humboldt, Alexander von. *Views of Nature or Contemplations on the Sublime Phenomena of Creation*. Translated by E. C. Otté. Edited by Henry G. Bohn. London: Henry G. Bohn, 1850.

Jacob, François. *The Logic of Life: A History of Heredity*. Translated by Betty E. Spillmann. New York: Vintage, 1976.

Jacobson, Brian R. "*Ex Machina* in the Garden." *Film Quarterly* 69, no. 4. (2016): 23–34.

Jaeger, Michael. *Global Player Faust oder Das Verschwinden der Gegenwart. Zur Aktualität Goethes*. Würzburg: Königshausen & Neumann, 5th edn, 2013.

Jonze, Spike, dir. *Her*. 2013; Burbank, CA: Warner Home Entertainment, 2014. DVD.

Kant, Immanuel. *Anthropology, History, and Education*. Edited by Günter Zöller and Robert B. Louden. Cambridge: Cambridge University Press, 2007.

Kant, Immanuel. "Conjectural Beginning of Human History." In *Anthropology, History, and Education* (1786), edited by Günter Zöller and Robert B. Louden, 163–75. Reprint, Cambridge: Cambridge University Press, 2007.

Kant, Immanuel. *Correspondence*. Translated by Arnulf Zweig. Cambridge: Cambridge University Press, 1999.

Kant, Immanuel. *Critique of Judgment*. Translated by J. H. Bernard. New York: Hafner Press, 1951.

Kant, Immanuel. *Critique of Pure Reason*. Edited by Paul Guyer and Allen W. Wood. Cambridge: Cambridge University Press, 1998.

Kant, Immanuel. *Critique of Pure Reason*. Edited and translated by Marcus Weigelt. New York: Penguin, 2007.

Kant, Immanuel. *Critique of the Power of Judgment*. Edited by Paul Guyer. Translated by Paul Guyer and Eric Matthews. Cambridge: Cambridge University Press, 2000.

Bibliography 319

Kant, Immanuel. *Kant's Gesammelte Schriften* "Akademieausgabe," Königlich Preußische Akademie der Wissenschaften. Berlin: Reimer/de Gruyter, 1900ff.

Kant, Immanuel. *Lectures on Logic.* Translated and edited by J. Michael Young. 1765–1800. Reprint, Cambridge: Cambridge University Press, 1992.

Kant, Immanuel. *Metaphysical Foundations of Natural Science.* Edited by Michael Friedman. Cambridge: Cambridge University Press, 2004.

Kant, Immanuel. *Prolegomena to Any Future Metaphysics with Selections from the Critique of Pure Reason.* Edited by Gary Hatfield. Cambridge: Cambridge University Press, 2004.

Kant, Immanuel. *Religion and Rational Theology.* Edited by Allen W. Wood. Cambridge: Cambridge University Press, 1996.

Katsafanas, Paul. *Agency and the Foundations of Ethics: Nietzschean Constitutivism.* Oxford: Oxford University Press, 2013.

Kayser, Wolfgang. *Das sprachliche Kunstwerk.* Tübingen: Franke, 1992.

Kayser, Wolfgang. "Kleist als Erzähler." *German Life and Letters* 8, no. 1 (October 1954): 19–29.

Kirksey, Eben, ed. *The Multispecies Salon.* Durham, NC: Duke University Press, 2014.

Kittler, Friedrich. *Austreibung des Geistes aus den Geisteswissenschaften. Programme des Poststrukturalismus.* Paderborn: Schönigh, 1980.

Kittler, Friedrich. *Baggersee: Frühe Schriften aus dem Nachlass.* Edited by Tania Hron and Sandrina Khaled. Paderborn: Wilhelm Fink, 2015.

Kleist, Heinrich von. *Sämtliche Werke und Briefe; vol. 3: Erzählungen, Anekdoten, Gedichte, Schriften.* Edited by Klaus Müller-Salget. Frankfurt a.M.: Deutscher Klassiker Verlag, 1990.

Kohlenbach, Margarete. "Transformations of German Romanticism 1830–2000." In *The Cambridge Companion to German Romanticism,* edited by Nicholas Saul, 257–80. Cambridge: Cambridge University Press, 2009.

Korsgaard, Christine M. *The Constitution of Agency: Essays on Practical Reason and Moral Psychology.* Oxford: Oxford University Press, 2008.

Korsgaard, Christine M. *Self-Constitution: Agency, Identity, and Integrity.* Oxford: Oxford University Press, 2009.

Ladewig, Rebekka. *Schwindel: Eine Epistemologie der Orientierung.* Tübingen: Mohr Siebeck, 2016.

Lakoff, George and Rafael E. Nunez. *Where Mathematics Comes From: How the Embodied Mind Brings Mathematics Into Being.* New York: Basic, 2001.

Larson, James L. "Vital Forces: Regulative Principles or Constitutive Agents? A Strategy in Germany Physiology, 1786–1802." *Isis* 70 (1979): 235–49.

Larubia-Prado, Francisco. "Horses at the Frontier in Kleist's *Michael Kohlhaas.*" *Seminar: A Journal of Germanic Studies* 46, no. 4 (November 2010): 330–50.

Latour, Bruno. *Facing Gaia: Eight Lectures on the New Climatic Regime.* Cambridge: Polity, 2017.

Latour, Bruno. "For David Bloor and Beyond ... A Reply to David Bloor's 'Anti-Latour'." *Studies in History & Philosophy of Science* 30, no. 1 (March 1999): 113–29.

Latour, Bruno. *Politics of Nature: How to bring the Sciences into Democracy.* Translated by Catherine Porter. Cambridge, MA: Harvard University Press, 2004.

Latour, Bruno. *We Have Never Been Modern.* Translated by Catherine Porter. Cambridge, MA: Harvard University Press, 1993.

Leder, Christoph Maria. *Die Grenzgänger des Marcus Herz: Beruf, Haltung und Identität eines jüdischen Arztes gegen Ende des 18. Jahrhunderts.* Münster: Waxmann Verlag, 2007.

Lenoir, Timothy. *The Strategy of Life: Teleology and Mechanics in Nineteenth-Century German Biology*. Dordrecht: Reidel, 1982.

Lennox, James G. "Darwin *was* a Teleologist." *Biology and Philosophy* 8, no. 4 (1993): 409–22.

Leopardi, Giacomo. "Dialogue between Fashion and Death." In *Essays and Dialogues of Giacomo Leopardi*, translated by Charles Edwardes, 19–23. Boston, MA: J. R. Osgood & Co., 1882.

Leroi-Gourhan, André. *Milieu et techniques*. Paris: Albin Michel, 1945.

Lesky, Erna, ed. *Franz Joseph Gall: Naturforscher und Anthropologe*. Bern: Huber, 1979.

Lesky, Erna. "Gall and Herder." *Clio Medica* 2 (1967): 85–96.

Lesky, Erna. "Structure and Function in Gall." *Bulletin of the History of Medicine* 44 (1970): 297–314.

Lewens, Tim. *Darwin*. London: Routledge, 2007.

Lilienthal, Georg. "Samuel Thomas Soemmerring und seine Vorstellungen über Rassenunterschiede." In *Die Natur des Menschen: Probleme der physischen Anthropologie und Rassenkunde (1750–1850)*, edited by Gunter Mann and Franz Dumont, 31–55. Stuttgart: G. Fischer, 1990.

Lindroos-Hovinheimo, Susanna. "Excavating Foundations of Legal Personhood: Fichte on Autonomy and Self-Consciousness." *International Journal for the Semiotics of Law* 28, no. 3 (2015): 687–702.

Look, Brandon C. "Blumenbach and Kant on Mechanism and Teleology in Nature: The Case of the Formative Drive." In *The Problem of Animal Generation in Early Modern Philosophy*, edited by Justin E. H. Smith, 355–73. Cambridge: Cambridge University Press, 2006.

Lotze, Hermann. *Allgemeine Pathologie und Therapie als mechanische Naturwissenschaften*. Leipzig: Weidmann'sche Buchhandlung, 1842. https://books.google.com/books?id=bZc_AAAAcAAJ&printsec=frontcover&source=gbs_ge_summary_r&cad=0#v=onepage&q&f=false.

Lovejoy, Arthur O. *The Great Chain of Being: A Study of the History of an Idea*. Cambridge, MA: Harvard University Press, 1936.

Luhmann, Niklas. *Introduction to Systems Theory*. Edited by Dirk Baecker. Translated by Peter Gilgen. Cambridge: Polity, 2013.

Luhmann, Niklas. *Theories of Distinction: Redescribing the Descriptions of Modernity*. Edited by William Rasch. Stanford, CA: Stanford University Press, 2002.

MacCormack, Patricia. *Posthuman Ethics*. New York: Routledge, 2012.

McCulloch, Warren S. and Walter H. Pitts. "A Logical Calculus of the Ideas Immanent in Nervous Activity." *Bulletin of Mathematical Biophysics* 5 (1943): 115–33.

Mahoney, James. "Path Dependence in Historical Sociology." *Theory and Society* 29 (2000): 507–48.

Malabou, Catherine. *Before Tomorrow: Epigenesis and Rationality*. Translated by Carolyn Shread. New York: Polity, 2016.

Malabou, Catherine. *The Future of Hegel: Plasticity, Temporality and Dialectic*. Translated by Lisabeth During. New York: Routledge, 2005.

Mann, Gunter. "Franz Joseph Gall (1758–1828) und Samuel Thomas Soemmerring: Kranioskopie und Gehirnforschung zur Goethezeit." In *Samuel Thomas Soemmerring und die Gelehrten der Goethe-Zeit*, edited by Gunter Mann and Franz Dumont, 149–89. Stuttgart: Gustav Fischer, 1985.

Maturana, Humberto R. and Francisco J. Varela. *Autopoiesis and Cognition: The Realization of the Living*. Boston, MA: D. Reidel Publishing, 1980.

Maturana, Humberto R. and Francisco J. Varela. *The Tree of Knowledge: The Biological Roots of Human Understanding*. 2nd edn. Boulder, CO: Shambala, 1992.
Mayr, Ernst and William B. Provine, eds. *The Evolutionary Synthesis: Perspectives on the Unification of Biology*. New edn. Cambridge, MA: Harvard University Press, 1988.
Mehigan, Tim. *Heinrich von Kleist: Writing after Kant*. Rochester, NY: Camden House, 2011.
Mehigan, Tim. "Legality as a 'Fact of Reason': Heinrich von Kleist's Concept of Law, with special reference to *Michael Kohlhaas*." In *Literatur und Recht*, edited by Bernhard Greiner, 153–70. Heidelberg: Winter Verlag, 2010.
Mehigan, Tim. "The Scepticism of Heinrich von Kleist." In *The Oxford Handbook of European Romanticism*, edited by Paul Hamilton, 256–73. Oxford: Oxford University Press, 2016.
Mehigan, Tim. "Kleist und die Tiere. Zur Frage des ausgeschlossenen Dritten in dem Trauerspiel *Penthesilea*." In *Penthesileas Versprechen. Exemplarische Studien über die literarische Referenz*, edited by Rüdiger Campe, 291–311. Freiburg: Rombach, 2007.
Meillassoux, Quentin. *After Finitude: An Essay on the Necessity of Contingency*. Translated by Ray Brassier. London: Bloomsbury, 2010.
Meillassoux, Quentin. *Science Fiction and Extro-Science Fiction*. Translated by Alyosha Edlebi. Minneapolis: University of Minnesota Press, 2015.
Meulders, Michel. *Helmholtz. From Enlightenment to Neuroscience*. Translated and edited by Laurence Garey. Cambridge, MA and London: MIT, 2010.
Millán-Zaibert, Elizabeth. "Alexander von Humboldt's View of America: A Break from Imperial Eyes." In *Humanism and Revolution. Eighteenth-Century Europe and Its Transatlantic Legacy*, edited by Uwe Steiner, Christian Emden, and Martin Vöhler, 209–26. Heidelberg: Universitätsverlag Winter, 2015.
Millán-Zaibert, Elizabeth. "Alexander von Humboldt's Interest in America: In the Service of Empire or of Humanity?" In *Raumzeitlichkeit des Imperialen/SpaceTime of the Imperial*, edited by Holt Meyer, Susanne Rau, and Katharine Waldner, 204–19. Berlin: Walter de Gruyter, 2017.
Millán-Zaibert, Elizabeth. *Friedrich Schlegel and the Emergence of Romantic Philosophy*. Albany: State University of New York Press, 2007.
Minsky, Marvin Lee. "Theory of Neural-Analog Reinforcement Systems and Its Application to the Brain-Model Problem." PhD diss., Princeton University, 1954.
Minsky, Marvin L. and Seymour A. Papert. *Perceptrons: An Introduction to Computational Geometry*. Cambridge, MA: MIT, 1988.
Monod, Jacques. *Chance and Necessity: An Essay on the Natural Philosophy of Modern Biology*. Translated by Austryn Wainhouse. New York: Knopf, 1971.
Moore, Cristopher. "Recursion Theory on the Reals and Continuous-time Computation." *Theoretical Computer Science* 162, no. 1 (August 5, 1996): 23–44.
Moravec, Hans. *Mind Children*. Cambridge, MA: Harvard University Press, 1988.
Morton, Timothy. "All Objects are Deviant: Feminism and Ecological Intimacy." In *Object-Oriented Feminism*, edited by Katherine Behar, 65–81. Minneapolis: University of Minnesota Press, 2016.
Morton, Timothy. *Ecology without Nature: Rethinking Environmental Aesthetics*. Cambridge, MA: Harvard University Press, 2007.
Morton, Timothy. *Humankind: Solidarity with Non-Human People*. London: Verso, 2017.
Morton, Timothy. *Hyperobjects: Philosophy and Ecology after the End of the World*. Cambridge, MA: Harvard University Press, 2013.
Moss, Lenny. "Detachment Theory: Agency, Nature, and Normative Nihilism of New Materialism." In *The New Politics of Materialism: History, Philosophy,*

Science, edited by Sarah Ellenzweig and John H. Zammito, 227–49. New York: Routledge, 2017.

Müller, Johannes. *Handbuch der Physiologie des Menschen*. Koblenz: Hölscher, 1833–40.

Müller, Johannes. *Handbuch der Physiologie des Menschen für Vorlesungen*. Coblenz: J. Hölscher, 1840–4. http://searchworks.stanford.edu/view/547162.

Müller, Johannes. *Über die phantastischen Gesichtserscheinungen*. Eine physiologische Untersuchung mit einer physiologischen Urkunde des Aristoteles über den Traum, den Philosophen und Aerzten gewidmet. Koblenz: Hölscher, 1826. http://www.deutschestextarchiv.de/book/show/mueller_gesichtserscheinungen_1826.

Müller, Johannes. *Zur vergleichenden Physiologie des Gesichtssinnes des Menschen und der Thiere nebst einem Versuch über die Bewegungen der Augen und über den menschlichen Blick*. Leipzig: G. Gnobloch, 1826. https://books.google.com/books/about/Zur_vergleichenden_Physiologie_des_Gesic.html?id=2x0_AAAAcAAJ.

Muth, Ludwig. *Kleist und Kant: Versuch einer neuen Interpretation*. Cologne: Kölner Universitätsverlag, 1954.

Nancy, Jean-Luc. *Hegel: The Restlessness of the Negative*. Translated by S. Miller and J. Smith. Minneapolis: Minnesota University Press, 1997.

Nayar, Promod K. *Posthumanism*. New York: Polity, 2014.

Neurath, Otto. *Philosophical Papers, 1913–1946: With a Bibliography of Neurath in English*. Edited by Robert S. Cohen and Marie Neurath. Dordrecht: Reidel, 1983.

Newhouse, Victoria. *Art and the Power of Placement*. New York: The Monacelli Press, 2005.

Nisbet, Hugh Barr. *Herder and Scientific Thought*. Cambridge: Cambridge University Press, 1970.

Nyhart, Lynn K. *Biology Takes Form: Animal Morphology and the German Universities, 1800–1900*. Chicago: University of Chicago Press, 1995.

Oehler-Klein, Sigrid. *Die Schädellehre Franz Joseph Galls in Literatur und Kritik des 19. Jahrhunderts*. Stuttgart: Gustav Fischer, 1990.

Oken, Lorenz. *Lehrbuch der Naturphilosophie*. Jena: Frommann, 1809.

Olby, R.C. "Charles Darwin's Manuscript of Pangenesis." *British Journal of the History of Science* 1 (1963): 251–63.

Osten, Manfred. *"Alles veloziferisch" oder Goethes Entdeckung der Langsamkeit*. Frankfurt a.M. and Leipzig: Insel, 2003.

Otis, Laura. *Müller's Lab: The Story of Jakob Henle, Theodor Schwann, Emil du Bois-Reymond, Hermann von Helmholtz, Rudolf Virchow, Robert Remak, Ernst Haeckel, and Their Brilliant, Tormented Advisor*. Oxford: Oxford University Press, 2007.

Page, Scott E. "Path Dependence." *Quarterly Journal of Political Science* 1 (2006): 87–115.

Parisi, Luciana. *Abstract Sex: Philosophy, Bio-technology, and the Mutations of Desire*. New York: Continuum, 2004.

Parnes, Ohad. "From Agents to Cells: Theodor Schwann's Research Notes of the Years 1835–1838." In *Reworking the Bench: Research Notebooks in the History of Science*, edited by Frederic L. Holmes, Jürgen Renn, and Hans-Jörg Rheinberger. New York: Kluwer, 2003.

Pepperell, Robert. *The Posthuman Condition: Consciousness beyond the Brain*. Bristol, UK: Intellect, 2003.

Phillips, James. *The Equivocation of Reason: Kleist Reading Kant*. Stanford, CA: Stanford University Press, 2007.

Bibliography   323

Pias, Claus. "Analog, Digital, and the Cybernetic Illusion." *Kybernetes* 34, no. 3–4 (2005): 543–50.
Pickering, Andrew. "Explanation and the Mangle: A Response to My Critics." *Studies in History and Philosophy of Science* 30 (1999): 167–71.
Platner, Ernst. *Neue Anthropologie für Aerzte und Weltweise.* Leipzig: Siegfried Lebrecht Crusius, 1790.
Pollock, Jackson. *No. 5, 1948.* Oil on fiberboard, 8 by 4 feet. Jackson-pollock.org. Accessed August 15, 2017. https://www.jackson-pollock.org/number-5.jsp.
Poulton, Mary M. *Computational Neural Networks for Geophysical Data Processing.* Edited by Mary M. Poulton. Oxford: Pergamon, 2001.
Pratt, Mary Louise. "Humboldt and the Reinvention of America." In *Amerindian Images and the Legacy of Columbus*, edited by René Jara and Nicholas Spadaccinieds, 585–606. Minneapolis: University of Minnesota Press, 1992.
Pratt, Mary Louise. *Imperial Eyes: Travel Writing and Transculturation.* London: Routledge, 1992.
Pross, Wolfgang. "Die Begründung der Geschichte aus der Natur: Herders Konzept von 'Gesetzen' in der Geschichte." In *Wissenschaft als kulturelle Praxis, 1750–1900*, edited by Hans Erich Bödeker, Hanns Peter Reill, and Jürgen Schlumbohm, 187–225. Göttingen: Vandenhoeck & Ruprecht, 1999.
Pross, Wolfgang. "*Ideen zur Philosophie der Geschichte der Menschheit.*" In *Herder Handbuch*, edited by Stefan Greif, Marion Heinz, and Heinrich Clairmont, 171–216. Paderborn: Wilhelm Fink, 2016.
Putnam, Hillary. *Mind, Language and Reality: Philosophical Papers,* vol. 2. New York: Cambridge University Press, 1975.
Putnam, Hillary. "The Nature of Mental States." In *Readings in Philosophy of Psychology*, vol. 1, edited by Ned Block, 223–32. Cambridge, MA: Harvard University Press, 1980.
Rang, Bernhard. *Identität und Indifferenz. Eine Untersuchung zu Schellings Identitätsphilosophie.* Frankfurt a.M.: Klostermann, 2000.
Rheinberger, Hans-Jörg. *An Epistemology of the Concrete: Twentieth-Century Histories of Life.* Translated and foreword by Tim Lenoir. Durham, NC: Duke University Press, 2010.
Rheinberger, Hans-Jörg. *Toward a History of Epistemic Things: Synthesizing Proteins in the Test Tube.* Stanford, CA: Stanford University Press, 1997.
Richards, Robert J. "Kant and Blumenbach on the Bildungstrieb: A Historical Misunderstanding." *Studies in History and Philosophy of Biological and Biomedical Sciences* 31 (2000): 11–32.
Richards, Robert J. *The Meaning of Evolution: The Morphological Construction and Ideological Reconstruction of Darwin's Theory.* Chicago: University of Chicago Press, 1992.
Richards, Robert J. *The Romantic Conception of Life: Science and Philosophy in the Age of Goethe.* Chicago: University of Chicago Press, 2002.
Richter, Simon. "Goethe's *Faust* and the Ecolinguistics of 'Here'." In *German Ecocriticism in the Anthropocene*, edited by Caroline Schaumann and Heather I. Sullivan, 45–64. New York: Springer, 2017.
Risse, Guenter. "Medicine in the Age of Enlightenment." In *Medicine in Society*, edited by Andrew Wear, 149–95. Cambridge: Cambridge University Press, 1992.
Ritter, Johann Wilhelm. *Key Texts of Johann Wilhelm Ritter (1776–1810) on the Science and Art of Nature.* Translated by Jocelyn Holland. Leiden: Brill, 2010.
Roden, David. *Posthuman Life: Philosophy at the Edge of the Human.* London: Routledge, 2015.

324 Bibliography

Roe, Shirley A. "Anatomia animate: The Newtonian Physiology of Albrecht von Haller." In *Transformation and Tradition in the Sciences*, edited by Everett Mendelsohn, 273–302. Cambridge: Cambridge University Press, 1984.

Rojas, Raul. *Neural Networks: A Systematic Introduction*. Berlin: Springer, 1996.

Rorty, Richard. *Objectivity, Relativism, and Truth: Philosophical Papers*. Cambridge: Cambridge University Press, 1990.

Rollin, Bernard. *Putting the Horse before Descartes: A Memoir*. Philadelphia, PA: Temple University Press, 2011.

Rosenbluth, Arturo, Norbert Wiener, and Julian Bigelow. "Behavior, Purpose and Teleology." *Philosophy of Science* 10, no. 1 (1943): 18–24.

Rotmann, Brian. *Mathematics as Sign: Writing, Imaging, Counting*. Stanford, CA: Stanford University Press, 2000.

Roux, Wilhelm. "Beiträge zur Entwickelungsmechanik des Embryo: Ueber die künstliche Hervorbringung halber Embryonen durch Zerstörung einer der beiden ersten Furchungskugeln, sowie über die Nachentwickelung (Postgeneration) der fehlenden Körperhälfte." *Virchows Archiv* 114 (1888): 113–53.

Roux, Wilhelm. *Der Kampf der Theile im Organismus: Ein Beitrag zur Vervollständigung der mechanischen Zweckmässigkeitslehre*. Leipzig: Engelmann, 1881.

Roux, Wilhelm. *Gesammelte Abhandlungen über Entwicklungsmechanik der Organismen*. Leipzig: Engelmann, 1895.

Roux, Wilhelm. *Ueber die Bedeutung der Kerntheilungsfiguren*. Leipzig: Engelmann, 1883.

Ruse, Michael, ed. *Philosophy after Darwin: Classic and Contemporary Readings*. Princeton, NJ: Princeton University Press, 2009.

Rüve, Gerlind. *Scheintod. Zur kulturellen Bedeutung der Schwelle zwischen Leben und Tod um 1800*. Berlin: transcript, 2008.

Sachs, Aaron. "The Ultimate 'Other': Post-Colonialism and Alexander von Humboldt's Ecological Relationship with Nature." *History and Theory* 42 (2003): 111–35.

Sarkar, Sahotra. "Models of Reduction and Categories of Reductionism." *Synthese* 91 (1992): 167–94.

Schaeffer, Jean-Marie. *Art of the Modern Age: Philosophy of Art from Kant to Heidegger*. Translated by Steven Rendall. Princeton, NJ: Princeton University Press, 2000.

Schelling, Friedrich. *First Outline of a System of the Philosophy of Nature*. Translated by Keith R. Peterson. Albany: State University of New York Press, 2004.

Schelling, Friedrich. *Ideen zu einer Philosophie der Natur*. In *Werke*, vol. 1, edited by M. Schröter. Munich: C. H. Beck, 1927.

Schelling, Friedrich. *Ideen zu einer Philosophie der Natur*. In *Sämmtliche Werke*, vol. 1, no. 2, edited by Karl Friedrich August Schelling, 1–343. Stuttgart: Cotta, 1857.

Schiller, Friedrich. *On the Aesthetic Education of Man in a Series of Letters* (English/German). Edited and translated by Elizabeth M. Wilkinson and L. A. Willoughby. Oxford: Clarendon, 1967.

Schiller, Friedrich. *Sämtliche Werke, vol. 5: Erzählungen, Theoretische Schriften*. Edited by Wolfgang Riedel. Munich, Vienna: Carl Hanser (Deutscher Taschenbuch Verlag), 2004.

Schlegel, Friedrich. *Friedrich Schlegel: Philosophical Fragments*. Translated by Peter Firchow. Minneapolis: University of Minnesota Press, 1991.

Schlegel, Friedrich. *Friedrich Schlegel Kritische Ausgabe (KFSA)*, 35 volumes. Edited by Ernst Behler et al. Paderborn: Ferdinand Schoeningh, 1958 ff.

Schleiden, Matthias Jacob. "Beiträge zur Phytogenesis." *Archiv für Anatomie, Physiologie und wissenschaftliche Medicin* 5 (1838): 137–76.

Schleiden, Matthias Jacob. *Über den Materialismus der neueren deutschen Naturwissenschaft: Sein Wesen und seine Geschichte: Zur Verständigung für die Gebildeten.* Leipzig: Engelmann, 1863.

Schleiermacher, Friedrich. *Hermeneutics and Criticism and Other Writings.* Edited and translated by Andrew Bowie. Cambridge: Cambridge University Press, 1998.

Schmidt, James, ed. *What is Enlightenment? Eighteenth-Century Answers and Twentieth-Century Questions.* Berkeley: University of California Press, 1996.

Schmidt, Jochen. *Goethes Faust, Erster und Zweiter Teil: Grundlagen—Werk—Wirkung.* Munich: C. H. Beck, 1999.

Schrödinger, Erwin. *What is Life?: With Mind and Matter and Autobiographical Sketches.* Cambridge: Cambridge University Press, 2012.

Schulte-Sasse, Jochen, et al., eds. *Theory and Practice: A Critical Anthology of Early German Romantic Writings.* Minneapolis: University of Minnesota Press, 1997.

Schwann, Theodor. *Mikroskopische Untersuchungen über die Übereinstimmung in der Struktur und dem Wachstum der Thiere und Pflanzen.* Berlin: Sander, 1839.

Scott, Ridley, dir. *Blade Runner.* 1982; Burbank, CA: Warner Home Video, 2007. DVD.

Seel, Martin. *Aesthetics of Appearing.* Translated by John Farrell. Stanford, CA: Stanford University Press, 2005.

Sembdner, Helmut. *Heinrich von Kleists Nachruhm: Eine Wirkungsgeschichte in Dokumenten*, vol. 2. Frankfurt a.M.: Insel Verlag, 1984.

Semper, Karl. *Die natürlichen Existenzbedingungen der Thiere.* Leipzig: Brockhaus, 1880.

Sharon, Tamar. *Human Nature in an Age of Biotechnology: The Case for Mediated Posthumanism.* Dordrecht, Heidelberg, New York and London: Springer, 2014.

Shaviro, Steven. *The Universe of Things: On Speculative Realism.* Minneapolis: University of Minnesota Press, 2014.

Shaviro, Steven. *Without Criteria: Kant, Whitehead, Deleuze, and Aesthetics.* Cambridge, MA: MIT, 2009.

Sherburne, Donald W. *A Key to Whitehead's Process and Reality.* Chicago: University of Chicago Press, 1981.

Siegert, Bernhard. *Relays: Literature as an Epoch of the Postal System.* Translated by K. Repp. Stanford, CA: Stanford University Press, 1999.

Simondon, Gilbert. *Du mode d'existence des objets techniques.* Paris: Aubier, 1958.

Smail, Daniel Lord. *On Deep History and the Brain.* Berkeley and Los Angeles: University of California Press, 2008.

Smail, Daniel Lord and Andrew Shryock. *Deep History: The Architecture of Past and Present.* Berkeley and Los Angeles: University of California Press, 2011.

Smith, John. H. *Dialectics of the Will: Freedom, Power, and Understanding in Modern French and German Thought.* Detroit: Wayne State University Press, 2000.

Soemmerring, Samuel Thomas. *Über die körperliche Verschiedenheit des Mohren vom Europäer.* Mainz: [n.p.], 1784.

Soemmerring, Samuel Thomas. *Ueber das Organ der Seele.* Königsberg: Nicolovius, 1796.

Soemmerring, Samuel Thomas. *Ueber die körperliche Verschiedenheit des Negers vom Europäer*. Frankfurt a.M.: Varrentrapp Sohn und Wenner, 1785.

Soemmerring, Samuel Thomas. *Werke* 15: *Anthropologie: Über die körperliche Verschiedenheit des Negers vom Europäer* (1785). Edited by Sigrid Oehler-Klein. Stuttgart: G. Fischer, 1998.

Sewell, William H. Jr. "Three Temporalities: Toward an Eventful Sociology." In *The Historic Turn in the Human Sciences*, edited by Terrence J. McDonald, 245–80. Ann Arbor, MI: University of Michigan Press, 1996.

Stahl, Georg Ernst. *Theoria Medica Vera, Physiologiam et Pathologiam* [1708]. Halle: D. Joan Junckeri, 1737.

Star Trek: The Next Generation, Complete Seasons Bundle. 1987–94; Hollywood, CA: Paramount Pictures, 2007. DVD.

Starobinski, Jean. "The Style of Autobiography." In *Autobiography: Essays Theoretical and Critical*, edited by James Olney, 73–83. Princeton, NJ: Princeton University Press, 1980.

Steel, Karl. "Medieval." In *The Cambridge Companion to Literature and the Posthuman*, edited by Bruce Clarke and Manuela Rossini. Cambridge: Cambridge University Press, 2017.

Stegmaier, Werner. *Philosophie der Orientierung*. Berlin: de Gruyter, 2008.

Steinke, Hubert. *Irritating Experiments: Haller's Concept and the European Controversy on Irritability and Sensibility, 1750–90*. Amsterdam: Rodopi, 2005.

Stiegler, Bernard. *Technics and Time, I: The Fault of Epimetheus*. Translated by Richard Beardsworth and George Collins. Stanford, CA: Stanford University Press, 1998.

Strathausen Carsten. *Bioaesthetics: Making Sense of Life in Science and the Arts*. Minneapolis: University of Minnesota Press, 2017.

Sullivan, Heather I. "Agency in the Anthropocene: Goethe, Radical Reality, and the New Materialisms." In *The Early History of Embodied Cognition 1740–1920. The Lebenskraft-Debate and Radical Reality in German Science, Music, and Literature*, edited by John A. McCarthy et al. Leiden and Boston, MA: Brill Rodopi, 2016.

Taylor, Charles. "The Concept of a Person." In *Philosophical Papers, vol. 1*, 97–114. New York: Cambridge University Press, 1985.

Taylor, Charles. "What is Human Agency." In *Philosophical Papers, I: Human Agency and Language*, 15–44. Cambridge: Cambridge University Press, 1985.

Thacker, Eugene. *In the Dust of this Planet*. vol. 1. *Horror of Philosophy*. Winchester, UK: Zero Books, 2011.

Temkin, Owsei. "Gall and the Phrenological Movement." *Bulletin of the History of Medicine* 21 (1947): 275–321.

Theisen, Bianca. "Der Bewunderer des Shakespeare. Kleists Skeptizismus." *Kleist-Jahrbuch* (1999): 87–108.

Thompson, Evan. *Mind in Life: Biology, Phenomenology, and the Sciences of Mind*. Cambridge, MA: Harvard University Press, 2007.

Thompson, Evan and Francisco J. Varela. "Radical Embodiment: Neural Dynamics and Consciousness." *Trends in Cognitive Sciences* 5, no. 10 (2001): 418–25.

Toscano, Alberto. "Fanaticism and Production: On Schelling's Philosophy of Indifference." *Pli* 8 (1999): 46–70.

Treviranus, Gottfried Reinhold. *Biologie, oder Philosophie der lebenden Natur für Naturforscher und Aerzte*. Göttingen: Röwer, 1802–22.

Treviranus, Gottfried Reinhold. *Die Erscheinungen und Gesetze des organischen Lebens, neu dargestellt*. Bremen: Heyse, 1831–32.

Turing, A. M. "Computing Machinery and Intellignce." *Mind* 49 (1950): 433–60.

Uexküll, Jakob von. *A Foray into the Worlds of Animals and Humans*. Translated by Joseph D. O'Neil. Minneapolis: University of Minnesota Press, 2010.
Uexküll, Jacob von. *Der Sinn des Lebens. Gedanken über die Aufgaben der Biologie mitgeteilt in einer Interpretation der zu Bonn 1824 gehaltenen Vorlesung des Johannes Müller "Von dem Bedürfnis der Physiologie nach einer philosophischen Naturbetrachtung"* mit einem Ausblick von Thure von Uexküll. Godesberg: Helmut Küpper, 1947.
Uexküll, Jacob von. *Umwelt und Innenwelt der Tiere*. Berlin: Julius Springer, 1909. https://ia700302.us.archive.org/27/items/umweltundinnenwe00uexk/umweltundinnenwe00uexk.pdf.
van der Laan, J. M. *Seeking Meaning for Goethe's* Faust. London and New York: Continuum, 2007.
Virchow, Rudolf. *Die Cellularpathologie in ihrer Begründung auf physiologische und pathologische Gewebelehre: 20 Vorlesungen, gehalten während der Monate Februar, März und April 1858 im Pathologischen Institut zu Berlin*. Berlin: Hirschwald, 1858.
Vogel, Carl. *Die letzte Krankheit Goethes*. Berlin: G. Reimer, 1833.
Vogl, Joseph. "Nomos der Ökonomie. Steuerungen in Goethes *Elective Affinities*." *MLN* 114, no. 3, German Issue (April 1999): 503–27.
Waldau, Paul. *Animal Studies: An Introduction*. Oxford: Oxford University Press, 2013.
Watercutter, Angela. "*Ex Machina* has a Serious Fembot Problem." *Wired*. Last modified April 9, 2015. https://www.wired.com/2015/04/ex-machina-turing-bechdel-test/.
Weatherby, Leif. *Transplanting the Metaphysical Organ: German Romanticism between Leibniz and Marx*. New York: Fordham University Press, 2016.
Wegmann, Thomas. *Tauschverhältnisse. Zur Ökonomie des Literarischen und zum Ökonomischen in der Literatur von Gellert bis Goethe*. Würzburg: Königshausen and Neumann, 2002.
Weismann, August. *Die Continuität des Keimplasmas als Grundlage einer Theorie der Vererbung: Ein Vortrag*. Jena: Fischer, 1885.
Weismann, August. *Ueber die Berechtigung der Darwin'schen Theorie: Ein akademischer Vortrag, gehalten am 8. Juli 1868 in der Aula der Universität zu Freiburg im Breisgau*. Leipzig: Engelmann, 1868.
Weismann, August. *Ueber die Vererbung: Ein Vortrag*. Jena: Fischer, 1883.
Wellbery, David. "Foreword." In Friedrich Kittler, *Discourse Networks 1800/1900*, translated by Michael Metteer, with Chris Cullens, vii–xxxiii. Stanford, CA: Stanford University Press, 1990.
Wenzel, Christian Helmut. *An Introduction to Kant's Aesthetics: Core Concepts and Problems*. Oxford: Blackwell, 2005.
West-Eberhard, Mary Jane. "Developmental Pasticity and the Origin of Species Differences." *Proceedings of the National Academy of Sciences* 102 (2005), supplement 1: 6543–49.
West-Eberhard, Mary Jane. "Toward a Modern Revival of Darwin's Theory of Evolutionary Novelty." *Philosophy of Science* 75 (2008): 899–908.
Wetters, Kirk. *Demonic History: From Goethe to the Present*. Evanston: Northwestern University Press, 2014.
Whistler, Daniel. "Schelling on Individuation." *Comparative and Continental Philosophy* 8, no. 3 (2016): 329–44.
Whitehead, Alfred North. *Modes of Thought*. Toronto: Free Press, 1968.
Whitehead, Alfred North. *Process and Reality. Corrected Edition*. Edited by David Ray Griffin and Donald W. Sherburne. New York: Free Press, 1978.

Wild, Markus. "Anthropologische Differenz." In *Tiere: Kulturwissenschaftliches Handbuch*, edited by Roland Borgards, 47–59. Stuttgart and Weimar: J. B. Metzler, 2016.

Wimsatt, William C. "Generative Entrenchment and the Developmental Systems Approach to Evolutionary Processes." In *Cycles of Contingency: Developmental Systems and Evolution*, edited by Susan Oyama, Russell D. Gray, and Paul E. Griffiths, 219–37. Cambridge, MA: MIT, 2001.

Wimsatt, William C. and James R. Griesemer. "Reproducing Entrenchments to Scaffold Culture: The Central Role of Development in Cultural Evolution." In *Integrating Evolution and Development: From Theory to Practice*, edited by Roger Sansome and Robert N. Brandon, 228–323. Cambridge, MA: MIT, 2007.

Wolfe, Cary. *Before the Law: Humans and Other Animals in a Biopolitical Frame*. Chicago: University of Chicago Press, 2012.

Wolfe, Cary. "Human, All too Human: 'Animal Studies,' and the Humanities." *PMLA* 124 (2009): 564–75.

Wolfe, Cary. *What is Posthumanism?* Minneapolis: University of Minnesota Press, 2010.

Wolfendale, Peter. *Object Oriented Philosophy: The Noumenon's New Clothes*. Falmouth, UK: Urabanomics, 2014.

Wolff, Christian. *Vernünfftige Gedancken von Gott, der Welt und der Seele des Menschen, auch allen Dingen überhaupt, den Liebhabern der Wahrheit mitgetheilet*. Halle: Renger, 1751.

Woodward, William A. "Hermann Lotze's Critique of Johannes Müller's Doctrine of Specific Sense Energies." *Medical History* 19, no. 2 (April 1975): 147–57.

Wubnig, Judy. "The Epigenesis of Pure Reason: A Note on the 'Critique of Pure Reason' B sec. 27, 165–167." *Kant-Studien* 60, no. 2 (1969): 147–52.

Wyhe, John van. *Phrenology and the Origins of Victorian Scientific Naturalism*. Aldershot: Ashgate, 2004.

Young, Robert M. *Mind, Brain, and Adaptation in the Nineteenth Century*. Oxford: Oxford University Press, 1970.

Zammito, John H. *The Gestation of German Biology: Philosophy and Physiology from Stahl to Schelling*. Chicago: University of Chicago Press, 2017.

Zammito, John H. "Kant's Persistent Ambivalence towards Epigenesis, 1764–90." In *Understanding Purpose: Kant and the Philosophy of Biology*, edited by Philippe Huneman, 51–74. Rochester, NY: University of Rochester Press, 2007.

Zöller, Günter. *Fichte's Transcendental Philosophy: The Original Duplicity of Intelligence and Will*. New York: Cambridge University Press, 1998.

Zöller, Günter. "Kant on the Generation of Metaphysical Knowledge." In *Kant, Analysen-Probleme-Kritik*, edited by Hariolf Oberer and Gerhard Seel, 71–90. Würzburg: Königshausen & Neumann, 1988.

Index

Note: Page references followed by "n" indicate footnotes.

actor-network theory (ANT) 113
Adorno, Theodor W. 145, 188–94, 197
aesthetics 120–3, 127–44, 185–90, 194, 200
Africans 45–7
Agamben, Giorgio 38, 46, 290
agency 73–4
    biological 55–6, 60–2, 68–76
    of matter 59–60
Allison, Henry 135
analogy, use of 180
Anderegg, Johannes 257 n.60
animal studies 37–9, 52
animality 38, 39 n.11, 52, 209, 215–16
anthropocene, the 106, 127, 127 n.2, 176
anthropocentrism 3, 7, 12, 39, 39 n.11, 41 n.19, 52, 58, 81, 96, 99, 108, 118, 129–31, 137, 165–6, 212, 244, 270, 279
anthropomorphism 72, 91, 111, 117–18
anti-humanism 2
Arendt, Hannah 287–8
Aristotle 20, 49, 170
art, theory of 128–9, 133, 144
art works 140, 144, 190, 193, 287
artificial death 280, 282
artificial intelligence (AI) 24, 146–7, 153, 164, 208, 220, 223–6, 229–34, 237–8

artificial life 244, 276, 280
autobiographical perspective 274–8
autopoietic systems 115 n.31
avatars 235–7

Bacon, Francis 276–7
Badiou, Alain 146, 158
Badmington, Geoffrey 124
Badmington, Neil 2, 226 n.10
Barad, Karen 54–5, 58–60, 73, 76, 220
Bateson, Gregory 8, 166–81, 290
Battlestar Galactica (TV series) 226–7
Baudrillard, Jean 243
beauty 8–9, 140–4. *See also* natural beauty
    of a particular object 136
Beiser, Frederick 184 n.3, 238–40
Benjamin, Walter 189, 300, 301 n.36, 302
Bennett, Jane 117–19, 124–5, 146 n.1
Bentley, Madison 48 n.47
Bergson, Henri 56, 136
Berners-Lee, Timothy 151, 152 n.15
Bigelow, Julian 224 n.5
Binswanger, Hans Christoph 258 n.64
Blade Runner (film) 226–7
Blamberger, Günter 209 n.18
Bloor, David 114 n.29
Blumenbach, Johann Friedrich 67–8, 116

Blumenberg, Hans 157 n.30
Boerhaave, Herman 32–3
Bogost, Ian 124
Böhme, Hartmut 192–3
Bois-Reymond, Emil du 6, 82
Bonnet, Charles 47
Bostrom, Nick 80
Botz-Bornstein, Thorsten 247
Bowler, Peter J. 53 n.1, 54 n.3
Braidotti, Rosi 2, 39 n.11, 54–5, 57 n.8, 59–60, 119, 270–2, 274 n.17, 275, 279, 281, 284–5, 292 n.12
brain structure and function 46–52
Brassier, Ray 107 n.7, 109, 306
Breidbach, Olaf 48 n.51
Brodsky, Claudia 261–2
Brown, John 273
Brugmans, Anton 290
Brüning, Gerrit 264 n.99
Bryant, Levi 119
Buffon, Georges-Louis Leclerc de 41
Bunge, Gustav von 69–71

Calarco, Matthew 39 n.9
Campbell, Donald T. 116
Camper, Pieter 43, 46
Canetti, Elias 243–4
Carnap. Rudolf 57 n.9
Caspari, Otto 54, 70–3, 76
Cassirer, Ernst 26 n.20, 204 n.6, 205 n.7
categorical imperative 118
Caygill, Howard 113
cell theory 6, 64–70, 76–7
Church–Turing thesis 21
cognition 43–51, 81, 86–7, 90, 94–5, 105, 121, 134–8, 147–8
Colebrook, Claire 11–12, 295 n.20
Coleman, William 65 n.40
color, theory of 249
Condillac, Étienne Bonnot de 47
Connolly, William 119–20
consciousness 5, 10, 18, 21, 23, 24, 26, 33–4, 44, 66, 80, 86–7, 89, 93, 105–8, 111–12, 136, 148, 161, 163, 168, 174, 177–8, 194, 207–8, 214, 220–1, 224–5, 230–5, 269, 289, 299. *See also* self-consciousness
constitutivism 56 n.6
constructivism 83, 93–5, 99–100
continental philosophy 56, 108
Coole, Diana 58 n.14, 59, 73
Copernicus, Nicolaus 129, 157
correlationism 86, 93–5, 108, 113, 121, 130, 137–40, 149
Crary, Jonathan 85 n.24
critical posthumanism (CP) 125, 244–5
Crutzen, Paul J. 127 n.2

Darstellung 279
Darwin, Charles 38, 53, 61–3, 69, 72, 76
Dassow Walls, Laura 194 n.30
Davidson, Donald 74 n.76
Davies, Martin L. 25 n.20, 33 n.48
Deacon, Terence 115 n.31
death
  concept of 269–72
  productive element to 272–3
  theories of 270–1, 275, 285
Deleuze, Gilles 56, 110, 120–4, 136 n.26, 140, 270–1
Depew, David 72 n.71
Derrida, Jacques 38, 40, 51–2, 124, 130, 148, 169
Descartes, René 38, 110
Dewey, John 221
Diderot, Denis 39
Dischner, Gisela 203 n.2
disembodiment 80
Dollimore, Jonathan 1
dream images 90, 92
Driesch, Hans 63, 69 n.58
Dyck, J.W. 203 n.2

ecology, terrestrial 176
Edmonds, Dean 19, 35
Eibl, Karl 248 n.14

embodied cognition 5, 90
embodied phantasy 87–99
embodiment, concept of 79–81, 82 n.12, 84–7, 93 n.55, 94, 266
embryology 6
Emden, Christian J. 55 n.5
Enç, Berent 74 n.76
energy, *general* and *specific* 85 n.22
Engler-Coldren, Katharina 82 n.12
Enlightenment thought 183–4, 205
Enoch, David 56 n.6
epistemology 7–8, 58, 107–13, 120–5, 130, 135, 138
  evolutionary 116
eugenics 281
Euler, Leonhard 142
Eurocentrism 184, 199
evolutionary theory 54, 61–4
Ex Machina (film) 223–41

fashion 11–12
Fechner, Gustav 24
feedback effects 73
Fichte, Johann Gottlieb 10, 204–6, 224 n.6, 225, 227, 230–3, 238–40, 253
film-making 225–7
Finger, Stanley 95 n.60
Firchow, Peter 184 n.4
Fischer, Bernd 204 n.6, 208 n.17
Foerster, Heinz von 28, 35–6, 82
Fontane, Theodor 218
Foucault, Michel 56, 119 n.49, 281
Franklin, Benjamin 282–3
Freud, Sigmund 24, 34 n.53
Friedlander, Eli 142–3
Frost, Samantha 58 n.14, 59, 73

Gaddafi, Muammar 281
Gall, Franz Joseph 6, 39–40, 44, 47–52
Galloway, Alexander 146
Galton, Francis 63
Garland, Alex 9, 223–7
Gasché, Rodolphe 130 n.9

Gehlen, Arnold 258–9
Geist concept 165–6, 169, 173, 177–81
Ghiselin, Michael T. 72 n.71
Girtanner, Christoph 68 n.55
Goethe, Johann Wolfgang 3–4, 7, 10–11, 83–4, 87–91, 92 n.53, 98, 99 n.74, 100, 170, 205, 273, 275, 280–4, 299 n.28
  Elective Affinities 288–92, 297–308
  "The Experiment as Mediator between Object and Subject" 297
  Faust 245–67
  Poetry and Truth 302
  Wilhelm Meister's Apprenticeship Years 280–1
Google 235, 236 n.35
grace 207
Graham, Elaine L. 2, 80 n.6
Graham, Ilse 216 n.36
Grant, Iain Hamilton 107 n.7, 170 n.9, 288 n.2
Gray, Russell 69 n.57
great apes 40, 43–5
great chain of being 40–2, 45–7, 50–2, 219
Greenberg, Martin 214 n.32
Greiner, Bernhard 205 n.7, 209 n.19
Grene, Marjorie 72 n.71
Griesemer, James R. 75 n.80
Griffin, Andrew 236 n.35
Griffiths, Paul 69 n.57
Grimm, Wilhelm 218
Grosz, Elizabeth 57 n.8, 60–1, 106, 119–20
Gruber, Thomas R. 150–4, 152 n.15
Grusin, Richard 3 n.4, 12, 106 n.6
Guattari, Félix 124, 270
Guyer, Paul 134–8, 142 n.46, 143

Hacking, Ian 71 n.66
Haeckel, Ernst 6, 64 n.35, 82

Index

Hagner, Michael 40 n.15
Haller, Albrecht von 26, 32–4
Hallward, Peter 124
Hansen, Leeann 26 n.20
Hansen, Mark 7, 8, 30 n.37
Haraway, Donna 2, 57–8, 149, 186, 229
Hardenberg, Friedrich von 179. *See also* Novalis
Harman, Graham 2, 8 n.9, 60 n.20, 107 n.7, 108–10, 113, 146 n.1
Harris, Errol E. 166 n.2
Hayles, N. Katherine 2, 7, 21–2, 79–82, 105, 148–9, 233, 243, 245, 246 n.8, 266–7, 269
Hebb, Donald O. (and Hebbian learning) 20 n.8
Hegel, Georg Friedrich Wilhelm 3, 7–9, 18, 166–81, 127–33, 137, 145–9, 155–64, 188, 190
  Encyclopaedia of the Philosophical Sciences 168–71, 175–80
Heidegger, Martin 56, 127, 145, 146 n.1, 260–2
Helmholtz, Hermann von 6, 82, 85 n.22, 86, 97, 99
Henrich, Dieter 239 n.42
Hepburn, R.W. 187 n.9
Her (film) 226–7
Herbrechter, Stefan 1–2, 80, 125, 203 n.1
Herder, Johann Gottfried 39–47, 51, 273
"Herr C" 206, 208
Herz, Marcus 5–6, 17–19, 22–7, 30–6
His, Wilhelm 64
Hitler, Adolf 118
Hoffmann, E.T.A. 291
Hölderlin, Friedrich 179, 187 n.10, 205, 301 n.36
Holland, Jocelyn 290 n.8
Houlgate, Stephen 166 n.2
Hufeland, Christoph Wilhelm 10, 271–85

Hui, Yuk 152 n.17
human condition and *conditioned-ness* 287–8
human faculties 37
human-ness 227
humanism 4, 81, 118–19, 125, 183–4, 190, 255, 271
  use of the term 183
humanity 9–10
Humboldt, Alexander von 9, 184–200
Hume, David 27, 110, 161, 205
Husserl, Edmund 136, 145
hylozoism 116
"hyper-Chaos" (Meillassoux) 159–60

idealism in philosophy 7, 25, 47, 76. *See also* transcendental idealism
  German 145, 147, 157
identity, law of (Fichte) 231
indifference 289–304
  in Goethe's *Elective Affinities* 297–304
  of the inorganic 291
  of naturephilosophy 292–7
  operations of 289–92
individuation, doctrine of 296
inorganic, *negative* and *affirmative* 291–2
intentionality 74, 90–2, 136, 220
Internet resources 141, 235–6
interoperability between "agents" 150–1
Irigaray, Luce 56

Jacobi, Friedrich Heinrich 26
Jacobson, Brian R. 225–9
Jaeger, Michael 255 n.51
Jonze, Spike 226

Kafka, Franz 221
Kant, Immanuel (and Kantianism) 2–8, 13, 17–18, 22, 25–39,

67–8, 99, 106–25, 127–47, 152–62, 170, 183–5, 188, 190, 195–6, 203–6, 219–21
Kästner, Abraham Gotthelf 18
Katsafanas, Paul 56 n.6
Kayser, Wolfgang 208 n.17
Kierkegaard, Søren 169
Kittler, Friedrich 17, 165, 167–8, 246
Kleist, Heinrich von 9, 203–9, 211 n.26
  "Das Bettelweib von Locarno" 216–18, 221
  "Das Erdbeben in Chili" 215
  "Die Marquise von O..." 212, 216, 221
  "Michael Kohlhaas" 210–16, 221
  Penthesilea 209, 215
  "Über das Marionettentheater" 220
Knapp, Lore 82 n.12
Kohlenbach, Margarete 189 n.15
Kohlhaas, Hans 211, 214 n.30
Korsgaard, Christine M. 56 n.6

Laan, J.M. van der 257 n.60
Ladewig, Rebekka 27 n.25
La Mettrie, Julien Offroy de 39
Larson, James L. 68 n.52
Larubia-Prado, Francisco 214 n.31
Latin America 9, 184–5, 189–90, 194–200
Latour, Bruno 61, 113–14, 119, 122, 186
Leder, Christoph Maria 25 n.20
Lee, Charlotte 82 n.12
Leibniz, Gottfried 94 n.58, 150, 152, 204
Lennox, James G. 72 n.71
Lenoir, Timothy 54 n.3
Leopardi, Giacomo 11
Levinas, Emmanuel 56
Lewens, Tim 53 n.1
life
  "higher purpose" to 283
  in relation to nature 296
life sciences 53–6, 61–5, 68, 70, 76, 86, 101, 244
Lilienthal, Georg 46 n.37
Lindroos-Hovinheimo, Susanna 224 n.6
Locke, John 7
Look, Brandon C. 68 n.52
Lotze, Hermann 85–6
Luhmann, Niklas 22 n.13, 28, 35, 148
Luther, Martin 211–12

MacCormack, Patricia 269–70
McCulloch, Warren S. 19–21
machine learning 25, 147
McLuhan, Marshall 246, 284
macrobiotics 271–85
Mahoney, James 75 n.81
Malabou, Catherine 115–16, 155 n.23, 157, 158 n.33, 160, 164 n.45
Mann, Gunter 44 n.31
Marx, Karl 56, 146–7, 170
Marxism 109, 147
materialism 7, 25, 32, 55, 57–8, 65, 70, 76, 80–1, 96, 98–9, 119, 129, 144, 146 n.1, 155, 160. *See also* new materialism; posthuman materialism
mathematics 21 n.10, 107 n.7, 108 n.11, 130, 146
Maturana, Humberto 23, 82, 115 n.31
Maupertuis, Pierre 282–3
Mayr, Ernst 62 n.26
medical life and death 281–4
Mehigan, Tim 205 n.7
Meillassoux, Quentin 2, 8, 81, 86, 93, 94 n.58, 98, 99 n.74, 107 n.7, 108, 129–30, 146 n.1, 149, 155–63
Mendelssohn, Moses 26
mental illness 178
mental representations 36

metaphor, use of 285
metaphysics 124, 145–6, 291
   special and *general* 150, 153
Meulders, Michel 88 n.38
Millán-Zaibert, Elizabeth 184 n.2
mind
   concept of 8–9, 166, 181
   human 115–17, 122
   theory of 125
mind/body dualism 23, 81, 84, 271
Minsky, Marvin 19–24, 28, 35–6
Monod, Jacques 116
Moore, Christopher 21 n.10
morality as distinct from legality 212–13, 216
Moravec, Hans 80, 234–6
Moritz, Karl Philipp 26
Morton, Timothy 2, 58 n.13, 100, 130 n.10, 186
Moss, Lenny 56 n.7
Müller, Johannes 5–7, 66, 81–101
Müller-Salget, Klaus 204 n.4, 210 n.20, 211 n.26, 214 n.32, 218
Muth, Ludwig 205 n.7

Nagel, Thomas 124
Nancy, Jean-Luc 181 n.48
natural beauty 127–34, 185–92, 195–7
natural selection 62–4, 72
naturalism, philosophical 76–7
nature
   laws of 90, 194
   processes of 191
naturephilosophy 10, 290–2
   indifference of 292–7
Nayar, Pramod 2, 80, 119 n.50, 266
necrophilosophy 269, 272
necropoetics 275–6
nerve energies 84–6, 96
neural mechanisms 19–20
Neurath, Otto 57 n.9
new embodiment 244, 266
new materialism 54–8, 81, 98 n.74, 99–100, 106, 117, 119, 125

Newton, Isaac 83
Nietzsche, Friedrich 3, 12, 56–7, 94 n.58, 114, 203
Nisbet, Hugh Barr 41 n.19
North Korea 120
Novalis 18, 179, 186, 205, 290–1
Nyhart, Lynn K. 54 n.3

Oehler-Klein, Sigrid 50 n.54
Oken, Lorenz 5, 38 n.7, 39, 54, 66, 69, 290
ontology 7–8, 27, 56, 58, 60, 77, 100, 107–13, 117, 119–25, 129, 145–6, 149–63, 290
   definition of 112–13, 150
   object-oriented 60, 81, 99, 106, 154
ontology engineering 152, 154, 160
optics 88. *See also* visual perception
organic and *inorganic* beings 293–7, 308
orientation, philosophical concept of 23–32, 36
Osten, Manfred 256 n.54
Otis, Laura 82 n.13, 89

Page, Scott E. 75 n.81
Papert, Seymour A. 24 n.18
Parsons, Talcott 28
path dependence 73, 75
phantasy and phantasmagoric phenomena 6, 82–4, 87–99
Phillips, James 205 n.7
phrenology 6, 47–8, 50 n.54
physicalism 57 n.9
Pias, Claus 7
Pickering, Andrew 2, 75 n.81
Pitts, Walter H. 19–21
Platner, Ernst 33, 35 n.57, 36
Plato 22
poetry 184–6, 194–5
   of nature 194
politics, posthuman 117–20

Pollock, Jackson 228–9
Popper, Karl 116
"post-" philosophies 269
posthuman materialism 57–61
posthumanism 1–13, 23–5, 28, 38,
    46, 52, 54–7, 76–7, 79–82, 96,
    105–6, 122–5, 127–31, 144,
    165–6, 183–4, 190, 200, 206,
    233, 243–4, 266–7, 269–70,
    274–5, 281, 285
  definition of 105–6
  first use of the term 105
  origins of 203, 209–16
  two senses of 148–9
posthumanist aesthetics 136–41
potencies, doctrine of 293–4
Poulton, Mary M. 20 n.8
Pratt, Mary Louise 194 n.30
pre-humanism 245–6, 249, 265,
    267
Pross, Wolfgang 41 n.17
Protevi, John 120
Provine, Wlliam B. 62 n.26
"psychic locality" problem 34 n.53
puppets' movements 206–7
Putnam, Hillary 224 n.5

racism 46
Rang, Bernhard 290 n.10
reason, human 72, 114–16, 152,
    183–4
recursion 21 n.10, 27–29, 35
reductionism 57 n.9, 69, 71
Reinhold, Karl Leonhard 206
representationalism 110
Richards, Robert J. 53 n.1, 68 n.52
Richter, Simon 256 n.55
Ritter, Johann Wilhelm 290, 298–9
robotics 9–10
Roden, David 80, 244 n.6, 266
    n.104
Roe, Shirley A. 26 n.23
Rojas, Paul 20 n.8
Rollin, Bernard 38 n.7

Romanes, George John 62
Romanticism 5, 38 n.7, 118, 184,
    189, 205–6, 253
Rorty, Richard 108, 119 n.49
Rosenbluth, Arturo 224 n.5
Rosenzweig, Franz 187 n.10
Rousseau, Jean Jacques 211
Roux, Wilhelm 62–6, 69
Ruse, Michael 38 n.7
Rüve, Gerlind 282

Sachs, Aaron 194 n.30
Sarkar, Sahotra 57 n.9
Schaeffer, Jean-Marie 127–8
Schelling, Friedrich Wilhelm 11,
    39, 170, 173, 179–80, 288–96,
    299–302, 306
Schiller, Friedrich 190, 205–8, 220,
    273
Schlegel, Friedrich 179, 184–6, 189,
    205
Schleiden, Jacob 5, 54, 65, 69
Schleiermacher, Friedrich 26,
    221 n.45
Schmidt, Jochen 264 n.102
Schöne, Albrecht 250 n.26,
    264 n.102
Schwann, Theodor 5–6, 54, 65–8,
    82
Scott, Ridley 226
Seel, Martin 189–90, 194, 197
self-consciousness 5, 23, 223–5,
    230, 232–3, 238, 240
Sembdner, Helmut 203 n.2
Semper, Karl 68–9
Sewell, William H. Jr 75 n.81
Shannon, Claude 151
Sharon, Tamar 2, 79–80
Shaviro, Steven 112 n.22, 118–23,
    136–41
Siegert, Bernhard 168 n.7
Simondon, Gilbert 56, 61 n.22, 152
    n.17
sleep, poetic meditation on 282

Smith, John H. 169 n.8
SNARC calculator 19–24, 28, 30
Soemmerring, Samuel Thomas 18, 34, 39–40, 44–7, 52
somnambulism 92
Sorgner, Stefan 80
species difference 40–52
speculative philosophy 31, 123, 129–30, 138
speculative posthumanism (SP) 80, 244, 266 n.104
speculative realism (SR) 7–8, 81, 86, 99, 107–13, 117, 123, 137–8, 144, 146 n.1, 149, 170 n.9
speculative reason 27–8, 156
Spinoza, B. 57, 177, 270, 304
Stahl, Georg Ernst 33
Star Trek (TV series) 226–7
Starobinski, Jean 274
Steel, Karl 1 n.1
Steinke, Hubert 32 n.47
Steppes, the 195–9
Strathausen, Carsten 115 n.31
subjectivity 1–3, 5, 79, 94 n.58 105, 119–21, 123–5, 169, 181, 184 n.3, 186, 200, 225, 227, 230–3, 236, 238–41, 248 n.14, 266 n.104, 274 n.17, 299 n.28, 300
Sullivan, Heather I. 99 n.74
systems theory 22, 30, 93 n.55, 106, 125, 244

Taylor, Charles 224 n.6
teleology 71–6, 84, 138
Temkin, Owsei 47 n.46
Thacker, Eugene 137 n.28
Thompson, Evan 86, 93 n.55
Tieck, Ludwig 214, 218
Toscano, Alberto 290 n.9
transcendental idealism 10, 28, 31, 155
"transcendental illusion" (Schein) 162

transcendental philosophy 107–8, 112–16, 130
transhumanism 81 n.8, 244, 267
Treviranus, Gottfried 54, 67–8
Treviranus, Reinhold 5
Trump, Donald 118
Turing, Alan 223. *See also* Church–Turin thesis
Turing test 223–7, 232, 238, 240
Tyson, Edward 43

Uexküll, Jacob von 7, 51, 83, 95–9, 144
ugliness 135

van Wyhe, John 50 n.54
Varela, Francisco 86, 93 n.55, 109, 115 n.31
vertigo 18–19, 22, 25, 31–6
Vienna Circle 57 n.9
Virchow, Rudolf 6, 65, 82
virtual reality 247, 253, 271
visual perception 88–93
Vogel, Carl 283 n.43
Vogl, Joseph 298 n.26
Vollmer, Gerhard 116
Voltaire 204

Wade, Nicholas 95 n.60
Wagner, Richard 258
Watercutter, Angela 230 n.21
Weatherby, Leif 35 n.57, 40 n.15
Weismann, August 63–4
Weismann, Hans 63 n.31, 64 n.35
Weitin, Thomas 261 n.83, 264 n.101
Wellbery, David 11, 248 n.14
Wenzel, Christian Helmut 130–1, 142 n.46
West-Eberhard, Mary Jane 69 n.57
Wetters, Kirk 302 n.41
Whistler, Daniel 295 n.23
Whitehead, Alfred North 56, 110–14, 120–3, 137–40

Wieland, Christoph 273
Wiener, Norbert 224 n.5
Wilson, Edward O. 111
Wimsatt, William C. 75 n.80
Wittgenstein, Ludwig 114, 235
Wolfe, Cary 2, 38, 39 n.12, 58, 60–1, 80–1, 100, 105–6, 119 n.49, 124, 148–9, 166 n.1, 183, 190
Wolfendale, Peter 109 n.13
Wolff, Christian 112, 150, 152, 204
Woolf, Virginia 274 n.17

Wubnic, Judy 115
Wundt, Wilhelm 6, 30 n.39, 82

Young, Robert M. 49 n.52

Zammito, John H. 53 n.1, 68 n.55, 116 n.37
Zimmermann, Rolf Christian 248 n.14

I Don't Wanna Be Pink

Dena Taylor

How a single, 39-year-old refused to let breast cancer and its fervent culture define her

outskirts press

I Don't Wanna Be Pink
How a single, 39-year-old woman refused to let breast cancer and its fervent culture define her
All Rights Reserved.
Copyright © 2019 Dena Taylor
v4.0

The opinions expressed in this manuscript are solely the opinions of the author and do not represent the opinions or thoughts of the publisher. The author has represented and warranted full ownership and/or legal right to publish all the materials in this book.

This book may not be reproduced, transmitted, or stored in whole or in part by any means, including graphic, electronic, or mechanical without the express written consent of the publisher except in the case of brief quotations embodied in critical articles and reviews.

Outskirts Press, Inc.
http://www.outskirtspress.com

ISBN: 978-1-9772-1164-4

Cover Art © 2019 Chad Otis. All rights reserved - used with permission.

Outskirts Press and the "OP" logo are trademarks belonging to Outskirts Press, Inc.

PRINTED IN THE UNITED STATES OF AMERICA

For Beth
We walked and talked for miles, and for a time,
up a long, steep hill in uncomfortable shoes

*It's all right
'Cause there's beauty in the breakdown*
— Frou Frou
"Let Go"

*All shall be well, and all shall be well and all manner of
thing shall be well*
— Julian of Norwich

AUTHOR'S NOTE

TO WRITE THIS book, I consulted my personal journals, appointment and procedure notes, and memory. I also tapped the memories of those who helped me along the way and did my best to check facts. A few names have been changed and identifying details altered to preserve anonymity. The medical tests, procedures, and treatment I underwent for breast cancer are personal, relevant to the time period in which the story takes place, and should not be considered medical advice. The choices I made were based on my individual diagnosis and risk tolerance, and do not apply to anyone else. There have been many advancements in breast cancer research and medical care. Consult a medical professional for the latest information.

Chapter 1

Today's the big day.
—Journal Entry

I WOKE UP in a surprisingly good mood. Tad anxious. Actually, I was manic. I thought about the impact a positive mental attitude can have and wondered if I could actually direct the day's events by being bright and cheerful. With time to kill before my dear friend Steve picked me up for my appointment, I decided it was worth a try. While I normally detest the perky morning set, I found myself bustling to the neighborhood coffee shop to join them—chirping my order to the barista, grinning too hard at a couple of cute guys, and flitting about the outdoor patio before taking a seat. I whipped out my laptop and emailed my sister, Tay, and best friend, Marit, and used lots of exclamation points and smiley emoticons. Back home again, while waiting for Steve, I told the cat how sweet she was, even when she barfed on my couch, and thanked the plants for living with me all these years. It was Wednesday, September 13, 2006.

I looked around my apartment and thought how different everything would or wouldn't be in a few hours' time; how most of what we do every day is done with this blind assumption that things will go pretty much how we expect them to. Unless you're a journalist or injury lawyer, no news really is good news.

I spent the last few minutes before Steve arrived sipping a bottle of Dos Equis beer and hanging a new hummingbird feeder on the deck. I don't typically drink beer in the morning, and I know little about birds. In a fit of hope, I told myself that if a hummingbird visited the feeder before Steve knocked on my door, my test results would be negative. But no hummingbird came, and the question lingered: did I or didn't I have cancer?

Of course I didn't. How could I? I was too active, healthy, and young. In fact, in thirty-five days I would be in Italy, celebrating my fortieth birthday with my best friend, a bottle of Chianti, and, if the stars aligned, some handsome, single, and psychologically stable Italian men. It was a big deal, this trip. It symbolized the end of a shaky decade. While I was behind much of the shaking—the crack at acting, the dim romantic choices, the two-thousand-mile move from Seattle to Austin without a job—not

CHAPTER 1

everything had been in my control. There were some surprises too, pink ones, by way of my mom's early-stage breast cancer and a suspicious growth in my own breast. But Mom prevailed, and my lesion was benign, and life went on. On the precipice of forty, I had begun to enjoy the fruits of risk and change. I was courting my new town, making friends, loosely dating (and dating loosely), performing in local theater, and earning just enough as a freelance copywriter to cobble together a birthday overseas. I was on a roll and was going to ride that roll all the way to Italy, dunk it in olive oil, and spend a week savoring every bite.

Or was I?

A routine mammogram had revealed a small mass in my right breast, which had led to a biopsy, and, according to my breast surgeon, Dr. Perry, a fifty percent chance that the results would be benign. So, I might have cancer. But I might not. I might go to Italy, I might not. I might live long enough to marry before my parents died, I might not.

Considering the odds in this way was useless and exhausting and made my head hurt. There are always exceptions, benign anomalies do happen, and that's what I decided to focus on until somebody told me different.

Except there had been some needling signs of malignancy along the way, too, thin but peculiar instances that I had noticed but brushed off, one by one.

The first came earlier in the summer by way of Marit's trepidation about our trip to Italy. "I just feel a little apprehensive," she said, over the phone one day. "I'm not sure if it's because of 9/11 or what, but in all the times I've traveled to Europe, I've never felt this way. It's like it's not the right time to go or something." After wondering aloud if we should go somewhere else, she acquiesced to Italy, and I didn't give it a second thought.

The second sign came in early September, during my mammogram, which, with all the adjusting and squishing, and stopping-dead for pictures, reminded me of a game of freeze tag, where your breast is always "it." After studying the last image of my right breast on the monitor, the technician turned abruptly and looked at me. Our eyes met, and I saw the slightest shift in her gaze, an almost undetectable beat in an otherwise unremarkable moment in time. She quickly looked back to the monitor and said she wanted to get just one more shot. I figured she was just being thorough and stepped up to the plates.

The last sign emerged during my consultation with Dr. Perry, when she described a mass she saw in my films as "dark with fuzzy edges." It wasn't just the ominous conglomeration of words, which sounded like something out of a Harry Potter novel; it was how they were delivered. It was as if she had read them and said them before: words belonging to the vernacular of surgeons with hundreds of

CHAPTER 1

biopsies and substantiated suspicions under their belts, words with weight. It was as if she knew exactly what was happening in my breast but protocol prevented her from saying it out loud.

On their own, each of these signs was a dusky, inconsequential lightbulb, but when strung together they cast a murky shadow. It seemed like Marit, the technician, and Dr. Perry all knew what was wrong. While riding in Steve's car on the way to Dr. Perry's office, I wondered if maybe I didn't know too, and my positive exterior started to crack.

Why is Steve taking you to the doctor? I thought. If you truly believe you're going to be okay, why didn't you drive yourself?

A pit formed in my stomach and began to dance, its steps quickening with every mile. Why all the Google searches and appointment recaps to family and friends? Why the forced bright side?

The pit went from a slow shimmy to a triple-time polka, and by the time we turned into the parking garage, to something out of Stomp the Yard. If everything is really going to be okay, why did you cry in the car after the mammogram? Why did you stop planning your trip to Italy—because you did simply just stop.

People say actions speak louder than words. I was minutes from finding out whether this was true.

It's a blur, but I'm certain Steve hugged me before I left him in the waiting room. It's something he would do. I wasn't alone per se, but it was still only me walking into that exam room, baring my flesh, perching my ass on the edge of the exam table, waiting. The dancing pit kicked its way into my throat and turned to stone, and I held it there, hard and tight.

I couldn't imagine having cancer, couldn't imagine adding that word to my daily vocabulary—Hi, I'm Dena Cancer, er, Taylor; Hello, I'll have a grande nonfat cancer, I mean, latte. It was a mouthful of marbles and peanut butter and shock. I couldn't imagine going so severely off course. And if I couldn't imagine it, it couldn't be real.

What I could imagine was Dr. Perry (whom I've nicknamed here for her uncanny resemblance to Journey's original lead singer, Steve Perry) entering the room with a smile and delivering good, noncancerous-fifty-percent news. Really?! I would reply. She would nod and I would hug her in gratitude. The stone in my throat would dissolve. Steve and I would bound to the Mexican restaurant across the street for margaritas. I don't even like margaritas but I'd drink one because that's what people in Austin do, and I'd be grateful to be there and not in an exam room, crying. I'd call my family and friends on the way home, and once there, I'd resume making plans for Italy, where I would turn forty and have nothing more to contend with than an inflated Visa bill and a hangover.

CHAPTER 1

There was a quick knock on the door and turning of the handle. Dr. Perry entered the room with my chart, which seemed heavy in her hands. She offered a feeble hello and wan smile. I countered with a bright if wobbly hello, dragging out the "o" and punctuating it with a question mark. Her manner was different than in our previous two appointments, quieter and more doctorly. She placed my chart on the counter, turned her back to me, and opened it. After looking at the contents one last time, either to remind herself of the pathologist's findings or to choose her words, she turned back around.

"You have invasive breast cancer," she said.

"Oh God."

"Given your family history, the benign abnormality you had in 2003, and the fact that you're only thirty-nine and we'd like you to see fifty," she continued, "I recommend a bilateral mastectomy."

She had me at "cancer." It roared through my head, forcing the rest of her words—the ones about living to see fifty and cutting off my breasts—to scatter and embed like shrapnel—malignant shrapnel, small and sharp. My stomach, the hinges of my jaw, and the backs of my eyes began to quiver with shock. The stone in my throat throbbed, making it nearly impossible to swallow. I wasn't in the noncancerous fifty percent. Everything wasn't okay.

She said something about a lumpectomy and radiation but said she thought the more aggressive bilateral mastectomy was more appropriate; if you removed all the breast tissue there wouldn't be anything for the cancer to come back to. There would be no room at the inn because there would be no inn.

"While you're under, we'll test a lymph node to make sure the cancer hasn't spread."

More roaring. More shrapnel. The stone dislodged, and lava-like tears welled in my eyes—hot, thick, and slow. Gravity pulled them down, along with the sinking feeling that comes when you realize that something really bad might actually get worse. I had cancer and it might have spread. I might die before my parents did. I might die having never been married. I might die.

I thought about the coffee shop I had visited that morning. How ridiculously I had behaved—chatting it up with the barista, smiling at handsome men, awkwardly inserting myself into the normalcy of a morning routine. I had strained to stay positive to prevent a self-fulfilling prophecy. Now that the truth was out, I could stop wasting the energy. My diagnosis was irrefutable. I was free to be consumed by shock.

"If the cancer has spread, we'll go back in later and remove any affected nodes. And I know chemotherapy will be recommended."

Dr. Perry was going too fast; she was so far ahead of me, seeding a vision of my future self—bald, pale, and nauseated, a plastic tube stuck in my vein, an

CHAPTER 1

ugly pink ribbon stuck in my lapel. I lagged behind, grappling with cancer. Fighting it, treating it, whatever they called it, whatever she was talking about, was beyond my comprehension. My hands were full with disbelief.

I had every right to tell her to stop, to give me a minute to wrap my head around the disease in my breast, to collapse in a heap of disposable exam cape, crinkly table tissue, and grief, but I found myself trying to keep up instead—or at least look like it. The person I had presented to her thus far was proactive and strong. During my consultation the week before, I had even made her laugh. A breakdown was imminent but it wouldn't happen in front of her. She could see my now-steady stream of tears and red, drippy nose, but there was no way she was going to see me lose my shit. I'd wait until she was gone.

Dr. Perry paused, but she wasn't done. She stepped toward me, began tapping my knees with her knuckles, and explained how chemo could affect fertility and how that was something I might want to think about if I wanted to have children.

Baby shrapnel—but it didn't hurt that much. I wasn't bent on having kids.

"Doesn't matter," I said. "I can barely find a man I want to have dinner with let alone get naked with. At the rate I'm going, I'll be pushing a walker down the sidewalk before a stroller."

There's always a joke. It may not be funny, but it's always there, ready to distract. It disrupted the tears, gave me a chance to gain some emotional ground, bought me time.

Dr. Perry half-laughed and reminded me that neither a partner nor sex was required to have a baby. She had plenty of friends who had kids on their own. I have those friends, too, I thought, but I don't want to have a kid by myself. And I don't want to have to decide right now. And I really don't want to have fucking cancer.

She went on to recommend reconstruction, the first phase of which could occur immediately following the mastectomy. I could wake up with (budding) (fake) breasts. It's how it's done these days.

"I can't believe I'm going to lose my breasts."

I had never been a big fan of my breasts. They were too small, too far apart, too pointy. They veered to the sides like a pair of shoes on the wrong feet. My relationship with them was one of tough love and digs. They looked like candy corn without the dye, profiles of Bob Hope's nose, piping bags of frosting, elf hats without the curling tip. A way bustier Marit and I often laughed about how when she spilled food it landed on her shirt. When I spilled food it landed in my lap. My breasts were out of proportion with my five-foot-seven-inch frame, wide-spanning hands, broad shoulders, and size ten feet. It was like they were meant for someone else—but

CHAPTER 1

they weren't, they were mine, and now, more than ever, I wanted to keep them around.

"And the nipples and areolas will be taken too," she added, "because they're made of tissue and that tissue puts you at risk. But your plastic surgeon can create new ones."

Out of what, I thought. Papier-mâché?

As Dr. Perry checked the incision site on my right breast—the breast where a cancerous tumor was growing, the one she had assaulted through a biopsy just two days before—she suggested I also get genetic testing to find out if I had mutations to the BRCA1 or BRCA2 breast cancer genes. If I did, I might be at increased risk for ovarian cancer.

Ovary shrapnel. Sweet Jesus, when does it end?

In the case of a mutation, removal of my fallopian tubes and ovaries might be recommended via a salpingo-oophorectomy, which sounded like something a Roman Catholic priest would chant while giving last rites. The test would cost thousands. Insurance might or might not cover it. The thought of talking this over with my crotchety, anal-retentive insurance company made me almost as sick to my stomach as my diagnosis did.

Dr. Perry asked if I had any questions. I had one. I wanted to know if everything she had just said was real.

"What was it again you said I have?" I asked incredulously. "Because I had this dream where you told me I didn't have cancer. You were wearing lip gloss and green eye shadow, and you said I didn't have cancer."

Sometime after first meeting Dr. Perry, I had fantasized about fixing her up with Marit's newly single sister, as if finding true love for my doctor might influence my test result. The color of her Crocs shoes—green for her alma mater—and my juvenile association between lip gloss and dressing up for a first date had also worked their way into my dream and, in this surreal moment, out of my mouth. It was a small interruption and final attempt to both grasp the truth and postpone being left alone with my broken breast and new reality. I left out the part about fixing her up with Marit's sister. I didn't want to push my luck.

She graciously chuckled and said she didn't think she had ever worn green eye shadow. Then she softly confirmed that it was cancer that I had. I had no reason not to believe her. Having grown up with a physician father, I had a general reverence for the profession. They knew things I didn't.

She encouraged me to take some time to absorb the news, write down my questions, and call her to talk. I thanked her. She had delivered the worst news of my thirty-nine years, and I actually said "thank you." It was automatic and respectful. She had done her job, blown the whistle on some ill-intentioned cells, and, somewhere in the mess of my emotions, I

CHAPTER 1

was glad, because the what-if-ing was over. Plus, as shallow as it sounds, I liked to be liked, especially when it came to someone responsible for removing a deadly tumor from my body. So I thanked her. If Dr. Perry liked me, maybe she'd pay extra special attention in getting every last one of those warped cells out. I wanted her to like me. I wanted her to save me.

"You're welcome," she said, and left.

Alone in the exam room, I stopped controlling and let the shock and fear take over. I cried with inflated gasps for air, like when you have your heart broken for the first time and think you'll be alone for the rest of your life. If only I had been upset about that. If only my ego had been shattered. A bag of chips, a few glasses of wine, a month, and I'd be fine.

I remembered that Steve was in the waiting room. Then I thought about all the people I had to call, all the appointments I would have to make, the genetic test I had to get, that cancer kills people.

The nurse came in quietly with the BRCA gene testing kit and a purple canvas bag from the local Breast Cancer Resource Center, filled with information for the newly diagnosed. Of course the center's logo was pink. That fucking pink ribbon had been nipping at my heels for years. I've never hated a color more.

I gathered my things and made my way to the lobby. On the way I could hear Dr. Perry in another exam room. She had delivered news that changed the course of my life and was on to her next patient. She did this for a living.

Steve took one look at me and knew.

"I have fucking cancer!" I screamed in the hallway. "Can you believe it?!" He trailed behind, absorbing the blow.

❖

Back home, I cycled through my copy of the pathology report and the treatment recommendations, tears alternating with calls to my mom; my dad and stepmother in Oregon; my big brother, Paul, in Alaska; and my sister, Tay, and Marit, both in Seattle. I squeezed trembling words through a throat constricted by disbelief and escalating fear. Everyone offered to fly down and help. I'd known they would, even thought they should—it didn't seem like a person who was just diagnosed with cancer should be alone. Part of me would have loved to have a spotter for my emotions, but another part of me needed room to process. I had never had cancer before; I didn't know what kind of help I needed. To say I was overwhelmed was like saying Keith Richards looks a little worse for wear. I had everyone hold off until I had a plan.

There was one exception to this holding pattern: Marit's and my trip to Italy. She had long suspected it wasn't a good time to go, and she had been right all along. We could have pushed back the dates, found a way to go later, but I couldn't see past the next twenty-four hours, let alone the next month. Cancelling our trip was an easy decision to make. She graciously offered to take care of it, and just like that, our vision of bliss was gone.

Just when I thought I could disappear into my couch, the phone rang. It was my sister calling back with an idea. Since it would take several weeks to get the BRCA gene test results, which would be needed to determine treatment, I might want to get the testing process started that afternoon.

"You might feel better knowing that you have that done," she said.

She spoke with the kind, wise voice she had used when helping me through the crises of my adolescence, like the time I started my period and needed her to explain how to use a tampon, or when I was fooled by a boy I liked and couldn't see why I'd be better off without his capricious affections. With four years on me, she had experienced pretty much everything first, and was more than happy to lend her advice. From my baby-of-the-family perspective, I sometimes found her bossy and know-it-all, but she was usually right. Her sincere loyalty to my welfare eased many of my growing pains.

But as we dug our heels into adulthood, parts of our lives diverged like chunks of ice drifting from a glacier, and I needed her advice a little less.

On the cusp of forty, I had done many things that she hadn't. I had some firsts now too, like traveling to England and running a half-marathon. But not having the exact same experience didn't mean she couldn't be supportive of my endeavors. She would do the same with my latest first—cancer—encouraging me to take action on the very day I was diagnosed.

I didn't want to be told what to do or to leave my apartment, not today. But something told me she was right, it might feel good taking a step. She had not had cancer, but she'd had plenty of scary experiences with serious food allergies and asthma. And she pushed herself when they threatened to block her from following her passions. She became an expert in her conditions and took charge of her life, graduating magna cum laude from Syracuse University, building a career in broadcasting in Chicago, and later in Seattle, where she moved with my brother-in-law, Rob. If I had some of her will in my blood, maybe I could push myself into going to the walk-in lab and getting the genetic testing process started. I could start doing something about my grave new problem—regain a tiny grip of control. I had all night to be devastated.

By this time, it was already 4:40 p.m. I called the lab to make sure they'd be open. I told the lady on the phone that I had just been diagnosed with cancer. She said it wouldn't be a problem.

CHAPTER 1

❖

Thirteen hazy minutes later, BRCA gene kit in hand, I was holding myself up in front of two women in blue scrubs behind a reception desk. The shorter, older woman greeted me with a calm and pleasant professionalism, and I recognized her as the woman I had spoken with on the phone. I told her I had just called and had come to get my blood drawn for the BRCA gene test.

The other, a large, surly woman, glanced at me and sighed then turned to her coworker. "Are we gonna do somethin' like this, this late in the day?"

"Listen, you mean, cold-hearted Amazon," I wanted to scream. "I was told you could fit me in. I have cancer, so fucking fit me in!"

Instead, I started to cry again, and like magic, the behemoth's gruff visage softened. She led me to a small room, put a needle in my arm, and pulled out my blood. She put it in the kit I'd brought and sent it off to the genetic testing facility. I was back home in minutes.

I called Tay to let her know that the test was on its way and, indirectly, that I had followed her advice. I used a flat, clipped tone, a passive-aggressive hint that I wanted to keep the call short; I wanted to sit in silence the rest of the night. She praised me for going to the lab and acknowledged how hard it must have been. I cut her off.

"I don't want to talk about it anymore,"
"I'm sorry. I love you."
"Love you too."

I hung up, did a few Google searches on breast cancer statistics, and took turns crying and staring into space.

Chapter 2

*I had a dream that I was on the table,
ready for surgery. I waited and waited.
Ready to roll. And no one came.*
—Journal Entry

THE NEXT MORNING, I opened my eyes, and for one fleeting moment nothing had changed. I was the same sleepy, non-morning Dena I had always been. I lay comfortably in my bed, under the security of my soft comforter, my head heavy on my pillow, a gorgeous smattering of sunlight shards streaming through the window onto my bedroom wall. Then that really awful thing that happened the day before came flooding back.

❖

There are two kinds of shock. The first is absolute, out-of-nowhere surprise, what you feel when you experience something that defies all logic, like discovering a lion cub in the dentist's parking lot or watching a steel tank crash into the kiddie pool. You couldn't have known there was a black-market exotic pet dealer in your community or that space junk had plummeted through Earth's atmosphere, but there it is. The second kind of shock is more of a wagered surprise. It's what you feel when something that usually happens to someone else finally happens to you, like getting struck by lightning or entering a local radio station contest and actually winning a trip to Mexico. My cancer diagnosis was like that, possible but unlikely.

Had I been sixty-nine instead of thirty-nine, it would have been more likely and less jarring. That was my mother's age when she was diagnosed with ductal carcinoma in situ (DCIS), a non-invasive breast cancer. She was in her golden years and had already had one hip replaced. It was just a matter of time before another condition, illness, or injury arose. On some level we could expect it; we just didn't know what it would be or when.

Not that her diagnosis wasn't upsetting, because it was. Maybe it was considered stage zero, "the good kind," she said, but to me cancer was cancer. Pink-ribbon cancer, I thought. People die from that. I had participated in my fair share of pink-coated fundraising 5Ks. I had seen the pink race bibs on which you could write "In celebration of" and name someone who had survived breast cancer or, worse, "In memory of" and name someone who hadn't. Pink was supposed to symbolize solidarity and hope, but as far as I was concerned, pink symbolized a threat: a ticking clock, a pounded nail.

Retired from the state of Oregon's child protective services division, Mom was living a full life in my hometown of Salem, Oregon. It had been nearly twenty years since she and my dad had divorced. She had recovered and evolved into a vivacious sixty-nine-going-on-fifty-nine-year-old social butterfly, avid hiker, traveler, and church choir soprano. I wasn't ready to reduce her to an "In memory of" name on a race bib.

Luckily, I didn't have to. She got a lumpectomy and radiation, and had an excellent prognosis. Even so, the pink wrench of mortality had been thrown into our family den. Her diagnosis meant Tay and I were at increased risk. It was recommended that we start getting annual mammograms at thirty-five, which we did. I didn't think either one of us would develop cancer; it was just the smart thing to do.

Yet there I was, just shy of forty, a tumor in my bed with me. And what, I thought, am I supposed to do about that, anyway? I had to do something, because continuing to sleep with it, eat with it, and run the trail with it felt lazy and reckless. If left alone, it would kill me. This wasn't unfounded hysteria but a fact I could cite and feel with increasing dread. I had to figure out what the next smart thing to do was. I had to get it out.

While Dr. Perry strongly recommended getting both breasts removed, she encouraged me to understand all of my options before making any decisions.

❖

Options are great unless you're indecisive like me. It's why I can't stand grocery shopping. Fresh or frozen, local or imported, conventional or organic, bulk or packaged, salty or low-sodium, sweetened or sugar-free, nondairy or full fat, scented or unscented, paper bag or be an asshole and take plastic? Toothpaste alone—whether cavity-protection, sensitivity formula, peroxide-whitening, or tartar control—is enough to give me a headache, in which case I can choose from aspirin, ibuprofen, acetaminophen, or naproxen in regular strength, extra strength, caplets, tablets, smooth gels, or liquid gels in either eight-hour or nighttime formulas. Jesus—if I thought shopping was hard, deciding on cancer treatment was going to make my head explode.

I could have the bilateral mastectomy, a unilateral mastectomy, or a lumpectomy and radiation. I could have breast reconstruction using saline implants, silicone implants, or tissue from my own abdomen, back, buttocks, or thighs. I could have nipples made out of my own skin or out of tissue and fat, or I could be injected with a poly-l-lactic acid dermal filler (poly-what?). And I could top everything off with some professionally inked areolas.

Or not.

I could choose not to have reconstruction at all and simply wear any multitude of prostheses from climate-control silicone forms to free-style athletic cups. Or, I could just be me—melon free.

Whatever I decided had to be the most-right decision for me. That meant taking the time to meet with specialists about my options, but I didn't know how much time I had or who I was supposed to consult. By nine that morning, I had calls into my general practitioner (GP) and Dr. Perry. Dr. Perry called back first.

"How long until I should have surgery?" I asked.

"About a month," she said. "It's very unlikely this type of tumor will progress in a matter of weeks. But we don't like to wait much longer than that."

Her voice sounded the same, but the tone of our exchange was different, mostly because it was in fact an exchange versus the one-way pummeling of bad news. I was asking questions and assembling answers, deflecting fear with an attempt to take control. It took the thud out of the previous day's diagnosis; the diagnosis was no longer the last word.

I hung up with referrals and a time frame in hand. If the tumor had been growing for a few years, what was another month? It gave me time to do my homework. Then again, letting it continue to fester was a nauseating idea and dangerous. By 9:20, I had an appointment with a radiation oncologist for the next day and another with a plastic surgeon for the following week. If I had my way, I'd be under the knife within fifteen days, and the malignancy would be gone.

Most of the morning, all of the afternoon, and the entire evening loomed before me like a cavernous tunnel with C-A-N-C-E-R L-A-N-D spelled out, one insidious letter at a time, over a gaping entrance. Passing through that entrance was the only way forward. Distracting myself with freelance work would be futile; the temptation to go online and torture myself with cancer statistics would be too great. Instead, I drove myself to the Breast Cancer Resource Center (BCRC), the place whose name was printed on the canvas bag that Dr. Perry's nurse had given me. I didn't know what I would do there, but I had to get out of my apartment and out of my head. I had to do something, anything, other than pretend I wasn't on the road I was on.

I didn't know it then but I needed to see the human side of cancer: not the doctor in a sterile setting or static words and numbers on a screen, but the I-was-shocked-too side. I needed to see what happens in between diagnoses and appointments and surgeries, to understand how mere mortals continue to function inside those scary, overwhelming moments when there is nothing to do but speculate and wait.

In the BCRC lobby, I was greeted by an elderly

CHAPTER 2

volunteer who, upon hearing I had just been diagnosed, informed me that she was a two-time survivor. I was both inspired—look at her, she survived, she's smiling!—and irritated: I just found out I have cancer, I'm centuries younger than you, how can you be smiling at a time like this? She ushered me into a library where I would wait for Sharon, the client services director, to come and tell me about the center's services.

One look at the bookshelves of cancer books, the circle of worn, empty chairs from the previous night's support group, and a single Kleenex box—stoic and ready—and I started to cry. It was the first of many sudden-tears moments to come. I was in the exact right place for it: no exam rooms or charts, just a low-lit homey space—and here was a tall forty-something woman dressed in kindness.

Within minutes of introducing herself, Sharon was sharing her own breast cancer story, and several soggy tissues later, I had shared mine. She explained some of the breast cancer lingo and acronyms I had stumbled over in my nascent attempts to understand the disease, like dorsi flap and HER2/NEU. She acknowledged the sadness, irritability, and sleeplessness that come with joining the cancer club, and she offered, if it would be helpful, to show me her reconstructed breast.

❖

I DON'T WANNA BE PINK

The last time I'd seen a woman's bare breast had been several years before in the bathroom stall of a Seattle pub. I was having drinks with my friend Sabine, filling her in on the antics that had taken place at our mutual friend Alice's recent bridal shower outside of Austin. Both Sabine and Alice were part of a special group of friends I'd made while working in the creative group at Starbucks Coffee Company. Alice had told me about her bridal shower earlier in the week: an all-girl weekend soiree. One of her friends had performed a mini (if rustic) burlesque show by taking off her bra, attaching matches to her nipples and lighting them on fire. She then shook her breasts to and fro to the delight of the tipsy bride-to-be.

Sabine and I were fascinated and confused.

"But how did she get the matches to stick?" Sabine wondered.

"I guess she licked them," I replied. Sabine spit up her drink.

"Did she bend them away from her skin before lighting them?"

"Maybe."

"How long until she had to blow them out?"

"Couldn't have been long."

"She could have burned her boob."

This line of questioning was typical of Sabine. It wasn't enough to know something worked—she liked to know how and why. This along with her robust imagination and razor-sharp wit ensured conversations that were never boring and rarely short. I always ended up with a laughter-stretched face and sore sides.

After a few cocktails we decided to find out for ourselves just how long one could go before blowing out a lit match stuck on one's nipples. We grabbed some matches from the bar and made our way to the women's restroom. Giggling like schoolgirls, we disrobed in the handicap stall, exposing two sets of breasts rife with disparity; if mine were like cupcakes Sabine's were like seven-layer tortes. We licked some match stems and tried attaching them to our nipples, and after several failed attempts, finally got some to stick. Then, very carefully, we lit the matches on fire. In what looked more like spasms than burlesque, we spent the next few seconds shaking our lit breasts to and fro before panic had us blowing them out. All the while, we tried to conceal our laughter from customers going in and out of the neighboring stalls. I'm pretty sure we botched that too.

❖

There was nothing funny about Sharon's reconstructed breast but there was nothing that unusual about it either. I had been afraid of what reconstruction would look like, imagining a misshapen, dented blob riddled with thick scars in various shades of flesh, like a wad of bread dough that had been kneaded by an osprey before being shoved into an oven. Sharon's breast hadn't endured wild talons; it had been carefully tended to by a skilled surgeon. As we stood in the library bathroom, her top and bra hanging on the doorknob, I examined it the way you might a restored porcelain vase, looking for patched cracks and replacement parts. But what I saw was a woman's breast. I could see scars but they had faded into the surrounding skin, proof of cancer come and gone. The breast itself hung as naturally as its sister, the latter slightly lower and larger, bearing the effects of weight and time. If both of my breasts ended up looking similar to Sharon's, reconstruction wouldn't be as devastating as I had thought.

I left the BCRC glad I had gone there. Another first step was behind me. There was solace in knowing what support was available but mostly in having a moment alone with someone who had trudged through Cancer Land—a moment to safely cry in front of someone who had walked through the tunnel and come out the other side.

❖

The next morning, two days after diagnosis day, I got a call from my GP's office. My GP wore flippy girly sandals and colorful crop pants to every exam. You'd think she was going to a garden party, not spelunking through my vagina to scrape what felt like a stubborn layer of wallpaper off my cervix. It was always spring when she was around, yet I always felt like a gray lump of clay, sitting heavy and shapeless on the tissue-covered table, telling her the same story I always seemed to tell her: no one had been downstairs in months.

It was my GP's nurse on the line, calling with a recommendation for a plastic surgeon. Then, like a bad joke, she told me my recent Pap smear results had come back abnormal. "There were some squamous cells present and we just want to check it again."

"You've got to be kidding me."

She said it wasn't urgent, but I scheduled an appointment for the following week, my brain connecting the dots with a big fat line from my breast to my cervix. The fear in my voice must have made an impression because she called back five minutes later to apologize for causing any anxiety. She'd spoken with my doctor, and she assured me that the squamous cells weren't related to the breast cancer. They weren't related to an STD either, in case I was wondering. I wasn't, but it was nice to know I didn't have to add Incurable Disease from Rare Wanton Sex to the list of things that gave me character.

Results from the second Pap smear would come back normal and I exhaled with relief.

❖

Less than an hour after hanging up with the nurse, I, my malignant tumor, and my STD-free squamous cells were sitting at a large conference table in the community room of a central Austin grocery store, surrounded by women in various stages of breast cancer treatment. Some were bald and wearing a wig, a scarf, or a hat. Some had new hair halos, while others flaunted sassy, short, post-treatment dos. There was a woman who was pregnant and going through chemo, and two sisters who had been diagnosed within the same year.

All were under forty-five and very much alive. They were members of a young breast cancer survivors support group, and this was their monthly luncheon. Sharon had mentioned the group to me the day before, and, still unwilling to spend an entire day at home alone with cancer, I thought it would be good to meet more members of the club. But once I got there it was like tenth-grade geometry all over again: everyone talking about solutions to the problem on the board while I, feeling like the idiot who wasn't getting it, prayed I wouldn't be called upon.

"When did you find out you had cancer?" the bald lady sitting next to me asked, between bites of her Asian chicken salad.

"Two days ago," I squeaked.

"Oh, wow! You just found out!"

I wanted to throw up. I knew I should bond with these women, but I didn't want to identify with

CHAPTER 2

them because I didn't want to have cancer like them. The way they were talking so openly about it—like you would a migraine or bladder infection—clashed with my current state of shock. I could barely utter the words "I have cancer" when I was alone with Sharon, let alone chat about its characteristics or plans for treatment in front of a group. I was still reeling, still raw.

I didn't want to talk about cancer because I didn't know how to talk about it. If anyone could appreciate my state of mind, it was these women, but they were miles ahead of me. They were fluent in the language, they knew how to be strong while being vulnerable. If there was a Toastmasters for cancer they had graduated cum laude. I hoped to catch up to them, but in that moment, in that room, stuck to that chair, it was all I could do to blink.

"I don't know if you were sitting across from me," one of the women would write in an email later. "But if that was you, you did have a deer-in-the-headlights look."

Underscoring it all was the fact that I was the only single person there. The others didn't know, and they wouldn't have cared. But I did. It was one more thing between us, one more way in which I felt clunky and inexperienced and completely out of place.

❖

Had you told me that getting cancer would be easier than finding a compatible mate, I wouldn't have believed you. What I'd believed was that by the age of thirty-nine, I would have a husband and maybe a couple of kids. But my romantic life had largely consisted of crushes and flings, which I went along with until my early thirties. Then I looked around and realized just how in the minority I had become. My siblings, and pretty much everyone I knew from high school and college, had paired off, started families, or both. In the Brazilian steakhouse of life, they had moved on to the carved meat, while I continued to circle the salad bar. Was there something wrong with me? Was I defective? Take the *I* out of *married*, and you had *marred*, which seemed about right.

I wondered whether love was evading me, or me it, and whether those were my only options, which prompted the bigger question about how I was supposed to be spending my time. With or without a life partner by my side, there were a million things I wanted to experience. Dying or, worse, living without seeing places like Italy, Australia, and Yellowstone, or trying my hand at comedy and writing, seemed tragic. I had never worried about cancer. I'd worried about dying without having fully lived.

When I was in my early thirties and going through what I call a third-life crisis, I turned to a therapist. Had it not been for the recommendations of trusted friends, I never would have made the call to Dr. Paulsen, a lanky Ellen Barkin look-alike who I nicknamed TheraPaul. What I knew of therapy was touchy-feely, icky, and, as Tay would say, oogy. Sharing feelings and talking about super personal stuff without sarcasm or a punch line was like skinny-dipping in a stagnant mountain pond or sitting next to the creepiest looking guy on the bus—physically unsettling with a high potential for rash. It just wasn't my family's style. We expressed feelings but not in any great depth. Feelings slid across the surface, like a disk across a shuffleboard table, thrust at varying speeds in accordance with their nature. Problems were swiftly fixed, changed, or sucked up, or, in my case, privately poured into a journal. To drag out a feeling hinted at weakness. The smarter, productive thing to do was to be strong and move on.

Too fast and with fidgety hands and a shifty seat, I told TheraPaul about my family's communication style and explained how after my parents' divorce, as I'd entered adolescence, my already sarcastic manner had thickened, maybe because of the divorce but maybe not. My high school grades had been average, but I had a smart mouth. I used it to make people laugh, and, when it worked, to make friends. I could be sweet and funny with my girlfriends. But when it came to the opposite sex, I felt snarky and insecure. I didn't know how to act around boys and wasn't sure I could trust them, so I kept my sarcastic shield handy. My closest friends were female. Many of them ended up with boyfriends. The boyfriend phenomenon, save for a two-week fling the summer before my sophomore year, was something that happened to other girls.

"I'm certain my sarcasm scared them off," I told TheraPaul. "Though not all of them."

There was one guy who liked my snark or more likely didn't care. He was an older kid who had graduated from another school a few years before. I met him my senior year at a party hosted by a friend whose parents were out of town. He worked for a sporting goods store and was sexy, bad-boy hot, a hard-to-get partier popular with the ladies. He was the least trustworthy guy I could find and thus I bestowed my virginity on him at seventeen in a haze of Miller beer and Camel cigarettes. I didn't know what an orgasm was at the time, and when I went home that night I still didn't. It's a fact, not a dig: a sad, first-intimacy experience and not without shame.

This drinking-too-much-and-having-sex-too-soon-with-an-unavailable-guy thing repeated itself off and on throughout my twenties. Not that I didn't encounter genuinely interested, quality guys, because I did, but those scenarios never seemed to work out. The guys I was most attracted to inevitably were the ones who didn't want a relationship, didn't live in the same town, or were about to move. Some simply weren't interested, which was always the hardest to take because it meant inadequacy—my inadequacy.

CHAPTER 2

It meant I was not able to offer what they wanted or had too much of what they didn't.

By the time I reached my early thirties (and TheraPaul's couch), my brand of humor was a large part of my personality. It was expected and largely entertaining but not always. On occasion, it came at the expense of others. "I feel sorry for the guy who marries you," a random man told me in a pub one innocuous Saturday night out with friends. I had made a quip, probably about men, and he didn't find it funny. I said I was kidding, but he was onto something and it stung. My choices and demeanor were at odds with what I was claiming to want: a healthy romantic relationship.

I hypothesized to TheraPaul that getting someone unavailable to stay, because he was inspired by or at least undeterred by my style, would prove I was worth staying for. It was textbook daddy-divorce stuff, so obvious and trite.

I was critical of my choices—especially the one I'd made when I was drunk at seventeen, which was stupid on so many levels—and worried that being a single woman slighted by love had become part of my identity. It seemed like a pattern, and I wanted the pattern to die. Maybe if I pointed and wagged the finger at myself first, TheraPaul wouldn't feel the need to concur; we could skip further analysis and get straight to the fixing. I didn't want to listen to her repeat back what was wrong with me, to drag those clunky feelings out. But further analysis of the past was necessary to move forward, and I braced myself for it. What I didn't brace myself for was empathy. TheraPaul empathized with my younger self as well as the person sitting before her, in a way I never had. I'm not sure I deserved it—on the giant spectrum of hardship my life had been a breeze—but I appreciated the kindness.

I found myself motivated to try what TheraPaul called "completing" my uncomfortable feelings. Incomplete feelings fester, probably grow warts, and contaminate their happier counterparts. But talk about them and you begin to understand them, diminishing their ability to cause further harm. This was easier said than done. With TheraPaul's help, I was willing to try.

Mom had a different idea. "Oh, Dena," she said, when I told her I had been seeing a therapist. "With all the money you're spending on therapy, you could go on a nice vacation."

Sure, I could've spent a week relaxing on a beach or in a mountain cabin, but I was banking on the effects of therapy lasting longer. And they would. With TheraPaul's help, I learned how to put my past into perspective, to let go of guilt, shame, and the idea that I wasn't fit to find love. I learned what it meant to embrace vulnerability—to be more open to possibilities and less limited by fear. There would be no overnight transformation, and those familiar old traps would always have a certain allure, but little by little, over the next two years, I began putting what I learned into practice. I stepped outside of my regular programming and got involved in theater, writing, running, and volunteering; I pushed past old limits and began living a more enriching life. I dared to hope that out of risk and change might come a romantic prospect or two, and certainly, as I graduated from my thirties, a healthy, long-term relationship.

But in mid-September 2006, as I sat rigid and wide-eyed in a room full of spoken-for cancer survivors, I was reminded that a romantic relationship wasn't meant to be. There would be no flirting with my witty boyfriend over lunch, no conspiring over frivolous weekend plans. There would be grasping for composure, restraining of tears, a yearning to escape, and Asian chicken salad.

❖

Being single had always been a sore spot. Now it was a sore spot with a noxious tumor in the middle. Taking away my breasts and pumping toxins into my veins might make that tumor go away; I was afraid it would take away any chance for lasting love, too. I bolted from the survivors' luncheon with repressed tears and a lie on my lips about attending next month. (One small lie, one giant setback for embracing vulnerability.)

Chapter 3

I need more time to digest and I have to get surgery soon. Pressure pressure pressure.
—Journal Entry

I WENT STRAIGHT from the luncheon to an appointment with a radiation oncologist. Dressed in a black t-shirt bearing Elvis's face, a white lab coat, and jeans, he sat across from me in the exam room and reviewed my preliminary pathology. I wanted to know whether a lumpectomy and radiation would be a viable alternative to complete removal of my breasts and possible chemotherapy.

He explained that the cancer cells in my breast looked closer to normal than not and that more-normal-looking cells were less likely to grow in lymph nodes. In other words, chances were good the cancer hadn't spread.

Good news.

It was also likely that the cancer would be

estrogen- and progesterone-receptor positive, (ER/PR). That meant it was slightly slower growing and should respond well to "hormone-suppression treatment," whatever that was. Unless my genetic test came back positive, he concluded, "it wouldn't be unreasonable" for me to have a lumpectomy and radiation. That cautious double-negative construct; it sounded like something my retired cardiologist dad would say, doctor-speak for "yeah, it could work."

"How am I supposed to decide?" I asked.

"It all comes down to risk tolerance and how you feel about your breasts."

Some women want to save their breasts, he explained, especially if removing them only reduces their risk of recurrence by a small percentage. Why give up whole body parts if you didn't have to? It was a dreadful decision for anyone to have to make. And yet it wasn't. I was emotional about my breasts but only because I knew their days were numbered. It was like ending a stale long-term relationship—you feel bad for your partner, about what others might think, about your quality of life without your partner around. But deep down, you know you're doing the right thing because staying together would be unhealthy. In my case, it would literally kill everyone involved.

If giving up my breasts would reduce my risk by even one percent, I would gladly hand them over.

❖

Three days later, my treasured friend Linda (Steve's wife) took me to my appointment at a plastic surgeon's office. If all went well, I would leave having decided on the type of reconstruction I wanted and the person for the job.

Linda was the first of my Starbucks' friends to become a friend for life. She started working for the company the week after I did. We shared a cubicle wall, and she was my saving grace: I had showed up on my first day with my dominant arm in a cast (clumsy ski fall the weekend before), and by that Friday I had contracted strep throat, suffered an allergic reaction to the penicillin I was taking, and was on the verge of breaking up with my then boyfriend. Instead of running from the white patches on my throat, the red hives coating my body, and my worried blather about being fired, Linda gave me rides to and from work and literally lent me her right arm. But her greatest gift was quashing stress with amusement. Our bond was quick, deep, and set for life. When she, Steve, and their two young sons ended up moving from Seattle to Austin a few years after I did, I was over the moon.

The walls of the plastic surgeon's office were covered with eerie, hollow-eyed mask art. There was a white porcelain number with black lashes, pastel accents, and yellow ribbons pouring out of its cheeks; there was a harlequin pair made of bronze papier-mâché—one looking tipsy, the other constipated; and there was one with an orangey, antique finish and sun-ray hair, reminding me of Donatella Versace and prompting me to use a sunscreen with a higher SPF. I wondered if the masks were molds taken from patients who never woke up from surgery.

"I hope it's not a sign of things to come," I told Linda.

But Dr. Mender, a wiry, forty-something in blue scrubs, seemed more assured than sinister. He introduced himself and invited us back to his office. We followed, passing under a befeathered Native American warrior mask.

There are many ways to go about reconstruction. Dr. Mender walked us through the pros and cons of each. Linda took copious notes.

Taking tissue from my back, belly, or rear would create the most natural look and feel, but surgery and recovery time would take longer, and I would end up with more scars. It could also affect physical activities, e.g., take muscle from the back, and, the back has less oomph for a hearty golf swing or curve ball.

Implants would be much easier to insert, the surgery would be easier to recover from, and it would leave fewer scars. But implants would look and feel like what they were, and would need to be replaced down the road.

"Given your weight, small cup size, and active lifestyle," he concluded, "implants are probably the way to go."

I cared much more about being active than about trying to replicate my breasts. Really, I just wanted the tumor out and my life back to as normal as possible. Plus, the time I would save on physical healing could be put to emotional healing, which I would need much, much more. I told Dr. Mender I would like to pursue reconstruction with implants, mentally checking the box on another big decision.

Reconstruction would immediately follow my mastectomy—same day, same operating room, under the same dose of anesthesia. After removing my breast tissue, Dr. Perry would hand the baton to Dr. Mender, who would insert deflated silicone-shell balloons called "tissue expanders" under my pectoral muscles. Then, over the next several weeks, he would inject them with saline, stretching my skin to make room for my permanent implants. It reminded me of stretching a pair of shoes; it would take a little time to get the right fit, but eventually they would be comfortable enough to put on and wear around.

Reconstruction wouldn't stop with implants. Areolas and nipples would have to be recreated too, the first via tattoos, the latter out of skin from the groin crease between my torso and thigh. I'd never heard of a groin crease and thought it sounded like a service you might get at Jiffy Lube, but if the doctor thought it could work, I was willing to give it a try. In fact, the only concern I had with the entire process was that I not end up with a massive, buoyant bosom.

"I just want a natural drop with nipples pointing toward the floor instead of the ceiling," I said. "Like they belong to someone my age."

Dr. Mender said it wouldn't be a problem; extra stretching of the skin would help create a natural droop. It sounded boring, but I didn't want to draw any more attention to my chest than necessary.

I had just one question left, maybe the most important one of the day: "So, what's your favorite barbecue place?"

In my recent desktop research, I had come across a post in a survivors' forum by a woman who had undergone a mastectomy. She said her surgeon wasn't particularly warm but she didn't care, because that wasn't what she was paying her for. I knew what she meant, but it sounded like a compromise she shouldn't have to make. When you have cancer and are faced with losing body parts, and possibly your life, you deserve a surgeon who is both excellent at what she or he does and compassionate about what you're going through. I knew Dr. Mender was recognized as one of the country's top plastic surgeons. I knew he would do great work. I didn't know whether he was the kind of person I wanted to bare myself to over the next several months.

He considered my question with a smile. "I'm not a big meat eater, but I do like the Salt Lick."

I liked it too.

As we made our way back to the lobby, Linda asked, "So what's the deal with the masks?"

"They're from a former patient," he explained. "He was severely burned and brings these masks to me from his travels around the world."

Chapter 4

You have been selected to travel to sunny Austin, Texas, for the first ever Bilateral Mastectomy Festival (BMF)!

- *Eat world-class vittles at St. David's Hospital—known nationwide for its tapioca surprise!*
- *Immerse yourself in floor after floor of full parking garages!*
- *Play hide-and-seek in endless hospital corridors!*
- *Discover the beauty of beige on beige interior design!*
- *Witness the rare "changing of the boobs" ceremony!*
- *Meet my crackerjack breast surgeon and my plastic surgeon, the first of whom I'm convinced is Steve Perry of Journey's twin, if not Steve Perry himself!*

This landmark event is taking place September

> *29, at the butt-crack-of-dawn. An opportunity like this comes along just once in a lifetime (we hope), so don't delay—pack your bags for BM Fest today!*
>
> —Email to Loved Ones

A WEEK AFTER my diagnosis, I had a medical team in place; a surgery date; the itineraries of family and friends who would be coming to help, starting with Mom and Tay; and a heartening show of support. It was the perfect time to put TheraPaul's vulnerability teachings into practice, but the need to appear like I had everything in control was hard to shake. To convince everyone I was okay, I took a lighthearted approach to my various progress communiqués. Mostly, I was trying to convince myself. Sometimes it worked, and other times it didn't. Just when I felt anchored by my treatment decisions and plan for recovery, I would open an envelope or email and lose my footing. People were taking the time to wish me well, and it was beautiful but also unsettling; it signified the seriousness of my situation and stoked my fear that the cancer would eventually prevail.

Among those expressing support were my clients, two of whom I was currently working with. There was no way I could finish their projects on time. I needed to conserve my energy for surgery, healing, and whatever emotional adjustments would be required to live in my altered physique.

CHAPTER 4

They were beyond compassionate. Still I worried, not about the projects—they weren't life or death—but about my livelihood. What if they found other writers to take over and liked them better? What if I was perceived as unreliable? What if breast tissue directly correlated with my ability to write a clever headline or succinct paragraph? What if copywriters with cancer were yesterday's news?

And if I didn't work for a few weeks or a month, how was I going to pay for the biopsy, surgeries, painkillers, follow-ups, and whatever ongoing treatment might be prescribed? I did have health insurance—through the individual market. To keep the monthly premium down, I had maxed my deductible. I was finally making a living as a freelance copywriter, but I wasn't prepared for a big medical expense. Unless I won the lottery, which, given my recent luck, didn't look promising, I would have to get back to work as soon as possible.

It was during this time, between finalizing and executing my plan, that my Aunt Steenie, my dad's only sister, passed away in her home state of Oregon, after being in a coma. She had only recently been diagnosed with cancer, but by the time it was discovered, it had spread to her bones. A biopsy confirmed that the cancer hadn't originated in the breast, but they never did pin down the source. In her obituary, she was noted for being a talented seamstress and artist, for her beautiful yard and her roses, for being a devoted mother and grandmother, and for her sense of humor, "which made her a joy to be around." She was seventy-nine years old and Dad's last living immediate relative.

I wondered what he was thinking.

Dad was the strongest, smartest, and most capable man I ever knew—part inventor, engineer, and builder; part hand-to-hand balancer (a form of acrobatics), U.S. Navy Seabee, doctor, holder of Brazilian jiu-jitsu black belt, and pilot. He was my living encyclopedia on weather, space, wildlife, and how to fix pretty much anything, including my health. It had been years since he'd left his medical practice for business, but to me he would always be a doctor. He had treated most of my ailments when I was growing up. When I was seven and cut my knee open on the school playground, he stitched it up. When I was ten and my eyes were swollen shut by a poison-oak-induced rash, he gave me shots of cortisone. And when I was fourteen and had a wart on my right middle finger (the envy of all my friends), he burned it off with electrocautery. He even pierced my ears. In every situation, he was unflappable despite my tears, assessing the damage, explaining why it was painful, how it could be alleviated, and how long it would last. His pragmatic and instructive demeanor in the face of my childhood injuries had a calming effect I would continue to lean on through the maladies of

CHAPTER 4

adolescence and adulthood, from an oozing spider bite in my late teens to that broken arm I brought to my first day at Starbucks.

He was always the fixer not the fixed, with few exceptions. Once, in his mid-sixties, he dislocated and fractured his shoulder skiing. He was helped by a medic but only after picking himself up and hoisting his skis, poles, and excruciating pain for a mile down the mountain. The only tears I ever saw him cry were when his mother, my grandma Ethel, died. Her death, and the preceding deaths of his father and elder brother, were now long past. He was living a good life with his wife, Janet, in Salem. And now his youngest child had cancer.

When I told him about my diagnosis, I could hear the cogs in his brain turning—assessing the pathology and Dr. Perry's recommendations. I was desperate for his assessment, for him to be in on the fixing, for him to approve the choices I made. They seemed to me to be the right, practical ones, the ones that would eradicate the disease and quash any possibility of it coming back. When he agreed, I knew I had chosen well.

I didn't know whether my dad ever tried to convince himself he was in control of life's hardships or whether he just was. I didn't know if his ability to endure pain came first or if pain was what cultivated his strength. Nor did I know the extent of his strength reserves; I just hoped enough of that strength had been passed down to me. I was working on being more vulnerable, but I also needed some of that staunch might to make it through surgery, to inhabit a revised body, to take cancer as it came.

Chapter 5

*Seems like I'll never get a boyfriend
now. Now I have "a thing."*
—Journal Entry

ALL THAT WAS to be done had been done. The research, the vetting, the deciding—all had been tended to with all I could throw at it; everything was in place for removal of the tumor, its hiding place, and the surrounding tissue that it was so hungry to occupy. I had a forty-eight-hour reprieve before my pre-op appointment and Mom and Tay's arrival in Austin: forty-eight hours to breathe. I could choose to spend this time getting sucked back into the Cancer Land tunnel—second-guessing my decisions and dreading the cutting away of my natural breasts and a future focused on outrunning the shadow of disease. Or I could channel my energy into forging some kind of confidence that my decisions were the right ones for me. This more positive spin wasn't something I would finish in two days' time, but it was a step.

When I booked my massage at the luxury spa downtown, I had none of this in mind, only gratitude to Tay for giving it to me (and making it a ninety-minute session instead of the routine sixty), and to Linda, who I suspected had recommended the establishment. I was looking to forget about fucking cancer for a while. But human touch is a powerful, powerful thing.

❖

The tobacco- and ivory-colored walls of the massage room were warmed by the reflection of dim lights and a single flickering candle. Tranquil, wordless music and a mint and lavender aroma worked in unison to create a shield from the outside world. Completely naked, I climbed onto the massage table and under the sheet, lying on my stomach with my face in the cradle, as instructed. Gravity wasted no time in flattening the tissue of my breasts and the intruder within against the bottom sheet.

"Anything in particular giving you trouble?" asked the female massage therapist.

Everything? But I left it at tightness in my shoulders and neck.

I was acutely aware of her first touch. After gently pulling back the sheet and brushing my hair off of my neck to expose my back and arms, she placed one hand to the lower left of my spine while lightly sweeping the other hand from the top of the spine down, as if she were cueing a symphony. Then she began.

I had been touched countless times that September in the way of supportive hugs from loved ones and clinical probes by medical staff. Both were emotionally taxing in completely different ways. My sister's gift of massage was an opportunity to enjoy touch for the sake of human touch. I had no personal investment in the woman doing the touching, nor she in me. I could tell her what muscles felt tense without also explaining why. I could just lie there, check out, and go emotionally numb.

But as the tension in my body loosened under the massage therapist's fingers, so did the anxiety that had been clinging to my bones. Research and decision making were only part of dealing with cancer. I had a lot of pent-up emotions to unravel. Instead of suspending all thought and visualizing peaceful beachscapes and blue skies when I closed my eyes, images of sorrow and fear—shrapnel of shock—broke loose and flooded my mind. I witnessed a mélange of what had come to pass—Dr. Perry holding my chart, unvisited Italian piazzas, Aunt Steenie sitting at her kitchen table—and what was to be—my body prostrate in a hospital bed, bandages across my chest, get-well cards. I tried to get back to the rhythm of the massage, to be present, but it was too late. Tears had formed.

On the floor below the face cradle was a small copper bowl filled with smooth, gray rocks and little white flowers—an intentionally placed bit of nature upon which to rest the eyes. I could have told the massage therapist I had cancer and was having an emotional moment, but I didn't want to prompt questions about my diagnosis. I didn't want to let cancer ruin my sister's gift. When it occurred to me that I could blame my sniffling on allergies and simply ask for a tissue, it was too late. The run from eyes and nose had dripped and splashed upon the rockery below, the slimy residue adding a dash of realism to the display.

For the last half of the session, I lay on my back. My breasts, which had recently been smashed, palpated, and scrutinized, were purposefully covered and left alone. The massage therapist was just following normal protocol. But it felt like she knew their days were numbered and was giving them space. The next time they would be touched would be the last, and it wouldn't be pretty. It would be with sterile precision—nothing messy, playful, or passionate.

❖

It had been two years since my breasts—and the rest of my body—had experienced physical passion with any kind of regularity, two years since my relationship with the Italian. We'd met in the checkout line at the Apple store in the mall. I commented on how we were buying the same iBook, and a conversation grew from there. Plus, I'd caught him looking at me. He had rich, brown eyes, equally brown tousled hair, smooth olive skin, and a sweet boyish smile. When he asked me not to coffee but "espresso," with his Italian accent, I was beside myself. Meeting a single, good-looking European during the day, sober—that never ever happens. I was totally in.

The Italian was a graduate student at the University of Texas at Austin and lived in a massive apartment complex behind a popular strip club called The Yellow Rose. Our second date was at his place for homemade mushroom risotto. Several glasses of red wine later, we were taking turns chatting and kissing on the couch. After a slurry exchange about the magnitude of American grocery carts (daunting when compared to those in a small Italian village), he stopped talking and gazed at me—all of me—for several loaded seconds. I felt so magnetic in that moment, so desired and ready to be devoured. I held his gaze, anticipating an invitation to his bedroom.

"You have such broad shoulders," he said. "I wish mine were that broad."

Part of me wilted, my expansive frame drooped. It's not like I'm linebacker material; I've never shopped the big and tall section of Macy's.

Another part of me, more aroused than offended, attributed his comment to a linguistic misstep and let it roll off my hulking back.

"Thank you," I tittered, inhibiting future gaffes with an uninhibited kiss.

On a mattress indented by the weight of my brawn, we went about unbuttoning, unzipping, and undoing anything that prevented the fever of skin on skin. Were Italians really better lovers? I couldn't wait to find out.

He whispered naughty Italian somethings in my ear. (At least that's what I'm telling myself because "I'm gonna lick every inch of your gargantuan shoulders" would have had the opposite effect.) The passion in his words and ferocity of his touch transported me to another world—a Mediterranean world—where savoring good food and delighting in the curves of a woman's body are second nature. I followed him there without question. They are the best lovers, I concluded. It's so very true.

But sensual delight wasn't enough for the long haul. After several weeks together, in and out of bed, we broke up, genially.

❖

The last time anyone outside of the medical community would see my breasts was later that night, when Linda and Alice came to my apartment to photograph me topless on my bed. I had read somewhere that you should take time to say goodbye to your breasts. With an idea to immortalize them through art, I asked these kindred souls for help.

I'd met Alice at Starbucks, too. And, as with Linda, the connection was instantaneous. Originally from Austin, with big blue eyes and lips always, and I mean always, the color of red poppies, Alice was an expert copywriter with a contagious enthusiasm for life. But it was her kindness and playful personality I loved the most. My transition to writing and the move to Austin (not long after she moved back herself) was largely inspired and aided by her. It was Alice who in 2003, eight months pregnant, had driven around Austin in hundred-degree temperatures to find an apartment for me. It was Alice who could make me laugh by dropping into any character voice at will, from Cockney tourist to whatever grackle or squirrel was crossing our path.

To have two such friends in the same city was a luxury. To have two such friends with natural artistic abilities—and a willingness to help me fulfill an awkward wish—was grace.

From the photographs they took, Alice created a classic charcoal drawing and Linda a hand-cut black-and-white silhouette. Both would immortalize my body in a way I couldn't have done myself. My breasts were unremarkable, but my friends made them seem flawless and forever, and with that, I found it a little easier to let them go.

Chapter 6

"Go, Speed Tracer, go!"
—Mumbled from Exam Table

THE SENTINEL LYMPH node is the Watchman of the Armpit. It's where breast cancer cells are likely to spread first. A biopsy of this node helps inform staging and treatment.

During surgery, Dr. Perry would remove my sentinel node for biopsy. Ensuring she would take the right one required a pre-surgery visit to the nuclear-medicine department of St. David's Medical Center, where a radiologist would stick a needle full of radioactive tracer and blue dye into my areola. The Watchman would soak up the blue tracer and, like an Irish sunbather on a Mediterranean beach, be easy for Dr. Perry to find.

I went in for the procedure the day before my mastectomy, bracing myself. Dr. Perry had said it would "hurt like hell." I shared my anxiety with the

CHAPTER 6

young female technician who assured me that the man performing the injection was the fastest around.

"Yeah, it's going to hurt?" she said in upspeak. "But only for, like, seven seconds?"

Just as I was counting to see how long seven seconds actually was, the radiologist, aka Nuke, was hovering over me, wielding a needle full of radioactivity—a hard sharp point that was about to pierce the most delicate and innocent part of my breast. Soft-spoken, fifty-something, and with wisps of gray peeking out of his scrubs cap, Nuke carefully described the procedure. I steeled myself.

When I was eleven years old, I stepped on a nail sticking out of a discarded board in a walnut orchard next to our house. The nail went through the sole of my tennis shoe and into the bottom of my foot. I screamed in pain and wailed for my parents to come help. It was excruciating—but nothing compared to what felt like a glowing, pitch-burned spear being plunged into my defenseless areola.

I cried out in agony.

"I'm sorry, Ma'am," Nuke replied. "Almost done."

Then, just as I was about to scream that he'd violated the seven-second rule, he was gone—and with him the pain. For the next hour and a half, I lay under a gamma camera, the blue tracer in my breast inching its way toward the Watchman while the young tech tracked its progress on the computer screen. I prayed its journey would be in vain.

That night, with the areola trauma behind me—a pinprick compared to the imminent surgical gashes—I picked up Mom and Tay from the airport. They had put their lives on hold to come and take care of me for the next few weeks. The rest of my family and Marit would come later, in a sort of tag team of care.

I was relieved to have them there—Mom, who would stay with me in my apartment, doting on me, and Tay, in a nearby hotel, making sure whatever needed to get done got done. Together, they would find humor in the quirks of the medical staff and postoperative dos and don'ts, and bring it to me with my dose of pain meds. Both were natural entertainers. They couldn't help but bust out a limerick, break into song, mimic whomever, or strike a clever quip. I expected I would also see them use these gifts against each other. Impatience, irritability, and stress would prod them (and me) to do everything from theatrical eye rolls to biting comebacks. But these moments would be short-lived, as they always were. We would toss them out at the end of the day, along with the coffee grounds, take out containers, and tissues.

Chapter 7

I was trying to memorize the shape of my breasts by tracing over them with my fingers. But I stopped and returned my hands to my sides. There was a tumor inside one of them. I didn't want to touch it.
—Journal Entry

"HAVE YOU SEEN the Marfa Lights?" I asked the anesthesiologist.

Incredibly early the morning after Mom and Tay's arrival, and fifteen days after being diagnosed, I was lying on a gurney in a pre-op room. The anesthesiologist was giving me a little something to relax. Mom and Tay looked on, grinning.

"Sometimes they can be blue and sometimes they're white...," I continued.

I had first seen the Marfa Lights in 2004, when Alice and I made the seven-hour drive from Austin to West Texas to visit her husband, John, who had been away for weeks working on the set of an upcoming Tommy Lee Jones' film. It was a clear, cool night when we huddled in the viewing area off Highway 90 to watch mysterious light forms appear, twinkle, and fade into the horizon between Marfa and Paisano Pass. There are many plausible explanations for these ghostly orbs. Still, they were the closest things to supernatural I had ever seen, and like a fresh Amway recruit, I was hell bent on spreading the word in what my sister refers to as my "happy-juice-stream-of-consciousness."

"You can drive out there one night and see 'em...."

"I'll administer a general anesthesia," the anesthesiologist said, redirecting his attention to Mom and Tay.

"And another night, not see 'em."

"She'll wake up within a few minutes after surgery."

"And! Planes have tried to find them by flying over...."

"We'll keep her back here for thirty to forty-five minutes," a nurse chimed in.

"Have you seen the Marfa Lights?" I asked Dr. Mender as I was being rolled into the operating room. It would be another three hours before Dr. Perry finished the mastectomy and passed him the baton, but he wanted to check in before I went under. I don't remember whether he said he had seen

CHAPTER 7

the Marfa Lights or not, but I remember looking up at him and seeing him smile. The last thing I remember was Dr. Perry hovering over me while my arms were lifted out to my sides like broken wings. Marfa Lights out.

❖

"OK, DENA. DOIN' ALL RIGHT?" came a voice in the distance. A clipped voice. "WHAT'S YOUR PAIN LEVEL?"

The voice became louder. So did the cacophony of the recovery room: rubber soles squeaking across linoleum, gurney and IV pole wheels rolling full tilt, privacy curtains being swished back and forth, beeping machines, and instruments and supplies being clicked, snapped, and fastened into place. Out of the haze of bobbing pink and blue shapes, the bustling bodies of nurses came into focus.

"C'MON HON," the voice came again, rushed. She was looking down at me now, waiting. "IT'S THE ONLY WAY I CAN GIVE YOU THE RIGHT AMOUNT OF...."

I muttered something about not feeling good.

"Okay, all right," she said, setting something plastic and crinkly under my left hand. "If you feel sick you can throw up in the bag, okay?"

I threw up in the bag.

❖

I DON'T WANNA BE PINK

"WHY IS IT SO FUCKING LOUD IN HERE?!" I growled into Linda's face. I was out of recovery and resting in my hospital room. She and Steve had come to visit. At the precise moment she was pressing a sweet, motherly kiss to my furrowed brow, a floor-waxing machine raged to life in the hallway outside my open door. It sounded like it was next to my bed. I couldn't focus on anything else. Between the noise and the nurses checking my vitals every ten seconds, a restful recovery seemed miles of unwaxed corridors away. Linda pulled back and squeezed my hand. Steve shut the door.

As evening rolled around, visiting friends took their leave, and the effects of the anesthesia slowly evaporated, I became more and more aware of the condition of my body. My chest was flat, bandaged, and tight. The bandages covered pain. What looked like two miniature beer bongs were taped to my torso, draining fluid the color of cognac. My left arm was hooked up to an IV, my right finger was clasped inside a pulse oximeter, and my calves were wrapped in compression garments to prevent blood clots. (In that moment, I didn't remember this, but my dad was responsible for the original research and development of these life-saving devices, and received a patent for the system while working at Salem Memorial Hospital in the late nineteen sixties.) Next to my left hip was a button for adding pain medication to my IV. Next to my right was a

CHAPTER 7

button to call the nurse.

Having to pee didn't help. The catheter I'd had in during surgery, I later learned, had been removed too soon. This aggravated my sour mood but was also motivating. A prerequisite for fleeing St. David's for the quiet confines of my own bedroom was clearly to be able to get up and go to the bathroom on my own.

The nurse suggested I start with a bedpan. As Mom looked on, Tay and the male nurse strategized placement.

"Do you think you can lift yourself up and we'll slide the bedpan underneath?" asked the nurse.

"I'll try," I said.

As I attempted to lift my hips into a yoga-like bridge pose, my weight sank into my upper body, which was still reeling from surgery. "It hurts!" I cried, letting myself fall back into the bed. I was going to get whoever took that catheter out. And when I did, he or she would be using it as a straw.

"Okay, Dena," the nurse said, calm and indefatigable. "We're going to lift your hips for you." It bugged me that he used my name. "Try not to put pressure on your upper body, and just let us do the work."

Always a fan of letting someone else do the work, I relinquished the weight of my upper body and within minutes the pan was in place and I was sighing relief.

I DON'T WANNA BE PINK

❖

At three a.m., Tay—who was spending the night on a whiny vinyl chair-bed—and I and everyone within a three-block radius were jolted awake by a fire alarm, which was later determined to be false. My irritation spiked; I couldn't take the noise; concerns about being too weak to go home dwindled by the minute. I renewed my resolve to pee alone.

Later that morning, after I'd progressed to the bedside potty-chair, Dr. Mender popped in. Wearing a Hawaiian shirt and a ready smile, he checked my chart and said he was happy with the surgery as well as the pace of my recovery. I could stay another night if I needed to, he said, but I should know that hospitals were breeding grounds for "mersa," i.e., MRSA (methicillin-resistant *Staphylococcus aureus*), i.e., horrifying staph infection that could lead to pus-filled boils and, in rare cases, spread to vital organs. It was the best reason yet to go to the bathroom on my own. By that afternoon, under the watchful eyes of my faithful sister, I was swinging my legs slow-mo over the side of the bed, pushing myself up, and shuffling to the bathroom, where I peed my way to victory.

❖

When the makers of Tupperware developed their colorful line of food storage products, I doubt

CHAPTER 7

they had vomit in mind. But dishwasher-safe plastic containers really come in handy when lingering anesthesia teases your stomach into reverse.

I had been home for less than twenty-four hours when the roiling began. "Mom," I begged, "please find something plastic for me in case I need to throw up." I was thinking garbage bag, but when she rushed into my bedroom she was brandishing an old fork-nicked, tomato-sauce-stained food container I hadn't seen since college. It was good enough. Except I couldn't position myself to use it. Without the luxury of an adjustable hospital bed I was stuck flat on my back. Rolling my bandaged and double-draining torso to the side was out of the question. I pleaded with Mom to push me upright. But this was easier screamed than done, and she was forced to call my sister for help.

My sister, after forty-eight hours of Dena duty with only a few naps in between, was fast asleep when we called. "I'll be there as soon as I can get some clothes on," she said, groggily, from her hotel bed. I felt bad about waking her up. Don't rush, I told her, the urgency in my voice betraying my words. I needed my big sister's help again; I needed the security of her presence.

After she arrived, she had me sitting upright and retching into the Tupperware in thirty seconds flat. That's the beauty of my sister; she goes all in and gets shit done.

Mom wasn't quite ready to relinquish control, though. "Do you want some water?" she asked.

"I think she just needs a few minutes," my sister said. I could hear the fatigue in her voice.

"Should we call the doctor?" Mom said.

"It's probably just the anesthesia wearing off," my sister said.

"Do you want some soup?"

"Mom! Soup is probably the last thing she wants."

"I wasn't asking you."

"MOM! Will you please just give it a rest?"

"I CAN HELP TOO, YOU KNOW!"

And with that, Mom stomped out of the room but not before sticking out her tongue behind my sister's back.

Things smoothed over quickly. Mom and Tay proceeded to wait on me until I could get around on my own. An acquaintance would later say I was brave to have gone through cancer alone. You know, as a single person. How she was able to find and strike the one unsevered nerve I had left was amazing. I felt defensive about it, compelled to stand up for myself and all single cancer people.

Like I had a choice, I wanted to say. Many of us with disease hadn't seen it coming, hadn't realized we needed to run out first and snatch up the love of our life, hadn't known that the havoc would be easier to manage with a mate in our corner. But thanks for pointing that out. Helpful.

My hands didn't have cancer. I imagined wiping away tears with one of them and using the other to punch her in the face.

The hurt side of me wished I wasn't her definition of "alone," but the practical side knew that having a significant other doesn't guarantee loving support. There are countless breakups in the wake of cancer, with women taking the hit. According to one study, women who become ill are significantly more likely to be abandoned by their partners than men in the same position.[1] Financial strain and the inability to cope with caregiving are partly to blame. I applaud anyone who has a supportive partner—an "us" with which to go through cancer or any of life's surprise tribulations. It sounds nice. And I challenge those people to acknowledge that mothers, fathers, siblings, friends, coworkers, clients, neighbors, nurses, exes, and even pets count, too.

Even when I wanted to be, and there were plenty of times, I was never alone.

I've considered that acquaintance's words many, many times. While I appreciate her discomfort with being unattached in an adverse situation, I've decided it's a personal projection and little to do with me.

---

[1] Glantz MJ, Chamberlain MC, Liu Q, Hsieh CC, Edwards KR, Van Horn A, Recht L.,Gender Disparity in the Rate of Partner Abandonment in Patients With Serious Medical Illness, *Cancer*, 2009 Nov 15;115(22):5237-42

❖

"I THINK MARK HARMON IS SOOOOO GOOD LOOKING!" Mom hollered from the kitchen while preparing dinner.

Given her delicate hearing and my loud air conditioning, my sister had bought her a cordless headset so she could enjoy NCIS, CSI, and other favorite televised acronyms during her stay. She looked like an air traffic controller without a tower, but at least she could listen to her programs.

"Yeah, he's pretty handsome," I replied.

"WHAT?"

"SHE SAID HE'S PRETTY HANDSOME!" my sister shouted.

"That's what I said!" Mom barked, shaking her head and wondering what in the hell was wrong with her girls.

By the end of that first week I was making strides, at least physically. I had my drains removed, I could get the mail by myself, and I could reach the bowls in the cupboard without feeling like I was pulling what was left of my chest through my armpits. Emotionally, though, I was treading water.

Before taking my first shower, I stood in front of the mirror naked and lost it. It wasn't that the surgeons hadn't done a wonderful job, it was just that not having breasts didn't look right. It was as if they had imploded, leaving debris: swelling, bruises, stitches, and stained bandages. I had also noticed several new and unpleasant sensations, the first being the reconstructive tissue expanders in my chest. Dubbed the iron bra, the expanders felt like having a couple of 14-ounce ceramic ramekins shoved under my pectoral muscles, the latter of which were then twisted into a knot and secured with several layers of duct tape. Either ramekins or a bike rack. But at least they were temporary. I can't say the same for the hot, tingly numbness I felt when anything rubbed against my chest. That was the residual effect of severed tissue and nerves. It was like having an SOS pad grazing a mild sunburn on a limb that had fallen asleep.

Dr. Perry's office called that week, confirming my pathology: the cancer hadn't spread to the Watchman of the Armpit; I was officially stage one. This was really good news—the best news possible. It didn't get any better than that. Yet I didn't feel like celebrating.

"Do you want to go to church with me, to give thanks?" Mom asked as we walked to the corner store. Mom was, had always been, and would always be Catholic. She didn't just *believe* in the teachings of Christ; deep in her heart, she *knew* them to be true. Emboldened by faith or, perhaps, blinded by love, she allowed herself to marry a nonbeliever. And look how that turned out, she would say. Her three children weren't practicing, either, despite the great lengths she'd gone to raise us in the Church. But her efforts weren't for naught—we all feel guilty about it to this day.

"Give thanks for what?" I grumbled. "For getting breast cancer?"

"That it wasn't stage four."

"Those were my only two choices?"

Chapter 8

I should be thrilled that the cancer is gone and I'm node-negative, but instead I hate everything.

I hate that I'm having trouble sleeping because I can't find a comfortable position and my back hurts.

I hate that I'm tired because of it.

I hate that I haven't had any time to myself except in the shower and in the middle of the night when I should be sleeping.

I hate that I feel bad about even wanting time to myself.

I hate the way my sticky underarms rub against my numb, tingly skin.

I hate the feeling of these tissue expanders.

I hate that I feel guilty for everything I'm feeling thanks to ingrained Catholic guilt.

I feel like I should be using this time to write some brilliant essay, yet I'm writing a bulleted list of everything I hate instead.

> *I'm also worried about money.*
> *And getting fat.*
>
> —Journal Entry

I kept being partly angry. I'd squeeze some of it out, throwing passive-aggressive comments like darts into various parts of the day, then water the rest of it down with guilt. It was like driving by pumping the pedal instead of maintaining a steady speed, which makes you both car sick and late to your destination. If I ever wanted to sustain a degree of hope and optimism, and I did, I would have to keep my foot on the pedal and complete my feelings first. It was something TheraPaul had encouraged.

I gave it a shot. It had only been a month since I'd been shoved into the Cancer Land tunnel and just days since my breasts had been lopped off. I had never asked to have cancer. I didn't want to deal with all the appointments and procedures. Nor did I want to spend the rest of my life afraid it would come back. Damn right I was angry and scared. I resented the pressure to be anything but. Masking anger, fear, and sadness, suppressing them to put everyone else at ease, felt taxing and dishonest. "I'm the one who had cancer at thirty-nine!" I wanted to shout. "Cancer kills people, remember? They die. And if I want to go all Sean Penn and wax angst for a while, I have every fucking right."

I didn't shout, but I did let loose in my journal,

CHAPTER 8

and cry, and go on long walks, and process pieces with my family and friends. Only when I had sifted through some of the anger and fear could I make room for something more positive, like my impending birthday, and some encouraging news.

"I *knoooow* they're going to recommend chemotherapy!" Dr. Perry had said on diagnosis day. "Mwah-ha ha!" Actually, she'd spoken gently, but my fragile and frightened mind distorted the tone. This is how I remembered what she'd said when it came time to find out if chemo was something I should pursue.

I didn't want chemo–didn't want to be sick, didn't want to lose my hair. Just thinking about being sick made me sick. I had just done a hard, hard thing having my breasts removed. The thought of soaking my insides in toxins was like reopening a wound. But if it would reduce the chance of recurrence, if it would kill even one microscopic fugitive cell, which I pictured wearing a ski mask and twirling a pocketknife, I would voluntarily open a vein.

❖

Two weeks after surgery and two days before my birthday, I consulted an oncologist to find out whether chemo was necessary. Linda and Tay, who was in town on her second tour of Dena duty, accompanied me to the appointment.

The three of us sat quietly while the tall,

soft-spoken oncologist with a German-sounding last name reviewed my pathology report. I was bracing myself for the dreaded chemo recommendation when, to my surprise, he looked up and said it might not be necessary after all.

"Your chance of recurrence may be low enough to render chemotherapy overkill," he said.

To help him decide, he would have my tumor examined using a test called the Oncotype DX. I'd get the results in early November.

The three of us left his office hopeful. Being able to bypass months of chemo would be a huge relief. It suggested my cancer wasn't as serious as we thought. What a glorious note on which to exit my thirties.

Two days later, on October 18th, I crossed the threshold to forty, emboldened by these maybe-wins and the warmth of loved ones. I had so wanted to be in Italy with Marit, to explore its history, taste its delights, and expand my mind in the way only travel can do. And I could have gone, could have postponed surgery and lugged my tumor from village to town, trying not to let it sour every moment of a celebratory trip. But I couldn't imagine looking back on it fondly with cancer photobombing every scene.

"Where was this taken?" I imagined a coworker asking, about a picture of Marit and me posing against a Tuscan landscape.

CHAPTER 8

"In Italy," I would reply. "When I turned forty."

"Nice!"

"You can't see it, but there's a tumor, right there, in the right breast. Cancer."

"Oh."

So I stayed stateside, within time zones that were accessible to the most important people in my life, all of who went out of their way to celebrate a profound birthday. From Homer, Alaska, my brother, Paul, who was born on the same day three years before me, and his fiancée, Melinda, made sure to call and sing (jubilantly shout, actually) and send their love. The rest of my family and other friends did the same. In Seattle, my dear friend Sara hosted a "check your boobies" party in my honor, gathering friends for a how-to on self-exams. And in Austin, Marit, who had flown in for the week to relieve my sister, joined me, Alice, and other sweet souls for a night at the fancy Vespaio Ristorante—dipping bread into little pools of olive oil and balsamic vinegar, savoring pasta stuffed with butternut squash, drinking red table wine, and appreciating every uncomplicated second. And, somewhere in Tuscany, I imagined a swarthy Giovanni and Antonio flirting with some carefree American tourists, the four of them reveling into the night, shutting down the bar.

Chapter 9

I always make my payments. I disclosed all my information. I don't smoke. I'm not overweight. But I get breast cancer so "let's make her suffer some more."
—Journal Entry

I HAD BECOME an obstacle slayer, confronting each threat as it appeared in my path:

- Obliterate tumor, remove breasts. Check.
- Reconstruct breasts (aka, faux-tas). Underway.
- Embrace an Austin birthday instead of Italy. Check.
- Find out if positive or negative for BRCA genes. Underway.
- Confirm chemotherapy unlikely. Underway.

But the one I dreaded the most still loomed:

- Make sure health insurance will pay for everything. Gulp.

CHAPTER 9

Like waiting in line at the DMV or attending a baby shower, health insurance is a necessary evil. Despite ever-increasing premiums and too-frequent errors (out-of-network penalties or miscoded procedures anyone?), it's good to have insurance when facing a major illness.

Unless you don't have it.

I thought I did. The unmarried self-employed person is responsible for obtaining his or her own health insurance. I couldn't imagine going without it, even for a few months, because I was certain that the minute I wasn't covered, something bad would happen and I'd be financially screwed. It was too risky. When I moved to Austin I enlisted the help of a local broker to secure an individual plan with a company I refer to as Jackhole Health. Aware of the horror stories surrounding pre-existing conditions, I was afraid that the breast cancer scare I'd had before my move would cause alarm. I imagined an eager young underwriter slapping one of those red Post-it flags on the pre-existing condition section of my application and handing it to his boss. The boss would laud the underwriter for putting a stopper in a potential money pit. She might even take him to lunch.

My fear was realized when Jackhole responded with an exclusionary Rider—a little "fuck you" written into my policy to prevent coverage of the one type of coverage I might actually need.

"This policy/certificate does not cover any loss

incurred…resulting from atypical ductal hyperplasia, papillomatosis, proliferative or atypical changes, tumor or malignancy of the breast, including treatment or operation therefore."

With an eye for discrimination and knowledge of my recent normal mammograms, my astute broker went to bat for me and asked Jackhole to remove the Rider. But Jackhole refused.

"Too risky," I imagined them saying. "If her pre-existing condition returns we'll be stuck covering what she pays us to cover."

They did, however, with my broker's prodding, amend the Rider to exclude only the bad breast:

"We have agreed to your request to rider only your left breast. We typically do not rider only one breast so new rider language was created to accommodate your request."

I typically do not purchase health insurance from jackholes, I wanted to say, but with so few choices, I'm stuck with a provider who misuses a noun as a verb to exclude crucial coverage. They made it sound like they were doing me a favor. I was paying them to cover me—all of me. The Rider was greedy and gross. I imagined shipping the underwriter my severed left breast. You'll be happy to know it's gone, I'd say. They're both gone, actually. Will you cover what's left now?

As insane as it was, partial coverage was better than nothing. In fact, given that the cancer had

CHAPTER 9

originated in my right breast, it was, ironically, fortunate.

It was in the middle of a sleepless, post-diagnosis night when I remembered the dark exclusionary Rider galloping in the distance. I felt sick thinking I had misread something, missed some detail and wouldn't have the coverage I needed. That I'd be paying off cancer bills for the rest of my life. I bolted out of bed, pulled the file and read the language over and over, making sure it said what I thought it did. While it seemed clear that my expenses for the right breast would be covered, I had to hear it from Jackhole's mouth.

My initial call to customer service was pleasant. From what the agent could tell, as long as the cancer had in fact originated in the right breast and my doctors deemed their services "medically necessary and FDA approved," it looked like the genetic test, mastectomy, and reconstruction would all be covered. Of course, I had to meet my $5,000 deductible first—a hefty sum I approved just five months before in an effort to lower my monthly expenses, and because I thought I was healthy.

It looked like Jackhole had my back. But as when reaching for a Band-Aid in a box of broken glass, I had to bleed a little first. Three days later, I learned that Jackhole had told Dr. Perry's office I had been terminated because I wasn't paying my premiums, which was impossible because they debited my account every month. I called them in a panic.

"You're covered, Miss Taylor," the agent chirped. "Perhaps the verbiage referencing that 'payment is contingent on premium being paid' and the fact that next month's payment hasn't yet posted was somehow misinterpreted as coverage coming to an end."

Right.

A week after that, Jackhole told Dr. Mender that reconstruction of my left breast wouldn't be covered because of the exclusionary Rider.

"Why would you let them put a rider on your policy?" he asked, perturbed.

"I'm self-employed. It was the only way I could get health insurance!"

My voice shook. No one seemed to get that I had gone out of my way to do the most responsible thing I could. I hadn't asked to have a breast cancer scare at thirty-six nor had I asked to be discriminated against because of it when the real thing came along. It was like blaming the split, charred tree for the lightning strike. What else could I have done?

Seeing my frustration, he softened and explained that he was simply astonished that anyone would take my health history and craft such a blatant denial. I was basically paying them to use an unforeseen, unpreventable, and tragic condition against me.

"Believe me, I know."

Back home, I scoured my policy for anything on reconstruction coverage and found the Texas Notice of Mandated Benefits for Breast Reconstruction in Connection with a Mastectomy. The notice clearly stated that in order to "achieve symmetrical appearance," surgery and reconstruction of the opposite breast was covered. I closed my eyes and exhaled.

The way I read it, insurance extended to my left breast. But Jackhole agent Charlene disagreed.

Two days before my surgery, Charlene had reassured me that only half of my surgery would be covered. Squeezing the handset as if it were her neck, I explained that according to the Texas Notice of Mandated Benefits issued by her Jackhole company, reconstruction of the left breast was covered under symmetrical appearance. Mean Charlene said the exclusionary Rider overrode the mandate. Her obstinacy fueled my own. Short of threatening to involve lawyers, CNN, and a bag of Asian hornets, I strongly suggested she review the issue with her Jackhole supervisor. Maybe the frustration, anger, and fear she caused could go toward my deductible.

Fifteen long days later, civil Sarah, the antithesis of Charlene, called to say reconstruction would indeed be covered as outlined in Jackhole's mandated benefits. By this time, my breasts were long gone, and I wondered if the underwriter responsible for "ridering" only my left breast might be gone too. I was relieved—relieved and glad I had pushed back for what I knew was right.

In the end, Jackhole covered everything—not

out of the goodness of their heart, but because it was what I had paid them to do and what the law required. What I didn't pay them for was added anguish during the most frightening time in my life. I have since wondered whether I should give thanks that the whole situation didn't turn out worse but then I think, for fuck's sake, haven't I given enough?

Chapter 10

*I don't want to make any more thoughtful
decisions. I just want to make out.*
—Journal Entry

HORNY, FRESH, FRISKY, feverish—call it what you will, but three weeks after surgery that familiar urge had returned.

I wasn't looking for a one-night stand, per se. I just wanted to go out, have some wine and flirt with an attractive man, like a regular person. Fall had come to Austin, and the cooler temperatures were ideal for drinks and titillating banter on an outdoor patio. Other people were doing it; the city's cafes and bars were teeming with smiling patrons looking strong in body, happy in mind. I wanted to join them and feel that confidence again, even for a few minutes, so that when the time came to put myself back in the dating world, I would be ready.

I needed an accomplice, an easygoing collaborator who wouldn't mind if a night out on the town backfired into a single drink, tortilla chips, and pajamas on the couch. Someone who understood that cancer can reverberate at will, pinching one emotion or another hard enough to kill a happy moment. Someone like Marit, patient and kind and funny.

Marit and I had met nearly ten years earlier, when a coworker invited me to join her and her "Viking friend" for happy hour at a bar in Seattle's Queen Anne neighborhood. A statuesque Norwegian beauty, Marit apparently had recently dated my ex-boyfriend, Rick, which was weird because I had only broken up with him a month or so before.

I was dying to know her Rick story and, thanks to a string of vodka lemon drops, didn't have to wait long to hear it.

"Sooo," I began without an ounce of subtlety. "When did you meet Rick?"

"Oh, that," she replied with a wry smile. "I had a party at my house in August and a mutual friend brought him along, to fix us up."

"That's funny," I replied, "because I broke up with him in August. When exactly was your party?"

We did the math and realized that Rick had agreed to be fixed up with Marit while he was still dating me. Not only did he show up at her house with the intent to meet her, he also rolled around in the grass with her in the park across the street from

CHAPTER 10

her house, kissing and whatnot. She was told he was single.

A week or so after they met, I just happened to break up with him for other chemistry-type reasons. He and Marit went out a couple of times thereafter, and then, without warning, he stopped calling. Blew her off. She was disappointed at the time, but now that she knew of his unholy ways, she was glad.

We have been best friends ever since.

Marit came to Austin for my fortieth birthday and stayed at my place through the weekend. We set our sights on a Saturday night in Austin's Warehouse District. I was emboldened by her company. We had sat on many a barstool in the decade since we met—in Seattle, in Europe, this one time on a yacht in the Caribbean—hashing through work, health, and relationship stuff. Sometimes we talked about nothing much at all. Whatever surfaced, it was always easy and welcome. As we got gussied up for our night in the District, I took comfort in the familiarity of our years-old routine, pulled it over my head along with my top, covering up the reconstruction site underneath. She didn't care; no one else would know.

We kept it simple. Instead of a loud club or pretentious lounge, we went to an Irish chain pub with Celtic relics populating the walls, a U2 cover band, and at least one bartender faking a lilt. We had been there before and had no trouble finding a seat outside. But as we settled in, I started feeling out of sorts. Austin, a college town and prized place to live, is full of young students, young professionals, and determined young transplants. Everyone looked so confident, so sure of themselves, so healthy—all probably highly orgasmic acrobats in the sack or whatever people mean when they describe someone as being good in bed. It took just one glass of red wine for me to go into my head and feel way out of my league. The thought of flirting felt like a lie; the suggestion of even a taste of intimacy, a sham. How would I explain the unnatural firmness of the tissue expanders underneath my top? The scars underneath my bra? Blood tests every four months? Random sudden tears from gratitude for life and fear of death?

I didn't belong. Mentally I battened down the hatches to protect my healing wounds. I would enjoy my time with Marit, might even manage another drink, but hope of forgetting about cancer, of sparking some repartee with an attractive man, was gone.

Then I spotted Donal. The small, hot flame flickered.

❖

I'd first met Donal at this very pub more than a year before. He'd been several pints into celebrating a local soccer league win when his punch-drunk teammate started serenading women at the bar, including my friend and me. Then, like a character

CHAPTER 10

from a playbook on how to pick up chicks, Donal swooped in and apologized for his friend's godawful singing. He was about six feet tall, with curly black locks and green eyes. The second I heard his seductive Irish brogue, I was hooked.

"Just don't quit your day job," I said to Donal's serenading friend with a smile. I glanced back at Donal, hoping he'd appreciate my sass.

He guffawed. The chemistry was electric. By night's end he had my number on a napkin in his pocket.

A month later, we bumped into each other at the same pub. He bought me a beer and apologized for not calling. I told him that if he wanted to ask me out, the answer would be yes. But if he didn't, he should stop saying he did. He blurted that he liked my hair. I had tried styling my wavy shoulder-length hair differently that night—straight with the ends flipping out to the sides—but the ends had bowed instead of flipped, creating a triangular Christmas tree shape that I openly poked fun at. Ever the charmer and savvy opportunist, Donal grinned.

"I want to be an ornament in your Christmas tree hair," he said before leaning in and kissing me on the lips.

A week later he called and we went on a date, one of only two he had been on since moving to Austin three and a half years before. About halfway through, with two glasses of wine under my belt, and two glasses of wine and four beers under his, I detected that Donal wasn't exactly relationship material. He didn't like living in the United States; he wanted to quit his job and travel to New Zealand, maybe end up in Thailand. Still, I was intrigued. I identified with his desire to be Somewhere Else—that magical place where life is always engaging, never monotonous. Where worry and disappointment are extinct, sleep is restful, love abundant, and sex never embarrassing. I'd thought Austin might be my Somewhere Else until romantic misfires, professional ups and downs, bills, and now disease showed me that life is geographically agnostic. Life's irritation and beauty, hurdles and wins, frustrations and fulfillment emerged wherever you went. The setting might look different, the dialect might sound lovely or strange, but no place was perfect. Newness was delicious but temporary.

Somewhere Else was an idea; its true potential came from within. Life without woe was unrealistic. I was learning that we could create joy, though, by carefully choosing how we spent our days and whom we spent them with; how we took care of ourselves; and how we viewed life. It wasn't a function of place but of conscious daily decisions.

But in the moment, I didn't dare go that deep. Romantic prospects had been few and far between. In fact, I hadn't met anyone of great interest since the Italian two years earlier. Why not indulge my

CHAPTER 10

attraction, have some fun?

That Donal and I would never amount to more than a fling was confirmed the second time we went out. After we'd tipsily agreed to go back to his place, he ushered me through his apartment door with, "Promise me you'll find a better man than I."

The dwindling sober part of me winced, dejected. The beer-logged rest of me shook it off, accepted the Red Stripe beer he proffered over the open refrigerator door, and made myself at home. Several Red Stripes later, we were lounging on his bed swapping travel stories, family anecdotes, and work complaints. And then, just after I switched from beer to water in hopes of regaining a modicum of composure, it happened: he put on Frou Frou's *Details* album, the one with "Let Go" on it—the urgent, ethereal track from the movie *Garden State*, and my pants practically undid themselves.

We fumbled our way through the first four tracks. By the time "Psychobabble" came on, we were fully immersed in drunk new sex, uttering our own unintelligible jargon. It was funny, sweet, and passionate—the noise of self-consciousness muted by Frou Frou's dreamy voice. I felt like a model in a music video, a mirage in which each body is flawless, no one smells, and mutual satisfaction is guaranteed.

By track number seven, fittingly titled "Shh," Donal was sleeping, and I was carefully disentangling myself from him to silence Frou Frou so I could sleep too.

A restless hour or two later, head pounding, dehydrated, and with a fierce craving for Tex-Mex, I put on the previous evening's ashtray-and-stale-beer smelling clothes, kissed Donal goodbye, and made the walk of shame to my car.

"Girls always want to have sex to Frou Frou," he would confess later. I had fallen for one of his seduction techniques. But I didn't care. It was good to be had.

Despite the absence of potential, I didn't run from Donal. It was more like a leisurely stroll with revised expectations. For the next several months we'd find each other here and there and indulge our mutual whim. Our times together were never long, always late at night, and weeks apart. He was a sweet Band-Aid of affection during an affection-deficit time. He was also the safe bet I needed that Saturday night out with Marit: a reliable reason to stay.

He was in line at the outside bar several feet from where we were sitting. He couldn't see us so I sent "Nice tie" via text message. I watched him read it then scan the patio for me before I walked up to him and said hello. He kissed my cheek and asked how I had been. While fine, good, great, or busy would have been more than acceptable, cancer was how I'd been and the only thing I could think of.

"Well, something pretty big has happened,"

CHAPTER 10

I said. "Do you really want to know?"

The color seemed to fade from Donal's cheeks. I have since wondered if he thought I was going to tell him I was pregnant, and was squeezing his brain trying to calculate the last time we'd seen each other and recall what protections, if any, had been in place. My awkward buildup didn't help.

"Yeah, what happened?" he asked.

"I had breast cancer."

There was no witty comeback this time. He simply said he was sorry. It didn't matter. I didn't need Donal to say anything of substance. I just needed him to still think I was fun and, if possible, sexy.

Another drink later, with Marit's blessing ("I have earplugs," she said), Donal accompanied us back to my apartment. She went to bed in my bedroom while Donal and I proceeded to crack open a bottle of wine and make out on the couch. It was just like old times, except nothing was the same. The kissing was just as relaxed and sweet, but when hands wandered, as they do, I found myself diverting traffic from the reconstruction under my blouse. I had largely healed by this time; it wasn't a matter of physical pain. It was not wanting to explain the lack of shape from tissue expanders that had yet to be expanded, the settling scars and missing nipples. It was physically safe to be touched but emotionally hazardous. I wouldn't be able to feel the pleasure I once did with this person, only sad numb pressure.

I wasn't ready to face this new reality.

"Maybe just avoid this area," I said, waving my hand over my chest.

"Okay," he replied.

Donal seemed largely unfazed by the diversion and my cancer news. Not that he was insensitive; he made a point of asking me how I was doing and if I was going to be all right. Maybe he didn't really care and was just being polite. Maybe it was as awkward as it seemed because we knew virtually nothing about each other. Probably a combo platter. Either way, I had no delusions that my recent struggle might jolt him into sobriety and elevate our hookup status to a relationship. I was far from relationship material myself. I just needed to know whether he still found me attractive, and since he didn't run for the door and continued showing me affection, I gathered that, to some degree, he still did.

Knowing that was enough. I thought about drinking more wine and having drunk sex with Donal—turning the lights off, leaving my bra on. But I didn't want to. I was physically and emotionally drained. I had cycled through so many feelings that night—convincing myself to go out, feeling like I didn't belong, convincing myself that I did belong and to stay and have fun, avoiding thinking about the unyielding expanders, feeling guilty about dragging Marit through my emotional roller coaster ride—it was exhausting. And watching Donal polish off his glass of wine, my glass of wine, and pour himself another, wasn't sexy. In fact, part of me resented that I had been handed this disease and was going to great, swift lengths to tackle it, while he appeared to have his own malady and wasn't even trying to get it under control.

I was done drinking, done kissing. For the first time since we started going on these late-night pleasure trips, my desire to rest outweighed my desire for Donal. So, I left him on the couch with the wine and went to my bedroom, relieved to curl up alone under the sheets of my bed while Marit slept on an air mattress a few inches away. Four hours later, I woke him up and drove him home. He was going to meet friends at a bar to watch a soccer match on TV, I was going to sip iced coffee with my best friend on her last full day in Austin—neither one of us wanted to be late.

My first kiss after cancer would be my last with Donal. Maybe the thrill of the handsome, witty Irishman had run its course. But the course had also changed. I would eventually visit many of my pre-cancer haunts, never quite capturing the lightheartedness I'd felt before. I had been diseased; a possible cause of my death had been identified, and I had never been so frightened or so eager to live. I wanted to strengthen my body and avoid health risks while the Donals of the world seemed hell-bent on seeking them out.

Five years my junior, Donal once told me he didn't think he'd live much past forty. But if you had the chance, I wanted to say, why wouldn't you want to keep living? Why wouldn't you try?

Chapter 11

KVUE is coming to interview me. I considered opening the door without my shirt on. I'm pretty flat right now so it would be like a shirtless guy. Plus, it's Halloween.
—Journal Entry

A FEW DAYS after my mastectomy, Mom and I went through pictures from the previous summer's family vacation. We paused when we came across a picture of me perched atop a bale of hay in Taos, New Mexico, looking glum. The Taos trip was one of many over the years starring Tay as captain of the rental car, my brother-in-law Rob as chief gas-tank-filler and roadside bathroom scout, and Mom and I as backseat grunts whose main duties were to keep our humming, candy wrapper rattling, and unhelpful commentary to ourselves.

This particular trip began in Reno, Nevada, wended through Arizona and New Mexico, and ended in Colorado Springs, Colorado. It featured such natural attractions as Grand Canyon Caverns, Bandelier National Monument, Red Rocks Park, and the historic La Hacienda de los Martinez in Taos, whose bale of hay I was sitting upon when Mom snapped my photo.

I remember the moment vividly. Some forty-five minutes earlier, Tay, Rob, Mom, and I had stuffed ourselves into the rental car, arriving at the historic hacienda before it opened. We loitered out front, like dozing cattle, cameras dangling from our wrists like cowbells, waiting to explore the hacienda's twenty-one rooms and two courtyards.

Having stayed up late the night before, I was two hours of sleep and three cups of coffee shy of being able to state my name and date of birth let alone comprehend the history posted on the hacienda's didactic placards. Pretending to be coherent, I walked through a few rooms and attempted to imagine what it would have been like to live there in the eighteen hundreds, but gave up when I realized none of the information on the placards was registering. That it was an important trade center for the northern boundary of the Spanish Empire and final terminus for the Camino Real, which connected northern New Mexico to Mexico City, wasn't enough to rouse me from the fog that is morning.

I stepped outside into the courtyard and spotted the bale of hay, beckoning me like a giant discarded

CHAPTER 11

block of shredded wheat. I was wearing a summer top from the Target clearance rack, faded, unflattering crop jeans, and some old woven Clarks sandals. The top was snug—I remember having trouble getting the side zipper past my ribcage—and my chest looked underdeveloped.

Mom looked at the photo and didn't miss a beat.

"See! You were as flat then as you are now," she said.

Sometimes Mom takes the short route to sentiment. This usually happens when she's motivated, which in this case was to try to make her daughter feel better. Had I not known my mother, her comment would have upset me. She meant well; the words just came out wrong. It was like the time she made me healthy oat-and-dried-fruit cookies that were burnt on the bottom.

"Just scrape the burnt part off," she'd snapped. "They're good for you."

Sometimes you have to do the same with words.

At the end of the day, Mom was right. My chest looked as flat on that bale of hay in Taos as it did after my mastectomy. But I knew that underneath that battening Target top I was wearing in the photo, there were breasts. Not curvy full breasts like my friend Sabine's but breasts nonetheless, and I was anxious to get some semblance of them back.

❖

Three weeks and 200 cc of saline later, my breasts were starting to rise.

Not that anyone could tell just yet; 200 cc is just under seven ounces—more than you can carry through airport security but less than a can of Red Bull. The saline was stretching the tissue expanders and the tissue expanders were living up to their name—making room for my future implants. We just needed a little more time.

The first 100 cc of saline had been injected along with insertion of the expanders immediately following the mastectomy at the end of September. In mid-October, I went to Dr. Mender's office for injection, or "fill," number two—a 30-minute outpatient procedure.

The nurse led me to the exam room and laid out a paper shrug. Aren't we past the shrug phase? I thought. I've got nothing left to hide. In fact, giving me something to hide is why I'm here. Yet, there I was, succumbing to formality; sticking my arms through the shrug-holes, pulling the ends together in front of my chest like you might a cardigan on a cool day.

Lying on the exam table, right breast exposed, right arm over my head, I held steady as Dr. Mender inserted a needle through my skin and into the tissue expander, slowly injecting it with 100 cc of saline. With my nerves severed from the mastectomy, I felt nothing more than a little pressure. Dr. Mender repeated the procedure on the left side, then I was free to go. Later that day, I felt a painful charley horse across my chest, and that's exactly what it was. Because the expanders sit under the pectoral muscles, their growth pushes the pecs away from the chest wall, causing them to experience separation anxiety and throw a tantrum, or spasm, if you want to get all technical. Aleve took care of the pain and I was able to appreciate the beginning shapes of my future breasts.

With Halloween approaching and my chest looking like Sally in *The Nightmare Before Christmas,* it occurred to me that I had a built-in costume. I would be Her Majesty Scarborella, Queen of Mastecta—a medieval empress toplessly roaming the centuries searching for the breasts that had been taken from her by the evil Carcinoma, nasty whore-skank of the despicable underworld, Diseasa. I'd definitely want to blow out my hair, get out the black eyeliner, and go Goth. I'd also want to carry a spear, and, as a symbol of hope, a special embroidered silk box in case I found my breasts and needed to carry them home for the mystical Reattachment Ceremony. TMZ would coin me ScarBo and track my every move.

Or, if I didn't want to go topless, I could always go as Mammotomb Raider. It would be apropos: a local television station was going to interview me that week about the Mammotome biopsy procedure.

The story was for Breast Cancer Awareness

Month—it was that time of year, everything draped in pink à la Christo and Jeanne-Claude—and it featured Dr. Perry describing the importance of biopsies in early detection. The reporter had asked Dr. Perry whether they might also interview one of her patients. The thought of being on the news made me nervous, but I couldn't not do it. Without early detection, my tumor would have continued to grow. If my story encouraged even one person to get checked, it was worth it.

The interview took place on my couch. It consisted of a few questions about my Mammotome biopsy and featured some cheesy lifestyle footage of a stack of cancer books on my dining room table and me pretending to type something important on my laptop with a moving closeup of my unmanicured nails hitting the keys. At least they didn't shoot me sitting in a corner, looking out the window, petting the cat.

The interview was broadcast a few days later, a small part of a brief segment. I was proud to take part, even though I had talked too much with my hands and wished I had worn a different outfit.

The very next day, I was back on Dr. Mender's exam table for fill number three. That brought the total to 300 ccs—the amount of half-and-half you'd need for a green-bean casserole.

It seemed like I was nearing my previous (and desired) size, though it was hard to tell without

CHAPTER 11

being able to smoosh my breasts around.

"You don't want to go larger?" asked Dr. Mender. He sounded surprised.

"Not really," I replied.

Somewhere between a big fake bosom and no bosom at all was where I wanted to be. Anything else felt extreme, like plastering a "Breast Cancer Was Here!" sign across my chest, the letters, of course, in pink. I wanted to look like I did before, to saunter through the grocery store undetected, to run the trail without fracturing my jaw.

But I was never going to get an exact replica of my original breasts, not within the parameters of my Jackhole insurance coverage. Implants are complicated. You don't just choose a cup size and pop it in. There are a million factors to consider, like how they will sit inside your reconfigured chest—one might be centered, the other slightly off to the side—and whether your skin will accommodate an ampler size without causing permanent stretch marks. The implants themselves have characteristics to consider such as texture, shape, and, most important, content, whether silicone gel or saline saltwater. (I liked the idea of chocolate mousse but they don't make those yet.)

The best I could do was make an educated guess and hope Dr. Mender got it right. I felt some sample implants, held them up to my chest and estimated the size. As far as whether to go with saline or silicone gel, the saline was firmer, the silicone gel squishier.

I'd read that silicone gel implants had once been banned by the FDA because of concerns related to auto-immune diseases. They were supposedly safe now, but the FDA still required implant manufacturers to conduct "post-approval" studies, and it recommended that women with these implants get routine MRIs to detect rupturing. The FDA's approach seemed backward to me. Shouldn't safety come before approval for use? And if the implants really were safe, why would I need to check for ruptures? Something didn't add up.

You'd know if a saline implant ruptured, because it would deflate. Its harmless contents would then be absorbed into your body and eventually flushed out via urination. The same couldn't be said for silicone gel, which leaked slowly and was too often associated with health risks. Saline was good enough for me.

"Then you're mostly done," Dr. Mender said.

That left one last fill of the expanders and two weeks of overstretching my skin to create the natural droop I wanted (I had never been accused of being perky; I wasn't going to start now). Around the end of November, I'd be ready to exchange the expanders for implants via surgery.

"Unless you have to have chemo," said Dr. Mender.

I had mentioned that the oncologist had said chemo was probably unnecessary, but that we were

CHAPTER 11

waiting on some test results to be sure. Dr. Mender didn't want to schedule my exchange surgery until the decision was made. Chemo made you more vulnerable to infection. Surgery would be too risky. We could proceed with the last expander fill, but if I did have chemo, the implants would have to wait.

❖

As my expanders rose, my life settled into a sort-of pre-cancer groove. Marit's departure after my birthday weekend marked the end of visitors. I'd miss the company but it was time to resume chores, errands, and cleaning the cat box on my own. I was able to resume work, too, and anxious to do so, what with a $5,000 deductible hanging over my head. By the beginning of November, thanks to some undaunted clients, I had projects on my desk. None were particularly complicated—ideal for easing back into the game.

On November 2, I reclined on Dr. Mender's exam table for my last expander fills.

"Any word on chemotherapy?" he asked.

"Any day now," I replied. "What's exchange surgery like?"

It was an outpatient procedure, he explained. The patient would be anesthetized, her expanders would be replaced with implants, and the doctor would stitch her back up. The whole thing would take about an hour.

Same as LensCrafters, I thought. LensCrafters for tits.

Without chemo, we were looking at surgery at the end of the month. I was so happy to see the light at the end of the tunnel, to bring at least part of cancer treatment to a close, that not even the ensuing Clydesdale-sized charley horse kicking across my chest could bring me down.

More potential good news came later that day when Dr. Perry's office called with the results of the genetic test. I was negative for the BRCA1 and BRCA2 gene mutations associated with breast and ovarian cancers. But the results were shaded with caution—a BRCA mutation could have been missed; a different, as-yet-unidentified mutation could be lurking; completely different cancers could still arise. All to say: I was still at risk. It was like winning the lottery and being handed Monopoly money, fun to think about, but you can't actually buy anything. We were still waiting for the Oncotype test results, which we expected to show a low chance of recurrence, making chemo unnecessary.

In theory, I was on a roll. I was excited and grateful that my predicament hadn't been worse. I also felt horrible that so many other breast cancer survivors didn't have it so easy. You should do something, I thought. You're one of the lucky ones, you should do something to help.

Guilt: The great motivator.

CHAPTER 11

❖

That night, I set aside my disdain for pink and registered on Austin's Race for the Cure website to walk in that weekend's event. When I reached the part of the form that asked if I was registering as a survivor, I surprised myself and checked "Yes." That meant that the volunteer who put my registration packet together would have to include a special survivor t-shirt—one that would publicly identify me as a bona fide member of the cancer club.

But I don't want to be a member of the cancer club, I thought. I'm not ready to go public.

Then uncheck the box, I countered.

I suppose I had already come out as a survivor when I did the interview with the local news station on the Mammotome biopsy. But that was from the safety of my own home. Only the reporter and cameraman were privy, and when they left I put my sweats back on and went back to being me. I would never have to see the faces of the viewers or hear them feel sorry for me.

The Race for the Cure would be different: live, uncomfortable, with scores of supporters cheering participants on, especially those in the special survivor t-shirts. We would symbolize strength and hope and, for some, bravery. But I couldn't get past my discomfort. I didn't feel sick, but wearing that shirt would label me as such and invite pity. I didn't want to be defined by cancer. Just thinking about it put me on the defensive.

Guilt pulled me back.

Just because they give you a t-shirt doesn't mean you have to wear it, I thought. And c'mon, t-shirt or no t-shirt, who's going to notice you anyway? Someone you passed on the freeway? The girl from Office Max? Your face will be one of hundreds. It's not like anyone is going to recognize you and think, "Oh my God! I know her! She bought a ream of paper from my store the other day, and now she has awful horrible cancer! Poor thing!"

I love rationalizing with myself, especially when I'm right. Countless people go to these events wearing every shade of pink conceivable, and a lot of them would be wearing the special t-shirt. If anything, I'd blend in. I was more of an adjunct survivor anyway; I had had early-stage cancer, no chemo—cancer lite at best. My role would be to support true survivors, not muddy their limelight.

Convinced it was safe to participate, that I could hide in the pink, and maybe even feel good about doing it, I submitted the registration form with the survivor box checked "Yes."

The next day, I went down to the event center to pick up my packet. Inside were a race bib and the special survivor t-shirt in dark fuchsia, a color you might see on the plumes of a burlesque dancer at the Flamingo in Las Vegas.

CHAPTER 11

Two days later, I walked from my apartment to Auditorium Shores, a park that runs alongside downtown Austin's Lady Bird Lake, heading for the Race for the Cure starting line. In a parking lot near the lake, some women got out of a minivan. They were all dressed in athletic wear, so I figured they were participating in the day's event. They noticed me, too.

"That's what the survivor shirts look like," one of them said, pointing in my direction.

So much for blending in. I kept a straight face, kept walking, wanting to say: I ran a half-marathon once. Been to Ireland and Spain; placed third in barrel racing at horse camp; performed sketch comedy in front of a live audience. Hosting a deadly disease before the age of forty wasn't something I was particularly proud of.

With hindsight, I would realize I was recoiling from an image lurking in my unconscious. It featured an enormous and faceless crowd of pink. I didn't want to join them because I didn't want to lose myself.

In the moment, I was oblivious to this source of aversion. All I knew was that other survivors seemed to have achieved a degree of acceptance and resilience I wasn't capable of. The survivor lunch ladies in particular seemed so in control and confident; there was no choice but to see them as individual people first and patients second, third, or even fourth. I wished I could channel their grip on cancer while protecting my identity, but I couldn't get past feeling embarrassed and angry, and, deeper down, afraid that I wouldn't live long enough to try. What I failed to consider was that this "grip on cancer" I so admired, hadn't just magically appeared. It was wrought with the same staggering emotional upheaval I was experiencing. These survivors were ahead of me in the process but no less affected. An inflated and unfair—albeit unconscious—characterization was stoking my anger and fear. I was ashamed of that, too, since I could have instead let myself be inspired by other survivors' dignity and personal power.

I resented my diagnosis and all the bad feelings that came with it: wondering why I got cancer, if it was karmic payback for something ugly I'd done. Quickly, I dismissed the thought as both ridiculous and insulting to anyone who has ever faced adversity. But genetic fuckery or bad luck wasn't good enough. I wanted something specific to blame, like a toxic exposure incident. Which I would never get; getting cancer would never make sense. I berated myself for not being more grateful for my stage-one pass, for seeing the day's event as glamorizing a hard and selfish disease, and for wanting to scrap the flimsy ribbons and thin balloons for Special Ops docs who would sneak up on cancer cells and snap their little necks so that I, the ladies across the parking lot, and everyone at Auditorium Shores could just go home.

Wearing the fuchsia shirt felt phony. But not wearing it would have felt like a betrayal of the volunteers and supporters, my fellow diagnosed, and the unsurvivors. So green and so blinded by pink, I saw only two paths—participate and stew with every step or not participate and deal with the guilt. I thought I was on the road to reconciling these jangled feelings, but being called out in public had yanked me back. I was adamantly against being seen as a survivor; I just wanted to be me.

I'm done trying to be good at cancer, I thought. After this event, it's time to move on.

❖

"Your Oncotype test results are higher than I expected," the oncologist said in early November.

He added: "Patients with your score have an Average Rate of Distant Recurrence at ten years of 20 percent."

He explained: "You're at the high end of the Intermediate Risk group."

As in a slow, methodical lashing, each sentence felt heavier than the last.

"I'm going to recommend chemotherapy," he said.

But, I thought, I'm only stage one. Ready for exchange surgery. Everyone's waiting for me to catch up, to move on.

Part of me felt like I was being held back in school, like I had to spend summer inside, face down in subjects I didn't understand, while all the healthy kids got to play outdoors. But what I really felt was that I was being punished for daring to think I was done with cancer, for not wanting to be part of the pink, for being excited to walk away. Underneath it all was dread that the cancer would come back and be terminal. My fear didn't allow for in-between scenarios; it bolted from recurrence to early death. That's how fear works. I was only stage one, but the test proved that the type of cancer I had was more serious than I'd thought.

Not so fast, said a voice in my head. Cancer may still be here. Slow down and do what you have to do to get rid of it.

I would step up to chemo the way I did surgery. Make it a project. Break it down into attainable steps that I could put behind me. I would follow the recommendations of the experts I trusted and do what had to be done.

Chapter 12

*Living referrals—a must-have when
shopping for an oncologist.*
—Journal Entry

IT DIDN'T OCCUR to me to not get chemo. I was more concerned with getting enough. The oncologist with the German-sounding name recommended four rounds of a two-drug therapy. But Dr. Tucker, from whom I sought a second opinion the very next day, and who was also surprised by my score, recommended a more aggressive six rounds of a three-drug therapy. He wanted to knock any chances of recurrence out.

"If it comes back," Dr. Tucker said, "it's not curable."

I hated those words so much. Hated that they came out of the mouth of an authority on the subject, riling and affirming my deepest fear. He might as well have said that without chemo I would die.

"I know, okay? I get it!" I wanted to shout. "I'll do the fucking chemo. I'll do anything."

"I'm good with the more aggressive approach," I said. "Let's do it."

Dr. Tucker came highly recommended by a colleague whose husband the doctor had treated ten years before. I liked that he had a living referral and that he had squeezed me into his schedule so quickly, though it meant going to the appointment by myself—no Linda or my sister coming along and taking notes. I liked his more aggressive recommendation—I would do almost anything to prevent recurrence—and his confidence that I was young and healthy enough to handle the side effects. I liked that he was smart and handsome with a dry sense of humor, and that he had married one of his former patients. He and his wife hadn't let cancer or a fear of recurrence stand in the way of love. Love post-cancer did happen.

The other thing I liked about Dr. Tucker was that he used email. That gave me a direct line to the person who would be in charge of adding years to my life.

"I was thinking about your case this weekend," he wrote in an email after I agreed to be under his care. "I think that 'chemo lite' would not be good enough. So, doing six rounds of chemo is more arduous than four, but I honestly think it is better for increasing the chance of cure as much as possible. I

CHAPTER 12

look forward to working with you."

Dad reviewed Dr. Tucker's bio and agreed with his recommendation. Dad was my personal expert, and his approval, as well as the consenting nods from the rest of my family and friends, confirmed I was doing the smart best thing.

I had an oncologist now; I was a chemo patient.

What I knew about chemo consisted of nausea and those pale, bald, pajama-clad kids in St. Jude's Research Hospital ads. And quilts. The rare movie or TV character going through chemo always seemed to be in a chair or bed draped with a quilt. The quilt was like the national flag for cancer. Countries drape flags over the coffins of their soldiers—a symbol of honor. Families drape quilts over the bodies of cancer patients—a symbol of anguish and love.

My limited chemo knowledge prompted a lot of questions. Should I be doing something to prepare for my first infusion or do I just show up? How long will it take? Should I bring my laptop or a book? Some Tupperware to throw up in? A quilt?

Between Dr. Tucker and a stack of patient handouts, I started to get a feel for how things went down.

The week before my first chemo, I would have a small plastic port surgically implanted under my collarbone. Like Platform Nine and Three-Quarters, the port allowed the chemo concoction safe passage into my vein. The actual infusions would take place at the cancer center where Dr. Tucker worked.

I would go once every three weeks for a total of six infusions over eighteen weeks. The first visit would take three to four hours, the remaining five about two hours each.

Side effects varied depending on the drugs and patient, but one thing was for sure, I would have them. Hair loss and nausea were just two of a smorgasbord of possibilities. In fact, reading the handouts on side effects was like perusing the menu at Denny's: something for everyone, but nothing you'd want to take home and reheat the next day. And despite the toll, most chemo patients continued going to work, making Friday a popular infusion day. The worst days in a chemo cycle were the first few after infusion, and getting infused on a Friday gave you the whole weekend to get most of what felt like the latest avian flu out of the way. Going to work on the following Monday might be crappier than normal but not as crappy as it could be.

I, too, planned on working through chemo. But I was lucky. Since I worked for myself, I wouldn't have to cram feeling crappy into my weekend. I could feel crappy pretty much any day of the week.

"The sooner you start the better," Dr. Tucker said. "If you can get the [port] in next week, we can start the Monday after Thanksgiving."

Getting the port in was just the beginning. Chemo required all kinds of preparation. In a matter of minutes, my to-do list, home to such banal and unhurried tasks as grocery shopping and getting a boot reheeled, was transformed into a measurable action plan with deadlines.

Pre-Chemo To-Do
- Schedule port surgery with Dr. Perry
- Sign up for Chemo 101 at cancer center
- Get tooth filled (to avoid infection!)
- Get anti-bacterial hand gel (see above)
- Get flu shot
- Get oyster crackers, ginger candy, ginger ale, ginger tea, ginger everything (for nausea)
- Call Jackhole re: insurance coverage for wig
- Really enjoy Thanksgiving (because it's all downhill after that)

I managed to get it all done in time, including a short but important visit with Dr. Mender, since having chemo meant postponing surgery for the expander/implant exchange.

"You can have surgery as soon as a week after your last chemo cycle," he said, sympathetically. "So, probably next April."

"Great!" I lied. As certain as I was that chemo was the right thing to do, I was not looking forward to hoisting the iron-bra expanders around for another four months. With the injections complete, at least it looked like I had breasts. They were just so hard and unforgiving, a constant reminder of the long road ahead.

Whether it was the rolling of my eyes, or combo scrunched-up nose and heavy sigh, Dr. Mender picked up on my frustration. "Come see me any time you want to vent or talk about it," he continued. And he meant it.

An oncologist who emails and a plastic surgeon who encourages me to vent? What next? A gynecologist who projects episodes of *Friends* onto the ceiling during a pap smear? Now, that would be something.

❖

Everyone in my family offered to come for the port surgery—or before, if I needed them. But deciding who to have come and when required careful thought. I worried that my scheduling choices would imply that I loved one person over another: You come first because I love you most. You come last because I love you least. The ways in which my actions might be perceived was one of a series of considerations—however unreasonable—that I cycled through before making any decisions involving family.

Avoiding conflict was something I had been doing for as long as I could remember. It had to do with being the youngest child, with wanting to keep the peace. It was most pronounced in the years after my parents' divorce, when I thought I could and should attend to the various chasms, divots, and

CHAPTER 12

dings that had arisen between certain family members in its wake—relationships strained by words and silence, resentment and miles. I hated the discord and thought I could fix things by being a neutral sounding board, translator, and messenger. I went as far as to think it was my job and that I could do it and come out unscathed. But it wasn't my job, and I wasn't good at it. If Mom was upset with my brother for saying her fancy new car was a waste of money, for example, I might say, "He's under a lot of pressure at work" and "I'm sure he didn't mean it." Then I might call my brother and gingerly say that Mom was hurt that he wasn't more excited about her car. While my intent would be to smooth things out, I would only make them worse. In this scenario, I would make Mom feel like she was overreacting while also letting my brother know that we were talking about him behind his back. Instead of just listening to Mom, I risked causing both parties to also be irritated with me, which I would then personalize and regret. Fun.

Who was I to try to change people and fix things? Everyone in my family was a grown-up, all with their own experiences and perceptions, their own personalities and desires, none any less important than my own. Harmony wasn't a fact of life and entertaining the notion that it ought to be was naïve. All I could do was maintain individual relationships with my family members, keeping tension at bay. It felt important to do this even when it came to planning my own cancer treatment. Old habits die hard.

My family was more than supportive; they would do whatever I needed them to do. It was all up to me, which meant it was all up to me. I wished the scheduling would take care of itself, but that wasn't realistic. It was up to me to coordinate the details. Like a bride planning her wedding, I wanted this special occasion to go down a certain way. Staying mindful of distance and availability, checkbooks, discomfort on planes, and the effects of being in an unfamiliar city, I submitted my requests. I trusted my family knew how much I appreciated them and that it would all fall into place. They didn't let me down.

On a Friday morning, ten days before I would start chemo, Dr. Perry spent a quick thirty minutes installing a port into my chest. If there was an award for the most forgettable surgical procedure, this might be it. The port, a hard, circular bump protruding from my chest, looked like something out of the *X-Files*, a kind of tracking device that was transmitting my every thought to the government, or worse, to my mom.

❖

The weekend following port surgery, Dad and Janet flew in for their turn at Dena Duty and an early Thanksgiving. At dinner one night, I tapped on the port as if it were a microphone. "Is this thing on?" I mused. They laughed. I winced because it was still pretty sore, but really because it was such a tired joke.

Their visit would be short but sweet and familiar. Our dinners together were always unhurried. They often featured Dad explaining an astronomical event or new tool in his shop, which he would support with a sketch on a napkin. We talked about their upcoming trip to Japan, his sister Steenie's passing, and my chemo plan. They expressed their support and complimented me on how well I was handling everything, but none of us let cancer dominate our conversation or our weekend together. I didn't want it to.

Chapter 13

Dear friends and family,

You've got your aromatherapy. You've got your massage therapy. But nothing says Happy Holidays quite like chemotherapy.

The oncologists have spoken, and chemo is the order of the day. Dena, who is now being referred to as Bad Ass Chemo-D, will undergo six cycles of chemo, once every three weeks. This has its risks (leukemia, heart damage, etc.) but they are teeny-weeny compared to the benefit.

Hair loss is guaranteed. I'm already looking into head cozies and an array of holiday adornments from popcorn garlands to antlers. Or perhaps a tattoo that simply asks, "Where's Hairdo?"

A kajillion thanks for your love, support, and prayers. Your kindness has brought me to tears and given me the confidence to fight this hairlessly head-on.

Please look for my new Holiday CD with

CHAPTER 13

such hits as "Here comes Chemo Claus" and "I'm gettin' Chemo for Christmas," and the release of "Six Cycle," my film collaboration with fellow-rapper Eminem.

—Email to Family and Friends

I'D HEARD THAT the discovery of chemo-induced hair loss can be unsettling, gruesome even, like stumbling upon a crime scene. Lifeless strands are found stuck to car headrests, stacked around shower drains, and sprawled on pillows, and the longer the hair the more striking the scene.

"There's a lot of hair here," the detective might say, "but where's the body?"

I decided to have my hair cut short—one more thing to add to my to-do list. An appointment was set for the day after Thanksgiving. My first infusion would be the following Monday. Since most people had the day off, I invited a few friends to meet me at the salon. I don't typically invite friends to my haircuts, but this one would be a *bon voyage* party for my hair and life sans chemo. "See ya next year!" I imagined my friends saying. "Can't wait to see pictures!" no one would say.

The night before my appointment, I gazed at my scalp in the mirror, noting the wiry coarseness of the occasional grays and the contrast they created. They seemed extra angry and defiant, like they knew what was coming. Their unwillingness to play twenty-eight embarrassed me. I wouldn't be sad to see them go.

The next day, I sipped white wine and gabbed with friends Suzanne, Ava, Alisa, and Linda at my local salon while stylist Francesca cut off nearly half of my hair and shaped what was left into an inverted bob. "I like your hair better short," said Alisa.

I was surprised they all showed up, reading into their presence the seriousness of my situation. With the exception of Linda, I had only known these women for three years, and here they were spending their day off watching their friend—the one who had the cancer—get a haircut. But what they did after they showed up was what struck me the most: they didn't give chemo the spotlight. They didn't pepper me with questions about treatment or tell me how sorry they were that I had to go through this horrible, awful thing. We swapped Thanksgiving anecdotes and talked about how we'd eaten too much, about the offbeat commentary by family members, and about what we were doing the rest of the weekend. There was no shortage of humor, which is what bonded me to each of these incredible women in the first place. They brought kindness but, more important, they brought their real, funny selves, transforming what could have been an emotionally charged event into a show of strength.

I was again reminded of the survivor luncheon ladies and how they talked about cancer with seeming ease. It wasn't that cancer was easy. At some point, they—we—had to find a way to balance the anguish of this disease with everyday life. We didn't have the choice to just stop. We had to wedge the doctor appointments, injections, and side effects among work, household chores, and haircuts. In a way, this wedging of cancer was a demotion. Cancer wasn't the ruling party but the stubborn, uninvited guest. I liked framing it this way and wondered if it was how the luncheon ladies got to where they were.

Chapter 14

Will people tire of me? When I'm on month two of chemo, who is going to listen to me without getting tired of it?
—Journal Entry

SHOWING UP FOR my first chemo was like forcing myself to go on a date with someone who gave me the creeps. Whether I doubted my instincts or felt overly judgy, I would talk myself into going. If nothing else it would make a good story.

"And then he hit me over the head and I woke up bleeding in a freezer!"

It would be good practice.

"I've gotten really good at detecting the subtle nuances of a bloodthirsty psychopath."

I'd grow from the experience.

"I've realized that basements and brooders do not a love nest make."

And that nothing good in life comes easy.

CHAPTER 14

"I may be a Xanax-popping claustrophobic but I got to wake up today. I'm alive."

❖

"Want something to take the edge off?" Dr. Tucker asked, before ushering me into the infusion room.

"No, thank you," I groaned, noting the irony of being offered drugs to ease the anxiety of taking drugs. Nothing was going to make the injection of a mustard gas derivative any less stressful. Honestly.

The L-shaped infusion room had all the trappings of a commercial office space: it was large and open with a bank of windows, rectangle after rectangle of overhead fluorescent lighting, and bathrooms with heavy wood doors and bronze-finish handles. But instead of cubicles lining the perimeter, there were gathering areas. Each of these areas was anchored by an oversized recliner flanked by IV poles, pillows, and blankets. With warm-toned carpeting, cushy armchairs, side tables adorned with boxes of tissue, magazines, dishes of candy, and a TV, each of these areas was like a mini drawing room. The only things missing were a grand piano and a sleeping Whippet.

I was led to a recliner and dutifully fell in.

Tay, who had returned for a few days to help me manage any side effects, joined Alice and Linda in kicking off my inaugural infusion. The three of them

I DON'T WANNA BE PINK

gathered around my chair, and as if it were kindergarten story time, we listened intently as the nurse told us tales of needles and IVs, of drugs so powerful they had to be injected by hand to prevent severe blistering, and of nadir, the seven- to fourteen-day window after an infusion when patients were most vulnerable to infection. Going to Target during nadir would be like covering yourself in *au jus* and walking into a swarm of yellow jackets—you'd be asking for it.

Story time sucked.

In an undazzling transformation from raconteur to master bartender, the nurse began preparations to serve me the concoctions that would save my life. She started with saline to flush my port.

Like an old pincushion or dartboard, I was getting used to being stuck with needles. That didn't mean I liked it. When I was offered a spray of lidocaine to numb my port before the nurse inserted the needle for the IV, I went for it. I watched, transfixed, as the needle disappeared into my chest without causing a twinge of pain. The nurse hung the clear plastic bag of saline from the IV pole and plugged me in, and just like that, I joined the ranks of the infused.

About fifteen of us dotted the infusion room that day, propped up in our La-Z-Boy-like thrones and tethered to IV poles from which dangled these transparent bags of drugs. It reminded me of a restaurant in my neighborhood, where plastic bags of

CHAPTER 14

water hung from the patio rafters to ward off insects. If only tumors were like bugs, I thought. If bags of water didn't keep a tumor away, you could just swat it with a rolled-up newspaper.

Among the patients were an elderly man dozing under the cover of a worn, navy-plaid quilt he must have brought from home; a middle-aged woman with a purple scarf around her bald head, knitting what looked like baby booties; and another middle-aged woman who stared blankly at the TV like you would a cup of coffee in the microwave or clothes in the dryer—waiting for the thing to be done, waiting to survive.

The nurses weaved their way from patient to nurses' station to pharmacist's window to patient, traveling inside a steady hum of instructive dialogue, ringing phones, cable news, and contained conversation. You rarely saw a doctor in the chemo room. This show belonged to the nurses.

After ten minutes of saline, the nurse returned with a round of pre-meds: anti-nausea to prevent Exorcist-grade projectile vomiting and steroids to prevent unsightly allergic reactions. It would take about an hour to down both bags, during which the ladies and I deflected first-timer awkwardness by swapping holiday plans and discussing the latest celebrity gossip, from a rock star's divorce to a surprise baby bump.

Following the pre-med aperitifs, it was time for

the strong stuff—three assassin elixirs, each so powerful that they had to be administered one at a time. For the first dose, the nurse had me confirm that the name and birth date on the label were mine. Then she ran the bag up the IV pole for a forty-minute drip. Feeling more settled, Tay, Alice, Linda, and I oscillated between small talk and retreating into our email or whatever issue of *Time Magazine* lingered nearby. It meant everything to have them there with me. Their presence calmed my nerves.

My second drug was the one we had been warned about during story time, the one so toxic it had to be injected slowly by hand to prevent leakage and blistering. For ten long minutes, I sat still, pushing away visions of bubbling, disintegrating flesh as the nurse pushed a fat syringe full of what looked like cherry Kool-Aid into my IV.

The third and final ingredient of my chemo cocktail was a mustard-gas derivative destined to slow or stop cancer cell growth. As it dripped into my vein, I imagined a Wudang warrior from *Crouching Tiger, Hidden Dragon*—slight, lithe, and undetectable, taking out slumbering cells with a single pass of her sword before backflipping out of their bedroom windows, somersaulting onto neighboring roofs, and spinning upside down into the night.

Thirty minutes into this hour-long drip, I rolled my IV pole into the bathroom, took a seat—and gasped. The cherry Kool-Aid drug that had been

CHAPTER 14

injected less than an hour before was coming out an electric shade of burnt orange. Austin is home to the University of Texas Longhorns whose official colors are white and burnt-orange. In fact, the whole town bleeds burnt orange on game days (and on regular days too). You'll find burnt-orange t-shirts, travel mugs, and ball caps for sale at the grocery store; your mechanic will drink his coffee out of a burnt-orange travel mug; and you'd be hard-pressed not to see at least three burnt-orange Longhorns decals or Hook 'em Horns bumper stickers during your morning commute. Now I was bleeding burnt orange too, which was insincere, considering I wasn't really a fan.

"Hook this!" I said aloud before reaching for the toilet handle and flushing it away.

With Alice and Linda off to pick up their kids from preschool (two each by this time) and my sister engrossed in a *National Geographic*, I spent the last twenty minutes of my drug drip studying the young couple across from us. I had noticed them earlier in the waiting room, partially because they were young—I'd guess early thirties—but mostly because of the wig the wife was wearing.

How does one know when someone is wearing a wig? It's subconscious at first; you know something isn't right but you're not sure what. I've experienced it dozens of times with older men, when the rich color of a toupee is at odds with the tone and character of a man's skin. You'd think it'd be less noticeable on a young woman whose skin is supple and unmarred by time, but then again, we were sitting in a cancer center where everyone's crown was up for grabs. The wig wasn't awful—a straight, brown, shoulder-length number with a part in the middle—but it hung lifeless and heavy. It reminded me of the wigs you see on those styrofoam heads in vintage clothing stores, waiting to become part of someone's story.

The most natural looking wigs are made from real hair, be it one's own or donated locks, and can cost upwards of thousands of dollars. The young woman and I had something in common. If I ended up deciding to get a wig, I wouldn't buy a real-hair one, either—even if I could afford it. It was too much for a temporary fix. I'd rather save my money for post-chemo clothes or a trip. So I would end up looking more or less like her, just older.

As the last dose of drugs dwindled into my port, I caught myself staring at the luster of the wigged woman's wedding band. I bet they hadn't been married that long and wondered which came first, the wedding or the diagnosis. It wasn't hard to imagine cancer fueling an expedited union, and when they looked up, I tendered a knowing smile, assuming that whatever the order of their lives' events, they had that unified front that many other couples seemed to lack.

I stopped short of initiating a conversation—something you want to be careful about doing in an infusion room. You have no idea what the other person might be going through. Imagine being stage one and pressing your infusion neighbor for their story, only to find out they're stage four. I'd feel pretty shitty whichever side of that conversation I was on. It's one thing for someone to elect to share a diagnosis, it's another to go digging uninvited.

In a way, cancer is like prison—people locked in a struggle with its own class system. There are those who have zero-stage cancer, those with middle stages, those with recurrence, those with secondary cancers, and those with mets (metastasized cancer). Some will have well-known cancers that receive a lot of public support (like the one drenched in pink), and some will have rare cancers that don't. And let's not forget varying ages and status: there are children, teens, young people, married adults with or without children, single adults, single parents, divorced adults, seniors, widowers. There are those with health insurance and those without; the list goes on and on. As in prison, you observe, find your people, and fall in line. It's the safest route through the mire. No one will ever understand a mets like a mets, a two-time survivor like a two-time survivor, a teenager with leukemia like a teenager with leukemia, or an uninsured patient receiving assistance like an uninsured patient receiving assistance. We all have this awful thing in common, but not quite.

With my drug bag flattened, I was unplugged

and free to go. The nurse advised me to call my doctor right away if any serious side effects occurred. You mean, I wondered, other than losing clumps of hair or barfing up an organ?

She meant the usual suspects: fever, bleeding, shortness of breath. I told her I would call if any of those arose and was elated that the only thing I felt as my sister and I walked down the sidewalk toward my car was a light tingling behind my eyes, awe at the surrealism of where I had just been, and a craving for sushi.

❖

Other than a mild headache and energy dip, I felt surprisingly good over the next few days, which meant Tay was off the hook as nursemaid. We went on walks and out to dinner. She regularly asked how I was feeling, but I had nothing much to report, and plain, noncancer topics crept into our conversations. Like taking your seat after barely catching the bus, it would take us a moment to relax into everyday minutiae. It was a reminder that while a crucial part of being sisters is supporting each other in times of need, the vast majority of the time—the glue—is about celebrity gossip, updates on each other's friends, and weird places to find hairballs (a slipper topped our list). Both of us were used to having our alone time, and we would retreat into our laptops—genealogy, Kauai, and Christmas planning for her;

CHAPTER 14

work, survivor diet, and exercise for me.

I was able to continue working on small projects, including a website for my friend Suzanne's design firm. I even met a pre-chemo commitment to be interviewed by Austin's *Downtown* TV show for an episode on local coffee culture. A friend who knew I did much of my freelancing in coffee shops had recommended me to the producers. At 9 a.m., just two days after my first infusion, I sat at the Halcyon coffee shop on 4th and Lavaca, answering the interviewer's questions and wondering if the camera was picking up on the toxic attack going on under my skin.

After my sister left, and with two and a half weeks until my second chemo, I went about my business as if I had been infused with Pom juice instead of poison. The emerging side effects, which included fatigue, a lone canker sore, and acid reflux, were nothing I hadn't experienced after a typical Austin happy hour of chips, queso, and beer. I even managed some running to clear my head and try to keep my body strong. My hair was suspiciously intact. Either the drugs were placebos, or I was going to be the only recipient of my type of chemo to not lose her hair.

Dr. Tucker was wrong, the handouts were wrong. I was sure of it.

But there's a reason I'm not an oncologist (several, actually). Within days of my thinking I was the great exception, my scalp started tingling, like I had been crowned with a ring of porcupine quills. Then, one day, after a walk on the local hike and bike trail, I pulled off my headband and a horde of hairs came with it. My pillow was covered too. When I tugged at my scalp, the follicles popped off like daisies.

To have this thing that I was warned would happen actually happen gave me a rush. It was like walking through the neighborhood after a violent storm and seeing the downed tree limbs and scattered debris: strangely exciting to witness. A powerful source was at work and I was in awe of what it could do. I was also relieved. There had been so much buildup to baldness, what it would be like, how it would look. I just wanted to get it over with. I didn't need any more surprises. The unknown was known. I could manage it from here.

From the privacy of my bathroom, I fervently plucked every gray hair I could find, no longer worried about a million more growing in their place. It was like stealing points in the last few seconds of a game you know you're going to lose; why not have some fun? Why not finish it on your own terms?

Within twenty-four hours of my scalp-tingling, I had an appointment to get my head shaved at a cancer-friendly wig salon. I was relieved to have Linda come along for the ride.

"You have a big head," the wig stylist said, stuffing the tape measure into her apron pocket. Apparently, underwear wasn't the only thing that could ride up. If you weren't careful, a wig could scooch its way up your big fat skull and pop right off your head. "We'll have to stretch whichever wig you end up getting."

Linda and I locked eyes in the mirror and laughed. With my massively broad shoulders and size ten hooves, hearing that I had a giant head wasn't all that surprising.

I might not have laughed had I been alone. But I wasn't alone; Linda was there, entertaining me with her opinions on the shop's various wig styles, even trying on a few herself. Linda was being Linda—silly, warm, optimistic. Her affable presence prevented me from going into my gargantuan head and getting upset about cancer and chemo and baldness.

So I have a big head, I thought, as the stylist fired up her tools and started shaving away my hair and Linda snapped photos. Big deal. Vanna White has a big head—a huge head, actually. So does Christina Ricci. They are very small women with extremely large heads. At least mine is in proportion to my body and oversized feet.

After the stylist finished, I looked in the mirror and a skinhead stared back. I didn't want to hang on to my sad, dying hair, but seeing my bare scalp with a five o'clock shadow was startling. Wearing an androgynous army green pullover didn't help. I looked militant, like Demi Moore in *G.I. Jane* sans the sleek physique and sexy confidence. My new look was bold by accident. For the next six-plus months—until chemo was done, my hair grew back, I could ditch the wig, and I was free to leave Cancer Land—sexy confidence was for other, healthier women. Anything remotely related to attraction and the opposite sex was a someday idea.

Linda said I looked more Sinead O'Connor than skinhead, and that I had a nicely shaped head. Either way, it was severe and would take time to process. In the meantime, I settled on looking like me without hair. Until I could hide under my wig, which would be ready the following week, I would have to endure the public dare-to-stare. That Linda was with me for round one made it possible to get through.

At the register, another stylist took my order for a brown, shoulder-length wig (a shorter version of the one the young woman at the cancer center wore). She told us that her mother had been in her thirties when she died of breast cancer. The stylist had had her own breasts removed to lower the chances of the same happening to her. I would have done exactly the same thing had I been the stylist. I got it. Giving up breasts and hair, absorbing toxins—it was a way of taking charge. It felt good, like some things were in our control.

The stylist handed me a white button with pink letters that spelled Fuck Cancer. I had seen this phrase before, and loved it. I loved how the two negatives made a positive—the word for the menacing disease pushed to the right by the crude word for defiance, the spirited stance that would inform every step of treatment. I loved how it was honest, angry, dismissive, and funny all at the same time. It felt even better to say. It was a good way to punctuate the shaving of my head. Along with Linda by my side, it inspired me to walk into the world with my bald head held high.

❖

That night, I was back at the mirror, scar-gazing. The halfway-reconstructed breasts were hard and unyielding, and now my head was hard and unyielding. This was how I looked now—rough: patchwork breasts, protruding port, and shaved head. Baldness was the ultimate public manifestation, the announcement that this body was under siege. It was hard not to cry. I tore myself away, forced myself into bed, reading pages from a book I can't remember in an effort to sleep with someone else's life on my mind. It didn't work. I dreamt that Daniel Craig was spending the night and we were going to have sex but I wanted to keep my sweatshirt on so he couldn't see the construction underneath. When I glimpsed myself in a dream mirror over the dresser, I looked like a troll. My hair was over-permed and thinning, my eyes were red and underscored with dark circles. I was horrified by what I had become.

Steve Hill — Compassionate friend on diagnosis day, fashionable travel companion à Paris.

Duane Taylor, MD — My amazing dad and the doctor whose opinion I value most, with his wife Janet, Salem, Oregon's 56th mayor, wedding weekend in Alaska.

Mom and sister Tay—They dropped everything to care for me post-mastectomy and lifted me up in every sense of the word.

Mom—Thoughtful, funny, caregiver; sometime air traffic controller.

My favorite Viking and would-be Italy companion, Marit, celebrating my 40th with me in Austin. Her support was everything.

Thomas Tucker, MD — Expert oncologist whose humor and personable approach gave me confidence that I could handle chemo.

CHAPTER 14

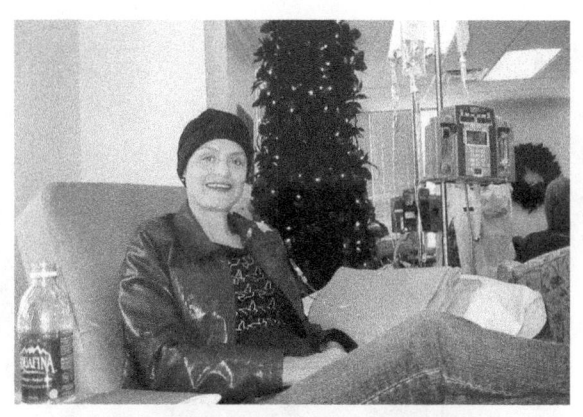

Chemo for Christmas—One of six chemo infusions, every three weeks, starting the Monday after Thanksgiving and ending the following March.

Once my hair gave way to chemo, Linda took me to the wig store for a shave and fitting, followed by pancake therapy at Austin's Kerbey Lane Cafe.

Allison, Linda, Alice and my itchy wig enjoy a night out—the latter's days were numbered. (L-R)

The result of not letting chemo get in the way of creating my annual holiday card.

End-of-chemo trip to Belize with Alice (pictured) and Allison—the first mindless respite since being diagnosed eight months before.

With Leslie Phinney of Phinney/Bischoff Design House—the folks behind the Walk for Dena— on a post-treatment visit to Seattle.

*Mom on our shore excursion in Copenhagen—
more fun than fundraising walks at sea.*

*My big brother, Paul, near his cabin in
Alaska, the place he feels most at home.*

*My sister-in-law, Melinda, with Bailey, in Alaska.
Her love and support meant the world.*

*With Steve and Linda in Paris, which "should
be part of every treatment plan."*

The drummer from New Orleans embracing the moment, in Post Park on the Peña Colorado River, West Texas.

Tay, Rob, Mom and I celebrating the holidays at the Gage Hotel in Marathon, West Texas, the trip that brought my unofficial post-treatment tour to a close.

On safari in Tanzania, Africa, embracing being, "spectacularly outside my comfort zone," and taking back my life.

Chapter 15

I'm so touched. Too tired to cry now but I did earlier. How do I thank these people? I don't know how to thank them.
—Journal Entry

I DON'T SPEND much time in the kitchen. I can make a few things, but cooking doesn't come naturally. I also find the best part, the eating, to be fleeting—bookended by the toil of preparation and drudgery of cleaning up. So December 23 was already an unusual day. It was the one day of the year I was actually in the kitchen baking.

Earlier in the week, I had received my second infusion and two shots of a bone-aching white-blood-cell booster. With the worst of the side effects behind me, and Christmas coming, I was inspired to make a batch of what I called Chemo Snap cookies. I was stirring the dough and talking on the phone to my dear friend Ruth, another beautiful soul from

CHAPTER 15

my Starbucks days, who still lived in Seattle, when FedEx delivered a package to my door.

"It's from Stephanie in Bothell, Washington," I said, reading the airbill aloud. Neither Ruth nor I knew of any Stephanies in Bothell, but it was clearly addressed to me, and I proceeded to tear it open. Inside was a frosty plastic envelope wrapped around a smaller iridescent green envelope with my name penned on the front. Enclosed was a custom-designed card that started: "Dena dearest—We froze our asses off just for you."

I was struck by the humor. Whoever was behind this knew how to get my attention. I read on.

"On a recent chilly Saturday morning in December—11 dogs and 32 people braved the cold and walked around Green Lake to show our love and support for you."

With Ruth patiently holding the line, I finished reading the card and attempted to comprehend the substantial numeric total of the two checks tucked inside—enough to cover my current and following year's health insurance deductibles. I was stunned and speechless (the latter, quite a feat). This already unusual day had just become extraordinary, and more than a little uncomfortable.

The gesture was grand, the moment surreal. I was in shock and embarrassed to have been the subject of an event I'd heard nothing about. I got that I was the recipient of a significant amount of money, but pieces were missing, like who was behind the surprise. The card was signed "your family and friends," but that was still anonymous. I needed to know whom to thank. The sooner I could properly acknowledge this enormous act of kindness, the sooner I could shove the mushrooming confusion of emotions out of my head.

"Was this part of Race for the Cure or something?" I asked Ruth. Ruth was a loyal and compassionate friend. We had watched each other's pets over the years and consoled each other when it came time to put one of them down. We had commiserated over the ups and downs of jobs and relationships, and found a way to laugh at life's sometimes absurd turns of events. She had been immediately supportive when she heard I had cancer, and it came as no surprise that she had participated in the very event we were discussing. Nor was it a surprise that when party to a secret, Ruth would keep it hidden. All she would say was that the walk had been organized to support my cause.

"It really was cold, though," she added. "My butt really did go numb."

Undeterred, I tapped an informant and found out that my former employer/friends at Phinney/Bischoff Design House in Seattle had coordinated a "Walk for Dena," a "freezing-our-asses-off-campaign" to help a freelance writer with some hefty medical bills.

CHAPTER 15

With the mystery solved, I was free to wrestle with feeling grateful, humbled, and ashamed. My vulnerability chord was struck and swelling. Asking for help was one thing, but to be seen as needing help—enough to motivate a group of people to subject their derrieres to bitter cold and part from their own hard-earned money—was an overwhelming other.

"But I'll find a way to pay things off—it'll be fine!" I exclaimed to Marit on the phone later. "I didn't complain about my ridiculous insurance deductible so that people would give me money. Complaining about insurance is just what people do. Bitching about customer service hold times, indecipherable policies, and clerical errors brings people together. Everyone knows that."

She humored me until I added, "I just feel like this should go to someone who really needs it. Like some little cancer girl."

"But Dena," she replied. "You are the little cancer girl."

Like most people, I would have much preferred being on the ass-freezing side of things to being the recipient of aid. It was a predictable reaction—hence the anonymity of the gift; not knowing where it came from eliminated the chance of giving it back.

I was running a charity double standard, okay to give but not to receive. My ego couldn't stand the thought of being perceived as less than strong and capable, a thought so self-absorbed and ugly it made me cringe. But there was a deeper emotion at work. It wasn't about perception; it was that I was still angry about having cancer. I was responding to it, stepping up to treatment, but I was far from full acceptance. I didn't need money as much as a swift kick in the ass. You have support, medical care, and now money to pay for it! I wanted to scream. You had cancer, but your situation could be so much worse. Please, for fuck's sake, get over yourself.

Had the tables been turned, had it been a friend of mine struggling to accept help, I would have told her that no one thought she wasn't strong or capable; rather, they thought she'd been dealt a bad hand and they simply wanted to help her get back on her feet. Wouldn't you do the same for me? I would ask.

I added Catholic guilt to my inventory of feelings. I didn't mean to sound like I thought I was too good for help. I love help! Any time someone wants to come over and vacuum the inside of my car or fix the crooked towel rack in the bathroom, they're more than welcome. But you can't dictate kindness. What you can do is honor it by accepting it with as much grace as you can muster.

I knew the people at Phinney/Bischoff were special, that they had made a habit out of giving back to the community in thoughtful, creative ways. But to be on the receiving end of their benevolence and

CHAPTER 15

to experience how it drew others in, some of whom I didn't even know, was magical, beautiful, and intensely humbling. It was another lesson in vulnerability—one I needed more than I cared to admit. One I would clumsily accept.

Chapter 16

*Every day I feel good is an honor.
It deserves my full attention.*
—Journal Entry

IT'S HARD TO jump out of bed and put your best self forward when you feel like you crawled out of a hole in Middle-earth and look like it too. But, when possible, during the months of chemo, I tried. Staying active in mind and body was key. For example, I was educating myself on links between lifestyle and my particular kind of cancer, with the goal of minimizing the risk of recurrence. Some risks, such as obesity, smoking, and alcohol, were well documented. I was good on the first two counts—was able to maintain my pre-cancer weight and easily avoided cigarettes—but when it came to drinking, I wasn't innocent. I worried that the excessive partying in my twenties had encouraged my cells to split. To think I could have brought cancer on myself was horrifying.

CHAPTER 16

Some survivors were adamant about giving up alcohol. "Continue drinking or add more years with my children?" they would say. "Dumb question."

I didn't want to be dumb. But then I learned about a host of other factors associated with breast cancer. I became both certain that alcohol couldn't be solely responsible and confused because no one thing probably could.

What I did learn was that what I put in my body and on my body, and breathed into my body, mattered. There was a lot of conflicting information. (Eat soy. Don't eat soy. Eat soy occasionally.) Still, it was empowering to know what was associated with cancer development and where the general consensus lay. My food, beauty, and household product choices were informed by the knowledge I was gaining. Adjustments were made. I would try to minimize exposure to things that messed with my hormones. Some were easy, like not eating food out of microwaved plastic containers, using cosmetics free of parabens and phthalates, and purchasing organic, low-pesticide produce. But when it came to drinking—giving that up would be tough. It was a part of my social life; I enjoyed happy hour with friends; I savored a cold beer on a hot day.

Somewhere I read that fewer than seven drinks per week, on average, was a good guideline, and I couldn't help but start to keep track.

I had a glass of wine on Sunday, I would note,

and two cocktails on Wednesday. That means I have three left for the weekend. So if I go out Friday, I can have two, which is only five total, which is good. I don't have plans for Saturday night, but if something comes up, I could have one and then switch to club soda. That'd be under seven, which is okay.

I would find myself saving up, making up, and feeling guilty if I approached seven. Then I would consider all of the other risks I'd eliminated and wonder if it all might be a wash. I scrub the bathroom with Bon Ami, I'd rationalize. I don't eat dairy with hormones. I walked for thirty minutes four times this week. I can have a mimosa on Sunday. Can't I?

The counting, the justifying, and the worrying that only an idiot would pour herself a glass of wine was exhausting and, thankfully, according to my doctors, unnecessary. When I ran my concerns by them, they were quick to point out the multitude of factors that had gone into each study, factors that might or might not apply to my situation. For alcohol to have a negative impact, for example, I would have to drink a lot more than I did, and for weeks and months and years on end. I had fitness, mastectomy, and chemo on my side, plus all of the other lifestyle amendments. Red wine in moderation, they said, had been shown to have health benefits—the stress around counting every drink, not so much. Their opinions made me feel less like an ignorant risk taker, and more like a survivor trying to find a happy medium between avoiding recurrence and ensuring quality of life. I could stop counting. I could try.

Exercise, however, was a no-brainer. It has always been part of my lifestyle, and it doesn't take much to get me outside and moving. I come from a family that went hiking, skiing, and walking along the Oregon Coast. I played tennis in high school. When I was diagnosed, I had two half-marathons under my belt. It was never about speed. Seeing if I could finish was the thrill. I would apply this approach to exercise during chemo. As soon as the bad days of infusion had passed, I would see how far I could walk before I needed to head home and rest. It might be a three-block slog to the old corner store, where the young, vacant cashiers looked like they had rolled out of bed into yesterday's clothes, or a Saturday trek with my long-walk-loving equal, Ava, up and down the foothills northwest of town. On my best days, I would run around Lady Bird Lake. It felt good to work my muscles, to remind them of their strength, to set them alight. My body was imperfect, but it could still take me where I needed to go. I never felt more empowered than when I reached a self-imposed finish line—street sign, fire hydrant, light pole, furry dead thing. Save for work, chemo-related fatigue, or melancholy, little kept me from heading out.

I didn't wear my wig on my walks or runs. I didn't want the added heat or to worry about it sliding off my head. Instead, I opted for a ball cap or lightweight hat. I didn't want to deal with making sure it was on straight or whether it was being ruined by my sweating head. Each time, before I left the house, I looked in the mirror. I thought I knew what I looked like when I laced up and went out—somewhat fit, female, average height, bald, with that distinct, ghostly chemo glow—but I couldn't be sure. Caps and hats don't cover the entire head. There's a reverse valance of baldness you can't get around. Passersby, I trusted, would be too engrossed in their own worlds to notice, unless they were observers, like me. I noticed people on the trail all the time—their outfits, body types, behavior. I noticed when outfits looked expensive or trendy, were snug or loose-fitting. Depending on the assembly and perceived attractiveness of its owner, an outfit could cause a shudder (not enough coverage) or admiration (not enough coverage). Long before and after my diagnosis, I would see buxom women runners and wonder if it hurt to run and if they wished they had less. And I wondered about smaller-breasted women, whether they felt efficient, whether they ever wished they had more. I was thankful when a handsome man would run past so I could enjoy his exterior in action, but I was repulsed if his contrail smelled of two-day sweat. I watched moms

CHAPTER 16

running while pushing kids in double strollers and knew they were better suited for the task than I. And I observed senior citizens walking with gentle strides, and hoped, now more intensely than ever, that I would be so lucky. Such trail study provided comforting perspective. We were one in our various shapes, ages, and sizes; we all belonged.

Of all the people I noticed on the trail that chemo December, one stood out. I was energized that day, the weather cool and sunny. I was running east; she and her companion were running west. In about twenty seconds we would pass each other.

She was tall, but there was something else. As the distance between us closed, it became clear. Along with her blue and white ensemble, she wore a white ball cap, skirted on each side with an absence of hair. Bald, like me. She could have had alopecia or some other condition, except that she had the chemo glow I was getting so used to seeing at the oncology office—pale with thinned lashes and eyebrows. I wondered what kind of cancer she had, what the stage and her prognosis were; whether she was done with treatment or just starting; whether she was into pink fundraising events, had a sex life, or went to survivor luncheons.

Time didn't stop when we passed each other. I didn't slow my pace or nod in allegiance. Both of us were wearing sunglasses; there was no way to know if there was mutual regard. But I did look back to check for a ponytail or hair peeking out from under her cap—there wasn't any—and to see if she would look back too. I can't remember if she did, but I know I wanted her to. As if we were expats intersecting in a foreign land, I wanted us to quietly confirm our kinship, to acknowledge that we were part of the trail, running amongst those who had yet to check a box on a health history form.

Ultimately, it didn't matter what I or anyone else looked like on the trail. Still, with such a dramatic change in my appearance, I couldn't help but feel self-conscious, and I often wondered what other people saw. If she was any indication, it wasn't bad at all. She wasn't just her chemo. She looked fit, determined, and stronger than many of the elite runners who occasionally whizzed past. I knew this wasn't an objective approach, of course. It couldn't be; I had lost the non-chemo lens. Whether anyone else noticed us was anyone's guess. For me, knowing she was there was enough. I felt empowered by her presence. If I got tired halfway through my run, if I felt like I couldn't complete the loop, I would think of her on the opposite end of the trail. If she could do it, I could do it too.

❖

Limiting unnecessary unpleasantries was also essential to my well-being. If a loud person sat next to me at the coffee shop, I would get up and move. If

CHAPTER 16

there was a clusterfuck in the Target parking lot, I'd come back another time. And, if something I wore pinched, poked, or scratched, I wouldn't wear it, which meant, more often than not, that the wig was left at home.

The few times I wore it out—to dinner with friends, the store, Dr. Tucker's office—I felt fake, like I was wearing a costume, pretending to be an undiagnosed version of myself. It itched, literally and metaphorically. I didn't want to broadcast my situation, but I didn't want to go to that much effort to conceal it either—especially not for the sake of fitting in. If I was going to take a few extra minutes getting ready, I'd rather spend them using makeup to add some color to my face than mess with a wig. The wig was impractical and inefficient. I appreciated the option, would encourage others to explore it, but for me, it was so much easier to wear a hat. If I didn't have one handy, I'd wear absolutely nothing at all.

That's what I did on Christmas Eve at the airport. I was about to board a flight to Oregon to spend Christmas with my family and Marit. It had promised to be such a public affair—the shuttle, airport, hours on the plane—that I had gone against my better judgment and donned my wig. Infected with the holiday spirit, I decided to give it another chance. It wasn't the wig's fault I'd had cancer. Maybe my scalp would be less sensitive, my pride less pride-y.

I DON'T WANNA BE PINK

Try and have fun with it, I thought. Make it yours. It's Christmas!

But no amount of sugarplum fairy could change the prickle. I endured it on the ride to the airport, through security, and on the walk to the gate, but the thought of five hours itching on a plane was too much. So I yanked it off in the airport bathroom, stuffed all $250 of it into my backpack, and said fuckit. I'd never felt more brazen or free. My scalp sighed in relief. It stopped struggling and relished the air.

My scalp wasn't completely smooth. There were a few stubby patches, shadows really, that had yet to fall out. They didn't look intentional, rather like something was off. I could have covered this up, a hat was buried somewhere in my backpack, but my scalp felt so good in the open air, I decided to leave it be. I felt a little edgy, a little in-your-face, exhibiting my affliction, but thought my makeup and upbeat holiday spirit offered an acceptable contrast. The hat would stay in the bag. Try and have fun without it! I thought. Make it yours. It's Christmas!

I took my seat in the exit row, and like a market researcher or detective without the one-way mirror, I watched the remaining passengers board. I was curious whether and how they would react. A handful of people did a double take and either smiled empathetically or quickly looked away, as if they were just anxious to find their seats. I figured it was

CHAPTER 16

a fragment of what people with unusual features or missing limbs must endure every day, and I'd learn to endure it too. Besides, maybe I wasn't being looked upon with pity. I could have been pegged for a Hare Krishna or the lead singer of a German punk-rock band.

To the weathered, coral-lipsticked flight attendant hovering over our row, I was just another passenger. Her matter-of-fact approach suggested years on the job, as far back as the Wright Brothers. She was more concerned about whether I was fit for the exit row than what happened to my hair.

"You there—Kojak," I imagined her saying. She'd eye my missing hairline. "Is that coming or going? If you're going to sit in the exit row, you have to be willing and able to help us out in the unlikely event of an emergency or water landing. So, you in, you gonna vomit, or what?"

"Ever heard of Yul?" I'd reply. "Vin? GI Jane? Damn straight I'm ready! I may be bald, lady, but I'm also badass! In the unlikely event of an emergency or water landing, I'll PULL UPPER HANDLE INWARD like nobody's business! Follicle-laden passengers will be awestruck by my ability to LIFT EMERGENCY DOOR UP AND OUT OF DOORWAY. The merely receding will look on with envy as I swiftly fling DOOR ON SEAT and execute the final step, the pièce de résistance, EXIT THROUGH DOOR TOWARD BACK OF PLANE!

I DON'T WANNA BE PINK

Whether sunlight or moonbeams are bouncing off my head, I'll lead my fellow passengers to safety. 'Follow Spalding!' they'll cry. 'She knows the way!' Once outside, whether amidst smoldering cattle or engine-fried fish, we'll huddle and pray and sing 'Kumbay, uh, what the fuck just happened, my Lord?'

In the unlikely event of an emergency or water landing, I will be the best goddamned exit row passenger to grace U.S. Airways, lady. Put that in your flotation device and smoke it."

But I simply said "yes." We took off without a hitch.

Chapter 17

*I hope we can look back on this many
years from now. Many, many years.*
—Journal Entry

AVA, A FINANCIAL planner and artist, was another of Alice's good friends whom I had the good fortune to adopt. She was single when Alice introduced us over drinks one Friday night, and it was only natural that we started to hang out and talk about men. At first, she was reserved. I wasn't sure if my sometimes overt playfulness (read: silliness) was her cup of tea. As I got to know her, I found this tall, natural beauty to be incredibly thoughtful, warm, and intellectually engaging. She wasn't one to bust out a limerick or impersonate a farm animal, as Alice and I had been known to do, but she loved to laugh—when she thought something was funny. And to make someone like Ava laugh, someone who didn't guffaw willy-nilly, felt like winning a prize.

Whether we were taking a long walk to the farmers market or drinking Lone Star beers at Ginny's Little Longhorn Saloon, her unique lens on life enriched hours of conversation, and I saw in her a friend for life.

The only thing I didn't like about Ava was her doctor.

On a Tuesday in early January, the day after my third infusion, Ava called to tell me she had recently found a lump in her breast and, not wanting to alarm anyone, quietly had it biopsied. She had a follow-up with her doctor the next day and wondered if I'd come along. "Of course," I said. My heart gave a little start, but I was glad she asked me to go.

As I hoisted my aching, queasy excuse for a body into her car the next morning, I assumed we were going to find out the results. But what Ava hadn't mentioned when we spoke the night before was that she already knew. Her doctor had left her breast cancer diagnosis on her voicemail.

"She left it on your fucking voicemail?" I seethed. "Who does that?!"

An effusive minimalist, Ava replied, "Maybe she doesn't have the best bedside manner."

When I met Frosty the Surgeon myself, this turned out to be an understatement. I practically got freezer burn just standing next to her. No amount of fleece, Gore-Tex, or alpaca wool was going to melt the permafrost of her demeanor. In addition to the

CHAPTER 17

cold hard facts, Frosty granted Ava a treatment recommendation and about two minutes for questions. I wanted to tell her that just because she was a good surgeon didn't mean she was allowed to be an asshole. You just diagnosed this woman with cancer, I wanted to say. At least pretend to care.

On the way home, Ava and I discussed the importance of second and third opinions. Eventually, she would drop Frosty for a compassionate crackerjack, aka my Dr. Perry.

❖

Having a close friend go through the drill on the heels of my own diagnosis was surreal. It was as if I'd given it to her or she was copying me because walking around ashen, bald, and queasy was the cool thing to do.

How do I respond? I wondered. If I welcome her to the club, it might come off like I'm glad she had cancer: "Ohmygawd, you're going to looove chemo. All your pubes are going to fall out! Do you know how much that would cost at a spa?"

If, on the other hand, I offered condolences, I ran the risk of sounding like there was no hope. "Ugh. That's so awful," I'd groan. "It's bad enough to have one of us suffering, but two? Say, did you ever see *Thelma & Louise*? Let me know what you think."

I settled for how it would be nice to have someone to barf with and left it at that.

Chapter 18

*I looked in the mirror and saw
Tolkien's Gollum—big-eyed, pale
and bald. Precious, indeed.*
—Journal Entry

PART BORED, PART curious, part should, I agreed to go to a local design firm's new office party with Suzanne. It was mid-January, nearly a month since I'd retired my wig in the airport bathroom. I had accumulated a collection of stylish, non-itchy hats, some gifts from compassionate friends, others purchased online. For the party, I picked a black cotton pull-on with accordion pleats. But no matter how chic one's chapeau, how sparkly one's dangly earrings, there's no getting around vanishing eyebrows, sparse eyelashes and missing wisps of hair. Chemo-D was in the house.

With fresh party potions in hand, Suzanne and I followed the waft of music to the back of the warehouse-cum-edgy design studio where a band of break dancers were popping and locking for a small crowd. Within seconds of our arrival, a lone belly dancer undulated her way onto the scene sporting red hair, red harem pants, and a gold coin bra. Her exposed midriff featured an innie belly button stretched flat into an oval the size of a Skittle. Her hips seemed to move independently of her body, causing every straight man in the room to untuck his shirt.

Just then I noticed a towering blond woman heading our direction. Instead of merging into the side or rear of the crowd, as is customary when one has the stature of a Redwood, she proceeded to stand right in front of us. She had that angsty-artsy look about her—like she was in turmoil over which textile she should use in her collage on the deconstruction of the symbolism of pregnant women in ancient Norse culture. While she was struggling with her hypothesis, we were struggling to see.

"That wasn't cool," whispered Suzanne, after the woman rooted in place, blocking our view. "You should tell her you have cancer."

Suzanne had a rapier wit. It's one of the reasons I agreed to go to the party with her—she would keep me delightfully distracted. She was also smart and probably right. Instead of cowering behind cancer, maybe I should be wearing it like a fucking badge. After all, I was a tumor-toter, a cancer-courier, a dark-fuchsia-shirt wearing *lesionnaire*. With that status came all the privileges pity and guilt could provide. Wielding the Cancer Card like a scythe, I could move to the head of the line at the post office, snag the coveted booth by the window at IHOP. Doors would be opened for me. Cups of coffee would be on the house, and my next beer would be—hello!—free!

I didn't tell the towering blond woman I had cancer, but I did manage to look past her trunk to spy a cute guy across the room. He didn't see me, which was best, given my Gollum exterior. Still, it was fun to imagine a healthier version of myself flirting with him in a dark corner, entertaining a what-if, even if for a moment.

❖

A month later, a more viable, platonic what-if presented itself.

"What if we went to Belize for a few days?" Alice asked over Thai takeout. "When you're done with all your chemo crap."

We had rolled into February, a week after chemo number four. I had managed a fifty-five-minute run earlier that day. Pad kee mao at Alice's house was my reward.

"We could go snorkeling, drink beer, sit on the beach. Get massages."

She had a client who used to live in Belize and loved it. But with three young kids, and her and

CHAPTER 18

her husband's variable workloads, she hadn't got around to planning a trip herself.

"John might have to work but I know Allison would go," she added. "And maybe Ava, once she knows if she has to have chemo. We could share hotel costs. When are you done again?"

"Mid-March, I think, with exchange surgery in April."

There was no way I was going to Belize. I had two more chemo infusions to go, the cumulative side effects of which might suck more than anything I'd experienced thus far. Then I'd go back to the O.R., where Dr. Mender would replace the obstinate expanders with more obedient saline implants and, hopefully, with Dr. Tucker's blessing, remove the chemo port. After that, I would need time to heal. I couldn't imagine frolicking in the surf of Belize, having just been sewn up and with nothing but nylon and spandex between my fresh scars and the hot rays of the Caribbean sun. There was also the matter of my giant head. Any new hair growth would be downy at best. I'd need an extra layer of sunblock or a new hat—wouldn't want to get skin cancer.

Besides, I had no business flitting off to Belize. Even if I could swing the airfare, shouldn't that money go toward the trip I longed for, the trip I'd been about to take before cancer hijacked my cells? The trip to Italy? Yes, but Italy seemed far away now. When I had imagined myself there, it was with my own breasts and a full head of hair, and without worrying about cancer or scars or money or recurrence. I'd imagined lingering there for at least two weeks, not a few days.

Italy bore a scar now too. Like an ex-lover's haunt, it reminded me of spoiled happy times. Going there, at least this soon, would not be joyful. Above all else, Italy wouldn't be able to live up to my pre-cancer expectations. My expectations would have to change, but I didn't have the energy or brainpower to retool them now. Not when I had yet to finish what cancer started. Like someone avoiding an ex-lover's haunt, I would have to find somewhere else to go.

"So, Memorial Day weekend?" Alice suggested. "That gives you more than a month to recover from surgery, and Allison and Ava can use a paid holiday."

"Okay," I said with budding enthusiasm. "Let's do it!"

I'd had every intention of saying no. But it was way more fun to chuck my cautious post-treatment plans and sad thoughts of Italy, and just say yes. Flitting off to Belize was impractical, and I deserved it. I might not frolic, per se, but I sure as hell could seize the opportunity to celebrate the end of cancer treatment on the shores of the Caribbean in the company of friends who could give a shit about my scars

CHAPTER 18

and gargantuan downy head. I floated the idea by Dr. Tucker at the following week's checkup, and he agreed.

Italy would happen someday, my way. For now, Belize was on deck.

Chapter 19

I'm not feeling funny. Maybe cancer isn't that funny, as one might think.
—Journal Entry

SURE, I HAD sexual fantasies. I starred as an enthusiastic and capable seductress with double-joints and no gag reflex. My costar was a strapping and tireless foreign man-god—a Javier Bardem or Idris Elba with an insatiable appetite and kempt fingernails. A typical vignette started with a chase on horseback, built to a passionate struggle in an abandoned seaside fortress, and ended with me riding my assailant through legendary pleasures.

But during treatment, feeling as sexy as a pair of Crocs with erogenous zones like dried lakebeds, I had more practical fantasies. Reprising his television role as Dr. House, a curmudgeonly Hugh Laurie would thrust me onto the bed, tear down my flannel pajama collar, and check my port for infection.

CHAPTER 19

Shoving up my top he would palpate my torso for tenderness and lumps. He'd stare wildly into my eyes in search of spots before making me open wide so he could check my mouth for canker sores. Unable to ward off his advances, I'd beg him to stop teasing and give me what I so desperately needed.

"Just don't puke on the sheets," he'd growl, handing me a glass of warm, flat ginger ale.

I'd savor each sip in relief. With the energy of a sloth and every bit as attractive, I couldn't muster much more excitement than that.

Despite my deficit of desire and low expectations for the impending Valentine's Day (it had been years since I'd received a Valentine from anyone other than my mom), February 14 still got under my skin. It's easy to dis it as nothing more than an insulin-spiking, commercial ploy, but if you're hoping to find love, it's hard to see the florist delivery guy make his way to someone's front door or watch couples sip effervescent whatever on a café patio without feeling a tinge of envy. I would joke that the flowers were unwanted, sent by a creepy ex, that the couples were on doomed first dates or masking worn-out, sexless marriages. Secretly, I thought it would be nice to receive a bouquet of flowers, deep coral peonies, perhaps, from someone whose company I adored, whose affections I craved.

Romantic love was like Italy, an unreachable world away. Until the injections stopped, the port was out, and hair reclaimed my scalp, I was a spectator only. That Valentine's morning, I sat on the couch and wept, feeling sorry for my bald, sickly-looking self. But the fruitlessness of self-pity made me restless. I had to replace it with something completely unrelated or go all in and find a way to have fun with it. I went with the latter, gathering scissors, glue, leftover fabric, my camera, and various objects from around my apartment.

The result was a Valentine email featuring an anecdote about unlikely lovers and uninhibited passion. It consisted of a brief foreword and three captioned photographs.

"It was Valentine's Day and expectations were low. So, you can imagine my surprise when an otherwise bland day took a cowboy turn down a dirty road. After a few drinks, one thing led to another, and the evening climaxed in a bed of sweet abandon."

The first photo introduced the protagonist, a white billiard cue ball draped in a pink muumuu with silk flower, and her seducer, a four-inch, guitar-strumming cowboy figurine flanked by a miniature bottle of Don Julio, a single green olive, and a morsel of cheddar cheese. The second photograph revealed Cue Ball stripped down to a black thong and surrounded by candy hearts. The third and final photograph was a close-up of Cue Ball resting atop a bed of candy hearts, completely nude save for a red lipstick mark front and center.

CHAPTER 19

"Valentine's Day is for everyone," I wrote in closing. "Hope yours is extra sweet." I addressed it to forty-three of the most good-humored people I could think of and clicked Send.

"So my question is this," my witty friend Dana fired back from Seattle. "Did he stay on for the full eight seconds?" I laughed out loud at her lightning double-entendre, until I realized she had replied to All. I wasn't sure how another, albeit funnier, email would go over with everyone else, especially my esteemed and very busy oncologist.

"I've stayed on for at least ten seconds!" Dr. Tucker wrote jubilantly to All.

"Ummm...not sure you should be bragging about that," quipped Dana to All.

"Oh. Gee, time seems to fly when you're having fun," Dr. Tucker replied to All.

"Okay...my Diet Coke just spewed forcibly out my nose and all over my computer," penned Ava. To All.

With forty-three email in-boxes in five states blowing up, I was about to call a truce. But Dr. Tucker beat me to the punch. "Then my job here is complete," he concluded. "It's kind of weird talking like this in front of all these people I don't know. Perhaps I should be more professional. Naah."

If the good doctor wasn't worried about decorum, then neither was I. Besides, what was Valentine's Day without a little dirty talk making you red in the face?

If I hadn't been laughing so hard I would have cried—not because of cancer or being single on yet another Valentine's Day or looking like a troll. It was because instead of chastising his patient for including him on a funny email chain, my very busy oncologist played along. He was the rare combination of medical expert and human being, someone I could trust with my emotions as well as my life. I hadn't thought I could like him any more than I did, but he proved me wrong.

Then there were the other people on the email chain, family and friends who responded to my creative expression, however therapeutic, not with clichéd well wishes, but with encouragement. They didn't just get my humor, they honored it by riffing off of it, sharing a laugh across network servers and states. In a brief moment in time, they showed me that when cells divide, relationships deepen. They accepted and supported me in whatever shape I was in. I treasured them in return.

Chapter 20

*Since starting chemo, I'm more irritated
more often. My neighbors in particular
bug me. Not because they're loud.
It's just because they're there.*
— Journal Entry

IT WASN'T UNTIL I was in the throes of my own cancer story that I became acutely aware of how we talked about cancer in the media. Whether it was a research hospital ad, a fundraiser brochure, or a local human-interest story on the news, the same small cadre of words were used over and over again, a single metaphor carrying the weight.

Jim is battling cancer.

Barb is fighting back.

Frank won the war.

And Kate? Well, she didn't just beat cancer, she defied all odds. She's a triathlete now. A medical miracle. A baffling phenom. A so-very-brave hero or whatever will tug people's awe-strings once they find out she overcame the dreaded cancer.

Maybe it was just me. Maybe at the end of February, after knocking out my second-to-last infusion with no particular fanfare and having one foot out the cancer-club door, I was simply tired of the cancer vernacular and hollow violence metaphor—as if survival depended on one's ability to throw a lightning punch or outrun an arrow. My eyes glazed over at the lack of creativity when it came to personal cancer-story headlines. If we absolutely had to stick with the whole battle-speak thing, could we at least replace the trite fighty verbs and synonyms with something—anything—more colorful?

- Jim obliterates opposition in melanoma melee.
- Barb bitch-slaps unruly cells in carcinoma crux.
- Kate bulldozes taciturn tumor in grueling duel.
- Dena to cancer: "I'm just not that into you."

Pretty easy for those on the winning end of the deal, but what happens if you're at the other end? We are inundated with lost battles and sad succumbings. I challenge reporters everywhere to describe a cancer-related death without declaring it a lost battle. Technically, we don't die from it anyway. We

CHAPTER 20

transform. In fact, when it comes to death by cancer, the biggest loser is cancer, which in killing its host blindly kills itself. Let's see a headline about that.

- Gluttonous cancer eats its way out of host and home, dies.
- Man reincarnates into frolicking otter while clueless cancer starves itself to death.
- Fed up with self-centered cancer, woman says "Later, dumbass," leaves body for peaceful plateau.

I loved the idea of an empowered epitaph, but it didn't mean I was okay with dying. I feared it greatly. I feared the profound sadness of a permanent goodbye as well as the potentially horrendous drawn-out manner by which it could come. Just the thought of fading in front of my family's eyes was devastating. The idea of death escorted by panic or torture: astonishingly worse. Dying peacefully in one's sleep—after a scrumptious dinner with loved ones, with resentments and regrets long unpacked and discarded, the cat fed and trash taken out, at a ripe old age—was the only way to go.

Did my fear of death stem from my limited experience? The closest I had come was when I was ten or so. Tardy to dinner, I hastened my way by sliding down the top rung of our home's split-level staircase. I miscalculated, flipped, hit my chin on the second rung, and landed on my back on the hard entryway floor. My family heard a thud and rushed to my side. My brother, Paul, went outside and cried. He thought I was dead. I was just stunned and really sore. "The second section broke your fall," Dad said. I knew what he was implying. I never slid on that or any other railing again.

That fall was a long time ago. The fear I experienced in the days and months afterwards had diminished with time.

Time had also diluted the effects of losing people I loved. It had been decades since my grandmothers had died, and in each instance I'd been too young or immature to understand what their absence meant for me, let alone for my siblings or parents. I have vague memories, out-of-order stills, of each of my grandmothers lying in a hospital bed, each of my parents with wet eyes, and long, quiet car rides home. I couldn't, nor did I try, to imagine what it would be like if my own mother died. I didn't make the connection. I don't recall how grief entered our home, but it must have been there, by the kitchen stove with Mom, in the leather recliner with Dad. Then life carried on, only without trips to visit grandma.

Classmates, coworkers, and family friends had died over the years, and most recently, Aunt Steenie, but whether it was because I hadn't known them very well or hadn't known them for very long,

CHAPTER 20

their deaths seemed more surreal than devastating. I might never see them again, but that didn't mean they had ceased to exist. They were just somewhere else, somewhere unknown but safe, a porous thought that allowed sadness to fade more quickly, the way rain evaporates on a hot sidewalk in summer.

Had I actually witnessed their deaths, as had happened with pets, maybe those feelings would have lingered. Nine months before I was diagnosed, I watched one of my sixteen-year-old cats die. His name was Cork, and he had renal failure. He would sit in front of his food and water bowls, and not eat or drink. He just stared at them. His sister, Dublin, would sniff him and walk away. It was time, the vet agreed, to put him down. That was on a Friday. I should have done it right away but selfishly put it off until the following Monday. That weekend, I had to squeeze his bladder in the bathtub to help him pee. I apologized to him repeatedly, through hot, messy tears, for prolonging his suffering. On Monday morning, I needed a friend, and Alice was there. The vet came shortly after. I placed Cork in his favorite chair. When I was ready, the vet injected him with a sedative and then with the drug that would stop his heart. In seconds, his fur collapsed, freezing in place along with his breath. I continued scratching lovingly around his ears, quietly murmuring that he was such a good boy, but he was gone. Alice wrapped my shoulders in a hug. Ava came by later with more hugs and flowers.

Cork didn't know what was happening, but I did. I felt horrible adding two days of discomfort to the end of his life. Alice, my family, Ruth, Marit, and others assured me I hadn't done anything wrong. We tearfully mused that he was chillin' with their deceased pets in that great window seat in the sky, but I'm not sure I believed it. There's no denying a lifeless body.

I mourned Cork by writing him a letter and wrapping his collar around the base of my bedside lamp. I was thirty-nine but felt like a child. If that was my response to the death of a pet, how would I manage the death of someone I was close to or my own final days?

❖

I fantasized about being unafraid of death, of being able to look it in the face and know better. That death wasn't the end of life but rather a kind of mountain ridge we must traverse to get to our next destination in the universe. I would refer to it as More, the next stop on our journey, a place where all the world's creatures were elevated and enlightened after their last earthly breath. There is always More, I would say. As with the Dalai Lama, my peaceful confidence would be a source of comfort to others as well as to myself. I would be a rock.

CHAPTER 20

But as much as I wanted to make peace with death, I wasn't sure how to go about it. Knowledge is power, I thought. Maybe learning more about the process of dying and stages of grief would diffuse some of my anxiety. There were plenty of articles and books to read but nothing compared to the firsthand accounts generously shared by friends like Hannah.

I met Hannah in Seattle through the graphic design community, and we kept in touch after I moved to Austin. Her empathy and humor while I went through chemo helped lighten the darker days; her willingness to talk about her mother's recent passing was gracious and profound. She walked me through bedside visits and vigils, and described how her mother's body changed with the progression of disease. She told me about the comforting presence of the hospice nurse, who explained to Hannah and her family what her mother was experiencing at each stage, told them when it was time to gather and say goodbye. Hannah's was a sad but beautiful story of people coming together and letting go. It spoke to the importance of accepting circumstances as well as support, and to the preciousness of relationships. That she shared such a personal story with me was a gift I would never forget.

❖

"What do you think happens after you die?" TheraPaul asked. It had been five years since our last session. She had helped when I sought a more enriching life; maybe she could do the same as I sought to dispel death. Our sessions now were over the phone.

"Oh, I don't know," I replied nonchalantly, as if she had asked where I wanted to go for summer vacation. "There's Heaven, Hell, and Purgatory, right?"

I equated Purgatory with waiting in a subway for a train that never comes while some guy with a guitar sings "Cracklin' Rosie" over and over. And all the vending machines are empty. Or was that Hell? Sounded like Hell. And Heaven? That was a religious idea that had really taken off. It was where souls from all over the world aspired to retire. Where generations of families reunited. Where God and Ben & Jerry's were headquartered. The eternal all-expenses-paid vacation destination.

I could sense TheraPaul getting irritated with me. She was trying to help, but I kept becoming uncomfortable and impatient and squirming my way to a joke. "Does everything have to be a joke?" she asked at one point. I felt like such a jerk, wasting her time, and apologized immediately. From then on, I tried to be a better student of death. But despite several calls with her, the mystery remained: what actually happens when we die? I didn't know where my grandmothers, Aunt Steenie, or Hannah's mother had gone. Looking for the answer only stirred the muddy mixture in me: my mother's faith in the Lamb of God and my father's trust in science. Heaven or black hole? I couldn't decide. And what if I did decide? Would my fear of death just disappear? Would the thought of dying become as mundane as a honey-do task—something I'd eventually get around to but was in no hurry to mark off my list?

- Change hallway light bulb.
- Clean out junk drawer.
- Return *Miss Congeniality 2* DVD to neighbor.
- Die.

Doubtful. And after several therapy sessions; after trudging through the dense and philosophical *Who Dies?: An Investigation in Conscious Living and Conscious Dying,* by Stephen and Ondrea Levine; after praying to the God of my childhood and the universe of my adulthood; and after consulting friends of all beliefs, I still didn't know. I decided to stop forcing an answer and try accepting not knowing. Maybe, the answer would find me if I let it.

❖

One thing I could do, however, was get my affairs in some kind of order. With the help of an estate attorney, I would attempt an estate plan. Maybe it was premature. But with so much downtime until

I finished chemo, why not try to figure some of this stuff out?

After an initial overview meeting, I was given ninety days to think about what I wanted my family to do with me should I be incapacitated by irreversible injury or terminal illness. What they should do with my body, money, and belongings should I die. How I wanted them to commemorate my life. It was an unpleasant exercise filled with dark, unpleasant places. I got emotional at the thought of never seeing my family and friends again, dying single, and never reclaiming that trip to Italy, not to mention all the other countries on my list. Then I rationalized that if I were in a coma or dead, I wouldn't be sad. I wouldn't be anything. It was my loved ones I had to consider. I imagined them hovering over my hospital bed, agonizing over whether they should pull the plug, unlocking my apartment door and wondering what in the hell they were going to do with the cat and all my crap, wading through my files trying to make sense of my finances, laboring over funeral proceedings and whom to invite.

I remembered the dread that came over me each time one of my parents wanted to talk about their own wishes regarding death. How I would weep in private. Just don't die, I'd thought. It'll be so much easier that way. But their presence of mind would ease the burden on an already grieving family, and I wanted to do the same for them, and for my sister

CHAPTER 20

and brother, should I be the one to catch an early flight.

I read through all the documents and started making decisions about executors, life support, beneficiaries, and remains, and realized why the attorney allowed clients ninety days to think things through. Hard as it was, being able to designate Journey's "Don't Stop Believin'" as the theme song for my memorial blowout made it all worth the trouble. It felt good to be certain about something.

Chapter 21

With Glade® Chemo Port Plug-ins, cancer never smelled prettier! Simply attach the plug-in to your chemo port and you'll be emanating the scent of fresh lavender, sea zest, or snickerdoodle in no time!
—Journal Entry

I LEARNED THE hard way not to schedule client work the same week as chemo. A few days after my second infusion, I went to do a voiceover for a local e-learning company. Seven minutes into a thirty-minute narration for elementary students, on the topic of the lunar eclipse, my stomach started twitching at the base of my esophagus, threatening to throw up my breakfast.

You can do this, I thought. Just a few more sentences. It'll pass.

As I stood in the booth, reading aloud from the script in my best History Channel voice, I couldn't

CHAPTER 21

get the vision of barfing on the mic out of my head.

After squeezing out the rest of the paragraph, I told the sound guy a lie about drinking a ton of water in preparation for the voiceover. In the bathroom, I stood in the stall the farthest from the door, closed my eyes, and rested my head against the laminate wall, willing my insides to settle down. Mind over matter. Deep breaths. Sips of water. Imagine the kids staring at their computer screens, entranced by your voice, inspired to explore the wonders of the universe. Little Stephen Hawkings in the making. Probably more like little Steven Tylers, but whatever! Get through it and you can go home, suck on some ginger chews, and finish watching Robin Williams in *RV*.

Somehow, I made it through the voiceover, suppressing the nausea, leaving the mic and booth unscathed. But from then on, I scheduled client interaction only on what I had learned were my best ten or so days between my tri-weekly infusions.

Working with clients who knew me was easy, since I'd kept them abreast (I know, I know) of my plight. They were unfazed by my appearance and knew me well enough to laugh when I mused that Weight Watchers was missing an opportunity by not incorporating chemo drugs into their meal plans. New clients, however, were a different story. I couldn't just sit down at a conference room table; say, "Hi, I'm Dena, the copywriter with cancer who's undergoing chemo"; and then expect to dive into their copy needs. When I entered the room, I brought an elephant with me—a smooth-scalped behemoth with eyebrows as sparse as the first mustache on a twelve-year-old boy. My appearance introduced doubt and I felt compelled to get the fact that I was going through chemo out of the way, to prove to them that though I looked like I was falling apart, I actually did have my shit together, that I was the best writer for the job.

I needn't have fretted. A copywriter working through chemo is a shoo-in for any project. Because really, what kind of an asshole says, "No we don't want a cancer patient on our team"? If the copy sucked, they would have good reason to get out of the relationship, but I would do everything in my power to make sure that didn't happen. I might have lost my hair, I might have days of debilitating nausea, but on good days I could still produce. Wasn't I managing to go running a few times a week? Hadn't I maintained a kind of social life, going to a movie or dinner a couple of times a week with friends? My work, my writing, wasn't going to be any different.

But even if the copy I provided clients was good, it was becoming harder and harder to deliver; finding the right words was like catching fish with my bare hands. They kept slipping from my grasp, along with the hours of the day.

Cancer experts call it chemo brain or chemo fog, symptoms of which include short-term memory lapse, slower thinking and processing, and trouble with concentration, word finding, and multitasking. At forty, I'd come to expect the occasional escaping synonym or celebrity name, but to spend three hours on a single sentence or a whole day on a paragraph, as was happening more frequently during chemo, was frustrating as hell. At its worst, I would cry and wonder if my craft was slowly eroding. Would I lose my clients' trust and my livelihood? The rest of the time I fought an intense proclivity to stare through the computer screen, lumbering through each copy project sentence by sentence, with a reliance on Thesaurus.com that bordered on abuse. I proofed completed drafts several times to make sure my impairment hadn't leaked onto the page. Only then did I attach it to an email and hit Send.

While I padded my turnaround times so that I'd have the extra time I needed to produce a decent product, I kept my struggle from my clients (and their invoices). I read that most patients recovered cognitive function after chemo. When I finished chemo, just a few weeks away, I planned to do the same.

❖

I spent most of the weekend before my sixth and final infusion with Ava, who was recovering from surgery. She'd had her tumor removed by Dr. Perry and a chemo port put in. Her first infusion was scheduled for the end of March, after which she'd endure weeks of radiation. I hated that she had to trudge through the muck of emotions and side effects that is Cancer Land, and empathized with her dread. "I'd do it again, though," I said. "For peace of mind." Easy to say when you're twenty-four hours away from vacating your infusion chair—but true. As eager as I was to get my hair back, disperse the mental fog, and blend into the crowd, I would endure all of it again—the puncturing needles, the sad clinical smell of the treatment room, the days of feeling sick in body and spirit—if it meant reducing the chance that the cancer would return.

Actually, I wondered whether it would be enough.

Ava felt the same way. We talked at length that weekend about whether the treatments we had chosen would really prevent recurrence. After receiving our diagnoses, we had done our homework—considered our options, sought expert opinions, pored over statistics—and made the best decisions we could. Yet we could only hope it would be enough. We hoped that decades from now, we'd look back on that fall in Austin when we both had breast cancer—and the following spring when her hair was falling out just as mine was coming in—and know we had chosen wisely. We'd be golden girls, bitching about our arthritis and wrinkles, proof that what we had gone through had been enough.

CHAPTER 21

The following Monday, March 12, I was injected with chemo for the last time. Shitty days still lay ahead, with the toxins wreaking havoc on my body—three weeks until the cycle was complete—but it was the end. If the first five infusions had been any indication, I'd walk away from treatment without any major setbacks. I was ready.

❖

Dear Chemo,

We're through. Our relationship has run its course. Some breakups come as a surprise—one lover secretly rehearsing "It's not you, it's me" while the other naively falls into what will be the last embrace, the last white lie about looking good in spandex. But you and I both knew this wouldn't last.

When we met, I was young and scared, and your penchant for killing turned me on. The skill with which you stalk and destroy cellular felons was exhilarating. You were like my personal Dirty Harry—a hired gun in a plastic tube. Much as I love your knack for annihilation, though, it's not enough to sustain a long-term relationship. I'm looking for someone to inspire me, desire me, light the fire in me! You make me want to puke.

I may feel vulnerable without you, but any more of you will surely result in my demise. Don't be sad. When one port closes, another one (unfortunately) opens. There's someone else for you and a million other places I'd rather be.

No longer yours,
Dena

❖

Suckers

One spring day after chemo, I read a post from one of the survivor luncheon ladies. That morning, after her chemo infusion, she'd spent some time lounging in a chair in her backyard. She'd watched as a mosquito landed on her thigh, sucked, and then keeled over and died. It kind of made my day.

Chapter 22

My hair is coming in. Looks really dark to me—gray dark. Like it's going to rain.
—Journal Entry

IF THERE'S SUCH a thing as bile-rrhea, I had it. Mysterious, bile-colored diarrhea perfectly timed for my reconstruction surgery the morning of April 13. It had to be nerves, a mélange of stubborn chemo remnants and nerves, about going back under the knife. I was afraid I would leak on the operating table and mortified at what the surgical team would think. In the way-off chance that my future husband was on the surgical team, thinking my Gollum get-up was quirky cute, the bile-rrhea would send him running. Meeting the love of my life, however, wasn't the day's goal. Finally getting my implants was. I didn't have energy for anything else, including worrying about something I couldn't control. I decided to come clean and make sure everyone involved in the surgery knew about the bile-rrhea—starting with my funny, patient chaperones, Linda and Ava, and ending with Dr. Mender, the nurses, two anesthesiologists, and a surgical assistant. All were involuntarily debriefed. In warning them, I absolved myself of all blame and humiliation. I was simply the messenger. Whatever happened on that operating table was not my fault, even if it did come out of my behind.

No one seemed too concerned.

"It's nothing to worry about," said a nurse.

"We've seen it all," said another.

"It's just nerves," Linda added.

"You just need to have faith," said the surgical prep assistant with a lisp that made "faith" come out as "faif." I almost laughed, but the sincerity with which he squeezed my hand kept me in check.

Over the next hour, Dr. Mender and his entourage went to work finishing the breast reconstruction they started five months before. Having done their job in stretching my tissue, the silicone expanders were swapped for permanent saline implants. What used to be hard, nearly flat expanders were now hard, small balloons. The team also cut tissue from a crease in my groin (one side of the V of my bikini line), to create nipples. My chemo port was removed, with Dr. Tucker's blessing.

❖

CHAPTER 22

My first thought when I awoke in recovery was to stay calm and work my way out of the anesthetic stupor so I could go home. My second thought was to brace myself for nausea. The nausea never came. My fingers wandered to the base of my scalp and caressed the new hair growing there—dark, baby-fine wisps emerging with the caution of newly released captives adjusting to light.

In a recovery bay across the way, a large man in his sixties was also coming to, grunting and trying to get out of bed. Two nurses tried to get him to settle down, telling him that he'd just woken up from surgery, that everything was all right, and that he should try to relax. I could see him straining to orient himself, to understand their words. We were both so vulnerable then—lying on our backs, IVs bored into our arms, mostly naked and incoherent and weak, at the mercy of strangers.

I asked the nurse how my surgery had gone. She didn't mention the bile-rrhea. She simply said I was "a delight." I doubted anything in the OR could be delightful, unless they were popping chocolate truffles in between incisions. But it was kind of her to say it, and I felt a tinge of relief.

Alice ditched her husband and two young children to spend the night with me in my apartment. That night an angry storm hurtled through Austin, and parts of central Texas were under a tornado watch. While the thunder, lightning, and wind duked it out overhead, Alice and I watched TV and messed around on our laptops, unplugging them when the lights started to flicker. At one point I thought the windows might break, but they weren't anything that couldn't be replaced. Hadn't I weathered worse?

❖

My recovery went according to plan. Some two weeks after surgery, the staples were removed, the stitches dissolved, the glue peeled. My groin incision had given way to a scab, which would give way to a scar, which would give way to the fading effect of time.

My new breasts were more buoyant than my old breasts, like those arm floaties for kids. They would always be accompanied by the numb, pulling sensation that comes with severed nerves, but it was much better than the unrelenting tightness of the iron-bra expanders. I no longer felt like I had granite stuffed in my chest. I didn't miss that feeling one bit. But having had those rigid expanders in for so long did help my new breasts hang more naturally. The round shape of the implants gave me a fuller appearance than my previous coned set, which was going to take some getting used to.

I didn't want to be busty. I just wanted to have breasts that went with the body I had known for the last forty years, the one I knew how to dress and move around in. While I was still far from busty, adjustments would have to be made. I would need to purchase a set of lightly padded bras to smooth out indentations from scars and ensure symmetry. The bras would mask something else, too, an embarrassing side effect I hadn't considered when deciding on reconstruction. With the implants sitting underneath my chest muscles, any contraction of those muscles might be visible, depending on what I wore. Say I met a friend at a coffee shop and needed to move a chair to our table. If I were to wear even a slightly snug shirt with my old thin bra, anyone who just happened to be looking would be able to see my chest muscles contract and my décolletage grimace in wrinkles, then relax back into place. That prospect only added to my self-consciousness. The new bras, including some flattening sports bras, would help cover things up. With trial, error, and time, I would discover that certain patterned and/or roomy tops covered me so well, I didn't have to wear a bra at all, like a Scotsman going commando under his kilt. Having nothing tight and binding against my numbed, scarred skin felt best of all. These types of tops would populate my closet over time.

❖

With the end of chemo and surgeries, I entered May armed with a five-year follow-up plan. The first two years were considered the "danger zone," requiring exams and blood tests every four months. If all went well, I could drop to every six months until I reached the five-year mark, after which I could return to annual exams.

My five-year plan would also include a daily dose of tamoxifen—the standard for pre-menopausal women with estrogen-positive breast cancer like mine. By blocking estrogen from connecting to cancer cells and growing, tamoxifen helps reduce recurrence. It's not without its side effects. Tamoxifen mimics menopause, with the hot flash as the most common and pronounced side effect.

My hot flashes started in the recesses of my torso as tingling portents of doom, before ballooning into head-to-toe blowtorches of flushing, sweaty heat. In the weeks before I regained a head of hair, I didn't just look like Gollum, I looked like Gollum during a habanero-eating contest—hot, red, damp, bald.

I felt like a walking sauna—opening pores, steaming vegetables, fogging windows, and melting bumper stickers off cars in my wake. The flashes could be so intense I thought I was going to self-combust. After just thirty days of taking tamoxifen, I logged twenty-one hot flashes in a twenty-four-hour period. That meant waking up several times a night to thrust the covers off and on my body, and shuffle into the bathroom to pee from all the heat-combating water I was drinking. But I didn't mind this sweltering side effect; every drop of sweat was proof

CHAPTER 22

that the drug was working to keep recurrence at bay. Having a hot flash, I decided, was like waving a big shiny cross in the face of an ugly demon.

But crosses can be heavy. A girl can go only so long without a good night's sleep before "Yay! The tamoxifen's working!" turns into "One more fucking hot flash and I'm going to explode!"

To help users and those scorched by association to better understand tamoxifen's various manifestations, I created The Tamoxifen Glossary. Torcherous terms include:

- Tamoxifanity—A pool of flaming expletives used to describe a hot flash, e.g., "It's so hot"; "Shit it's hot"; "It's too damn hot, dammit."
- Tamoxifender bender—What happens when sweaty hot-flashing hands slip off the steering wheel.
- Tamoxifeng shui—The pleasing arrangement of an industrial-sized fan and ice block next to one's bed.
- Tamoxiferno—What's happening between a hot-flasher's buttocks.
- Tamoxifetish—An obsession with pressing bags of frozen peas onto one's naked flesh.
- Tamoxifoe—That skinny coworker who is always cold and turning up the heat.
- Tamoxifree—How Stella gets her regular temperature back.
- Tamoxifun—This word not found.

When Ava eventually joined me on the Tamoxi-train, after a difficult course of chemo and radiation, I dubbed us the Tamoxitwins. When Tay signed up on a prophylactic basis, we indulged in the occasional Tamox-à-trois. There's an upside to everything.

You'd think I would have been happy when, some six months after I'd started tamoxifen, the flashing subsided. Instead, I worried that the pharmacy had been duped with tamoxifen placebos or that my estrogen was making a comeback. Equating a degree of suffering with security is one of the mind-fucks of cancer treatment. It's like Stockholm syndrome, where you fall in love with your captor, except you can take showers and go out in public without a disguise.

Another side effect of tamoxifen is irregular periods. All in all, I hadn't had a period in nine months, and it would be hard to know whether one was coming. Without breast tissue, I wouldn't get the tenderness tipoff, and with tamoxifen side effects mirroring PMS, other signs of an impending period had become commonplace. Soon, though, I'd realize that the flash deficit was the only sign I needed. I just didn't know for sure until the morning it all came together in a gushing red downpour, like Niagara Falls after a hurricane. I didn't mind the deluge. Like cleaning out the refrigerator or preparing my taxes, it wasn't my favorite thing to do, but at least I knew how to do it. The familiarity made me feel normal, something I hadn't felt since Dr. Perry told me I had a malignant tumor over a year before.

I had three periods in a row before the end of 2007, when they stopped, the hot flashes recommenced, and I resumed tossing and turning through the night. It was eleven months until I had another period. This estrogen seesaw would be typical as long as I was popping tamoxifen. I learned to live with it because I was, in fact, living. And that was worth losing sleep over.

❖

The end of chemo and launch of my five-year plan was a weird place to be—exciting because my summer didn't include appointments at the cancer center but daunting because I was merging back into the world completely unsupervised. I felt as if I were standing on a riverbank and admiring all the people floating and playing in the water. I wanted to shed my scarred skin, jump in, and join them, while hesitating to leave the safety of shore, worried that I would sink. I had Dr. Tucker's permission and encouragement to resume a full life, but not being monitored for cancer every few weeks was scary. What if it returned and we missed the chance to contain it? Unlikely, but the anxiety was a real and taut thread sewn into my post-treatment mind. I trusted Dr. Tucker and our follow-up plan. Still, as crazy as it sounded, I had to push myself to accept that I was healthy enough to move on.

My upcoming trip to Belize with Alice and Allison would help. It seemed like ages since Alice had suggested it in February, and our departure date was now just days away. I was getting excited. Travel planning and the promise of discovery were a welcome distraction. I would also be going to Alaska in early September for my brother and Melinda's wedding. After more than a decade together, they were finally tying the knot. My whole family would be in attendance.

The more I thought about getting away from the places I had sat with cancer—my couch, the chemo chair, the exam rooms, Austin—the more I wanted to leave. I booked two more trips, one to the Pacific Northwest at the end of June and a ten-day cruise to the Baltic with Mom at the end of July. I would take work with me when I could and cross my fingers that I wouldn't lose out on anything when I couldn't.

❖

Six weeks after my exchange surgery, Allison, Alice, and I arrived in San Pedro, on Ambergris Caye, the largest island in Belize, for Memorial Day weekend. Ava, whose passport hadn't come in time, remained in Austin, minding her body and spirit as she recovered from treatment. I was a country away from cancer and hoped to create some emotional distance too, inserting fun new memories in front of

CHAPTER 22

the anxiety-filled old.

Twenty-five miles long and mostly a mile wide, Ambergris Caye boasts all the elements of a tropical paradise. The skies are sunny, the palm trees are tipsy, and the shores of white coral sand doze nakedly against a startling mix of jade and sapphire water topped with diamond sprinkles.

San Pedro is the only town in Ambergris Caye and the island's central hub. It's chock-a-block with colorful condos, lodgings, shops, and restaurants, none of which exceed four stories in height per city limits. Resident San Pedranos and tourists pepper the hard, sand-packed streets in bare feet or flip-flops, or on bikes or golf carts—the most popular mode of transportation. The shores are lined with jetties that stick out like antennae and transmit a bevy of ocean delights, from deep-sea fishing to scuba diving along the adjacent Belize Barrier Reef.

We stayed in a bright white boutique hotel with a matching patch of boutique beachfront—boutique being touristese for "tiny." It was clean, with a pool and a handful of options for reclining on the beach in the sun or shade. Allison and I were staying through Tuesday, and we shared a room. Alice would be on her own until her husband John came on Monday for three days, after which they'd fly back to Austin.

By this time, Elizabeth Gilbert's *Eat, Pray, Love: One Woman's Search for Everything Across Italy, India and Indonesia* was out in paperback. I spent my island downtime devouring it. Her story had elements of my own: both of us had grappled with emotionally devastating circumstances and struggled with how best to respond. And both of us had to find a way to go on living. This was where our paths diverged, for she went about eating her way through Italy while I ventured to San Pedro to slather my body with a greasy blend of sunscreen and mosquito repellant. I call it "Swat, Sweat, Swim: One Woman's Search for Some Fucking Relief in San Pedro."

❖

Swat. The thing about mosquitoes is they don't know how to queue. They're focused, which looks great on a resume, but mosquitoes are narcissistically so, and impatient. Always hungry, always in a rush, always rude; it's all about them, all the time. The mosquitoes in San Pedro are no exception.

We couldn't have met them under more perfect conditions. Not only was it the beginning of the rainy season, with all of Ambergris Caye serving as an equatorial KinderCare, it was also dusk—happy hour for what Australians call "mozzies" looking for quick eats on the cheap.

We had only been on the island for a couple of hours when we boarded a golf cart to go to a restaurant for dinner. Everyone else on the island seemed to be heading to dinner too. The congestion forced the golf cart to a crawl, transforming it into a virtual food court, each of us an item on a menu of tantalizing North American fare.

We had spritzed ourselves with bug spray before leaving the hotel, but the mozzies were unfazed. We waved them away with our hands. They pointed their proboscises at us and laughed.

You're lucky I'm not full of chemo, I thought. Watching you suck and die would be worth the itch.

For every one we managed to kill, another hundred were whining in its place. We were screwed, outnumbered, bitten. We scratched our ankles at the dinner table.

Dreading another four days of mozzie swatting, I almost reconsidered my choice of DEET-free repellant, relinquishing part of my strategy to stop exposing myself to so many dangerous chemicals.

DEET isn't linked to breast cancer, but it does have neurotoxic potential. It can also dissolve plastic. When used as directed, it's considered safe and effective. With my luck, I'd end up frying my remaining uncut nerves. If we were at significant risk of getting West Nile virus or malaria in Ambergris Caye, I'd reach for DEET. But we weren't so I didn't. I'd rather suffer a few bites from San Pedro's mozzies than steep my skin in N,N-diethyl-meta-fucking-toluamide.

I was on my high school tennis team. I knew how to swat.

❖

Sweat. I used to pride myself on being low-maintenance. I was the girl who didn't need an hour to get ready just to go to coffee in the morning. I could throw on jeans and a pullover and go. Pick any restaurant, I'd find something to order. Sleeping bag in a tent? No problem! I could even poo in the woods if I had to, and men would find this attractive. But with age and disease and treatment's hormonal fuckery, those easygoing days were gone. I wore makeup to look less sickly and approached menus as if they were a game of Clue, sleuthing for murderous ingredients. And, thanks to tamoxifen, there would be no pullovers; only zip-up hoodies or cardigans—easy off, easy on. I was more than willing to go camping and travelling, but until the end of my five-year prescription, sleep would be snagged in between hot flashes, sips of water, and trips to the bathroom.

I had high hopes for sleep our first night in San Pedro. I was tired from our day of travel, and the air-conditioned room I shared with Allison was nice and cool.

After washing our faces and brushing our teeth, we crawled into our individual beds, scratched our mozzie bites, and turned out the lights. I curled up under the covers into a fetal position—one foot firmly clamped upon the other, legs squeezed together, arms up hugging the pillow tight—and closed my eyes. My body exhaled into the mattress, prey for

CHAPTER 22

sleep. But instead of drifting off, I warmed up. Sweat gathered on the tops of my hands, at the backs of my knees, and in the crevices of my nose. My clamped-together feet and thighs slid apart; my chest, back, and neck radiated heat. I thrust the covers off. I turned on my back and jutted my left leg out of the bed like a plank. I looked over at Allison. She was fast asleep.

The room, which had been so light, airy, and open during the day, was blaring, sterile, and mocking at night. Tiles, walls, bedding—everything was a variation on white. The curtains too: white, inviting the light from the outdoor fixtures to stream in, taunting my melatonin into hiding.

After a minute or so, the flash dissipated. The air-conditioned air I'd just been relishing began to bite. I pulled the covers on and resumed the fetal. The room was too cold now, the bedding too lightweight, the bottom sheet damp.

I'd have two more flashes and one complementary trip to the bathroom before daybreak.

What man wouldn't want a piece of this?

Sleeplessness gave me plenty of time to obsess about my lack of a love life. The desire for a relationship was there—buried under the events of the last eight months—but there. Between sweating and freezing, I worried (while Allison comfortably slumbered), that my temperature swings would spoil my chances at affection. A new manfriend would either have to love me enough to look past them or be too oblivious to notice. Or—call me crazy—maybe he could have a great sense of humor and compassion. How about that? I deserved that, didn't I? Just entertaining the thought of love seemed like a good sign. It meant that somewhere, in the rubble of disease, was a sense of self-worth. Somewhere, deep down I believed I was a good and lovable person, someone who could enhance another person's life, as he would mine. When I was ready—had my hair, eyebrows, and eyelashes back, and a few more miles in my reconstructed body—I'd put myself out there, and this man and I would finally meet.

❖

Swim. Dr. Mender had said I was healed. My port and reconstruction scars were shut, and if I wanted to immerse myself in the Caribbean (in a swimsuit with padded cups), I could. So, on Saturday, Allison, Alice, and I boarded a snorkeling tour boat.

Despite the swatting and sweating, Belize was the first mindless respite I'd had since being diagnosed. Add the previous day's deep tissue massage and leisurely pace, and I didn't think I could be more relaxed. Yet the minute the boat left the dock, another layer of tension dissolved into the ocean air that swept across my face.

Some fifteen minutes later, we stopped in Hol Chan Marine Reserve. This roughly three-mile break in the Belize Barrier reef comprises coral reef, seagrass beds, mangroves, and the annexed Shark Ray Alley. Teeming with marine life, from bright corals to large sea turtles and vibrant fish, Hol Chan attracts snorkelers and divers the way Taco Bell attracts drunk college students.

We anchored with the other tourist boats near the coral reef and listened to a safety briefing before donning our squeaky snorkel masks and fins and sinking in to the sea.

If contentment floated above the surface, nirvana lay below. Everywhere we turned, something was swaying, floating, darting, gliding, or—if you looked closely—peering out from holes in the coral. There were other snorkelers, schools of jacks, bluestriped grunts, parrot fish, yellowtail snappers, a queen angelfish cruising solo, and a kaleidoscope of coral and sponges in fantastical shapes and sizes worthy of Dr. Seuss. In this underwater wonderland, I felt like a kid again, floaty and weightless, my breath reverberating in my head, the water swirling silkily with each kick of the fins and flutter of arms, and sunlight filtering through the ripples in rolling patterns.

Here and there, I popped my head up to make sure Alice, Allison, and the boat were within view. But mostly I stayed submerged.

I was admiring some fanning coral and seagrass when I noticed something large and slow, moving half in and half out of the shadows some seventy feet ahead. I swam closer to get a look. Too plump to be a stingray. No shell, so not a turtle. Too gray to be a human, unless it's been here awhile….

When I was within thirty feet, the creature came into full view. It was maybe eight feet long, plump, with fins, and a short flat tail. Its small eyes were far apart, its snout whiskered, its demeanor passive. It was a West Indian manatee, or "sea cow," but I thought it looked more like the lovechild of a seal and a Shar-Pei dog.

You know how you're not supposed to look dogs or mall kiosk clerks in the eye to avoid provoking an attack by the former or your purchase of a bedazzled cell phone case from the latter? I hoped the same wasn't true for the manatee because I couldn't help but stare. I had never seen anything like this prehistoric-looking creature so close up nor felt a greater thrill than when a few seconds later, it glided past me, its husky mass brushing against my leg.

What was that about sweaty hot flashes, famished mosquitoes, and itchy bites? About swimsuit padding and surgical scars? In that moment, all my human problems were forgotten. I felt nothing but cool, immaculate wonder. I wished Ava could have been there to feel it too. The natural world was far more beautiful than cancer was ugly. I would hate to leave it but if I ever had to because of cancer or some other aligned chaos, there was some peace in knowing that creatures like manatees would carry on.

❖

The afternoon tour-group lunch on an uninhabited island and that evening's dinner with my travel sisters were lovely. But the manatee moment reigned supreme. Snorkeling was the antidote. It was a safe house from menacing mosquitoes, a hot-flash protection program, a legal stimulant for the sleep-deprived. The tour operators hadn't mentioned any of this in their brochures. They really should have.

The next day was Memorial Day, Allison's and my last full day in San Pedro. We spent it sitting with Alice on our hotel's patch of beach, until her husband arrived and we all went to dinner.

Having finished *Eat, Pray, Love*, I was ready to head home. I wanted to get back to work, earn some money, and prepare for my next trip, to the Pacific Northwest. Coming to Belize in the company of such empathetic souls had been a good inaugural post-cancer adventure—proof that travel is its own kind of medicine: broadening minds with perspective, mending wounds with sheer wonder, and if the stars align, thrilling travelers with a brush by a manatee.

Chapter 23

My left nip is almost flat. I am not happy.
—Journal Entry

I HAD A lame reconstructed nipple; a sort of teat squatter I would refer to as my gimple. She melted into herself a little every day until the end of June, when, just as I was preparing for my trip to the Northwest, she went completely flat.

I had accepted the imperfections that come with reconstructed breasts, but did it make sense to have one nipple project and the other flat? All I wanted was for my breasts to look like they were siblings; an imperfect set. What lay beneath my bra already made me self-conscious. This added a vexing layer of shoddiness, like securing a loose bumper on your car with duct tape when all you really want is a whole new car. A whole new breast wasn't realistic, but a new reconstructed nipple was. I would have to go back to Dr. Mender and see what my options were.

CHAPTER 23

But I had more traveling to do, starting with my first trip home since finishing chemo three months before.

❖

"Greg?"
"Dena! Wow, I didn't recognize you!"
Maybe it was my third-degree pixie cut. Or maybe it was not having seen each other in over eight years. But chances are, Greg didn't recognize me, standing next to the cereal aisle in the Fred Meyer superstore in northwest Seattle, because my face was a pulsating shade of red and glistening with sweat. I was having an outstanding hot flash.

"Sorry," I stammered. "I'm totally, uh, sweating for some reason. Ha!" I wiped the perspiration streaming down the creases of my nose and tops of my forearms, nonchalantly.

"How have you been?" he asked.

❖

All things considered, I was doing pretty well. Following a lovely visit with Mom and then Dad and Janet in my hometown of Salem, Oregon, I was on the Seattle leg of my Northwest trip—enjoying the company of Marit; Tay and her husband Rob; and beloved friends, none of whom cared what I looked like, and all of whom made me feel loved. I had also secured new work, which, when combined with the generous funds from the Walk for Dena, made paying the year's health insurance deductible possible and my financial situation less stressful. I was making my way back to regular life, and it felt really good.

It felt so good that when I went to Freddy's and saw Greg, whom I had always liked, I eagerly flagged him down. It wasn't until we were face-to-face that I remembered what I looked like. I had to convince him (and myself) that everything was fine.

"Doing great!" I replied, too exuberantly. "Living in Austin. Freelancing as a writer. How are you?"

Greg and I had worked together at Starbucks. He was slight in stature but powerful in mind. He was the guy who had no problem walking out of a meeting when the bullshit was too thick. He had walked out of one of my meetings once. Seven of us had been sitting around the table reviewing the contents of a brochure. Greg disagreed with a suggested revision to a section that fell under his expertise. After several minutes of futile discussion, he abruptly stated it was fine as written. "We're splitting hairs," he said. "This is a total waste of time." He then walked out, leaving the door open. It was the stuff of network television, except we weren't on television; we were on South First Street in Seattle, hawking coffee beans. Later, he would apologize. I agreed with his position on the revision, though, so I hadn't minded in the first place. It was good to have

CHAPTER 23

him on my side.

Greg said something about his job and growing family, but I was too busy deciding whether I should tell him about my cancer to catch the details. I imagined him at home later, telling his wife about running into a former coworker at Freddy's and learning she had cancer.

"She's our age," he'd say. "She's fine now. Oddly red-faced and sweaty, but I guess fine."

"I'm glad she's okay," his wife would reply. "Did you remember the milk?"

It's not that I thought Greg or his wife wouldn't care. It was that there was nothing to gain from their knowing. Greg and I, while we may have liked each other as colleagues, weren't personal friends or even friends of personal friends. My health history was inconsequential to their daily lives, and their knowing was inconsequential to mine. There was always the chance that someone they knew had had breast cancer, possibly even Greg's wife, but in that moment, on the fly, at peak hot flash in a department store, I didn't want to out myself just to find out if that might be the case. I remembered the time I'd told my Irish fling about having cancer. No, it would only force Greg into issuing obligatory sympathy and me into scraping a still-raw wound. I was enjoying my time away from cancer. I was trying to not let it rule my every move. It felt good to go to the store without being on guard, wearing my big-girl survivor pants, and I wanted to hang on to that feeling. I wished Greg well and went back to Marit's house.

This exercise in deciding whom to share my cancer with wasn't something I had expected. Had I gotten engaged or bought a house, I wouldn't have hesitated to tell Greg—or the Freddy's cashier, for that matter. Those things were the sort of upbeat, relatable, comfort-zone news we can all respond to with ease. "Congratulations!" we say. "When's the big day?" "What part of town?" Cancer is different. Heavy and dark. A stepping-stone on an uncertain path. All-too relatable for some, scary to everyone else. "I'm sorry," we say. "Hang in there." We adjust our words to fit the weight of the news, but it's never quite right.

The people who I needed to tell about my cancer already knew. I could always add to that circle if the conditions were right. Until then, need-to-know was the way to go.

❖

By the time I returned to Austin in early July, I had not seen a doctor in two months, the longest run since I'd been diagnosed the previous fall. Even the most willing need a break. The change of scenery via my travels to Belize and the Pacific Northwest had been therapeutic. I was counting on the upcoming Baltic cruise with Mom to have the same effect.

CHAPTER 23

But I was still walking around with one nipple. No one had noticed but me, but that was enough. I wanted it fixed.

In mid-August, after the cruise and before my brother's wedding, I would have my first follow-ups with Drs. Tucker and Perry. All eyes would be back on my chest. Might as well add the resurrection of your nipple to the list, I thought. I liked the idea of getting my appointments over with in a sort of dog days breastival. I also liked the idea of celebrating my brother's wedding without a bunch of doctor's appointments hanging over my head.

I scheduled an appointment for mid-August, Tay's birthday. Maybe sharing a birthday with my sister would bring my nipple good luck. Reborn under the zodiacal sign of Leo, known for ambition, strength, and a flair for the dramatic, maybe she would roar forth and embrace the limelight that was my left breast. Maybe she would be magnificent.

Chapter 24

*The effects of chemo can last for years.
The nutritionist says I'm still going
to experience fatigue and chemo brain,
and to not be too hard on myself.*
—Journal Entry

IF BELIZE WAS a tropical escape and the Pacific Northwest home sweet home, the Baltic cruise was a culture sampler on the sea, each port a brief but flavorful encounter. Over ten days, we ventured into towns, museums, and palaces, stuffing our brains with local history and our stomachs with local fare, dashing through souvenir shops lest we miss our bus back to the boat.

No one on board the ship knew that Mom and I had had cancer. It wasn't just that we left our sandwich boards at home. It was also that we didn't look or act the part. My now nearly two inches of brown curly hair looked intentional, my eyebrows

CHAPTER 24

established, my cheeks kissed by the summer sun. I had hot flashes, but I doubt anyone noticed. Mom, at seventy-seven, looked sixty-seven, her eight-year-old scars well hidden, her health history mum. By all appearances, we were healthy, engaged passengers, going on shore excursions, attending onboard cocktail parties, and joining the line for the all-you-can-eat buffet. Cancer was our little secret. We didn't even talk about it to each other. Not really. Mom rarely brought up her DCIS or lumpectomy, the latter of which had been a disappointment. The surgeon had left her misshapen, she said. He could have done a better job. No point in reliving it. Best to leave it alone.

It was a practical response and not that surprising for someone who grew up under the strains of the 1930s and 1940s. To dwell on the Depression, the war, and, in Mom's case, the loss of her father when she was thirteen years old (he went missing after an explosion on board the USS *Abner Read* in the Aleutian Islands) was futile. The whole world had been suffering; her and my grandmother's loss was one of millions, and by any measure it could have been worse. Being sad and idle helped no one. So Mom adapted, immersing herself in school and books, acquiring knowledge, and keeping her grief to herself. In her later years, though only on occasion, Mom did tell me what it had felt like to learn the men in her life—her dad, then my dad—weren't coming home. These were brief conversations, but I could hear the resentment and sorrow in her voice.

It was different with cancer. Even when pressed, she didn't want to talk about her diagnosis or crude cutout. I could only conclude that cancer frightened her, made her think about recurrence and suffering and death. "And why would anyone want to sit around and talk about that?" I imagined her saying. "Let me tell you about the nutty choir director at church. She left all the sheet music at home. She's really losing it."

Maybe she would correct me one day, tell me cancer hadn't scared her at all. "You have it all wrong," she'd say. I'd like that. I'd like to be wrong.

I followed her lead and kept the cancer talk to a minimum, and our relationship remained as it had been. I had other outlets, so it wasn't that hard to do, especially on the cruise. I was more interested in visiting Baltic cities and eating.

❖

Somewhere between St. Petersburg and Stockholm, probably in a dark wetsuit in the dead of night, a pink ribbon crawled on board, a benevolence bandit intent on wrangling passengers into a three-mile walk for the cure. The walk would be held on our last port-free day at sea. For a small fee, participants would be given a t-shirt and wristband, and after twelve laps around the Sports Deck, a glass of

CHAPTER 24

pink lemonade. The majority of the proceeds would go to a well-known breast cancer foundation, which, I had read elsewhere, had a history of applying less than half of donations to actual research. Passengers were encouraged to join the fight.

I'm not opposed to combining goodwill with travel, but a walk for the cure on a boat in the middle of the Baltic Sea? How about something more relevant, like sending an impoverished Estonian family a couple of goats?

Besides, the last time I participated in a walk for the cure, just four weeks after my mastectomy, I wound up feeling defective, deflated, and angry. I hadn't traveled five thousand miles so that I could go through that again. Hadn't I done my share of "fighting?" This was my summer reprieve from cancer. This was my attempt to transition back to life. I had not come here to be led around the deck of a cruise ship on a pink leash.

At least you're well enough to travel five thousand miles, my guilty conscience said. Think of all the people who aren't. Think of Ava! While you're traipsing around Northern Europe and taking a second trip through the taco bar, somebody somewhere is sitting in a chemo chair, steeping in a mustard gas derivative and feeling like crap. They might even be stuck watching *The View.* In less than sixty minutes of your day, you could show people that cancer doesn't give a shit about age and build support for the cause. So own up, show up, and do your part!

"We're survivors, we should go," I said to Mom.

"I don't like calling attention to it," she said.

I signed us up anyway.

The morning of the walk, Mom and I had breakfast with a couple from Florida. They looked exactly like a retired couple from a cruise ship brochure: lightly tanned, trim, and neatly dressed in casual sportswear you might find at Land's End. The woman had a friendly and patient smile that I guessed came from years of taking a back seat to her husband's overzealous demeanor.

"You fell for me!" he pronounced after I tripped in front of him one day on the Lido Deck.

"If I were younger and not married," he said now, at breakfast, "I'd marry you."

I wondered what went through his wife's mind when he openly flirted with younger women, what intimate knowledge she had from their years together, tests passed and failed, that made it possible for her jaw to remain relaxed enough to enjoy another bite of French toast. Maybe it was just an empty, silly shtick, and she had mastered the ability to tune it out.

"Are you doing the walk later?" he asked.

"We are, actually," I said.

A month before, in Seattle, when my five-o'clock-shadowed scalp and raging hot flash were demanding explanation, I hadn't brought myself to tell Greg that I had had cancer. Being in the middle of the Baltic Sea, with no outward signs of cancer and in the company of total strangers, had the opposite effect. Not only did it feel safe to blurt out Mom's and my cancer history, I also got a peculiar rush from anticipating the couple's reaction.

"We've both had cancer," I said. "And my friend Ava just finished radiation. So yeah, we're walking."

Whether I'd regret revealing our secret hung in the balance. It was too late to take it back.

"I'll do the walk for you," the husband said.

It was the perfect response. Without apology, comment about my being too young to have had cancer, or anecdote about a relative who died of cancer, he had acknowledged our story with a simple commitment to participate in the walk. I can't speak for Mom (despite having just done so without her permission), but this retiree from Florida showed me that revealing my cancer didn't guarantee shock or pity. An emotional chain reaction wasn't always going to occur. I wasn't sure I'd be making a habit of it, but this one time, in the middle of the ocean, it turned out okay.

That afternoon, as the ship sailed toward Denmark, Mom and I, and about forty-five other passengers, including the man from Florida, gathered on the sports deck for the twelve-lap/three-mile walk for the cure. Sunny, warm, with calm seas and a light wind, the weather was ideal.

Mom winced when I added "Myself, my mother, and Ava," on the "In celebration of" line of my event bib, and "Myself, my daughter, and Ava," on hers. When it was time to pin them on our shirts, she pursed her lips and sighed through her nose. She didn't want everyone knowing her personal business. Leaving mention of her off the bibs would have been less irritating. I didn't give her that choice.

I was glad she'd come, even though she didn't want to be there. We hadn't participated in a cancer fundraiser together before, and as we crossed the starting line, I was proud to have this smart, funny, and beautiful lady by my side. Together we could strengthen the cancer community, build support, inspire hope! We weren't just doing a good thing, we were doing the right thing.

Mom dropped out after the second lap. "It's too hot," she said. She plopped down on a nearby lounge chair, took her bib off and cracked open a book she had stuffed in her fanny pack. "Come get me when you're done."

I would pass by her another ten times.

I doubted that Mom and I were the only survivors among the forty-five or so passengers who did the walk. Yet mine was the only bib that included "In celebration of Myself." If I had written "In celebration of not having to wax my bikini line for five months," no one would have been the wiser. It's not that people didn't care, it just wasn't that kind of

CHAPTER 24

event, not that kind of trip. No one, including me, had booked this cruise to read cancer-walk bibs or dwell on life's hardships. We were here to relax, eat 24/7, and explore a new part of the world. This well-intentioned fundraiser was just one of a variety of onboard activities to choose from, something to do during the odd long day at sea. In fact, actually walking all three miles was optional, and more and more people dropped out with every lap.

When I finished lap twelve, it wasn't to the cheering of a crowd of spectators waving pompoms and handmade signs that said, "You rock,"—or, my favorite, "Fuck cancer!"—but to a handful of lounging passengers glancing up from their books and some ship staff wearing pink ribbons on their lapels.

"Good job!" said one of the walk coordinators.

"Woo!" said another.

And that was it. I didn't feel defective or angry, nor was I inspired to take up ranks in the fight against breast cancer. I did, however, feel relieved that my obligation to support the cause while on vacation had been satisfied, and I could resume not thinking about it. I also felt like taking a shower. There was an alumni happy hour in ninety minutes, and Mom didn't want to miss another free glass of champagne. Being on time was the least I could do after pressuring her into the walk. I crumpled up my bib and I went to get her, putting our secret back in the box.

The last few days on the boat were a blur, the walk for the cure a streak fading from pink to peach to gray. By the time we disembarked on Sunday, we had visited seven cities in six countries in ten days, and I had had a hot flash in every single one of them.

Chapter 25

*The mammogram tech said my
reconstruction looks really good.*
—Journal Entry

A "DECREASE IN nipple projection" is the most common problem following nipple reconstruction. Dr. Mender thought a simple fat grafting might do the trick. Fat cells would be hoovered from one part of the body (liposuction) and injected underneath the flat nipple (lipoinjection) via syringe, to help it stick out. Kind of a job relocation program for fat.

The procedure was straightforward, would be mostly painless, and could be done in thirty minutes. There was a good chance the fat cells wouldn't survive the move or might be absorbed into the body, but it was worth a shot. On August 16, after wishing my sister a happy birthday, I went to Dr. Mender's office to give the gimple a second chance.

It was an awkward errand, stopping by the

doctor's office to pump my nipple with fat the way you might pop by Les Schwab to get air in your tires. The brevity of it, that it could be fit between trips to the post office and pet store, didn't match the emotional exertion that had brought me there in the first place. I was so grateful for health care, but using it to fix such an intimate part of my body was embarrassing. As I lay on the exam table, mauve paper shrug on top, jeans on the bottom, waiting for Dr. Mender and the nurse to start the procedure, I couldn't help but break the silence.

"Good luck finding any fat," I said, sarcastically. I hadn't lost or gained weight since being on tamoxifen, but far be it from me not to force a joke when I was feeling self-conscious.

"You can have some of mine!" the nurse replied with a laugh.

It was kind of her to play along.

The procedure went exactly as predicted. But, fat being fat, it took only a few days for the grafted cells to succumb to gravity and sink into recesses unknown (probably my ass), forcing the gimple to drop like a ball on New Year's Eve.

So much for a roaring comeback.

Maybe it's not meant to be, I thought. And maybe I don't care. But I did care. I cared a lot. How was it that we could restore pre-Columbian pottery, transplant a human kidney, send a man to the moon, but not create a standing nipple? I understood the complications associated with this detail of reconstruction, but it was still frustrating. How many more attempts to fix it would I have to endure? Was a fix even possible?

I fell into my insecurities around intimacy: I dreaded having to explain my flat nipple to a potential partner and then worry that his interest in me would fade. Would it be possible to meet someone who didn't care? It was one thing to already be invested in a relationship whose foundation of friendship, love, and mutual respect could get you through life's challenges. But to have a cancer history and blemished erogenous zone right out of the gate—in the tender stages of dating, when something as simple as unfashionable pants could inspire a blocked phone number—that was quite another.

I imagined the big reveal. In the heat of the moment, the guy would pull my top off, unhook my bra, and say something stupid, like "Whoa, what happened here?"

"Oh. Cancer?" I'd stammer.

I think, that's what I would say; I don't know. But I would definitely shut down. Or maybe I'd lie and say I felt nauseated from mixing beer with wine at happy hour. Either way, I'd go home or send him home or whatever was necessary to end the scene. When I was safe and alone, I would cry and feel sorry for myself and hate cancer more than I thought possible.

There had to be men who didn't care. That was what I hoped for, anyway. I imagined sitting around a fire with the man I loved, and maybe even with a couple we were close to, reminiscing about the early stages of our relationship. We would chuckle about how it took him several sleepovers to even notice my reconstruction, let alone a flat nipple. "What can I say," he would reply. "I was caught up in the moment." He would wink at me and squeeze my hand. The imperfections of my body wouldn't be any more or less significant than his own. None of it would matter.

❖

Before I'd left Dr. Mender's office the day of the doomed fat transfer, he'd asked how everything else was going. I told him about some impending appointments—my first mammogram since being diagnosed, my first follow-ups with Drs. Tucker and Perry since finishing chemo. Everyone would be looking for signs of disease. I was scared they would find something. The fear caused my voice to tremble.

"You're waiting for the other shoe to drop," he said.

"Yeah. I guess I am."

He sighed, then bent down, took off one of his worn, brown, tasseled loafers and threw it against the wall.

"There." he said. "Everything's going to be okay."

CHAPTER 25

❖

"I've seen a lot of reconstructed breasts," said the technician after performing the digital mammogram. "Yours look great." She didn't have to say anything, but I was glad she did. It made up for her initial comment that I was too young to have had cancer in the first place.

A few days later, Dr. Perry reviewed my mammogram films and performed a manual exam. Everything looked normal, she said. Normal! I was almost convinced, except looming the next day was the final test with Dr. Tucker—checking my blood for signs of a tumor.

He would be looking for increased levels of a certain antigen, aka tumor marker, which could signal cancer. It could be elevated in healthy people too. So a higher level didn't necessarily mean you had cancer, and a normal level didn't mean you didn't. Frustrating as hell. With a cancer history comes constant, justified worry. I couldn't fathom feeling confident in my body again, never worrying that something was growing deep inside. What had it been like to feel good about feeling good? I couldn't remember.

"Don't obsess about the tumor marker," Dr. Tucker said. "It has to be weighed in conjunction with all the other test results." Easy for you to say, I thought, as I left his office to commence forty-eight hours of thinking about nothing else. Being called back for more tests, another biopsy, a shocking diagnosis, was all too fresh and easy to imagine. While I waited for the results, I leaned on my family and friends to distract me with encouragement and humor. As always, they came through, diluting my dread with bright flecks of optimism.

❖

When I was younger, I was average in sports and at school. Middle-of-the-road-Joe, that was me. I always wanted to excel in one direction or the other, but at the time they didn't have grades for animal voices or sarcasm. They just called in the school psychologist or held you after class. But now that I've had my four-month-follow-up-tests-since-finishing-chemo, I'm celebrating being painfully average. There's not a sign of abnormal activity to be found anywhere.

Wanted to share this celebration with you since you have been such an amazing source of support this past year. Thank you for that. In addition to being lackluster, I'm incredibly lucky.

—Email to Family and Friends

❖

CHAPTER 25

After getting universal normal results, I felt intense bits of everything: incredibly relieved they hadn't found anything but so afraid they had missed something; truly confident in my treatment but seriously worried hidden abnormal cells would grow with a vengeance. It was a pendulum of emotions that would hijack my mammograms and blood tests for years to come. For now, I was given the green light. I could pass Go. I could blend back into the fold as if nothing was wrong. As if.

❖

"Congratulations!" Linda said. After getting my test results, I had stopped by Steve's and her house for an impromptu toast. The three of us were gathered around the table on their back deck.

"Makes this year's birthday pretty special," she continued. "October is just around the corner. Have you thought about how you want to celebrate?"

The last time I'd thought about celebrating my birthday I'd ended up with cancer.

"Not really," I said.

"Let's go to Paris," Steve said.

It wasn't the first time the subject of traveling together had come up. It would be great to go anywhere with Linda and Steve. They were so easy to be around. Cancer or no cancer, they never wavered from being their genuine, kind, and funny selves. Having a standing invitation into their hearts and home had been crucial to my recovery and was why I treasured theirs as one of the greatest friendships in my life. The thought of spending time with them out of cancer's shadow, archiving worry to make room for another distracting adventure, sounded divine. Plus, with Steve's fluency in French, Paris would be ideal. Knowing we could call on him to inquire about a larger size of lacey thong and where the bathroom was, would be like having our own personal guide.

"I wish," I said. "But with all the traveling I've been doing and my brother's wedding in Alaska this weekend, I can't take time off in October, or really afford it."

"Well, wait," said Linda. "What if we go for just a week? Maybe in November. That gives us more time to plan. We could share a place to cut costs, maybe with a kitchen so we can save on food. Could be fun!"

It would be fun, I thought. And spontaneous. With my recent test results, why stop with Alaska? What better place to indulge my hot flashes than the City of Light?

The more we talked about it, the more I looked forward to a belated birthday celebration in Paris in the company of two of my closest friends. By the end of the night, we had hatched a plan for November.

Chapter 26

*I loved the Crazy Sexy Cancer documentary.
She married her cameraman. Where's
my cameraman, who will love me and
all the damage I have to offer?*
—Journal Entry

BARING MY RECONSTRUCTED breasts to those charged with safeguarding my health was one thing. Exposing them to someone outside a clinical setting was unfathomable. The thought of being intimate with someone made me cringe, but the thought of not being intimate with someone made me cry.

I like kissing. I like sex. I like leaning into my boyfriend at a coffee shop on a Sunday morning, still glowing from the romp we had just an hour before. The thought of a life without love and affection trumped the elation I should have felt from making it through the hardest challenge of my life.

I couldn't imagine a man finding my scarred

breasts a turn-on. I'd catch myself making eye contact with a cute guy at the gym, then quickly look down to make sure my top covered my muscles as they contracted over my implants. What are you doing? I would think. What's the point? Other days, I would tell myself: If some guy doesn't like you because you have reconstructed breasts, he can go to hell. Nobody's perfect.

I had to remind myself to slow down. I was only a few months out of chemo. I had only just started to merge back into regular life with my new status as cancer survivor, lockstep with the fear of recurrence. I wasn't ready to start dating, let alone mess around with physical intimacy. During that safe first kiss with Donal, the Irishman, almost exactly a year before, our clothes had stayed on. More than kissing felt out of the question. I'd have to be really drunk, I thought. Drunk and somewhere far away, somewhere I could leave if things didn't go well.

To my surprise, all of these conditions would be met—and my fear of venturing beyond a kiss tested—at my brother's wedding in Alaska.

❖

Mom, Tay, Rob, and I arrived in Anchorage at the end of August and spent the night in a dumpy Best Western overlooking a parking lot. The next day, we packed the rental car and hit the Seward Highway for the approximately four-hour drive to Homer,

CHAPTER 26

where Paul and Melinda were getting hitched. We stopped along the way to take in the beauty of the Cook Inlet's Turnagain Arm just as a school of beluga whales were passing by. We stopped again outside of Homer and spotted a pair of adolescent brown bears fishing across a river. Talk about into-the-wild. We couldn't believe our luck.

Paul had always wanted a remote cabin in the woods. Where some saw loneliness and hardship, he saw freedom and adventure. When he was thirteen, Dad took him to Alaska to go fishing. A few years after that, the whole family went, rumbling up the Alaska-Canada highway, or Alcan, in a truck-towed travel trailer until we reached the city of Kenai, where Dad had a commercial fishing business, and where, a week in, I had my very first period—in our trailer, next to a fish cannery.

When Dad wasn't fishing, we explored the surrounding area. We ate fresh salmon and crab. We visited a town called Soldotna. We bought packages of chocolate candy dubbed "moose droppings." We panned for gold and saw bear and moose and eagles. We were constantly accosted by Alaska's beauty. But in the years after we returned, it was Paul who kept going back, until 1998, when he drove his camper up the Alcan, with Melinda and his beloved black lab Mike in tow. He's lived in Alaska ever since.

After meeting my brother and future sister-in-law at their house northwest of town, we headed down the hill toward a large rented guesthouse overlooking Kachemak Bay. With multiple floors, numerous bedrooms and baths, an expansive kitchen, living room, and a massive backyard, it was more like a compound than a guesthouse, perfect for accommodating wedding guests or a band of polygamists. We would be staying in the upstairs apartment while Melinda's family and a few close friends stayed in the main house. Dad and Janet settled into a hotel a few blocks away.

While the apartment was cozy, the main house had the big bay window with the big bay view. So the next morning, wearing my best baggy-bottomed pajamas and a paint-splotched University of Oregon sweatshirt, I wandered downstairs to set my gaze upon the Greatland.

I had the place to myself for nearly an hour until somewhere a door opened. Then another. Out of their dens shuffled a few fellow wedding guests, making their way toward the kitchen in search of caffeine and sustenance.

"Hi, I'm Dena. Paul's sister," I said to the pack leader.

"Hey, I'm Nathan. Friend of the fam," he replied. Swimming in his own pair of baggy-bottomed pajamas, with distinctive red-and-white skull motif, and faded Beastie Boys t-shirt, Nathan was cute, personable, and old enough to have voted in at least one presidential election. He also had some seriously

CHAPTER 26

deep brown eyes. I chuckled at the repartee between Nathan and Melinda's cousin Jeremy as they attempted to operate the coffee maker and concoct breakfast. Throwing back a few beers with these two was going to be fun.

The kitchen/dining area of the main house was lined with stacks of supplies, boxes of decorations, and bulk packages of food and drink. Just outside the kitchen door, on the deck, sat a variety of storage containers, some tent poles, and a rolled-up awning. And yet it wasn't until early afternoon, when the place was bustling with family and friends tearing open boxes, hanging decorations, and assembling party rental equipment in the expansive backyard, that I realized the compound was also the site of the next day's wedding. How this key bit of information had eluded me, I don't know. I blamed it on chemo brain, picked up a roll of streamers, and started decorating.

I've always felt less inhibited when I travel. There's comfort in knowing you have an out should calamity arise. You can get rid of the memory like you would an itchy sweater, stuff it in a bag, drop it in a donation box, forget you ever had it. Should I make a drunken fool out of myself at Oktoberfest in Munich or back up the toilet on a ferry in Sydney harbor, I can just up and leave incognito, never to be seen again.

I felt socially rusty post cancer, but with each

new encounter, whether I was known as a survivor or not, I found meeting people and engaging in conversation easier. Come Saturday night in Alaska, three thousand miles from home, I really started to loosen up.

While playing cards with Nathan, Jeremy, and Rob, I couldn't help but notice just how cute and funny Nathan really was. The stubble, the tousled blond locks, and the lightheartedness that comes from being less than a decade out of high school were really sexy and became more so with every beer. When he went outside for a cigarette, I suspended my distaste for smoking and invited myself along. And when he casually put his arm around my shoulders to keep me warm, I sank into him with ease. The attention felt great, but knowing my devout Catholic mom was just a flight of stairs away gave me pause. Don't get too carried away, I thought, especially the night before the wedding. Once we were back inside, I excused myself and went to bed.

❖

Since my parents' divorce over twenty years before, this wedding was only the second time that my entire family had been in the same room. Part of me worried about minor collisions, incomplete emotions emerging as they do under the influence of major life events and alcohol. The naïve child in me wished that we would all get along, maybe even

CHAPTER 26

share a laugh or heartfelt embrace. There was, instead, a gracious sharing of space. We left our individual worlds (and as best as I could, all things cancer) and, for a brief moment in time, gathered to watch my big brother and his best friend promise to love and cherish one another until death did them part.

After the ceremony, everyone streamed into the backyard for a reception full of food, conversation, music from a stereo speaker wedged in the living room window, and a crackling bonfire. Relieved by how well everything had gone, from the flight and weather to the absence of familial strife, I let myself imbibe a few drinks. I flitted between various members of my family, the bartender, and Nathan—at one point standing so close to him we couldn't help but hold each other's hands. I saw at least one family member grimace at the gesture, but I didn't care. My hand hadn't been held in a very long time, and it felt warm and sweet.

A few hours later, with the newlyweds off to their hotel suite and most everyone else off to bed, Nathan invited me to his and Jeremy's room to "watch a movie." With Jeremy passed out on another bed just a few feet away, Nathan and I snuggled up on his bed. Taking my face in his hands, he told me I was beautiful. In that moment I felt like maybe I was. Then, without knowing the significance of the moment, he kissed me. I kissed him back, and for the next fifteen minutes, we made out like eighth graders. For the first time in a year, I was getting felt up for the simple thrill of being felt up, not being checked for lumps. It felt good. At a far and safe distance from home and sleeping family members, I gave in to the moment.

Nathan wanted me. I felt it in the depth of his kiss and the hardness in his jeans. This guy thinks you're beautiful, I thought. This guy thinks you're hot. I felt sexy, confident even, and with each deepening kiss, I let go a little more. When his hand moved to my waist and pushed up my shirt, a little more. And when he squeezed my breasts through my bra…

"They're so firm," he whispered.

And there it was, that precarious moment before the moment of truth, the chance to bail before the assembly of twigs you called a raft hits the rapids, to leave the room before the shit hits the fan. Everything that had been leading me into a carefree reverie came to a screeching, sobering halt, and everything that was real rushed forth: Jeremy snoring; menacing background music from the movie we weren't watching; and me lying in a bed with a younger man I barely knew, just one push of a bra cup away from revealing my recent past, my undisclosed present, summoning a story I hadn't planned on telling—a story I thought I'd left back home.

Guilt had pushed me to expose my survivorship

on the Baltic cruise, but reticence would prevail here. There would be no moment of truth. I would run.

"I'm so sorry," I said gently, intercepting Nathan's hungry hand with my own. "But it's been a long night. I really have to go."

Nathan said he wished I would stay, but he didn't press. I got up, went into his bathroom and shut the door. I looked in the mirror and saw a night of drinking on my face. I made some sense of my hair, smoothed out my clothes, and breathed a sigh of relief at having kept my secret. I kissed him goodnight and eagerly climbed the stairs to my family's apartment, slipping into my bedroom and my thoughts.

Nathan was a sweet and safe first test, a toe-dipping foray into post-treatment intimacy. But what if I met someone with whom I wanted to pursue a serious relationship—what would I do then? Not tell him I'd had cancer? Never take off my bra? That wasn't realistic. If there existed a dating protocol seminar for cancer survivors, I wanted to sign up. Do we tell a potential mate about our cancer on the first date or wait until our first make-out session? Is it disingenuous, I would ask the instructor, to wait until we establish a certain level of trust? Are our chances of finding a lasting love lower than that of the general population?

A man turned off by reconstructed breasts would be a shallow man, I told myself. He wouldn't be someone I'd want anyway. But rejection is rejection. It would sting. I would be upset. Even if a man I was seeing ended our relationship for a completely different and valid reason, I wouldn't believe him. I would blame the breakup on my weird, nicked bosom and unsolicited cancer, and doubt whether I would ever be worthy of romantic love. (And should a widower ever ask me out, I'd have to say no. He wouldn't want to date a cancer survivor and risk another devastating loss, nor would I want to be brought any closer to the reality of death. Just thinking about it made me anxious.)

The whole thought of dating made me anxious but if I really wanted a fulfilling relationship, to love and be loved unconditionally, I would have to put myself out there and take the chance. There was no other way.

Someday, I thought. Someday I'll meet someone special and have the strength to tell him that I have reconstructed breasts because of cancer, but not tonight. Tonight, I'm just a girl who went to a party, got a little drunk, and had a good time.

❖

After a few weeks back in Austin, I was ready to complete the final phase of my reconstruction, the areola tattoo to simulate the bagel-like ring surrounding the human nipple. Having never had a tattoo, I wasn't sure what to expect when I went back

CHAPTER 26

to Dr. Mender's in mid-September. Waiting for me in the exam room was Fernando the tattoo guy, wearing a worn white lab coat over a bright yellow t-shirt and black hemp drawstring pants, the kind you see on folk-festival goers and Woody Harrelson. He looked more like a herbalist than a tattoo artist, but friendly all the same. Soft-spoken and deliberate, he asked that I disrobe so he could see his "canvas."

"Your doctors have done really nice work," he said. "I've seen many post-mastectomy patients, and they don't always turn out so well." He told me about one client in particular whose reconstructed left breast jutted awkwardly portside, hovering more over her hip than her ribs. It was so extreme that he encouraged her to go back to her surgeon or, better yet, find a new one, to reconstruct it properly.

I took it to heart. I had been lucky.

He described my left breast as positioned forward while the right leaned a bit too right.

If only you leaned right, I imagined my conservative mother saying.

But Fernando was an illusionist. He explained how tattooing the right-breast areola slightly inward would make the whole breast appear more balanced. He went on to describe how the ink could also be used to make my flat nipple appear to protrude and, with a subtle blurring of the lines, create a natural-looking contrast between nipples and areolas, and areolas and surrounding skin. The tattoos would look hard and dark at first, he said, but in a month they'd settle into shades that would match my skin tone.

With my consent to create these optical illusions, Fernando instructed me to sit up straight while he took a black felt-tip pen and dotted a pattern on each of my breasts. I then lay back on the table; useless paper shrug crumpled to my sides. With small quick movements, he went about pressing a shiny silver tattoo gun into my numb, scarred skin. Other than an occasional sting, I didn't feel a thing.

I learned a lot about Fernando during our time together. He was divorced. As a child, he'd had a foot operation for serious overpronation. He had seven sisters. His dad had died of cancer. He considered himself an artist and if a tattoo didn't complement a person's body, he wouldn't do it. He'd started tattooing reconstructed breasts at the request of a surgeon many years ago, and once he got into the plastic surgery world his name got around. He averaged one reconstruction client a week. At first he only worked with older women, but by now he had seen every age, most recently a twenty-three-year old. Whenever he thought he had a problem, he would meet someone like me and it gave him perspective.

I groaned internally. Please don't use my problem to make your problems seem small, I wanted to say. Not out loud with me in the room. I'm an example of life's surprise crap, I get it. And I know you mean well, but maybe leave that part out. It might make you feel better, but it makes me angry and sad.

"Perspective is good," I said.

Fernando had me stand so he could assess his work and mark me up a little more, then resumed tattooing. This cycle repeated itself for two and a half hours until he was done. He told me to avoid moisture and picking at the tattoos when they started to peel.

"Let them come off on their own," he said.

With the areola tatts indelibly inked onto the skin of my reconstructed breasts, I had officially reached the end of my breast cancer-related procedures. I was eager to have them behind me. But as nice a job as Fernando did in inking a protruding nipple, a flat nipple is a flat nipple. I thought about the late-night encounter with Nathan in Alaska, the almost intimacy. If he hadn't made the comment about the firmness under my bra, how much longer would I have stayed, how much more would have happened? I imagined his hand exploring underneath the light padding of my bra, searching in vain for an erogenous adornment that wasn't there, and was glad I had left the room.

If there was a way to create a resilient, protruding nipple and minimize some of the awkwardness I'd have to bear in the bedroom, I was willing to endure one more procedure. Before I left the office, I told Dr. Mender that the fat transfer had failed. There was one last option, he said. Something synthetic he wanted to try. He was enthusiastic. Feeling a new tinge of hope, I made another appointment for the end of October.

❖

At a coffee shop later that afternoon, I thought about the mix of graffiti and scars under my clothes and wondered about the markings my fellow patrons might be sporting under theirs. Beyond intentional tattoos, I was curious about marks of an unintentional kind—scars from childhood accidents, shadows of rashes, fierce bites and worried stings, notches and grooves from surgeries gone right and sports gone wrong, burns and birthmarks and violence. Evidence of life in and out of control. We all had this in common.

Chapter 27

Positive encounters with people today — the artist, receptionist, parking dude, coffee and grocery people, fish guys. You're doing okay, even if you feel completely isolated and freakish.
—Journal Entry

IT WAS OCTOBER again. A full year had passed since I'd found out I had cancer, scrapped my birthday trip to Italy, and had the flesh of my breasts removed. It was also Breast Cancer Awareness Month. The whole town was bleeding shades of cats' paws, Pepto-Bismol, and those rectangular erasers from grade school. There seemed to be a breast cancer walk, run, or ride every weekend. Fundraising luncheons, dinners, and galas saturated the calendar, and local news stations featured special reports on Central Texans "battling cancer." I couldn't make a trip to the grocery store without being accosted by tiny pink ribbons. Like an explosion of mutant mosquitoes, they fluttered through the aisles and clung to yogurt containers, cereal boxes, and packages of maxi-pads, whining in my ears and biting me at check out.

"Would you like to donate a dollar to breast cancer?" the cashier would ask.

"I already gave," I replied.

Despite the constant reminder of what I was trying so hard to forget, I had benefited from the funding and from the awareness that came as a result. My crappy year would have been worse without the shared experiences of fellow survivors, the access to nonprofit resources, and the research-informed treatment, not to mention the humbling Walk for Dena funds from Phinney/Bischoff (and total strangers) to help pay my medical bills. Survivor's guilt or not, the least I could do was pick up the pink torch and pay it forward.

This same mélange of guilt and a sense of duty had motivated me to walk in the Race for the Cure almost exactly a year before, and I hadn't forgotten how much I'd hated being called out as a survivor. I'd vowed to never do it again. But I'd been too raw then, a pink greenhorn. I knew my ports from my boosters, now, my tracers from my receptors. Despite an embedded fear of recurrence, I was stronger. I hadn't just made it through treatment, I had topped it off with world travels—had even walked in a breast cancer fundraiser while cruising

CHAPTER 27

across the Baltic Sea and had disembarked emotionally unscathed. I was in better physical shape and a healthier state of mind than I'd been in months. When a local shopping center asked survivors to model merchandise during a breast cancer fundraising event, I signed up.

For a donation of fifty dollars, shoppers would receive a twenty percent discount at participating stores the night of the event. Some of these stores would feature a survivor who would model merchandise and stamp the shoppers' raffle cards. Completed cards would be entered into a prize drawing at the end of the night.

The minute I walked into the luxury department store to pick up my store assignment, I knew I shouldn't have come. I'm not comfortable in a world where a miniskirt costs more than my rent. And, despite my initial confidence, I felt increasingly apprehensive about putting my personal survivorship on public display. This underlying tension would pinch every interaction I had until it was time to go home.

"Are you one of the survivors?" the volunteer coordinator asked. Her voice was high in pitch, her words placed with care.

"I am," I said. One of *them*.

"We really appreciate you being here."

She handed me a rubber stamp and inkpad along with a goody bag for my trouble. The apologetic smile was free.

Unlike the fundraising walk on the Baltic cruise, where you could count on low turnout and losing the few spectators to post-breakfast dozing, I couldn't do my bit for the cause unnoticed. I was the cause.

At least my store assignment was tolerable. In fact, it couldn't have been more perfect: an edgy jeans store where tight, distressed, torn, and disheveled was the fashion statement. I felt right on brand.

The handsome young manager with a flair for fashion outfitted me in a pair of dark, boot-cut jeans that threatened to cut off my circulation while forcing my belly to mushroom over the waistband. A roomy watermelon-colored top covered the roll and I planted myself by the front door, waiting to stamp cards.

After I'd spent several excruciating minutes dreading my first encounter (and wishing I had stayed home in my loose, drawstring pajamas), a shopper approached.

"Sooo, are you a cancer survivor?" she asked.

She was about sixty with metallic carrot hair and a Southern drawl. She wore a long bronzy tunic over skinny white capri pants and strappy heels. She studied my face, awaiting my reply, her beaded necklace dripping lazily over a cavernous freckled cleavage.

"Yeah, I'm a survivor," I replied with a weak smile. "Can I stamp your card?"

"But you're doing okay now?" she asked. She was nodding her head as if to will an affirmative response, yet squinting her eyes in suspicion, the way you might when asking someone with dementia if she'd remembered to turn off the stove.

"If I say yes, will you leave?" I wanted to ask. It was bad enough that I was on parade for having been afflicted with cancer. The last thing I needed was an inquisition by the Ya-Ya Sisterhood. "Yep-doing-great-have-a-good-night!" I said, quickly stamping her card and bringing our strained exchange to a close.

She had likely endured tragedies of her own—might have been a cancer survivor herself for all I knew. Instead of considering how we might be alike, I was consumed with how we were different. She could have been a source of comfort, but I felt only chagrin. I imagined her at Bunco the next night, enjoying a glass of Chardonnay with friends, and describing the cancer survivor she'd met at the charity function the night before.

"She was too young to be dealing with all that," she would say.

"Just terrible. Good of you to help out, though," a friend would reply.

All the women would nod in agreement and continuing playing the game.

The thought of this stranger and her friends casually discussing my misfortune, of being the target of their pity, caused a mess of emotions to swell. That this was an imaginary scene didn't matter; what mattered was the fear that it could happen. I would never not be a cancer survivor. There was so much more to me than this diagnosis but I was afraid the diagnosis was all the lady with the Southern drawl saw—and was how I'd forever be seen. My cancer status was what separated us in that moment in the edgy jeans store, permitting her to inquire if I was "doing okay now," and pressing me to supply a response. I felt violated, and yet I had volunteered to be there. I had signed up. That was what pissed me off the most.

When she was gone, I turned toward the mannequins in the window display. Between their plastic heads and the ceiling, in the rays of the overhead lights, I saw cobwebs and dust particles. I watched the particles float, my eyes welling up with tears.

"Allergies," I said to the next stamp-seeking shopper, mid-sniff. "Something in my eye," I said to another. "These strangler jeans are choking my uterus," I said to nobody.

Most of the remaining shoppers were twenty-something women who came and went without incident. I liked them best. They were too absorbed in their new duds to look at me funny. Eventually, shoppers stopped coming at all, and the raffle card stamping came to an end. I was making my way to the dressing room to peel of my jeans and free my genitalia when the manager approached.

"You can keep those," he said, glancing toward

my jeans with an empathetic smile. "My aunt had breast cancer."

"Oh," I replied, not wanting to know whether she had lived or died.

"She's okay now," he said. "It was just hard to watch her go through it."

I said something about being glad to hear it, thanked him for the clothes and proceeded to feel like shit for not wanting to be in the same demographic as his aunt, for seeing the clothes as more of a handout than a purely compassionate gesture.

On the way to my car, I stopped and watched the shoppers gather for the big raffle drawing. They clapped and cheered as each winner was announced—fine restaurant gift cards and cashmere sweaters egging them on. I stared at them from afar, feeling both relieved and forgotten.

What exactly, I asked myself, would you have them do? Cry?

Well, no. But maybe they could tone it down a little. Be less happy, less wealthy, less…tan.

Nothing they do is going to change the fact that you had breast cancer. They're having fun while donating to a good cause—your cause. They're doing what they're supposed to do. You should be grateful.

I should have been grateful. But I went back to feeling defective and angry—angry that they were enjoying an evening of shopping, winning free stuff, and having fun while I sweated under the heat of a pink spotlight, warding off tears. I was angry that I'd had stupid fucking cancer in the first place, and there was no one to blame. I was marked for life, would forever worry about recurrence, and it wasn't anybody's fault.

I wish I could have been more Sheryl Crow or Olivia Newton-John about the whole thing—more confident and gracious, less apprehensive and emotional. But just six months after chemo, I had more impatience than fortitude. I hadn't come to terms with cancer. Instead of taking however much time I needed to heal, I kept exploiting my still tender self in the name of "gratitude" and "doing my part," resented it, and then had the nerve to feel guilty about resenting it.

For me, participating in fundraising events was a bad investment—pain without the gain. But then everything about the formula was wrong: the goal (assuaging survivor guilt) was wrong, and the currency (me) was wrong, so of course the return in shitty feelings was wrong. If I was going to suffer, I needed the promise of a better payoff. Sweat enough times at the gym and I'd strengthen my body. Suffer enough awkward dates and there was a good chance I'd meet someone compatible. But putting myself on display as a survivor was never going to make me feel better about cancer or less afraid of recurrence. Nor would it allay the guilt attached to my prognosis. I couldn't see what would.

Chapter 28

I really need to be at peace with myself.
And with the pieces of myself.
—Journal Entry

DR. MENDER HAD an idea. He wanted to inject my flat nipple with a synthetic material used to plump up areas of facial fat loss, like sunken cheeks and hollow eyes. This method had also been used to treat deformities in breast reconstruction and to combat the effects of aging. It would be quick and painless, and despite my growing impatience with all things reconstruction, worth a try. I had hope of more normal looking nipples and whatever amount of confidence their symmetry might provide. So, on October 31, a week after the fundraiser, Dr. Mender, clad in scrubs printed with faded pumpkins, witches, and ghosts, injected the synthetic, gave me some candy, and wished me a happy Halloween.

In a matter of days, the synthetic material disappeared into my own little Mammary Triangle, flattening my flimsy nipple and my last nerve. This time, I decided to let her stay that way. I was disappointed and tired of being disappointed. Nipple projection was a common problem in reconstruction, so I wasn't alone. Women with partial nipples, no nipples, and even no reconstructed breasts at all, were carrying on with their lives. If they had found a way to move past what was beginning to feel like a superficial imperfection, I could too. Why should my happiness hinge on perfect nipples? If my smooth left breast bothered anyone, i.e., a potential lover, that would be his problem. I wouldn't want to associate with someone that shallow anyway. My feelings might get hurt, and my sister, Marit, or Linda might need to cheerlead for a bit and help me reboot my confidence, but I'd get over it. There were better, more meaningful ways to spend my time. When life gives you lemons, you make spiked lemonade. When it gives you one nipple, you take it to Paris.

Steve, Linda, and I—and now Ava, with passport in hand and treatment behind her—had a plane to catch.

❖

If Belize was a tropical escape, the Pacific Northwest home sweet home, the Baltic cruise a cultural excursion, and Alaska a trial run at intimacy, Paris was a romantic delight. Arc de Triomphe and Musée d'Orsay. Jardin des Tuileries and Champs-Élysées. La Seine, Eiffel Tower, Notre Dame, and Sacré-Cœur. Everything in Paris was so old and so new and so not cancer. It was like the City of Light existed to make up for malignant disease. For every nasty side effect I had endured, every hot flash, there was a bewitching iconic attraction or sensory experience to be had. Whether I was contemplating the Winged Victory of Samothrace at the Louvre or the chocolate ganache soul of my morning's croissant, a second cup of café crème or fine leather boots at the boutique de chaussures, I certainly wasn't worrying about recurrence or the leveled nipple under my bra. I was out of my head in Paris with three of my favorite people.

"Paris should be a part of every treatment plan," I told Linda. "Paris, Beaujolais, and warm chocolate croissants."

❖

Focus Grope

On a sunny January Sunday, while golfing with Suzanne and her coworker Mitch, I expressed worry about a potential boyfriend being turned off by the firm feel of my reconstructed breasts. Suzanne suggested I let Mitch, a stand-up guy familiar with my story, give them a test drive.

Throwing worry to the wind, I asked him. At the sixth hole, he obliged.

"I wouldn't be able to tell," he said after a gentle squeeze. "As long as we have something to play with, we really don't care. And just so you know, I have a third nipple." He actually did have a third nipple — and a fiancé, too. If she didn't care that her future husband had a third nipple, maybe I could find a man who didn't care that I had just one.

Chapter 29

*I just don't want everything to
be about breast cancer.*
—Journal Entry

WITH SOME DISTANCE between me and a pivotal year, I know two things for certain: you can't rush acceptance and there's no right way to respond to cancer.

When I ask Mom why she never talks about her cancer experience, she says it's because it's private. "You keep personal things like that to yourself. You take care of it, and you move on."

But the main reason Mom disses cancer?

"Because I don't want to think about it."

Other than telling me her mammogram has come back clear—after an appointment of which I'm made aware only after the fact—she lives a life *not* according to cancer. She may donate money to breast cancer research, but she doesn't go to fundraisers or pin pink ribbons on her lapel. She does wear pink from time to time, but that's because it complements her silvery curls and big blue eyes. Her response may be part generational, part only child who learned to fend for herself early on after losing her father to WWII, but mainly she just doesn't want to be reminded of a particularly shitty time in her life.

For some, cancer has been "the best thing that ever happened," even "a gift," bearing the fruit of epiphany. But then, how come people aren't chomping at the bit to get it? The companies cashing in on Breast Cancer Awareness Month certainly seem to dig it; selling everything from pink tennis shoes to ninety-six-gallon garbage carts, drills, and—wait for it—handguns, exploiting survivorship in the name of a cure but donating little to actual research and patient care.

Cancer isn't something to aspire to; misattributions matter. If it was a gift, it's certainly the worst one I've ever received—a terrifying and expensive disruption of life that I refuse to be thankful for.

But, someone might ask, what about the outpouring of love and support it inspired? What about your deepened appreciation for family and friends, your reinvigorated commitment to travel? That happened because of cancer.

No. It didn't. The people who were kind and thoughtful to me are kind and thoughtful people; cancer didn't make them so. They would have been

CHAPTER 29

just as supportive had my house burned down. And if I spend more time with my family and friends or vacation in Paris, it's because I choose to, not because cancer gave me an ultimatum.

No, I don't have to be a poster child for breast cancer if I don't want to. And I don't. I don't wanna be pink. I have years of tamoxifen and follow-ups with Drs. Tucker and Perry to contend with. I don't want to give cancer any more of my time than is absolutely necessary. I don't want it to be the first thing I share about myself when I meet someone new, especially when there are a million other things they should know, like where I grew up, how many siblings I have, what I do for fun, and that I think the breakfast taco is one of the greatest inventions ever made.

Nor do I want cancer to be the first thing people think of when they run into me on the street, like when I bumped into an acquaintance at happy hour months after finishing chemo. Instead of accepting my "I'm doing great" at face value, he usurped it with a suspicious "Yeah? Health-wise too?" as if he didn't believe me, as if I was a ticking time bomb, which would've made for a more interesting exchange. Imagine making it through a nasty divorce and having someone second-guess your "I'm back on my feet."

"Really?" the person might ask. "Are you sure? Because, that was pretty awful what your ex did and with such a hot guy. But hey, good for you!"

Allowing any more pink into my life would be like keeping my breasts in a jar on the mantle, a constant reminder of loss, pain, and fear, a reminder of how things will never totally be the same. But while I don't wanna be pink, I don't wanna be a heartless freeloading ingrate, either. I just need to find my own way to support the cause without letting it dominate my life. I'm working on it.

My response isn't better or worse than someone else's but it's mine, and that's okay. Comfort is where you find it, and like Mom, I find it in living an unpink life, taking back October as my favorite month. It's the month my brother Paul and I were born in, the time of year when the air turns crisp and fresh and the leaves burst into the most brilliant shades of red, orange, and gold.

❖

The thing about surviving cancer when you're younger is that you have that much more time for it to come back. So while survival is a formidable feat (or stroke of luck), managing the fear of recurrence poses another, slightly less jarring, but ongoing, challenge.

There are two types of recurrence: local (in or near the original site) and distant (in another organ). The majority of local recurrences are said to occur within the first two years of initial treatment.

CHAPTER 29

My risk of a local recurrence was greatly reduced by mastectomy and, we hope, risk of distant recurrence, at ten years, knocked down by chemo. But no one can say for sure. What we do know is that for most people, the risk of recurrence goes down over time and the prevalence of fear along with it.

Dr. Tucker gave me a good prognosis and believed I would live "for a very long time." I could get on with life between follow-ups—four-months at a time. Easier said than done. Getting caught up in the hysteria of what recurrence would mean has its own sick allure, like pulling off to the side of the road to see what all the vultures are fussing about. But I want to live an unpink life—one not dominated by breast cancer and fear of recurrence.

❖

The year after I finished treatment, my brother-in-law, Rob, landed a job in Dallas. He and Tay moved to a suburb north of downtown, just a four-hour drive from Austin. I loved being close to family again, being able to hop in the car for a weekend visit. It made holidays easier, too. That Christmas, Mom flew down from Oregon. The four of us celebrated at the historic Gage Hotel in Marathon, Texas, near the state's massive Big Bend National Park. It was the unofficial conclusion of my post-chemo travel tour.

This far west region has the kind of sweeping desert landscape I originally thought all of Texas looked like. I'd imagined a young Clint Eastwood on horseback here, rounding a mesa, all squinty-eyed and vigilant. We had an amazing time exploring the vastness of the park, looking across the Rio Grande, riding horseback, and having cocktails in the Gage's White Buffalo Bar. Like the other places I had visited since finishing chemo, the Big Bend area has the power to take you out of your problems and into the world. It's a reminder that the land, the limestone, the river—it was all here before us and will endure long after we're gone.

One afternoon we drove to nearby Post Park on the Peña Colorado River, home to a secluded pond, popular among birders. We had the entire place to ourselves except for a single young man banging away on a drum set in the dry, brown grass. It was peculiar and wonderful, and I was compelled to find out who he was and why he was there.

"I just needed a place to practice," he said.

His name was Pete. He was a drummer from New Orleans. He didn't say whether he still lived there, was just passing through, or had moved to Texas. It didn't matter. What mattered was that he allowed himself to go there, to embrace an opportunity to indulge his passion. Why not? I thought. Why not bang your drums right here, next to a river surrounded by the Los Caballos Novaculite Mountains, under the giant blue skies of West Texas? Until we showed up, he wasn't bothering anyone (save for

CHAPTER 29

some trembling birds). Why should Pete settle for a basement or garage when this natural open-air auditorium was sitting here, empty?

I thought of how often we get in our own way, how we are our own stumbling blocks to really experiencing life. Pete made hauling out your drum set in a birding park in the middle of nowhere look like an everyday occurrence. No big thing, but the kind of thing a guy like Pete would do.

What kind of thing does a girl like me do? I wondered. Cancer or no cancer, what do I naturally gravitate toward? If I could get out of my own way, where would I go, how would I spend my time?

Three months later, I put down a deposit on a trip to Africa.

Chapter 30

*I can't wait for my trip. I won't be
so in my head. It won't be about me.
The world's a much bigger place.*
—Journal Entry

I WAS ASKED to do some more work with the Livestrong Foundation; this time developing copy for their Livestrong Challenge website. The year had begun with a hearty plateful of projects and I was grateful to add this one to the mix.

When I was meeting with my client in her office one day, a screensaver popped up on her laptop. It was of a photograph of a tall, slender woman with long, tawny-colored hair like my client's. She was wearing a white blouse and a long skirt and walking down a dirt road. Flanking her were ten or so elementary-age children, each wearing what looked like a hand-me-down school uniform, each with the deepest ebony skin. All were photographed walking away from the camera toward a great mountain that loomed in the distance.

I wanted to walk that road.

"Is that you?" I asked.

It was. She'd been in Tanzania when the photo was taken, working with a school as part of a volunteer vacation. The mountain in the background was Kilimanjaro. She described her experience as enriching and rewarding, and couldn't say enough good things about the organization that made the trip possible, Cross Cultural Solutions, CCS for short.

So I followed in her footsteps. I could have spent weeks researching and comparing volunteer vacation organizations and yo-yoing on which developing country I should visit, but that was too much work. I just wanted to do something spectacularly outside of my comfort zone. I trusted my client, she trusted CCS and she had the enlightenment to show for it. So why not go to Tanzania? Malaria, terrorist attack, being maimed by a Maasai warrior with a spear to grind came to mind. But were any of them more likely than recurrence of cancer?

I decided that a volunteer vacation in Africa was exactly the kind of thing a girl like me would do. I would leave in September.

In the months leading up to my departure, I was busy planning for my trip, working to pay for it, and hanging out with friends. I still worried about cancer-related things like the results of my next blood test or how fake my breasts did or didn't look under my snug yoga top, but little by little, prickly thoughts such as these were losing ground.

Ava, who was also on the four-month follow-up plan, was experiencing a similar shift, as the prospect of marrying her new boyfriend and buying a home together filled her thoughts. While I'd never wish breast cancer on anyone, I was thankful that she and I spoke the same language. When I complained about the swelter of tamoxifen, the quagmire of medical bills and health insurance, the permanence of numbness and scars, she knew what I meant. Above all, I was relieved she had an equally good prognosis.

❖

The focus of my energy was slowly shifting away from cancer. I was spending less time dwelling on what I had endured and more on embracing the company of friends. I went on long walks with Ava; had green chili cheese fries with Alice, who had just welcomed baby number three; and crashed Linda and Steve's dinner table on Sunday nights. As spring warmed to summer, I attended my first ever Wilco concert in Austin and saw Radiohead in Dallas. A few weeks later, during a rambunctious weekend in Vegas with Marit and Dana, I wound up on stage with entertainment wonder Wayne Brady; during one of his shows, I became an audience volunteer,

CHAPTER 30

and impressed him with my ability to mimic the sound of blowing wind. (For the record, he called me a freak while we were waiting in line after the show to get our pictures taken with him, which I'm pretty sure was code for, "I'd rather hang out with you than a double-nippled model any day!" At least that's what I'm telling myself.)

Then came July and the guy.

We met at a Fourth of July patio party that one of Austin's new downtown condo developments was hosting for residents and their guests. I'd come with my friend Heather, who, as a prospective buyer, had been invited to attend.

Heather was a friend of Suzanne's from business school. We were often at the same group functions and eventually built up a rapport. The more I got to know her, the more I was drawn to her vivacious spirit and whip-smart mind. Equal parts lighthearted and nerd, one minute she'd be laughing about how she'd tripped in front of a packed sidewalk café, the next she'd be setting friendship aside to ruthlessly crush her opponents in an otherwise simple game of Scattegories. Heather's insatiable curiosity about the world and deep compassion for humanity made her a persuasive conversationalist and teacher. Time flew when we were together.

We were sitting in wicker chairs near the entrance, watching people and drinking complimentary cans of Heineken, when he walked by. I couldn't help but stare, not because of his six-foot-two ensemble—an easy conglomeration of baggy blue gym shorts, snug black t-shirt and black sneakers that screamed a weekend of corner take-out and ESPN—but because his deep brown eyes, high cheekbones and hint of mischievousness at the corner of his full lips were simply magnetic. When he caught me looking, I was flushed, powerless to look away.

Without slowing his pace, he held my gaze with a knowing smile, as if to say: Oh, I see you looking. And I'm looking at you, too.

Thirty-minutes of fireworks later, this magnetic man was introducing himself. His name was Luke, and he had just bought a condo in the building. He wondered if I'd like to get together sometime. I gave him my number, hoping like mad that he would call, and he did, the very next day, just as I was driving to the airport to catch a flight home to visit my folks and Marit. He was refreshingly forward about his interest in seeing me again. We set a date for the end of the month, when I'd be back in town.

❖

I boarded the plane to Portland giddy to get back to Austin. For the entire flight, I was immersed in my journal, rehashing the moment Luke and I met and wondering what our first date was going to be like. I rounded out the journey with a six-dollar beer and playlist of songs I associated with sex, starting

CHAPTER 30

with "Let Go," by Frou Frou.

It had been nearly a year since I hadn't exposed my reconstructed breasts to Nathan in Alaska. Could I go there now? I thought maybe I could. Regardless of whether I had met my soul mate or was merely captivated by his ridiculous good looks and playful repartee, I couldn't stop thinking about him—and impurely, at that. For the first time in years, I was fantasizing about a real person, not a celebrity I'd never meet but someone I was actually going to have a date with. A person who had told me he wanted to see me again, not under the influence of Chimay or Chivas, but at high noon, sober. Maybe it was due to my good prognosis or maybe it was due to complete denial, but the thoughts I was allowing myself to indulge in were the carefree thoughts of a pre-cancer Dena—someone who never had a malignant tumor, never had a decommissioned erogenous zone with a scar running through it, or breasts that felt, as Nathan so aptly put it, so firm. It felt good, focusing on the exciting beginning of this story instead of jumping to a bitter end.

I spent the first part of my trip in Salem visiting Mom, who, after some forty-five years in my hometown, was preparing to move to Texas. It was a major decision. Salem was where she raised her family, built her career, and cultivated deep friendships. But it was also where she endured divorce, breast cancer, a hip replacement, and the loss of two dear friends. As she got older, she wanted to be closer to her kids. Tay, Rob, and I all lived in Texas. My brother, Paul, and his wife, Melinda, rooted and thriving in Alaska, were supportive of the move, knowing the future held visits to our respective states and get-togethers somewhere in between. Mom's resilience, optimism, and sense of adventure would be inspirational at any age. That she was in her late seventies made them extraordinary.

A few days later, while on the train to Seattle to visit Marit, I received a call from Luke. With as much cool surprise as is humanly possible when wetting one's pants, I asked him to hold and galloped like a pony to the precarious unpopulated gangway, where I could speak freely. He said he was between meetings and just calling to say hello, but before I could say it was good to hear his voice, the train entered a tunnel followed by several miles of no-signal terrain. Usually I loved this leg of the trip, cruising along the stunning Puget Sound south of Tacoma, Washington. Now I couldn't wait for it to pass.

As soon as I had a few bars back, I sent Luke a text explaining what happened. He replied "LOL" and said he'd call me later. In the car on the way to her house, Marit and I shook our heads at the callousness of timing and tunnels after years of sexual deprivation.

A few beautiful Seattle summer days later, I returned to Salem to see Dad and Janet. A year shy of

CHAPTER 30

eighty, Dad never ceased to amaze me. His retired physician's hobby of creating exact reproductions of antique Harley-Davidson motorcycle parts was now a burgeoning small business, and he was fast becoming the go-to guy in the industry. Janet, also not one to be idle, was entrenched in her fifth year as Salem's mayor, working tirelessly to promote growth and vitality.

Dad wasn't keen on me going to Tanzania; talk of my upcoming trip was met with silence. With Janet's encouragement, I tried to allay his fears. I talked about the credibility of CCS and emphasized that Tanzania was not among the countries listed on the Travel Warnings page of the State Department website, that hundreds of volunteers had returned with nothing but stories of enrichment and awe. I think he felt more informed, but it was clear that he wouldn't be fully at ease until I was safely back at home. He wasn't the only one who felt this way. That was okay. I knew the concern was out of love.

Chapter 31

Wow!
–Journal Entry

PERCHED ON THE edge of a blue couch in his condo overlooking downtown, Luke seized the awkward lull, threw it to the ground, and kissed me.

Our date had begun on the roof of the historic Speakeasy Lounge. It was the end of July and ninety-five breezeless degrees out when he rounded the corner in his pinstripe suit, baby-blue button down, and dizzying smile. My legs would have given out at the sight if I hadn't been so preoccupied with the wad of skirt caught up in my fanny, thanks to a low-real-estate thong. We quickly moved inside, where there was air conditioning and gin. Before long, I was on his couch, thumbing through pictures of his recent trip to Patagonia.

Minutes later, as his hand slid under my skirt,

CHAPTER 31

the Voices of Should spit forth their warnings—but distantly:

"You should not let him see your scars; they will turn him off."

"You should not expect too much; your cancer crap will scare him away."

"You should not give the milk away for free."

"You should leave."

"Now!"

Instead of feeling apprehensive or insecure as I had that night in Alaska, I felt overwhelmingly happy, deeply excited, and inexplicably confident. I could think of no good reason to shut this party down. Did astronauts go half way to the moon? Did U2 stop in the middle of "Beautiful Day"? Did Jon Stewart set up a joke without delivering the punch line? Every inch of me was delirious with attraction to this man, to his smile, to this playful fumbling of hands, to the promise of whatever uninhibited deliciousness would emerge as the evening thundered on. It was just one moment, but it was all I really had—all any of us have if we're paying attention—and I wasn't about to take it for granted.

I kissed him back, fervently. The disparaging "shoulds" and bits of faux-pearled wisdom gave way to unabashed cheers:

"Take it off!"

"You can do it!"

"Get some, girl!"

My cancer experience was a fact, not a hindrance. It would only get in my way if I let it. More and more, in the sixteen months since treatment, it had been taking a backseat to every other aspect of my life. Intimacy in the form of sexual delight was the final showdown. With every piece of clothing we flung to the floor, vestiges of fear left me. I was about to give the milk away for free. I couldn't give it away fast enough.

Having sex with a man like Luke was just the kind of thing a young-ish and, dare I say, healthy woman like me would do. So I did, a couple of times that night and with an unabashed enthusiasm that surprised me. It was passionate, fun, and rewarding. As lovely Ava had said of her own first post-cancer sex, "it's good to know all your parts work."

❖

Somehow, in all the tumbling about, and without protest from Luke, I managed to keep my bra on—just like they do on daytime soaps. But the next morning, as the Texas sun flooded through his floor-to-ceiling windows, I entertained the idea of throwing it on the floor with the rest of my clothes. In my mind, a reveal would call for an explanation, but I was feeling victorious—invincible, even. With everything to gain, not the least of which was more sex, I decided to concede my truth.

"I have something I want to tell you," I started,

sitting up in his bed clasping my hands together under the sheets.

"Okaaay," he said, propping himself up on one arm.

Had the roles been reversed, a million things would have been running through my mind, none of them good: he's married, has twin boys with an ex-girlfriend, needs to borrow money. I had to cut to the chase, and fast.

"So, I had breast cancer." I tried to slow down my words by fixing my eyes on a pack of gum resting on top of his dresser. "I went through chemo, lost my hair…. And there was a bilateral mastectomy with reconstruction, so…implants and scars. You know, things don't totally look like you might expect."

Clearly, I had not rehearsed. I might go home having overcome the last of my post-cancer hurdles, but I wouldn't be hearing from Luke again. That was certain.

"What's your prognosis?" he asked with a command of the vernacular that suggested I wasn't the first person in his life to experience the big C.

"Good!" I said. I was surprised and encouraged by his calm response. "Stage one, node-negative." I added that I was on tamoxifen, which gave me hot flashes, which is why I kept flinging the covers off and on all night.

He half-chuckled, then said he was sorry for

what I'd gone through but glad I was okay.

Then he kissed me.

To "let go, let God" or "give it up to the Universe" is to relinquish one's worry or problem to a higher power in hopes that He, She, or It will resolve it for you or at least bestow upon you the solution you seek but are unable to see. It's hard to let go of fear, anger, and other negative feelings, especially if they've been carried around for a while—they can become part of your identity. But for all of the possibilities it opens up, it's worth trying.

Somewhere in the tangle of sheets that morning with Luke, I gave my bra up to the Universe; threw it wantonly across the room and set my breasts free. Without any unnecessary fanfare—for which I'm forever thankful—Luke went about introducing himself, and within seconds everyone was getting along beautifully. In fact, while the mastectomy had left most of the area numb, my sense memory was on high alert, allowing me to relive the erogenous sensations in my mind. Seeing and feeling the pressure of Luke's touch was essential. Lovelier still, he didn't stop to get a good look at my scars, inquire about my implants' buoyancy, or do anything that would make me feel awkward—not then and not during the next five nights we spent together.

Luke thought his calves looked like chicken legs. True, they were lean, but I didn't care. I still liked him and still wanted to spend time with him. Was

CHAPTER 31

it any surprise that although my breasts looked like something out of a Tim Burton movie, in my mind anyway, he still liked me, still wanted to spend time with me?

Love, marriage, kids—it was happening for plenty of other people post-cancer. I just wasn't sure if it would happen for me. I wouldn't be off tamoxifen until I was forty-five and couldn't imagine, nor was I really interested in, having a baby at that age. But the love business—I was very interested in that.

It was too early to know what role Luke would play in my life. If nothing else, he bolstered my confidence and gave me hope. I, too, could find love.

❖

In the afterglow of our week together and with preparations for Tanzania less than a month away, I almost forgot about my impending annual mammogram and four-month follow-up.

Almost forgetting was a good sign. Then again, as each appointment approached, that familiar tinge of anxiety took hold and the what-ifs clocked in for duty. What if they find something suspicious? What if the cancer is back? What if it's not treatable this time? I would have to cancel my trip, cancel Luke. Those little fuckers harassed me until the results of both exams came back normal. Then they rolled their eyes and evaporated. Whoever said anxiety around recurrence gets easier with time might have been right, but I was still in the danger zone. I had a long way to go, although, with consecutive positive checkups, I felt like I was headed in the right direction.

❖

Two hundred and twelve hours later:

I was sitting in the air between Amsterdam and Kilimanjaro, surrounded by people from all around the world.

"I cannot believe I'm going to Africa," I said under my breath. "I can't believe I'm really doing this."

With eight hours left of a nearly twenty-four-hour travel day, I bounced between listening to Swahili lessons on my iPod, studying Tanzanian dos and don'ts, scanning the side effects of my antimalarial medication, and eavesdropping on fellow passengers (a man on his twentieth hunting trip, a couple about to climb "Kili"). But mostly, I was reliving my nights with Luke, over and over again.

When we landed at Kilimanjaro airport it was night; the sky dark and the stars bright in the absence of light pollution. The airport didn't have jetways, so we deplaned onto a set of stairs, after which we stepped into Tanzania—into Africa!—the furthest I had ever been away from home, and walked toward the terminal.

I had wanted to go spectacularly outside of my comfort zone. Tanzania didn't disappoint. For three weeks, I volunteered at an elementary school, a minority in a sea of Swahili speakers. I joined fellow volunteers on cultural excursions, an REI-clad stranger bumbling through a Maasai village. I went on safari, a camera-slinging tourist gawking at elephants, giraffes, and more zebras than you can shake a Victoria's Secret teddy at.

It was intimidating, exciting, heartrending, and at times confusing.

In a classroom bursting with more than a hundred kids—a few of whom had lost a parent to AIDS, and many of whom were in sore need of clothing, school supplies, and a regular lunch—I found myself doing exactly what Fernando the tattoo guy had done that had irritated me so much: comparing my hard luck with theirs in the name of perspective. Only, it didn't make mine seem less hard, just hard in a different way.

I was a forty-one-year-old cancer veteran working for free in one of the poorest countries in the world. Perspective was the soup du jour every jour—hot, plentiful, and free. In the end, it wasn't about determining whether one situation was worse than another. It was about embracing empathy and inspiring action. I think that's all Fernando was trying to do that day in the exam room when I was so irked—express compassion while helping to make my reconstructed parts look more natural.

"It's so clear to me," I would write in my journal

on the flight back home. "I don't need to build a home, tend a garden, raise a child—I just need to travel. It's a relief to know I'm not missing something but embracing what there is, and all of it."

❖

Some 2,688 hours (sixteen weeks) after that:

Tay, retracing the journey she'd made for me five-and-a-half years earlier, moved Mom to Texas, into a house just three miles from her own and two hundred and thirty miles from where I lived in Austin.

"You made it!" I said to Mom over the phone. We had both made it, with unwavering support and our own depths of resilience.

It was now nearly two years since the chemo port had been removed from my chest. I was living the life I had set out to live. It was less about living unpink than being unencumbered by fear and guilt. Acceptance and time had made the former possible, and I achieved the latter by supporting organizations focused on reducing environmental carcinogen exposure. I also found myself sharing my story and baring my reconstructed breasts to friends and acquaintances newly diagnosed with breast cancer and unsure of how to respond.

One of the benefits of being a freelance writer is the ability to close shop and travel. Waiting for retirement or for the economy to improve, or for jet fuel to get cheaper or the dollar to get stronger—none

CHAPTER 31

are good enough reasons to wait. Time is my currency and I haven't a clue as to how much is left in my account.

Best to spend it wisely.

Italy, here I come.

Cortona, Italy—The time was finally right. Thanks to Heather Kennedy for being an amazing travel companion and friend.

ACKNOWLEDGMENTS

WRITING THIS BOOK was agonizing, exciting, and something I had to do. It took a while, which I attribute to having absolutely no idea what I was doing and a fierce commitment to what I call living-as-you-go. The thought of putting my life on hold for, say, two years, to focus on nothing but producing a finished manuscript wasn't an option. I was constantly striking a balance between living in the moment and moving the next, better draft forward. So, I wrote but I also traveled a lot, dated some, performed with a sketch comedy group, moved twice, changed jobs twice, and spent invaluable time with friends and family. At last, and with massive, joyful gratitude (and relief), this baby's done.

Thank you to the legendary Alan Rinzler for helping to shape the unshapely first drafts. Your expert and straightforward approach is exactly what was needed. Seeing you take my Fiat for a spin at the Writers League of Texas Conference, was an unexpected honor. Pretty sure its resale value went way up.

To Wendi Aarons, Alice Meadows, and Liz Castro, thank you for taking time out of your full lives to read early pages. You are particularly funny, smart, and thoughtful women and your feedback was crucial. And heartfelt appreciation for Wendi (again), along with Diane Mapes and Kee Kee Buckley—all published, talented writers—for endorsing this story.

I wrote most of the book within the walls of apartments in various cities, but for the times I needed to switch up the decor, I'm delighted to have found a comfortable seat in Austin's Caffe Medici, Mozart's, and The Flightpath coffee houses, and in Denver at the Denver Bicycle Cafe, Wash Perk, and Stella's coffee houses, as well as a certain beautiful and quiet floor in the Denver Central Library.

It was a true honor to talk about my book on *Good Grief with Cheryl Jones* on VoiceAmerica Talk Radio Network. Cheryl takes grief head on, interviewing people who have found strength and teaching through devastating loss. You are warm, funny, and compassionate, and the best person for the job. And thank you to my favorite pen-pal Sharon Schmidt and her husband Mike for the quiet office space in which I could call in to Cheryl's show.

Without Denver's Lighthouse Writers Workshop, I never would have met Sarah Gilbert, a fellow

ACKNOWLEDGMENTS

writer, exceptional human, and my for-Evernote confidante. I cannot imagine finishing this book without your humor and encouragement across the miles. By the way, are you Catholic?

Without Sarah Gilbert, I never would have met the incredibly gifted author and book coach, Shari Caudron. You have a magical way of calming nerves and instilling confidence. Your understanding of the story I was trying to tell and guidance in how to tell it in a more resonant way made all the difference.

I'm incredibly appreciative that Rebecca Berg, Ph.D, was available to lend her editing prowess and readerly insights. You made this little book better. To Kathleen Atkins and Stephanie Vandenack, thank you for catching all those little annoyances. You cleared the way for a better read. And thank you to the team at Outskirts Press for your help in getting this into readers' hands.

To have talented illustrator Chad Otis create the cover was an amazing gift. (I see a margarita in your future.) And thank you to Cathy Shoaf, Chad's beloved and my friend, for connecting the dots. I thought you were a great supervisor that one time at that .com, but your friendship means so much more.

My deepest gratitude to my family for your constant love, smarts, humor, and support—during that cancer time and always. We are a resilient bunch, and we like projects. This story reflects both of those things. I wouldn't have it any other way.

Lastly, to my smart, funny, thoughtful friends, from Seattle to Austin and the in-betweens, thank you for listening to me talk about "my fucking book" all these years. Your encouragement, humor, and friendship are truly everything. There are too many to name, but you know who you are. I would, however, like to call out: Steve Hill, Linda Glass, Marit Nordbo, Heather Kennedy, Alice Meadows, Angie McKenzie, Gina Mizner, Beth Bertin, Ruth Kapcia, Dave Hime, Sara Eizen, and Carol Hoffman. XOXO.

RESOURCES

Breast Cancer Action
www.bcaction.org

Breast Cancer Prevention Partners
www.bcpp.org

Environmental Working Group
www.ewg.org

Dena Taylor is a humorist and copywriter, and microwaves a mean Amy's burrito. Her work has been published in *Austin Woman* magazine and on *Fresh Yarn*, and recognized by *HOW* magazine, *PRINT* magazine, and *Graphic Design USA* magazine. She has written and performed with Austin's Gag Reflex sketch comedy group, and was hailed a "freak" by megawatt entertainer, Wayne Brady, after mimicking the sound of wind as a volunteer in one of his Las Vegas shows. She lives in Seattle surrounded by loving friends, gifted creatives, and a commotion of fur called Bridget. *I Don't Wanna be Pink* is her first book.

@denagram16
www.idontwannabepink.com
www.denataylor.com